DEATH'S DOOR

Acts of Attention: The Poems of D. H. Lawrence

In the Fourth World: Poems

The Summer Kitchen: Poems

Emily's Bread: Poems

Blood Pressure: Poems

Wrongful Death: A Memoir

Ghost Volcano: Poems

Kissing the Bread: Poems 1969–1999

Belongings: Poems

The Madwoman in the Attic: The Woman Writer and the Nineteenth-Century Literary Imagination *(with Susan Gubar)*

No Man's Land: The Place of the Woman Writer in the Twentieth Century *(in three volumes, with Susan Gubar)*

Masterpiece Theater: An Academic Melodrama *(with Susan Gubar)*

Shakespeare's Sisters: Feminist Essays on Women Poets *(editor, with Susan Gubar)*

The Norton Anthology of Literature by Women: The Traditions in English *(editor, with Susan Gubar)*

The House Is Made of Poetry: Essays on the Art of Ruth Stone *(editor, with Wendy Barker)*

MotherSongs: Poems for, by, and about Mothers *(editor, with Susan Gubar and Diana O'Hehir)*

René Magritte: *La Victoire* (1939).

DEATH'S DOOR

Modern Dying

and the Ways We Grieve

❏

Sandra M. Gilbert

W. W. NORTON & COMPANY

New York · London

Copyright © 2006 by Sandra M. Gilbert

All rights reserved
Printed in the United States of America
First Edition

For information about permission to reproduce selections from this book, write to
Permissions, W. W. Norton & Company, Inc., 500 Fifth Avenue, New York, NY 10110

Manufacturing by The Maple-Vail Book Manufacturing Group
Book design by Dana Sloan
Production manager: Julia Druskin

Library of Congress Cataloging-in-Publication Data

Gilbert, Sandra M.
Death's door : modern dying and the ways we grieve / Sandra M. Gilbert.
p. cm.
Includes bibliographical references and index.
ISBN 0-393-05131-5
1. Death—Social aspects. 2. Grief. 3. Mourning customs. I. Title.
HQ1073.G54 2005
155.9'37—dc22

2004065430

W. W. Norton & Company, Inc., 500 Fifth Avenue, New York, N.Y. 10110
www.wwnorton.com

W. W. Norton & Company Ltd., Castle House, 75/76 Wells Street, London W1T 3QT

3 4 5 6 7 8 9 0

For D. G., who brought new life

Anyone can stop a man's life, but no one his death; a thousand doors open on to it.

—Lucius Annaeus Seneca, *Phoenissae*

. . . if everybody did not die the earth would be all covered over and I, I as I, could not have come to be and try as much as I can try not to be I, nevertheless, I would mind that so much, as much as anything, so then why not die, and yet again not a thing, not a thing to be liking, not a thing.

—Gertrude Stein, *Wars I Have Seen*

CONTENTS

Part One

ARRANGING MY MOURNING: FIVE MEDITATIONS
ON THE PSYCHOLOGY OF GRIEF

Part Two

HISTORY MAKES DEATH: HOW THE TWENTIETH CENTURY
RESHAPED DYING AND MOURNING

LIST OF ILLUSTRATIONS

PREFACE

A Matter of Life and Death

A paradox: The days that really live in our public memories aren't birthdays, they're death days. These are the days we're talking about when we say *Where were you when . . . ?* Each of us of course has indelible memories of personal joy or triumph—successes in love and work, marriages, the births of children, special festivities. Yet our communal history may be most deeply shaped by memories of collective trauma that are at least as powerfully inscribed in our minds as the official holidays that mark the turnings of the calendar year. A whole generation of people over seventy remembers where they were and what they were doing when Japanese planes bombed Pearl Harbor. Several generations of people over fifty know where they were when John F. Kennedy was shot in Dallas while most people over twenty have similarly vivid recollections of the day Princess Diana died in a car crash in Paris. And now masses of people over, say, the age of ten know just exactly where they were and what they were doing when the twin towers of the World Trade Center, along with a wing of the Pentagon, were destroyed on September 11, 2001.

Why is public pain so lastingly woven into the fabric of our remembrance? It seems likely that confronting terror together at impossible-to-forget times, we experience as a society, if only for a moment, what the French philosopher Georges Bataille called "disintoxication," a brief awakening from the "projects" of love and work that function, thought Bataille, like "narcotics" to help us repress the consciousness of our own mortality.[1] On these occasions, in other words, the fearful knowledge that we're usually (and rightly) good at evading erupts into our dailiness as death's door swings so publicly and dramatically open that we can't look away.

That door, and the shadows it casts on our private lives as well as on our collective memory, will be at the center of my thoughts here, as I examine what seem to be distinctively modern ways of dying, mourning, and memorializing that have evolved in the course of the last century.

This book began nearly a decade ago as a project meant to return me to the practice of literary criticism after a long period of preoccupation with a grave personal loss. Invited in 1996 to deliver a special lecture on my own campus, I decided that I'd attempt to theorize contemporary renderings of the elegy and its close cousin the grief memoir, two forms to which I'd devoted most of my energy following the unexpected death of my husband in 1991. I drafted and delivered a talk on late-twentieth-century elegies and laments titled "The Handbook of Heartbreak," then developed my ideas further in a prospectus for a book that was to be called *The Fate of the Elegy: Mourning, Modernity, and Poetic Memory*. Here I proposed to consider a number of aesthetic and cultural issues as I addressed a central question in recent literary history, namely, how do poets mourn in an age of mounting theological and social confusion about death and dying?

As I explained to various granting agencies, I planned to argue in a fairly traditional academic mode that the fate of the elegy as a genre has been significantly affected by the cultural forces that have constructed what Wallace Stevens called "the mythology of modern death," and in doing this, I expected to explore the revisionary laments with which poets have for more than half a century responded to both "modern death" and modern modes of mourning while tracing some of their strategies back to at least the nineteenth century. My book, I told myself and others, would analyze texts by writers from Elizabeth Barrett Browning and Walt Whitman to Wallace Stevens, Sylvia Plath, and others, contextualizing them with analyses of the crises bred by the disappearance of a traditional God, the testimonial imperatives fostered by the traumas of global warfare, the privatization of death associated with the increasing medicalization of dying, the new technologies of film and video that allow the dead to "live" on-screen, and the male/female dialectic out of which modernism itself was in part constituted.

When I started to research and write the book I'd outlined, however, I soon found myself in the midst of an enterprise that was, on the one hand, more autobiographical than the one I'd planned and, on the other hand, more ambitious in scope. I'd always realized that my interest in the poetics of bereavement was rooted in a need to reflect on my own practice as an elegist, and I also understood that my concern with the cultural was as personal as it was literary. Yet I was, and still am, somewhat startled by the continuity among the personal, the poetic, and the cultural that has infused both the style and the substance of what was an ostensibly *im*personal professional project.

To explain how my meditations on the poetics of bereavement originated in musings on my own practice, I should begin by noting that I hadn't been able *not* to write the poems of grief that I collected in a book of elegies for my husband, nor had I been able to evade what I experienced as an urgent responsibility to draft a memoir about the medical cataclysm that ended his life. And I'd had to write both books with a testimonial passion that took me by surprise. Thus in the memoir I became a witness as well as the commentator I'd have been in a literary-critical work; in the poems I became not just a witness, as poets often are, but a journalist of my own sorrow, carefully dating and placing a number of my verses as I rarely had in the past. Why and how had my own writing been redirected in these ways? And if, as I supposed, I wasn't unique but at least in some respects representative of many contemporaries in my literary responses to bereavement, why and how was I representative?

Through the process social scientists sometimes label "introspection," I came to speculate that the insistence of my need to formulate the loss my children and I had suffered while producing a detailed narrative of the events in which our pain had originated was at least in part a protest against what I then only half realized were a set of social and intellectual commandments "forbidding mourning," to quote from the title of a famous poem by John Donne.[2] I think I felt driven to *claim* my grief and—almost defiantly— to *name* its particulars because I found myself confronting the shock of bereavement at a historical moment when death was in some sense unspeakable and grief—or anyway the expression of grief—was at best an embarrassment, at worst a social solecism or scandal.

I don't mean here to complain that my family didn't receive sympathy and support in our sorrow. It's hard to imagine that mourners could have encountered a more compassionate community of friends than the network surrounding and sustaining my children and me for months, indeed years. No, I'm thinking, rather, of a persistent, barely conscious feeling that I had throughout the worst days of grieving, a feeling that in my sorrow I represented a serious social problem to everyone except my circle of intimates, confronting even well-wishers with a painful and perhaps shameful riddle. I didn't at the time realize that this sense of embarrassment, even disgrace, was fairly common among the bereaved. It wasn't until several years after I'd entered my own tunnel of grief that I encountered C. S. Lewis's 1961 confession of the curious public anxiety that beset him when he was mourning the death of his wife, Joy: "An odd byproduct of my loss is that I'm aware of being an embarrassment to everyone I meet. . . . Perhaps the bereaved ought to be isolated in special settlements like lepers." Yet these words exactly described an important aspect of the mystifying oppression that had settled over me in my bereavement.[3]

I was wounded, yes, by my loss, and grieving because I was wounded, but at the same time I had a strange and strangely muffled sense of *wrongness*—"of being an embarrassment"—as though I incarnated something people would indeed like to isolate in a "special settlement." It was thus in reaction against my intuition of a pervasive social imperative to silence, isolate, or forbid mourning that I was driven to assert my grief, to name and claim my sorrow and my children's pain and above all my dead husband's suffering. And I believe other contemporary elegists have written out of these same impulses.

Precisely how, though, are literary responses to bereavement affected by barely spoken strictures against mourning? And how are such repressive forces, along with the elegiac gestures of defiance they elicit, related to the historical phenomena I'd all along meant to consider (though in a subordinate way) in my book: the crises bred by the disappearance of a traditional God, the traumas of global warfare, the privatization of death, the medicalization of dying, and so forth?

These questions turned me not only toward work that scholars in my own discipline have done on the elegy but also toward more general studies of death and dying, bereavement and mourning in Western cultures, especially the United States and other Anglophone societies. That the poetry of grief—exemplified most famously in the prestigious subgenre of the pastoral elegy (for instance, Milton's "Lycidas," Shelley's "Adonais," Arnold's "Thyrsis")—has changed radically since the mid-nineteenth century is a point that's been explored in scrupulously nuanced volumes authored by such critics and literary historians as Peter Sacks, Jahan Ramazani, Gail Holst-Warhaft, and Melissa Zeiger. And that our (Western) cultural attitudes toward death and dying, bereavement and mourning have also been radically transformed, perhaps especially in recent centuries— that, as I myself will put it here, history makes death just as surely as death makes history—is a phenomenon that's been investigated by a range of historians, sociologists, and anthropologists, including most notably Geoffrey Gorer, Philippe Ariès, and Zygmunt Baumann, while certain significant continuities have recently been examined by the literary scholars Robert Pogue Harrison and James Tatum.[4]

Whether or not the twentieth century was an age of "death denial" is, to be sure, an issue much disputed among journalists, social scientists, medical workers, and literary historians. Yet certainly there's consensus that by the second half of the century procedures for grieving were at the very least blurry and confused while cultural attitudes toward death and dying were so conflicted that in the 1990s a number of major social organizations began addressing the issues surrounding what both PBS and the Soros Foundation called "Death in America." By the year 2001, in addition to the usual self-help books by pop psychologists, television spiritualists, and other media "personalities," a number of serious volumes on dying, death, and bereavement had gained considerable attention. They included Sherwin Nuland's best-selling *How We Die*, Jerome Groopman's *The Measure of Our Days*, Marie de Hennezel's *Intimate Death*, and Studs Terkel's *Will the Circle Be Unbroken?: Reflections on Death and Dignity*.

Yet despite this new, multifaceted attention to death and bereavement, I was persuaded, as my research advanced, that no one had yet examined in depth the intersections among the personal, the cultural, and the literary that I was struggling to understand. Some literary critics had enriched their textual analyses with cultural observations, a number of social scientists had considered the impact of class, faith, and ethnicity on the expectations of the dying and their mourners, and a few of those who investigate death and bereavement had acknowledged that changes in elegiac modes are among the symptoms of sociocultural metamorphoses. But few thinkers had sought to synthesize different generic and disciplinary approaches to the emotional, aesthetic, metaphysical, and societal problems posed by what in the course of the twentieth century came to be called the "end of life."

Then, of course, nine months into the new millennium, as the twin towers of the World Trade Center exploded, flamed, and collapsed with "a slow, building rumble like rolling thunder" that roared through millions of television sets around the world, death itself seemed to have drilled a black hole in the American psyche, a gaping wound out of which a new awareness of mortality and even some new ways of mourning emerged. The very subject I'd been researching was now in flux around me, and it would be almost impossible for me to think of this book as primarily an "academic" enterprise.[5]

Thus, even as I began to organize the material that emerged from critical reflection and scholarly research into the book I'd proposed, I found myself writing in an unexpected way, fusing memoir and meditation with exposition and explication. Precisely the same testimonial urgency that had inspired my earlier poems of grieving and my memoir of personal loss was still infusing my work; there was evidently no going back, no chance of a full-scale retreat from personal witnessing to impersonal commentary. Because not only I but many of my contemporaries were living with considerable public drama through the very dilemmas I was studying, I couldn't sufficiently detach myself from the pressure of immediate experience to be wholly dispassionate. The solution? Either abandon the project or attempt what would be, for me, an unusual melding of the testimonial with the analytic, the personal with the professional.

Finally, I've had to understand that the book you're reading now is in some sense experimental, mingling the techniques of different genres (autobiographical narrative, cultural studies, literary history) in an effort to ground my investigation of the poetics of grief in the complexity and richness of what, for want of a better word, I'll name "the real." Along the way, as I pursued this investigation, I saw that taken as a whole, my completed study could no longer be titled *The Fate of the Elegy* because it had broadened into an examination as much of contexts as of texts. I was not only analyzing the lamentations that mourners utter when they find themselves stranded at death's door but also exploring the rapidly changing beliefs and customs that shape such lamentations as well as my own experience of such beliefs and customs.

Although throughout this volume I use the techniques of the three different genres I just mentioned, each does to some extent dominate a section of its own.

Every chapter in "Arranging My Mourning," Part One of *Death's Door*, begins with autobiographical narrative, and all five meditate, in one way or another, on what seem to be timeless and universal aspects of grief and mourning: the common belief in death as a plausible place, the haunting persistence of the very idea of haunting, the special meaning of widowhood in many societies, the widespread need to commemorate the date(s) of death and mourning, the (probably) transhistorical, perhaps even transcultural desire to communicate with the dead, and, inevitably, the ubiquitous urge to question and berate death. Throughout all five I juxtapose reflections on my personal experiences of mourning with discussions of poems that have illuminated those experiences for me along with analyses of the fears and hopes that seem to be broadly shared in human confrontations with mortality.

If the chapters of Part One begin with memoir, those in Part Two, "History Makes Death," are predominantly shaped by the techniques of what scholars now call cultural studies, with each drawing on the insights of sociologists, anthropologists, and historians to illuminate the particular aspects of death and dying as well as the specific procedures for grieving that seem to be distinctively "modern," sometimes even unique to the millennial moment we inhabit. Nevertheless, throughout these five chapters I continue to illustrate my points both with autobiographical reflection and with readings of individual poems, while examining in depth some of the topics with which I'd originally proposed merely to contextualize my study of the elegy: the crises bred by the disintegration of redemptive religious faith in many quarters, the traumatic impact of global warfare, the medicalization of dying, the effects of film and video on mourners, and the evolution of burial customs from the communal rituals of the country churchyard to the electronic rites of the "virtual cemetery" and memorial practices from the traditional requiem mass to the currently fashionable "life celebration."

Finally, in Part Three of *Death's Door*, titled "The Handbook of Heartbreak," I employ literary-critical strategies to explore what I called in my original book proposal "the fate of the elegy" in our time. But even here, as I consider the ways in which modern and contemporary poets in Britain and America have reshaped inherited modes of mourning in verse, I've felt impelled to test my readings of elegies and laments on my own pulse, through memoir and meditation, while also situating major elegiac works in the cultural settings I've sought to analyze throughout this project. Perhaps poets aren't really "the unacknowledged legislators of the world," as Percy Bysshe Shelley so extravagantly claimed, but I think many readers will sympathize with my belief that the achievements of twentieth-century figures from Wilfred Owen and Siegfried Sassoon to Robert Lowell, Allen Ginsberg, Sylvia Plath, and a host of others really do respond to, and thus dramatize, a kind of half-conscious, communal "legislation" that the world doesn't fully acknowledge in the prose of dailiness.

Writing this book has felt urgently necessary, felt, in fact, like a matter of life and death, so I'm particularly eager to thank the institutions and foundations that aided my research and writing as well as the many colleagues and friends who have advised and encouraged me. For crucial financial support, I'm grateful to the National Endowment for the Humanities, the Soros Foundation's Project on Death in America, and the University of California President's Fellowship program, along with ever-helpful administrators at the University of California, Davis. For beautiful spaces in which to think and write, I thank the Rockefeller Foundation and the Bogliasco Foundation; I'm grateful that they welcomed me to, respectively, the Villa Serbelloni in Bellagio and the Centro Studi di Ligure outside Genoa. For sterling research assistance, I thank Christopher Sindt, John Beckman, and especially Augustus Rose, facilitator, factotum, friend and adviser nonpareil. And for in-depth, detailed, and extraordinarily incisive readings of countless drafts, I thank in particular Joanne Feit Diehl and Marlene Griffith Bagdikian, while for meticulous help with individual chapters, I'm grateful to Bill Daleski, Anita Desai, Sharon Kaufman, Shirley Kaufman, John Murray, and Alex Zwerdling, and for enthusiastic advice about my title, I thank Joan Schenkar.

Ideas, encouragement, useful information, and illuminating comments also flowed from Leah Asofsky and her late husband, Richard Asofsky, along with Wendy Barker, Burton Benedict, Kevin Clark, C. Abbott Conway, Dorothy Gilbert, Christina Gillis, Donald Gray, Susan Gubar, Marilyn Hacker, Nancy Miller, Gregory Orr, Nancy Gilbert Phillips, Kathleen Woodward, the late and much mourned Ilinca Zafiripol-Johnston, and all the members of my Berkeley poetry group—Chana Bloch, Peter Dale Scott, Jeanne Foster, Diana O'Hehir, Phyllis Stowell, Mark Turpin, and Alan Williamson—as well as from my ever-resourceful children, Roger, Kathy, and Susanna Gilbert, along with my daughter-in-law, Robin Gilbert-O'Neil. For helping me learn to mourn and to understand mourning, I thank Toni Morrison and Ruth Stone. For cross-cultural hospitality and invaluable instruction, I am grateful to Sheila Lahiri-Choudhury, Masako Hirai, Hulya Adak, and Ahmet Alkan, along with a number of warmly responsive audiences in Japan, India, and Turkey. For comparable hospitality in France and Italy, I thank Ginette Roy, Michael Hollington, and Massimo Bacigalupo. For sustained and enlivening attention to the many questions raised by the topics listed in my subtitle, *Modern Dying and the Ways We Grieve*, I'm deeply grateful to the participants in the Berkeley "Life and Death Potluck" group, in particular Guy Micco, Sharon Kaufman, Tina Gillis, and Patricia Benner. For careful, supportive attention to the fate of my manuscript, I'm grateful to my agent, Ellen Levine; my editor, Jill Bialosky; and her sterling associate Evan Carver. For a great job on the index, I thank Cohen Carruth, Inc. For ceaseless inspiration, consolation, and sheer joie de vivre, I salute my grandchildren: nearly grown-up Val Gilbert, just-started-out-on-the-road-to-growing-up Aaron Gilbert-O'Neil, beginning-to-walk Stefan Gilbert-O'Neil, and just-arrived Sophia Rosette Gilbert. And for patiently reading every single draft of every single chapter while also attending (for the most part patiently) to me and my peculiarities, I'm endlessly grateful to David Gale, my companion in daily life and *bien aimé*. A genial mathematician and jovial jazz buff, he has cheerfully joined me on more tours of cemeteries, memorials, and mortuary exhibitions than he may care to remember.

—*Berkeley/Paris, 2005*

ACKNOWLEDGMENTS

Excerpts from this book have appeared, usually in slightly different form, as follows. "Death Opens," in *Seeing the Difference: Proceedings of the Townsend Center, 2001*; "Widow," in *Critical Inquiry* (Summer 2000); "Yahrzeit," in *Triquarterly* (Fall 2001); "Writing Wrong," as "Writing Wrong," in *a/b: Autobiography Studies* (Summer 1999) and in *Extremities: Trauma, Testimony, and Community*, ed. Nancy K. Miller and Jason Tougaw (Urbana: University of Illinois Press, 2002), and as "Writing/Righting Wrong," in *Accountability: Patient Safety and Policy Reform*, ed. Virginia A. Sharpe (Washington, D.C.: Georgetown University Press, 2004); "Rats' Alley," in *New Literary History* (Summer 1998). In addition, portions of "E-mail to the Dead" appeared in the *Michigan Quarterly Review* (Spring 1998); portions of "Technologies of Death" appeared as "'Unreal City': The Place of the Great War in the History of Modernity," a preface to *World War I and the Cultures of Modernity*, ed. Douglas Mackaman and Michael Mays (Jackson: University Press of Mississippi, 2000); portions of "On the Beach with Sylvia Plath" appeared in *Field* (Fall 1998); and portions of "Was the Nineteenth Century Different, and Luckier?" under the titles "American Sexual Poetics" and "Now in a Moment I Know What I Am For," appeared in, respectively, *Reconstructing American Literary History*, ed. Sacvan Bercovitch (Cambridge: Harvard University Press, 1986), and *Walt Whitman of Mickle Street*, ed. Geoffrey Sill (Knoxville: University of Tennessee Press, 1994). I am grateful to all these journals and presses for permission to reprint.

PART ONE

Arranging My Mourning:
Five Meditations
on the Psychology of Grief

The universal . . . presence of funeral rites and ritualized
commemoration of the dead has been one of the earliest . . .
discoveries of comparative ethnography. No form of human life
. . . has been found that failed to pattern the treatment of
the deceased bodies and their posthumous presence in the
memory of the descendants. Indeed, the patterning has been
found so universal that discovery of graves and cemeteries is
generally accepted by the explorers of prehistory as the
proof that a humanoid strain whose life was never observed
directly had passed the threshold of humanhood.

—Zygmunt Bauman,
Mortality, Immortality and Other Life Strategies

I

Death Opens

Paris. November 1, 2000. Today is All Saints' Day, and tomorrow will be the day of All Souls, also called the Day of the Dead. Once, before the Catholic Church embarked on a program of sanitizing and sanctifying, these days marked the Celtic Samhain, a holiday when, according to some, the walls between this world and the "other" are "most transparent," the souls of the dead driven toward us in multitudes, like swirling leaves. But even now Christian festivals preserve a trace of the old mysterious connections between the realm of the flesh and the realm of spirits that shaped this time for centuries. All Saints' Day, writes one cleric, "commemorates the holy ones of all ages and stations whose names are known only to God," while All Souls' Day celebrates "those who have died but not yet attained the presence of God." And there is "an old Scottish belief that anyone born on All Souls' Day will have 'double sight': he will be able to see the spirit world about him and have command over the spirits he sees."[1]

On this feast of All Saints it's exactly nine years, eight months, and twenty-one days since the sunny February morning when two orderlies arrived to wheel my husband of thirty-three years into the Northern California operating theater where he had a routine prostatectomy from which he never recovered. Though he was in robust health apart from the tumor for which he was being treated, Elliot died some six hours after my children and I were told that his surgeon had successfully removed the malignancy. And for the first six months after he died, death suddenly seemed plausible, not a far-off threat but urgently close, as if the walls between this world and the "other" had indeed become transparent or as if a door between the two realms had swung open. For the first six weeks after he died, death seemed

1

not only rational but right, or at least appropriate, as if I were already standing in its doorway and need merely keep walking toward where my husband
now was.

This death whose door suddenly swung so surprisingly open wasn't of
course my first encounter with the mortality of people I loved. My father,
my grandparents, and a specially cherished aunt all had died in or, as the
saying goes, "before" their time, and perhaps most shockingly so had my
first child, born prematurely when I was twenty-one years old and just six
months pregnant, in an era when it was remarkable if a baby boy who
weighed only two pounds could survive, as this one did, for three days. I
mourned those deaths and was, indeed, so devastated by the loss of the
child I was never allowed to hold in my arms and whose tiny body I never
saw after he died that I now realize I spent two years of my early twenties in
a state of what's lately been called clinical depression. Yet death remained
intransigently alien, sealed off, impermeable. In fact, I suspect that as I
struggled to accommodate my losses, I was stunned and grieved by precisely
the hermetic impermeability that had engulfed my baby and my father, my
grandparents and my aunt.

What had now opened the door of death, made its otherness so strangely
plausible? Such a transformative psychological event can no doubt have
many causes, but for me, at this point, a certain conjugal logic flung down
or anyway began dissolving a wall between the realm of the living and the
"other world" inhabited by the spirits to whom the Church dedicates All
Souls' Day.

If he who had been bone of my bone, sinew of my sinew, could do this
mysterious thing called dying, then so could (and clearly *should*) I. Not, I
have to add, as a ceremonial acknowledgment of widowhood, a form of sati
or a heroic gesture like the act said sometimes to have been chosen by a
bereaved wife in "imperial China . . . who arranged to hang herself publicly
on the death of her spouse [in] the presence of local dignitaries," a self-
immolation "not regarded as suicide but as a heroic victory over death."[2]
No, my queer and utterly surprising sense of the plausibility of death had
little in common with the "heroic" leap toward oblivion of the loyal Chinese
wife or with the willing or unwilling sati of the Hindu widow, or even,
indeed, with any fantasy of suicide, as I understand the term. It was more, I
think, like a move in a board game, an eerily competitive mirroring of
another player's strategy: "if *you* can do that, so can I." But without the hostility implied by the word "competitive," with, instead, a kind of eager, helpless mimicry. As in "Oh, I see, so *that's* what's next! Thirty-three years ago

we got married, bought a turn-of-the-century brass bed, wrote disserta-
tions. Now we're going to die."

Or perhaps, to offer an alternative explanation, my sense of the nearness
of death was akin to the protective feeling reported by the journalist Lisa
Schnell, a grieving mother who notes that just after the death of her
eighteen-month-old daughter she and her husband "wanted to be with
Claire right then, cradling her perfect soul as we had cradled her imperfect
little body all her brief life. We wanted to be dead with her." Adds Schnell:
"I wasn't suicidal—I didn't want to *make* myself dead—I just wanted to be
dead with Claire. I raged at the injustice of the fact that though she had
needed me to give birth to her, she didn't need me to die with her."[3]

As soon as I read Schnell's words, I recognized their uncanny rightness.
Of course! Elliot and I worked, traveled, ate, slept, dreamed together. Wasn't
it perfectly rational to suppose, just after he died, that we should be dead
together?

Nor are Lisa Schnell and I especially unusual in these yearnings not so
much toward death as to enter an open doorway into death and *be* dead
with someone much loved. Perhaps my earlier notion of death's impermeability had been merely a way of repressing an intuition of its dangerous
proximity to the bereaved, for certainly major poets and novelists—
Shakespeare, Hardy, Lawrence, and others, along with many, more recent
writers—have explored such a sense of death nearing and opening. "In its
first stages, grief is a kind of madness," speculated the Italian philosopher
Benedetto Croce, noting that after a loved one has died, "we feel guilty for
living, it seems that we are stealing something that doesn't belong to us, we
would like to die with our dead." But to the newly bereaved the need to die
with the dead seems to have a motive better explained by the strange, shadowy opening of death's door. In an account of his thirty-four-year-old
wife's death from breast cancer, the memoirist David Collins summarizes
with poignant precision the rationale underlying his feeling that "I wanted
to die too—so I could be with her." Explaining "so freshly present she
seemed [that] I had this thought: *I could follow her*," he adds, "I just wanted
to go after her, not let her get away. I wanted to find her again. Hadn't I
found her once?"[4]

I suppose a half-conscious trace of a similar impulse remains with me
even after nearly a decade, for right now, as All Saints' Day draws to a close
here in Paris, soon to blend into its close cousin, All Souls' Day, I'm
reminded again of the close yet invisible threshold toward which so many
mourners are drawn. The streets are almost sepulchrally still this afternoon.

Toussaint is a holy day for the French, as for the Germans (*Alleheiligen*) and the Italians (*Tutti i Santi*). Almost everything's shut today, even the bakeries where at this twilight hour people would usually be lining up for baguettes and croissants, but perhaps this *fermeture* signals the nearness of a mysterious door that might at any moment swing ponderously open.

According to a Web site I just found, medieval priests instituted the feasts of All Saints and All Souls because they feared the charisma of Samhain, a harvest festival whose acolytes celebrated this primordial Halloween and the next day, All Hallows' Day, as the doorway into "the season of death revels, the period of misrule from dusk on October 31 to the Winter Solstice, when light again pierces the dark business of the hag of winter, Cailleach."[5] Celebrants of such morbid revels hung lanterns, perhaps the ancestors of our jack-o'-lanterns, to guide wandering spirits, and to nourish the ghosts there were "soul cakes," maybe the forerunners of the "treats" we give today to would-be tricksters.

In contemporary Mexico, of course, *El Día de los Muertos*—the Day of the Dead—continues to be, if anything, more carnivalesque than the old European Samhain. The physician-essayist Frank Gonzalez-Crussi has eloquently described the altars known as *ofrendas*, cloth-covered tables "bearing fruits, dainties, beverages, and votive lamps," with which all over his native land the living seek to lure the dead "to descend upon the earth and enjoy the celebration in the company of friends and relatives." Like our Halloween, he notes, this traditional holiday is "a mestizo custom" that melds Catholic rituals imported by the Spanish conquistadors with pre-Christian practices, in this case festivals in honor of the Aztec mother goddess, who represents "the creative and destructive functions of the earth." For in Mexico, explains Gonzalez-Crussi, perhaps as in the pre-Christian Europe of Samhain, "the dead are not quite gone, and death remains a living personage, the bearer and harbinger of itself."[6]

But because in the New World, as in the Old, such potentially blasphemous revels couldn't be entirely repressed, the Catholic clergy had to make them less threatening. Samhain, like the pre-Christian festivals Gonzalez-Crussi describes, acknowledges the power of death and the dead over us. The Church had to convert each of these holidays into its opposite, a day when we have power over the dead, for as always, the Christian mission is to conquer death.

Whereas, for instance, the ancient Celts sought to honor the dead with offerings of soul cakes (and the Aztecs to appease the divinities of death with human flesh), the Church's attitude toward those on the "other" side is both more austere and more ambitious. According to the *Catholic Encyclopedia*, the "theological basis for the feast [of All Souls] is the doctrine that the souls which, on departing from the body, are not perfectly cleansed from venial sins, or have not fully atoned for past transgressions, are debarred from the Beatific Vision, and that the faithful on earth can help them by prayers" and other holy acts.[7] Perhaps in keeping with this injunction, some of my Paris neighbors are going now among the tombs of Père Lachaise with flowers and Ave Marias. And a damp gray with a hint of winter in its breath unfolds a chill in the little court I'm looking out on, though there are still impatiens cascading from tubs flanking the doorways, geraniums bursting from our window boxes. With its belated blooms, its wintry mist, the court itself seems an emblem of the "transparence" between the worlds of the living and the dead that supposedly defines these days, whether they're Christian or pagan feasts. At such a time, in such a place, it seems right to try to understand what it meant for death, suddenly, to seem "plausible," as if it had out of nowhere, unnervingly, opened itself to me when my husband was drawn through its doorway.

A DOOR OPENS

"I think this is finally the bitter river crossed," D. H. Lawrence wrote to a friend on December 12, 1910, the day of his mother's funeral. "It certainly feels like one of the kingdoms of death, where I am."[8] And "Death opened, like a black tree, blackly," Sylvia Plath declared as she remembered the shock of her father's death when she was seven.[9] A bereaved adult, I too was astonished when after years in which I'd mourned other deaths by distancing or repressing them, I crossed the "bitter river" into death along with my husband or when, to put it differently, my husband's death opened and unfolded itself like the chill in the court, as if it must now be part of a quotidian "season of death revels" leading to a new turning of the year.

Well, certainly not *revels*! When my daughters and I were led into the pale hospital cubicle where Elliot lay after what must have been a terrible six-hour battle to survive the surgery that killed him, we found ourselves at first, as we stared at the silent stone version of himself that he had become, in a space that was bleakly filled by corporeal substance. This death that had suddenly, gigantically, opened around us—opened perhaps rather more like a huge black umbrella rapidly unfurling than like a stately black tree unscrolling its branches—*this* death was hardly the soothing presence that Walt Whitman once described as a "dark mother always gliding near with soft feet," a "strong deliveress."[10] Serious and *material* rather than maternal, this death forced me, horrifyingly, to confront the metamorphosis of a body I had loved into a dead thing that now appeared to be the substance of fate itself.

Yet at that first dazed moment, as I gazed at the uncannily familiar image of Elliot—not at what *had been* "Elliot" but at what *still seemed to be* "Elliot"—death itself was made eerily plausible by my husband's lingering presence in the midst of it: by the slight rueful smile on his face (which might have been the relic of a grimace of pain or fear); by the tilt of his head that was even now so customary, so comfortingly *known*; by his shaggy eyebrows, as unruly as ever; by his hands (carefully folded on the white coverlet, maybe by a thoughtful nurse) that were still, though so frighteningly motionless, *his* hands.

He wasn't there, but he was *there*. And his thereness, his presence at the center of massive absence, was what made death plausible, what flung it open like a door into an all too easily accessible space or like a black umbrella defining an indisputably real circle of shadow into which it would be frighteningly simple to step.

From a "primitive" perspective, "the dead man is the double of the living," or so the French theorist Jean Baudrillard once wrote, a comment that points to the confusion of the animate and the inanimate that bound me in a sort of spell as I crouched, stunned, over my husband, and, certain that he *was* there, *could* hear, began speaking to him in low, rapid tones.[11]

Atavistically crossing myself (in acknowledgment of his death) even as I murmured to the person I felt sure was still alive, I was of course too stunned to remember how often, in a long career as critic and teacher, I'd read the words of others struggling to describe such a paradoxically vivid feeling of presence-in-absence, a feeling perhaps explained by an intuition that, as Robert Pogue Harrison puts it, despite "its grave stillness[,] there is nothing more dynamic than a corpse" since it incarnates "the event of passage taking place before our eyes."[12] My first serious critical work had been a dissertation that eventually turned into a book on D. H. Lawrence's poetry, and I now realize that what I experienced, gripping the iron hospital bedrail and gazing in shock at my husband's body, was a sensation Lawrence had often explored in the wake of his mother's death, when he mused that he had been dragged across the "bitter river" Styx into the realm the ancients called Hades.

Now I also realize, though, that I'd never understood just how incisive Lawrence's analyses of this sensation were. In a poem called "The Bride," he describes his adored mother as looking " like a girl" as she lies dead, adding, in a beautifully enigmatic line, "And her dead mouth sings / By its shape, like thrushes in clear evenings." But maybe when I first tried to understand this poem, I hadn't really considered how the attribution of *song* to the shape of stillness that is death implies a potential for mystical communion, emphasizing again that for her bereft son the dead woman is still somehow *there* even in the midst of death's otherness, *there* because he imagines himself as at least on the threshold of "one of death's kingdoms."[13]

Death's kingdom: as I meditate on this odd sense of the plausibility of death that I think Lawrence dramatizes in "The Bride" and that my husband's death so astonishingly bestowed on me too, I see that such a feeling must account for traditional images of dead people "living," as it were, on the "other side" of a sometimes permeable, at least semitransparent barrier. So-and-so is "gone," we say. But gone where? When one "goes," one goes *somewhere*. Somewhere plausible, which is to say *feasible*, practicable, indeed (paradoxically) *livable*.

Death's door opens, and one goes into a *place*. Death's kingdom, Hades, purgatory, the "other side": it doesn't matter how one imagines the place; what's important is that it's a *place* and that given the weird familiarity of the body of the dead one—its quality of both being and not being the beloved—the place where the dead one has "gone" must also be weirdly familiar. Geographically, I suspect many mourners may feel at that moment of deathly nearness, death must be as plausible as any hitherto foreign country to which one might move. Not travel, but *move* with all one's goods of memory and stores of thought and trunkloads of hope. As if, in other words, "going" into death were like uprooting oneself and resettling, say, in France, death being, after all, "just," in Hamlet's words, another "undiscovered country."

In that case, given the logic of the metaphor, death-as-plausible-country must also be or have a language that one might struggle to learn, the way one struggles to learn French. If (or, rather, when) you move to death, you'll learn its language through the educational process known as total immersion.

Prayer, the Church would say—especially on this *jour de fête* of *Toussaint*—is the tongue in which one addresses the dead and the tongue in which one speaks of them, whereas the celebrants of Samhain would argue that we signal those on the "other side" of the frontier between here and there, our country and their misty place, with pumpkins and turnips carved into lanterns or with hilltop bonfires and perhaps rattling calabashes. For in

8   SANDRA M. GILBERT

many cultures, "mere noise"—"explosions, the firing of guns, the beating of gongs"—is considered the proper way to talk to the dead, either to invoke them or to still them.[14]

Whether one whispers prayers, shouts imprecations, tolls a solemn bell, or bangs a drum loudly, though, one is seeking to speak the language of death, to address those who seem so indisputably *there* on what George Eliot, writing of the nonhuman world, called "the other side of silence." Nothing but a symbolic "piece of silk . . . separates us from the next world" and its inhabitants, remarks a character in W. G. Sebald's elegiac *Austerlitz*.[15] The dead were once of the human world, yet now they too are on the other side of silk, the other side of silence—right there, like trees, fish, flowers, butterflies—to be addressed in solemn apostrophes or to respond in what rhetoricians call prosopopoeia, the imagined speech of those who may appear to be absent or unreal but who are *truly* there because they are present to poets and other, perhaps more pious interlocutors.

"*There in the tomb stand the dead upright*," wrote William Butler Yeats, imagining the skeletal alertness of a troop of soldiers buried in a Celtic cairn. Nearing his own death, he fantasized the loyal speech of "the men of the old black tower"—"Stand we on guard oath-bound!"—and groped for a paradoxical image of the *living* of the dead on the other side of silence:

> There in the tomb drops the faint moonlight,
> But winds come up from the shore:
> They shake when the winds roar,
> Old bones upon the mountain shake.[16]

But in his earlier "All Souls' Night," the verse epilogue to his mystical prose work *A Vision*, Yeats constructed a more personal, richly described *ofrenda*, in which at midnight he ritually set out "two long glasses brimmed with muscatel," whose aroma a ghost might drink since "His element is so fine / Being sharpened by his death" that he need merely imbibe "the wine breath." Yeats longed for the dead to visit him at the solemn hour when he heard "the great Christ Church Bell / And many a lesser bell sound through the room," because he was certain he had learned the secrets of the spirit world, so on that night of the old Celtic Samhain he struggled like a neophyte sorcerer to summon the spirits of special dead friends. Yet despite his boasts of occult knowledge, the Irish poet seems to have been left stranded among the living, disconsolately confessing that he'd be willing to discuss his "mummy truths" with any ghost who might be delighted by the "fume of muscatel."

The bereaved are often far more certain of deathly presences and hence of the plausibility of death itself. Living in Italy in 1912, Lawrence continued to mourn his beloved mother, now several years dead and buried in the faraway heart of England, and he transcribed his own private ceremony for the dead in a poem that he too wrote about "the banner of death, and the mystery" that we celebrate on the feast of All Souls. Here in Italy, he noted sorrowfully, the "naked candles burn on every grave," although on his mother's grave "in England, the weeds grow." Yet now, as the thought of her death once more opened to and in him, he himself entered the day's solemnity, declaring that his own body was a candle and the "world is your grave" on which that body "is burning off to you / Its flame of life, now and always," for "It is my offering to you" since "every day is All Souls' Day."[17]

Like Lawrence and his Italian "village folk," Mexican believers enter passionately into the rituals of their *Día de los Muertos*. Frank Gonzalez-Crussi describes the naive hospitality of one old Mexican woman who would put together her altar for the dead, "diligently tidy up the house, and make sure that the table was set before the church bells started sounding. Then, on the afternoon of the second of November, she would go out to the street and actually talk to the invisible souls in these terms":

"Come in, blessed souls of my father, my mother, and my sisters. Please, come in. How did you do this year? Are you pleased with your living relatives? In the kitchen we have tamales, tostadas, pumpkin with honey, apples, oranges, sugarcane, chicken broth, a great deal of salt, and even a little tequila, so you may drink. Are you happy with what we have? My sons worked very hard this year so we could offer you this feast, as usual. Tell me, how is Saint Joseph? Did he receive the Masses we ordered for him?"[18]

And though our own society lacks such an institutionalized ceremony, countless North American grievers no doubt construct comparable rituals of intimacy with the dead.

Following the discovery in 2002 of scandalously *un*burned, rotting bodies on the grounds of a Georgia crematorium, one victimized mourner reported, for instance, that she'd set what she believed to be the urn containing her mother's ashes on the mantel in her living room and had lit candles "in front of it every Sunday without fail" while talking "to what she thought were her mother's remains." She would tell her mother " 'how we missed her,' " this aggrieved young woman explained, and "how we hoped she was resting in peace," but " '*Now we come to find out she wasn't.*' "[19] Of course the dead mother wasn't "resting in peace" because she wasn't *there*, where she was supposed to be—in the urn on the mantel—but instead was flung down among the bodies stacked helter-skelter at the criminal crematorium.

In an account of her six-week-old infant son's death and her own subsequent "journey through grief," the memoirist Carol Henderson relates what's essentially the obverse of this story as she meditates with bleak humor on her decision *not* to "view" her baby's body in the hospital chapel: "If I held Malcolm, how would I ever be able to give him up, turn him back in, like a library book. My son, the unfinished story. How could I say to a nurse: 'Here! Take him!' Knowing it was for keeps. If I saw him, I'd have to shove him into my purse and rush out of the hospital with my bundle. And then what? Keep him . . . forever?"[20]

"Keep him . . . forever?" Even while Henderson fearfully imagines an impulse to fetishize the lifeless body that evokes the Georgia mourner's ritual conversations with what she believed were her mother's ashes, her grotesque yet impassioned little fantasy recapitulates the curious sense of "still" aliveness in death that Lawrence dramatizes in "The Bride." Whether we seek to stay in touch with the dead symbolically, by offering real food to their disembodied spirits, or literally, by somehow feasting our eyes on their actual bodies, we grievers often fear we can't survive the inexorable severings we face.

Sometimes our fear of such severings reinforces the desirous belief that we haven't really lost all connections with those we've physically lost. As highly educated and as bitterly ironic as Henderson, Sylvia Plath was an unusually sophisticated mourner—far more self-conscious than, for instance, either the resentful Georgia woman or the pious Mexican villager—yet throughout the twenty-two years she lived after her father's death "opened, like a black tree, blackly," the dead Otto Plath was in the same way almost inescapably present to her. As she wrote in "Daddy," her love/hate elegy for this parent who had been figuratively reincarnated in her faithless husband, Ted Hughes, Otto's voiceless voice incessantly "worm[ed] through" what his daughter envisioned as a "black telephone" that she had to cut "off at the root."

More lovingly, more hopefully, Thomas Hardy believed he heard his dead wife Emma "calling" to him after her "great going" into death. "Woman much missed," he mourned in one of his finest elegies, "how you call to me, call to me." As he'd confessed some years before Emma's death, this poet-novelist had long "lived with Shades" and often, he claimed, "talked to them" as they led him "through their rooms / In the To-Be" of the grave. But after his wife's "going" into that "To-Be," he was inspired to meditate more particularly on its contours. Years after Emma died and he'd remarried, he was still speculating on the paradoxical life-in-death of the dead, noting in 1923 that Einstein's theory of relativity might mean that "things and events always were, are, and will be" so that "Emma, Mother and Father are *living still* [emphasis added]," albeit "in the past."[21]

Yet even Hardy was tormented by uncertainties. Although Emma called to him from the ever-present shadows of death and the past, from precisely where did she call, how, and in what form? "Can it be you that I hear?" he wondered in "The Call," demanding, "Let me view you then," and, by implication, commanding (as Horatio commands the ghost of Hamlet's father), "Speak, speak. I charge thee, speak."

ON THE THRESHOLD

Hardy's indecision about his wife's prosopopoeia dramatizes the mystery of Hamlet's "undiscovered country" even while his attention to what at least *might* be her "voice" emphasizes the plausibility of that paradoxically unknown and familiar place. His stanza beginning "Can it be you that I hear?" is followed by utterances of skepticism and near despair in which he confesses his fear that all he hears is "the breeze, in its listlessness / Traveling across the wet mead." But his own situation, as he follows what might or might not be the dead woman's voice, also inspires dread. He's "faltering forward, / Leaves around me falling, / Wind oozing thin through the thorn from norward," as he eagerly listens to "the woman calling." And surely such "faltering forward" into a vortex of oozing wind is dangerous! Surely, as he stumbles after the all too plausible "calling" of the dead woman, Hardy risks staggering across the threshold or border into death itself, that all too near country.

Hamlet's companions Marcellus and Horatio grasp this peril. When the prince, recognizing his father's ghost, declares, "I'll follow it," they seek to restrain him. "What if it tempt you toward the flood, my lord," demands Horatio, "Or to the dreadful summit of the cliff . . . ?" And Plath too encountered such a threat, famously confessing to her dead father in "Daddy" that "At twenty I tried to die, / And get back, back, back to you."[22]

Nor is a silent ghost less dangerously seductive. Even if the "black telephone" is off the hook, even if the "calling" seems to cease, the plausibility of the dead one draws the mourner like a magnet, as Plath imagines herself to have been urged "back, back, back" at the time of her first suicide attempt. Dead King Hamlet is speechless at first, until his distraught son cries, "Whither wilt thou lead me? Speak." Haunting his lost wife's childhood home in Cornwall, Hardy echoes the Danish prince, as he picks his way, half blinded, among the misty moors and cliffs of the past, writing in "After a Journey":

> Hereto I come to view a voiceless ghost;
>   Whither, O whither will its whim now draw me.
> Up the cliff, down, till I'm lonely, lost,
>   And the unseen waters' ejaculations awe me.[23]

Was my dead husband an Orpheus leading me, his Eurydice, not out of but *into* the kingdom of death? Perhaps, through the process of unconscious revising and reversing that Freud describes in *The Interpretation of Dreams*, the old myth has the plot backward. Perhaps the story of the poet and his lost beloved isn't a tale of a failed attempt at resurrection, with Orpheus striving to lead his bride away from the lower depths of Hades into the upper air of the living, but rather a myth of immolation, in which the mourner follows the dead one down into the increasingly real shadows of the grave, unwittingly straying across the border between life and death just as, during Samhain's "season of death revels," a traveler who has missed his path might be tricked into crossing the frontier between this world of the "too too solid flesh" and that "other" one, the one that only *seems* to be insubstantial and fantastic.

Mourning his mother, Lawrence felt the boundaries between life and death dissolving as if the very categories of the living and the dead had lost their usual meanings when he crossed the bitter river into what he experienced as death's kingdom. In *Sons and Lovers* he examined this grievous blurring of the lines that usually separate those who are still *here* from those who have "gone" into another somewhere: "In the country all was *dead still.* . . . There was no Time, only Space. Who could say his mother had lived and did not live? She had been in one place, and was in another, that was all. And his soul could not leave her, wherever she was. Now she was gone abroad into the night, and he was with her still [emphasis added]."[24] Though earlier in the chapter from which this passage is drawn Lawrence spoke of the battle between life and death raging in Paul Morel, there's a striking calmness in this vision of the mother and son entering death together. That she "was gone abroad into the night and he was with her still" seems like a serene statement of fact rather than a depressive fantasy.

In his first months of bereavement, Lawrence later confessed, even the town in which he lived began to "glimmer" with "subtle ghosts," who might be the dead walking among the living or the living appearing in the guise of the dead they must inevitably become. Addressing his lost mother in "The Inheritance," he claimed his grief as a gift of enhanced perception, almost like the privilege of "double sight" that supposedly belongs to anyone born on All Souls' Day. "I am dazed with the farewell," he admits, "But I scarcely feel the loss," for:

> You left me a gift
> Of tongues, so the shadows tell
> Me things, and the silences toss
> Me their drift.[25]

In another poem, the eerie "Troth with the Dead," he sees a "broken . . . half a moon" lying "on the low, still floor of the sky" as an emblem of his own fidelity to his dead mother, the "troth with the dead" that he is "pledged to keep." Half of this "broken coin of troth" lies hidden with his mother, but half still flickers within his own body so that he feels himself "lit beneath my heart with a half-moon, weird and blue."[26]

Yet such a troth with the dead is as perilous to this poet as the half-blinded, "faltering" pursuit of Emma might have been to Hardy, or as Plath's efforts to get "back, back, back" to her daddy surely were to her. The keeper of such a vow knows even better than Hardy did what Horatio and Marcellus fear: the "calling" of the dead one so eloquently described by Hardy may be not just dangerous but mortally threatening. It may indeed be a "Call into Death," as Lawrence confesses in a poem of that title, in which he admits to his dead mother that he "would like to come / And be lost out of sight with you, like a melting foam."[27] It's disturbing, then, when in another poem the young writer fantasizes his own passage through death's door:

> I look at the swaling sunset
> And wish I could go also
> Through the red doors beyond the black-purple bar.
>
> I wish that I could go
> Through the red doors where I could put off

    [my flesh] . . .
Like luggage of some departed traveler
    Gone one knows not whither.[28]

VOICES

For the young Lawrence, then, as for many other mourners, the dead beloved was an Orphic singer, uttering a breathless call into what once seemed all a darkness but has now become unexpectedly luminous. But what if the mourner fears that the dead are struggling to voice their needs and *they aren't heard*? Perhaps the survivor intuits a nearness from the "other side," the estranged dimension that spirits supposedly inhabit, yet the call from the dead is inaudible. Imagine, then, the frustration of the despairing spirit, speaking without sound or substance! In "The Haunter," one of the most poignant examples of elegiac prosopopoeia, Hardy evokes the pain of his ghostly wife, who cannot "let him know" how close her dead self is to his living one:

> *He does not think that I haunt here nightly:*
>   *How shall I let him know*
> *That whither his fancy sets him wandering*
>   *I, too, alertly go?—*
> *Hover and hover a few feet from him*
>   *Just as I used to do,*
> *But cannot answer the words he lifts me—*
>   *Only listen thereto! . . .*

> *What a good haunter I am, O tell him!*[29]

In a very different but equally bittersweet gesture of prosopopoeia, Dante Gabriel Rossetti inscribes the words of a dead woman just as her lover, left behind on earth, must himself imagine them (even though, as the poem eventually concedes, he can't really hear her). Rossetti's "blessed damozel" presses so fervently against the golden bar of heaven, a celestial barrier between herself and her still-living beloved, that her bosom "warm[s]" it as if she were still alive with fleshly desire. And standing, yearning, "on the rampart of God's house," she longs, beatifically, for her lover's death:

"I wish that he were come to me,
  For he will come," she said.
"Have I not prayed in Heaven?—on earth,
  Lord, Lord, has he not pray'd?"

About Edgar Allan Poe's famous "The Raven," Rossetti once declared, "I saw that Poe had done the utmost it was possible to do with the grief of the lover on earth, and so I determined to reverse the conditions [in "The Blessed Damozel"], and give utterance to the yearning of the loved one in heaven."[30]

Yet as in "The Raven," a perpetual chilly "Nevermore" provides a kind of ground bass to the utterances of mutual longing that cross the gulf between the lovers. Although in the gaze of heaven and in her own thoughts, the damozel "scarce had been a day / One of God's choristers," her survivors know she's been dead ten years, and her grieving lover, feeling her death has already lasted "ten years of years," intuits her presence as a powerful absence:

. . . Yet now, and in this place,
Surely she lean'd o'er me—her hair
  Fell all about my face. . . .
Nothing: the autumn fall of leaves.
  The whole year sets apace.

"Good" haunters or not, Hardy's Emma and Rossetti's blessed damozel can't break down the barriers between us and them, here and *there*—whatever or wherever that "there" may be.

The very concept of *haunting*, though, with its implications of shared obsession (we're haunted by the dead because we obsessively miss them; they haunt us because they obsessively need us) implies that from time to time ghostly desire just might disrupt what we consider intransigent physical reality. Hamlet's father *must* make his wishes known to the heir who ought to set things right. And in Toni Morrison's *Beloved*, the contemporary work that most brilliantly imagines what would happen if a yearning spirit burst through death's door, the "crawling-already?" baby ghost, weirdly grown into a sleepy-eyed young woman with "new skin, lineless and smooth," rises from the turbulent waters of "rememory" to haunt and harry her tormented mother, Sethe. "Tell me, how did you get here?" asks her sister Denver, at one point. "I wait; *then I got on the bridge* [emphasis added]," Beloved replies. "I stay there in the dark, in the daytime, in the dark, in the daytime. It was a long time."

What built "the bridge"? Sethe's desire or Beloved's—or their mutual yearning? And what urges some across the bridge while leaving others in a place that the grown-up "crawling-already?" baby ghost describes as "Hot. Nothing to breathe down there and no room to move in" because a "lot of people is down there"?[31]

Perhaps we require the ambiguous consolations of fantasy because those who seem so near, whose country has become so incontrovertibly real to the mourner, are yet so far: they're inhabitants of a distant land that is nevertheless absolutely ours. And perhaps the impulse to elegy itself arises from our sense of the simultaneous nearness and farness of their place, arises because we sometimes feel the dead are so near that we must speak *to* as well as *about* or *for* them—because, that is, we wish to converse with them as if we were in their presence while lamenting what, at least intellectually, we understand to be their absence.

To readers who have never fully mourned in quite this way, the elegist's intimacy with death must seem like ghoulishness. Such apparently bizarre intimacy may be what frightened the Church about Samhain, with its welcoming rituals of lanterns and soul cakes, or about the practices underlying *El Día de los Muertos*. But those who summon the beloved dead while intuiting and perhaps resisting their calls into death know that it is essential to speak of death and the dead because if those who have died are still part of us even while they are part of death, then death is part of us too.

It isn't surprising, I suppose, that Sigmund Freud, modernity's foremost investigator of thought and feeling, theorized this last point in his own way. Writing in his classic "Mourning and Melancholia" about what he defined as the "work" of mourning, he noted that when a "testing of reality" has proved that "the loved object no longer exists," the griever must withdraw "libido . . . from its attachments" to this lost beloved. But against "this demand . . . a struggle arises" that "can be so intense that a turning away from reality ensues, the object being clung to through a hallucinatory wish-psychosis." And though the "normal outcome is that deference for reality gains the day," Freud observed that reality's imperative "behest cannot be at once obeyed." In fact the task of detachment that is "the work of mourning" is "carried through bit by bit, under great expense of time and cathectic energy, *while all the time the existence of the lost object is continued in the mind* [emphasis added]."[32]

This internalized *being* of the dead beloved is no doubt what inspires the mourner's intense, uncanny, and ultimately, of course, fantastic sense that death has opened "the red doors behind the black-purple bar" when it's really, we, the living, who have opened in our grief and admitted the dead into the very center of ourselves, where they "speak"—in the prosopopoeia of Hardy's Emma, the lurid hissing of Plath's daddy's "black telephone," the purgatorial tones of Hamlet's father, the curiously sinister baby babble of Beloved—or anyway *seem* to speak, as if they still had independent ghostly existence.

Was it a measure of Lawrence's "success" or "failure" in mourning that he described the dynamics of this process Freud called introjection even before the great psychoanalyst himself drafted "Mourning and Melancholia"? It was in fact in Italy, on the shores of Lake Garda, where he had first commemorated the holy day of All Souls, that the poet stood "in the sloping shadow / The mountains make" and assured his mother that though he could no longer "gather" his thoughts "one by one / And bring them to you," he had discovered a new and "ghostly truth":

> *I know you here in the darkness.*
>   *How you sit in the throne of my eyes*
> *At peace, and look out of the windows*
>   *In glad surprise.*[33]

Perhaps in the end such knowledge "in the darkness" freed the young writer of the kinds of "hallucinatory wish psychos[es]" that variously gripped Rossetti, Hardy, Plath, Hamlet, and, in an even more hyperbolic way, Morrison's Sethe. Yet wouldn't it be a mistake altogether to dismiss as "psychotic" the yearning that brings the dead back to life and into *our* lives, inspiring us to ventriloquize their words and even, as in *Beloved*, to embrace the (hypothetical) presences they *might have had* if they'd lived and grown among us?

A famous passage from the Song of Songs summarizes the sometimes uncanny nexus of love and death that underlies such urgent desire to bridge the gulf of loss:

> *Set me as a seal on your heart,*
>   *as a seal on your arm;*
> *For stern as death is love,*
> *relentless as the nether world is devotion.*[34]

I have to confess here, however, that although my husband's death made death itself so eerily plausible, he never sang to me from beyond the grave, nor did he call me in formal verse. He simply put death *there*, in the middle of my life, because he was there himself, in the center of death. Once, yes, maybe a week after he died, he did appear to me in a dream, looking forlorn. "It's so cold here, sem," he complained, giving me my college nickname. "So cold." He had been exiled, so it seemed, in the mysterious but suddenly plausible ring of darkness that had unexpectedly opened around us both. He was shivering and sorrowful.

How many of us, dreaming or waking, imagine the dead living—*vulnerably* living—in the midst of their death! As she describes her own grief, Carol Henderson pauses to relate the plaintive confession of another mother mourning a newborn child: "Right after we buried Carolyn, it started raining. . . . All I could think about was how Carolyn was going to get wet out there, buried in the ground. I got hysterical about it and wanted to go out and put a tarpaulin and a baby blanket on her grave."[35] And in a powerful, surrealistic scene near the end of Ingmar Bergman's *Cries and Whispers*, a film the director himself subtitled *Reflections on Life, Death, and Love*, a young woman who has just died desperately calls on her two sisters to console her as she enters the ice of her death.

"Can't you hold my hands and warm me? Stay with me until the horror is over?" Agnes begs first Karin, then Maria, piteously explaining, "It's so empty all around me."

But both sisters refuse, and only the family servant, Anna, stays with the dead woman, cradling Agnes at her bared breast—in a posture of *pietà*—all through the long first night of death's endlessness.

In almost every culture around the world, writes the anthropologist Nigel Barley, it is "above all the dead that feel desperate grief and loneliness."[36]

At the close of Rossetti's poem, the not-so-blessed damozel yearns down from the suddenly vertiginous steeps of heaven, strains against "the golden barriers," and weeps.

"I heard her tears," confides her lover.

"For stern as death is love." Though even the sad words of elegies, burning like candles on the graves of All Souls, must falter and fail to cross the borders of mortality, countless living mourners cluster at death's door, hoping to console the mournful dead.

How could I not have wanted, in those early days of grief, to follow my husband through that door, to warm him, to comfort him, to "be dead with" him?

2

Widow

PHONE CALL

April 21, 1964. 2:00 A.M. When the phone rang, Elliot and I were sublimely asleep, striped pajamas and flowered nightgown drifting side by side in syrupy billows of sleep, the kind of luxurious sleep perhaps known only to the parents of small, demanding children, in this case three under four, the youngest just a month old.

The wonderfully serious brass marital bed we'd bought for a song in the late fifties was flanked by rickety orange-crate nightstands, on which we'd precariously stood the kind of electrified oil lamps that went with our fin de siècle bed. But an up-to-date white Princess phone sat next to the lamp on Elliot's side.

He picked up the phone, dropping it only once.

"Well, I'm a widow," my mother said. Her voice was high, shrill, with a metallic edge. Pressed close to the safety of my husband's shoulder, I could hear her hysteria beginning to leak out of the receiver. "I knew it would happen. Ah, but I didn't think it would be so soon. I'm a widow, I'm a widow, I'm widowed."

My father had been ill for what I then, still in my mid-twenties, considered a long time. Three years earlier a heart murmur, left by a childhood bout of rheumatic fever, had turned out to be the sign of a damaged mitral valve that started to deteriorate badly. My father was a relatively young man—only fifty-four when this problem was diagnosed—but the doctors were gloomy about his prospects. They said his heart was sick, couldn't pump properly. Without the artificial mitral valve cardiologists had only recently devised, they said he'd certainly die of heart failure within a few years. So far the valve replacement surgery was 80 percent successful, meaning, in those early days of cardiac operations, that it had a mortality rate of 20 percent. My father, who had a master's degree in civil engineering, had refused the surgery because he didn't like those odds.

"They just called me, he had a heart attack, he was trying to push the button for the nurse, they just called me right now, they must have just found him." I could still hear my mother's voice—a Sicilian voice on the verge of a scream—spilling out of the receiver.

"Oh, I'm so sorry, Mother," my husband said very slowly, as if by speaking in a calm, slow way he could calm her also. "But here's your daughter; let me put Sandra on."

"I'm a widow, Sandra, a widow now," my mother cried into the phone as I sat up in bed, gripping the receiver with one hand and the bedclothes with the other. "A widow!" Her voice finally broke into the wail that had been building since her first minute on the phone.

Only that afternoon I had visited my father in the hospital, where he'd spent the last two weeks with what we were told was a cardiac infection. I went that day not merely for an ordinary visit but to show him a copy of a letter offering me a fellowship for the following year. I was an only child—hence, perhaps, a symbolic son as well as a cherished daughter—so maybe that's why my father had always wanted me to go to graduate school, why he was furious when I married at twenty and went to live near a German army base instead of accepting an earlier offer to continue my studies in English. Now, after a detour that included the calamitous loss of a premature baby—my first child—and the joyful births of three others, who were thriving, I was back in school and sure my award letter would make him happy.

That afternoon my father was gaunt, pale, and clammy in his white hospital gown, but I imagine he thought, as we all did, that this El Greco look was only temporary; it was the way a person looked who had to take endless diuretics in order to get down to what his doctors defined as "dry weight" so his heart could pump more efficiently. Then, when the person recovered—for surely this unpleasant episode through which he was passing wasn't the promised end—and left the hospital and drank the proper fluids, surely then he'd resume his usual shape, like one of those Japanese paper flowers that unfold and thicken if you put them in water.

When I handed him my letter, he was sitting so taut and high in his bed that I could all too easily see just how emaciated he was. "I can't wait to get out of here, Sandra," he'd said, not looking at the letter, "can't wait to get home." He seemed to have so much excess nervous energy that his fingers were twitching on the starchy hospital counterpane, plucking at the crisp white cotton.

"Maybe you can go home tomorrow, daddy," I'd said hopefully. (But I really believed it.) "Isn't it nice about my fellowship?"

"Yes, it's nice, it's nice," he said, his fingers still twitching. "I've got to get out of here!"

Maybe a year later, when I reread *Henry V* for an exam, I understood what had been happening. " *'For after I saw him fumble with the sheets, and play with flowers . . . I knew there was but one way,' "* says the hostess, describing the death of Falstaff. *He fumbled with the sheets and he plucked at the counterpane, as the dying often do.*[1]

"I knew it would happen, but I didn't think it would be so soon," my mother lamented again. "I'm a widow. So soon! So soon!"

What did I do when she and I finally got off the phone? Snuggled down next to Elliot probably, burrowed into the warmth of our bed like an animal going to cover. By now we'd turned on the lights. Outside, the blackest part of the night hung beyond the windows, the after-midnight blackness when there were no cars on the long avenue outside our big, shabby old house. It was warm and still in the lamplight; I could hardly see the wallpaper roses that looped around our room, but I must have felt that, like Elliot, they were holding me close, safe in my coupledness, safe in my milky young maternity, though yes, there was some secret sickening knowledge they were holding at bay too.

At that moment my father's death had almost less reality for me than the death of my baby, *the* baby, as I always called him even after my other babies had been born. Or it had the same status. Both deaths were implausible, ridiculous. A three-day-old shred of life named Stephen Michael shouldn't have been born prematurely in the first place—and certainly shouldn't have died—and a fifty-seven-year old man, nervily alert and twitching with energy: What could it mean to say such a man had *died*? Why was my mother keening on the phone? I was stony-hearted, numb.

KEENING/KISSING

The death became more real to me, a day later, when I saw my father in his coffin at the funeral "home" just up the hill from our house, although at first the body laid out in the stuffy "parlor," surrounded by reeking masses of flowers, didn't look very much like my real father but instead like a wax effigy of the man I'd known all my life, and an angry effigy at that. There was a hard twist to the mouth, as if someone had just erased a reproachful grimace, and a blankness to the brow, as if the same kind soul had smoothed away a scowl.

To my mother, though, my father must have looked perfectly real and plausible. All day she sat near his body, next to his eighty-year-old Russian mother, who also sat there all day. As if by mutual agreement they sat one on each side of the polished mahogany casket where the effigy of my father lay, humiliatingly exposed to prying eyes in all his stony almost-anger.

Every once in a while my grandmother, round and small in swaths of black, would get up and go to the head of the coffin and stroke my father's forehead and kiss it, as if she were trying to comfort him, as if she were the one who had been smoothing away his scowls. It was her right as a mother, her gesture seemed to say, to pet him this way. Her strokes were tiny yet not tentative, quick tiny capable touchings like the urgent licks a cat gives her kittens, and as she stroked, I could see that she was almost inaudibly muttering something to herself, probably one of the Russian prayers I had heard her say so often during my childhood.

In such a way, like such a mother-animal, I soothed my own children when they were frightened or feverish. In such a way I would have soothed *the* baby who died, had he not died too soon for me ever to have touched him after the long night of labor in the army hospital and the terrible dawn in which he was expelled from my body.

When my grandmother went to the head of the coffin to comfort my father with her quick touches, my mother often also rose and went to the coffin—to *speak* to him. "Alex, Alex*ei*," she cried, in the high metallic voice of Sicilian keening that we had first heard on the phone that night, "Alex"—giving the first syllable theatrical weight—"*Ollex*,"—as if by addressing him so dramatically she could best communicate with him, "*Ollex*, you were too young, it was too soon, I wasn't ready . . ." and then maybe some words in Sicilian that I didn't understand.

"*I* wasn't ready." "*I'm* a widow."

Why did she emphasize herself that way? I wondered. Why did she keep reiterating the fate of the *I* who was doing the lamenting rather than the sorrowful end of the *he* who was the subject of the lamentation?

While my mother half shrieked at my dead father—melodramatically, it seemed to me—my little black-shawled grandmother stood silently at the head of the coffin, still quickly, urgently stroking his forehead or now and then dipping her lips toward his brow to give him a tiny kiss in a gesture that looked almost like *sipping*, as if grandma were sipping or tasting what was left of her beloved only son.

My grandmother was making these stroking-kissing-sipping movements as I entered what I sardonically considered the "so-called parlor" of the "so-called home." A wave of sickly perfume from the masses of "so-called floral tributes" surrounding the coffin seemed to break over my head, shocking and frightening me with its hint of vegetable decay.

Like most young people of my generation, my century, my country, I'd had hardly any experience of death. When my baby died, the nurses snatched his minuscule body out of sight, whisked it off to some refrigerated holding station and thence into the small white coffin that was all I ever saw of him again, a gleaming box about the size of the ones florists use for roses.

Panicky and embarrassed, I stared at my grandmother, who was kissing and stroking my father as if licking her young. Perhaps kissing was the thing to do.

"Oh, daddy." I approached the coffin nervously, leaned toward my father, looking yet not looking at his angrily twisted mouth, his bizarre pallor, and let my mouth rest a minute on his forehead.

Stone. Shock of stone, taste of cold stone even through closed lips. Ice on the tongue, steel in the throat.

I was astonished. How could grandma be kissing, stroking, sipping at *that*? What was *that*? Surely *it* was nothing to do with me, not my warm, funny father, not the jokey ex-altar boy who used to begin our dinner preparations hovering in the doorway of our closet-size Jackson Heights kitchen, martini glass in hand, lowering his chef's apron over his head, and hilariously intoning, "*In nomine patris et filius et spiritus sanctus.*" Oh, in the name of the Father and the Son and the Holy Ghost, this was not *that* father.

Yet my mother too seemed to recognize this effigy, this *thing*, as something to which she was related, leaning toward *it* and crying hysterically *at* it, "Alex, Alex*ei*, it was too soon, I wasn't ready."

Why "*I* wasn't ready"? Why not "*you* weren't ready"? Stonyhearted and shocked by the stone of my father's body, I was utterly alienated from my mother's grief and, worse, the sense of doom implicit in her "*I* wasn't ready," with its assertion that death had somehow happened to *her* as well as, or even rather than, my father. Maybe in fact the shock of the kiss that had seemed to coat my lips with some kind of toxic ice had alienated me from my father's death too, as much as from my mother's lamentations. In a few weeks I was to write a poem in which I struggled to measure the distance between me and the fearful thing I had encountered in the coffin dominating that "so-called parlor."

"I am far away from you," it begins, and then a stanza later goes on to formulate what I now realize was numbness, repression, denial:

I am astonished by my calm.
Have you really left me no pain?
The enormous sky, floodlit by thunder,
recalls your cold home—

the comforting grass,
the black socket of stone
in which you are fixed
like a blind eye, directionless.[2]

Death had sealed my real father away from me, closed his eyes to me, and lured him off in a "directionless" direction I couldn't and wouldn't recognize.

But now I think I know that death had opened for my mother, opened and become not only a plausible but an inescapable part of her just as it had, in a different way, for my grandmother. My grandmother kissed and stroked her son as if by proffering enough caresses, she could take him back into the heat of her own life, the body that had given him birth, and, by incorporating his death into herself, console him, redress the insult to his heart, even reconceive and rebear or repair him. My mother cried out again and again to my father because she didn't imagine him as a "blind eye, directionless": his eyes were open to her as hers were to him; she was *with* him in his death, addressing him directly as, in her dialogue (not monologue) of lamentation, he directed his dead gaze back at her. In her mind, he answered her apostrophes of "Alex, Alexei, I wasn't ready" with a silent prosopopoeia, a speech of absence that she heard as presence.

Maybe, then, my mother's "I'm a widow" wasn't, as I crankily felt at the time, a narcissistic self-dramatization that disregarded the suffering of the dead man, but instead an acknowledgment of the "reality of death" for the one who has lost the *other* and in particular for the woman who has lost a man. According to the *Oxford English Dictionary*, the word "widow" comes from the Indo-European *widhwe*, meaning "to be empty, to be separated," to be "divided," "destitute," or "lacking." Death has entered the widow, this etymology implies, and she has entered death, for she is filled with vacancy and has dissolved into a void, a state of lack or non-being that is akin to, if not part of, the state into which the dead person has journeyed, fallen, or been drawn.

What my mother knew, then, what she was saying as she cried, "I'm a widow," with that metallic edge of amazement at discovering herself in a new *place*—the place of death—was what I wasn't to discover until more than a quarter of a century later, when *my* husband died and death so surprisingly opened its dark doors to me too.

PLATH'S ETYMOLOGY

Of course a poet needn't be herself a widow to try to grasp the widow's special relationship to loss, the bereaved wife's sense of death's plausibility. In 1961, a few years before my father died, Sylvia Plath had drafted a poem on which I was to brood repeatedly over the years, as I thought about my mother's grief. Perhaps it was Plath's early, traumatic loss of her own father—or perhaps, even more likely, it was what evidently became her embittering intimacy with her own mother's mourning—that caused this acolyte of the thesaurus and the dictionary to focus the piece (simply entitled "Widow") so intensely on the dreadful etymology of the very word we use to define a woman whose husband has died.

"Widow. The word consumes itself—" is how Plath's poem begins, "consumes itself" perhaps precisely in the sense of vacating itself or emptying itself out, and she goes on to describe the word as a "dead syllable, with its shadow / Of an echo."[3] "Wid" or *widh O* is what she must have been thinking of. And thinking too that *widh* leads to the French *vide*, meaning "empty," or indeed, in an English word that chimes with it, "*void.*" "*Vide–Oh!*" says the poet. Or "*Void, oh,*" maybe even "*Shad-ow*" or "*Shade-oh!*" Yet the shade, says Plath also, is *with* the widow, in her and on her, as she enters the "dead syllable" of her newly empty life, "with its shadow / Of an echo." For "Death is the dress" the widow "wears," adds Plath, "her hat and collar," as if the death of the husband has annihilated, *nullified*, the wife too. Did all those growing-up years with a widowed mother, years haunted by depression and deprivation, teach this poet that?

In her fifth stanza, Plath confronts the metaphysical implications of such philology even more directly:

Widow: that great, vacant estate!
The voice of God is full of draftiness,

Promising simply the hard stars, the space
Of immortal blankness between stars
And no bodies, singing like arrows up to heaven.

For the author of "Ariel," that mad gallop in verse, life had to be all forward motion, all urgency and drive. Esther Greenwood, the heroine of *The Bell Jar*, wanted to shoot off like a set of arrows into the future. Widowhood must have seemed at the very least the "stasis in darkness" of "Ariel," at worst the "O-gape of complete despair" that settles over "The Moon and the Yew Tree," a piece (written a few months after "Widow") in which, as if in an echo of the dead echoes that must have shaped her mother's grief and perhaps her own, the poet encounters a place inhabited by "[f]umy, spiritous mists," a place "[s]eparated from my house by a row of headstones."[4]

"Fumy, spiritous mists": the widow both longs and fears to confront such manifestations of the lost one who may be reaching toward her from the realm of the dead. Plath's "Widow" ends, eerily, with an examination of such ambivalence, zeroing in on the way the widow, "a shadow-thing" herself, yearns toward the disembodied shade her husband has become. "A bodiless soul could pass another soul" in the "clear air" of "immortal blankness between stars," the poet worries, "and never notice it—." This, she concludes, is the deepest fear the widow has: the fear that her dead husband's soul "may beat and be beating at her dull sense" like an invisible messenger, beating hopelessly outside the window of a "gray, spiritless room / It looks in on, and must go on looking in on." Remember Nigel Barley's anthropological observation: in many cultures around the world, it's, "above all[,] the dead that feel desperate grief and loneliness."[5] They miss us, need us, and struggle to "look in on" us, perhaps in the sense of paying us desperate visits—like, say, Hamlet's father—as they "go on looking in on" the kingdom of the living from which they've been banished.

"I am thy father's spirit, / Doomed for a certain term to walk the night." So Hamlet learned. Doomed to look "in on, and . . . go on looking in on" our unattainable lives. So Plath may have decided. Thus, doomed to look "in on" and perpetually "go on looking in on" the life that seeks unavailingly to go on looking back at them, such shades invade Plath's widow with the shadow of their own emptiness, draining her soul of its own being so that ultimately she herself becomes an incarnation of *nothing*: a "gray, spiritless room."[6]

"Spiritless," though? My mother—keening, calling—was, if anything, fuller of animation than usual. "Alex, Alex," she cried, as if in "waking" the dead with her wails of dismay, she suddenly understood herself to be some-how living, now, not for the one that was herself—*had been* herself—but for the two that she had become, a double self that incorporated the being of my dead father into her own being. Yes, death opens to the widow, becomes plausible in ways I didn't understand as I listened, vaguely scandalized, to what I considered my mother's half-mad dialogue with my dead father. But the speech I heard wasn't coming from a "spiritless" place. Surely some of the emptiness Plath attributes to the "great vacant estate" of the widow as she follows the etymology of the word to a dark, only half-legitimate root in *vide-oh!*—surely some of this emptiness isn't what the widow herself experiences when death opens its door to her, surely it's what her culture tells her and those around her that she's experiencing or *ought* to be experiencing.

Standing by my father's coffin, keening her lament to his dead *being*, my mother wasn't gray or vacant. She was a cage crowded with a thousand birds shrieking their grief and anger—hers *and* his. Reproaching my husband for his untimely death, as I was to do a little more than a quarter of a century later, I myself wasn't a gray and spiritless room either—more, rather, a chamber of rage and despair, mine *and* his.

For after all, it's the society that defines the maiden as an empty cipher, a virginal blankness, and the matron as a feme covert (Angelo-Norman for the French *femme couvert*), a woman concealed or enclosed in the blanket of her husband's authority. Surely it's this society that asserts the widow's emptiness and not the widow herself. "Man and wife is one being," says the ancient English law, "and *he* is that being." "By marriage," wrote the eighteenth-century jurist William Blackstone, "the very being or legal exis-tence of a woman is suspended, or at least it is incorporated or consolidated into that of the husband, under whose wing, protection, and cover she per-forms everything, and she is therefore called in our law a *feme covert*."[7]

And Blackstone was merely rephrasing a concept that had governed the lives of women since the Middle Ages. Sometimes, in fact, in both England and America, marriage was called "civil death". But if the husband is dead, then the wife must be dead too. Or at least she must be a gray, spiritless room, a vacancy yearning toward numbness, annihilation.

This is how William Carlos Williams portrays the widow in his sensitive and lovely "Widow's Lament in Springtime," a lyric written for his mother not long after his father's death:

> . . . *Thirtyfive years*
> *I lived with my husband.*

The plumtree is white today
with masses of flowers . . .
but the grief in my heart
is stronger than they. . . .
Today my son told me
that in the meadows,
at the edge of the heavy woods
in the distance, he saw
trees of white flowers.
I feel that I would like
to go there
and fall into those flowers
and sink into the marsh near them.[8]

SATI

I would like to sink into that marsh. Does this notion of the widow's helpless passivity—her nullity—explain the vexed, now nearly nonexistent but always terrifying Indian practice of *sati*? In *Sati: Widow Burning in India*, an incisive exploration of this custom, the Bombay journalist and writer Sakuntala Narasimhan has noted that since in traditional Hindu culture "a woman's salvation lay in the service of her husband, it followed that she lost her *raison d'être* the moment her husband died [so that] widowhood came to be seen as the worst calamity that could ever befall a woman . . . because it practically invalidated her continued existence." In some Indian languages, adds Narasimhan, "the word for widow is an insult and a curse . . . in Tamil euphemism, a widow is referred to as a woman 'who does not live anymore' (even if she is alive)."[9] Shades of the Indo-European *widh O*, or of Plath's implied *vide-oh!*, the moan of the daughter-onlooker observing the "great vacant estate" of widowhood!

Is the lady for burning, then, because she's useless as used-up stationery, nuller than yesterday's news? I now realize that Plath's poem actually begins with a reference to sati: "Widow. The word consumes itself—/Body, a sheet of newsprint on the fire." But as commentators on the concept of sati have observed, the woman bent on such self-immolation is not strictly a *widow* but still a *wife*, since she's determined to die with her husband rather than endure what Plath (and the transcultural precepts that must have helped shape Plath's thought) define as the "vacancy" of widowhood. In a study of "Sati Tradition in Rajasthan," the anthropologist Lindsey Harlan writes that "when a woman utters her sati vow, she places herself in the context of a vivid temporal fiction. Time is condensed, so that she becomes a *sahagamini*, 'one who goes (*gamini*) together (*saha*) with one's husband.'"[10]

In *this* death narrative of female grief, then, the lady's not for burning because she *is*, already, burning. Adds Harlan: the "Rajput *sativrata's* death is thought to be a manifestation of her goodness, her *sat* . . . which is a moral heat. . . . It is said that when [she] learns of her husband's death, this heat begins to consume her body. So the woman who has taken a sincere *vrat* of sati quite literally becomes too hot to touch." Not only too hot, though, but also too eerily potent. "During the period between the *sati vrat* and the sati's death, a woman is considered extremely powerful. Because she has renounced life, she has in a sense progressed beyond life. She possesses special powers, among them the power to curse[,] . . . the power to establish prohibitions," and ultimately, when she is transformed into a *satimata*, a kind of saint, the power "to protect her earthly household" from her special place in eternity.[11]

But from a Western perspective too, there's something alarmingly apocalyptic in the burning rage and grief of the bereft wife. Consider, after all, the paradoxically empowered and exultant lament that Richard Wagner wrote for Brünnhilde, the warrior woman who is the heroine of his great *Ring* cycle. Remember, here, that Brünnhilde is an *ex*-Valkyrie; once, along with her Valkyrie sisters, she was an immortal who collected the bodies of heroes dead in battle, but she lost her divinity when she defied her father, the god-king Wotan, and was thereby condemned not just to mortality but to the humiliations as well as the pleasures of human love. Now, though, as she commands the lighting of her husband Siegfried's funeral pyre, she sings in triumph of her ecstatic reentry into the other world of the gods— and the dead:

Greetings, Grane, my horse.
Do you know, friend,
Where I am leading you?
In the blazing fire
Lies your master, . . .
Feel how my breast also burns . . .
To be wed
In the most powerful Love!—
Hi-ho! Grane!
Greet our friend!

Siegfried! Siegfried!
Let my greeting bless you.[12]

And of course we know what's going to happen. We know that the sheer fire of Brünnhilde's grief is going to consume the world and, most terribly, Valhalla, the heavenly home of the father god who cursed her. *Götterdämmerung*, the name of the last opera in Wagner's *Ring*, means "twilight of the gods," but this is no gentle gray-blue evening; *this* twilight issues in an explosion of female passion, a vengefully blazing sunset.

Is it the power, not the emptiness, of the widow that unnerves the world, not just her rage and grief but the sudden, mysteriously privileged access to the other world that such rage and grief bestow? Did I sense something alarmingly uncanny in my own mother's keening, her weird address to what I myself merely perceived as the absence graven on my father's icy forehead? In many cultures, writes the classicist Gail Holst-Warhaft in a fine study of the relationship between traditional female lamentation and Greek literature, "women and men are perceived and expected to mourn in different ways." Men, she argues, tend to defuse and politicize grief in public eulogies or else, as I myself have argued elsewhere, in ceremonial elegies. Thus, although both women and men "weep for their dead . . . it is women," declares Holst-Warhaft, "who tend to weep longer, louder, and *it is they who are thought to communicate directly with the dead through their wailing songs* [emphasis added]."[13]

THE WIDOWER'S EXEQUY

Not that widowers don't also grieve, often in deeply personal, intimate language. (The word "widower" here should really stand for any man who mourns a dead beloved.) C. S. Lewis's *A Grief Observed*, one of the twentieth century's classic bereavement texts, is a record of one man's sorrow at his wife's death and of his insight that grief "feels like fear" or "like waiting," giving "life a permanently provisional feeling," as the survivor merely endures "pure time, empty successiveness" while hopelessly anticipating the return of the one who has traveled to the other side of silence.[14] And before Lewis mourned the death of the wife so tellingly named Joy, Thomas Hardy struggled to get beyond the wall of silence, to "communicate directly with the dead" through the "wailing songs" he included in his *Poems 1912*, another classic text of modern grief. In "After a Journey," he even convinced himself that he was really *looking at* the specter of his dead wife Emma.

"Hereto I come to view a voiceless ghost," he began that poem, as we've seen. The first draft of the piece is still more explicit in its determination to cross the border between the living and the dead. "Hereto I come to *interview* a ghost [emphasis added]" was Hardy's initial assertion, as, in one critic's words, he called "out to a nearby but unseen spirit, asking it to pull him onward" as well as to show itself to him.[15]

Douglas Dunn, Peter Davison, Paul Monette, Ted Hughes, Donald Hall—these are only a few of the recent male poets who have elegized lost beloveds, and especially the latest of these writers—Monette, Hughes, Hall—have at times strained with a passion very like Hardy's to address the invisible dead, if not exactly to "interview" them. But weren't Hardy's elegies for Emma innovative precisely because they swerved significantly from much masculine grief-work, at least as it has come down to us through a literary tradition in which a man mourns in highly structured, eloquently styled, and clearly resolved modes (the public eulogy, the pastoral elegy) and usually in fact mourns for another *man* rather than for a woman? Unresolved—*never* resolved—struggles to get beyond the grave, Hardy's poems take on certain qualities of the female-authored lament as opposed to the male-crafted elegy, reminding us that the English word "widower" is a back formation on our word "widow" and one of the few such formations in a language in which "actress" is generated from "actor," "poetess" from "poet," and so on.

In spousal loss, women are primary, men secondary. What change of title, after all, is required for a widow*er*? *He* was Mr. John Doe before the death of Jane and continues thus ever after. The widow, though, was Mrs. *John* Doe before her husband's demise and after his death reverts to a part (but not the whole) of her single, unadorned self, or so Emily Post admonishes her to do: *John* having departed this earth, his widow must now be Mrs. *Jane* Doe, unless a Bill or Joe Doe or Smith or Jones comes along to replace the lost John. And as many sociologists have observed, her loss of her husband and at least part of the name he bestowed on her is reflected by a loss of social status that isn't paralleled by any comparable loss of position for the widower.

In Samuel Beckett's *Krapp's Last Tape*, the gloomily aging protagonist, musing on his mother's death following a "long viduity," becomes so obsessed with the word "viduity" that he looks it up in "an enormous dictionary":

> KRAPP: (*reading from dictionary*) State—or condition—of being—or
> remaining—a widow—or widower. (*Looks up. Puzzled.*) Being—or

remaining? . . . (Pause. He peers again at dictionary. Reading.) "Deep
weeds of viduity." . . . Also of an animal, especially a bird . . . the vidua or
weaver-bird. . . . Black plumage of male. . . . (He looks up. With relish.) The
vidua-bird![16]

"Black plumage of male": the "vidua-bird" of Krapp's ruminations, and the
relish with which Krapp contemplates his finery, should remind us too that
when widower's weeds aren't borrowed from a historically female tradition
of lamentation, they draw on other, historically masculine funeral
traditions.

Maybe the most famous utterance of a widower poet was the
seventeenth-century "Exequy" that Bishop Henry King produced after the
death of his much-loved young wife, a highly stylized and prayerful statement that the twentieth-century British poet Peter Porter copied generations later in an "Exequy" of his own, for *his* much-loved young wife. Unlike
Hardy, or those writers like, say, Monette and Hall, who have followed in
Hardy's "falteringly" confessional footsteps, King is lavishly ceremonial.
And clearly he expects neither reply nor "interview" from the "Matchless,
Never-to-Be-Forgotten Friend" in whose honor he writes:

> *Accept, thou shrine of my dead saint,*
> *Instead of dirges, this complaint;*
> *And for sweet flowers to crown thy hearse,*
> *Receive a strew of weeping verse.*

Unlike Hardy, King speaks not to a ghost but to a structure, a "shrine." And
though Porter doesn't distance his dead wife quite so thoroughly, he is certainly frank about his adoption of the ritual flourishes that marked his carefully chosen precursor's verse:

> *This introduction serves to sing*
> *Your mortal death as Bishop King*
> *Once hymned in tetrametric rhyme*
> *His young wife, lost before her time.*

Maybe the distinction between the ceremonial mode of these exequies
and the more personal genre of lamentation lies in the etymologies of the
words that define the genres themselves. "Exequy," meaning "funeral rite,"
very likely originates in the Indo-European *sekw*, "to follow," while "lamen-

tation," meaning "an expression of grief," probably comes from the Indo-European *la*, meaning "to mutter," "to lull," to "sing a lullaby," or even "to talk." So the exequy is a ritual of *following* and in fact *distancing*; it is public, performative, oratorical, while the lamentation is intimate, private, oral, informal. The widower, in his "black plumage," often stands apart from his loss, enshrining it in solemn measures, while the widow more frequently mutters or croons a lullaby to the lost one.

Yet don't the genres of exequy and lament ultimately refer not just to loss and not primarily to the *dis*embodied ghost but to the body itself, the corpse of the departed, whose washing is in most cultures the business of women? In traditional Greek villages, Holst-Warhaft tells us, "At the wake, when females related . . . to the deceased surround the coffin, squabbles may break out over both singing and sitting positions."[17] (Can this be why my mother and my grandmother sat one on each side of my father's coffin, warily balancing each other?)

"The women," adds Holst-Warhaft, "demonstrate their closeness to the deceased not only through . . . song or spoken testimony, but by direct physical contact, touching and caressing the hair or head of the corpse or holding the forehead." (Does this explain the kissing, even the apparent *sipping* my Russian grandma did? The keening and caressing my Sicilian mother did?) But when "the male relatives enter to pay their respects, their behavior is strikingly different. They remain in small groups on the margin . . . or wait at the entrances [for in] 'contrast to the linguistic, emotional and tactile intimacies of the women, men (including the priest) maintain a purely *visual* relation to the dead [emphasis added].' "[18] (Is it possible, then, that even Hardy's yearning toward "interview," with its overtones of expressive, "female" lamentation, comes from a "male" orientation to the visual?)

THE WIDOW'S LAMENT

Perhaps it's because in so many cultures women are so physically as well as psychically close to the dead that, according to Holst-Warhaft, one anthropologist has found in some settings "an underlying fear of laments as magic songs," sinister lullabies. Perhaps these female cries and whispers of loss seem to "open up perilous channels of communication between the living and the dead" as the lamenter becomes a "medium through whom the dead speaks to the living," a "shaman who leads the living to the underworld and back."[19]

Holst-Warhaft gives as an example of such a risky song the famous Irish "Lament for Art O'Leary," which was "composed by O'Leary's widow, Black

Eileen, for the second burial of her husband, who died in 1773 . . . shot on the run as an outlaw." In the stanzas quoted here, Eileen discovers and begins to lament O'Leary's death. "My friend and my love!" she cries:

> *I knew nothing of your murder*
> *Till your horse came to the stable*
> *With the reins beneath her trailing,*
> *And your heart's blood on her shoulders*
> . . . .
> *I struck my hands together*
> *And made the bay horse gallop*
> *As fast as I was able,*
> *Till I found you dead before me*
> *Beside a little furze-bush. . . .*
> *Your heart's blood was still flowing;*
> *I did not stay to wipe it*
> *But filled my hands and drank it.*
>
> *My love you'll be forever!*
> *Rise up from where you're lying*
> *And we'll be going homewards.*
> *We'll have a bullock slaughtered,*
> *We'll call our friends together,*
> *We'll get the music going.*
> *I'll make a fine bed ready*
> *With sheets of snow-white linen,*
> *And fine embroidered covers*
> *That will bring the sweat out through you*
> *Instead of the cold that's on you!*

Not only disturbingly tactile and erotic but scandalously oral, the "drama of Eileen's ride . . . leads to an act that fills us with horror [her drinking of O'Leary's blood] and breaks the boundaries between the living and the dead," notes Holst-Warhaft, "enabling the lamenting woman to call up her husband and invite him to feast and lie with her again."[20]

Even today women poets who have been widowed dramatize moments of transgressive communion with the dead that bear a striking similarity to Eileen's fierce address to her murdered husband. Plath, after all, drafted "Widow" from the position of a daughter, repelled by what she experienced as the "vacancy" of her mother's "estate," just as Williams composed his "Widow's Lament in Springtime" from the position of a son, (re)constructing his mother's grief. But two recent American writers, Tess Gallagher and Ruth Stone, speak specifically as widows themselves. The impassioned elegies for Raymond Carver that Gallagher collects in *Moon Crossing Bridge* (and note the boundary breaking, the border *crossings*, implied by that title) record moments of strange conjugal dialogue, silent but full of meaning.

"Three nights you lay in our house," recalls Gallagher in a lyric entitled "Wake," "Three nights in the chill of the body," but:

> In the room's great dark
> I climbed up beside you onto our high bed. . . .
> There was a halo of cold around you
> as if the body's messages carry farther
> in death. . . . We were dead
> a little while together then, serene
> and afloat on the strange broad canopy
> of the abandoned world.[21]

Two equally erotic elegies by Ruth Stone are perhaps even more shocking in the powerful candor of their dialogue not just with the dead but in a sense with death itself. In her openly necrophiliac "Habit," for example, Stone confesses to her husband, twenty years dead:

> Every day I dig you up
> And wipe off the rime
> And look at you. . . .
> Your waist drops a little putrid flesh.
> I show you my old shy breasts.

And in "Becoming You" Stone's fantasy of devouring her dead husband, of literally *incorporating* him into herself, even more directly recalls Eileen's drinking of O'Leary's blood. Burning with an intensity that parallels Brünnhilde's passion, this piece is marked by a frankness that might be terrifying were it not so loving:

> I think about territory
> And how you invaded my skin.
> Now, I shall grow

Until I encompass you.
There in your box,
Barefoot in your best suit. . . .
I am everywhere growing larger . . .
As, taking my time,
I come on digesting you.[22]

In her voracious desire to cross the bridge between the living and the
dead and incorporate her husband's ghost into her own, does the widow-
poet seem to become a kind of shaman? But in that case, if she's thought to
have special access to the supernatural, the widow has to be defined as
"empty"—*Vide-oh! Shade-oh!*—because she's less dangerous that way.
Brünnhilde burns up the world and brings down the gods. Eileen O'Leary
crosses borders between life and death. Even contemporary women like
Gallagher and Stone appear weirdly empowered to speak to ghosts. My own
mother frightened me, shrieking beside my father's coffin. Perhaps onlookers shiver at the widow's uncanny access to the other world in the same way
that culture shudders, more generally, at woman's potency, as if the power
to give birth must be matched by an equal power to take back the gift of life.

THE WIDOW'S DESIRE

Think of the "black widow" spider, devouring her mate in a paroxysm of
necrophiliac abandon. Think, for that matter, of Juana la Loca, Renaissance
queen of Spain and Flanders, whose mind supposedly "snapped under the
strain of [her husband's] death" so that she "would not be parted from his
coffin." Do some of us secretly believe that grief induces spasms of perverse
desire in bereft women? As if in imitation of Juana, the infamous nineteenth-
century Princess Belgiojoso, whom Mario Praz called a "'cracked vessel' [suf-
fering] from profound nervous disorders," was found in 1848 to have kept
"in a cupboard" of her villa "the embalmed corpse of her young secretary
and lover . . . who had died of consumption a short time before."[23] And the
perhaps misunderstood principessa herself had a number of fictional mim-
ics, ranging from the protagonist of Rider Haggard's *She* to the subject of
William Faulkner's "A Rose for Emily," grievously erotic (and apparently
*neu*rotic) women who fetishistically possessed and were possessed by the
bodies of dead beloveds. Have such women been culturally defined as
heiresses of the black widow spider's cunning—and "her" murderous
desire?

At the same time, though, almost as troublesome as the monstrous desire of the "black widow" may be the possibility that the unnervingly self-possessed widow feels *no such desire*! What if, like the infamous "merry widow," she is just, cheerily, *for* and *in* herself, *of* herself, *to* herself? In other words, what if the widow is utterly delighted to be relieved of that burden called a husband and freed, instead, to be a seductress of whom it might be said, as Oscar Wilde put it about one of his more lubricious female characters: "Her hair has gone quite gold from grief"?[24]

Indian widows are admonished to wear white, sleep on straw mats rather than in beds, and avoid meats and spices, any food that might "heat the blood" and, by implication, stir desire. The purity of the dead man's wife must be guarded with caution, this custom suggests; otherwise her raging sexuality, awakened in marriage, might be given to some interloper who would take unto himself the libido that was destined only for her lawful husband.

As if to comment on the problems posed by mature female sexuality (and the vulnerability felt by men of all ages), Maxine Hong Kingston offers in *China Men* a parable of how death came into the world. Maui the Trickster, she explains, sought "immortality for men and women by stealing it from Hina [the goddess] of the night." So he "dived into the ocean, where he found great Hina asleep. Through her vagina like a door, he entered her body. He took her heart in his arms. He had started tunneling out feet first when a bird [laughed] at the sight of his legs wiggling out. . . . Hina awoke and shut herself, and Maui died."[25]

In her grief and fury, the widow wants only to speak to the dead one, to sustain and preserve him. But from the perspective of those outside her grief, her desirous speech is both awesome and awful. If she seeks to absorb her dead husband, she is as mad as Juana, as perverse as Princess Belgiojoso and Faulkner's Emily! And maybe she can swallow up life too—like Hina, like Brünnhilde! At the same time, suppose she just wakes up from the long dream called marriage, "shut[s] herself," and goes back to dreams of her *own*, perhaps disturbingly fierce pleasures.

Those of us still safe in our dailiness fear such voracity just as men often fear female power. In a psychoanalytic commentary on Lindsey Harlan's examination of the sati tradition in Rajasthan, Karen McCarthy Brown observes that when the sativrata "mounts the funeral pyre [she] takes the body of her husband into her lap, in a breastfeeding posture," at which point her body supposedly "explodes into flames." Thus, argues Brown, as "he feeds on her, she eats him up and, most important, devours herself as well. The nurturing woman and the devouring woman become one through a process in which fire transforms the [potentially] rapacious, willful bad mother"—the mother who curses and destroys—"into a self-devouring good mother." And even if this primarily psychocultural analysis doesn't sufficiently decipher the complex meanings that the very notion of sati has taken on in India over the centuries, in a Western context it helps explain some of the ambivalence associated with the status of the widow as a grieving woman who seems to have been simultaneously emptied of her former social role and filled with a new power to mediate between the ordinary human world of the living and the mysteriously *in*human world of ghosts.

But in her scary stance between the quick and the dead, the widow takes on some of the morbid glamour that the great American modernist Wallace Stevens attributed to the earth mother in "Madame La Fleurie," one of his most eccentric and moving late poems. In this grim text, the poet offers readers what he calls a "handbook of heartbreak" in which he elegizes a dead friend who has been swallowed up, like Maui, by the death mother. "He looked in a glass of the earth and thought he lived in it," the poet writes, but "Now, he brings all that he saw into the earth, to the waiting parent." Yet the dead man's "grief is that his mother should feed on him, himself and what he saw," as if earth in "her" role of mother goddess were really "a bearded queen, wicked in her dead light."[26]

A transgressive and *phallic* (bearded!) mother: is that what the widow becomes in the misty places of the cultural unconscious? Must we therefore define her as empty precisely because we fear she's full? Or worse, has her fearsome fullness made her coextensive with death itself?

MR. LOWELL AND THE SPIDER

The ferocious conclusion of Robert Lowell's "Mr. Edwards and the Spider" actually makes such a claim. Throughout this brilliant monologue Lowell has drawn on imagery from the writings of Jonathan Edwards (his early *Of Insects*, his sermon entitled "Sinners in the Hands of an Angry God") to replicate the impassioned evangelism of America's most eloquent Puritan. The piece opens, in fact, with a paraphrase of the young Edwards's observations of spiders that "die / Urgently beating east to sunrise and the sea," then gradually develops a link between spiders that die with "no long struggle" and sinful souls with "abolished will." Yet in the poem's final stanza Lowell transforms the spider image, explicitly sexualizing death in a way Edwards did not. The Puritan preacher's formulation of an angry God's ultimate threat to the sinner is followed by the twentieth-century poet's own explosive interpretation of the darkness implicit in that threat, as Lowell links the infamous viduity of the "hourglass-blazoned spider" to the horrific blaze of consciousness that is eternal hellfire:

> *. . . picture yourself cast*
> *Into a brick-kiln where the blast*
> *Fans your quick vitals to a coal—*
> *   If measured by a glass,*
> *How long would it seem burning! Let there pass*
> *A minute, ten, ten trillion; but the blaze*
> *Is infinite, eternal: this is death,*
> *To die and know it. This is the Black Widow, death.*[27]

Lowell's leap away from Edwards's original text is as disquieting as it is dazzling. For even while the poet may well have intended simply to surface the misogynistic madness to which Edwards was heir, that brief, abrupt last sentence is thickened and darkened by countless cultural hints that what widowhood itself supposedly means (*to mourn and know it*) might at any moment dissolve into an awareness of obliteration (*to die and know it*) inexplicably fostered by the raging murderousness of the one who grieves (*to kill and know it*).

"I'm a widow, a widow, it's too soon, Alex, it's too soon," my mother told my father, wailing beside his coffin. Listening to her, I was embarrassed, bewildered, oddly anxious. Did I fear that shadows had already invaded and nullified her? Or did I secretly suppose that her keening signified the sudden immanence of "the Black Widow, death"?

3

Yahrzeit

WHY IS THIS DAY DIFFERENT FROM OTHER DAYS?

Paris. February 10, 2000. Nearly midnight. Nearly February 11, the ninth anniversary of Elliot's death. Tomorrow David and I are leaving for a month in the little Italian town of Bogliasco, just outside Genoa, where I have a residency at a villa that's been converted into a study center for artists and scholars, so I dash off a last e-mail to my kids back in the States, giving them our itinerary for the next three days, then add: "It seems very odd & sad to be starting on this journey on Feb. 11, but even if it's an inauspicious day perhaps it's not inappropriate, since I'm going to this place to work on my elegy book, now renamed 'Death's Door.'"

We're going to drive slowly to the Mediterranean coast, through Bourgogne, Switzerland, and northern Italy, not just so we can see some sights along the way but because I'm worried that overcome by a fog of mourning and melancholia, I might fall asleep at the wheel. What if, even though I'm distracted by beautiful villages and glittering Alps, I have what's called an "anniversary reaction" and get narcoleptic from grief? That's happened to me before. Many times, especially in the first months after Elliot died, I'd pass out in my chair, as if not only I but the world were sinking into sleep, poisoned by misery. When Keats wrote, "My heart aches and a drowsy numbness pains / My sense, as if of hemlock I had drunk," he wasn't suffering bereavement, unless it was anticipatory grief for his own rapidly approaching death, yet the narcoleptic feeling he records in "Ode to a Nightingale" is one I often associate with mourning: body and soul not wanting to stay awake, to be conscious. Clearly that's no state in which to be at the wheel, especially not in the Alps. So we'll go at a careful pace because David will do most of the driving, and I don't want him to have to keep at it eight hours a day.

David and I have been together for nearly seven years now, and he's always kind about the impulses to mourn that still master me from time to time. He understands quite well, I think, that one can love and grieve for the dead person who shaped the past even while loving and living with a new person who's central in the present. But as a "hard" scientist, a mathematician who theorizes games and economic strategies, he has trouble understanding what he considers my mystical tendency to brood on the chronological milestones that mark my personal narrative of loss. So I won't remind him of "the anniversary," although he knows the meaning February 11 has for me; over the years we have spent six such days together, with me usually planning each one well in advance.

But perhaps David's right to be skeptical about the anxiety with which, each year, I meet and meditate on this date. Why, after all, *isn't* this day a day like any other?

Mah nishtanah halailah hazeh,
Mikol haleilot? Mikol haleilot?

Sheb'chol haleilot, anu ochlin,
Chameits umatsah, chameits umatsah,
Halaylah hazeh, halaylah hazeh kulo matsa.
Halahlah hazeh, halaylah hazeh kulo matsa.

Why is this night different from other nights?
Why this night? Why this night?

On other nights we eat leavened bread,
Leavened bread and cakes,
But on this night, this night we eat matzoh,
On this night, this night we eat matzoh.

How is this day different from other days? And "*why is this night different from other nights?*" There was always an ironic edge in Elliot's voice when now and then, as a joke about something or someone, he used to intone those words from the Haggadah that structure the Jewish Passover ceremony. *On other nights,* Jewish parents tell their children, *we eat leavened bread. But on this night,* they say at the first evening meal of the seven-day feast that memorializes the journey of their ancestors across the Sinai, *we eat unleavened bread—matzoh—the raw stuff of affliction that we snatched from the ovens just before our flight out of Egypt, the flat bread we baked in the harsh sun of the desert. And on this night we eat bitter herbs, to remind us of the bitterness of our slavery and suffering in Egypt.*

Is commemoration—in particular the commemoration of suffering—a specifically Jewish theme? Certainly anniversaries of death, desperation, and disaster are built into ceremonies I came to know quite well through Elliot, secular though his Judaism was. Every winter, for example, on the anniversary of his father's death a Yahrzeit card (and sometimes, in the early days, a candle) arrived in our mailbox, courtesy of the Riverside Funeral Chapel, which had arranged Harry Gilbert's burial in 1970. At first I wasn't sure what this signified—*Yahrzeit? What's that?* I asked my husband—but after a while the ritual remembrance of ending, the commemoration of the *deathday*, began to seem as reasonable as the annual celebration of beginning, the commemoration of the *birthday*, with which we're so familiar.

The Yahrzeit—literally, in Yiddish, the "yeartime"—writes one chronicler of Jewish customs, "is the yearly anniversary of the death of a father, mother, [or other] relative [and there] is a universal Jewish custom to light a special candle which burns for at least 24 hours on the day of the *Yahrzeit*. This is an act of respect for the deceased." Equally important, on the day of the Yahrzeit the recital of the Kaddish, the ancient Hebrew prayer for the dead, can help the departed one "rise to higher levels in Gan Eden"—the Hebrew paradise—while because the Yahrzeit "is a time of judgment for the deceased," good deeds done on behalf of the dead person can also help the journeying soul.[1] For the marking of the Yahrzeit is part of a complex procedure that the living must undertake in order to ease the passage of the dead from our world toward the other, mysterious realm into which we imagine they must travel.

In Jewish mourning practice this procedure begins immediately after a death, when, for the first week, the bereaved "sit" shiva (meaning "seven") in their home, concentrating for seven severely focused days on their loss while sharing their grief and their memories of the dead one with visitors from the community. According to one commentator, the shiva candle, "*symbolic of the soul of the deceased* [emphasis added]," is "lit immediately on returning from the cemetery" to mark the beginning of this period, during which all must "sit low as a symbol of 'being brought low' in grief"; there must be "no 'luxurious' bathing or cutting hair" since "these are signs of vanity"; mirrors must be covered "for the same reason as not bathing"; "sexual relations are forbidden," as is almost any other "business as usual"; and "wherever possible," services are held in the household. On the morning of the seventh day, however, the ceremonial shiva candle "is blown out in silence," and the mourners go for "a walk around the block," not just "as a way of taking a first step back into the world" but also *to escort the soul out of the house*," demonstrating that the survivors *"are going to be all right"* in its absence (emphasis added).[2]

Yet still the Jewish soul would seem to be in transition from here to there, from "our" place to another one, for the seven-day period of shiva is followed by a second period of mourning called *Sheloshim* (meaning "thirty"), during which mourners avoid festive events and say Kaddish as often as possible, to speed the departing spirit on its way to "Gan Eden." And interestingly, some "follow the custom of not visiting the grave until after *Sheloshim*" (though others only wait until "after the Shiva period") as if, in a sense, the dead person had not at first quite settled into the tomb.

For those who have lost the most intimate relatives, moreover, there is yet another eleven-month period of grief, during which Kaddish must be recited, which rounds out to a year the time of *Avelut*, or mourning. During this period—or often at its conclusion, on the first anniversary of the death or funeral of anyone close—a *matzevah*, a tombstone or marker, is "placed on the grave and dedicated in a ceremony called 'unveiling' [during which a] cloth is removed from the stone in the presence of the immediate family and friends. . . . The top of the stone often has the Hebrew letters pay and nun standing for 'Here lies buried.' On the bottom are five Hebrew letters, tuf, nun, tzadi, bet, hay, meaning 'May his [her] soul be bound up in the bond of life eternal.' "

Now the dead one is in and of the earth and, it is hoped, has found some sort of rest there as well as in the bonds of a "life eternal" that is not just of the earth but, somehow, beyond or *without* the earth. Now too, or so this sequence of ceremonial practices implies, the living can free themselves from their anxieties about the fate of the wandering soul that was for a time so helplessly dependent on the prayers of survivors for aid on its journey.

CARING FOR THE DEAD

That we who are still alive must perform certain obligatory tasks so as to care for the needy dead is a powerful, nearly universal human belief, as numerous anthropological studies have suggested. The Chinese "feed" their ghosts with real or paper food and supply them with paper houses and paper automobiles, while those among the ancient Egyptians who had the means housed the bodies of their dead in solider mansions, elaborately furnished with the equipment of quotidian life. And from Africa to Oceania, Asia, and Alaska other peoples offer nourishment to the "departed," a term that in itself reminds us of the equally widespread impulse to imagine death as a journey that might well require material as well as spiritual provisions. "Have you built your ship of death, O have you?" asked D. H. Lawrence, anticipating his own death in a late poem that drew on Etruscan as well as Egyptian iconography. "O build your ship of death, for you will need it.

> O build your ship of death, your little ark
> and furnish it with food, with little cakes, and wine
> for the dark flight down oblivion.[3]

Yet surely the jobs we do for the dead are also jobs we do for ourselves— to reassure ourselves of our own worthiness, to ensure that others will take care of *us* when we are "gone" on the same journey, and, perhaps most important of all, to persuade ourselves that we're still somehow in *touch* with our vanished travelers and even, in a way, in *view* of them. Is the Yahrzeit, then, another way of staying connected to the dead, of imagining that we might pierce the cloud of unknowing that separates us from them? Does one feel, on "the anniversary," the nearness of the dead, as on All Souls' Day, when the veils or walls between "us" and "them" are thought most permeable?

I've always planned what I do on February 11 so carefully, hour by hour, because each hour evokes all too vividly the events of February 11, 1991, events I can't help recalling throughout the day, just as in a larger liturgical context Catholics trace the stations of the cross on the walls of churches. Maybe, like the stations of the cross, the sad plot of February 11, 1991, exists for me in a kind of eternal present that has to be ceaselessly reenacted with every annual recurrence of the fateful date: 6:00 A.M., now an orderly arrived—has again arrived!—to take my husband down to the surgery suite; 6:15 A.M., now he's once more saying good-bye to us; now, at 7:30 A.M., they once more, as in my mind they do every year, cut into his body, and now, at 11:15 the surgery is over and someone is moving him into the corridor, and now, yet again, it's 3:30 in the afternoon and he's alone in the recovery room, *now* he must be starting to bleed internally (though no one realizes), and now it's 6:30 in the evening and he's beginning to die (a nurse has noticed this and called for help), and now it's 7:30, the sky has gone dark, he's dying (though *we* don't know it, for my daughters and I are innocently waiting in the hospital lobby), and now, at 8:15, he *has* died, *now* he's dead.

Do I secretly believe, then, that if I recall and rehearse each of these events, hour by hour, I can somehow alter the configuration of the day through an act of remembrance so clear and fierce that it will revise the story of the death itself? At 3:30 in the afternoon, he's alone in the recovery room, starting to bleed internally—*but someone notices!* At 6:30 in the evening, he's *not* beginning to die—the doctors and nurses are hovering at his bedside, transfusing him with clean new blood! At 8:15 P.M., the girls and I are in his room, hugging him in the yellow glow of a lamp that beats back the shadows beyond the tall window; we're congratulating him on his narrow escape from death, celebrating his survival!

Yet surely such revisionary hopes don't shape the "drowsy numbness" that "pains my sense" throughout the anniversary day. On the contrary. Recurring annually, February 11 bespeaks finality. The gloom of the Yahrzeit reminds us of the reality of the death it commemorates. The card that came in the mail each winter, commemorating yet again the death of Harry Gilbert, was a thick, white square of cardboard, a kind of *slab* of cardboard, edged in black. The card told us that we should light a candle for the soul of Harry Gilbert, wayfaring alone in some cryptic distance, because there was now no way we could bring him back to us; the tiny signal of the candle, said the card, was the only communication possible between us and my husband's father—and a frail, chancy one at that. The card told us how irreversible were the events of the day that had killed Harry Gilbert. In this sense the Yahrzeit card was like—metaphorically, indeed, the Yahrzeit card *was*—the stone that marked the grave of Harry Gilbert.

GRAVESTONES

Maybe it's no coincidence that according to Jewish custom, the gravestone itself must be "unveiled" by or at the first Yahrzeit. The concept, as well as the moment, of "unveiling," is surely significant. We want the veil between us and the dead to be lifted; we yearn toward the beings (and what we hope is the *being*) "beyond the veil." Yet what is unveiled and revealed on the grave, at the first Yahrzeit, is the enigmatic factuality of the stone itself, the crypt that symbolizes the materiality of death. The very moment we look at the stone is, arguably, *the* moment of recognition (or re-cognition) when we know or relearn what has happened: here is the name of the dead one, the collection of symbols that remains to remind us that he *was* and is no more; here—ineradicable—are the dates of his life, *these* numbers telling when it began and *these* telling not just when but *that* it has ended.[4]

In the wistfully autumnal poem "Medlars and Sorb Apples," written some years before his "Ship of Death," D. H. Lawrence announces the theme of the journeying soul that he was so poignantly to elaborate in the later work. Meditating on the "exquisite odour of leave-taking" and the pilgrimage of Orpheus down "the winding, leaf-clogged, silent lanes of hell," he celebrates what he calls the "[i]ntoxication of final loneliness" that is or should be experienced by each soul "departing with its own isolation."[5] Yet the loneliness of the departed soul, as it continues "down the strange lanes of hell, more and more intensely alone" on the other side of the silence that divides it from the living, must of course be matched by the loneliness of the living, forced to acquiesce in their irrevocable separation from the dead. This separation, this ontological loneliness, is what the stone re-presents to us, for in recording (and thus remembering or re-evoking) the date of loss, the stone becomes a signifier of loss and thus, in a way, an incarnation of the Yahrzeit whose recurrence tells us, over and over again, that to go on living is to go on living with loss.

And doesn't the word "grave" itself express the congruence between loss or separation and the *writing* of loss that the gravestone preserves? My *American Heritage Dictionary* tells me that both "grave" meaning an "excavation for the interment of a corpse," a "burial place," and "grave" meaning to "sculpt or carve; engrave," to "stamp or impress deeply; fix permanently, as words or ideas" derive from the Indo-European root *ghrebh*, meaning to "dig, bury, scratch." In Western culture, at least, the inscriptions on stone that mark the hollows where we bury our dead strikingly parallel the trenches or hollows en-graved—inscribed—in the earth where the urns and coffins of the dead are actually interred. And if to inter is to engrave, then perhaps to engrave is to inter. Thus the dates engraved or inscribed on the Yahrzeit card, or on the stone whose herald it is, manifest the crypt or grave of the dead one, the hollow beyond time in which he is hidden away from us, forever inaccessible, hard as we may struggle to rend the veils that divide us from him.

Poets have of course repeatedly brooded on graves and their engraving—not a surprising point, given the connection between the mystery of death and the mastery of language that is as implicit in the philological history of *ghrebh* as it is in the story of Orpheus's journey to Hades. And the "epitaph" or "inscription on a tomb" (from the Greek *epi-taphos*, writing *epi*—"over"—the *taphos*—"tomb") is a time-honored poetic genre.[6] Tennyson's *In Memoriam*, however, has a special place among meditations on what I want to define as the epitaphic moment: the moment, perhaps, when a mourner fully recognizes the reality of loss. This elegiac sequence—not really a single poem but a series of related verses—was produced by Tennyson in the course of more than fifteen years, during which he struggled to come to terms with his grief over the unexpected death of his beloved friend Arthur Hallam. Indeed, the structure of the poem emphasizes the enmeshing of what we now call grief-work in the turnings of the year, while the poet's self-consciousness about the problems of memory and memorializing is implicit in the title of the work. But maybe, in connection with epitaphs and anniversaries, it's most interesting that *In Memoriam* focuses at key points on the torment of the veil that separates us from the dead and on the haunting enigma of the stone that both certifies and symbolizes the lost friend's death.[7]

"Behind the veil": this almost too well-known phrase was originally Tennyson's. "O for thy voice to soothe and bless!" he cries out to Hallam in section 56, after lamenting humanity's entrapment in evolutionary processes dominated by "Nature, red in tooth and claw," but then concedes that his yearning for communication beyond the grave is as hopeless as his wish for "redress" of what seems to him at this point the cosmic injustice that condemns living things to die. "What hope of answer, or redress?" the poet wonders, then answers, resignedly, "Behind the veil, behind the veil." Eleven verses later, however, in section 67, he confesses to a recurrent nighttime vision of the "commemorative marker on the wall of the church above the vault" in which Hallam was buried:

> When on my bed the moonlight falls,
>   I know that in thy place of rest
>   By that broad water of the west,
> There comes a glory on the walls;
>
> Thy marble bright in dark appears,
>   As slowly steals a silver flame
>   Along the letters of thy name,
> And o'er the number of thy years.
>
> The mystic glory swims away;
>   From off my bed the moonlight dies;
>   And closing eaves of wearied eyes
> I sleep till dusk is dipt in gray:

And then I know the mist is drawn
A lucid veil from coast to coast,
And in the dark church like a ghost
Thy tablet glimmers to the dawn.[8]

Why does a "silver flame"—a "mystic glory"—light the very stone that signifies loss? And why is the mist that's later, with the gray of dawn, "drawn" (opened? closed? sketched?) "from coast to coast" a "*lucid* veil"? At the least, I suppose, the poet finds some comfort in the factuality of history. Although Hallam *is* no more, the "mystic glory" of Hallam *was*, as the silvery tablet testifies in the tenuous moonlight of memory. After all, terrible as the epitaphic moment may be, with its reiterated reminder that the lost beloved will "nevermore" return, fate might deal even more hardly with the bereaved if there were *no epitaph*, leaving behind what Whitman called "the terrible doubt of appearances," specifically the doubt whether who and what "was" really *was*. Perhaps, then, though the veil of mist that's drawn "from coast to coast" at the end of this section is ambiguous, it gains its oxymoronic lucidity from the "mystic glory" buried in the vault of the past to whose reality the tablet bears glimmering witness.

At the same time, however, I have to confess that my own puzzlement at the "mystic glory" is rooted in a skeptical "postmodern" feeling that there's something inauthentic about all this talk of glory. Sorrow and pity are what we mostly feel today when we contemplate the dead; "mystic glory" is alien to us, isn't it? And didn't Tennyson himself confess that he hadn't in fact viewed his friend's memorial tablet when he wrote these lines? "I myself did not see Clevedon [Hallam's burial place] till years after the burial of A. H. H.," the poet noted, adding that after visiting Clevedon, he substituted the somewhat pessimistic phrase "dark church" for the more devoutly Christian term "chancel" (meaning the space around an altar) that he'd used in his original draft of this passage.[9] Maybe the lines "in the chancel like a ghost / Thy tablet glimmers to the dawn" would have attributed almost a priestly role to the spectral Hallam, hovering before the altar near which his body lay, while a glimmering "in the dark church" is more akin to a fading in and a fading out in a darkness of theological mystery we twenty-first-century readers find more congenial, though hardly more comforting.

By the end of *In Memoriam*, in any case, the past whose reality is represented in letters engraved on tablets like the one that Tennyson at least *seems* to see in section 67 becomes the stony foundation on which the present can move forward into the future. The sequence that began with the death of the friend who was engaged to the poet's sister Emily ends with the wedding of the poet's sister Cecelia, here pictured standing at the altar,

> Now waiting to be made a wife,
>   Her feet, my darling, on the dead;
>   Their pensive tablets round her head,
> And the most living words of life
>
> Breathed in her ear.

Standing above a vault like the one in which Hallam is buried, the bride is surrounded by "tablets" like the one that commemorates him: the dead are below and around the living, as the newlyweds move forward into a future that, as Tennyson reminds us through an allusion to the ceremonial *inscription* of their nuptials, must include their own deaths. "Now sign your names," he admonishes the happy pair, noting that these will be read by "village eyes as yet unborn" in years to come. As the joyful wedding bells begin to peal, he adds, "The blind wall rocks, and on the trees / The dead leaf trembles" at that sound.[10]

"*The blind wall rocks. . . . The dead leaf trembles. . . .*": *In Memoriam* concludes with a vision of a new child conceived on the bridal couple's wedding night, a child who will "live in God," as Hallam did and does, heralding the "one far-off divine event, / To which the whole creation moves."[11] And yet— the blindness of the wall, the tremor of the dead leaf! Though Tennyson claims that on this exultant wedding day even "the grave is bright for me," his own rhetoric betrays him for a moment. The "lucid veil" has become a "blind wall," the "mystic glory" of the dead man no more than a "dead leaf," as if, at least temporarily, the stones that signify loss had closed around the "dark church," sealing the poet off from his hope of reunion and communion with the dead man just as they seal the dead away from him.[12]

Tennyson's literary descendants are still more grim about the epitaphic moment that is entombed in the bleakness of the Yahrzeit. In a wry poem meditating on a "Disused Graveyard" that appeared some three-quarters of a century after Tennyson published *In Memoriam*, Robert Frost muses that though "The living come with grassy tread / To read the gravestones on the hill," the dead themselves don't do the same. In fact, "no one dead will seem to come" either to be buried in this "disused" cemetery or to view its "marble rhymes" with their messages of death. Why is that? Frost disingenuously wonders, remarking:

It would be easy to be clever
And tell the stones: Men hate to die
And have stopped dying now forever.
I think they would believe the lie.[13]

For if the graveyard Frost describes is literally "disused" because it's too full of death and the dead to offer space to more corpses, metaphorically it's "disused" because, as he sardonically notes, not even the dead to whom it's dedicated will "come" (back) to it. Yet there will be more and more dead bodies to populate (and not come back to) *other* cemeteries, since only (or maybe not even) a stone would believe the second (lying) half of the claim that "Men hate to die / And have stopped dying now forever." In Frost's view, human will (we hate to die, yearn *not* to die) and human fate (we can't stop dying and can't stop dying *forever*) are hopelessly at odds, issuing in a harsh conundrum to which the "disused" graveyard mutely testifies.

Bitter though it may be, however, to cope with the intransigent absence of the dead, wouldn't it be worse to imagine them somehow *present* within their death? Isn't there some comfort in reflecting that "the graveyard draws the living still, / But never any more the dead?" Certainly, if we construe Frost's line differently, we can find some consolation in believing that the dead have journeyed away from death, into that better place most cultures construct for them through myth and ritual. "Peace, peace," exclaims Shelley in "Adonais," in an effort to reassure himself that Keats "is not dead, he doth not sleep—/He hath awakened from the dream of life." Yet what if as we gaze at the grave in which we want to believe the dead are *not*, we can't keep from thinking that they are *not* "not here"? What if the dead aren't just figuratively "beyond the veil" but literally trapped behind the stony facade of the "blind wall" that seals them away from us? And what if our horror at the imperviousness of that wall is really a displacement of the deepest horror we feel, a horror at the stony imperviousness of the dead body itself, behind which the soul of the one we love may be trapped, unable to escape or speak or cry for help? What if the dead body itself *is* "the veil" beyond which the dead somehow still *are*?

THE BURIED LIFE

I suspect that the ultimate horror of paralyzed life-in-death, sometimes clearly formulated, sometimes not quite conscious, shapes countless poems that focus on what I've been calling the epitaphic moment, as if the contemplation of the tomb were really a way of meditating on the sheer terror evoked by the dead body itself. And maybe the old, old fear of living burial (intended or accidental) really masks a fear related to this terror, the fear that *any* burial is a form of "burial alive."[14]

Apparently ironic and resigned, Thomas Hardy's "Rain on a Grave" records a tentative confrontation with this fear, as the poet meditates on what his buried wife is presumably not (but by implication *might be* and therefore maybe *is*) feeling:

> Clouds spout upon her
>   Their waters amain
>   In ruthless disdain,—
> Her who but lately
>   Had shivered with pain
> As at touch of dishonour
> If there had lit on her
> So coldly, so straightly
>   Such arrows of rain:
>
> One who to shelter
>   Her delicate head
> Would quicken and quicken
>   Each tentative tread
> If drops chanced to pelt her.[15]

How alive, and how fearfully vulnerable, the dead woman becomes in the course of these lines that begin so matter-of-factly! "Clouds spout upon her"—upon *her* who had so disliked the rain, who had felt so "dishonoured" and so urgently sought shelter if "arrows of rain" had dared insult her "delicate head"! And she is helpless, now, to "quicken and quicken" her "tentative tread," helpless because although she may still suffer the dishonor of the rain, she is not among the quick but among the dead.

This last thought of his lost Emma's helplessness is so dreadful to Hardy that he suddenly casts about for a remedy, something, anything, to do to make things better. "Would that I lay there / And she were housed here!" he exclaims, adding that it would be better still if the two were together,

> . . . folded away there
> Exposed to one weather

We both,—who would stray there
When sunny the day there,
  Or evening was clear.

If living husband and dead wife could just, *at least*, be "folded away"
together, even if they were both exposed to the pitiless rain—if they who
once had strayed together through sunny days and clear evenings could
now weather the awful climate of death together—the two might perhaps
shelter or anyway solace each other.

As it is, Hardy can only turn at the poem's end to what seems here like
a cold comfort, even though it's a traditional one:

Soon will be growing
  Green blades from her mound,
And daisies be showing
  Like stars on the ground,
Till she form part of them—
Ay—the sweet heart of them.
  Loved beyond measure
  With a child's pleasure
  All her life's round.

"Soon will be growing / Green blades from her mound": the thought of the
biological processes through which death (re)generates life fails to comfort
in this context because the curious animation the writer attributes to his
wife's body makes the thought of such a transformation distinctly unpleasant. What must the shivering Emma, with her "delicate head," have to go
through in order to "form part" of a constellation of daisies? How ironic
that she, who loved such flowers with an innocent, childlike pleasure
throughout her lifetime, should now have fallen into a state where she will
become no more than the "sweet heart"—and maybe the unwilling, dishon-
ored *sweetheart*—of the inanimate!

I remember that when the rains came in March 1991, and the drought
that had settled over California that winter suddenly ended, I was almost
distraught. I'd often read the brief elegiac verses in which Hardy mourns his
first wife, but I certainly hadn't "read" "Rain on a Grave" as I do now. At
first, in fact, I'm not sure I knew what was bothering me about the tumultuous sheets of water that began to spill from the sky just a few weeks after
Elliot died. Then I understood my anxieties. He was *out in the storm*! How

could I have left him on the western slope of a chilly California hillside where "arrows of rain" could torment him? Like the bereft mother whose misery Carol Henderson records in *Losing Malcolm* ("All I could think about was how Carolyn was going to get wet out there"), I think I really believed the one I mourned was suffering through the weather just as Hardy seems to imagine Emma is suffering. And perhaps, I feared, I was to blame for his woe; perhaps I shouldn't have "left him" out there!

"Out there"—or *down there*—is after all where terrible transformations begin. "Full fathom five thy father lies," declares Ariel's famous song from *The Tempest*:

> *Of his bones are coral made;*
> *Those are pearls that were his eyes:*
>   *Nothing of him that doth fade,*
> *But doth suffer a sea change*
> *Into something rich and strange.*

Ah, but to the one who mourns, the sea change that the beloved must undergo seems awful rather than awesome. What if he *feels* his bones turning to coral, his eyes becoming pearls? Think of how the dead must suffer in being made "rich and strange." As for "the buried life" of those bodies more prosaically planted in graveyards on chilly hillsides, many a poet has reflected anxiously on that sad condition. Writing to her husband a year or so after his death, Edna St. Vincent Millay asked what may be a representative question: "Ah, cannot the curled shoots of the larkspur that you loved so . . . Instruct you how to return through the thawing ground and the thin snow. . . ?" And she answered with the resignation to which all mourners must come:

> *I fear that not a root in all this heaving sea*
> *Of land, has nudged you where you lie, has found*
> *Patience and time to direct you, numb and stupid as you still must be*
> *From your first winter underground.*[16]

Perhaps the gloom of the anniversary has a special connection to this morbid, physical dread that the epitaphic moment sometimes evokes. For if the dead one is entombed in the Yahrzeit—or any way the Yahrzeit annually "engraves" in memory the interment of the dead one—then that anniversary time is not just a time for speaking to the spirit of the dead that's journeying (we hope) away from the desolation of the material world and onward into a "better place" behind the veil but also a time for addressing the *body* of the dead in the "resting place" where it's helplessly immobilized.

In "R. Alcona to J. Brenzaida," a dramatic monologue Emily Brontë wrote so her fictive heroine Rosina Alcona might utter her grief for her dead beloved, Julius Brenzaida, the author of *Wuthering Heights* specifically linked the inexorable recurrence of anniversary after anniversary of the deathday that severed the lovers with fears of the torments weather might bring to the dead:

> Cold in the earth, and the deep snow piled above thee!
> Far, far removed, cold in the dreary grave!
> Have I forgot, my Only Love, to love thee,
> Severed at last by Time's all-wearing wave? . . .
>
> Cold in the earth, and fifteen wild Decembers
> From those brown hills have melted into spring—
> Faithful indeed is the spirit that remembers
> After such years of change and suffering![17]

Like Hardy's dead wife (or Millay's husband), Julius Brenzaida seems almost to be wakeful in this poem, as he endures the exhausting passage of "fifteen wild Decembers." For though the phrase "such years of change and suffering" overtly refers to the transformations experienced by the surviving Rosina, who faithfully remembers her dead lover despite the forces that have reshaped her life, the reader shudders to contemplate, and half fears Brontë may be contemplating, the "change and suffering" that the dead Julius has undergone, trapped in his grave on a wintry hillside.

And *can* "Time's all-wearing wave" sever us from the dead? Brontë's emphasis on the ever-increasing interval that separates Rosina from Julius reminds us that what is buried in the grave isn't just the body of the beloved but the body of the past itself that the lovers shared. Judith Wright's "Rosina Alcona to Julius Brenzaida," a moving revision of Brontë's poem, brilliantly surfaces the notion that as T. S. Eliot brooded in "Burnt Norton," "Time present and time past" coexist and that "both [are] perhaps present in time future." To survive into mid- or late life, Wright observes, is to witness the ways in which the past is interred in the present, for to live a long time is to contain "archaean levels / *buried yet living*" [emphasis added]." To dramatize this point, she recounts a moment of epiphany when, "rushing forward" along a new freeway, she suddenly catches sight of "the old wooden pub / stranded at the crossways" where she and her dead lover once drank and laughed "in a day still living, / still laughing, still permanent."

At that moment, as "Present crossed past / synchronized, at the junction," the poet insists, "Three faces met"—the "vivid" living face of her lover as he once was, his corpse's "face of dead marble," and her own—so that as the past rises from its grave, the poet finds herself weeping "undryable tears" that seem to arise from "artesian" depths below "the strata that cover you, / the silt-sift of time." Here, as if to parallel the momentary resurrection of dead love, Wright invokes "dead Emily," the writer whose love song of "R. Alcona to J. Brenzaida" this twentieth-century poet is also, as it were, resurrecting:

> Have I forgot, my only Love, to love thee,
> Severed at last by time's all-wearing wave? . . .

> The pure poem rises
> in lovely tranquillity . . .
> from the soil of the past,
> as the lost face rises
> and the tears return.[18]

THE BURIED SELF

But if any moment of memory can resurrect the past in which we lived with, instead of without, the one whose absence we now lament, how much more compelling is the regular, mournfully recurring Yahrzeit, with its reminder not only of the other we have lost but of the self we have lost or buried in the irretrievable past. Marking anniversary after anniversary, key moments at weekly or monthly as well as yearly intervals, Donald Hall's poignant *Without*, a collection of elegies for his wife, Jane Kenyon, struggles to revive at least the shadow of the person he himself was, even at the disease-haunted end of his married past, while ruefully tracing a lonely pilgrimage forward into grief. As Hall notes in "Independence Day Letter" that "I undertake another day / twelve weeks after the Tuesday / we learned that you would die," his funereal language ("I *undertake* another day") emphasizes the irony of "Independence" while his perpetual evocation of the events leading up to his wife's death dramatizes his continued inhabitation of the time when he lived with, rather than *without*, the dead woman.

Yet over and over again the past keeps dying in Hall's elegies; over and over again Jane Kenyon is buried; over and over again the poet studies the marker on her grave, as if repeatedly straining to decipher its meaning. In "Independence Day Letter," he confesses:

> *. . . I go to bed early, reading*
> The Man Without Qualities
> *with insufficient attention*
> *because I keep watching you die.*
> *Tomorrow I will wake at five*
> *to the tenth Wednesday*
> *after the Wednesday we buried you.*

Not too many Wednesdays later, in "Midsummer Letter," he is still dwelling on and, as it were, in the interstices of the calendar, as he observes that the polished granite of his dead wife's gravestone "reflects the full moon of August" on another anniversary, "four months from the day / your chest went still." And in "Midwinter Letter" he surfaces one of the imperatives that shape these poems, noting that just as "Remembered happiness is agony; / so is remembered agony," so that "I live in a present compelled by anniversaries and objects."[19]

For the mourner compelled by the "remembered . . . agony" incarnate in "anniversaries and objects," however, there are two key moments around which the calendar of grief is organized, as the Yahrzeit ritual itself suggests: the moment of burial that the first Yahrzeit commemorates and the moment of death commemorated in each later Yahrzeit. Although he isn't Jewish and doesn't allude to Jewish procedures for mourning, Hall's poems are shaped by his inescapable awareness of the (endless) moment of death and of the (unending) fact of burial. In "Letter from Washington"—significantly undated—the poet confesses that during a professional meeting with "distinguished patrons / and administrators / of the arts," he was really "elsewhere," in the eternal present (and eternal presence) of his wife's never-ending dying, "in that room I never leave / where I sit beside you listening" for the last sound of "your altered breathing." Finally, in "Midwinter Letter" and "Letter after a Year," the poet describes hiking to his wife's grave through deep snow and explains the urgency that motivates his visits:

> *All winter*
> *when ice and snow kept me away*
> *I worried that you missed me.*
> *"Perkins! Where the hell*
> *are you?"*[20]

"Perkins! Where the hell / are you?" The voice from beyond the grave is uncannily colloquial, cranky, wifely; the dead woman addresses her husband by his pet name, frets at *his* absence, and nags as if the two were safely, still, alive together. But if the wife is in fact (as we know) "beyond the grave"—"behind the veil!"—does this mean the husband too is somehow "beyond the grave," spiritually, if not physically, incorporated into the mysterious other world where his beloved has now so dreadfully settled? An eerie line from "Letter in Autumn," a poem recording the "first October of your death," fleetingly implies as much:

> *I sleep* where we lived and died *[emphasis added]*
> *in the painted Victorian bed*
> *under the tiny lights*
> *you strung on the headboard . . .*
> *The lights still burned last April*
> *early on a Saturday morning*
> *while you died.*[21]

That the couple "died" in "the painted Victorian bed" is no doubt in one sense a sexual fact, alluding to the "little deaths" achieved throughout what other poems in Hall's sequence testify was an erotically joyous marriage. Yet the deliberate repetition of "died" at the end of this passage—"while *you* died"—underlines the double meaning of the phrase "where *we* lived and died." When the wife died, the coupledness of the couple died; thus, when the couple-as-couple died, the husband at least symbolically died too. Now, just as Hardy longed to be "folded away" with his dead wife, "Exposed to one weather / We both," so Hall yearns to be assimilated into the natural setting in which *his* wife is lodged. There in the New England graveyard, he enviously notes, the trees, indifferent to the griefs of autumn, "go on burning / without ravage of loss or disorder," go on, that is, in an oblivious fullness of being without the pain of knowing how much they are (in his title word) *without*. Declares the poet:

I wish you were that birch
rising from the clump behind you,
and I the gray oak alongside.[22]

How inevitable it is, this wanting to join the beloved in death, this wild or wistful sense of death's plausibility, especially at those times—All Souls' Day, the Yahrzeit—when the door of otherness seems to open and the lost voice speaks, sometimes crossly ("Perkins! Where the hell / are you?"), sometimes woefully ("It's so cold here, sem"). Perhaps, then, the metaphorical death the mourner dies with every glance at the beloved's gravestone, every recurrence of the deathday or the day of burial, inevitably evokes the "time future" that is as implicit in "time present" as is "time past"—the time when the mourner too will be not just figuratively but literally at death's door.

The epitaph has of course traditionally been as much a memento mori for its reader as a reminder of the one whose death and burial it confirms. This is especially true when the spirit of the dead seems to speak in an icy prosopopoeia devised by poet or stone carver (or perhaps planned in advance by the one who was to die). "Look on my works, ye mighty, and despair," pronounces the ghost of Shelley's "Ozymandias," once a "King of Kings." "Cast a cold eye, on life, on death / Horseman, pass by!" commands William Butler Yeats on the tombstone that he asked to have planted "Under Ben Bulben." More ironically, "Life is a jest; and all things show it. / I thought so once; but now I know it," declares the Restoration playwright John Gay, author of the scathingly cynical *Beggar's Opera*, while more plaintively (but perhaps most persuasively) one Master Elginbrod inscribes a public prayer on his stone:

Here lie I, Master Elginbrod.
Have mercy on my soul, O God,
As I would have if I were God
And thou wert Master Elginbrod.

How desperately the dead seem to want to instruct us—or even God—from beyond the grave![23]

Such instructive epitaphs, however, record the terms of a generalized fate rather than a specific destiny; they're addressed to all who fear the *dies irae, dies illa* of death and judgment, which is to say, they're addressed to *all*. But to the husband or wife, lover or child, sibling or parent of a singular, much-loved dead person, the tombstone speaks with greater particularity, unveiling the mystery of "time future." And sometimes the loving mourner struggles, himself or herself, to unveil that mystery. In 1641, for instance, Lady Catherine Dyer caused the following epitaph to be engraved on the monument she erected to her husband, Sir William Dyer, in Colmworth Church, Bedfordshire:

> My dearest dust, could not thy hasty day
> Afford thy drowzy patience leave to stay
> One hower longer: so that we might either
> Sate up, or gone to bedd together?
> But since thy finisht labor hath possest
> Thy weary limbs with early rest,
> Enjoy it sweetly: and thy widdowe bride
> Shall soone repose her by thy slumbering side.
> Whose business, now, is only to prepare
> My nightly dress, and call to prayre:
> Mine eyes wax heavy and ye day growes old.
> The dew falls thick, my beloved growes cold.
> Draw, draw ye closed curtaynes: and make room:
> My dear, my dearest dust; I come, I come.

By turns erotic and rueful, gently chiding and delicately resigned, Dyer's epitaph is also—isn't it?—subtly chilling: "Mine eyes wax heavy and ye day growes old. / The dew falls thick, my beloved growes cold." Physically cold in death, the husband grows emotionally colder as he journeys away from his wife into death's forgetfulness, and as the day of her life draws to its end, the "widdowe bride" prepares for the only consummation she can now imagine: a (re)union with what is now, though dear, no more than "dust."[24]

Our contemporaries are perhaps even fiercer in their transcriptions of the mortal truths learned through incursions and recursions of the epitaphic moment. In *The Father*—a series of passionate elegies for her father, who comes, in the course of the collection, to represent the flesh that is "father" to all of us—Sharon Olds records a graveside education in the sheer materiality of death. "One Year," for instance, examines the literal revelations displayed above, beside, and below the "marker" unveiled at the Yahrzeit. Sitting on the stone over her father's grave, Olds comments, seems at first "like sitting on the edge of someone's bed." But as she broods on the spot, she sees the ants that run "down into the grooves of his name" along with the "coiled ferns, copper-beech blossoms." Finally, after lying down "on my father's grave" to drowse in the sun ("the powerful / ants walked on me"), she wakes to

> ... *think of his body*
> *actually under me, the can of*
> *bone, ash, soft as a goosedown*
> *pillow that bursts in bed with the lovers.*
> *When I kissed his stone it was not enough,*
> *when I licked it my tongue went dry a moment, I*
> *ate his dust, I tasted my dirt host.*[25]

Intensely detailed, Olds's communion with the eucharist of earth—the "dirt host" that is her father and in which her father is embedded—is relatively serene, as the poet wills herself to come to terms with the meaning of her own impending termination as well as her father's. Yet for every poem that is a least ostensibly "griefless" or even (like those by Hall, Hardy, Dyer) sadly desirous in its contemplation of the epitaphic moment in which each mourner must inexorably become the one who is mourned rather than the one who mourns, there are notable others that explore the *timor mortis* whose perturbations have preoccupied poets for centuries. Ted Hughes's "The Stone," for instance, examines the historicity that groups deaths together, forthrightly linking one inscription to another in what we might think of as an epitaphic chain. The gravestone (that will bind his name to another's, presumably a wife's), writes Hughes, "Has not yet been cut. / It is too heavy already / For consideration," yet "Soon it will come," with "horrible life" transporting "its face . . . To sit over mine." And locking him into an eternal *Liebestod*, "It will even have across its brow / Her name."[26]

When my children and I were ordering the stone that was to mark my husband's grave, we were given the option of inscribing my name too, as well as my date of birth, on the polished granite. Some people make that choice, said the solicitous representative of the Sunset View Cemetery, in El Cerrito, California, to save time and money "later." The kids were, I think, appalled at such an "option." And I? I was frightened and, I guess, somewhat taken aback by the certainties implicit in the gesture, not so much the frank formulation of the inescapable certainty that I'd someday die as the curious certainty that we could foresee, if not when, then *where* and *how* I'd die (somewhere safely within reach of the Sunset View Cemetery, not in a plane crash, a shipwreck, or a distant jungle, or, or—). Maybe we were even bemused by the implied certainty that California wouldn't be ripped apart by the earthquake ("the big one"!) that everyone fears, the certainty that the Sunset View Cemetery itself wouldn't tumble into the Pacific. So we said, "No, thank you," to the man who was taking our order for Elliot's stone. "No thank you, *just leave a space.*"

And there's a dark space on the stone, a blank to be filled in, a blank I see every time I visit my husband's grave. T. S. Eliot's words return again:

> *Time present and time past*
> *Are both perhaps present in time future*
> *And time future contained in time past.*

Those metaphysical musings here and now suggest that in a sense time past and time future are both implicit in the annual, mournful recurrence of the Yahrzeit. Thus if this day when I contemplate the bread of affliction is, like the first night of Passover, a time when I reenact "remembered agony," it's also a time where a premonition of my own future is buried—a day on which, willingly or unwillingly, I'll have to say, "My dear, my dearest dust; I come, I come."

4

———

E-mail to the Dead

THE HYPOTHETICAL LIFE

B erkeley. February 9, 1991. Late afternoon, the sky just beginning to darken outside the windows of my husband's study, but the lamp in the corner was casting a cheery glow on the big yellow poster—DÉTECTIVE PRIVÉ!—that he found a few years ago, just by accident, in Nice.

Tomorrow Elliot would enter the UC Davis Medical Center for surgery, and he'd decided that he should make a last-minute effort to teach me how to do home banking just in case his hospital stay should be longer than the week he anticipated. He was showing me how to get "online" (a mysterious technique, from my point of view), running through his "Payee" list, and imparting other aspects of what seemed a truly arcane operation.

Now, more than a decade later, the bewilderment I felt that day about the very meaning of the word "online" appears odd. Yet despite Elliot's expertise at contacting the Bank of America's "system," he too appears from my postmillennial vantage to have been peculiarly ignorant. For although he'd been banking electronically for six or seven years, neither he nor anyone else we knew "did e-mail," as the saying goes.

Elliot paid bills in the garage we'd long ago converted into a study for him, using a clunky old Kaypro whose CP/M operating system was even then obsolete. But the machine was one of the first to come with an internal modem, which my husband attached to a phone line that he'd moved so it emerged rather oddly from the floor, as if it were an umbilical cord linking him with a host of buried accountants. Sometimes when I picked up the phone in my own study inside the house, I could hear the cadenza of tones, hasty and decisive, that said his computer was dialing the Bank of

America. More often my receiver was clogged with the high-pitched wail that meant somebody was online.

Nevertheless, I understood little about what he was doing, even though I often boasted at parties about his mystifying prowess at home banking. I understood still less but was even more impressed when he learned how to access our campus library's online catalog and was actually able to print out useful lists of reference books for both of us.

Yet though I believed he knew such a lot about what to do with a modem, Elliot died before he could really grasp the nature of the tools he was using, much less their implications. He'd heard of e-mail, for example, but assumed he'd have to be in his office to "do" it, not realizing that for the price of a local call the same clunky home computer he used to reach his bank could telnet him to our university and thence around the world.

Of course, his ignorance (and mine) hardly mattered at that point in the early nineties because only the most advanced of our colleagues had the slightest interest in the oddly disembodied mode of communication called e-mail. Indeed, even the notion of faxing seemed remarkably twenty-first century and sci-fi to most of us. My husband was then the chair of our department, and I remember trying without much success to persuade him that he ought to ask the dean for funds to buy a fax machine for the office. His administrative assistant advised that this was an extravagant request, he told me firmly. How could he have imagined that within a year or two of his death such equipment would be considered not only a sine qua non but a rather old-fashioned one in most academic departments?

Sometimes it seems to me that as a way of thinking grief has much in common with speculative fiction. Both, after all, are about alternative lives—past, present, or future. *What if*, cries the griever, just as the sci-fi writer does. *What if* the calamity hadn't happened, the survivor broods, *what if* the dead one I loved were still alive? What would my life be like today? How would *he* be living, and how would I? The writer of speculative fantasy asks similar questions. Three or four decades ago, for example, storytellers publishing in *Fantasy & Science Fiction*, the most widely read magazine of its kind when I was growing up, might have wondered *what if* the sentences we have for centuries inscribed on stacks of recycled forest fiber should dematerialize and whiz off around the globe at almost the speed of light?

Along with the sci-fi writer, the fantasist, and the teller of ghost stories, the griever is always on the edge of another universe, a cosmos that aches with possibility like a phantom limb.

What if the surgeon's knife hadn't slipped (as perhaps it did), I ask myself on the most perilously speculative days, *what if* the residents had been more competent, *what if* my husband had lived with me through the long years that have followed his disastrous operation? On the seventh anniversary of his death—the seventh Yahrzeit, a special time, given the biblical connotations of the number seven—I even wrote a poem exploring this last *what if*, in which the coupledom of Elliot-and-me is reconstituted in a fantasy of the hypothetical life we might have lived, were it not for the slipped knife, the incompetent residents, the *who knows what*. The poem began with a glint of light that opened into a momentary bliss of vision: "[a]fter a week of rain, the sky / shedding its thousand mystery / meanings" and "a flood of sun" lighting up "the twigs the branches / of the hypothetical life" through which "we've walked caressed / and quarreled all these seven years," still man and wife like "Papageno/Papagena" and feathered with "the delicate matching / plumages of marriage."[1]

Yet it's sad that this life in which my dead husband and I are together is led in the fairy-tale precincts of Mozart's *Magic Flute*, where we masquerade in the feathers of Papageno, the bird catcher, and his enchanted bird bride, Papagena. Maybe in postulating such a charmed alternative world, I was unconsciously influenced by a story Elliot always liked, Rudyard Kipling's "They," a lyrical tale in which a band of dead children frolic in the beautiful gardens of a Tudor mansion set deep in the English countryside. Tended by the lady of the manor, a blind spinster who is a kind of maternal sorceress, the child ghosts are invisible to most visitors, though their aura frightens the few *bad* interlopers who sense their presence. But their happy giggles and "bright heads" are just barely discernible to, and much loved by, those, like the story's narrator, who have themselves lost children.

Elliot was a Kipling scholar who produced a number of books about the sometimes controversial author of *Kim* and the *Just So* stories, but one of his favorite projects had been an edition of R. K.'s letters to his children that he titled *O Beloved Kids*, in an allusion to the charming salutation with which this exceptionally loving father addressed his young daughters and son. The letters are especially poignant because two of the three children died very early: Josephine, the eldest, of pneumonia in 1899, at the age of seven; John, the youngest, in 1915, in combat during the First World War, at eighteen. "They," first published in 1904, memorializes Josephine. Just two years before he produced the tale, Kipling had purchased Batemans, a Tudor mansion hidden among the woods and dales of Sussex, and there he wistfully resurrected his little girl, in the alternative world toward which most mourners yearn—the realm where the dead live and laugh just as if they were still alive: "A child appeared at an upper window, and I thought the little thing waved a friendly hand. But it was to call a companion, for presently another bright head showed. Then I heard a laugh among the yew-peacocks, and turning to make sure . . . I saw the silver of a fountain behind a hedge thrown up against the sun [and] caught the utterly happy chuckle of a child absorbed in some light mischief."[2]

Tudor topiary and flashing fountains: Kipling imagines a realm of romance for his dead daughter to inhabit. But of course we survivors, enmeshed in the fleshly solidity of our ongoing lives, can't really dwell in that other "reality," though we may dwell *on* it so obsessively that it does indeed begin to seem in some weird sense a "reality." For as the mourner discovers over and over again, with each minute during which the dead one is absent from our dailiness, the bliss of the conditional is impossible to sustain. The light fades in the garden, and the hypothetical life vanishes once more, as the quotidian replaces the visionary world.

And the dead themselves take on a fictive quality, which is no doubt, from any sensible perspective, quite healthy. At the end of "They," the story's narrator—surely a surrogate for the bereaved Kipling—concedes that though it might be "right" for the sorceress who presides over the child-haunted house to remain with her supernatural charges, he himself, as she agrees, must "never come here again!" It "would be wrong," Kipling implies, for the mourner to stroll with the dead in the fantasy realm where they still live and laugh, wrong no doubt because, on the one hand, those who are bereaved must come to terms with grief by acknowledging the irreversibility of loss and, on the other hand, we must (willingly or unwillingly) travel away from the increasingly dreamlike past.

"They shut the road through the woods, / Seventy years ago," brooded Kipling in a poem about haunted Sussex that's almost a companion piece to "They." "And now you would never know / There was once a road through the woods":

> Yet, if you enter the woods
> Of a summer evening late . . .
> You will hear the beat of a horse's feet,
> And the swish of a skirt in the dew,
> Steadily cantering through
> The misty solitudes,
> As though they perfectly knew

The old lost road through the woods. . . .
But there is no road through the woods.[3]

No road through the woods: though we intuit vague rumors of what was—
"the beat of a horse's feet," "the swish of a skirt in the dew"—as we survivors
journey into our own futures, the dead become provisional, hypothetical.
Did they ever exist? Was there ever a road through the woods? If even our
memories of the living blur with age, our recollections of the dead grow still
more tattered, scenes from the past increasingly improbable.

In a section of his long late poem "The Rock" entitled "Seventy Years
Later," Wallace Stevens meditated movingly on this *im*plausibility of the
past, noting that with the passage of decades even moments of great intensity in one's personal history take on a curiously phantasmagoric quality.
Beginning with a radical comment on the increasingly imaginary quality
that the past accrues as one ages ("It is an illusion that we were ever alive"),
he focused on the particular unreality that had come to envelop what had
once been a passionate exchange between lovers. "The meeting at noon at
the edge of the field," he declared, now seems like "An invention, an embrace
between one desperate clod / And another. . . *A theorem proposed between
the two* [emphasis added]." And if the "real" through which the dead once
actually moved begins to seem like an "invention"—a "proposed" but
unprovable "theorem"—the *what-ifs* out of which we constitute an alternative world for those we mourn inevitably grow even more tenuous.

Nonetheless, how strangely reasonable the hypothetical life becomes in
those brief seconds when it tears through all that muffles it: the veils of forgetfulness, the fabric of dailiness. Sometimes, indeed, especially quite soon
after someone deeply loved has died, the wishful, wistful world of *what-if*
seems even more plausible than death. "Yesterday I caught sight of you / in
the Kearsarge Mini-Mart," Donald Hall matter-of-factly tells Jane Kenyon in
"Letter at Christmas," not "I *thought* I caught sight of you" but "I caught
sight of you." In the next line of his poem, though, his fantasy is subverted
by the inescapable truth of his bereavement, as he adds, still matter-of-
factly, "The first snow fell seven months / from the day you died."[4]

Tennyson is everywhere less prosaic than Hall and Hall's contemporaries, but in section 14 of *In Memoriam* he too meditates on this uncanny
reasonableness that gives body, as it were, to the hypothetical life of the
dead. Imagining the return of the "man I held as half-divine" as virtually a
normal event, he muses that if someone should tell him that his friend's
ship had just docked and if he'd gone to meet it and encountered what

seemed to be Hallam himself disembarking, "I should not feel it to be strange."[5] Perhaps, Tennyson implies, it's odder that Hallam should be *dead* than that, like any other traveler, he should return from his luckless Continental tour full of questions and solicitude. Yet like the brief, provisional epiphanies recorded in their different ways by Kipling and Hall, and like my own fantasy of the hypothetical life, the Victorian poet's hopeful fabrication quickly falters. In sections 15 and 16 of *In Memoriam*, he struggles to master the "fancies" that animate his alternately "calm despair" and "wild unrest," wondering what has "made me that delirious man / Whose fancy fuses old and new, / And flashes into false and true, / And mingles all without a plan?"[6]

If, then, in addition to the twin Yahrzeit visions of the spirit journeying away "behind the veil" of the dead body and the body painfully corrupting "behind the veil" of the tomb, many mourners nurture dreams of an alternative universe in which the dead go on living as usual, such visions are for the most part painfully evanescent, and they often darken as the dream of life turns back into the nightmare of bereavement. Secreted "behind the veil" of the routines enmeshing us in the "ordinary" universe we necessarily occupy, those we loved circle us in fantasies whose texture is often familiar and familial. But in many of these visionary narratives—for narratives they often are—the familiar quickly dissolves into the unfamiliar, into that which is *unheimlich* in the sense of both "uncanny" and "uncomfortable."

In Thom Gunn's eerie, virtuoso "Death's Door," for instance, one of the elegies for friends lost to AIDS included in the powerful volume entitled *The Man with Night Sweats*, the dead dwell, to begin with, in a realm that wittily mirrors the technologically adept world they'd once inhabited:

> After their processing, the dead
> Sit down in groups and watch TV,
> In which they must be interested,
> For on it they see you and me. . . .
>
> Thus they watch friend and relative
> And life here as they think it is
> —In black and white, repetitive
> As situation comedies.

Note that at first, perhaps precisely because it so accurately mirrors "our" world, the realm of the dead becomes somehow realer than that of the living in the course of this poem. Obliviously conducting our "life here as *they* think it is," we who survive become ourselves hypothetical—fictive characters not unlike Stevens's unlikely, "desperate" clods, reiterating the same old lines in "black and white" sitcom situations, as each of the side-by-side universes, the land of the living and the realm of the dead, questions the reality of the other.

But alas, by the end of Gunn's poem the two universes, both equally provisional, have canceled each other out, as a blizzard of amnesia overwhelms the dead, who simultaneously forget and are forgotten in a conceit that elaborates a likeness between the "snow" on a TV set and the Arctic white stuff that numbs and chills. For even as they watch our world, the dead

> . . . *woo amnesia, look away*
> *As if they were not yet elsewhere,*
> *And when snow blurs the picture they,*
> *Turned, give it a belonging stare.*

All too soon, then, as this snow "blows out toward them," the now-indifferent souls enter a "snow-landscape" in which they find themselves with "all the dead" from every age who ring our world in an "archaic host." And we? In a frostily prophetic metaphor prefiguring the fate we too have in store, we live and move on a screen where "snow blurs the picture": the snow of oblivion that will eventually engulf us too.

Equally quotidian in its setting, Ted Hughes's "Freedom of Speech," one of his *Birthday Letters* to Sylvia Plath, is differently nihilistic in its concluding vision of the hypothetical life and different from Gunn's poem too in plotting an alternative afterlife that the quick and the dead inhabit together. Rather than gaze across a gulf only bridgeable by a fantasy TV, mourner and mourned here dwell side by side in a hypothetical life that's one logical outcome of their "real" life, as Hughes narrates the events of the sixtieth birthday party Plath never had. "Ariel sits on your knuckle," he tells the dead woman, noting that although she herself is "solemn," almost everyone else at the party—friends, relatives, her children, her "Mummy" and "Daddy"—are laughing. "Only you and I do not smile," he adds.[7]

At the purely theoretical age of sixty, Plath is "solemn," as if she understood at last the devastation wrought by the book / god Ariel, perched on her knuckle. In Hughes's fantasy she and her husband (for in this poem he is probably still her husband) brood unsmiling in the homely glow of a candle-studded birthday cake bizarrely set at the center of a net of laughter that stitches together the animate and the inanimate, the living and the dead, the young and the old, excluding only the couple themselves. Yet why the laughter here, and why, for that matter, the solemnity of "you and I," amid so much joy? Hughes is vague on both counts, but perhaps the laughter suggests the absurdity of the fact that life goes on and even, at times, goes on merrily despite the devastations of death, while the solemnity hints at a guilt that he needs to deny because he doesn't want to formulate the extent to which he and his dead wife may be complicitous in culpability. As the author of much of the misery that inspired *Ariel*, after all, the writer of this "birthday letter" is in a sense *co*author of the bitterness his wife's book both recorded and inspired.

Yet the action of the birthday letter surfaces what Hughes leaves unsaid. For while the rest of the world surges forward with paradoxical good cheer, the poet and the long-gone Plath are fixed in an unalterable moment of dreadful, unsmiling consciousness. As if Hughes had set out to illustrate T. S. Eliot's insistence that "What might have been and what has been / Point to one end, which is always present," the birthday party that "might have been" is shadowed by the betrayals enacted in a past that really *has* been, so that the hypothetical life the poet constructs for himself and Plath disturbingly parallels the real, disastrous life the pair had lived together thirty years earlier. Because it's no more than a set of untested (and untestable) postulates, the alternative world that "might have been," says Eliot, is no more than "a perpetual possibility . . . in a world of speculation." But if that is the case, then the only alternative universe available to the needy dead must be one in which they continue somehow to move through the *same* plot that shaped their lives. So, at any rate, Hughes appears to suggest with his representation of surviving husband and dead wife trapped in a realm where they're condemned to remain exactly who and how and *as* they unsmilingly were.

PURGATORIES

William Butler Yeats explored such entrapment in the unalterable past in some of his grimmest imaginings, works that portray the dead as doomed to relive the bleak particulars of their lives again and again. In the Irish poet's terrifying play *Purgatory*, for instance, an old peddler and a boy (who we eventually learn is his son) stand before the ruin of a burned-out mansion suddenly ablaze with the light and life of a past that ceaselessly reen-

acts itself. Here, the old man asserts, he was conceived on the night his wayward young mother gave herself to a drunken "groom in a training stable,"
and here, he declares bitterly, the sexual conflagration of that union will be
repeated, for on this "anniversary / Of my mother's wedding night, / Or of
the night wherein I was begotten" the bride and her loutish lover must dramatize their passion yet again in a phantom marriage chamber.[8]

Or is the marriage chamber the mind of the survivor whose memories
are the sole remaining tokens of the past? Haunted by oedipal rage and
guilt, Yeats's aged, half-mad protagonist hears ghostly hoofbeats that the
boy to whom he's speaking cannot detect and "sees" or seems to see the sordid primal scene recycling itself once more. Like Dante, who interred the
dead in self-defined punishments from which they could never (in the
Inferno) or only after painful aeons (in the *Purgatorio*) escape, Yeats envisions an alternative realm that is a purgatory in which the soul is bound on
the wheel of its own chosen misfortunes. And is there any more horrible
hypothetical life, any more dreadful *what-if* that the mourner might
imagine?

Perhaps only the provisional hell of the will, in which it is the dead
themselves who force themselves not only into but *out of* the alternative
realm of the afterlife we fantasize for them and appear as ghastly revenants
in our own real world. One such figure is the "crawling already?" baby girl
who transforms herself into the implacable haunter of Tony Morrison's
Beloved. Another is the eponymous heroine of Edgar Allan Poe's "Ligeia," a
learned and beautiful woman who brings herself hideously back to life
through sheer passion for the husband who, though mourning her, has
unaccountably rewed himself to "the blue-eyed Lady Rowena Trevanion of
Tremaine." As the unloved Rowena languishes unto death, the obsessive
Ligeia takes her place, inhabits her corpse, and finally shakes off "the fetters
of Death," rising from the bier as a vengeful figure who might almost be a
precursor of Sylvia Plath's more sardonically imagined "Lady Lazarus."[9]

"Who knoweth the mysteries of the will, with its vigor?" mused Poe, citing Joseph Glanvill in the epigraph to this story. "Man doth not yield himself to the angels, nor unto death utterly, save only through the weakness of
his feeble will." And not long after the author of "Ligeia" explored these
mysteries, Emily Brontë also examined them in *Wuthering Heights*, whose
heroine, Catherine Earnshaw Linton, is just as fierce as Poe's character and
rises almost as terrifyingly out of the grave—at least from the point of view
of the novel's effete narrator, Lockwood. In a famous scene near the beginning of the book, the horrified Lockwood struggles to tear Cathy's icy hand

from the window of her old room at Wuthering Heights, to which, in the form of a child ghost, she frantically clings. "[My] fingers closed on the fingers of a little, ice-cold hand! The intense horror of nightmare came over me: I tried to draw back my arm, but the hand clung to it, and a most melancholy voice sobbed, 'Let me in—let me in! . . . I'm come home: I'd lost my way on the moor!' As it spoke, I discerned, obscurely, a child's face looking through the window. 'It is twenty years. . . . I've been a waif for twenty years!' "[10] As a "waif" wailing outside the house she once inhabited, Cathy is dissolving into the same annihilating snows of the past into which the newly dead were gradually drawn in Gunn's "Death's Door," while Lockwood, half asleep in the bed that once was hers, can barely comprehend the history she represents. In a way, then, the window to which she clings functions symbolically as a kind of window from the past into the present—a boundary impossible to cross, as Lockwood quite reasonably asserts: "'Begone!' I shouted. 'I'll never let you in, not if you beg for twenty years.' " Yet though she admits that " 'I've been a waif for twenty years,' " Cathy willfully refuses to release her "tenacious grip" on the world in which she no longer has a place.

TEXTUAL RESURRECTIONS

Dying, John Keats formulated the more than mortal passion for human connection—for love, or anyway, for *relation*—that so radically (re)animates Morrison's dead baby girl, Brontë's desperate heroine, and Poe's desirous Ligeia. The Romantic poet anticipated too the revulsion with which most living onlookers—like, for instance, Agnes's two sisters in Bergman's *Cries and Whispers*—respond to such ferocious hauntings:

> *This living hand, now warm and capable*
> *Of earnest grasping, would, if it were cold*
> *And in the icy silence of the tomb,*
> *So haunt thy days and chill thy dreaming nights*
> *That thou wouldst wish thine own heart dry of blood*
> *So in my veins red life might stream again,*
> *And thou be conscience-calmed—see here it is—*
> *I hold it towards you—*

Like Ligeia and Cathy, Keats is driven by an almost unearthly sexual passion; his poem was drafted in the fevered fury of the tuberculosis that was consuming him at the age of twenty-five and was intended to rebuke what he experienced as the heartlessness of his beloved Fanny Brawne. *You'll be sorry when I'm dead:* that's, in a vulgar sense, the gist of what he seems to want to say. Yet Keats *is* dead, was all too soon dead after writing these words, and so his purely speculative *what-if*—what if this "living hand" should reach toward you from the "icy silence of the tomb!"—takes on an uncanny verisimilitude as we read his words. It is now *as if* the dead poet, eerily resurrected on the page, were speaking to us from beyond the grave, holding out his hand in a woeful motion of "earnest grasping."

Maybe such literary hauntings are the only visitations from the hypothetical life of the dead that most writers can truly imagine, though even these essentially textual resurrections are as rare as they are strange. Surely the master of the genre was the American bard Walt Whitman, who prophesied and in a curious way enacted his own return from the dead—or at any rate his own perpetual, if indefinable, presence among the living—in poem after poem. "Who touches this book touches a man," Whitman famously declares at one of the many points in *Leaves of Grass* in which he implies that through a weird process of transubstantiation, his flesh and blood will metamorphose into paper and ink, offering his devoutest readers a chance at communion with "the origin of all poems" incarnated on his pages. "To die is different from what any one supposed, and luckier," insists Whitman in "Song of Myself," and in elaborating this theme, he made himself into the oracle of a new (albeit enigmatic) vision of mortality—and immortality:

> *Has anyone supposed it lucky to be born?*
> *I hasten to inform him or her it is just as lucky to die, and I know it. . . .*
> *I am the mate and companion of people, all just as immortal and*
> *   fathomless as myself,*
> *(They do not know how immortal, but I know.)*[11]

Unlike Ligeia and Cathy—even, for that matter, unlike Keats—Whitman presents himself as a grand personage whose attitude toward his own survival is fueled by a serene metaphysics far less personal than the sexual fury Poe, Brontë, and Keats transcribe. Still, what does Whitman "know" about immortality that the rest of us don't know? For one thing, he tells us in his mystical and mysterious "Crossing Brooklyn Ferry" that in order to enter a hypothetical future in which he can speak from the dead to the living, he knows he must first surrender himself to death, or anyway, to a hypothesis of death equal to his hypothesis of an afterlife. Through a skillful manipulation of grammar the poet imagines his own annihilation in this extraordinary poem by writing about his own life in the past tense as if he were already dead and then turning to the future tense to predict both his demise and his survival.[12] And because he is willing to write, as it were, from beyond the grave ("I too liv'd . . . I too had receiv'd identity by my body")—willing to write, in other words, *as a dead man*—the uncanny intimacy with which the speaker of "Crossing Brooklyn Ferry" addresses us convinces us that though he is dead, he is nonetheless talking to us as we read, conversing with us in what he quickly insists is an eternal (though speculative) present.

The emphases in the passage below are mine:

Closer yet I approach *you,*
What thought you have *of me* now, *I* had *as much of you—I* laid *in my stores in advance,*
I consider'd *long and seriously of you* before you were born. . . .

Who knows, for all the distance, but I am as good as looking at you now, for all you cannot see me?

"I agree with you that I am dead," Whitman has said in effect, but now he adds a crucial question: "Yet how do you know that even though I'm dead I'm not in some sense alive too, in an alternative dimension, and here with you right now?" And his very willingness to concede the death that our common sense tells us he must have experienced authenticates his hypothesis that he may, at the same time, be somehow alive and "enjoying this." Fantastic as it is, this tentative textual resurrection has a power that even the most unpoetic (often, indeed, *anti*poetic) undergraduates tend to acknowledge; many a skeptical sophomore is willing to admit that the author of "Crossing Brooklyn Ferry" may be "as good as looking at [us] now." Because the poet has died on the page, we can acquiesce in the premise that he may be hovering, like an aura, around the book that has become his only surviving "body."

PSYCHIC RESEARCH

For countless mourners, however, what I've been defining as a textual resurrection doesn't suffice, nor do the tenuous hypotheses implicit in Keats's and Whitman's poems, or for that matter Kipling's, Poe's, and Brontë's sto-

ries. The conditional is, after all, so—well, so tentative, so *conditional.*
What if frays around the edges as it dissolves into *if not.* No wonder, then,
that so many who are bereaved have over the years turned to spiritualism—
to mediums and Ouija boards and the investigations of the Society for Psychical Research—in their efforts not just to hear what the dead might have
to tell us about the alternative realm they inhabit but also to reach them and
speak *back,* actively interrogate them about their well-being, reassure them
of our devotion. Perhaps the most notable of all spiritualists was Sir Arthur
Conan Doyle, creator of the hardheaded Sherlock Holmes, who became an
increasingly fervent advocate of what he called "the new revelation" after
the death of his son in the First World War.

Examining what he called "the great argument" in one of several books
he wrote on spiritualism, Conan Doyle summarized the movement's central
premise with the admirable lucidity that one would expect from a master of
that supremely rational genre the detective story. "The physical basis of all
psychic belief," he explains in *The Vital Message* (1919), "is that the soul is a
complete duplicate of the body, resembling it in the smallest particular,
although constructed in some far more tenuous material." After death, this
lighter, "more tenuous" body peels away from its heavy shell, or "cocoon,"
which "the world" buries "with much solemnity but taking little pains to
ascertain what has become of its nobler contents."[13]

But if the spirit body is in every particular except weight "a complete
duplicate" of the physical body, doesn't it stand to reason—isn't it indeed
"elementary, my dear Watson"?—to suppose that the world in which the
spirit dwells is also "a complete duplicate" of the realm once inhabited by
the physical self? In that happy case, the "new revelation" of spiritualism
brings "tidings of great joy" to those who mourn, not only because it assures
us that our loved ones are still alive and well somewhere but because it gives
this usually all too vague "somewhere" a "local habitation and a name" that
are singularly comfortable and comforting.

Sometimes merely referred to as the "other side," the spiritualist afterlife
is just as often known as Summerland. And this brave new world of the
dead is one in which, Conan Doyle assured his readers, "Our loved ones
have their own pleasant tasks in their new surroundings" and "are very busy
on all forms of congenial work," for the "world in which they find themselves is very much like that which they have quitted, but everything keyed
to a higher octave." Indeed, claimed Conan Doyle, every "earthly thing has
its equivalent" on "the other side," including (although "scoffers have guf-
fawed") alcohol and tobacco, for "if all things are reproduced it would be a

flaw if these were not reproduced also" (though neither is "abused, as they are here"). Moreover, "Let no woman mourn her lost beauty, and no man his lost strength or weakening brain. It all awaits them once more upon the other side," which is, perhaps most consolingly, a realm in which "Happy circles live in pleasant homesteads with every amenity," including (among other things) beautiful gardens and "domestic pets."[14]

Heavenly—and saccharine—as it may sound, this utopian realm of what Conan Doyle rather charmingly called "the long rest cure" was conceived as part of a distinctly nineteenth-century effort to postulate an afterlife that would be "consistent with gradual evolution and with the benevolence of God." Averring that "those extremists [who] pictured with their distorted minds an implacable torturer as the Ruler of the Universe" were essentially blasphemous, Conan Doyle insisted that his new creed "abolishes the idea of a grotesque hell and of a fantastic heaven, while it substitutes the conception of a gradual rise in the scale of existence without any monstrous change which would turn us in an instant from man to angel or devil."[15] Like a number of other spiritualists, too, he contended that his claims about the afterlife he hypothesized for the dead could (and should) be scientifically investigated and that if this were done, they'd be empirically proved.

Probably the most respectable group to undertake such investigations was and is the Society for Psychical Research, one of whose major missions, according to its twenty-first century Web page, "has been to examine the question of whether we survive bodily death, by evaluating the evidence provided by mediumship, apparitions of the dead and reincarnation studies." Founded in England in 1882, the society has branches on both sides of the Atlantic and continues to proclaim the academic disinterestedness with which—even in our credulous New Age of channeling, past life therapy, and magic crystals—it supports the assessment of "*allegedly* paranormal phenomena in a scientific and unbiased way [emphasis added]."[16] That the society has also investigated "near-death and out-of-the-body experiences" should remind us that this institution is hardly superannuated. Many contemporary physicians, and certainly a slew of recent journalists, take quite seriously the often lyrical twentieth-century reports of so-called near-death experiences that notably parallel Conan Doyle's accounts of weightless but "complete duplicates" escaping from the bodies of the dead.

In the 1960s, for example, Martin C. Sampson, M.D., quoted a patient who described his brush with death as utterly ecstatic: "My pain was gone, and I couldn't feel my body. I heard the most peaceful music. . . . God was there and I was floating away. The music was all around me. I knew I was dead, but I wasn't afraid." And a few years later, in 1971, the highly reputable *Canadian Medical Association Journal* included a piece entitled "Cardiac Arrest Remembered," in which a patient offered a more detailed narrative of his near-death experience: "I saw myself leave my body, coming out through my head and shoulders. . . . The 'body' leaving me . . . was somewhat transparent, for I could see my other 'body' through it. Watching this I thought 'So this is what happens when you die' [and my] next sensation was of floating in a bright, pale yellow light—a very delightful feeling." Perhaps not surprisingly, the coauthors of this piece, both cardiologists, comment: "The delightful feeling of floating in space and the tranquillity, the yellow light . . . associated with [a] wish of not wanting to be brought back again, may provide comfort and reassurance to patients suffering from coronary artery disease as well as to their relatives."[17]

But if some recent medical practitioners have studied the near-death phenomenon as seriously as Conan Doyle studied the "etheric bodies" of the "other side," a number of contemporary poets and novelists have struggled almost as diligently to communicate with spirits in less aggressively scientific fashions. Elizabeth Stuart Phelps and Elizabeth Barrett Browning, two of the best-known nineteenth-century spiritualists, have a range of descendants. From William Butler Yeats to Ted Hughes, Sylvia Plath, and most recently James Merrill, these artists have sought to peer "behind the veil" and in doing so have sometimes found their way to meetings of the Society for Psychical Research as well as, more often, to the spiritualists' fabled Summerland.[18] Yeats, probably the most famous of these researchers, was a founding member of the mystical society known as the Golden Dawn, a disciple of the Theosophist Madame Helena Blavatsky, and an apparently convinced spiritualist who regularly attended séances throughout most of his life. When in 1917, just after he'd married George Hyde-Lees, his interest in his bride momentarily faltered, the young woman undertook automatic writing and for many years transcribed the messages from "ghostly instructors" that became the foundation of the mystical manifesto he entitled *A Vision*.

Indeed, where even Conan Doyle refused to go so far as to grant erotic fulfillment to the "lighter bodies" of the dead (on "the other side," he admitted, there "is no physical side to love and no child-birth, though there is close union between those married people who really love each other"), Yeats fantasized that at least a privileged few of the spirits in *his* hypothetical afterlife might enjoy fabulous sexual pleasure beyond the grave. In "Ribh at the Tomb of Baile and Aillinn," a poem about a pair of legendary Celtic star-crossed lovers that he included in the cycle he entitled "Supernatural Songs," Yeats dramatized a Yahrzeit moment of sexual consummation that was actually out of this world. "Transfigured to pure substance," no longer mere "bone and sinew," the ghostly Baile and Aillinn do everything better than those of us they've left behind:

> . . . *When such bodies join*
> *There is no touching here, nor touching there,*
> *Nor straining joy, but whole is joined to whole;*
> *For the intercourse of angels is a light*
> *Where for its moment both seem lost, consumed. . . .*
> *Here on the anniversary of their death.*[19]

Perhaps no other twentieth-century poet hypothesized so sexual a Summerland, but Plath and Hughes did undertake joint experiments with a Ouija board, one of them recorded by Plath in a relatively early piece titled "Dialogue over a Ouija Board" that she never chose to publish. Here the two poets, allegorically disguised as Sibyl and Leroy, a kind of prophetess and a royal being (le *roi*), manage to get in touch with Sibyl's dead father, a stand-in for Plath's "daddy," who informs them via a spirit they call Pan that he is "in plumage of raw worms."[20] Later, although Hughes never made a public statement on the subject, he indicated to the critic Ekbert Faas his fascination with "emissaries from the underworld," and in particular with the salvation of a "desecrated female in the underworld who then becomes [a] bride." As for James Merrill, throughout the 1970s he and his companion, David Jackson, spent so much time at the Ouija board that their "sittings" yielded Merrill a 560-page collection of poems entitled *The Changing Light at Sandover*.[21]

Of course, unlike the highly professionalized Society for Psychical Research, the twentieth century's spiritualist poets and novelists were for the most part as amateurish and even playful as they were mystical. Despite its grandiose pretensions, after all, the Ouija board was conceived and marketed as a toy, and for many writers communication with "the beyond" is really a kind of game, albeit one they often take quite seriously. For some, in fact, the spirit world provides, or is provided by, the very substance of literary art. Yeats conceded, in one of his cooler moments, that the "ghostly instructors" who spoke to him through his wife came to bring him "metaphors for poetry," and Merrill's adventures on the Ouija board gave him, he reported, news from a host of aesthetic precursors, ranging from Yeats himself to W. H. Auden, whose afterlife chatter he recorded in dryly witty, stylishly polished verse.

By comparison, Conan Doyle and his spiritualist contemporaries might be considered *technologists* of the afterlife. It was crucial to Sherlock Holmes's author, for example, that the "real science which has examined the facts [of the spiritualist claim] is [a] valid authority," and he staunchly maintained that incontrovertible evidence for "the great argument" of spiritualism—namely the existence and integrity of the "etheric body"—was provided by photography.[22] Cameras, he asserted, had repeatedly recorded the phenomenon known as ectoplasm, "a strange white evanescent dough-like substance" that was "exuded" as one of the "properties of mediumship" and was "frequently photographed by scientific enquirers in different stages of its evolution" during séances. Just as tellingly, Conan Doyle declared, cameras had frequently captured on film the images of "etheric bodies," as part of the enterprise known as spirit photography.[23]

How much more plausible the hypothetical life becomes if our hopeful *what if* can somehow gain empirical support from those instruments of science to which we regularly trust our lives! After all, most of us never "see" blood cells or bacteria, yet we believe the testimony of physicians who claim they have encountered such microscopic marvels. Nor do most of us understand how atomic particles manifest themselves to the eyes of physicists, yet we know what such particles can do when what we are told is a nuclear reaction has been unleashed. Why, then, shouldn't phenomena "produced" by, or expressing the *being* of, the dead be discernible by mechanisms like those that analyze and calibrate the secrets of biology, chemistry, and physics, or indeed by au courant instruments of communication like portable phones and Palm Pilots? Not long ago the American medium James Van Praagh, author of the spiritualist best seller *Talking to Heaven: A Medium's Message of Life after Death* (1997), affirmed that ghosts are increasingly making use of television and computer screens to communicate news from the spirit realm, but as early as 1904 Rudyard Kipling published a story, "Wireless," postulating that the alternative world of the dead might be accessible through what was at that time the very up-to-date technology of radio waves.

If "They," written in the same period, was a fairy tale about unnamed, elliptically glimpsed child ghosts, "Wireless" is a sci-fi fantasy about one particular grown-up ghost, the very John Keats who had so yearned to hold his "living hand" toward his beloved while it was still "warm and capable / Of earnest grasping." On a dark and stormy night, when the narrator and some associates have undertaken "Marconi experiments" with the "magic" of "what we call Electricity," the "Powers—whatever the Powers may be— at work—through space—a long distance away" somehow select a tubercular young pharmacist named Mr. Shaynor, who works in the shop where the experiments are being conducted, as a vehicle for the thoughts of that other tubercular young medical worker named John Keats. Now presumably "cold / And in the icy silence of the tomb," Keats mysteriously broadcasts portions of several stanzas from "The Eve of St. Agnes" to the "receiver" that Shaynor has become. That *John* Shaynor is courting a girl named *Fanny* Brand, that he and she walk out into the darkness near *St. Agnes's* church in the bitter cold of a night about which the young pharmacist confesses, "I shouldn't care to be lying in my grave a night like this," and that the sick man studies catalogs of medicinal plants: all these points prepare him to transcribe perfectly the passage from "The Eve of St. Agnes" in which Keats describes the delicacies his hero, Porphyro, sets by the bedside of his heroine, Madeline. Notes the tale's narrator wonderingly, the supple, sensuous stanza that begins "Candied apple, quince and plum and gourd" came "away under his hand as it is written in the book—as it is written in the book."[24]

Yet of course none of the similarities between Shaynor and the true author of "The Eve of St. Agnes" can explain the twentieth-century pharmacist's bizarre "reception" of these lines from his nineteenth-century precursor. Kipling isn't, after all, writing the famous probabilistic story of the roomful of typewriting monkeys who, given aeons of random keystrokes, would type out *King Lear*. No, he's writing about what one of his experimenters calls "the Power—our unknown Power—kicking and fighting to be let loose" as he installs electrical connections and "with a rending crackle . . . streams of sparks" fly into the air. What might such a "Power" mean? the scientists wonder, and in a disheartened moment they compare their Marconi session to "a spiritualistic séance . . . odds and ends of messages coming out of nowhere . . . no good at all." But "remember," observes the youngest and most enthusiastic of the group, "we're only at the beginning. There's nothing we shan't be able to do in ten years."[25]

LETTERS TO THE VIRTUAL WORLD

And in a century? E-mail *to* the dead? E-mail *from* the dead, whose shadowy faces might appear on our computer screens, who might even, eventually, set up their own Web sites? Such speculations obviously comment on the mysteries of the technology that has overtaken us with such astonishing speed that one begins to believe even the inconceivable might be conceivable or might, perhaps should, be *postulated*. In the conditional realm of *what if*, there are of course a range of not so interesting hypotheses available to me as I mourn the death that engulfed my husband. *If* the surgeon's knife hadn't slipped (supposing that's what happened), *if* the residents had been competent (supposing their incompetence was the problem), I might well have lived a more serene and equable life throughout the 1990s, which isn't a terribly fascinating idea, though for me it should go without saying that it's piercingly poignant. A more amusing *if*, though, centers on the technology of communication that's our equivalent of Kipling's "wireless": since everyone in my department now has an e-mail address, *if* Elliot, our chair in 1991, had survived the surgery, he would now have an e-mail address.

And just the way, for the sheer fun of it I sometimes thought, Elliot used to log on to his home banking system too often, with a clatter and scuttle of life across the keyboard of the Kaypro, so he'd now check his e-mail three or four (or more) times a day, inscribing a newer, faster computer with his user name —"elgilbert," I imagine—and a secret password whose contours will alas always have to stay secret. (Would it be "Kipling" or "Dickens," in honor of authors whose works he studied? Would it be, like his ATM password, our two sets of initials put together to celebrate our marriage? I'll never know, but I can virtually see the rapid two-finger technique with which he'd deliver that magic word into cyberspace.)

I can *virtually* see: in a contemporary revision of Kipling's Marconi fantasy or, for that matter, in a variation on Conan Doyle's obsession with spirit photography, when I'm most bemused, I feel as though the hypothetical cosmos in which we who are bereaved live out the lives we would or should have had *if* the chance of grief had not been dealt to us is itself comparable to the virtual realm into whose unseen folds we aim our daily e-mail. Grief constructs invisible interlocutors, absent presences who read the stories we send into air, into thinnest air, and who are our cherished companions in the imaginary rooms of what might have been. Ever since the day when my husband's life was severed from mine, I've talked to him "in my head," as we mourners often put it. But once I realized he'd have an e-mail address by now, I found myself standing before the glittering screen of the night sky and posting messages toward the virtual, though cryptic, space where I wish he'd be waiting to read them.

That I'm not alone in writing my fantasy e-mail to the dead is evidenced by a whole new mode of elegiac verse that's flourished in the century since first Tennyson and then Hardy tentatively penned what might be considered missives to those they mourned. Donald Hall's *Without*, which includes ten poems frankly titled "letters" as well as a "postcard," articulates the weirdness of this genre. In "Letter after a Year," the poet tells his dead wife that "years before we met," he'd rented a room where he had found and been mystified by a bundle of letters that an earlier tenant had written to a lover who had been killled in a plane crash.

> *In my thirtieth year, with tenure*
> *and a new book coming out,*
> *I read the letters in puzzlement.*
> *"She's writing to somebody* dead?"[26]

To those who are innocent of death's plausibility, to those who haven't been radically bereaved, the hypothesis that one might speak or write to the dead is absurd. "She's writing to somebody *dead*?" *Is she crazy?*

But for the mourner the letter to a virtual world beyond the grave is earnest, insistent, and desperate for news of what the Victorians quaintly called the "beyond." In the first of his letters to Jane Kenyon, "Letter with No Address," Hall is specifically obsessed with the hypothesis of an afterlife:

> *You know now*
> *whether the soul survives death.*
> *Or you don't. When you were dying*
> *you said you didn't fear*
> *punishment. We never dared*
> *to speak of Paradise. . . .*[27]

Ted Hughes also meditated on this subject. The late Poet Laureate of Britain apparently wrote the verse epistles to Sylvia Plath that he included in *Birthday Letters* for more than thirty years, marking perhaps the Yahrzeit of her death, certainly the anniversary of her birth, with scrupulous regularity.

Like Hall, Hughes wanted to tell his dead wife about himself: his latest doings, his grief, his regrets. But he also wanted information about the hypothetical world "beyond" ours. In a poem ironically titled "Life after Death," for instance, he relays sad facts about his and Plath's children's lives after her death, describing their baby son's weeping (his eyes became "wet jewels") and their little daughter's pallor from a "wound" she "could not see or touch or feel." But plainly this always mystical, onetime Ouija practitioner masks a pressing, if barely formulated, question with his news of the living: "What can I tell you that you do not know / Of the life after death?"

ALLAS THE DEETH

Supposing, though, we knew for sure that we *could* communicate with the dead, as Conan Doyle believed and as the channeling practitioners of our New Age assert. Would we truly want to? Perhaps the most dazzling contemporary work on spiritualism, A. S. Byatt's 1992 novella "The Conjugial Angel," meditates on just this question. Set in 1875, in the south England seaside town of Margate, this tale focuses on Emily Tennyson Jesse, the sister who'd been engaged to *In Memoriam*'s much-mourned Arthur Hallam not long before he shockingly and unexpectedly died in Vienna. Now married for some thirty years to a sea captain, Mrs. Jesse is one among a group of mourners attending séances led by a pale young adept named Sophy Sheekhy and a more robust, older medium named Lilias Papagay. Deeply influenced by Mrs. Jesse's brother's famous poem, like just about everyone else in Victorian England, the little group of spiritualists continually hopes to make contact with Hallam's ghost. Yet Emily Jesse herself is also curiously distressed by the "chill, terrible little lyrics" in which her brother expressed his "unappeasable longing" for the dead man to whom *she*, not he, had been betrothed.[28]

On the one hand, Byatt explains, Hallam's grieving onetime fiancée admires "Arthur's monument," for "it expressed *exactly* the nature of her own shock and sorrow." On the other hand, Tennyson's sister feels excluded by "Alfred's masterpiece," for "Alfred had lived with his grief, and worked upon it [but she] had married Richard [Jesse] and closed her mourning"— or at least "closed" it publicly. Privately, however, in company with her husband, several other spiritualist citizens of Margate, and the semiprofessional practitioners Sophy Sheekhy and Lilias Papagay, Emily does eventually receive tidings from "behind the veil." On one occasion, Sophy, the most receptive of the group, transcribes messages from a creature that seemed "to be made up of huge golden eyes the way a mass of frogspawn is made up of jelly." Making her "feel alternately hot and cold," this manifestation of the other world dictates disturbing fragments to the medium, including allusions to *In Memoriam* and trailing off into stammeringly misspelled Chaucerian quotations from Hallam's own letters to Emily: "'Allas the deeth. Allas min E. Allas.'" And at other times, similar messages have been indited at the séances—for instance, "I have somewhat against thee, because thou hast left thy first love," and "Your silliness o'ercasts me much with thought."[29]

That these "faintly threatening," wistful, and reproachful messages come from the dead Hallam and are destined for the living Mrs. Jesse quickly becomes clear to all in the little group of spiritualists. But Mrs. Jesse is after all no longer Emily Tennyson; over the years she has become a new and different person. And Arthur Hallam, though still in some sense himself in spirit, is at the same time *not* himself, for in the world of the living he is a dead man. His first manifestation, in which he appears to Sophy Sheekhy as a sort of huge "decanter or flask" that "gives off a kind of bright *fizzing* sort of light [from countless] golden eyes," emphasizes the otherness of his afterlife being, which is utterly unlike the definitions of the "etheric body" offered by Conan Doyle and other psychic researchers. Peering and staring, *this* "etheric body" represents both the exclusion from the human ordained by death and the desperate yearning—the piercing gaze—with which the dead regard the living. In a second manifestation, moreover, Hallam appears to Sophy as the dead, not the "etheric," body that is the only physical body he actually has.

> There was a sudden gust of odour, not rose, not violet, but earth-mould and corruption.
> "You see," said the harsh, small voice. "I am a dead man, you see." . . .
> She saw dark glass, and she saw him struggling, it seemed to her, to keep his appearance, his sort-of-substance, together, with a kind of deadly defiance.
> She knew immediately that he was the man [Hallam]. . . . She saw that his brows and lashes were caked with clay. He said again, "I am a dead man."[30]

The lesson that the medium Sophy Sheekhy learns from this encounter is dreadful but, Byatt implies, severely necessary. "He wanted to feed off her life, and was invading the very fibre of her nerves with his death," she realizes, deciding "that she would never again, never again try to come into the presence of the terrible dead," among whom Hallam-that-was is "being unmade, undone," so that "he had no more face, or fingers, only clay-cold, airless, stinking mass, plastering her mouth and nostrils." And tellingly, this is a lesson that the principal mourner—Emily Tennyson-that-was—also learns, for as Sophy transmits a final desperate message from her dead lover ("Emilia. I triumph in conclusive bliss. Tell her. We shall be joined and made one Angel"), the middle-aged Mrs. Jesse decisively disengages herself from the little ring of spiritualists, turns to her living husband, and admits prosaically, "I consider that an extremely unfair arrangement, and shall have nothing to do with it," for, she explains, although "I do love him"—Hallam—"[i]t is hard to love the dead. It is hard to love the dead enough."[31]

It is hard to love the dead. Seemingly so simple, that sentence surely has several meanings. It's hard to love the dead because it's an ordeal to love the dead, to think of them dead, to feel the ordeal of their death ("allas the deeth") and their dying, and our loss and lonely survival without them. But it's hard to love the dead too because we're living, and they're ("allas the deeth") dead, and irrevocably so, at least to us and in the terms of the only life we can evidently know.

I do "love the dead." I love Elliot and have written him so much imaginary e-mail that if in the unknowable folds of the virtual cosmos where I hypothesize that he might read it, he *can* read it, he must be happy to have such a full mailbox from the woman who was his wife. I've told him about our children and our grandchildren, brought him up-to-date on the politics of our department and of our country, sent him some of my poems, and, yes, told him a little about my relationship with David, the man I've lived with, at this point, for more than a decade.

But can I, even virtually, tell him who and how I am now? In my new life, changed by countless new experiences, including a love that flourishes side by side with my abiding love for my dead husband, I'm not only older than Elliot was when he died but also no doubt very different from the person I was then. Different in part *because* of his death and different because of a whole range of other encounters with the world.

Maybe if I could "communicate" with Elliot at a séance tomorrow, I'd be as transformed, perhaps as incomprehensible, to *him* as he is ("allas the deeth") unknowable to me.

At the same time, I want to think that like me, he'd still remember with a certain rueful approval the feisty remark a particularly notable literary heiress once made to us both. When he was researching the writings of Rudyard Kipling, we went to visit the author's only surviving offspring, his daughter Elsie Bambridge, who still lived in a vast Jacobean mansion in Cambridgeshire—vaguely reminiscent of the haunted Tudor house in "They"—that her father had bought her when she'd married many years earlier. She showed us around graciously enough but was plainly impatient with scholarly investigations of her family. As we stood gazing at the dusty private chapel that was an integral part of the great estate, she turned fret-

fully toward us. "Why are you so interested in *them* at all?" she asked, meaning her father, her mother, her brother, her sister. "Why aren't you more
interested in *me*? They're *dead*! I'm *alive*!"

Of course we're "interested" in every sense in the dead; invested in our
memories of them, wondering about their fate, we long to reach them in
their hypothetical world. But though we yearn, though we mourn, don't we
have to concede that "they're *dead*," we're *alive*, and admit too—with the
grieving Kipling himself—that there is "no road through the woods"?

Writing Wrong

KEYNOTE

Berkeley. May 11, 2000. Just one day back from Paris and a bit jet-lagged, I'm wearing "conference clothes"—a dark suit set off by a scarf I've tried to knot with vaguely Gallic chic—and I'm standing before an auditorium full of doctors, nurses, bioethicists, lawyers, and "risk management" consultants, along with a few interested academics. I'm at a conference on medical error where I've been asked to represent the perspective of patients and their families, so I reiterate the story of my husband's death following routine surgery, noting that to this day no one from the hospital has really told us how or why he died. Thus, I comment, using the words of the poet Ruth Stone about the mysterious death of *her* husband nearly a quarter of a century ago, "I am still at the same subject, / Shredding facts."[1]

Through painful investigation, I explain, my children and I discovered that my husband evidently bled to death because someone in the recovery room inexplicably failed to get the results of a hematocrit, a simple test that would have detected what may have been a massive postoperative hemorrhage. When we filed suit for negligence, therefore, our lawyer won a settlement just two days after he deposed the attending surgeon. Although, as in most settlements, the hospital admitted no guilt, my husband had clearly been the victim of what researchers call a "negligent adverse event": an event defined by one writer on the subject as "an injury caused by the failure to meet standards reasonably expected of the average physician, other provider, or institution." Eventually, I conclude, I wrote a book that focused on the story I've just summarized for the conferees. In doing so, I observe, I understood that I was writing (recording) as well as seeking to right (to rectify) wrong, and now, as I retell the tale, I realize that "I am still at the same subject," still engaged in the same fearful and fierce activity—writing and seeking to right a mortal wrong.

That the effort to write (record) and right (rectify) wrong involves both fear and ferocity is at the heart of what I want to say to my listeners at the medical error conference, but I speak to them specifically about the aid I think patients and their families need when doctors or nurses make mistakes, outlining some steps that health care professionals might take to help sufferers—or their survivors—cope with such error. I'm addressing questions that I consider crucial. To begin with, how can caregivers who have erred bestow at least a minimal feeling of empowerment on those who suffer from their mistakes? And are there other ways to guide the victims of error or negligence as they confront suffering? Further, how can health care professionals assume responsibility for their errors while helping sufferers or their survivors *not* to feel guilty for having made bad medical choices, for complaining, or for just plain being sick? As part of this process, how can health care professionals construct a narrative of a "negligent adverse event" that isn't merely self-serving or self-centered? Just as important, how can they help the victim of medical error produce an equally coherent and legitimate narrative? Finally, how can, and why should, doctors and nurses encourage patients to complain of medical error when we live in a world that's inevitably fallible?[2]

Though on this occasion I cast these questions in medical terms, I realize that ultimately, in unfolding this line of thought, I'm developing five linked propositions about the problems implicit in the very process of writing wrong, an activity that is as much a process of remembering, testifying, and reorganizing as it is of reiterating and striving to repair or readjust. Just as important, I've come to believe that these five propositions about writing wrong are intimately connected with what have come to be called procedures for grieving and thus too with procedures for elegizing.

Like mourning, like elegizing, the processes that are part of writing and striving to right wrong generate a range of fears and awaken a host of angers, all of which are likely to evoke in both the mourner and the would-be writer some kind of ferocity—ferocious defiance, fierce stubbornness—in order for her to persist in her efforts to transcribe and transform the wrong on which she meditates. Yet such anger can't solace or banish sorrow, even though at first, in a flash of angry inspiration, the mourner or elegist may experience its momentary flush of energy as a way of doing something for, with, and about, even the deepest sorrow.

WEEP AND WRITE

Here is my first and perhaps most draconian proposition. Writing wrong is, or ultimately becomes, wrong—or at the least problematic—because it's a hopeless effort at a performative act that can never in fact be truly performed. You can't, in other words, right wrong by writing wrong, even though you are engaged in the writing because consciously or unconsciously you believe that your testimony will reverse, repair, or undo the wrong you're reporting. You may think, for instance, that your witnessing will trap the culprit in the case you're describing, whoever "it" or "he" or "she" may be. Or more fantastically still, you may think your *act* of witness will change the story itself!

"DÉTECTIVE PRIVÉ?" Did the black and yellow poster that still hangs on the wall of what was once my husband's study summarize the secret project underlying my effort to write wrong? Looming over us in the lamplight during my home banking lesson two days before Elliot's death, the poster shows a masked, fedora-hatted film noir private eye, coat collar turned up, clutching a walkie-talkie and ready to undertake *toutes missions*. Was this whom I thought I might become, as I struggled to assemble the fragments of what I knew about my husband's death into a coherent narrative?

If that was so, mine was a mission impossible, as Elliot's ghost might have advised me. It was because he'd been seriously analyzing the genre of the detective novel that my husband had acquired that charmingly sinister poster some years earlier, on the French Riviera. But his professional view of mystery fiction tended to be skeptical. "One of the limits of detection most often explored [is] the difficulty of converting knowledge into proper action," he'd once written, adding that a "work of detective fiction is constructed to lead up to the revealing of some previously hidden truth [but] the actual business of converting that truth into action—into, say, the capture and punishment of the criminal and the 'healing' of society"—is problematic, for "there's no necessary connection between the ability to discover knowledge and the ability to apply it."[3]

If I thought my written (re)construction of a or *the* story of his death might bring some culprit to justice, he might have wanted to remind me from beyond the grave that I was deceiving myself.

Nevertheless, it may be significant that I began trying to write the story on precisely the day my children and I had our first meeting with the attorney who represented us in our lawsuit. Even though Elliot may have imbued in me a proper doubt about the possibility of a just denouement to his "case," I may have unconsciously had even more unrealistic beliefs about the powers of righting implicit in any act of writing wrong. I may in fact have secretly believed that in some sense the "performance" of the narrative my children and I had just outlined to our lawyer would somehow reverse or at the least revise the script in which we were trapped.

Did I feel that if I could *tell* the whole "true" story, it might end differently? Or did I suppose that if I got *that* story out of the way, it might be replaced by another? And do other, comparable modes of mourning reflect similar needs to reconstruct the narrative of death in the covert hope that such a reconstruction might facilitate a reshaping of the tale itself?

Just as I never of course confessed to such a dream in the book I wrote, so I certainly didn't indulge there in grandiose fantasies about revising the "plot." On the contrary, I offered a conventional expository paragraph explaining that I wanted to document the real-life impact of medical negligence for people who get angry at "greedy" plaintiffs and for doctors who deplore the escalating costs of malpractice insurance.

Earlier, though, I'd speculated, "Do I still believe that the lawsuit will, if only temporarily, resurrect my husband?" Did I, I'd now add, believe that by recounting the story of both the negligent, adverse event and the lawsuit to which it led, I could subtly change its ending? Such a sense of authorial potency may be akin to the feeling some people have (I'm one of them) when watching films of great catastrophes—the assassination of JFK, for instance—that if it were only possible to run the film backward or freeze a crucial frame, the inexorable plot of what-has-been might magically modulate into what-didn't-happen. The motorcade would take a different route; the grassy knoll would turn out to be just *grassy*; the young president and his pink-suited wife would return triumphantly to Washington.

By the time I was ending the book, I have to admit, I was more moderate, conceding that I'd decided to write this story because "sad as it is, there isn't and wasn't and never was anything else to do." Nothing to do, I was conceding, but testify, bear witness, swear to the truth of this account I hereby proffer to you, the reader. Nothing to do because once the calamity has happened, it is of course inexorable; it will *always have happened.*

Such a sense that catastrophe can't be averted, I now understand, is ultimately as central to the impassioned questions that mark so many ceremonial elegies as are the hopeless dreams of transformation and the futile protests against fate that mark the lamentations of great and small alike.

"Where were ye, nymphs, when the remorseless deep / Closed o'er the head of your loved Lycidas?" demands Milton, but he soon has to concede that not even the interventions of divinities could have changed the plot that shaped the death of Edward King, the drowned schoolmate whom he mythologizes as Lycidas. But "Ay me! I fondly dream," he quickly concedes.

> *Had ye been there—for what could that have done?*
> *What could the Muse herself that Orpheus bore,*
> *The Muse herself, for her inchanting son*
> *Whom universal Nature did lament,*
> *When by the rout that made the hideous roar,*
> *His gory visage down the stream was sent . . . ?*

If not even the muse Calliope, great mother of the fabled poet Orpheus, could save her son from savage dismemberment by the maddened Bacchantes, how could a few nymphs—sprightly nature goddesses though they might be—have altered the story of Edward King?[4]

A century and a half later Shelley echoed Milton's questions in the ritual interrogation with which he begins "Adonais," his thunderous elegy for Keats:

> *Where wert thou mighty Mother, when he lay,*
> *When thy Son lay, pierced by the shaft which flies*
> *In darkness? Where was lorn Urania*
> *When Adonais died?*

But again, as the poet realizes all too fully, the mother goddess—in this case Venus Urania—cannot intercede with death to save her doomed son, here called Adonais.[5]

What remedy is there then? What charm against immovable fate? Both Milton and Shelley confront an abyss of despair as they lament their losses, an abyss embedded at the center of the elegiac genre itself. Even writing as an act of witnessing begins to seem pointless. Confesses Milton:

> *Alas! What boots it with incessant care*
> *To tend the homely slighted shepherd's trade,*
> *And strictly meditate the thankless Muse?*

Why write wrong if the writing won't right the wrong?

And I? Where even Milton faltered, what could I have dreamed my own small act of writing might perform? Yes, I was going to write a book because there never was anything else to do. But a sentence later I can see that in some part of myself I must still have had grander ambitions. If I couldn't inscribe a spell that would heal or resurrect, then I wanted to spell out words that would damn and destroy those guilty of the crime that left my husband bleeding to death in the recovery room of a modern medical center. Thus I quoted Elizabeth Barrett Browning's scathing diatribe against slavery, "A Curse for a Nation":

Weep and write.
A curse from the depths of womanhood
Is very salt, and bitter, and good.[6]

Was I unconsciously evoking Milton, who halfway through "Lycidas" imperiously (and rather mysteriously) curses those "Blind mouths! That scarce themselves know how to hold / A sheep-hook"—corrupt clergy who have wrongly survived the righteous Edward King? Or was I influenced by the raging Shelley, who sought to blast the anonymous reviewer on whom he blamed Keats's death as a "deaf and viperous murderer"? Storms the author of "Adonais":

Remorse and Self-contempt shall cling to thee;
Hot shame shall burn upon thy secret brow,
And like a beaten hound tremble thou shalt—as now.

Yet where these curses uttered by the great elegists were as majestic as they were cathartic, leading to moments of transformation when rage and grief yielded to visionary consolation, my own anger was more anxious, less salutary.

A humbler mourner, a lamenting widow and an end-of-the-skeptical-twentieth-century memoirist rather than a ceremonial elegist, I drew on Barrett Browning to claim that my curse was "very salt, and bitter, and good," but clearly it frightened me, for not insignificantly, I withdrew from my own anger. "I didn't want to curse. I don't," I insisted in an open letter to all the doctors who'd been associated with my husband's care. I just "want to *talk* to you. I want you to hear me. . . . And I guess this is the only way."[7]

Yet what *did* I have in mind when I ended this meditation by evoking Barrett Browning's admonition that "THIS is the curse. Write"?

THIS IS THE CURSE. WRITE.

My second proposition: writing wrong is wrong, or at least problematic, because it's not only painful but *writing* pain—pain that as I've just claimed, can't really be righted or sedated. On the contrary, to write wrong, whether in memoir or elegy, is to drive oneself into the heart of fear, pain, rage. Barrett Browning's sentence to slaveholding America was also a sentencing *of* slaveholding America. "THIS is the curse. Write." Consider the ambiguity of this phrase, which can surely be taken to imply *that the act of writing is itself a curse* inflicted as much on the accuser as on the accused, as much on the writer as on the target of the writing.

Of course, even to bring a lawsuit, that would-be performative motion of accusation always hurling itself toward the judicial words "I now *pronounce* this or that culprit guilty," even to bring such a suit is to suffer the inscription of pain. You, the witness and accuser, do testify before the clerkly attorney-at-law who records your statements. "BE IT REMEMBERED," begins the standard deposition form, "that on _____ day, at the hour of _____ of said day, at _____ (place name), before me, _____ (name of notary), a Notary Public, personally appeared _____ (name of deponent), who was examined as a witness in said cause." The ancient formula has hardly changed: "Comes now before me so-and-so and deposes"—which is to say, "puts down her word"—"and says."

Maybe I shouldn't have been surprised, then, at the number of people who wondered how I could stand to bring a lawsuit ("How can you keep on reliving it again and again?" they asked) and, worse, how I could stand to write a book about such loss and grief—and such anger. How could I bear, they seemed to be asking, to bear witness over and over again, both before the law and on the page? How could I bear to see it again and to say it again?

My answer, always affirmed by my children, was always the same, to questions both about the lawsuit and about the book: we're bringing the suit because we have to, he'd want us to; I'm writing the book because I have to, he'd want me to. He'd want! How could we possibly know what or how he'd "want"? Yet we were haunted by the remorselessness of a subjunctive we ourselves—I in particular—created. Perhaps such a subjunctive was a way of keeping the dead one alive; "he'd want," after all, was only a grammatical step away from "he *wants*." Somewhere, in another dimension, another shape—perhaps in the "virtual" world of the dead—there he is, *wanting* his survivors to go to a lawyer or write a book. Surely such a confident hypothesis helped us relieve the pain of reliving the pain.

At the same time, I was troubled by the no doubt well-meant comments of people who assumed that either the lawsuit or the writing was "therapeutic." From my own perspective, certainly, I was undertaking what I believed to be actions that would have consequences *outside* myself, although I did indeed understand that one always engages in acts one considers moral for the sake of one's own conscience as well as for the effect such actions will have on the world beyond the self. But even the concept "my own conscience" wouldn't really altogether define the *consciousness* I was trying, darkly, to assuage.

Yet what of the fear not just enacted but elicited by the writing of this, or any, wrong—or indeed by the memorializing and consequent remembering of this or any death? As one commentator has put it, a memorial functions, in some respects, "as a boomerang," for "Traumas and losses are like boomerangs—one cannot throw them away, rather the attempts to get rid of them effect their very return."[8] I'd be deceiving myself and others if I denied the pain that surrounded the very process of transcribing what I knew to have happened and, worse, *what I didn't know about what had happened.*

"That which you fear the most, that you must do." I said this sentence to myself over and over again, like a mantra, as I tried to narrate the story I've still never been told, the story of the moments of my husband's death. In order to imagine something of that event, I had to quell my fear of the hospital records I'd been given and struggle to assemble at least an approximation of a death scene. That which I feared the most, as I bleakly put it to myself, was what I had to confront, and I had to confront it precisely because in order to stand the pain of my loss, I had to strive to stand *up* to the pain and loss, strive to *with*stand them by looking at them.

"DÉTECTIVE PRIVÉ?" Here too did the black and yellow poster depict the figure I longed—albeit shiveringly—to become, as I sought to narrate for myself that unspoken and perhaps unspeakable scene in the recovery room? But again mine was a mission impossible, for even if some nurse or orderly who'd been in that recovery room should now, suddenly, step forward to fill in the gaps in the records, such a bystander could obviously never tell the tale from the perspective I care most about, that of the dying man, though I've repeatedly tried to envision his experience for myself, both out of obligation to him and as a crucial gesture of lamentation.

Of course I realize that this aspect of my procedure for grieving may be disconcerting to those who want to shield themselves as well as me from suffering. As I argue later in this book, we live in a culture where grief is frequently experienced as at the least an embarrassment and sometimes even as a sort of illness or a disorder from which one "recovers," as from alcoholism. The surgeon who came to tell us of my husband's death was accompanied by a woman wearing a badge that said "Carolyn, Office of Decedent Services"; she carried a large folder labeled "Bereavement Packet." Lacking traditional strategies for solace, we're so dumbfounded by death that we'd rather leave the pain to professionals.

Thus I know that in recent years, as I've spoken personally as well as generally about the topics at the heart of my memoir—medical calamity, death, grief, elegy—I've probably embarrassed or distressed a number of listeners. To be frank, I myself am sometimes troubled by the words I have to say out loud when I tell the story of error and sorrow that I tell. Often I go through a kind of performance anxiety very different from the nervousness ordinarily associated with public speaking. Have I required too much sympathy from my audience as I reiterate my script? In describing my writing of a wrong, as well as in the very act of writing about this wrong, have I done something *socially* wrong—turned myself into a "loser," a "whiner," a "complainer"?

YOU MUST BE WICKED TO DESERVE SUCH PAIN

Such remarks lead to proposition three about writing wrong: writing wrong may be wrong or at least problematic because you, the writer, may actually be the one who is wrong, either in your perception of events or in your response to them. Perhaps people are embarrassed or distressed by your assertion that you've been wronged because you're asking them to judge the merits of a case they can't evaluate. Perhaps you, the writer, are a wrongdoer who has leveled your *J'accuse* against an innocent person. Or perhaps, just as bad, writing wrong is an effort to exploit (and thus intensify) a wrong.

This last notion of course underlies public scorn for those so-called ambulance-chasing lawyers and greedy plaintiffs who are together held responsible for the escalating costs of malpractice insurance and thus (so some commentators insist) the rising cost of medical care. But it's probably also at the center of the distaste some people seem to feel for what is called confessional poetry and indeed the disgust many express for any kind of tell-all memoir writing that can be characterized as sensational and hence exploitative.

Grace under pressure, we're taught, is "cool." Writing wrong, then, may be *uncool* as well as uncouth. "Revenge is mine," saith the Lord, not any mere *writer's*. In the face of pain, one should be stoic, unflinching, even, if possible, courteous. Perhaps, then, to protest suffering is to earn or even merit suffering. Or perhaps the suffering itself is and always was a sign that suffering was *warranted*.

My husband, a Victorianist, was always especially fond of the skewed logic manifested by the eponymous speaker of Robert Browning's "Childe Roland to the Dark Tower Came." Catching sight of a "stiff blind horse, his every bone a-stare," Browning's "Childe Roland" comments that the creature "must be wicked to deserve such pain."[9]

How many woeful mourners, wailing grievers, sufferers of injustice or absurd mischance haven't at one time or another considered this possibility? *I think I have been wronged, but I must be wicked to deserve such pain.* How write wrong, then—how inscribe pain—if the pain and wrong are themselves stigmata of guilt?

A HOLE IN THE HEART

Proposition four: writing wrong is wrong or anyway problematic because after all, as contemporary theory would tell us, if you can write it, you've written it wrong.

This proposition, to be sure, can be applied to the writing of any memoir. Haven't I already confessed that what I feared the most was that I had to *imagine* (which is to say, I had in some sense to write *wrongly*) the, for me, crucial moments of my husband's death, the moments whose truth I never had a chance to witness? "Art is a lie one tells in order to tell the truth," declared Picasso, who was in fact not just serene but seraphic about rearranging faces, bodies, curves, and angles. But Defoe said—and his comment is darker, scarier—"Supplying a story by invention . . . is a sort of Lying that makes a great Hole in the Heart."[10]

There's a hole in my heart where I had to supply the story of my husband's wrongful death by lying—that is, by imagining what I hadn't seen and thence by writing wrong. And what of the "true," supposedly real-life, episodes to which I declare I *have* borne witness? Have I transcribed them rightly or wrongly, wrong*fully*? Can an elegist at one and the same time mourn and produce an accurate account of the loss that shapes the plot of grief?

Even when and if I think I have gotten the story somehow *right*, surely it's wrong; surely I haven't said all there is to say. The story itself, as any memoirist knows but perhaps as the traumatized writers of wrong particularly know, continually recedes into an infinite, untellable distance, as does the pain at the center of elegy. That's the point of "Something Deeper," the Ruth Stone poem

I quoted earlier. And the something deeper, as Stone observes, seems always to have been there, like a question behind or beyond appearances:

> *I am still at the same subject—*
> *Shredding facts—*
> *As old women nervously*
> *Pull apart*
> *Whatever is put in their fingers . . .*
> *Tearing the milky curtain,*
> *After something deeper*
> *That did not occur*
> *In all the time of making*
> *And preparing.*

"Something deeper" always there but untellable: it isn't surprising that my sense of such a deeper, unreachable story gives me a feeling of affinity with other poets—rememberers and questioners—that's often powerfully confirmed. But maybe in a strange way it's fortunate for me that in my own case another writer has corroborated the practical as well as theoretical conundrum proffered by my husband's death. Robert Pinsky's beautiful "Impossible to Tell" was in part composed in memory of Elliot and includes the same kind of effort at writing the wrong of his death that I myself have made, though from the perspective of someone outside the situation. Pinsky begins by observing that often a joke he liked "was Elliot's." Then, about a particular joke he'd heard at one point, he notes: "The doctors made the blunder / That killed him some time later that same year," adding, farther on in the poem: "It was a routine / Procedure. When it was finished the physicians // Told Sandra and the kids it had succeeded . . . They should go eat," though when they—*we*—returned, "The doctors had to tell them about the mistake."[11]

Yet still, admits Pinsky, though he has narrated this story, like so many other "true stories," it is ultimately "impossible to tell" because yes, there's some other story one is always trying to uncover in telling this tale or any other tale of wrong and woe.

IMPOSSIBLE TO TELL

Here, then, is my fifth and final proposition. Isn't that "other" story the story of storylessness, the story of death, loss, grief—the story we don't want to tell because we can't tell it? Writing wrong is wrong— problematic, painful, guilt-inducing, or all of these—because it is *writing death*, writing *the* absence that can't be written. In the course of his poem, Pinsky tells a joke about a dead man that he says he learned from my husband. It's a kind of miniature Jewish folk tale about a rabbi who struggles with naive stubbornness to resurrect a dead man with blessings and incantations in a host of different languages:

> *"Arise and breathe," he shouted;*
> *But nothing happened. The body lay still. So then*
> *The little rabbi called for hundreds of candles*
>
> *And danced around the body, chanting and praying*
> *In Hebrew, then Yiddish, then Aramaic. He prayed*
> *In Turkish and Egyptian and Old Galician*
>
> *For nearly three hours [until]*
> *Panting, he raised both arms in a mystic gesture*
>
> *And said, "Arise and breathe!" And still the body*
> *Lay as before.*

"And still the body / Lay as before." The motionless body—the unalterably factual body of death and the dead—lies at the center of Pinsky's poem, as it so differently lies at the center of my husband's joke. "Impossible to tell / In words how Elliot's eyebrows flailed . . . Like shaggy mammoths" as he dramatized this joke, the poet comments, but of course what makes this point "impossible to tell," just as it makes Pinsky's poem almost impossible for me to read, is the brute truth that Elliot's once-mobile eyebrows have now been incorporated into the corpus of unspeakability here, the unknowable corpse that is ultimately *the* "impossible to tell" certainty at the heart of all story.

"Death," wrote the critic Walter Benjamin, "is the sanction of everything that the storyteller can tell. He has borrowed his authority from death."[12] By this, he must have meant something like what the philosopher Michel de Certeau means when he declares, "Discourse about the past has the status of being the discourse of the dead," or when he adds, "The dead are the objective figure of an exchange among the living"—both the subjects and *shapers* of narrative.[13] For death is the end of all story as well as the mysterious blank out of which story starts and against which it sets itself while at the same time it is what is "impossible to tell."

Yet the protest against death is what must be "told," as the beads of a rosary are told, and what must be written, even if it's written wrong. Pinsky's poem rises to a crescendo as this contemporary poet segues into a series of quasi-Miltonic or Shelleyan curses, *his* complaints at the injustice of muses, demons, gods, divinities whose indifference to human fate makes death possible while leaving it "impossible to tell." Addressing the "immortal / Lords of the underground and afterlife, / Jehovah, Raa, Bol-Morah, Hecate, Pluto," he asks an eternally unanswerable question:

> *What has a brilliant living soul to do with*
> *Your harps and fires and boats, your bric-a-brac*
> *And troughs of smoking blood? Provincial stinkers,*
>
> *Our languages don't touch you.*

Nor will our languages ever touch that wrong. Our languages, all of them, lie and leave a hole in the heart, even though there is surely a sense in which, as Benjamin wisely insists, "a man's . . . real life—and this is the stuff that stories are made of—first assumes transmissible form at the moment of his death," the moment when the narrative reveals, in several senses, its "end."

That Benjamin's own death by suicide was shaped by the barely speakable, often "impossible to tell" circumstances of the Holocaust has a grim irony here. For there's a sense in which almost all the efforts at writing and righting wrong on which I've been meditating evoke the concept of testimony as it's defined by Shoshana Felman and Dori Laub in their absorbing collection of essays on Holocaust witnessing. Felman and Laub's *Testimony* is a psychohistorical study focusing primarily on the devastating experiences of European concentration camp survivors, but its analysis of the relationship between trauma and acts of witnessing has considerable relevance for any theoretical overview of what I've described as "writing wrong." In fact, as Felman defines "testimony," it is the fragmentary product of a mind "overwhelmed by occurrences that have not settled into understanding or remembrance . . . events in excess of our frames of reference" not unlike those mystifying events on which the mourner of a sudden, calamitous death so hopelessly and helplessly broods.[14]

Holocaust survivors have of course had to confront a trauma of such magnitude that it dwarfs almost any other, becoming in a sense a paradigm of collective as well as personal nightmare for the era in which we live. Yet anyone who has suffered the shock of a death that is unexpected or experienced as wrongful has had to engage with what is impossible to tell yet somehow essential to speak, if only stammeringly. Sylvia Plath was another poet who repeatedly made such halting efforts at rendering an account of the unspeakable, especially as she struggled to define the grief for her father that had made a hole in the heart of her childhood. Toward the end of her cryptic "Little Fugue," for instance, she struggles to evoke the lost "daddy." Confessing "I am lame in the memory," she confides that all she can really remember consists of "a blue eye, / A brief case of tangerines" and notes, "This was a man, then!," as if marveling that the whole of a human being could somehow be represented by such fragments. But though she adds, in a dark comment that I continue to find extraordinarily resonant, "Death opened, like a black tree, blackly," she concedes that she has had to endure her pain and find ways of organizing experience: "I survive the while, / Arranging my morning."[15]

"I survive the while, / *Arranging my morning*": these two lines define what is perhaps the only thing that I'm sure is deeply right about writing wrong. Though the lost loved one keeps on being dead Yahrzeit after Yahrzeit, though curses fail to blast and no blessing will resurrect and letters to the virtual world beyond the veil go undelivered, writing wrong is what there is to do. Perhaps, for some of us, all there is to do. And yes, that's sad, indeed worse than sad, given the ways in which losses are so much "like boomerangs" that every effort at inscription returns and revitalizes them.

Yet facing the chaos of loss, the continual undoing that opens "like a black tree" behind what Ruth Stone sees as the "milky curtain" of the quotidian, I have to join others in believing that even though writing wrong won't right wrong, this grievous task is a special way of arranging not just the beginning of each of my days but my *mourning*—the untellable sorrow out of which I strive to bring some order, some meaning. And because such arrangements of mourning are the primary work of elegy and lamentation, my project throughout the rest of this book will be an attempt to study them in all their variety while seeking to understand how history and culture have shaped and reshaped them in our own time.

PART TWO

History Makes Death:
How the Twentieth Century
Reshaped Dying and Mourning

Death has its history. This history is biological, social, and mental. . . . Every historical era, every society and culture have had their own understanding, iconography, and rites of mortality. It may well be that all mythologies and religious or metaphysical systems and narratives are a mortuary, an endeavor, often ingenious and elaborate, to edify a house for the dead.

—GEORGE STEINER,
GRAMMARS OF CREATION

6

Expiration/Termination

"MODERN DEATH"

There's a story, perhaps apocryphal, that Wallace Stevens, among the most skeptical of modern poets, was converted to Roman Catholicism not long before he died. A lawyer, Stevens had a "day job" with the Hartford Insurance Company, where some of his associates apparently had trouble believing that he wrote verse, let alone that he was an extraordinarily distinguished author, so conventionally corporate did he seem. Perhaps they'd have found it equally difficult to imagine a connection between this seemingly prosaic coworker's daily business and the metaphysical brooding of which his alleged turn to the Church would have been a final sign. Yet Stevens's hypothetical deathbed conversion may itself have been a form of insurance, not unlike the notorious "wager" proposed by the seventeenth-century mathematician-philosopher Blaise Pascal: "Let us weigh the gain and the loss in wagering that God is. . . . If you gain, you gain all; if you lose, you lose nothing. Wager, then, without hesitation that He is."[1]

If, as the conversion story suggests, Stevens did yearn to "gain all" in a Catholic afterlife, it's important to consider that such longing coexisted with the nihilism expressed in this poet's disturbing "Madame La Fleurie," where as we've seen, the fate of one who has died is to bring "all that he saw into the earth, to the waiting parent," to have "his crisp knowledge . . . devoured by her, beneath a dew." Here, as in so many other Stevens poems, death is, as the writer put it elsewhere, "absolute and without memorial." Even if the earth is personified as a sort of goddess (a flowering "Madame," maybe a genteel one but maybe the doyenne of a not so respectable bawdy house), "she" eats up consciousness as surely as she devours flesh and bone, leaving behind not a shred of spirit and certainly not what's traditionally been called soul.[2]

Stevens's friend William Carlos Williams, a physician in *his* "day job," imagined life's end as even more inexorably material. With clinical coolness, he stripped the subject bare in a poem entitled "Death," describing a dead man as "a godforsaken curio / without / any breath in it," a *thing* that in its stiffened state of rigor mortis can lie like a board between one chair and another, with eyes

> *rolled up out of*
> *the light—a mockery*
>
> > *which*
> *love cannot touch—*
>
> *just bury it*
> *and hide its face*
> *for shame.*[3]

Stevens himself never produced quite such an unflinching sketch of a body from which the breath of life has departed. Whereas Williams's career in medicine taught him to look at the dead with scientific "objectivity," the author of "Madame La Fleurie" usually dressed death in flourishes and at times sought to treat it whimsically.[4] Yet the photographic gaze at the center of Williams's "Death" is also at the secret center of "Madame La Fleurie" as well as at the heart of many other Stevens poems. Moreover, if Williams had been professionally hardened to cope with the anxieties induced by such a sight, Stevens, like most of us, was less equipped by training or temperament, despite the bravado to which he sometimes aspired.

No wonder, then, that Stevens may have finally been drawn, as Pascal was, toward the Christian promise of transcendence and transformation through communion with a redemptive divinity. If he did accept a holy wafer on his deathbed, that's because he was struggling to deny a vision of absolute annihilation that was to become increasingly common throughout the twentieth century. "*Modern* death," Stevens called this view of mortality in an elegy for a close friend in which he sought to outline a "mythology" that might bring some comfort to those who mourn.[5] History, this phrase implies, is constituted as much by a series of different deaths ("classical," "romantic," "modern") as by a series of different lives. Each death changes the world even while each way of dying, each different imagination of death, has itself been changed by the world's changes. There's a sense, then, in which we might say history makes death, even while there's also a corresponding sense in which death makes history.

Death makes history. Both literally and figuratively, history can be seen as a product of death in the same way that language is a product of loss. Just as language stands for that which is not *there*, with, say, the word "rose" evoking an absent flower for us, so history records the past presence of that which was (once) there.[6] Indeed, even colloquially the word "history" is now interchangeable with the word "death," as in the sometimes playful but occasionally murderous phrase "So-and-so is dead; he's *history*." But of course death doesn't make history only in the abstract. Death makes history in the most particular and poignant sense, makes not just that history of each individual summarized by birth and death dates but the histories of individual lives that subsist within those parentheses. Thus the deaths of charismatic leaders, the dissolution of old ideas, the destruction of traditional customs, the disintegration of antiquated social structures—all these demolitions of the past prepare and constitute the cultural transformations we call history even while the history they beget shapes what we call the modern and its notions of death.

But as this last point implies, *even while death makes history, history makes death*, makes and remakes it as it has been continually reimagined from age to age and place to place. As the French historian Philippe Ariès was one of the first to document, different eras have had radically different views of death and dying, just as different cultures around the world imagine both the fate of the dead and the grief of the living in strikingly diverse ways. Thus, with all the confusions and contradictions of belief or disbelief surrounding it, the death we confront today in the industrialized West is always in some sense a form of Stevens's "*modern* death," an end to life surrounded by assumptions and customs significantly unlike those that shaped life's end in, say, the Middle Ages, the Renaissance, or the Victorian period.

This modern death is, perhaps most strikingly, a demise many of us would rather not think about. As I began researching contemporary modes of mourning and recent ideas about mortality, I found a remarkable anecdote in a volume by a fellow investigator of the subject. When he asked the American Cancer Society for permission to include some of its materials in a scholarly book entitled *Confronting Death: Values, Institutions, and Human Mortality*, reports the sociologist David Moller, its representative responded with a statement that's distinctively "modern": "Absolutely not. In no way do we want to be associated with a book on death. We want to emphasize the positive aspects of cancer only." It isn't easy to imagine such words coming from a medieval theologian or even a Renaissance physician, either of whom would have defined the confrontation with serious illness as an opportunity to acknowledge the urgencies of mortality, but the Cancer Society's reaction tellingly illustrates what another observer has called the "peculiarly twentieth-century" concept of "death as an unmentionable, almost unnatural, subject."[7]

Yet of course, if a dead person is "a godforsaken curio," a material *thing* whose "crisp knowledge" is going to be eaten by "the waiting parent" known as "mother earth" (for which read also "worms"), if death is merely ending, terminating, what right-minded, upbeat person—indeed, what well-intentioned charitable organization—would "want to be associated" with it? Death as a rising of the soul, an expiration into the arms of the Church—that would be a different matter, wouldn't it, or at least slightly better? "The mind blanks at the glare," wrote the British poet Philip Larkin in the late seventies, in a poem ironically entitled "Aubade," as he contemplated "the dread / Of dying, and being dead. " The mind, he meant, "blanks"—almost redundantly—at the blankness of "total emptiness for ever, / The sure extinction that we travel to / And shall be lost in always." And like Stevens, Larkin understood his nihilistic vision to be peculiarly "modern." Noting that he was defining a fear of death that "is a special way of being afraid / No trick dispels," he admitted: "Religion used to try" to dispel our dread, yet *now* we are forced to see religion as merely a "vast moth-eaten musical brocade / Created to pretend we never die."[8]

With Stevens, though (if not Williams and Larkin), many of us who confront "modern death" oscillate between two views of dying. The first, which I'll label "expiration," is a wishful, often wistful imagination of life's end that has been clothed in the "musical brocade" of traditional religious belief; the second, which I'll call "termination," is a self-consciously "modern"and austere vision of dying that has been almost willfully stripped of theological embroidery. In my own experience, those two views were painfully but dramatically summarized by two deaths—well, really, two ways of *telling* death—that now, after considerable reflection, I see as having represented two ways of thinking about death.

"EXPIRATION" VS. "TERMINATION"

The first of these deaths occurred in 1958, at an American army hospital in Fürth, Germany, a town that had been bombed out during the Second World War, before which it had been a thriving suburb of Nürnberg.

Twenty-one years old, six months pregnant, I'd been admitted to this hospital with strong contractions, and though the doctors at first refused to acknowledge it, I was in labor with a premature baby boy, to whom I gave birth in the chill of a September dawn.

Three days later, as my husband and I paced the corridor outside the nursery where the child was being cared for, a young nurse came up to us and murmured, "Your baby has taken a turn for the worse."

Would we like her to baptize him? she wondered. She'd noticed that I'd checked off "Roman Catholic" in response to the religious affiliation question on the hospital admissions form. She was a Catholic herself, she told us, and any layperson can baptize "in an emergency."

I surprised myself by murmuring, "Yes, please."

Pascal's wager? Probably it was, just as my checking off the box that said, "Roman Catholic," had been. When I was a third grader in "religious instruction," I was taught by the nuns that unbaptized babies have to spend an eternity in limbo, a shadowy nowhere land to which no mother would consign her infant. As Stevens probably did, I was taking out an insurance policy.

An hour or so later the same nurse reappeared to say, again in a muted, regretful tone, "I'm sorry, he just expired."

Expired. Breathed out the breath of life he had only days earlier taken in. Expelled, so it suddenly seemed to me, the soul, that had so recently entered and animated him.

Just a third of a century later, in July 1992, my husband's doctor was deposed in our wrongful death lawsuit. Reporting the circumstances surrounding the "code"—the moment when Elliot went into cardiac arrest and a "team" arrived to try to resuscitate him—the surgeon claimed that he knew rather little about what happened because, he said, "I arrived when he was just terminating. I arrived before he terminated, but he had not responded at that time."[9]

Terminated. Arrested. Not even he *"was* terminated." *He* "terminated." *He* ended himself. His heart stopped; his breathing ceased. He himself produced, as it were, an absolute finale.

Because the word "expire" has roots in the Latin *spiritus* (meaning "breath") in which our concept of spirit originates, it means both "to breathe out" and "to breathe one's last" but also implies "to breathe out the spirit or soul." In many medieval and Renaissance depictions of what was traditionally called the Triumph of Death over mortals—the all-powerful sway of death that gives us the very word "mortality"—it's possible to see representations of this soul just emerging from the mouths of the dying. For instance, in the magnificent *Trionfo della Morte* that occupies several walls of what was once a monumental cemetery in Pisa, tiny person-shaped puffs of breath ascend like miniature balloons from the mouths of those who have been stricken by death's unresting spear, some (the souls of the damned) destined to be trapped by the pitchforks of vigilant devils, others (the souls of the blessed) rising straight up to the celestial blue, where angels are awaiting them. In a number of medieval and Renaissance crucifixions too, the two thieves whose crosses flank Christ's die exhaling miniature versions of their human selves, spirits winging their way from mortal flesh to moral fate [fig. 1].

With their inherent allusion to an ongoing spiritual existence, these visions of the expiring soul give the word "expiration" a positive overtone

1. Collégiale Saint-Martin: detail of *La Crucifixion* with expiring souls as homunculi (c. 1400).

that the word "termination" lacks. If he really died in the bosom of the Church, Stevens no doubt did so because he wanted to *expire* into blessedness, wanted to escape a lifetime in which he had tried but failed to come to terms with the depressing concept of termination. For the word "termination" originates in the Latin *terminus* for "end" or "boundary" and means simply to "reach a terminus" or "come to an end in time."

The one who "expires" wins Pascal's wager. The one who "terminates" is the loser. And it seems to me that the "mythology of modern death" whose assumptions shape our ends increasingly depends on a definition of death as termination rather than on a conception of death as expiration. Because of this, moreover, for at least the last century, most of the serious writings in which we represent death have refused to solve the problems of loss and grief in traditionally comforting ways. Where, for example, the great elegists of the English language trusted for centuries in the radiant reality of a transcendent realm into which the souls of those they mourned might *expire*, most poets mourning "modern" deaths have sought to cope with the intransigent blankness of *terminations* that lead nowhere and promise nothing.

ASH WEDNESDAY

Ashes to ashes, dust to dust. Dust thou art, and unto dust thou shalt return.

When I was a little girl studying the ways of the Catholic Church every Wednesday afternoon during what the New York City school system rather curiously designated as "released time," I was frightened and vaguely sickened by Ash Wednesday. Since those of us who were "released" to learn more about the faith into which we had been born were in any case spending each Wednesday afternoon at the parochial school associated with our local church, it was easy to lead us in a solemn, if straggly, line from the classroom where we'd been taught that God was infinite, omnipotent, and immortal to the altar where we were to be reminded that we ourselves were finite, powerless, and mortal.

Still in winter coats or jackets, breath still marking the cold not-yet-spring air with little clouds of our own warmth, we stumbled from the brightness outside into the dark of the church, which seemed especially gloomy on this especially scary day. The priest, in liturgical purple, signifying death and grief, loomed behind the railing that surrounded the sanctuary. I remember how his thumb dug into my forehead, marking it with a cross of ashes. I remember the grim satisfaction with which, so it seemed to me, he muttered his sacred Latin phrases—words in an indecipherable undertone that were said to mean "Ashes to ashes, dust to dust," or "Dust thou art, and unto dust thou shalt return," or both, I was never sure which.

"On this day," the *Catholic Encyclopedia* tells us, "all the faithful according to ancient custom are exhorted to approach the altar . . . and there the priest, dipping his thumb into ashes previously blessed, marks the forehead— or in case of clerics upon the place of the tonsure—of each with the sign of the cross, saying the words 'Remember man that thou art dust and unto dust thou shalt return.' "

On these occasions, as I recall, I brooded a good deal on my relationship to "dust," which I visualized as the little gray balls of fluff that my mother's mop retrieved from under my bed. Was *I* originally made of such dust? Was I destined, then, to drift off or down (under a bed, for instance) as mere fluff?

At the same time, there was the question of ashes. These I imagined, the way any city child of the time probably would have, as the smelly gray-white leavings of cigarettes and cigars that were heaped in ashtrays after the grown-ups had finished smoking their Old Golds or Pall Malls or Havana Specials.

Comical as my puzzlement may seem now, I don't remember finding it funny *then*. Though I may have misunderstood the symbolism of dust and ashes, I knew from the hollow feeling I got as I stood before the altar, as the hand of the priest descended toward my head, as he said his strangely incomprehensible words, just what the occasion meant.

You started out as next to nothing, you came from nothingness, and you'll end up as next to nothing again on your way back to nothingness.

"The ashes used in this ceremony," adds the *Catholic Encyclopedia*, "are made by burning the remains of the palms blessed on the Palm Sunday of the previous year."

The palms of victory will become the ashes of defeat. Entering Jerusalem in triumph, Christ Himself, son and body of God, exited bearing the cross on which He Himself was destined to journey toward the pall of death.

Even what Philip Larkin derided as the "vast moth-eaten musical brocade" of the Church that was presumably created "to pretend we never die" could not conceal the terror of extinction toward which the priest's ashen finger, his sepulchral words, pointed us annually. *Timor mortis conturbat me*, complained the medieval poets and clerics, even the most faithful among them. "The fear of death confounds, dismays, *perturbs* me!"

And did I believe that after I had dwindled into a bit of fluff under the bed or a heap of ashes in a little dish, some part of me would "expire" into the bosom of a transcendent Father? So, arrayed in celestially white organdy, I told the bishop, daunting in his sacerdotal costume, on the day I was confirmed. Like the priest's on Ash Wednesday, yet very differently, his holy finger came down onto my forehead, carving in the sign of the cross, this time in godly oil, to mark me as one of the saved.

To be saved, though, I had had to memorize the knotty narrative of the Apostle's Creed, with its rush of clauses, its piling on of theological pointers. And perhaps because at heart I was a "modern" child, imbued with an increasingly modern dread of an increasingly tenuous, indeed absent "hereafter," I suffered at this task, stumbled in my recitation, couldn't seem to make dramatic or rhetorical sense of what I was saying:

> I believe in God, the Father Almighty, Creator of heaven and earth; and in Jesus Christ, His only Son, our Lord; Who was conceived by the Holy Spirit, born of the Virgin Mary, suffered under Pontius Pilate, was crucified, died, and was buried . . . descended into hell . . . arose again from the dead . . . ascended into heaven . . . sits at the right hand of God . . . shall come to judge the living and the dead. . . . I believe in the Holy Spirit . . . the resurrection of the body and life everlasting. Amen.

If someone had asked me as I fidgeted in the procession of children, did I truly believe in the *Credo* I was enunciating, I'm not sure what I'd have said. How did I imagine the risen Christ? What did I think, to come right down to it, about the possibility of an ultimate restoration of my own body? And did I suppose that if I died in a "state of grace" at that sacramental minute of confirmation, I'd go straight to some sort of heaven?

Meditating on these questions now, I can barely begin to construct answers. Good Friday frightened me, much as Ash Wednesday did. We children had been told that as Jesus hung on the cross, in the afternoon hours between three and five, God the Father was so displeased that the sky blackened and the earth quaked and gave up its dead. This all seemed quite right to me; brooding in the darkened church, I contemplated the sufferings of Our Lord with pity and anxiety, and sympathized too with the onlookers who were flung about like straws in the wind by the divine wrath that was causing rocks and tombs to tremble. But the Risen Christ? Maybe because my family wasn't truly religious, I pictured Him as standing in a kind of gigantic sugar egg, the whole festooned with candy roses, for baskets and sweets, rather than spirits and miracles, signified Easter to me.

Yet in thoughts of my own resurrection I was relatively provident, as I recall, and remained so for many years, always wondering what would happen if I lost a limb or, once organ donation became common, gave up a kidney or liver. How, then, could I rise radiant and whole on the latter day? Did I truly believe, though, that at some point, soon after death but long before my bones could be reassembled, I'd fly upward into a dazzling empyrean? Perhaps in some yearning part of my mind I had visions of a place not unlike the ancient Greek Isles of the Blessed, about which I read in Bulfinch's *Mythology*, where things were edged with lines of light and everyone strolled in a glow of satisfaction among friends and relatives. But if I did somehow have that vision, it wasn't very compelling.

I think I must almost always have had a terror of "modern death." Puzzling over *dust thou art and unto dust thou shalt return*, I had fallen, as no doubt most of my contemporaries had or eventually would, into a skepticism that was already animating the art of countless poets whose names I hadn't yet learned. In a 1983 review of *The Oxford Book of Death*, a compendium of epitaphs and elegies that draws heavily on traditions shaped by the long-standing Christian view of death-as-expiration, Philip Larkin dramatizes the blend of scorn and panic that underlies such skepticism:

> *Several recognizable attitudes emerge from [the anthology's] chorus of voices. First of course, death isn't going to happen ("One short sleep past, we wake eternally"). Or if it does happen, it is by definition something we needn't worry about ("so long as we exist death is not with us; but when death comes, then we do not exist"). Or if it does happen, it is jolly nice and comfortable ("in a sleep deeper and calmer than that of infancy, wrapped in the finest and softest dust"). Or, finally, life would be very dull without death ("it is immeasurably heightened"). . . .*
>
> *What might with some justice be called the majority view, however— death is the end of everything, and thinking about it gives us a pain in the bowels—is poorly represented.*[10]

"The majority view," so Larkin assures his readers, "gives us a pain in the bowels" not unlike, I guess, the awful feeling I had as I stood before the priest in his purple raiment and felt his hand descend to inscribe my forehead with ashes. It is a vision of death as termination rather than expiration.

TIMOR MORTIS

For centuries a "majority view" of death certainly included fear and trembling. Lamented the Scottish poet William Dunbar in the sixteenth century:

I that in heill was and gladness,
Am troublit now with great seikness,
And feeblit with infirmity:
Timor mortis conturbat me.[11]

The *fear* of death (*timor mortis*) disturbs and distresses me (*conturbat me*). The fear of death, indeed, plunges me into despair and trembling.

Half a century later Dunbar's English counterpart, Thomas Nashe, expressed comparable terror in his "Litany in Time of Plague":

Rich men, trust not in wealth,
Gold cannot buy you health;
Physic himself must fade.
All things to end are made,
The plague full swift goes by;
I am sick, I must die.
Lord, have mercy on us!

"The plague full swift goes by," and therefore, understandably, "*Timor mortis conturbat me*"!

Part of what confounded Dunbar and Nashe, presumably denizens of an age of faith, was anticipation of the pangs of mortal illness—fear of what was almost ritualistically called the death agony—as well as terror of *some* kind of termination, an ending, at least, of the material world ("All *things* to end are made"). At the same time, when their near contemporary Hamlet muses on the disconcerting mystery of that "undiscovered country, from whose bourn / No traveler returns," he articulates an anxiety they too must have shared. The crypt is, after all, so *cryptic* that from the moralizings of the Hebrew Talmud to the maxims of the seventeenth-century *philosophe* La Rochefoucauld, its fated finality has often been defined as too dangerous to be thinkable by the wise. Warns the Talmud: "Whosoever speculate[s] on these four things, it were better for him if he had not come into the world—what is above? what is beneath? what was beforetime? and *what will be hereafter?*" Decrees La Rochefoucauld, "*Comme le soleil, la mort ne peut être regardée fixement*" ("Like the sun, death can't be looked at steadily").[12]

Nonetheless, the language of time and space ("hereafter," "undiscovered country") implies an assurance of *being* rather than *nothingness*. Hamlet confides his "dread of something *after* death," and Nashe calls on the Lord to "have mercy," as if there were both a divinity to make a difference in the afterlife and a difference that could be made. The fears these writers formulate are generated by a universe of spirits alternately malign and benign. Thus though a range of medieval and Renaissance complaints prove that, alas, it was never given every mortal to believe he could penetrate—as, say, Dante did—the theological thickets that separate this realm of substance from whatever insubstantial realm abides beyond the grave, most poets, even the terminally sardonic, assumed that to die was to "expire" into some kind of somewhere else—assumed, in other words, that as I too had almost instinctively felt, death "opens" and one goes into it as into a "place."

And the medieval man in the street? The Renaissance lady by the fire? The endless swarm of peasants in the fields, eternally "digging and delving," as Virginia Woolf once described them? Philippe Ariès scrupulously examined the permutations of Western attitudes toward death and dying from the Middle Ages to the present, recording through studies of funeral customs the subtle ways in which what he called the "tame death" (the humbly anticipated, essentially impersonal death marked by "familiar simplicity") modulated into the deaths he defined as "good" and "beautiful" (the "untamed," more personal, theatrically "triumphant" deaths achieved in a "state of grace"). In addition, as he explored these metamorphoses, Ariès showed how the medieval notion of death as a serene sleep that finally ends with the great awakening of the Last Judgment was gradually transformed into a nineteenth-century concept of death as expiration into an immediately blessed or damned afterlife. Yet the French historian flatly noted that until "the age of scientific progress, human beings accepted the idea of a continued existence after death," reminding us that particularly in "Pauline Christianity, life is a dying into a state of sin, and physical death is access to eternal life."[13]

My boiling down, here, of thousands of years of history may seem clichéd or platitudinous, yet the nature of the anxiety with which at this skeptical millennium we contemplate life's end requires a reminder of just how different we are from our precursors. *Timor mortis*, yes, was what our forebears felt, but it was evidently a *timor*, precisely, of the rigors of *mortis*—the moment of mortality—rather than of what followed it, a fear that finds its contemporary echo in Woody Allen's well-known remark "I don't mind dying. I just don't want to be there when it happens!" A more apposite recent formulation of this point, by the philosopher Thomas Nagel, poses a counterargument: "I should not really object to dying if it were not followed by death."[14] The worries of the average medieval or Renaissance thinker are probably best summarized by Johan Huizinga, who notes: "Nothing betrays more clearly the excessive fear of death felt in the Middle Ages than the popular belief, then widely spread, according to which Lazarus, after his resurrection, lived in a continual misery and horror at the thought that he should have again to pass through the gate of death."[15] The *dying*, not its aftermath, was the problem. For us, the opposite is the case. As one commentator wrote in the early seventies—in a necessary statement of the obvious about contemporary sensibility as concise as Ariès's comment on the views of Pauline Christianity—our preoccupation, "which began in the nineteenth century and has steadily intensified since[,] [is] with death without an after-life."[16]

How did it really feel, though, to fear the act of dying so much more passionately than the fact of death itself? For those of us to whom such a mindset is problematic, only representations and symbolizations can offer answers (and those only provisional) to that question. An especially dramatic representation, which may stand for countless others, is the great *Issenheim Retable* that has been attributed to the sixteenth-century artist Matthias Grünewald. Housed in the Musée d'Unterlinden in Colmar, this elaborate altarpiece, with its complex system of panels to be opened and closed at various points in the liturgical calendar, has rightly been called a— perhaps *the*—*monstre sacré* of Western art, maybe precisely because it so theatrically summarizes the contours of what was long the Church's holy writ on death and resurrection.

What is "monstrous" about the *Retable*, though, is what seems truest about it from a modern or postmodern perspective: the hideous image of the Crucifixion central to the panels of the altarpiece that were shown in the darkly admonitory days of Lent, between Ash Wednesday and Good Friday. Never has the body of Jesus, agonizingly suspended from the cross by clawed fingers, seemed both so enormous, as if expanded by suffering, and so distorted, as if defiled by abuse [fig. 2].

Scored and scarred by whiplashes, the flesh of the doomed man is greenish gray, exposed in a chilled nakedness splashed with blood, dotted with pustules, studded with thorns, the same that shape the grotesque crown beneath which the head is helplessly bent, eyes shut, forehead twisted in agony, mouth open and thirsting. If this is what it is, Grünewald seems to be telling the viewer, for Our Lord to die the death, what must it be for those of us less staunch, less noble—in short, less divine? Indeed, in another compartment of the altarpiece, the Temptation of St. Anthony is folded away, but when it is opened for display at the saint's celebration, it will show the holy man surrounded by a chorus of bestial demons and at his feet a

2. Matthias Grünewald: detail of *La Crucifixion,* from the *Issenheim Retable* (c. 1515; Musée d'Unterlinden, Colmar).

sufferer from the disease called St. Anthony's fire—a stripped figure whose maimed limbs, bloated stomach, and festering sores reiterate the horror of embodiment manifested in larger scale in the terrifying vision of the Crucifixion.

Yet the viewer cannot turn away from the image of crucifixion central to the *Retable*; instead all eyes are voyeuristically drawn to its literal and fig-urative enormity, for in the panel in which Christ hangs on the cross—as in the panel, below it, in which He's being entombed—the god who became human, like the sufferer from St. Anthony's fire, is both swollen and weighted with sheer materiality. For us "modern" onlookers, these images are riveting because to most they convey what we fear is inescapable: a purely physical death. For Grünewald's contemporaries, however, these images must have been riveting because they summarized all those fears from which an ultimate expiration into heaven offered escape.

And what an escape! In the panels that were opened at Christmas, Easter, and all the feasts of the Virgin, the congregation privileged to share in the most ecstatic moments of the Issenheim altarpiece could gaze not only at the otherworldly glamour of the Annunciation and the Nativity, but also at an astonishing vision of the Resurrection [fig. 3].

In this last panel, whose image of divine rehabilitation prefigured what its original viewers must have hoped for their own ultimate transforma- tions, Christ rises in a circle of almost blindingly intense light over a tomb whose stones are flung about helter-skelter and above armored soldiers tumbling down with amazement or terror. He's gone up and away with such a rush of brilliance that His bluish greenish shroud still trails below Him, though His feet are getting clear of it as, posed with upturned arms and out- turned palms displaying the stigmata of His recent suffering, He rises, serene and entranced, into the Mystery that lifts Him ever higher.

And those hands whose palms bear (like His feet) the small, sacred blood spots that along with a dark streak on His right side where the spear went in are almost the only lingering marks of his recent crucifixion—those hands, like that side, are white and supple, smooth and rounded. All seems designed to prove that as the fourteenth-century theologian Ludolph of Saxony wrote in his influential *Vita Christi*, the "Saviour's Resurrection was not destruction but transformation of His adored flesh; its substance was not another but the same, perfect," for possessing, now, "the four most important principles of grace, clarity, agility, subtility, and impassivity," the risen Lord had become a paradigm of "the glory which surrounds the bod- ies of those chosen to be resurrected in general."[17]

"One short sleep past, we wake eternally": so proclaims John Donne in one of the heartening selections from *The Oxford Book of Death* at which Philip Larkin took particular umbrage. Our "majority view" of that suppos- edly "short sleep," the twentieth-century poet declares, is actually sickening ("gives us a pain in the bowels"). For, Larkin insists, we don't in general believe that we've been "chosen to be resurrected." Yet we're haunted by that belief. Our churches and museums are emblazoned with representations like Grünewald's, depicting the triumphant transformation of the "adored

3. Matthias Grünewald: *La Resurrection,* from the *Issenheim Retable* (c. 1515; Musée d'Unterlinden, Colmar).

flesh" of our Lord into a spiritual balm meant to inspire viewers with the hope that they too will expire into a heaven of eternal glory. And our anthologies—not just *The Oxford Book of Death* but countless others—are crammed with poems implying that for centuries the "majority view" of the problem death poses might be summarized with the tersely optimistic final sentence of Donne's sonnet: "Death, thou shalt die."

Consider, after all, the prestigious genre of the pastoral elegy. This traditional mode of poetic mourning persisted in English-language verse at least into the mid-nineteenth century, and it not only records but is structured by a confident vision of death as an expiration that issues in salvation. In "Lycidas," for instance, perhaps the most famous and influential of elegies, John Milton adopts the highly literary mask of an Arcadian shepherd to mourn his dead schoolmate Edward King, who was drowned "in his passage from Chester on the Irish Seas, 1637." Milton shudderingly imagines the terrible fate of his lost friend's physical self—bones perhaps "hurled . . . beyond the stormy Hebrides" or sunk to "the bottom of the monstrous world"—and as we've seen, he angrily reproaches the spirits of nature for their apparent indifference. Ultimately, however, the author-to-be of *Paradise Lost* and *Paradise Regained* assumes that the hapless King breathed out a spirit that would mount "high, / Through the dear might of him that walked the waves." Like (and because of) the risen Christ, the dead man has entered "the blest kingdoms meek of joy and love" where "all the saints above" will forever sing to him in "solemn troops and sweet societies."

Nor was Milton's elegy the last to seek comfort in a vision of death as expiration rather than termination. Despite the increasing secularization that the Enlightenment brought to Western culture, nearly two centuries after Milton penned "Lycidas" Percy Shelley grieved for the death of his fellow Romantic John Keats in another ceremonial elegy that balances the terror of mortality with a luminous vision of immortality. In fact, although Shelley doesn't share Milton's Christian confidence in heavenly consolation, his ritual lamentations for "Adonais" issue in a differently triumphant assertion of transcendence—"He lives, he wakes—'tis Death is dead, not he"— that echoes Donne's "Death, thou shalt die." Not only that, but the expiration of "Adonais" / Keats into "the white radiance of Eternity" facilitates an aesthetic transaction in which the expiration of one poet leads to the inspiration of another. Because Keats has breathed out his spirit, Shelley implies, a prophetic "breath" descends on him as survivor so that by the end of the elegy his own "spirit's bark is driven" toward the immortality already achieved by the dead Adonais, whose soul, "like a star, / Beacons from the abode where the Eternal are."[18]

In "Lycidas" too, though Milton modestly defines himself as an "uncouth swain," the poet is sufficiently inspired by his comrade's expiration to imagine regeneration in "fresh woods, and pastures new." As the critic Peter Sacks notes in a fine study of the elegy in English, the author of traditional pastoral elegies almost always comforts himself by drawing attention "to his own surviving powers," and his compensation for loss as well as for performing proper rituals of bereavement usually involves what Sacks calls "consoling identifications" with creative powers often incarnated in the spirit that is grieved for.[19] In fact the traditional elegy ends with hope precisely because it arises as directly from a mythology of expiration as does the risen Christ in the *Issenheim Retable*. In this connection even the etymology of the term "elegy" has special force. Scholars tell us that the word derives from the Greek *elogoi*, referring to couplets traditionally accompanied by an "oboelike doublepipe called *auos*," and that the earliest meaning of "elegy" was "flute song of grief."[20] Symbolically, then, or so this derivation suggests, the elegist inspires and is inspired to breathe (out)— *expire* into—a wind instrument whose melodies mourn the expired but implicitly imperishable breath of the dead one.

How did the sorrowful yet ultimately auspicious grandeur of those "flute songs of grief" produced by Milton and Shelley and so many others turn into no more than what Larkin calls a "vast moth-eaten musical brocade / Created to pretend we never die"? Even if, like Stevens, we seek the afterlife insurance offered by Pascal's wager, many contemporary mourners—especially, with a few notable exceptions, most "modern" literary intellectuals—suspect that death is merely termination. Like Larkin, we tend to fear "sure extinction," the "anaesthetic from which none come round." Like Williams, we're inclined to represent a dead person as "a god-forsaken curio / without / any breath in *it*" rather than as a *being* whose breath has "gone" to or toward a redemptive god. Indeed, even when we imagine those figures that "poetic license" licenses us to call gods, we're more likely to blame them for their power to inflict "sure extinction" than we are to praise them for the "dear might" through which they help us, like Lycidas, to "moun[t] high." As Robert Pinsky puts it in "Impossible to Tell," if there are gods whom we can name, they're useless to us since they all too often appear to be "provincial stinkers" who are either indifferent or malevolent.

From the Renaissance to the present, of course, a slew of scientists and philosophers forced the gods to dwindle into demons or, just as infamously, to disappear entirely. By the early twentieth century most thinkers had abandoned any conception even of the watchmaker deity of Enlightenment faith, the First Cause that set the universe in motion and then withdrew behind a mask of the material to let us work out our destinies in a clockwork system where, painful though things may be, "Whatever Is, Is Right." Wrote Bertrand Russell in his 1903 *A Free Man's Worship*: "Man is a product of causes which had no prevision . . . his origin, his growth, his hopes and fears, his loves and beliefs are but the outcome of accidental collocations of atoms. . . . [T]he temple of man's achievement must inevitably be buried beneath the debris of the universe in ruins." And the British logician was sounding a theme that countless others developed as they laid the foundation for Stevens's "mythology of modern death." For as the historian of philosophy Jacques Choron put it in 1963, in his magisterial *Death and Western Thought*, "Nihilism has become the heritage of modern man."[21]

Asserting that "Man is little more than a chance deposit on the surface of the world, carelessly thrown up between two ice ages by the same forces that rust iron and ripen corn," the American historian Carl Becker formulated such nihilism, and it was similarly expressed by the French zoologist Jacques Monod, who insisted that "Man . . . is alone in the universe's unfeeling immensity, out of which he emerged only by chance." But perhaps the American physicist Steven Weinberg makes the same point most powerfully in the conclusion of *The First Three Minutes*, his influential survey of contemporary cosmology. Noting with a certain sympathy that "[i]t is almost irresistible for humans to believe that we have some special relation to the universe," Weinberg nevertheless claims that "human life is . . . just a more-or-less farcical outcome of a chain of accidents reaching back to the first three minutes" and then adds tersely that the "more the universe seems comprehensible, the more it also seems pointless."[22]

From such a perspective, the world itself, like the cadaver at the center of Williams's "Death," is little more than "a godforsaken curio." We have here entered the realm of Samuel Beckett's *Waiting for Godot*, where "one day we were born, one day we shall die, the same day, the same second," the realm where "[t]hey give birth astride of a grave, the light gleams an instant, then it's night once more" because "[d]own in the hole, lingeringly the grave digger puts on the forceps."[23]

GHOSTS OF HEAVEN

To be sure, the holy ghosts of religion still linger throughout Western culture, especially in the United States, whose citizens continue to honor the theological origins of the Thirteen Colonies by perpetually pledging spiritual allegiances. With its "faith-based initiatives" and its fervent invocations of what sounds like a politically partisan deity, the "born again" administration of George W. Bush is hardly anomalous. American presidents have always gone rather theatrically to church, where they're frequently and reverently photographed. Nor does their churchgoing seem in the least odd to their constituents. The phrase "under God" was, after all, added to the Pledge of Allegiance during the 1950s, although Dwight D. Eisenhower, the president who presided over the revision, wasn't a proseletyzing evangelist but just a solidly pious American whose views on God, life, and the afterlife were—and still are—representatively mainstream. For according to a

Time/CNN telephone poll of 1,018 adult Americans conducted in March 1997—years before so-called "moral values" became a rallying cry of the evangelical right—81 percent of those queried "believe in the existence of heaven, where people live forever with God after they die" and of those, 67 percent "think of heaven as something that is 'up there'" while 93 percent expect to find angels on the premises, 79 percent imagine they'll encounter St. Peter, 43 percent suppose there will be harps present, and 36 percent also anticipate halos.

More recently, Bill Moyers reported on a 2002 *Time*/CNN poll that found that "59 percent of Americans believe that the prophecies found in the book of Revelation are going to come true [while nearly] one-quarter think the Bible predicted the 9/11 attacks." Noted Moyers in addition: "[T]he best-selling books in America today are the twelve volumes of the left-behind series written by the Christian fundamentalist and religious right warrior, Timothy LaHaye." Those who subscribe to the literal truth of LaHaye's tales of "the Rapture" expect that they will sooner or later be "lifted out of their clothes and transported to heaven [where] they will watch their political and religious opponents suffer plagues"—and to many intellectuals their certainty may appear as comical as Hollywood's fleshly renditions of the hereafter's harps and halos often seem. But the 2004 presidential election in the United States proved that the Christian fundamentalist movement is no joke, just as the Islamic and Hindu fundamentalisms sweeping other parts of the world are equally serious—and equally powerful.

Nevertheless, even the special issue of *Time* that featured the 1997 poll on the afterlife approached the concept of expiration into a traditional heaven or hell with notable uneasiness. One somewhat disaffected theologian is quoted as explaining that from the contemporary Roman Catholic Church's point of view, "we should [do good] because we *should* do good," so that thinking about heaven is "sort of like cheating." Another is said to speculate that clerics "want to stay off the subject [of heaven] because they're going to have to climb a wall of popular skepticism." Even the famously Christian writer C. S. Lewis succumbed to doubt when he was mourning the death of his wife, Joy. "Can I honestly say that I believe she is now anything?" he wondered in 1961. "The vast majority of the people I meet, say, at work, would certainly think she is not." As *Time*'s David Van Biema concluded more than thirty years later, a "robust conception of heaven [may] be the victim of an unbelieving era"; perhaps, he added, the "biblical heaven [is] a victim of its own, centuries-long hype; so much has been claimed for it, much of it contradictory, that our literal-minded age overloads and calls the whole thing a wash."[24]

In a similarly devotional special issue that also appeared in 1997, the *New York Times Magazine* recorded comparable ambivalence toward the old theology of expiration and reward. Citing "a recent study by the National Opinion Research Center in Chicago" that showed that "74 percent of all Americans believe in an afterlife," the *Magazine* jovially "asked some forward-thinking folks to ponder where they might expect to find themselves after they're gone." And most of the responses were as cleverly ironic as the question itself. "I don't believe in an afterlife. I don't even believe in *this* life," said "Fran Lebowitz, writer," while "Ross Bleckner, artist," declared that he would like "to be ground up and have my assistants mix my ashes in a vat of oil paint" to be distributed to "my 10 favorite painters," who would "use the mixture . . . to make art that'll hang in a group show. . . . That'll be my afterlife, a group show." In the same tone, "Marilu Henner, actress," confessed, "I don't know what it is, I don't know what it looks like, but I do know I'm taking my credit cards with me in case there's a Gucci's." Even those respondents who were slightly less insouciant were equally skeptical. "My hereafter is here," proclaimed "Frank McCourt, writer." "I am where I'm going, for I am mulch." And "Tommy Smothers, comedian," asserted that "my kids [are] my afterlife . . . how a little bit of me is going to survive."

Oddly enough, only "Geraldo Rivera, talk-show host" approached the question with a frank anxiety analogous to Larkin's "pain in the bowels." "I hope something *does* happen," he confessed. "Anything. Any kind of consciousness. My fear is that nothing will." Although a minute later Geraldo was joking too ("I'm not sure what a Heaven would be like, but Hell, Hell might be interesting—a lot like the news business"), the nervousness he was willing to expose undoubtedly shaped even his fellow respondent's light-hearted lines about group shows and credit cards.

Less superficially tough thinkers might seek to allay their fears by joining a host of distinctively "modern" cults, ranging from the St. John Coltrane African Orthodox Church (which "treats Coltrane as a patron saint attracting Christians and curious Coltrane fans from all over") to members of the New Age Unarius Academy of Science (who "herald the future arrival of [their] 'space brothers' ") and participants in the Cryonics Institute (who believe in the actual resurrection of the flesh through techniques of "low temperature physics" that supposedly allow the preservation of cadavers until some future day when they can be brought back to life).[25] Yet no matter how we struggle for belief, we suffer from "the curse of never really knowing anything for sure," as another *Times* story put the problem of reconciling traditional spirituality with scientific materialism. Thus, though the "teachings of any religion ultimately come from ancient revelations by people who said they were prophets and heard the voice of God," we inevitably wonder: "What if the prophets turn out to be wrong? Or nonexistent?"[26] From Beckett's Gogo and Didi (for whom *Godot* will never come) to the maestro of the evening news (who isn't sure what to believe), what were once glad tidings of great joy have disintegrated into the hopeless, hapless quackings of Beckett's Lucky, for whom the hypothetical existence of "a personal God quaquaquaqua with white beard . . . outside time" evokes merely "the earth abode of stones in the great cold" and "the skull the skull the skull."

NADA

"I'm going to *die*, I can't get it out of my head," Billy, a character in a story by John Updike, says to his friend Nelson. Nelson genially reassures him, in the mode of the *Times'* afterwords on the afterlife, that "[i]t's like a nap, only you don't wake up and have to find your shoes." But the plaintive metaphysician persists; he can't get over the fact that he's "really going to die. I mean *really*, totally–zip–zero . . . *nada*." His comforter admits: "It's a concept the mind isn't constructed to accept. So stop trying to force it to." Still, masses of modern minds have struggled to "accept" just such a concept— "zip–zero . . . *nada*"—of termination. Even for those who believe in a transcendent deity, the concept of posthumous spiritual survival became increasingly problematic throughout the twentieth century. Gertrude Stein spoke for many when in *Everybody's Autobiography* she remembered her distressing youthful decision that even if "There was a God there was eternity," there nonetheless "was no future life and I found how naturally that worried me." And even more radically, in his short story "A Clean, Well-Lighted Place," Stein's sometime acolyte Ernest Hemingway produced a famously bitter parody of the Lord's Prayer: "Our nada who art in nada, nada be thy name thy kingdom nada thy will be nada in nada as it is in nada."[27]

Despite the "faith-based" credos that dominate so much of American political discourse, nihilistic concepts of death and dying akin to those expressed by Stein and Hemingway have lately entered the book-buying mainstream. *How We Die*, a frequently clinical dissection of the processes of morbidity produced by a Yale University Medical School professor, became a major best seller in the mid-nineties despite (or perhaps because of) its definition of death as not just "an event in the sequence of nature's ongoing rhythms" but in fact "a series of destructive events that involve by their very nature the disintegration of the dying person's humanity."[28] But even in the nineteenth century just such a "disintegration" of humanity was dramatized in Leo Tolstoy's classic "The Death of Ivan Ilyich," the tale of a man who dies what is, at least until the very last moments of his life, one of the first "modern" deaths.

The confrontation with annihilation that Updike's Billy dreads and that his friend defines as "a concept the mind isn't constructed to accept" is brilliantly figured by Tolstoy through Ivan Ilyich's imagining of terminal oblivion as a "black sack": "It seemed to him that he and his pain were being thrust somewhere into a narrow, deep black sack, but though they kept forcing him farther and farther in they still could not push him to the bottom. And this horrible state of affairs was accompanied by agony. And he was frightened and yet wanted to fall into the sack, he struggled and at the same time co-operated." More powerfully still, the suffering man's final loss of control and surrender to death are represented through the severance of human bonds dramatized by his rejection of his wife ("Go away, go away. Leave me alone!"), which issues in "the screaming" that begins and continues for three days and is "so awful that one could not hear it through closed doors two rooms away without horror."[29]

"The screaming" is, of course, Ivan Ilyich's screaming, but it's more fittingly described by a general article than by a personal, possessive pronoun. Unlanguaged and uninflected ("He had begun by screaming 'I won't!' and so had gone on screaming on the same vowel sound 'o' "), this scream is an animal howl that belongs to no one—and to everyone. In a sense, it's an inevitable consequence of "that black sack into which [Ivan Ilyich is] being forced by an unseen, invincible power."[30] Eventually, by recounting its protagonist's redemption through human gestures of sympathy and forgiveness, Tolstoy's tale retracts the deadly dehumanization that the screaming signals, so that as in some New Age accounts of "the near death experience," "In place of death there [is] light." But from a "modern" or postmodern perspective, what's surely most striking in the narrative is its account of a proud man's—a *judge's*—reduction to a prelinguistic state where "he" is no more than a shriek of pain and fear. For in telling such a story the nineteenth-century novelist outlined a conception of death that was to become central to the twentieth century's "construction" of death as termination.

Death "sits on the divide between nature and culture, a continual reminder of our embodied human nature," declares the British sociologist
Clive Seale in a recent book whose title, *Constructing Death*, reflects precisely the metaphysical uncertainty summarized by the *New York Times'*
piece on religion and science as "the curse of never really knowing anything
for sure." Although for centuries death would have been seen by theologians
and physicians alike as one of the immutable realities of human existence,
from a postmodern perspective it is just another "constructed"experience,
or so Seale's title implies. And most contemporary readers would probably
agree that what's constructed is how we feel and think about dying itself as
well as the beliefs and customs surrounding death and its consequences.

Here, paradoxically, Seale's location of death "between nature and culture" is singularly "modern" in its emphasis on "embodied [rather than *disembodied*, transcendent, or spiritual] human nature." This is the nature that
we share with animals rather than with angels, and it is surely the nature given
voice in *the* screaming that possesses Ivan Ilyich as he is stuffed into the "black
sack" of the grave. "In crisis or 'marginal' situations, such as those engendered
by a death," notes Seale, drawing on the work of several other prominent sociologists, "society provides a type of 'sheltering canopy' that defends against
experience which would otherwise reduce the individual to a 'howling animality.'" Yet ultimately, he argues, we all do, must, succumb to "howling animality" as, in a crossing of the divide, the "ageing, dying, grieving, embodied
individual [experiences] a final fall from culture." For, adds Seale, "[i]n spite
of symbolic attempts to transform death into hopes of immortality, to create
a sheltering canopy of culture against nature, for people facing death these
human constructions appear fragile. Disruption of the social bond occurs as
the body fails, self-identity becomes harder to hold together and the normal
expectations of human relations cannot be fulfilled."[31]

That "hopes of immortality" are simply "human constructions" appears
to Seale self-evident, showing how definitively we've moved from a conception of death as expiration (in which the characteristics of an afterlife might
at least be debated) to a notion of death as termination (in which ideas
about an afterlife are just part of "a sheltering canopy of culture" or, for that
matter, shreds of "a vast, moth-eaten, musical brocade" in which we clothe
ourselves so as to ward off what Beckett's Lucky calls "the great cold" of a
godless universe). Moreover, that as mortals we're basically talking animals
plainly seems to Seale just as self-evident. In a post-Darwinian world (as
Ivan Ilyich's wordless screaming implies), facility with grammar rather than
the possession of a soul divides us from the beasts. Once we lose language

we become no more than animals or even, as in the popular formulation about comatose patients, "vegetables."

Experientially, of course, we don't ordinarily feel ourselves to be merely the organic stuff—whether animal, vegetable, or (ultimately) mineral—to which such notions reduce us. As the philosopher Maurice Merleau-Ponty once noted, human beings are those creatures who paradoxically seem both to *have* and to *be* bodies since mental consciousness doesn't perceive itself as identical with physical being. In the early twentieth century William Butler Yeats articulated the increasingly urgent anxiety this paradox posed for an aging writer facing "modern death." In "Sailing to Byzantium," one of his most widely anthologized poems, he prays that the "sages standing in God's holy fire" might "consume" his "heart" away, defining this self or "heart" as "sick with desire / And *fastened to a dying animal*" [emphasis added]—that is, fastened to but therefore presumably *separate from* the "dying animal" that is the body. And not long after formulating the problem so metaphorically, he addressed it more directly, declaring in a poem aptly entitled "Death":

> Nor dread nor hope attend
> A dying animal;
> A man awaits his end
> Dreading and hoping all.[32]

In his succinct meditation on this last point, Yeats was condensing an argument that was also, at around the same time, traced by the German philosopher Martin Heidegger, in his magnum opus *Being and Time* (*Sein und Zeit*, 1927) and elsewhere, and that much later was articulated by the French thinker Maurice Blanchot. Claiming that it's specifically the consciousness of (ultimately) impending death that makes human beings human, Heidegger wrote that "[m]an dies constantly until the moment of his demise," adding—as if to gloss Yeats—that "[o]nly man dies. The animal perishes [because] It has death neither ahead of itself nor behind it." Similarly, expanding these ideas, Blanchot comments that "man only knows death because he is man, and he is only man because he is death in the process of becoming."[33] And the words of these two influential theorists both summarized and shaped a stance toward mortality that has characterized concepts of "modern death" for more than a century.

At the same time, however, although most of us may still await our ends "dreading and hoping all," we're now more likely to imagine ourselves as dying animals than as transcendent beings fastened to animals. More-over, many of us believe ourselves as dying animals to be wholly organic matter, part of an intricate ecology in which no particular species or phy-lum can or should be privileged. A recent literary work that makes this point with extraordinary verve (and I use the vivacious word "verve" advis-edly) is oddly not a poem but a novel, the British writer Jim Crace's elo-quently elegiac *Being Dead*, first published in the United States in the millennial year 2000. Here, as he traces what might be considered the life-in-death of a middle-aged couple murdered while making love on a remote beach, the author celebrates the nature of a natural world that "embraces and adopts the dead," a realm in which dying animals turn "to landscape, given time" because "gulls die. And so do flies and crabs. So do the seals. Even stars must decompose, disrupt and blister on the sky. Every-thing was born to go."

As if entering into a vigorous dialogue with the "special way of being afraid" recorded in Larkin's "Aubade," Crace's novel begins briskly with a light verse epigraph drawn from Sherwin Stephens's "The Biologist's Vale-diction to His Wife":

> *Don't count on Heaven, or on Hell.*
> *You're dead. That's it. Adieu. Farewell.*
> *Eternity awaits? Oh, sure!*
> *It's Putrefaction and Manure*
> *And unrelenting Rot, Rot, Rot,*
> *As you regress, from Zoo. to Bot.*

And after devoting just a few paragraphs to the senseless (and never solved) murder of the protagonists, Celice and Joseph, who are themselves both "doctors of zoology," the narrator offers a commentary on traditional mythologies of expiration that is notably different from, on the one hand, Larkin's scorn for the Church's "moth-eaten brocade" and, on the other hand, the anxieties expressed by Beckett's characters at the absence of a *God*ot who refuses to arrive. "Should we expect their spirits to depart, some hellish cart and its pale horse to come and take their falling souls away to its hot mines, some godly, decorated messenger, too simple-minded for its golden wings, to fly them to repose, reunion, eternity?" he demands, and answers his own question with a kind of equanimity Larkin never achieves: "Celice and Joseph were soft fruit. They lived in tender bodies. They were vulnerable. They did not have the power not to die. They were, we are, all flesh, and then we are all meat."

What meaning, then, is there in our mere materiality, our sheer *meatiness*? "I have come to believe that it is the flesh alone that counts," declares the physician-essayist Richard Seltzer in a fine meditation on "The Exact Location of the Soul," yet it's hard to imagine that Crace's protagonists, decomposing, would find this thought consoling. Chronicling the decay of the couple's corpses as beetles, gulls, crabs, and flies feed on their flesh and then as cells degenerate, molecules loosen, Crace at first writes with just the icy objectivity about "sure extinction" that gave Larkin "a pain in the bowels." Yet, as if to affirm Seltzer's notion that a "philosophers' stone" might be found "in the recesses of the body," the conclusion of *Being Dead* is curiously celebratory in its affirmation of a mythology of termination: "All along the shores of Baritone Bay and all the coast beyond, tide after tide, time after time, the corpses and the broken, thinned remains of fish and birds, of barnacles and rats, of molluscs, mammals, mussels, crabs are lifted, washed and sorted by the waves. And Joseph and Celice enjoy a loving and unconscious end, beyond experience. These are the everending days of being dead." It's almost as if, here, termination itself equaled a kind of redemption, as if there were a mystic union with the absolute available only when bodily death is the *sole* (not the soul's) afterlife. Indeed, just as there's a mysterious paradox implicit in the description of a "loving and unconscious end, beyond experience," so there's a powerful oxymoron built into the very title of Crace's book. The phrase "being dead" suggests that death itself, in its neverending everendingness, *is* a kind of existence or being.[34]

Joseph and Celice are of course going to be recycled; in fact they're being recycled (in the systems of birds and insects) throughout the novel that tells their story. And is such recycling the only road to redemption? No doubt for many areligious or even antireligious contemporaries that may be the case; certainly some of the *Times Magazine*'s afterwords suggest as much. Frank McCourt expects to be "mulch" and hopes that "in my mulch-hood I may nourish a row of parsnips," while Tommy Smothers hopes for no more than to live on as part of his children. Yet recently it has begun to seem that there's yet another way for nervous thinkers to come to terms with termination and more particularly with their fears of "howling animality." For some, the very "dying animal" to which Yeats complained of being "fastened" is itself an ensouled, rather than a merely material, creature.

THE SOULS OF ANIMALS

The question of animal souls is, to be sure, a long-standing philosophical and theological issue, one that for centuries was almost as pressing as the question (on which Plato and Aristotle, among others, meditated) whether women and slaves have souls. St. Thomas Aquinas, for instance, claimed in the twelfth century to follow Aristotle in deciding that "the souls of brute animals," who have no "understanding," aren't logically conceivable because among crucial "operations of the soul" (which include various forms of "sensation" as well as reason or "understanding") understanding alone is performed "without a corporeal organ." And five hundred years later René Descartes concluded that an "animal lives . . . as a machine lives."[35] In the fifteenth century, however, about halfway between the moments when these weighty thinkers formulated their views, a now-nameless Renaissance master painter produced a charmingly ambiguous canvas entitled *Le Miracle de la résurrection des poulets rôtis* ("The Miracle of the Resurrection of the Roast Chickens") that simultaneously assumes and parodies precisely the theology of expiration represented in so many religious paintings of that period [fig. 4].

With suitable, though no doubt unintentional, irony, *Le Miracle* hangs in the Musée d'Unterlinden, home of Grünewald's great *Issenheim Retable*, not far from one of the many fifteenth-century paintings of the Crucifixion in which the expiration of the two thieves who flank the dying Christ is dramatized through depictions of tiny, translucent souls escaping from the mouths of the two. As if to echo the theme of these works, the painter of *Le Miracle de la résurrection des poulets rôtis* shows a richly dressed couple ensconced at their dining table, attended by several servingmen, a little dog, and a maid, who sits by the hearth near a spit on which three savory-looking chickens have almost finished roasting. But lo! Above the very spit that turns the bodies of the browning birds, three pure white ghostly chickens rise, expiring toward heaven in the spirit, if not the flesh! And at this presumably astonishing turn of events the onlookers appear relatively unfazed, with the possible exception of the little dog, which looks up at the flying chicken souls in evident surprise.

Did the painter of *Le Miracle* intend comedy? Parody? A reductio ad absurdum of Christian theology that would deflate the hopes of true believers? Or a loving joke about the impossibility of chicken redemption that would reinforce the expectations of *human* redemption fostered in viewers by the neighboring painting of *La Crucifixion* along with the many works (like the *Issenheim Retable*) portraying Christ's resurrection? The last of

4. Painter unknown: *Le Miracle de la résurrection des poulets rôtis* (n.d.; Musee d'Unterlinden, Colmar).

these interpretations—the painting as loving joke—is most likely, given the theology of human expiration/animal termination that dominated the century in which this particular master produced his wonderful work.

   To some of us, however, comic as *Le Miracle* seems, the idea of animal expiration (rather than termination) may be no joke. For as if to counter the possibility that death-as-termination threatens us with a "fall from culture" into "howling animality," our contemporary definition of ourselves as talking animals has meant a revaluation of the "dying animal" as, at least hypothetically, an ensouled creature. In 1999 the South African novelist J. M. Coetzee produced an absorbing meditation on this subject that proposes an even more radical revision of our place in the ecosystem of nature than the view offered in Crace's *Being Dead*. Elizabeth Costello, the central character in Coetzee's *The Lives of Animals*, is an aging novelist and animal rights polemicist, who passionately repudiates Descartes's definition of an animal as "no more than the mechanism that constitutes it," arguing instead: "To be alive is to be a living soul. An animal—and we are all animals—is an embodied soul."

We are all animals—and if we are all animals, then animals are *all us*. So this assertion implies, as it turns the concept of "howling animality" upside down in order to redeem the animal that is in us, or that *is* us, along with the animals who live alongside us. That Coetzee is considering the complexity of these implications becomes clear when, in the very last scene of *The Lives of Animals*, Costello's son realizes that she has "become so intense about the animal business" because she is terrified by the prospect of her own nearing death. Taking "his mother in his arms," he "inhales the smell of cold cream, of old flesh. 'There, there,' he whispers in her ear. 'There, there. It will soon be over.'" What underlies her protest against, for instance, human carnivorousness—against what she sees as kitchens filled with "fragments of corpses . . . bought for money"—is her recognition that she too is part of the food chain. But how can an ensouled creature be food for another ensouled creature? Shouldn't the ensouled eat only the soulless?

Or if the ensouled *are* destined for material consumption, aren't they at least entitled to the spiritual resurrection promised by expiration? Shouldn't dead animals rise and in some sense live again, like the spiritual chickens who have ascended from the *poulets rôtis*? This is a view at least in part espoused by another of Coetzee's characters. Having fled a personal and professional scandal in Johannesburg, David Lurie, the protagonist of the Booker Prize–winning novel *Disgrace*, has withdrawn to his daughter's farm in the countryside, where he begins working at an "Animal Welfare" clinic. There, among other tasks, he has the weekly job of administering deadly injections to "superfluous canines." And rather than second Yeats's conviction that "Nor dread nor hope attend / A dying animal," he becomes certain that "the dogs know their time has come . . . the dogs in the yard smell what is going on inside" the room where they are to be killed. "They flatten their ears, they droop their tails, as if they too feel the disgrace of dying." Eventually, moreover, he decides that when the animals enter the death chamber, they encounter, among its "rich, mixed smells," one that is new to them: "the smell of *expiration*, the soft, short smell of the released soul."[36]

As the new millennium opens wider, have we come full circle from a nihilistic view of death-as-termination to a redefined mythology of modern death as expiration, even for those dying animals who are ourselves and our companions in mortality? To be sure, Coetzee's David Lurie associates the released souls of the dogs he's killing with a "soft, *short smell*" and fails to speculate on what may follow that brief terminal phenomenon. Does he imagine disembodied canines ascending into the heaven toward which the airy spirits of the Renaissance painter's *poulets rôtis* may be flying? That seems unlikely, but nevertheless it's clear that his vision of ensouled animals, like Elizabeth Costello's in *The Lives of Animals*, represents a new stance not just toward life but toward death. Whereas for centuries we considered ourselves superior to the beasts because we were spiritual and transcendent while they were material and immanent, we now understand ourselves to *be* beasts—but we hasten therefore to attribute the souls we once considered uniquely our own to the animals whose fates we share.

This current solution to the old expiration/termination polarity has a range of implications, some whimsical, some serious. The last of the *Times Magazine*'s afterwords on the afterlife comes from "Elliot Erwitt, photographer," who muses that "[o]ne pleasant thought is to come back as a golden lab," reminding us that Eastern theologies of reincarnation have always emphasized the continuity between animal and human life that Western thinkers from Plato and Aristotle onward sought to deny. But in the course of the twentieth century a spectrum of writers have sought to insure themselves against Stevens's dread of being "devoured by [earth], beneath a dew" through strategies very different from the turn to the Church taken by the author of "Madame La Fleurie." Like Crace, for instance, the British children's book author Philip Pullman produces anti-Christian tales proclaiming "the absolute primacy of the material life, rather than the spiritual or the afterlife," insisting that "the angels envy our bodies—because our senses are keener our muscles are stronger." And like Coetzee, the American poet Mark Doty reappraises what used to be considered the "lower" order, struggling to cope with his lover's death from AIDS by meditating on their shared ownership of Beau, who is, yes, a golden retriever and represents for both the dying man and his partner a kind of redemption through "the restless splendor, / the unruly, / the golden, / the *animal*, the new [emphasis added]."[37]

Perhaps, though, James Dickey's lovely meditation on "The Heaven of Animals" is the most daringly fantastic of these efforts even while it shares the piquant ambiguity of *Le Miracle de la résurrection des poulets rôtis*. "Here they are," proclaims the American poet as he describes this paradise, for even though he concedes that animals have "no souls, they have come, / Anyway, beyond their knowing." Here, he observes, though predators are "[m]ore deadly than they can believe," those "that are hunted" accept their destinies because they can fulfill "themselves without pain," so that

At the cycle's center,
They tremble, they walk
Under the tree,
They fall, they are torn,
They rise, they walk again.

Would such a vision of animal expiration and resurrection assuage the terminal terrors of Wallace Stevens or, for that matter, of Philip Larkin or of Samuel Beckett's unlucky Lucky? What is the reality status, as some philosophers might put it, of such fantasies in a "literal-minded age," when "the biblical heaven [seems to be] a victim of its own, centuries-long hype"? If Stevens and Beckett couldn't really answer, how can we? Maybe the most we can do is assent to the charisma of fictions that mirror our deepest desires. After all, as Rudolf Steiner, one of the last fin de siècle's more eccentric philosophers of the "invisible world" once put it, it's possible to "think these thoughts without believing them."[38]

Technologies of Death

EXTERMINATION

On a sunny afternoon in the last third of the twentieth century a plump and jovial-looking peasant of about sixty-five stands by a railroad track, talking to a camera.

"Since the world began"—he pauses, shrugs, smiles faintly with a certain embarrassment—"since the world began, no one ever murdered so many people this way."

There is a silence, broken only by distant birdcalls and a sort of breathing sound, maybe the soughing of the wind in the branches behind him, maybe the whirring of a tape recorder.

Over his head looms a sign that says TREBLINKA.

One of his interrogators, an interpreter, turns to the camera herself, and amplifies his remarks in French, with English subtitles. "At first it was unbearable," she explains. "Then he got used to it. Now he thinks it was impossible."

Again he grins sheepishly, as if the pain he describes—whether his own pain at witnessing the event or the pain of Treblinka's victims—had been a social solecism.

Cut to a long shot focused on the famous gate of Auschwitz, where the camp orchestra played Brahms and Schubert while thousands of skeletal prisoners in striped pajamas marched to their slave labors beneath the arch with its admonitory motto: ARBEIT MACHT FREI. Now a middle-aged Polish housewife is talking to the camera. Perhaps she's standing not far from the gate, next to the stretch of track where the trains slowed or screeched momentarily to a halt before passing under the arch, under the watchtowers, to the dead-end platform where the locked boxcars discharged cargo destined for the crematoria.

The filmmaker nods toward her, addressing one of the interpreters. "Does she know what happened to the Jews of Auschwitz?"

"I think they all ended up in the camp," the housewife answers.

"That is, they returned to Auschwitz?"

"Yes. All kinds of people from everywhere were sent here. All the Jews came here . . . to die."

Here again an empty sighing in the background—or a mechanical whirring—suggests that what the viewer might once have taken for wind no longer evokes the breath of God, the breath of life, or indeed any breath at all. Into what heaven could the soul expire as the body rose in smoke from the assembly lines of death that were fabricated at Auschwitz? The American poets Naomi Replansky and William Heyen speak for countless other twentieth-century elegists as they deplore celestial indifference. Writes Replansky in "The Six Million": "No gods were there, no demons. / They died at the hands of men."[1] And in "Blue," a poem based on Eli Wiesel's description of a "lorry [delivering] its load—little children. Babies!"—to a pit for burning, Heyen explicitly addresses an opaque "Lord of blue, / blue chest and blue brain," to help him decipher the smoke sign made by "murdered children . . . flaming in their rags," children "of bone-smolder."[2]

"Since the world began, no one ever murdered so many people *this* way." Embarrassed and bemused though he was, the farmer whose comments Claude Lanzmann captured in *Shoah* was defining a physical event whose implications were ultimately metaphysical. For *this* way—this technology of extermination—is surely the twentieth-century innovation that sealed the transformation of what had for most been a hopeful vision of death-as-expiration into what was now more likely to be a nihilistic view of death-as-termination. Arguably, in the century just past, the extraordinary phenomenon of mass *ex*termination helped facilitate the devolution of "expiration" into "termination."

To be more chronologically precise, redemptive visions of "expiration," already blurred by several centuries of mounting theological doubt, probably began to expire in the rats' alleys where the bodies of dead soldiers festered throughout the First World War, and *then* the gate of a "heaven" into which the soul could "expire" locked when the gate of Auschwitz engraved the irony of ARBEIT MACHT FREI not just in the consciousness of contemporaries but in the center of the West's cultural unconscious. For as countless witnesses and commentators have lamented, the skeleton in the trench of No Man's Land and the skeleton in the mass grave of the European Holocaust point down to the muck, not up to the sky, and the human smoke belched out by the chimneys of the crematoria dissipates in vacancy.

"What is the meaning of death in the twentieth century," asks the religious studies scholar Edith Wyschogrod, "when millions of lives have been extinguished and the possibility of annihilating human life altogether remains open?" And she goes on to wonder if the only adequate response to "the emergence of the numberless dead" is the primal "gasp of horror, the scream, that in Greek tragedy accompanies the revelation of things unspeakable."[3] For inevitably, as her comment suggests, the technology of modern killing shaped and shadowed "the mythology of modern death." Indeed the trenches of the Great War and the mass graves of the Second World War represent only two of the last century's instances of what Wyschogrod has chillingly defined as "death events" in which "scale is reckoned in terms of the compression of time"—that is, *the efficiency*—with which "destruction is delivered." If we add to these catastrophes such other "death events" of the 1940s as the atomic bombings of Hiroshima and Nagasaki, the firebombings of (among other cities) Dresden and Tokyo, and the siege of Leningrad, along with "the 160 wars that have been fought since the end of World War II," then, estimates the critic Margot Norris, "the twentieth century was the bloodiest in human history," marked, as it was, by "the killing and wounding of well over a hundred million people in a hundred years' time—the equivalent of decimating a nation the size (in people) of Belgium, Chile, or Greece every ten years for a century."[4]

But even if we focus chiefly on the technologies of death delivered at the front during the First World War and in the extermination camps of the Second, we must wonder if the technical sophistication of twentieth-century mass murder shaped the view of so many scientists that as Steven Weinberg puts it, human life is merely "a more-or-less farcical outcome of a chain of accidents reaching back to the first three minutes" so that the "more the universe seems comprehensible, the more it also seems pointless."[5] Though such a professionally depersonalized concept of life *and* death may not have been directly influenced by the atrocities of history, it is at the least a literalization of the philosophy learned in and from the First World War, the Holocaust, and the many other "death events" that scarred the landscapes of the last century. Such a literalization, too, shadows the worldview of Beckett's Pozzo, whose apparently hyperbolic assertion in *Waiting for Godot* that "one day we were born, one day we shall die, the same day, the same second" becomes no more than a statement of fact in the context of, for instance, the many eyewitness reports of births in concentration camps, where neonates who would otherwise have been consigned to the gas chambers "were routinely killed by [inmate] nurses"—were in fact, with the kindest of intentions, "poisoned, strangled, dropped into cisterns, smothered with pillows." It was not, after all, Samuel Beckett but a onetime (inmate) doctor at Auschwitz who wrote that the "fate of the baby always had to be the same. . . . After taking every precaution, we pinched and closed the little tyke's nostrils and when it opened its mouth to breathe, we gave it a dose of a lethal product."[6]

Because Auschwitz has become a paradigm of the twentieth-century "death event" marked by a fusion of "the death-world and the technological world," it perhaps can't be noted too often that the space in which new life was so summarily converted into new death was a zone of contradictions in which immediate annihilation threatened almost everyone but unquestionably awaited anyone who failed to grasp the system of absurdity that manufactured corpses out of babies, gold bars out of dental fillings, "industrial felts and threads" out of human hair.[7] Filip Müller, a Jewish survivor who recounted his experiences on camera for Lanzmann as well as in his *Eyewitness Auschwitz: Three Years in the Gas Chambers*, describes a representative incident that illustrates this point. Watching the *Kapo* of his unit ruthlessly assault his fellow prisoners, a righteous lawyer—a decent and "respectable citizen" who simply doesn't "get it" even after quite some time in "camp"—exclaims, "This is intolerable! These are innocent people who are being put to death!" At which, of course, he is himself truncheoned into oblivion. "He had failed to realize," Müller explains, "that in Auschwitz the values and laws which formed the basis of civilization were obsolete."[8]

Primo Levi tells the same sort of story quite early in *Survival in Auschwitz*, a little narrative that might have been just as well have been constructed by one of Beckett's characters: "Driven by thirst, I eyed a fine icicle outside the window, within hand's reach. I opened the window and broke off the icicle but at once a large, heavy guard prowling outside brutally snatched it away from me. '*Warum?*' I asked him in my poor German. '*Hier ist kein warum*' (there is no why here), he replied, pushing me inside with a shove."[9] No *why*, no law, and grotesquely enough no useful distinction between life, as one had previously understood it, and death, as it had traditionally been defined.

CONDITIO INHUMANA

In a careful analysis of the distinctively modern phenomenology of the concentration camp, the Italian philosopher Giorgio Agamben notes: "What happened in the camps so exceeds the juridical concept of crime that the specific juridico-political structure in which those events took place is often simply omitted from consideration. The camp is merely the place in which the most absolute *conditio inhumana* that has ever existed on earth was realized."[10] But through what revisions of traditional Western jurisprudence did such a setting for "death events" come into being? That there were no laws for prisoners doesn't, after all, mean that Auschwitz-as-paradigmatic-camp was a lawless place. It had, on the contrary, its own endlessly nihilistic regulations—precisely the rules of an "absolute *conditio inhumana*"—yet how and why were these devised?

To begin with, Agamben argues that "in the biopolitical horizon that characterizes modernity," camp inmates were implicitly defined as "no longer anything but bare life" because (whether Jews, Gypsies, homosexuals, criminals, mental defectives, or undesirable "politicals"), all were instances of "life unworthy of being lived." This last phrase is both curious and crucial. At first glance it might seem an awkward translation of the German *lebensunswerten Lebens*, which would surely sound more idiomatic in English as "life not worth living." Indeed Agamben tracks the phrase back to the writings of presumably high-minded, well-intentioned theorists of euthanasia and eugenics, thinkers who were regularly concerned with when and why life isn't "worth living." But as the Italian philosopher's further development of his thesis suggests, "life unworthy of being lived" implies a negative judgment of the one who is living that life, whereas the more usual English "life not worth living" connotes, instead, a deprecation of the nature of the lived life itself, the life as a state of existence, while leaving room for sympathy with the one who lives it. And as Agamben goes on to show, human " life unworthy of being lived" becomes in the very context of such a definition life that is not only hardly human—what the writer calls "bare life"—but life that must be exterminated.[11]

Agamben is vehement about the precision with which he uses the word "exterminate," emphatically reminding his readers that, as Hitler did in speaking of the Jews, he is consciously evoking the standard dictionary definition: "to get rid of by destroying completely; extirpate: [as in] *a new spray to exterminate insects.*" In his view, Agamben insists, the "wish to lend a sacrificial aura to the extermination of the Jews by means of the term 'Holocaust' was . . . an irresponsible historiographical blindness," for the "Jew living under Nazism is the privileged negative referent of the new biopolitical sovereignty [and the truth is] that the Jews were exterminated not in a mad and giant holocaust but exactly as Hitler had announced, 'as lice,' which is to say as bare life. The dimension in which the extermination took place is neither religion nor law, but biopolitics."[12]

Both the establishment of the Nazi *Lager* and its nature, then, were functions of a particular definition of those whom such a camp was intended to imprison. Historically, Agamben demonstrates, the Third Reich's declaration of "a state of exception" or emergency made "legally" possible the quarantine, as it were, of those whose lives were "unworthy of being lived" along with their consequent reduction to something like the "howling animality" described elsewhere by Clive Seale. And with a circularity that sealed their doom, precisely "because [the Jews and other prisoners] were lacking almost all the rights . . . that we customarily attribute to human existence, and yet were still biologically alive," notes Agamben, "they came to be situated in a limit zone between life and death, inside and outside, in which they were no longer anything but bare life." As for the camp, moreover, "*The camp is the space that is opened when the state of exception begins to become the rule* [emphasis added]. In the camp, the state of exception, which was essentially a temporary suspension of the rule of law on the basis of a factual state of danger, is now given a permanent spatial arrangement, which as such nevertheless remains outside the normal order."[13]

In an illuminating historical aside, Agamben traces the history of the concentration camp as this *kind* of place to the last fin de siècle and situates it squarely in the narrative of imperialism:

> *Historians debate whether the first camps to appear were the* campas de concentraciones *created by the Spanish in Cuba in 1896 to suppress the popular insurrection of the colony, or the "concentration camps" into which the English herded the Boers toward the start of the century. What matters here is that in both cases, a state of emergency linked to a colonial war is extended to an entire civil population. The camps are thus born not out of ordinary law . . . but out of a state of exception and martial law.*[14]

For the most part, to be sure, the colonized peoples who fell victim to Western depradations weren't systematically and scientifically exterminated as if they were mere lice, "bare life," though they were almost always obliterated by the thousands in wars of conquest. But definitions of colonized "others" as less than human—as, in Agamben's words, "bare life"—were certainly common, and the notion of extermination is made possible by such definitions.

In fact during the very decade when, Agamben says, the concentration camp came into being as a space to which entire populations might be relegated, Joseph Conrad was at work on a novella that dramatizes a shocking decline of apparently noble sympathies to openly scandalous sentiments not unlike the series of "biopolitical" redefinitions of *lebensunswerten Lebens* that were to make Auschwitz possible a half century later. The passage in *Heart of Darkness* where Marlowe recounts his reading of Kurtz's writings begins with the comment that "[a]ll Europe had contributed to the making of Kurtz; and . . . most appropriately, the International Society for the Suppression of Savage Customs had entrusted him with the making of a report, for its future guidance" and adds that what he'd written constituted an eloquent "appeal to every altruistic sentiment" until it reached a conclusion as shocking as "a flash of lightning in a serene sky: 'Exterminate all the brutes!' "[15] But suppose that instead of being headquartered in a jungle, Conrad's antihero had been lodged in a modern industrial capital. Then, just as "all Europe had contributed to the making of Kurtz" as would-be philanthropist, so all Europe—from the Enlightenment to the Industrial Revolution and on—would have provided him with a technology of extermination far more sophisticated than the methods he used in constructing walls of "heads on stakes."

In a sense, if we follow the bizarre logic Agamben explores, we can imagine Auschwitz, Treblinka, Buchenwald, and the other camps as the cities Kurtz might have founded: cities (or perhaps, more accurately, anticities), eerily modeled on the great factory towns that had sprung up everywhere around Europe's dark Satanic mills, with their highly specialized divisions of labor, their elaborate manufacturing equipment, their squalid housing for workers. That the chief business of these "cities" was extermination, that dead bodies were their principal products (though many had as a sideline the manufacture of *by*-products from those products), contributed of course to the absurdity that Müller's respectable lawyer couldn't comprehend. But as everyone familiar with the chronicles of the twentieth century knows, the grisliness of such municipal employment never detracted from the diligence with which these cities went about their business. In its way, Auschwitz was as industrious as Mainz, Manchester, or Pittsburgh. As one commentator puts it, the camp was "a mundane extension of the modern factory system" though "the raw material was human beings and the end-product was death, so many units per day marked carefully on the manager's production charts."[16]

Summarizing these points in *Modernity and the Holocaust*, the sociologist Zygmunt Bauman proposes with chilling plausibility to "*treat the Holocaust as a rare, yet significant and reliable, test of the hidden possibilities of modern* society [*sic*]," and in doing so he draws on analyses of this "death event" as " 'not only the technological achievement of an industrial society, but also the organizational achievement of a bureaucratic society.' "[17] In support of this notion it's worth quoting the eyewitness testimony of Filip Müller as he expounds the intricately enmeshed jobs of extermination:

> *The prisoners of the motor transport team . . . repaired and serviced the trucks belonging to the SS which carried not only the materials for building work in the camp, but also the living and the dead to the crematorium. The building team made the concrete posts for the endless fences and the fitters put up the barbed wire. The electricians wired it up for high tension, thus drawing ever more tightly the net in which they and their fellow sufferers were entrapped. The wooden gate to the crematorium and the great door which hermetically sealed the gas chamber had been made by prisoner carpenters. Prisoner plumbers had laid a water-pipe inside the crematorium and repaired it when necessary to prevent the death factory from going out of operation. . . . Prisoner carters with their horses and carts fetched coke and wood for the cremation of the murder victims and carried away their clothes and belongings.*[18]

Arbeit macht frei—and the absurdity of the *Arbeit* around which the city of death was organized was merely intensified by the fact that the supposedly *lebensunswerten Lebens*—the "bare life" whose extirpation was the object of all these labors—nevertheless had the ingenuity to carry out the many tasks connected with "its" own obliteration.

Ultimately, of course, such phenomena force us to question many of our assumptions about both "civilization" and "modernity" since in Bauman's words, they remind us that the Holocaust "was not an irrational outflow of the not-yet-fully-eradicated residues of pre-modern barbarity" but instead was "a legitimate resident in the house of modernity; indeed, one who would not be at home in any other house."[19] At the same time the paradoxical abjection that what we might call the Holocaust's industrial system forced victims to inflict on themselves redefines both life and death, most deeply for those who experienced the camps directly but also for those like, say, the viewers of *Shoah* or the readers of Müller and Levi, who confront the camps from a safe historical distance. For after all, to redefine humanity as *lebensunswerten Lebens* is to re*construe* as well as to reconstruct both life and death.

Levi is astute in his analysis of such revisions. Remembering his induction into Auschwitz—"[we] find ourselves . . . in the blue and icy snow of dawn, barefoot and naked, with all our clothing in our hands, with a hundred yards to run to the next hut"—he explains, "We are transformed into . . . phantoms," and adds:

> *Then for the first time we became aware that our language lacks words to express this offence, the demolition of a man. In a moment . . . the reality was revealed to us: we had reached the bottom. . . . Imagine now a man who is deprived of everyone he loves, and at the same time of . . . everything he possesses: he will be a hollow man. . . . He will be a man whose life or death can be lightly decided . . . on the basis of a pure judgement of utility. It is in this way that one can understand the double sense of the term "extermination camp"; and it is now clear what we seek to express with the phrase: "to lie on the bottom."* [20]

The double sense of the term "extermination camp" refers, Levi implies, to the death factory's double function: the simultaneous extermination of "bare life" and human values, or perhaps, more accurately, the inhuman extermination of bare life made possible by the virtually surgical excision of human values. For the man who "lies on the bottom," psychically annihilated in preparation for physical annihilation, is one who has been figuratively as well as literally dislodged not only from possessions-as-values but also from values-as-possessions.

Perhaps, indeed, our grief at witnessing the abandoned belongings of the camps' victims is often so intense because possessions-as-values so movingly reflect values-as-possessions. Meditating on *Shoah* in an introduction to the text of the film, Simone de Beauvoir confesses that she "found one of the most heartrending sequences a heap of suitcases, some unpretentious, others more expensive, but all carrying name and address tags. Mothers had carefully packed into them milk powder, talc, baby food. Others had packed clothes, food, medicines. But no one ever had any need of them." Nor, Levi might add, of the love they enclosed, or of the identities to which their tags once seemed so unproblematically to refer. What those who entered the camps had to leave behind were what the American poet Sylvia Plath, herself obsessed with the Holocaust, once described as suitcases "Out of which the same self unfolds like a suit / Bald and shiny, with pockets of wishes." For there were few "suits" of moral *value*—not even "[b]ald and shiny" ones—and no pockets, no wishes, in the twentieth century's cities of extermination, the almost grimly parodic towns where *Hier ist kein warum.* [21]

ANNIHILATION IN HISTORY

The human history of inhumane extermination is of course long and varied, and even the most murderous practices don't seem for the most part to have been incompatible with the religious assumptions that underlie a mythology of death-as-expiration. After all, much of the history of human annihilation of other humans features the killing of sacrificial victims in an effort to appease or celebrate the gods. From, say, Agamemnon's immolation of his daughter Iphigenia and Abraham's effort to immolate his son Isaac to the ritual slaughters practiced by Aztecs, Mayans, and countless other peoples, "violence and the sacred"—to use René Girard's phrase—have had a time-honored relationship. Indeed, if we take into consideration such bygone scandals as the Crusades, the Spanish Inquisition, and the Salem witch burnings, the human annihilation of other humans evidently all too often took place in just those theological contexts that would seem to have been obliterated by the twentieth century's murderous anticities.

Even when violence wasn't frankly deployed in behalf of the sacred, it coexisted nicely enough with religious values. Certainly the grisly "spectacles of death in ancient Rome" that one classicist recently studied in a book of that name don't seem to have offended any god-fearing citizens. On the contrary, this narrative of public bloodshed situates "the development and diversity of Roman spectacles of death," including "corpses and carcasses as food—Christians: persecutions and disposal," squarely within the framework of a devout Roman belief system. Quoting Seneca's observation that "Romans saw the turning of a man into a corpse as a 'satisfying spectacle,' " the author notes that "homicides in Roman spectacles" can be "understood as ritualized or sacralized killings . . . associated with gods or spirits of the dead."[22]

Everywhere in the world too, within countless belief systems analogous to ancient Rome's, the most exquisite techniques, indeed *technologies* of torture were (and are) as regularly features of internecine political battle as of international warfare. From the medieval strappado—the so-called Queen of Tortures—to the horrific "interrogation" practices at Abu Ghraib and Guantánamo, military *and* civilian interrogators have applied inhuman force to dehumanized prisoners. Even today the contemplation of such procedures isn't always offensive to the masses. Snuff films? S&M movies? Digital videos of anguished victims? Maybe such entertainments are comparatively rarefied, but to judge from the box-office draw of slasher flicks (including updated "spectacles of death in ancient Rome"), Torturers R Us. And though the more sensitive may be distressed by the agony of others, we aren't necessarily disillusioned. Some onlookers, indeed, draw moral strength from the fortitude of sufferers, like the American traveler who commented, after touring a European "museum of torture," that he hoped "anyone that has the opportunity to visit this site will renew their resolve to make love for their fellow man the rule of their life as Jesus taught 2000 years ago."[23]

To the extent that torture, physical as well as psychological, has long been part of what we might call the execution process, many cultures have always granted it pride of place in moral systems. Though extracting an eye for an eye and a tooth for a tooth may seem vindictive to some, others consider such an exchange perfectly just. Rome's ingeniously devised executions "included exposure to wild beasts, crucifixion, and burning alive [and the] victim's lasting agony and death provided [an] exemplary public spectacle."[24] Of course similar "acts of social vengeance" are still widely accepted in contemporary America, where executions are often defined as events that will bring the relief of "closure" not just to society in general but to the families of murder victims in particular.

In June 2001, in fact, the attorney general of the United States arranged for the filming of Timothy McVeigh's death on closed-circuit TV in order to accommodate the many out-of-town mourners who insisted that their grief would achieve "closure" if they witnessed the on-screen annihilation of the Oklahoma City bomber. And the fifty-six-page Execution Protocol issued by the Bureau of Prisons was as scrupulously bureaucratized as the arrangements for the video spectacle were high-tech. "The Final 30 Minutes," for instance, included a series of carefully planned steps, among them the removal of "the condemned individual . . . from the Inmate Holding Cell by the Restraint Team"; his strip search "by the Restraint Team"; the removal of "ambulatory restraints" in the Execution Room; the opening of "drapes covering the windows of the witness rooms"; and the "prearranged signal" that "will direct the executioner(s) to administer the lethal injection." Though the procedures described might not be out of place in a snuff film, they're sanctioned by many in the clergy and the state, whose representatives would probably say that they've been altruistically designed to bring comfort to grieving survivors while mitigating the suffering of the condemned.[25]

Altruistic "values" might even be said to motivate the use of human subjects in deadly medical experiments, a Nazi practice that constituted a particularly outlandish subset of procedures for torture. Agamben devotes a crucial section of *Homo Sacer* to the fate of the so-called VPs (short for the

German *Versuchspersonen*, or "human guinea pigs"). "At the Nuremberg trials," he reminds us," the experiments conducted by German physicians and scientists in the concentration camps were universally taken to be one of the most infamous chapters in the history of the National Socialist regime." Still, he adds, such tests on human subjects can be traced back to "experiments on prisoners and persons sentenced to death [that] had been performed several times and on a large scale in our century, in particular in the United States (the very country from which most of the Nuremberg judges came)." Like camp inmates, Agamben argues, convicts selected for such treatment were definitively excluded from "the political community," and precisely because they had no rights "and yet were still biologically alive, they came to be [seen as] no longer anything but bare life." Nevertheless, some ethicists claimed that their treatment was consistent with traditional systems of moral value because it was part of a "fight against the misery and death caused by [malaria and other diseases that were] a scourge of the natural order."[26]

Nor does a history of human intimacy with human "corpses and carcasses" appear to have threatened abiding visions of expiration from mortality into immortality. Indeed, the opposite was sometimes the case, as Philippe Ariès has perhaps most persuasively shown. For although, as the French historian observes, "the ancients feared the proximity of the dead and kept them out of the way," Christian "faith in the resurrection of the body" meant that "the dead ceased to frighten the living, and the two groups coexisted in the same places and behind the same walls." For centuries, for example, the Catholic cemetery functioned as a place of sanctuary and as a "public meeting place" that elicited neither fear nor revulsion.[27] Clearly intimacy with death does not trivialize it or intensify its fearsomeness—or redefine cultural ways of mythologizing its theological meanings.

In the course of the twentieth century, though, every one of the already dreadful phenomena just listed—state- and even church-sanctioned individual or mass annihilation, death as spectacle, torture as a technology, dehumanizing medical experimentation with human subjects, corpses as quotidian familiars—came together in a new definitional space, as it were, that contributed significantly to the construction of what Stevens called the "mythology of modern death." That new space was the camp, or *Lager*, that was bureaucratically organized in the service of extermination as well as enslavement.

Despite etymological differences, the linguistic associations of both the English word "camp" and the German *Lager* are buried in the nature of the concentration *camp* or *Lager* as it evolved in the 1930s. Our English "camp" derives from the Latin *campus,* meaning "open field," and has long been associated with temporary military shelter. Similarly, *Lager* denotes military lodgings, but the word has other senses that complicate its connotations— for example, "storehouse, warehouse, depot, dump" and (of animals) "lair, den, hole, cover," as well as "dregs, sediments."[28] As if to bring together multiple meanings, the cities of death founded at Auschwitz-Birkenau, Bergen-Belsen, Treblinka, and elsewhere throughout Germany and eastern Europe ended up as *storehouses* or *dumps* established by military authorities for the imprisonment of dead and dying human beings who had been redefined as *animals* or social *dregs.*

Yet how did the military camp solidify into the heavily industrialized, quasi-urban site represented in countless images of the European Holocaust? If we review the twentieth century's history of extermination(s), we can trace the rise of the deadly anticities that dominated the Second World War directly back to the First War.

THE GREAT WAR AND THE CITY OF DEATH

Among the curious military relics in the Imperial War Museum, which has long occupied the grounds where London's notorious Bedlam once stood, is an old-fashioned double-decker bus, painted olive drab to blend into the ruinous territory through which its occupants were to be transported. For as if to dramatize the strangeness of the space into which they were about to step, the soldiers of 1914–1918 were often ferried from the apparent normalcy of the home front to the extraordinary hell of the western front in what would otherwise have been the most ordinary of vehicles—the lumbering buses that plied the streets of the British capital, knitting homes, pubs, shops, schools, and hospitals into a pattern of placid urbanity. Now, dislodged from their peacetime contexts, the buses journeyed, as in some surrealistic nightmare about London transport, toward the even more surrealistic realm of the trenches.

Yet despite its oddness, such a use of London buses was singularly appropriate, for the complicated network of trenches in which the Great War's combatants were buried alive for four long years itself constituted an unnerving parody of a modern city, as is suggested by some of the names the troops bestowed on key routes or intersections (Half Moon Street, Dublin Castle) in the "labyrinth" they inhabited. The "muddy maze of trenches," declared one Major Owen Rutter, was "Worse to find one's way about in /

Than the dark and windy subways / Of the Piccadilly tube are," so that it made sense to map them as if they were part of an extended cityscape. But again, the bleak "city" into which the soldiers were bused was notably eerie, indeed, as the historian Eric Leed has explained, uncanny (*unheimlich*) in Freud's sense of the word, for this weirdly urban battlefield was " 'empty of men' and yet it was saturated with men."[29]

"Trenches rise up, grey clay, three or four feet above the ground," wrote one observer. "Save for one or two men—snipers at the sap-head—the country was deserted. No sign of humanity—a dead land. And yet thousands of men were there" like "rabbits concealed" or like dwellers in some diabolical underground township. No wonder, then, that Wilfred Owen compared No Man's Land to those paradigmatic cities of evil "Sodom and Gomorrah" and "Babylon the Fallen," that Rudyard Kipling called the vast British war cemeteries "the silent cities," and that an entrepreneurial travel agent declared that once tourists saw the ruins of Ypres the "ancient ruins of Pompeii . . . will be simply out of it."[30]

Armies have always of course been traveling communities, so that there is a sense in which any war can be figured as a ferocious city. Too, the "city of dreadful night" has always itself been a trope for ultimate social perversion, the hell of human inhumanity. At least one analyst of the Great War's literary impact has noted the relevance of Northrop Frye's theories of "demonic" imagery to the self-wasting of culture so often symbolized through representations of the war's infamous No Man's Land. The "demonic human world," writes Frye, is archetypally portrayed not only as deserts or waste lands but also as cities "of destruction and dreadful night" characterized by emblems of "perverted work" like "engines of torture, weapons of war [and] images of a dead mechanism [that] is unnatural as well as inhuman."[31] In the violent psychodrama of our era's first "war to end all wars," these long-standing cultural stereotypes came together not with a whimper but a bang, constructing a demonic cityscape that marked the "epochal event" of the twentieth century because it effectively ended the very history that might produce so naive a concept as a "war to end all wars."

As early as 1915 that shrewd cultural analyst Sigmund Freud meditated on this issue, remarking that before the war, "he who was not by stress of circumstance confined to one spot, could confer upon himself . . . a new a wider fatherland, wherein he moved unhindered [but] now that civilized cosmopolitan [stands] helpless in a world grown strange to him—his all-embracing patrimony disintegrated . . . the fellow-citizens embroiled and debased." More recently, the British poet Philip Larkin made the same point in his poignant "MCMXV," through a description of the innocence of the unwary prewar city, with its "long uneven lines" of volunteers "Standing as patiently / As if they were stretched outside / The Oval or Villa Park . . . Grinning as if it were all / An August Bank Holiday lark."[32]

To be sure, the "moustached archaic faces" of Larkin's beaming enlistees, ingenuously regarding the guns of August as harbingers of a kind of extended "Bank Holiday lark," were visages of working-class city dwellers, while, cultivated and urbane, Freud's cosmopolitan traveler needed no such liberation but was a connoisseur rather than a prisoner of cities, perhaps a kind of Baudelairean flâneur. Both worker and flâneur, however, were still at that point denizens of the largely prosperous city that Baudelaire saw as the type and image of "modern life" in the nineteenth century. "For the perfect flâneur, for the passionate spectator," enthuses the French poet in "The Painter of Modern Life," "it is an immense joy to set up house in the heart of the multitude," adding that this artist of the quotidian "marvels at the eternal beauty and the amazing harmony of life in the capital cities."[33] However, "Never such innocence again," one is tempted to exclaim, for arguably the city of the war permanently contaminated those peacetime cities of which it was a murderous reflection.

Its combatants immobilized in endless miles of trenches on both sides of No Man's Land, the war that began as an "August Bank Holiday lark," a way of getting out of the workaday city, soon began to feel permanent as a city, with what A. A. Milne described in a bitter jingle as the "same old bodies out in front, / Same old strafe from 2 till 4, / Same old bloody War" established like a stain on the horizon of modernity. Its citizens stripped of peacetime identities and re-created as virtually nameless ciphers, this entrenched city of dreadful night was also alienated from what had been "normal" cities, as the gulf between western front and home front suggests, with its construction of the front as a kind of countercapital to the capital itself.[34] Most tellingly, this deadly city of war was so highly industrialized that, as two recent historians have commented, "some wicked perversion of the factory system" seemed to have evolved into "the killing fields of the Somme, Verdun and elsewhere." With its trenches surrounded by barbed wire; its ceaselessly rattling machine guns, bursting shells, and constantly roaring cannons; its swarms of trains, ambulances, even double-decker buses, and even too its newly swooping planes; its stammering radios and hissing gases, the city of the (First) War looks retrospectively not just like "the negative realization" of those quintessentially urban products "Enlightenment and Industrialization" but also like "the spring board to what 1918 would ultimately lead the world into: a second war where death was still more scientifically and industrially delivered" *in* the murderous cities of Auschwitz and Bergen-Belsen as well as (very differently) *to* the cities of London, Dresden, Berlin, Tokyo, and Hiroshima.[35]

It was in the First World War's city of death, indeed, that the casualties of technology first became even in death bizarre tools of technology. Writes the historian David Cannadine, "the combat zone might remain littered for weeks with bodies [and new] trenches might be dug through them; parapets might be made of them," pioneering the grisly efficiency that was to be far more systematically exploited in the concentration camps of the next war. Noted one combatant describing such a cadaverous parapet, in this structure "the heads of two men could be seen," with their teeth "showing so that they seemed to be grinning horribly down on us." Yet often, remarked the same writer, the dead were even more immediately useful; in the infamous Battle of the Somme in 1916, the ground was "hardened by the sun and difficult to dig" so that when "a man was killed . . . he was used as head cover and earth thrown over him" by his surviving mates, a maneuver that "saved the lives of [many] men that were digging themselves in."[36]

Despite (or perhaps because of) their utility, however, such scenes were often difficult to decipher. The German combatant Ernst Jünger commented, on the sheer unreality of the charnel house with which he and his men were confronted, that "we had to stare again and again at these things that we had never seen before, without being able to give them any meaning. . . . We looked at all these dead with dislocated limbs, distorted faces, and the hideous colors of decay, as though we walked in a dream through a garden full of strange plants, and we could not realize at first what we had all round us." Not only had "the Romantic pastoral" been transformed into a grotesque, even surreal landscape ("a garden full of strange plants") but the Romantically inspired Baudelairean city was gone too, to be replaced by the "Unreal City" of the Eliotian waste land, with its "hooded hordes swarming / Over endless plains, stumbling in cracked earth" among "Falling towers."[37]

And "stumbling in cracked earth" through the damned and doomed city of the Great War the once-joyous Baudelairean flâneur became a sort of voyeur *maudit*, a desperate spectator/participant, whose wartime observations were scribblings in a journal of death marked by an ironic precision that would influence generations of writers in every European language. The painter Fernand Léger succinctly formulated the paradoxes of this anticity in one of his letters home from the front near Verdun:

On est entre dans la terre, on est absorbe par elle, on se colle dessus pour
éviter la mort qui est partout. . . . On se cache derrière un tue. On vit avec
les morts en bon camarade. On ne les enterre même pas. À quoi bon? Un
autre obus les deterrera.[38]
[You're entered into the earth, you're absorbed by it, you stick yourself
to it in order to avoid the death that's everywhere. . . .You hide behind
someone who's been killed. You live with the dead like good friends. You
don't bury them. What's the use? Another shell would dig them up (my
translation).]

But with its bitter allusion to Horace's "It is sweet and proper to die for
one's country," Wilfred Owen's famous depiction in "Dulce et Decorum
Est" of one soldier's death by gas perhaps most vividly illustrates the horror
experienced by this new kind of Baudelairean poet-as-stunned-witness:

GAS! GAS! Quick, boys!—An ecstasy of fumbling,
Fitting the clumsy helmets just in time;
But someone still was yelling out and stumbling,
And flound'ring like a man in fire or lime . . .
Dim, through the misty panes and thick green light,
As under a green sea, I saw him drowning.[39]

In the city of death that was the front, most normal categories of experience
were transformed—turned upside down or polluted. "Buildings" above-
ground were fabricated from the bodies of the dead while the "life" of the
living, such as it was, subsisted beneath the earth, in the underground world
to which the dead would ordinarily have been consigned. Rats lived with
humans, and birdsong was drowned by the "anger" of guns. Double-decker
buses traveled from the "real" world of London into the surreal realm of the
trenches. And with the technological innovation that made possible the
introduction of deadly gases as weapons of combat, the air that ought to be
the very breath of life brought death instead.

The most pernicious of the poisons used in combat during the Great
War, mustard gas, was first used by the German Army in September 1917.
The skin of its victims blistered, they were generally blinded, and the gas
caused internal and external bleeding while attacking the bronchial tubes,
stripping off the mucous membrane. "In the face of gas, without protection," comments the British historian C. R. M. F. Cruttwell, "individuality
was annihilated; the soldier in the trench became a mere passive recipient

of torture and of death. A final stage seemed to be reached in the whole tendency of modern scientific warfare to depress and make of no effect individual bravery, enterprise, and skill."[40] The British memoirist Vera Brittain, who served as a nurse's aide at the front, described the horror of witnessing such torture and death in terms not unlike Owen's, writing passionately that she wished those who "glibly" defined the conflict as a "holy war" could "see the poor things all burnt and blistered all over with great suppurating blisters" and hear them "saying their throats are closing and they know they are going to choke."

The "strain [is] very great," Brittain added in this dispatch from what seems to have been the center of hell. "The enemy within shelling distance . . . —ambulance trains jolting into the siding, all day, all night—gassed men on stretchers, clawing the air—dying men, reeking with mud and foul green-stained bandages . . . dead men with fixed, empty eyes and shiny, yellow faces."[41] But the war went on, and rather than being a war to end *all* wars, as the rhetoric of the time proposed, it functioned as a pale prototype for cities of death yet to come.

HELL ON EARTH

Here is Filip Müller describing one of his experiences as a traumatized member of the *Sonderkommando* that tended the crematoria at Auschwitz:

We left the mortuary and came to a huge iron-mounted wooden door; it was not locked. We entered a place which was in total darkness. As we switched on the light, the room was lit by bulbs enclosed in a protective wire cage. We were standing in a large oblong room measuring about 250 square metres. Its unusually low ceiling and walls were whitewashed. Down the length of the room concrete pillars supported the ceiling. However, not all the pillars served this purpose; for there were others, too. The Zyclon [sic] B gas crystals were inserted through openings into hollow pillars made of sheet metal. They were perforated at regular intervals and inside them a spiral ran from top to bottom in order to ensure as even a distribution of the granular crystals as possible. Mounted on the ceiling was a large number of dummy showers made of metal. These were intended to delude the suspicious on entering the gas chamber into believing that they were in a shower room. A ventilating plant was installed in the wall; this was switched on immediately after each gassing to disperse the gas and thus to expedite the removal of corpses.[42]

Like much of Müller's testimony and that of countless other death camp witnesses, this passage depicts a reality that seems either too gothic to be true outside the realm of fiction or too infernal to be imaginable in *this* world rather than in a hypothetical afterlife. Indeed, as George Steiner long ago remarked, the "concentration camps of the twentieth century . . . are *Hell made immanent . . .* the transference of Hell from below the earth to its surface," as if they were "the deliberate enactment of a long, precise, imagining," embodying, "often down to minutiae, the images and chronicles of Hell in European art and thought from the twelfth to the eighteenth centuries [*sic*]."[43]

Just as heaven was historically figured as a bejeweled celestial city, so hell was often represented as a city where the damned burned alive in terrible furnaces or boiled in awful cauldrons, while demons skewered them with pitchforks. Translated into earthly terms, heaven is the city toward which Western reason strives, a metropolis that offers the apotheosis of the modern urban planner's vision of perpetually accessible light, warmth, and water (electricity, efficient heating, and plumbing), broad boulevards, flowering parks, fine buildings, comfortable clothing, rapid transit, and, more generally, health and safety. Heaven, in other words, is a city in which the Baudelairean flâneur would be at home, perhaps idling along streets made possible by rational industry, a city like the better parts of fin de siècle Paris, London, or Berlin. Hell, however, is that dream capital's antiself, a place that looks like a city but in which perversions of reason have labored to destroy or defile every one of the categories of comfort and safety through which Western civilization defines itself. Hell is the city in which the machinery devised by reason annihilates rather than alleviating, torments and denies rather than assuring and sustaining.

If Paris and the other great capitals yearned to emulate heaven, Auschwitz and the other camps were "Hell made immanent" in parodic industrial cityscapes crisscrossed by stony "streets," studded with concrete blockhouses, and "served" by precisely the sorts of trains and trucks, furnaces and chimneys that ensured the comfort of the European flâneur. Here the grotesque lineaments of the front that were entrenched in the First World War were built upward and outward, reified, elaborated. Here unarmed civilians rather than armed combatants were immured. Here a poison gas like the kind that had been an experimental weapon in the earlier "death event" became a final solution to what was seen as a species of industrial problem. And here, in this unlikely urban setting, as if in a weird allusion to the great frescoes onto which the preindustrial imaginations of the Middle Ages and the Renaissance projected dreams or nightmares of the Last Judgment, the "damned" were naked, while the "saved" were clothed; the "damned" were reduced to animal materiality, to filth and pollution, while the "saved," though hardly elevated in a glow of angelic cleanliness, were nonetheless suited and booted with military efficiency.[44]

Nakedness was in fact essential to the hellishness of the all-too-real unreal cities erected by the Nazis. As Primo Levi explained:

> *One entered the Lager naked. . . . [T]he day in the Lager was studded with innumerable harsh strippings—checking for lice, searching one's clothes . . . as well as for the periodic selections, during which a "commission" decided who was still fit for work, and who . . . was marked for elimination. Now, a naked and barefoot man feels that all his nerves and tendons are severed: he is helpless prey. Clothes, even the foul clothes distributed, even the crude clogs with their wooden soles, are a tenuous but indispensable defense. Anyone who does not have them no longer perceives himself as a human being but rather as a worm. . . . He knows that he can be crushed at any moment.*[45]

Terrence Des Pres and Tsvetan Todorov, two of the most astute commentators on the strategies deployed throughout the Nazi Holocaust, note that this particular degradation, like a number of other techniques of depersonalization, was a social tool, a technology of control, ultimately "aimed at helping the guard forget the prisoner's humanity." Supplementing Levi, Todorov observes that former guards "have testified that it became impossible for them to identify with their victims once those people became a mass of nude bodies: clothes are a mark of humanity."[46] As Todorov and Des Pres also remark, however, for the camp inmate the "process of being stripped bare culminates when the past and present are torn apart, as if some actual rending, some intimate severance of the self from prior roots, has occurred." Todorov quotes the report of one survivor: "There were still naive prisoners among us who asked, to the amusement of the more seasoned ones . . . if they could keep a wedding ring, a medal or a good-luck piece. No one could yet grasp the fact that everything would be taken away."[47]

Even language was in many cases a crucial component of the "everything" that was "taken away." A number of commentators have pointed out that "in order to murder their victims, the Nazis had to murder the German language first, associated as it was with high culture, rationality, and philosophical thought."[48] Thus Todorov explains that in order to "condition" the guards to "do what they did," each inmate had to be stripped not only of clothing and history but also of his or her name, "that cardinal sign of human individuality, and given a number." For the same reason, he suggests, the guards avoided "using words like *people* or *men*" when speaking of their prisoners, instead defining them as "pieces" or "items." In *Shoah*, two gravediggers recall at one point that "the Germans even forbade us to use the words 'corpse' or 'victim.' The dead were blocks of wood, shit, with absolutely no importance."[49]

But if linguistic references *to* the prisoners, the so-called *Häftlinge*, were debased, the state of animallike speechlessness imposed *on* some prisoners constituted a different and perhaps more hellish degradation. Confides Levi:

> We immediately realized, from our very first contacts with the contemptu-
> ous men with the black patches, that knowing or not knowing German was
> a watershed. Those who understood them and answered in an articulate
> manner could establish the semblance of a human relationship. To those
> who did not understand them the black men reacted in a manner that
> astonished and frightened us . . . the blows fell, and it was obvious [that
> the] use of the word to communicate thought . . . had fallen into disuse.
> This was a signal: for those people we were no longer men.[50]

This reduction to a minimal existence divested of history, identity, language was exacerbated by what Des Pres terms "excremental assault," for as he puts it, "prisoners were *systematically* subject to filth. . . . [Defilement was] a condition of life from day to day." Indeed, since it was often dangerous or impossible to void, quotidian misery was intensified "by the mineral movement of life itself. Death was planted in a need which could not, like other needs, be repressed or delayed or passively endured." Testified one survivor: "Urine and excreta poured down the prisoners' legs, and by nightfall the excrement, which had frozen to our limbs, gave off its stench. We were really no longer human beings in the accepted sense. Not even animals, but putrefying corpses moving on two legs."[51]

"Not even animals": Filip Müller describes the visits of SS doctors to the crematorium, where, like "cattle dealers[,] they felt the thighs and calves of men and women who were still alive and selected what they called the best pieces before the victims were executed," then, after the executions, "proceeded to cut pieces of still warm flesh from thighs and calves and threw them into waiting receptacles." Only later, he explains, did he and his companions learn that "these buckets of living flesh were taken to the Institute of Hygiene at Rajsko where it was used in the laboratories for the growing of bacterial cultures." Adds Müller wryly: "Once I heard *Oberscharführer* Quackernack remark: 'Horseflesh would do, but in war-time it is too valuable for that sort of thing.' "[52]

Only in medieval representations of hell (perhaps not even in those representations) could one encounter such transgressions of the categories through which the rational mind distinguishes culture from nature, speech from mere sound, clean from unclean, human from animal, life from death. Detailing the abyss of pollution into which the survivors of Auschwitz—immured among the diseased, the dying, and the dead—had sunk at the time the camps were liberated, Primo Levi laments that "it is no longer man who, having lost all restraint, shares his bed with a corpse."[53] Yet of course this willful obliteration of humanity was as functionally necessary as the stripping away of clothing and history. Just as "the gas chamber was invented to avoid . . . 'human' reaction" and to "keep the members of the *Einsatzkommandos*, who shot prisoners by the thousands, from losing their minds" (for once "the machine had replaced the man, the executioner could avoid all contact with the victim"), so the absolute abjection of its victims was diabolically rational, facilitating their transformation from people to "items," dead human beings to "blocks of wood" or pieces of "shit."[54]

In a meditation on the dynamics through which such confounding of traditional epistemological categories redefined the essentials of the world itself, Des Pres examines the distinctions between what we expect from "ordinary" life and what became the quotidian existence of *Häftlinge*:

> *Prisoners in a concentration camp would eat anything, at any time they could get it, in almost any state of rawness or decay. We, on the other hand, eat the kind of food we choose, when we choose, after it has been achieved aesthetically through cooking, and upon occasions rich in ritual observance. And thus too, the dead in the camps were stacked naked in piles, rammed into ovens, tossed every which way into ditches and pits. But the man or woman who dies in normal circumstances becomes the object of complicated ritual procedures which confer meaning and dignity upon his or her death and thereby humanize it. The primacy of death is denied symbolically. . . . Death is no longer thought of as death, just as animal flesh is no longer thought of as animal flesh after it has been transformed by cooking and table rites.*[55]

As many writers on the First World War have noted, trench warfare also frequently forced combatants to confront the unmediated "primacy of death": soldiers sharing muddy holes with rats and cadavers had few chances to undertake "ritual procedures" that would "confer meaning and dignity" upon the deaths of their comrades. Yet at least the men at the front could imagine their predicament as one component of a cultural emergency in which the spectacle of unburied human flesh was simultaneously traumatic and "normal."[56]

But what does it mean for an understanding of "modern death" that in the cities of hell encrypted at the center of the twentieth century the "primacy of death" could not be "denied symbolically"? Human consciousness usually seeks to evade awareness of death even when modes of symbolic denial (elegy, ritual, theology) are largely unavailable. But when twentieth-century history confronted millions of direct witnesses—as well as the readers and viewers of their experiences—with the unburied dead "stacked naked in piles," it became necessary, at least symbolically, to assert rather than deny the "primacy of death." But with the heaven of expiration transformed into the hell of extermination, victims and witnesses inevitably experienced death as little more than the cessation of an already horrifying material existence. Yet the human need to symbolize and summarize trauma endured, and that need produced the highly specific narratives of annihilation constructed by Müller, Levi, and countless others, each of which constitutes, in its way, a detailed version of what Wyschogrod describes as "the gasp of horror, the scream, that in Greek tragedy accompanies the revelation of things unspeakable."

That "gasp of horror" at the unspeakable is also a form of testimony in just the sense that Shoshana Felman and Dori Laub define in their illuminating study of the ways in which the mind, even when it's been "overwhelmed by occurrences that have not settled into understanding or remembrance . . . events in excess of our frames of reference," nevertheless seeks to gain some control over chaos. For though the authors, a literary critic and a psychoanalyst, entitle their book *Testimony:* Crises [emphasis added] *of Witnessing in Literature, Psychoanalysis, and History*, they demonstrate that in Felman's words, agonized testimony, however fragmentary, is a "crucial mode of our relation to events of our times."

Arguably, such witnessing can be traced back to the often maddened and frantic reports sent from the front by First World War combatants. But as deployed by survivors of the Shoah, the very genre of bearing witness became even more urgent than the testimonials that issued from the Great

War. As Felman notes, the testimonial imperative implies that to "testify—to *vow to tell*, to *promise* and *produce* one's own speech as material evidence for truth—is to accomplish a *speech act*, rather than simply formulate a statement," a speech act analogous to those hurled by countless witnesses from front to home front or from concentration camp to courtroom. But whereas soldiers returning to England from, say, the Battle of the Somme could expect to be believed by their interlocutors, many victims of the Holocaust feared that even if they survived to testify against their oppressors, the scenes they had witnessed were nearly unspeakable because barely credible.[57]

In any case the Nazis didn't believe that their victims would live to tell the tale of the immolations they had witnessed. Des Pres records a Dachau survivor's report of the SS guards' "pleasure in telling us that we had no chance of coming out alive, a point they emphasized with particular relish by insisting that after the war the rest of the world would not believe what happened [because] people would conclude that evil on such a scale was just not possible." Also, as Todorov observes, it's "unbearable to recall having been reduced to existing only to eat, to living in one's own excrement . . . just as it is unbearable to recall the time when one did not do all one could to defend one's dignity [or] care for others."[58] Yet in its insistence on accumulating the minutiae of horror, even the smallest details of humiliation, the testimony of such writers as Levi and Müller asserts the terrible facts of modern death, of extermination and termination. Indeed, just as the death camps appear to have been structured by the typology of hell as the European imagination has traditionally figured it, so the testimony of Holocaust survivors seems to have been shaped by the prophetic or even apocalyptic assertions of the Bible, from the earliest books of the prophets to (even) the New Testament book of Revelation. "I, John, saw" becomes "I, Filip Müller, saw" or "I, Primo Levi, saw."

Yet what John saw and transmitted to centuries of readers was a vision of one whose "eyes were as a flame of fire" and who declared, "I am he that liveth, and was dead; and behold, I am alive for evermore," and visions too of those who "serve him day and night in his temple" and "shall hunger no more, neither thirst any more," while what the twentieth century's most impassioned witnesses saw was only "the bottomless pit; and . . . a smoke out of the pit, as the smoke of a great furnace; and the sun and the air . . . darkened by reason of the smoke of the pit," as if the bowels of the earth had opened to disclose the death immanent in all life.[59]

THE GERMAN REQUIEM

Paris, November 21, 2000. The terrifying second section of the Brahms *Deutsches Requiem* has just begun its funereal march of prophecy and admonition. *Denn alles Fleisch, es ist wie Gras und alle Herrlichkeit des Menschen wie des Grases Blumen.* "For all flesh is as grass, and all the glory of man as the flowers of grass." Led by the Belgian conductor Philippe Herreweghe, the orchestra and chorus seem especially dark in their warnings, the pounding of the muffled drums unusually sinister. *Denn alles Fleisch, es ist wie Gras.* With what the program notes describe as "a sarabandelike rhythm"—curiously, for a march, this piece is in three-quarters time— these opening words seem to limp or stagger toward us with strange determination, as if the members of the Collegium Vocale are a mass of prisoners, chained together and advancing into the audience as they thunder Brahms's setting of the Bible's stern reminder. *Das Gras ist verdorret und die Blume abgefallen.* "The grass withereth, and the flower thereof falleth away."

. . . und die Blume abgefallen . . . "and the flower thereof falleth away."

So seid nun geduldig, liebe Brüder, bis auf die Zukunft des Herrn. "Be patient, therefore, brethren, unto the coming of the Lord."

The biblical words of encouragement seem sickly sweet, spurious. *Siehe, ein Ackermann wartet auf köstliche Frucht der Erde und ist geduldig darüber. . . .* "Behold, the husbandman waiteth for the precious fruit of the earth and hath long patience for it."

Even the tormented, funereal approach of Brahms's marching mourners feels wrong, though not as ironic as the counseling of patience. Behind the darkening strings, banging drums, and blaring horns, I suddenly sense the macabre rhythms of Paul Celan's famous *Todesfuge*:

> *Black milk of daybreak we drink you at night*
> *we drink you at midday and morning we drink you at evening*
> *we drink and we drink*
> *a man lives in the house your goldenes Haar Margareta*
> *your aschenes Haar Shulamith he plays his vipers*
> *He shouts play death more sweetly this Death is a master from*
> *   Deutschland*
> *he shouts scrape your strings darker you'll rise then as smoke to the sky*
> *you'll have a grave then in the clouds there you won't lie too cramped*[60]

"Tango of Death" is what Celan called this poem when he first published it in Romanian, a title alluding to the "Death Tango" that the SS forced Jewish musicians to perform at Auschwitz and elsewhere when groups of prisoners were executed, as well as "during marches, grave-digging [and] tortures."[61]

It is as if Brahms has been polluted—and how could he not have been?—by my months of immersion in Holocaust writing. As if even the Salle Pleyel, in whose grandiose thirties space we're now seated, has been contaminated by the shadows of extermination that gathered throughout the very decade when this Parisian concert hall was constructed. As Felman puts it, "A 'life-testimony' is not simply a testimony to a private life, but a point of conflation between text and life, a textual testimony which can *penetrate us like an actual life.*" And Margot Norris adds, "Reading testimony can therefore alter us, inhabit us, haunt us, augment us more profoundly than other acts of reading."[62]

Slouched in a plush orchestra seat, I'm neither survivor nor witness, not even a true scholar of the extremities that sliced so darkly through the heart of the twentieth century, though I'm trying, in my way, to grope toward an understanding of how those horrors have shaped modern modes of mourning.

What of the "real" theorists? What, for instance, of Theodor Adorno, who so notoriously declared that "to write poetry after Auschwitz is barbaric," then revised his claim to make an even more radical assertion: "Perennial suffering has as much right to expression as a tortured man has to scream; hence, it may have been wrong to say that after Auschwitz you could no longer write poems. But it is not wrong to raise the less cultural question whether after Auschwitz you can go on living."[63]

The part of me that's a poet wants to resist both these extravagant generalizations. To the first, I want to reply, with the British poet Tony Harrison, that "[t]here can be only poetry after Auschwitz" or at least, with the American poet Lyn Hejinian, that "[i]t is, sadly, in the context of atrocity" that one must attempt to "subvert [such a] declaration of the impossibility of poetry."[64] To the second, I want to respond that poetry isn't, anyway, analogous to the scream of torture.

But the part of me that's a reader and critic—the person who's right now discomfited by Brahms's all-too-German *German Requiem* with its tidy assurances of redemption—this person wants to argue that it is poetry, indeed any art, *before* Auschwitz that now appears "barbaric," or at least bitterly ironic in the scalding light of a history with which one begins to fear such art might have been in some way complicitous.

As for poetry *after* Auschwitz, such work, whether or not the poet consciously realizes it, must inevitably be an art inflected by Auschwitz and by the other traumas that made and marred the history of the last century and that are still marking the era in which we live and mourn our dead. Shaped by the testimonies to "death events" produced throughout a murderous age, the poetry of mourning in particular must be a poetry of witnessing, even if the act of witness is understood to be an act of artifice and even if the speech of witnessing is a speech of the unspeakable.

Following Adorno, a number of other theorists have meditated on what has come to be defined as the "unrepresentability" of the Holocaust. Some have argued, for instance, drawing on the tenets of poststructuralism, that it's naive to assume the "trustworthiness and authenticity" of "testimony," since, in the words of Robert Scholes, we don't in any case "imitate the world, we construct versions of it. There is no mimesis, only poeisis. No recording, only construction."[65] At the same time, many have claimed that there is in any case no "narrative frame" that would facilitate the "telling" of the Holocaust, even if a "realistic" telling were theoretically possible. Since "the mechanism of survival" often "forced inmates to kill the self in order to keep the self alive," comments Ernst von Alphen, the "capacity to narrate is lacking. When one [has] had to kill the self, one is no longer able to tell. One lives on, but the voice has been struck dumb. In Charlotte Delbo's words, 'I died in Auschwitz but no one knows it.' "[66]

At the least, as Geoffrey Hartman defines the problem, the very horror of the events to be narrated makes narrative difficult, if not impossible, because the tales to be told are so incredible. Writes Hartman: the "nature of what was experienced and could hardly be believed needs our attention" because "it has a similarity to what transpires in Shakespeare's *Troilus* when he sees before his eyes Cressida's infidelity and is tempted to renounce his eyes rather than give her up. Such trauma leads to a splitting of the image which is like a splitting of identity: we too could say of our tainted civilization, 'This is, and is not, Cressid.'"[67] Uneasy in my comfortable seat, grappling with the *German Requiem*, shall I consider that "This is, and is not, Brahms"?

Yet if narrative were impossible and the Holocaust unrepresentable, I wouldn't be struggling with these anxieties, would I? Nor would the magnificence of Brahms's funeral march be polluted by such an ironic consciousness of the future into which his mourning multitudes were fated to stagger.

The French memoirist Charlotte Delbo did, we should remember, produce a powerful account of her experience in Auschwitz, a narrative that includes her straightforwardly paradoxical *telling* of the way "I died in Auschwitz, but no one knows it." And countless other witnesses, observers, historians, novelists, poets, playwrights, filmmakers, artists, and composers have essayed the same subject, as if driven by the belief that it would be barbaric *not* to record such suffering. In some cases, indeed, the proliferation of high-gloss media attention that the camps have received confirms another concern of Adorno's, a fear that representations of the Holocaust will elicit a prurience that shamefully replicates the humiliations inflicted on the victims of the event—a fear that, as a tersely cynical observation said to be current among Israeli survivors has it, "There's no business like Shoah business." When the Holocaust "is turned into an image," wrote Adorno, "it is as though the embarrassment one feels before the victims were being violated. The victims are turned into works of art, tossed out to be gobbled up by the world that did them in."[68]

Yet again, that every theme has its degraded and degrading variations doesn't mean we should abandon art. Does the mass marketing of the latest Holocaust sitcom inevitably problematize the words of Levi or Delbo? Those words were, yes, wrung from violation, yet in their testimonial urgency they transcend the whirlwind out of which they were born. *I alone am escaped to tell thee.* Delbo may have "died in Auschwitz" in a way that "no one knows," yet she has also escaped Auschwitz in order to *tell* her own death—and the deaths of others. As in the passage below in which she and her companions, standing at mute attention during a seemingly endless "roll-call," frozen in what feels like "a block of hard, cutting ice, transparent like a block of pure crystal," watch as a truckload full of condemned prisoners "moves silently" past them on the way to the gas chamber:

> *The women pass by near us. They are shouting. They shout and we do not hear anything. This cold, dry air should be conductive in an ordinary human environment. They shout in our direction without a sound reaching us. Their mouths shout, their arms stretched out toward us shout, everything about them is shouting. Each body is a shout. All of them torches flaming with cries of terror, cries that have assumed female bodies. Each one is a materialized cry, a howl—unheard. The truck moves in silence over the snow, passes under a portico, disappears. It carries off the cries.*[69]

After the visionary precision of this passage, after its icy light and silent shouts, Brahms has a new meaning—is and is not Brahms—as his chorus of mourners, sounding a warning (*Denn alles Fleisch, es ist wie*

Gras) made *different* by a century's trauma, seems to march across the stage of the Salle Pleyel, a space that itself gradually becomes a monitory image of the decade that produced it. And if the *Deutsches Requiem* has been changed by the cries that move silently past us or, for that matter, by an era in which, as Celan put it, "*der Tod ist ein Meister / aus Deutschland*," so too our notion of death has changed utterly—changed in the terrible chambers of the history that makes and remakes death.

8

Technologies of Dying

Mysterious clickings and hissings. Inexplicable beeps. Sometimes half darkness dominated by a shadowy monitor alive with enigmatic tracings. Sometimes fluorescence that forbids any sleep other than the stupor of sedation.

The late-twentieth-century/twenty-first-century setting of medical crisis, particularly of illness-unto-death, is one we all know, if not from personal experience, then from television, movies, newspapers.

Here's the journalist Molly Haskell on how it felt to visit her gravely ill husband at a New York City hospital in the 1980s. The ICU, she reports, was "like an airship, suspended in space [with] only the whirring and clicking of machines surrounding mummylike patients [who were] lined up side by side, with tubes of the most expensive lifesaving machinery in the world reaching like tentacles into every orifice, and with their faces, peering out from oxygen masks, unrecognizable as to sex and age. They weren't humans, but cyborgs, half man–half machine, new arrivals on display from the planet of near-death."[1]

Of course, as a layperson Haskell might be expected to feel astonishment on encountering such a space. But even doctors and nurses who spend much time in similar zones of technologized life support often seem bemused by the ICU and more generally by the modern hospital of which the ICU has become symbolic. The pulmonologist John Murray, for instance, begins *Intensive Care: A Doctor's Journal* with a scrupulous description of how he imagines a half-alive, half-dead ICU inhabitant must look to an outsider, a description that's also, clearly, an account of how the sick man looks to him if he defamiliarizes the sci-fi sight before him: "The patient appears tethered by the cat's cradle of tubes emerging from plastic bags that hang from stainless steel poles surrounding his bedside. . . . Wires sprout from his chest . . . and they all converge at a large television monitor mounted on the wall. . . . Apart from the flashing signals that his heart is beating and his blood pressure exists, propped up by powerful drugs, there are no signs of life."[2] And in a prose poem entitled "Euthanasia," Belle Waring, a nurse-poet, offers an equally defamiliarized sketch of "neonatal intensive care": ". . . ventilators snap and blow, monitors glimmer with QRS-respiration-&-pressure, IVs tick, computers clack STAT lab reports, chest tubes boil . . . knots of doctors confer and work under pitiless banks of fluorescent lights—a hospital spaceship."[3]

"A hospital spaceship": the superhigh-tech setting that reminded Haskell of an airship transporting patients from "the planet of near death" gives pros too the sense that they're actors not so much in an episode of *ER* as in a segment of *Star Trek*. It's a setting that, as the French historian Philippe Ariès explained several decades ago, evolved in the course of the twentieth century when "advances in surgery . . . brought parallel advances in resuscitation and in the reduction or elimination of pain and sensation" that could be not merely used postoperatively but also "extended to all the dying, in order to relieve their pain."[4] Ironically, however, it's precisely this life-sustaining technology that allows physicians not just to stave off but to administer death, as if it were simply another sedative. In fact it is most often into the "hospital spaceship" of the ICU that doctors come to "do the death" of a "terminal" patient.

I first heard about the practice of "doing" death—arranging, administering, or managing someone's demise—from a friend who works on ethnographies of health care and has lately been studying the ways in which hospitals deal with the dying. We were on a plane to New York, where we'd both been invited to attend a meeting of a research project on death and dying.

Many hospital deaths, my friend told me, take place at the end of the day, around five-thirty or six o'clock.

Is that, I wondered, because the life force flickers or fails in the dying patient at that hour?

Oh, no, she replied. It's because that's when doctors and family members usually get off from work and are free to assemble at the bedside, ordinarily the bedside in the ICU.

For a minute I was puzzled, but then, as the plane continued evenly through a steep blue sky, I understood what she was telling me. She was saying that as one commentator puts it, the "production of death in the hospital setting, especially intensive care, has been documented ethnographically in recent years and the fact that deaths in such sites are orchestrated, negotiated, and timed is by now well-known."[5]

Obviously I already knew that people decide to "withdraw life support" from loved ones, sometimes even beg doctors to "pull the plug," "disconnect the tubes," whatever. In the mid-seventies I myself had urged the staff at Memorial Sloan-Kettering "just" to "let" my favorite aunt, at age sixty-six riddled with late-stage colon cancer, "die in peace." Yet I guess I hadn't quite understood how efficient the process of "letting" someone die has now become, at least in those instances in which patients have been "intubated"—that is, have been breathing with the aid of a ventilator. Sharon Kaufman, a medical anthropologist, insists on the importance of "the cultural transformation that has accompanied and followed the changes in hospital practices brought about by the ICU and the mechanical ventilator. The cultural expectation of waiting for death and knowing it would come that had historically characterized health professional, family, and patient responses to dying [has been] replaced in many cases by decision-making . . . regarding when and how to end a life."[6] By the time my friend and I landed in New York I realized that I'd known about this sort of decision-making too, just hadn't quite grasped what it meant.

For instance, a seventy-five-year-old friend, a distinguished Renaissance scholar in shaky health, had been hospitalized following a series of strokes. When his condition worsened, he was transferred to the ICU, where he could breathe only with the help of a ventilator. Soon, as his wife and daughters later told me, those who loved him had to confront what is now a familiar question: when should he be "extubated"—when, considering that "extubation" almost certainly equaled what would amount to asphyxiation? After some days had passed, the family decided, as countless others do, that life on the ventilator was as pointless as it was unpleasant. While his wife held his hand and his daughters stood by, the scholar was "extubated." He was made comfortable, cradled in kindness, but nothing more was or could have been done. And his death, after several hours of slowed-down breathing, was as "good" a death as possible, his widow later told me.

And a death carefully planned, controlled, *administered*.

Not exactly like my aunt's death in 1976. Because mechanical ventilation wasn't what kept her alive, there was no significant life support to withdraw, so she lingered on a minimal saline IV until her own system shut itself down. But the scholar's death was like the demise, a few years ago, of one of my favorite cousins, a sixty-seven-year-old sufferer from emphysema who begged for extubation after unsuccessful lung volume reduction surgery. A research biologist and poet, he knew that the ventilator was making a "cyborg" of him, and he desperately wanted to escape "the planet of near death." "I've had a good life," he wrote in a note to his family, "now let me go." And they did, gathered around his bedside at an appointed time as by prearrangement he breathed his last.

Meditating on these incidents, I again feel sure that our "mythology of modern death" has been shaped not only by the technologies of killing that made possible the mass "death events" of the twentieth century but also by the technologies that surround dying—whether staving it off or facilitating it. Indeed, I think such technologies are as implicated in our ideas of modern death as are our disputations about a hypothetical afterlife. For after all, just as a society that has perfected bizarre techniques of extermination is likely to transform long-standing assumptions about the possibility of the soul's expiration into a welcoming heaven, so a culture that has developed nuanced modes of termination is likely to alter such assumptions.

Indeed, the more I study the daunting technologies of the contemporary hospital, the more I begin to see why a patient confined in its life-supporting but often depersonalizing realm might, in extremis, associate that space with the life-destroying, always depersonalizing arena of the prison camp. Molly Haskell reports in fact that as he hovered between life and death during his excruciatingly uncomfortable stay in the ICU, her husband, the ordinarily lucid and incisive film critic Andrew Sarris, became "very confused, insisting that he was in Auschwitz."[7]

QUESTIONS OF TECHNOLOGY

"Look around your hospital," demands Lawrence Martin, the chief of pulmonary and critical care medicine at Mount Sinai Medical Center, Cleveland, addressing young doctors in *The House Officer's Survival Guide*. "Did it always have a pulmonary function laboratory? An intensive care unit? Facilities for cardiac catheterization? A computerized laboratory?" Not unless it was built after the 1950s, he declares. For since World War II came to an end, "there has been a technologic revolution in patient care," which means that "we use machines, prescribe drugs and perform operations inconceivable a few decades ago." Martin is referring to a whole range of "hospital spaceship" devices, but in particular the mechanical ventilators, feeding tubes, IVs, and monitors that so impress outsiders like Molly Haskell when they first enter an ICU.

To put things in perspective for the neophytes who study his handbook, Martin recounts the circumstances surrounding René Laënnec's invention of the "cylinder" or "stethoscope" in 1816. Consulted by a female patient whose diseased heart he couldn't hear because of her "great degree of fatness," Laënnec found that "by rolling a sheaf of paper into a cylinder and placing one end over her heart," he could "thereby perceive the action of the heart in a manner much more clear and distinct than I had ever been able to do by the immediate application of the ear." As Sherwin Nuland observes, however, "Every scientific or clinical advance carries with it a cultural implication, and often a symbolic one." Thus the introduction of the stethoscope "set in motion the process by which physicians came to distance themselves from their patients," perhaps in part because many doctors don't "feel at ease with an ear pressed up against a diseased chest" but perhaps too because this simple tool represented medicine's new power to penetrate the hidden recesses of a human being not just through dissection of a dead or unconscious body but through instrumental examination of a living, conscious person.[8]

This uncanny power of penetration was to be elaborated in countless modern medical strategies, from such unprecedented diagnostic instruments as X rays, CAT scans, and MRIs to methods of organ supplementation (intubation, dialysis) and procedures for joint or organ replacement (prosthetic implants and transplants of all kinds). Most dramatic, perhaps, was the comparatively recent development of a "fully contained artificial heart" that "whirs" instead of beating. Its first recipient was a fifty-nine-year-old man with the allegorical name Robert *Tools*, who died five months later from complications following a stroke but claimed to savor the additional life the device offered him. Although he admitted that this new "plastic-and-titanium pump the size of a small grapefruit" was a "little heavy," Tools commented that the "biggest thing is getting used to not having a heartbeat."[9]

Given the fanfare with which late modern society has greeted most of these innovations, it's one of the many paradoxes in the history of science that what some observers define as contemporary medicine's "technological imperative" has issued, among other things, in a new sort of *timor mortis* even while it has enhanced most people's expectations of survival. Noting that death's "old savagery" has crept back "under the mask of medical technology," Philippe Ariès remarked in the 1970s that the "death of the patient in the hospital, covered with tubes," had already, by the time he produced his masterful history, become "a popular image, more terrifying than the transi or skeleton of macabre rhetoric." As he pondered the irony of what he considered a "correlation between the 'evacuation' of death, the last refuge of evil, and the return of this same death," he wondered how some of the very instruments that bestow or at least preserve life had come to symbolize death.

But perhaps the irony is more apparent than real. For one thing, many patients welcome the supposedly macabre instruments of life support. There's a long history, for instance, of polio patients composing hymns of gratitude for the iron lungs, precursors of today's mechanical ventilators, that made sheer existence possible for them even following severe paralysis. One particularly talented patient, the late Mark O'Brien, used a mouth stick and a computer to produce several volumes of verse, a memoir, and a considerable body of writing while he was immobilized in such a cylinder of steel.[10] Keenly aware of the toll exacted by his "cyborgification," O'Brien nevertheless devoted much energy to battling exponents of euthanasia from the well-intentioned "physician-assisted suicide" activists in Oregon to the notorious Dr. Jack Kevorkian. Under the law that was finally passed in Oregon, O'Brien noted, " 'terminally ill' is defined as anyone a physician expects to die within six months. Sounds reasonable, until you notice the absence of the phrase 'without medical intervention.' Without medical intervention in the form of my iron lung, I would die within six hours." Although O'Brien was often sardonic about the machine he called his Metal Mom, he frankly admitted: "*I labor like a stevedore to keep the connection* [emphasis added]."[11]

It might be argued, of course, that O'Brien had years in which to adjust to his "Metal Mom," whereas most mortally ill patients, never having lived with disability, may find technological interventions traumatic. Even toward the often tormenting ventilator, however, many are more welcoming than popular commentary might suggest. Following a devastating stroke, the French editor Jean-Dominique Bauby suffered from what's called locked-in syndrome. A quadriplegic, utterly dependent for life support on a feeding tube and a respirator, he could communicate only by blinking his left eyelid. Yet he claimed at one point that "for now, I would be the happiest of men if I could just swallow the overflow of saliva that endlessly floods my mouth," and after devising an ingenious method of alphabetic "dictation," he produced an eloquent memoir of his illness, *The Diving Bell and the Butterfly*.[12]

Speaking for the so-called vegetables "locked in" by catastrophic medical events, Bauby asked not for "death with dignity" but requested instead a "niche" for "us, broken-winged birds . . . who have made our nest in a dead-end corridor of the neurology department." And he recorded with grace and wit the long days he'd spent tracing the flight of "the butterflies" of thought "that flutter inside my head"—days that might well have seemed pointless to unwitting observers.[13]

To be sure, Bauby dreamed of improvement until he died just four days after *The Diving Bell and the Butterfly* appeared. "In the long term, I can hope to eat more normally: that is, without the help of a gastric tube," he wrote, and eventually, he mused, "[P]erhaps I will be able to breathe naturally, without a respirator, and muster enough breath to make my vocal cords vibrate."[14] But even patients who are more obviously terminal frequently welcome the sort of technological intervention Ariès associates with the dying person whose entanglement in tubes suggests "the skeleton of macabre rhetoric." Among other case histories, for instance, Sharon Kaufman examines the story of "Carol Jones," a fifty-four-year-old woman dying of cancer who had been intubated for so long (three weeks) that her ICU doctors wanted to extubate her because they feared complications from pneumonia and other side effects of intubation. While explaining their plan, though, they added that because "of the underlying disease, for which there is no cure, if problems occur when the tube is out, we don't want to put it back in," and, turning to the patient to be sure she agreed, one physician asked, "Does that make sense to you?"

To which the patient, "very alert and focused at that moment, shook her head 'No.'"

"Carol is a fighter," commented her sister; "she wants to live."[15]

But in fact, according to one group of researchers, family members often misunderstand what the terminally ill "really" want, with relatives sometimes reporting that the sick person would prefer "comfort" to "aggressive" intervention while "many patients wanted more treatment, even at the risk of discomfort."[16] In a poem entitled "My Death," Raymond Carver insouciantly protested the frequent misunderstanding of patients' wishes, declaring: "If I'm lucky, I'll be wired every which way / in a hospital bed. Tubes running into / my nose." But "try not to be scared of me, friends!" he urged, explaining that from his perspective, "this is okay. / It's little enough to ask for at the end." More generally, comments John Murray, "What the patient wants and what society thinks is warranted are often incongruent." In "one survey," he continues, "although many of the patients [questioned] had poor functional status and/or inferior quality of life . . . *only eight percent were unwilling to undergo intensive care again to achieve any prolongation of survival* [emphasis added]."[17]

Asked his first thoughts after a perilous seven-hour-long procedure during which two cardiac surgeons together with "a team of 14 nurses, perfusionists, physician assistants, anesthesiologists and other support staff" implanted the experimental mechanism that would now keep him at least provisionally alive, Robert Tools "smiled. 'I was happy to wake up and see people, to know I was alive,' he said. 'And to know I got that far.' " This despite the heaviness of his whirring heart.[18]

Still, Tools's relatively positive experience is one of the more cheerful case histories to have emerged from several years of experimentation with the AbioCor artificial heart. More representative may have been the ordeal of James "Butch" Quinn, who died in discomfort and disillusionment some nine months after the device had been installed in his body. By the time his doctor actually unplugged his AbioCor, Quinn and his wife had been on the verge of suing the group of physicians who had presided over what a *New York Times* reporter described as "an experiment that ethicists say raises serious questions about the participation of dying patients in medical research." Notes Sheryl Gay Stolberg: "Mr. Quinn . . . said that if he had to do it all over, he would stick with his natural heart. 'This is nothing, nothing like I thought it would be,' he said. 'If I had to do it over again, I wouldn't do it. No ma'am. I would take my chances on life.' "[19]

As these conflicting tales of technologized hospital death suggest, the instruments of medical salvation are widely considered both tools of reification and sources of torment even while their intervention is often devoutly wished. To begin with, some of the major instruments of analysis employed by biological science reduce the living patient to a series of body parts that are really mere *things* exposed to what Michel Foucault called the clinical gaze, the dispassionate, dehumanizing gaze of the laboratory worker.[20] But in addition, many of the procedures associated with the saving of lives threaten to destroy lives. Cardiopulmonary resuscitation often breaks ribs and collapses lungs. Chemotherapy poisons the patient along with her tumor while inducing dreadful symptoms of its toxicity. Radiation sometimes burns the healthy flesh of the sufferer as well as any malignant mass on which it's trained. Surgically implanted defibrillators, designed to correct abnormal heart rhythms, can "prolong misery" for the very heart patients they're meant to cure. The AbioCor appears to have induced numerous strokes along with various lung problems in its recipients, and it was in any case designed to last only a year.[21] But perhaps most dramatically because most persistently exposed to public view by visitors and other patients, intubation with a mechanical ventilator seems to create a curious kind of compound being.

To many onlookers as well as to patients themselves, the intubated patient does become what Haskell calls a cyborg—half human, half machine—because she and others experience her relationship with her ventilator as in a sense reciprocal. Perhaps, just as the ventilator becomes necessary to the patient, almost a part of her, so the patient appears to become part of the ventilator—not only the object of its solicitude but in a sense, as the body on which it works, its appendage. But the machine that is dehumanizing the patient by "cyborgifying" her is also depersonalizing her. As the boundaries of her body open or even dissolve to accommodate objects of steel, plastic, and rubber, her body itself metamorphoses into a figurative as well as literal home for nonsentient things. What or where, then, is that sentient self she formerly experienced as intact and cohesive?[22]

At the same time, in another paradox produced by such technology, the very instruments of life support that help the patient at least temporarily to evade death and ultimately to control its timing become symbols of an out-of-control existence. To the question What kind of person inhabits—or is "tethered" to—an artificially constructed body?, further questions are added. What kind of self can't breathe for itself, can't feed itself, can't excrete its own waste? What kind of body can't circulate its own blood? Even while it emblematizes modern control of disability, the dependency of the "cyborgified" patient masked by a ventilator and imprisoned in a "cat's cradle of tubes" evokes the dependency of the paralytic or the infant—or indeed the inanimate machine itself, which must be plugged in, equipped with batteries, or in some other way refueled in order to move and seem to "live."

Numerous medical researchers and bioethicists have discussed the dilemmas of definition along with the moral problems posed by comatose patients or by those in what is called a persistent vegetative state—that is, patients who "have an eyes-open unconsciousness" and thus seem to be "awake, but unaware." Situations like the famous cases of Karen Ann Quinlan, Nancy Cruzan, and Terry Schiavo—all irreversibly brain-damaged patients whose continued existence on life-support became the subject of extended legal and even, in the case of Schiavo, political debate—raise crucial issues about medical technology's contribution to a kind of existence that, as the word "vegetative" suggests, tests the limits of the "human." But what Ariès describes as the "macabre" image of the patient "covered with tubes" is likely to terrify observers even more when the sufferer is imagined to be conscious of her dependency than when she's thought to be oblivious of it. In the second case, to be sure, she's a monitory example of the abjectly exposed living body reduced to utter vulnerability, but in the first, she's an instance of helpless, awake-*and*-aware torment—the abjectly embodied self that is all too conscious of its own abjection.

The human being who is coupled with a machine but doesn't know it presents a category problem, but the human being who knows she's coupled with a machine both asks and embodies a phenomenological question that at its simplest can be reduced to: which is in charge, the person or the machine? Though he labored "like a stevedore" to "keep the connection" with life that his iron lung made possible, O'Brien also fulminated against that "Metal Mom," while Bauby recorded with horror the moment when he understood that he was irrevocably quadriplegic and thus permanently dependent on (at best) a wheelchair, tellingly likening his realization of "the frightening truth" to two of technology's most sinister products: "It was as blinding as an atomic explosion and keener than a guillotine blade."[23]

Modern poets have long explored the experiential dilemmas represented by human bodies whose functions have been in part replaced by machine-controlled processes. In fact the fantasy of evading death through becoming, or in some sense merging with, a machine or artifact can be traced back at least as far as William Butler Yeats's "Sailing to Byzantium," one of the twentieth century's most famous discussions of the relationship between aging and what philosophers call the mind-body problem. Well into his sixties when he drafted this classic poem, the great Irish writer was anxious about physical decline not just because he was aging but because, aging, he was married to a much younger wife and was the father of two small children. At the same time, as he explored the uneasy links between the fragile human body and its insubstantial tenants—on the one hand, the personal consciousness he called "self" and associated with heart and sensuality and, on the other hand, the transcendental consciousness he called "soul," meaning abstract mind or spirit—Yeats was developing a theme that had long haunted him as well as countless other artists. What were "self" and "soul" to do when the flesh on which they were dependent began to fail?

The first three stanzas of Yeats's four-stanza poem outline his pain and begin to hint at the remedy of which he dreams. "*That* is no country for old men," he exclaims, perhaps sorrowfully, perhaps scornfully, for *there*, in the land of the living, all that "is begotten, born, and dies" is caught "in *sensual* music [emphases added]." "An aged man" like himself is therefore "but a paltry thing, / A tattered coat upon a stick, unless" his "soul" or abstract mind finds a way to transcend the tatters of "its mortal dress." As for the "heart" that symbolizes his personal self, in one of the poem's most memorable passages Yeats prays the "singing-masters of his soul" for deliverance from that troublesome organ, urging them to "Consume my heart away" because it's "sick with desire / And fastened to a dying animal"—sick with desire for further life, but tethered to a decaying (animal) body.

Yeats's solution to the problems faced by "heart" and "soul" when they were "fastened to a dying animal" was mystical and allusive, drawing on traditions from around the world. Imagining medieval Byzantium—the city that was later to evolve first into Constantinople, then into what is now Istanbul—as a sacred city of art, the poet defined his "singing-masters" as the haloed figures that decorate the walls of so many Byzantine churches and urged them to redeem him from the "tatter[s]" of his "mortal dress" by transforming his flesh into a more durable substance that might partake of "the artifice of eternity." Since the "sensual music" of youth was no longer available to him, he decided, he no longer wanted to be a human being. Rather, he prayed Byzantium's "sages" to *change* him by metamorphosing him into something utterly different: "such a form as Grecian goldsmiths make / Of hammered gold and gold enameling."

What sort of object or creature could such a "form" be? After studying the poem's last stanza, most readers assume that Yeats was imagining himself as a golden bird, like the legendary emperor's artificial nightingale:

> *Once out of nature I shall never take*
> *My bodily form from any natural thing,*
> *But such a form as Grecian goldsmiths make*
> *Of hammered gold and gold enameling*
> *To keep a drowsy Emperor awake;*
> *Or set upon a golden bough to sing*
> *To lords and ladies of Byzantium*
> *Of what is past, or passing, or to come.*[24]

But though the poet does hope that in his new embodiment he'll be "set upon a golden bough to sing" as a bird might, he's otherwise vague about the shape he longs to assume; indeed, since he says he doesn't want to take his "bodily form from any natural thing," and since a bird is a "natural thing," it's likely that the dream machine into which he longs to be transformed might look as abstract as a Brancusi sculpture or, to be anachronistic, as sheerly functional as Robert Tools's whirring heart.

When I first began teaching "Sailing to Byzantium" in the late sixties and early seventies, my earnest, hip undergraduates used to find the poem's conclusion rather horrifying. "He wants to be a golden *bird*, Professor Gilbert?

Why doesn't he want to be a *person*?" I sympathized with them in those days. But now I realize that I myself was still too young to understand how awful it would be to experience oneself as "fastened to a dying animal." Older and more anxious now, I can more easily grasp how comforting it might be to escape the dying animal body by adopting a shape of "hammered gold and gold enameling" that could transcend nature by being "*out of nature.*"

An iron lung, a ventilator, a cat's cradle of tubes—even these are mechanisms with which one might yearn to merge, machines one might wish to *become*, in one's flight from the endlessly multiplied deaths signified by the word "nature"!

As early as the 1970s, long before Robert Tools's whirring heart was a gleam on anyone's computer, the radical psychiatrist Thomas Szasz sarcastically proposed that the "final medical solution to human problems" might simply be to "remove everything from the body that is diseased or protesting, leaving only enough organs which—by themselves, or hooked up to appropriate machines—still justify calling what is left of the person a 'case'; and call the procedure 'humanectomy.' "[25] In its visionary way, such a humanectomy is rather like what Yeats's Byzantine fantasy evoked.

Yet as Szasz's bitter neologism—*human*ectomy—intimates, where is the sentient human "self" when it merges with a machine, even a machine of "hammered gold and gold enameling"? Can the "I" that I experience as "me myself" live on as a golden bird? Who or what would the living William Butler Yeats be if he were actually to merge with such an object?

In 1939, a little more than ten years after he wrote "Sailing to Byzantium," Yeats died of emphysema, without ever (to my knowledge) having heard of an iron lung, much less of a ventilator. Except in a few poems about dead or dying friends, the Irish master rarely acknowledged in verse the existence of doctors, hospitals, and what we now know as life support systems. Yet in "real life" he was by no means immune to the sort of technological imperative that's implicit in "Sailing to Byzantium." Less than a decade after he produced that masterpiece, romantically involved with several women even younger than his young wife and still distressed at the sexual deficits of old age, he submitted to a form of vasectomy known as the Steinach operation, in the hope of renewing his potency. Medically the surgery failed, yet the poet exulted that at least it had renewed his *desire*, an abiding passion for "sensual music" to which he returned as if to acknowledge that he'd rather have himself as he was than replace his failing body with a golden "form," would rather be a man than a machine.[26]

Although the twentieth-century poets who are Yeats's descendants have spoken more realistically than he did about the details of decrepitude as well as the problems and possibilities of artifice, their works have often dramatized the same conundrums on which he brooded, exploring in particular the experiential dilemmas of bodies that pose such questions as Who are *you* when you take your "form" from "out of nature"? and Who, in such situations, is in charge, the person or the machine? Writing both from the perspective of outside observers and from what they construct as the perspectives of the sufferers themselves, Thom Gunn and Sylvia Plath, for instance, are frank about the ambiguities of medical technology. In "Lament," one of the strongest works in his prizewinning *The Man with Night Sweats*, Gunn addresses a much-loved friend whose death from AIDS he characterizes with tough understatement as a "difficult, tedious, painful enterprise." As he reviews this patient's exile from normalcy—his "martyrdom / In the far Canada of a hospital room"—he recounts key details, dwelling on the depersonalizing presence of the mechanical ventilator. For a minute, he notes, a "gust of morphine hid you," but then:

> . . . *Back in sight*
> *You breathed through a segmented tube, fat, white,*
> *Jammed down your throat so that you could not speak.*

Then, in "Still Life," a third-person meditation on what he's witnessed, he confesses:

> *I shall not soon forget*
> *The angle of his head,*
> *Arrested and reared back*
> *On the crisp field of bed,*
>
> *Back from what he could neither*
> *Accept, as one opposed,*
> *Nor, as a life-long breather,*
> *Consentingly let go,*
> *The tube his mouth enclosed*
> *In an astonished O.*

How succinctly Gunn summarizes the patient's quandary here! The ventilator is what the dying man doesn't wish to accept (since he's presumably opposed to artificial life support) but what, at the same time, he can't agree to renounce, since (in a magisterially ironic phrase) "as a life-long breather" he can't not breathe. On such equivocal terms, therefore, the patient astonishes even himself by acquiescing in an unwilling marriage to the machine around which his mouth forms a linguistic as well as an anatomical O.[27] In this posture, however, he replicates the qualities of a "still life": both a person who is still alive and a motionless object like the subject of the sort of genre painting that's called in English a still life but (more appropriately here) in French a *nature mort*.

More openly striving to enter the "cyborgified" patient's consciousness, Sylvia Plath speaks from the center of such a "still life" in a late poem entitled "Paralytic." The first line of the piece summarizes precisely the abject helplessness that underlies the question Which is in charge, the person or the machine? "It happens. Will it go on?—"[28]

"It" happens? *What* happens? Breathing, to begin with, "happens"— happens, for this paralytic speaker who is enclosed in an iron lung and perhaps also in an oxygen tent. (Plath was writing in 1963, sometime before the mechanical ventilator came into widespread use.) But *being* happens too—"the world occur[s]," as Plath puts it in another poem—and will *that* go on?[29] From moment to moment the motionless man-in-the-machine can neither predict nor control, so he confides that not just his body but his *mind* is "a rock," that he has no "fingers to grip, no tongue," and is at the mercy of a kind of "god," the iron lung that pumps his "two / Dust bags in and out." And perhaps it's *because* the lungs are "dust bags" (bags made out of dust and bags for the collection and processing of atmospheric dust) that the mind metamorphoses into a rock; as the body is reified, the mind or self rigidifies and merges with the machine that has become, half in an exclamation and half in a statement of fact (like Gunn's "astonished O"), "My god."

Yet even in this poem of deathly extremity, as in the case of Gunn's "life-long breather" or Kaufman's "Carol Jones," the patient at the edge of the end of existence, appears at least in part to want to go on just for the sake of going on. Writes Plath (and is this her comment or the patient's?):

The claw
Of the magnolia,
Drunk on its own scents,
Asks nothing of life.

Like the last stanza of "Still Life," "Paralytic" is brilliant in its formulation of the ambiguity that surrounds the technology of life support. Reduced to little more than a body part—a "claw"—and a vegetable one at that ("claw / Of the magnolia"), the immobilized speaker nevertheless claws onward, clutches and clings to being, enamored of his own "scents" and, punningly, "sense(s)." He seems in this way to ask "nothing [more] of life" than life itself.

At the same time, though, describing himself as a "Dead egg" who lies "Whole / On a whole world I cannot touch," the speaker is suicidal because he "Asks nothing of life." Asks, that is, for nothingness. For no more machines, perhaps, and therefore no more breath. And in asking this even while he cherishes his own "scents" with the senses that make him human, he too adopts the attitude of Gunn's friend, "Arrested and reared back" from the life-giving tube "his mouth enclose[s]."[30]

Am I myself or "the iron lung / That loves me," myself or the tube my mouth encloses? Or if I'm gazing at someone who has long been my lover, friend, child, or parent, who is he—the man he was or the machine with which he's now coupled? That such questions haunt not just dying patients but the onlookers who love them emerges in one of John Murray's case histories, when he describes a nurse's turning off the monitor "that displays [the patient's] blood pressure, heart rate, and electrocardiographic tracing" as she prepares for the "doing" of a death by withdrawal of life support. "Why are you doing that?" Murray reports one of the man's brothers asking. " 'We don't need this information any longer,' [the nurse] replies. . . . But [she] does not disconnect the monitor at the central nurses' station because we must know what is going on at all times. She turns the bedside monitor off because we have learned that relatives and friends tend to pay more attention to it than to their loved one. People become obsessed watching the electrocardiographic squiggles that announce each heartbeat marching across the screen."[31] In a sense, this story implies, the "electrocardiographic squiggles" don't just represent the patient; they become his last breaths, the final beats—or, as the case may be, the final whirs—of his heart.

THE INHOSPITABLE HOSPITAL

"A hospital spaceship." "The far Canada of a hospital room." Whether it's characterized as an extraplanetary vessel or as unknown, freezing wilderness bizarrely enclosed by four walls, the space that surrounds these eerie transformations of dying patients is as alien as the events its walls witness.

In *A Whole New Life*, an account of his nearly fatal struggle with a spinal tumor in the early eighties, Reynolds Price describes an "excruciating" series of neurological tests, X rays, and probes that leave him with a "growing sense of being consumed by a single vast live idiot creature concealed throughout this enormous building. The creature had just one blank eye of the keenest focus and not one atom of self-awareness or even remorse at its endlessly accumulating knowledge, its power over the building's inhabitants—sick and well—and its impotence or refusal to help them."[32] But even in the not-so-high-tech 1940s, John Gunther remarked in his classic memoir *Death Be Not Proud*, the poignant tale of his seventeen-year-old son's death from a brain tumor, that he and his family had been "sucked . . . into the vast mechanism of a modern hospital, with all its arbitrary and rectilinear confusion."[33]

No wonder, then, that as we round the corner into the twenty-first century, even experienced viewers of *ER* are struck not just by the institution's sci-fi sights and sounds—its loudspeakers; its flashing, squealing, and beeping instruments—but by its sheer size and apparent depersonalization. "One of the most disturbing aspects of being in a hospital," writes one commentator before she's even begun to consider the place's elaborate technologies, "is the disorientation one feels in the maze of hallways, waiting rooms, elevator banks, and patients' rooms."[34] Like Jonah in the belly of the whale, the hapless seeker after health fears that she's been engulfed by the "vast" yet idiotic "creature" whose tentacles these cavernous spaces are.

To be sure, the relationship between the "hospital spaceship" and the hospital as unnerving space isn't coincidental. As one sociologist of medicine observed more than a third of a century ago, "Since the introduction of modern technology, the hospital has lost its aura of being a place of comfort and has instead become an establishment resembling a factory, where illnesses are taken care of, rather than human beings."[35] Hospitals are huge, mazelike, and disorienting precisely because this modern institution is, as Gunther put it, a "vast *mechanism*" designed to process a universe of illnesses in a range of specialized ways. The artist Robert Pope, who suffered from Hodgkin's disease but ultimatly died from the effects of the treatment he received, portrayed the X-ray department of a hospital as a room with a "surreal quality" that "could be a scene from *Star Trek* where Mrs. Smith becomes no more than a piece of film." Noting that the hospital-as-factory (or as space station) both reflects and contributes to an increasingly specialized medical profession, several sociologists have also observed that in such a system the patient, like Pope's "Mrs. Smith" who is "no more than a piece of film," becomes not just an "illness" but an abstract "unit" moved from department to department, so that each can exercise its specialized function with dispatch and efficiency" [fig. 5].[36]

The debilitating alienation that so many people associate with the actual space of the hospital—its crowded impersonal lobbies as well as its long, sterile corridors, anonymous cubicles, mechanized examination and "procedure" rooms—is of course on a primary level an effect of the vulnerability, often the desperation, patients and their families inevitably feel when illness forces them into the space of medicine itself. But in addition, consciously or unconsciously, most postmodern citizens perceive a crucial connection between the medical technology that reduces them to objects of analysis and the bureaucracy that diminishes them to ciphers. On the one hand, you *are* your X rays, your CAT scan, your MRI result. On the other hand, you're your computer file. Indeed, to go back to Price's conceit of the hospital as concealing "a single vast live idiot creature," this creature's "one blank eye of the keenest focus" allows it to merge the "you" that is your test

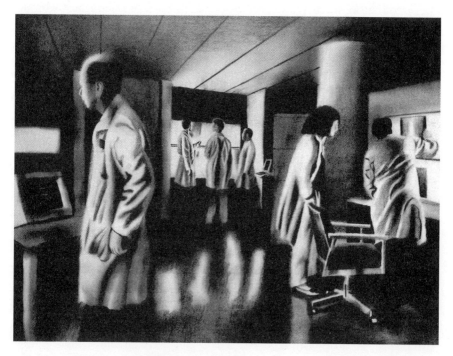

5. Robert Pope: *X-Ray Viewing Room* (1991).

results with the "you" that has become part of the "endlessly accumulating knowledge" in its high-tech banks of electronic records.

Given these unsettling aspects of the hospital, there's a certain irony in the etymology of our word for this now highly specialized site at which doctors perform or oversee the processes that either transform the sick into the well or fail to arrest the metamorphosis of the sick into the dead. According to the *American Heritage Dictionary of the English Language*, "hospital" in the modern sense of an "institution that provides medical, surgical, or psychiatric care and treatment for the sick or the injured" has an archaic meaning of a "hospice for travelers or pilgrims," deriving from the "Latin *hospitalis*, of a guest, from *hospes, hospit-*, guest," which in turn descends from the Indo-European *ghos-ti*, meaning "Stranger, guest, host; properly 'someone with whom one has reciprocal duties of hospitality.'"[37]

Doctors, nurses, even clerks in the admissions office as "hosts"? Ill or dying patients as "guests"? The concept of "hospitality" appears absurd in this context. Yet if we reimagine patients as figurative "travelers or pilgrims" journeying toward health or death and medical staffers as a specialized order, like nuns or monks, with particularized knowledge and a highly defined mission, then the hospital can indeed be understood as a sort of temporary refuge, albeit a frequently unpleasant one. In the hospital for an appendectomy, Sylvia Plath wrote in "Tulips" that as she stared at the vivid blooms a visitor had brought her, she felt the flowers seemed to come "from a country far away as health." Always a keen student of etymologies, she understood herself to be en route to such a dominion, though briefly halted—"a thirty-year-old cargo boat"—at a rest stop for the ill. Some years earlier T. S. Eliot had used the concept of hospital in this double sense of medical center and temporary refuge even more elaborately when in "East Coker," the third of his *Four Quartets*, he produced a passage comparing the world itself to a hospital with Christ as a "wounded surgeon" seeking to cure us of our sins and God as a "ruined millionaire" who has put us here to care for us, despite ourselves: "The whole earth is our hospital / Endowed by the ruined millionaire."[38]

If we turn Eliot's conceit around, however, and meditate on the implications of the analogy between this (transient) earth and a (medical) hospital, it's clear that even if we put aside the intersections of bureaucracy and technology that make the hospital a defamiliarizing location, precisely its earliest definition as *temporary*—a "stopping place" for passing travelers—accounts for some of the feelings of alienation it imposes on its "guests." Because the hospital is a temporary refuge, it both signifies mortality and is by definition *not home*. Thus in the deepest sense it's associated with those unnerving qualities that Freud attributed to the "uncanny"—the *unheimlich*, the "not homelike." In fact, the feelings of estrangement that so many patients experience in hospitals are at least in part caused by the ways in which, like Freud's *unheimlich*, this temporary "home" is a potentially lifesaving but also potentially fatal border zone that both is and is not familiar. (*"Unheimlich*," declared Freud, "is in some way or other a sub-species of *heimlich*.")[39]

The hospital does, after all, share some qualities with the hotels, motels, and inns that we now define as actual refuges for travelers. Certainly, like these structures, it replicates "home" in its accumulation and organization of the spaces and furnishings we think we require in daily life, from bathrooms and bedrooms to dining and recreation areas, from beds, chairs, tables, linens, and dishes to telephones and television sets. But whereas most hotels actively strive to mimic the "comforts of home," the hospital offers mostly stripped-down, anonymous—in effect defamiliarized—versions of both places and things: mechanized beds that are and aren't like "real" beds; rolling tray "tables" that are and aren't ordinary tables; cubicle curtains that function as "walls" but aren't really walls; "gowns" that don't fasten in the usual ways; lights that never go out; "aprons" made of lead; hallways that don't seem to lead anywhere usable or familiar; "tables" on which people are placed like objects; examination "rooms" that turn out really to be machines; and so forth.

Of course, to the extent that these unfamiliar versions of familiar furnishings are associated with what may be lifesaving "procedures," their uncanniness may often take on phantasmagorically beneficent qualities. The chair in the treatment room that rises or lowers at a touch, the table that similarly ascends or descends, the surgical lamps that are so much brighter than ordinary lights, the mysterious "instruments" that gaze, pierce, or probe—it's understandable that those yearning toward "a country far away as health" would invest all these objects with magical powers. And of course, as mortal illness weakens and infantilizes those who will never again attain that land of well-being, childlike wishes for salvation further intensify fixations on fairy-tale cures, miraculous tools of healing. In moments of hope, the bed that is and isn't like an "ordinary" bed, the table that is and isn't a table, the walls that are really curtains—all may well seem like properties of a Wonderland where the patient is an Alice who will soon be delivered safely back to the ordinary, the "real," through the ministrations of the extraordinarily unreal.

"I have given my name and my day-clothes up to the nurses," writes Plath in "Tulips," adding with relief: "My body is a pebble to them, they tend it as water / Tends to the pebbles it must run over." For someone who passes through the hospital en route to health, she implies, its odd blankness ("how white everything is, how quiet, how snowed-in") betokens a childlike purity, "swabbed . . . clear [of] loving associations."

As hope fades, though, precisely the magical objects on which the desperate fixate in their hunger for transformation become sinister, and the infantile helplessness of the patient—"scared and bare on the green plastic-pillowed trolley" to nowhere—dramatizes paralyzing vulnerability. Finally, engulfed by the uncanny spaces of the hospital—mazelike spaces akin to those in a gothic novel, where the quotidian world is and isn't itself—the dying patient is all too often afflicted not only by the pain her dis-ease produces but also by the un-ease the *unheimlich* fosters.

Even from the perspective of healthy outsiders—relatives or friends, for instance, who come to visit the ill—the characteristics of the site are unnerving. Sharon Kaufman quotes the comments of one such visitor, who struggles to define the alienation and defamiliarization she has experienced merely as an onlooker. "The hospital is like an airport," she speculates,

> but it's not. It's like a supermarket you've never been to before. It's disordered. The space is disordered. Two in a room is disordered, especially when your relative is lying next to a dying person. Even the cleaning process is disordered—this is crucial. You're not supposed to hear certain conversations, or see bodily fluids. But there is nowhere not to. It is a place of smell, sound, space, and time disorientation. You see these tubes, bags, fluids, and overflowing waste baskets, with unsettling debris, with blood. And it is all over the place. Swabs and waste are everywhere. And old food trays, waiting for someone to take them away. It's a boundaryless place. There is no classification, yet it is all about classification—charts, bureaucracy. . . . The patient is moved here, tested there. Social workers, case managers, have the script—which you don't know ahead of time.[40]

If the hospital looks and feels like this to the *well*, how must it seem to the mortally ill?

Perhaps the most striking rendition of the terrors induced by what we might call hospital gothic appears neither in the relatively upbeat American TV series *ER* nor in the more melodramatically scary miniseries *Stephen King's Kingdom Hospital* but in the ambitious Danish series entitled *The*

Kingdom (on which the King work is based). Here the innovative director Lars von Trier filmed the strange doings in a Copenhagen hospital whose technology is haunted by death. The tormented spirit of a murdered child lingers in the elevator shaft; a phantom ambulance glides nightly toward the emergency room; a resident sets up tiny crosses in trays of sand to mark the deaths and injuries caused by medical error; even doctors get lost in endlessly intertwining corridors; and as if to acknowledge what often seem to laypersons to be frightening parallels between scientific expertise and black magic, a wicked neurosurgeon actually undertakes to study voodoo, while most of the other staffers are initiates in a sinister "lodge."[41]

Two young sufferers from Down's syndrome, ceaselessly washing dishes in a surreal hospital kitchen serviced by giant conveyor belts, comment oracularly on the phantasmagoric action in *The Kingdom*. Asks one, "Is the building crying?" and the other replies, "The building began crying long ago." Why? "There are things that can't be washed off"—namely, "Some blood can't be washed off." And though these remarks are as hyperbolic as the visions of health care implicit in von Trier's whole series, they would no doubt resonate with many of the frightened, mortally ill patients dizzied by the literal and figurative labyrinths of the modern medical center.

Yet it is to this weird final "stopping place" that for at least the last third of a century most people have come to die. Explains Sherwin Nuland: "Eighty percent of American deaths now occur in the hospital. The figure has gradually risen since 1949, when it was 50 percent [and the] increase is not only because so many of the dying have needed the high level of acute care that can be provided only within the hospital's walls. The cultural symbolism of sequestering the dying is here as meaningful as the strictly clinical perspective of improved access to specialized facilities and personnel, and for most patients even more so." Both in emphasizing the need for "acute care" and in noting the "cultural symbolism of sequestering the dying," Nuland is drawing on the work of Ariès, whose detailed research into the history of death and dying led him to suggest that by the midtwentieth century the "tame death" of the Middle Ages and the "beautiful death" of the nineteenth century had evolved into the memento mori incarnated in the patient's dying what this scholar rather shockingly called the "dirty death."

In our simultaneously squeamish and medicalized era, according to Ariès, death "turns the stomach, like any nauseating spectacle. [It is] no longer acceptable for strangers to come into a room that smells of urine, sweat, and gangrene, and where the sheets are soiled. . . . A new image of death is forming: the ugly and hidden death, hidden because it is ugly and dirty." Thus, both Nuland and Ariès argue, what is now half-consciously defined as the polluting spectacle of death has been transferred to the hospital. Explicitly people in urbanized society might claim that "the presence of a terminal patient [makes] it very difficult to provide home care and carry on a job at the same time," but implicitly the hospital offers "families a place where they can hide the unseemly invalid whom neither the world nor they can endure."[42]

On the surface, there's something rhetorically excessive about Ariès's characterization of the "unseemly invalid whom neither the world nor [the family] can endure." Surely most of us don't regard our dying loved ones as "unseemly" or unendurable. Yet at the same time most would probably agree that the "termination" threatening these patients is "unseemly" in its construction of a decaying, leaking, ultimately filthy body, and unendurable in its reduction of the once-autonomous human being to "howling animality." To ensure an end of life that's both clean and painless, we believe the dying patient requires special care that (particularly in an age of specialization) most of us don't know how to give. In *Patrimony*, an unflinching memoir of his eighty-six-year-old father's death from a brain tumor, Philip Roth describes an episode when the old man lost control of his bowels and his literary son was confronted with the problem of cleaning up a bathroom in which, "nearly blind and just up out of a hospital bed . . . he had managed to spread the shit over everything": "The bathroom looked as though some spiteful thug had left his calling card after having robbed the house. As my father was tended to and he was what counted, I would just as soon have nailed the door shut and forgotten that bathroom forever. 'It's like writing a book,' I thought—'I have no idea where to begin.' "[43]

In her eloquent *Bequest and Betrayal: Memoirs of a Parent's Death*, a series of incisive readings of such autobiographical accounts (including Roth's) as well as a memoir of her own parents' deaths, the critic Nancy K. Miller tells a similar tale about her own aged father, whose fingers had on one occasion "grown so rigid that he couldn't, as he put it, 'snare' his penis," though "he wanted to get up and go to the bathroom. It was late and I wanted to go home. So looking and not looking, I fished his penis out from behind the fly of his shorts and stuck it in the urinal. It felt soft and a little clammy."[44] Like Roth, in caring for the dying, most of us "have no idea where to begin," yet like Miller, many of us find ourselves "looking and not looking" at scenes of frightening disintegration. Is it surprising that we often feel a need to "sequester" terminal patients who evoke such anxiety and ambivalence?

Still, when he comments on the "acute care" that the dying ought to have, Nuland isn't primarily referring to their toileting problems. Rather, in claiming that those who are dying need "improved access to specialized facilities and personnel," he's arguing that the dying require high technology and thus hinting that death itself is an event that demands processing. Such processing, as we've seen, entails not just sequestration but a level of bureaucratization whose depersonalizing tendencies may best account for a widespread sense that the hospital is one of contemporary society's most inhospitable spaces. The sociologist David Moller notes that in the belief "that the vital needs of human beings are reducible to technologically manageable components," medical institutions justify "the depersonalization of patients" as "'worth the price" when good "results" are obtained.[45]

But what if death is the only "result" possible? Would a more modest and "low-tech" space of sequestration perhaps be preferable? Nursing and "assisted living" homes seem on the surface to offer the option of smaller, more personalized spaces for the dying. But as all too many aged and terminally ill patients discover, sick people who find themselves in these institutions encounter problems that are sometimes even more disturbing than those posed by hospitals. Jeanie Kayser-Jones, who has researched end-of-life care in nursing homes, observes that most of those who die in such facilities "have limited access to palliative care": pain isn't often properly controlled, and other medical interventions that might make patients more comfortable (e.g., special beds to prevent so-called pressure ulcers—bed sores) are rare. Worse still, the most basic human needs for food, cleanliness, and sleep are often unmet.[46]

In the "homes" she studied, Kayser-Jones reports, residents were crowded into small, multibed rooms with "little privacy" and sometimes "no chairs [or] recliners for families who wanted to stay all night with a dying relative." Television sets were played night and day at a high volume to distract the staff, who turned them on when they entered rooms to provide care but then rarely turned them off. Food trays were left in positions that bedridden patients couldn't reach. Similarly, residents "often stated that they were thirsty [because] containers of water were often out of reach" or caregivers simply didn't bring them. Patients weren't bathed or turned in their beds; many died with multiple pressure ulcers, and even oral hygiene was often so minimal that one observer recorded visiting a dying woman whose lips were "dry, severely cracked [and] covered with blisters."[47]

Accounting for this neglect was the situation of the staff, most of whom were overworked, underpaid, and barely educated for the work they did: as a rule they were neither RNs (registered nurses) nor LPNs (licensed practical nurses) but at best CNAs (certified nurse's assistants). They had to deal with inadequate equipment and supplies (Kayser-Jones notes that a "resident suffering from nausea asked for an emesis basin and was given the metal plate cover from her tray [while] a bunch of grapes had been placed at [another] resident's bedside in an emesis basin"). And in almost every case there was such a heavy patient load that as one family member remarked to Kayser-Jones, "I see people lying in feces and urine for hours." A patient who actually "survived" a nursing home of this sort later summarized the horror of the situation she'd encountered. "All day and all night," she told Kayser-Jones, she'd heard people "crying out 'Help me, help me,'" so that, she confessed, "I literally thought I had died and gone to hell."[48]

Even the hospital as a kind of factory for processing "illnesses" would seem to be preferable to the anti- or (at best) a-technological "hell" of such nursing homes. Yet although, as Nuland noted, the modern medical center offers terminal patients "improved access to specialized facilities and personnel," when it functions as a place in which to "sequester" the dying, it seems to some, at its most depersonalized, like a sort of death-and-dying factory. Both Reynolds Price and Andrew Sarris survived their nearly fatal illnesses, but Price nevertheless imagined the hospital as a huge "idiot" organism without an ounce of goodwill, and Sarris hallucinated the ICU as "Auschwitz." How malign, then, the space of high-tech medical sequestration might feel to those who are really dying!

Because it's meant to serve life rather than deal death, the hospital is, to be sure, an *anti*-Auschwitz. In addition, whereas Auschwitz was the setting of the mass killings that Edith Wyschogrod shrewdly designates "death events," the anti-Auschwitz that is the modern hospital is often, on the contrary, what Ariès calls "the place of the solitary death," a place where instead of being exterminated in an anonymous crowd, the isolated patient "terminates" in the clicking and hissing loneliness of a tiny cubicle. Yet nightmare visions of the technologized modern hospital may have been planted in the mind of sufferers like Price and Sarris by the very urgency of the wish to escape from "the planet of near-death."

For one thing, whether one imagines the place as a "vast mechanism" or an "idiot" organism, the contemporary medical center is in fact a kind of surreal city, frequently housing thousands of inmates (patients) most of whom can't leave until they're "released," employing a giant staff, and often complete with a number of "wings" or outbuildings, storage areas, and its own morgue.

Like a small city, the hospital can be self-sufficient for a while: it has its own backup electrical supply, its own platoons of guards and cleaners, and its own often confusing clerical systems. And the dread evoked by the size of this sur-real city may be intensified in the minds of some patients not just by their desperation to survive but also by a concomitant fear that the inhospitable hospital isn't just depersonalizing them but actively destroying them.

Equipped with mysterious, sometimes pain-inflicting instruments for the analysis of the human body, the hospital's examining rooms are frequently more frightening than comforting, while patients who have experienced the side effects of chemotherapy frequently become ill at the mere sight of the innocent-looking "infusion" rooms where toxic substances are administered to the mortally ill. Similarly, people already sick from radiation treatment sometimes experience the spaces where huge machines train X rays on immobilized bodies as related to that most awful of twentieth-century tech-nologies, the nuclear science that gave us not only radiation but radiation sickness. Because he was "being burned, good flesh and bad," Reynolds Price reports "joking" that "I was going to Hiroshima every day for lunch."[49]

More generally, the hospital's labyrinthine corridors, some unnervingly empty but some jammed with immobilized patients, seem either to go nowhere at all or else to dimly or searingly lit treatment and examining rooms whose purposes are as mystifying to the layman as their location. And as the patient surrenders her "real-world" identity to become a com-puter file and a set of X rays while putting on a hospital "gown" indistin-guishable from the garments worn by all the other sick people in the medical center, she is threatened with an obliteration of her unique self-hood that matches the physical annihilation against which she is struggling. "I am nobody," Plath declared in "Tulips," musing: "I have given my name and my day-clothes up to the nurses / And my history to the anesthetist and my body to surgeons." More sardonically, the British philosopher Gillian Rose, who died of ovarian cancer at the age of forty-eight, described the anonymous "hordes of people" dispiritedly waiting in the depersonalizing lobby of the Dudley Road Hospital, Birmingham, as looking like " 'Mussul-men,' the working prisoners of labor and death camps who give up the will to live."[50]

Dwarfed by the social as well as physical architecture of the institution on which he must depend for survival, the sufferer often feels vulnerably stripped, simultaneously divested of the clothing that covers physical nudity and the identity that shapes ontological nakedness. New York Times reporter Benedict Carey begins "In the Hospital, a Degrading Shift from Person to Patient" with a horrifying anecdote:

Mary Duffy was lying in bed half-asleep on the morning after her breast
cancer surgery . . . when a group of white-coated strangers filed into her
hospital rom.

Without a word one of them—a man—leaned over Ms. Duffy, pulled
back her blanket, and stripped her nightgown from her shoulders . . . while
his audience, a half-dozen medical students in their 20's, stared at Ms.
Duffy's naked body with detached curiosity, she said.

After what seemed an eternity, the doctor abruptly turned to face her.

"Have you passed gas yet?" he asked.

Reynolds Price recounts an experience just a little less demeaning, lying
on a stretcher in a crowded hallway, wearing only one of those backless hip-
length gowns designed by the standard medical-warehouse sadist." He was
in this abject position, he bitterly notes, rather than in the comparative
safety of a private room, when two doctors breezily informed him that he
had a life-threatening spinal tumor even while "like all such wearers [of
hospital gowns] I was passed and stared at by the usual throng of stunned
pedestrians who swarm hospitals round the world."[51]

Finally, this stripping that radically divides the dying patient from the
customs and costumes of ordinary life is exacerbated by the glaring imbal-
ances that separate the patient and the doctor, the shocked or bewildered
sufferer and the at least apparently hardened attendant. While the patient is
nearly naked, immobilized, frequently in pain, either partly or wholly ignorant of the implications of his illness, and basically unable to control his
own condition, the doctor is clothed, mobile, healthy, educated in the
meanings of illness, and at least superficially in control of the situation. At
best, this asymmetry may replicate the relationship of infant to parent, with
the patient in the role of helpless child and the physician playing the part of
wise caregiver. But of course such a relationship of power to powerlessness
can rapidly disintegrate into something more sinister. Whereas the patient
is emotional—fearful, angry, needy—the doctor is detached, abstract,
"objective." The patient, indeed, may be *im*patient, but the doctor may well
appear unnervingly *clinical* in the dictionary sense that means "very objective and devoid of emotion; analytical . . . austere, antiseptic."

THE DOCTOR'S DETACHMENT

In "Lady Lazarus," her by now notorious fantasy of volcanic resurrection,
Plath surfaced the most alarming implications of this disturbing
doctor/patient power ratio, caricaturing the "Doktor" she associated with

her German "daddy" as a menacing fascist scientist by melodramatically addressing him as "Herr Doktor . . . Herr Enemy" and "Herr God, Herr Lucifer."[52] Indeed, from Mary Shelley's *Frankenstein* to Robert Jay Lifton's *The Nazi Doctors*, writers have documented the misdoings of medicine. With Faustian ambition, Shelley's Victor Frankenstein uses body parts he exhumes from a nearby cemetery to vivify a cadaverous monster who seeks love but, denied that, deals out death. Even more grotesquely, the infamous doctors to whose "scientific" aspirations the Third Reich gave free rein sterilized, castrated, starved, froze, infected, vivisected, and otherwise murdered countless human subjects who were ostensibly their patients.[53] Though they may sometimes seem distant or preoccupied, most contemporary doctors certainly can't be compared with scientists who carried experimentation to such Grand Guignol extremes. Yet to the mortally ill patient who is likely to have been painstakingly and often painfully examined as well as "cyborgified," the physician's imperturbable professional facade often appears no more sympathetic than stone or steel.

Bauby, for instance, describes an encounter with an ophthalmologist who inexplicably sews his right eyelid shut, then, "in the tones of a prosecutor demanding a maximum sentence for a repeat offender, [barks] out: 'Six months!' " The man, comments the author, was "the very model of the couldn't-care-less doctor: arrogant, brusque, sarcastic . . . thoroughly evasive in dealing with ghosts of my ilk, apparently incapable of finding words to offer the slightest explanation."[54] Similarly, Price recalls encountering a radiation oncologist who told "me, with all the visible concern of a steel cheese-grater, that my tumor was of a size that was likely unprecedented in the annals of Duke Hospital." After another meeting with this "frozen oncologist," he yearns for the "humane doctors of my childhood and youth [who] in their willingness to visit patients' homes, had agreed to expose themselves to the context of patients' lives" and who therefore met "the sick as their equals, their human kinsmen, not as victim-supplicants broiled in institutional light and the dehumanizing air of all hospitals known to me." And to the artist Robert Pope the impassive power radiating from teams of physicians made them seem to "loom over the patient like giant white ghosts," inhuman, inhumane, and perhaps *super*human[fig. 6].[55]

Is the "dehumanizing air of all hospitals" the source of what in some cases seems like a physician's scandalously impersonal stance? Or is the "clinical objectivity" of doctors a cause rather than an effect of that "dehumanizing air"? In the view of David Moller and other medical sociologists who have studied the "technical detachment" of physicians, the very nature of the

6. Robert Pope: *Doctors* (1991).

"bureaucratic ethos by which the hospital organizes its daily activities" sustains such detachment because it "continually impresses on the physician" qualities of "detachment" and "objectivity" that were learned in medical school. For as Moller goes on to note, "the primary effect of bureaucratic consciousness in technological civilization is the management of emotionality."[56]

But if the hospital as a bureaucracy, or, for that matter, a sort of factory assembly line designed to process illnesses rather than people, fosters a steely clinical demeanor, it's important to remember that this demeanor is actually *formed*, and later encouraged, by the nature and structure of medical training. The virtually ritual dissection of a "first" cadaver in the anatomy lab is not only a learning experience but a rite of passage for the neophyte physician. "The medical school curriculum still starts with the dead and moves slowly towards the living patient, encouraging students to develop clinical detachment on the way, " note the curators of a Wellcome Institute exhibit tellingly entitled *Doctor Death: Medicine at the End of Life.*[57]

And for the doctor in training, a "first" death is often just as ritual an experience as a first confrontation with a cadaver. Sherwin Nuland begins his best-selling *How We Die* with an account of the "first time in my professional career that I saw death's remorseless eyes." Explaining that "it was my unsettling lot to encounter death and my very first patient at the same hour," Nuland caps his tale of the "strangled heart" from which "James McCarty" dies with a frank admission of his own distraught response to the event ("I was crying, in great shaking sobs"), followed by the words of wisdom that the intern who was his senior spoke while sitting him down "as if we were actors in an old World War II movie": " 'Shep, now you know what it's like to be a doctor."[58] This last statement is interestingly ambiguous, however. Because though "what it's like to be a doctor" does mean to be a witness of death, "what it's like to be a doctor" (as Nuland's subsequent narrative reveals) *doesn't* mean to cry "in great shaking sobs" every time one is forced to face "how" and why "we die."

In fact, as Nuland himself observes, to be a doctor is all too often to abandon the dying and the inexorable triumph of death of which they are quite literally mementos. When faced with evidence of their inability to conquer mortality, writes Nuland, "[e]motionally, doctors . . . tend to disappear; physically, too, they sometimes all but disappear." Why? Nuland offers a range of explanations, including the possibility that medicine especially attracts "people with high personal anxieties about dying" along with his own perception that doctors, fearing failure (as well as death), have an unusual "need to control" and thus deal badly "with the consequences [of their own] impotence" in the face of mortality.[59] But whatever the reasons, medical and non-medical observers alike agree that countless doctors "put on the roller skates," in one clinician's succinct phrase, when a patient is "terminal." The "tendency to flee from death typifies physician responses to the nearing of death," explains David Moller, adding: "All too often dying patients and isolated pockets of loved ones are left to their own resources . . . at a time when they are highly vulnerable and their personal and social selves have been reduced to a point of insignificance."[60]

Even when doctors remain physically present to the dying, they frequently seem emotionally absent. Like a number of other writers, Moller examines the facade of objectivity that many physicians maintain despite what are clearly the overwhelming psychological needs of their patients. In one case, a doctor coolly informs a patient's weeping husband that his dying wife "won't make it through the night" so that now "nothing can be done for her except to try to make her as comfortable as possible." This conversation, comments the sociologist, "lasted for approximately two minutes" and was accompanied by "a noticeable straining on the part of the physician to exit from this death scene as quickly as possible." In another, even more egregious case, Moller records an encounter between a doctor surrounded by first-year medical students and another anxious husband seeking information about his wife's condition:

The physician told the patient's husband . . . that his wife had a serious form of cancer and that her life expectancy was about one to two years. The

husband began to cry and continued to cry [while] insisting that the doc-
tor lie to his wife about her condition; [but the doctor] very calmly, ratio-
nally, and without any recognition of or attention to the husband's
emotional outpourings [emphasis Moller's], convinced him that his wife
should be told of the cancer, but that the emphasis in the discussion would
be on treatment modalities.

Dropping his own air of dispassionate professionalism, Moller exclaims
"[W]hat an introduction to detachment and objectivity these first-year students received!"[61]

In one sense, such behavior is a function of the ways in which medical
education together with the specialization fostered by hospital bureaucracy
encourages the physician to avoid mortal anxiety by fragmenting the whole
person who is a patient into a series of problematic "bodily parts and
processes," thus making it possible to "organize dying within a technological framework."[62] In another sense, however, the physician's real or apparent
indifference to the feelings of the dying person (and that person's companions) is also a function of his or her self-definition as a warrior who has
undertaken a battle against the inimical disease that inhabits the patient.

Nuland's heated descriptions of cancer, together with his characterization of the surgeon's stance toward the illness, represent an important strain
of medical metaphorizing. "Of all the diseases they treat," he comments,
"cancer is the one that surgeons have given the specific designation of 'The
Enemy,'" and they've done this because the disease "pursues a continuous,
uninhibited, circumferential, barn-burning expedition of destructiveness,
in which it heeds no rules, follows no commands, and explodes all resistance in a homicidal riot of devastation. Its cells behave like the members of
a barbarian horde run amok—leaderless and undirected, but with a single-
minded purpose: to plunder everything within reach."[63] If through a process
of psychological displacement and synecdochic replacement the patient
seems to become her illness, then perhaps what the doctor sees when he
gazes at the dying patient is not a human being in extremity but rather an
alien marauder who has been an indomitable foe. In that case, it isn't surprising if he treats the sufferer coldly, even with some hostility.

This last point may seem extravagant, but it's certainly true that many
terminal patients rationalize the physician's absence or indifference by
internalizing a verdict of failure, as if they sense that the doctor is judging
them somehow to have been not just inadequate warriors themselves but in
some inexplicable way collaborators with the illness whose victory they

incarnate. In a memoir of his sister's death, the poet Alan Shapiro percep-
tively summarizes the dynamics by which his sister gradually came to view
her doctor as "not just her potential savior but also her potential judge":

> *When she was doing well, meaning when she responded well to the treat-
> ment he prescribed, he bolstered her self-esteem by saying he was proud of
> her, she was his best patient, she was his favorite patient. But if he were the
> benevolent deity when she was doing well, responding to his treatment, he
> became the deus absconditus when the cancer had metastasized, and it was
> clear that she was going to die. . . . On top of all her mortal grief and ter-
> ror, Beth toward the end of her life also felt a wholly artificial and unjusti-
> fied sense of guilt about her body and her illness.*[64]

"You've done beautifully! You're really *doing* well!" We've all heard these
well-intentioned lines from our doctors—statements clearly meant to
encourage further efforts to struggle toward "a country far away as health."
But of course the active verb "to do" has a double edge in such a context. If
you aren't "doing well"—if you're actually "doing badly"—who is to blame
but you, the *doer* of the illness and hence the *undoer* of yourself?

And what if you yourself were the ultimate, if not the proximate, cause of
your own deathly illness because of your "bad habits"—poor dietary choices,
smoking, drinking, failing to exercise properly, even choosing the wrong job
or home? The "media" flood us with warnings about, on the one hand, substances we should avoid (toxins, carcinogens, innocent-seeming and not-so-
innocent chemicals or foods) while, on the other hand, urging the need for
regular exercise and emotional stability, not to mention continual medical
vigilance. Commenting on the way in recent decades "mortality [has] been
deconstructed into diverse events of private death, each with its own *avoidable* cause," the sociologist Zymunt Bauman argues that in our time death has
come "perilously close to [being] declared a personal guilt" and cites a comment made by sociologist Robert Fulton in 1965: "We are beginning to react
to death as we would to a communicable disease. . . . Death is coming to be
seen as the consequence of personal neglect or untoward accident."[65]

More alarming still, even conscious efforts at hygiene, exercise, and vigilance may not have sufficed to save the patient from responsibility for a
death unconsciously wished. From Georg Groddeck and Wilhelm Reich to
Bernie Siegel, some twentieth-century theorists of cancer have elaborated
Freud's notions of the connection between psyche and soma to urge the
mortally ill to "do well" by curing themselves through meditation, visualiza-

tion, biofeedback, "a positive attitude," and a host of other "alternative ther-
apies." Claimed Groddeck in 1923: "One must not forget that recovery is
brought about not by the physician, but by the sick man himself. He heals
himself, by his own power, exactly as he walks by means of his own power,
or eats, or thinks, breathes or sleeps." Consciously most oncologists would
repudiate this claim. In some part of themselves, though—in, let's say, the
medical unconscious—those who deploy the rhetoric of "doing well" subtly affirm Groddeck's point.[66]

But if there is a barely acknowledged view in some medical quarters
that the sick can cure themselves, the converse is also true: not only are the
sick considered *as* their illnesses, but they're frequently considered the
causes of their illnesses, not only because of bad personal habits they
should have controlled but because of psychic habits they could not have
controlled. As Susan Sontag pointed out in *Illness as Metaphor*, "Supporting
the theory about the emotional causes of cancer, there is a growing literature [announcing] the scientific link between cancer and painful feelings."
Some thinkers have sought to outline the characteristics of "the cancer personality" while others have even labeled death itself "a psychological phenomenon." According to Groddeck, "He alone will die who wishes to die, to
whom life is intolerable." Musing on popular theories about the origins of
the ovarian cancer that would kill her, Gillian Rose proclaimed that she
could "compose" an "anthology of aetiologies," including "Nature's revenge
on the ambitious, childless woman" and "the wrong kinds of relationship
with men" as well as "too much whiskification" and " too little red wine and
garlic," for, she noted, the "cancer personality," as "described by the junk literature of cancer, covers everyone and no one. Characteristics: obesity,
anorexia, depression, elation," and so forth.[67]

No matter what the supposed cause of death is, then, from this blame-
the-victim perspective, the real cause is suicide or at least some sort of self-
destructive behavior that could be construed as suicidal. Perhaps the
cruelest formulation of this view appears in W. H. Auden's early ballad
"Miss Gee," the presumably "rollicking" tale of a sexually repressed spinster
who develops an incurable cancer as a consequence of her life of self-denial.
Comments her doctor, "Cancer's a funny thing,"

> "Childless women get it,
> And men when they retire;
> It's as if there had to be some outlet
> For their foiled creative fire."

Finally, in a climactic representation of medicine's technological triumph, if not over an illness, then over a patient troublesomely and (in the view of the physicians) willfully inhabited by disease:

> *They laid her on the table,*
> *The students began to laugh;*
> *And Mr. Rose the surgeon*
> *He cut Miss Gee in half.*[68]

It's hard to imagine a terser summary of the abjection that every patient fears—abjection linked to a process of medical reification that transforms a person not just into an object, not just into an object of indifference, but even into an object of indifferent laughter and scorn.

WHAT VIVIAN IS BEARING

Arguably, Auden's "Miss Gee" was reincarnated in the mid-1990s as Vivian Bearing, the protagonist of Margaret Edson's Pulitzer Prize-winning play *Wit*. An unmarried English professor who specializes in the writings of John Donne, Vivian, who has lived entirely for her research, eschewing any human contact, is now enduring ("bearing") an experimental course of chemotherapy for late-stage ovarian cancer. But as the play traces her terminal decline, it becomes clear that the treatment is useless. Vivian has no chance of being revivified. Rather, like Miss Gee, she has become an object of analysis for doctors and students (in her case one of her own former students). Unlike Miss Gee, however, to whom Auden never grants a point of view, Vivian can and does voice her feelings about the state to which she has been reduced by the joint workings of the hospital-as-factory and the medical technology it houses:

> *Yes, it is mildly uncomfortable to have an electrocardiogram, but the [agony] of a proctosigmoidoscopy sweeps it from memory. Yes, it was embarrassing to have to wear a nightgown all day long—two nightgowns!—but that seemed like a positive privilege compared to watching myself go bald. Yes, having a former student give me a pelvic exam was thoroughly degrading—and I use the term deliberately—but I could not have imagined the depths of humiliation that—*
> *Oh, God—(VIVIAN runs across the stage to her hospital room, dives onto the bed, and throws up into a large plastic washbasin.)* . . .

*Now, watch this. I have to ring the bell . . . to get someone to come and
measure this emesis, and record the amount on a chart of my intake and
output. This counts as output.*

By the end of the play Vivian understands not just that she's been humil-
iated by medical technology but also how thoroughly she's been depersonalized by science itself. Though they've failed to cure her, her physicians
are going to write "her" up in an article, which won't be about her but
rather about parts of her body—her ovaries and peritoneal cavity—and
about the traces, excretions, or representations of that body. For what
"we have come to think of as me is, in fact, just the specimen jar, just
the dust jacket, just the white piece of paper that bears the little black
marks."[69]

As many reviewers have observed, the death of this tormented patient
dramatizes most of the horrors of the medicalized "termination" facilitated
by the twentieth century's technologies of dying. Her doctors are stereotypically "clinical" in their stance toward her ("bedside manner" is a "colossal
waste of time for researchers," comments one); she's isolated in a standard-
issue hospital room; at a moment of ultimate agony she's sedated with a
morphine drip that renders her unconscious rather than a "patient-
controlled analgesic" that might alleviate her pain without obliterating her
awareness; and she's almost subjected to a full, rib-cracking "code" in which
a "team" of medics begin cardiopulmonary resuscitation (CPR) in a "whirlwind of sterile packaging and barked commands." From Ariès's historical
point of view, in fact, Vivian's demise is a paradigm of modern death:
"dirty," "sequestered," "solitary." And from Moller's sociological perspective,
her end is equally paradigmatic. On the one hand, she's "faced with suffering through the human indignities of the total institutional hospital"; on
the other hand, she isn't "able to receive the full benefits of modern medical
technology, i.e., recovery." Thus, like countless other dying patients, she's
"subjected to a double failure: the technical failure . . . and inability of modern medicine to effect a cure along with a structurally rooted neglect of
[her] personal and social needs."[70]

How might Edson's protagonist have died a "better" death? From Cicely
Saunders, Elisabeth Kübler-Ross, and Marie de Hennezel, on the one hand,
to Derek Humphry, Jack Kevorkian, and less radical advocates of physician-
assisted suicide, on the other hand, medical theorists as well as self-defined
political savants have proposed alternative modes of dying and settings for
death. But the range of their suggestions, and the fact that most nonviolent

deaths still occur in hospitals, imply the intransigence of the problem they confront.

Saunders, the founder of the modern hospice movement and coauthor of, among other pioneering works, *Living with Dying*, and Kübler-Ross, the author of the influential *On Death and Dying*, have long advocated revisionary returns to traditional customs. "Hospice" is structured either as an in-home nursing service or as a "homelike" residence for those who need more special facilities, and *Living with Dying* is a *Guide for Palliative Care* in such a setting. Famously charting five "stages" of dying—"denial," "anger," "bargaining," "depression," and "acceptance"—through which the sufferer not only does but, ideally, should come to terms with mortality, *On Death and Dying* is essentially a kind of how-to book for health care professionals and their terminal patients. More recently, the French psychologist Marie de Hennezel has offered in *Intimate Death* an eloquent account of her own caring visits to dying patients, which employed a therapeutic stance mixing approaches advocated by Saunders and Kübler-Ross. Thus, in their different ways, Saunders, Kübler-Ross, and de Hennezel seek to gentle death, to domesticate it, to detechnologize it by renouncing extreme interventions like those of the ICU in favor of often quite sophisticated palliative care— drug therapy that treats pain but doesn't promise to cure the disease that is the cause of pain.[71]

Humphry and Kevorkian, however, both proponents of euthanasia and in particular of physician-assisted suicide, return technology to the deathbed scene. In his *Final Exit: The Practicalities of Self-Deliverance and Assisted Suicide for the Dying*, Humphry produced a technical how-to manual quite unlike Kübler-Ross's more spiritualized contribution to the "human potential" movement. As for Kevorkian, his *Prescription Medicide: The Goodness of Planned Death* was written to justify his ongoing use of the "Mercitron," a "suicide machine" that he invented and has deployed as part of a self-promoting campaign to end the sufferings of more than thirty supposedly terminal or near-terminal patients. And to the most impassioned acolytes of the "right to die" offered by these proponents of euthanasia, it doesn't seem terribly troublesome that Humphry's volume, ostensibly intended to promote peaceful dying for the fatally ill, has also become useful to healthy people with suicidal personalities and that Kevorkian's "Mercitron" may have aided the terminations of patients who weren't, by most medical definitions, "terminal." By comparison, physician-assisted suicide (now legal in Oregon and, overseas, in the Netherlands and Belgium) is a measure available to patients only within very narrowly prescribed circumstances—specifically, only when an illness can be scrupulously documented as terminal. Nevertheless, like the "Mercitron," it's an end-of-life option whose opponents, most notably members of the disability advocacy group Not Dead Yet, consider dangerously subject to abuse.[72]

When I reflect on the range of interventions these distinctively different thanatological savants prescribe, it seems clear that only a few of their methodologies would have given Edson's Vivian Bearing a more bearable death. Kevorkian would have gassed her with his "Mercitron," a feat of medical engineering presumably kinder and gentler than the toxic chemotherapy that killed her, but nonetheless a device with the conscience of a "steel cheese-grater" and one that is eerily reminiscent of the strategies of euthanasia practiced by doctors at Auschwitz. Humphry would have instructed her in the uses of a simpler tool or set of tools: pills stirred into a "Seconal pudding," perhaps, abetted by a plastic bag "moderately loose [but] firmly tied around the neck with either a large rubber band or a ribbon," a homemade technology of the kitchen that, for better or worse, would have been hard to manage in her state of extremis. And Kübler-Ross would have quieted her through "counseling" until she made "the dying transition" with the requisite placidity of "acceptance," a numbed "decathexis" from the things of this world leading to a state "without fear and despair." Only Saunders and de Hennezel might have helped her find an environment where she could in some way remain herself—perhaps fearful, perhaps fretting over Donne or over what she herself had left undone—while receiving "comfort care," the end-of-life palliation that an increasing number of medical organizations have begun to advocate.[73]

At its best, hospice in particular might have helped Vivian Bearing confront her death in familiar surroundings, with minimal pain and little cant, for in many communities its caregivers help patients die in their own homes, among friends and family. Rebecca Brown's *Excerpts from a Family Medical Dictionary*, a brilliantly understated but excruciatingly detailed account of her mother's death from metastatic cancer, names as heroes the "oncology and hospice folks" associated with the local medical center. Although Brown's narrative of their intervention is brief and dispassionate ("The day after we met with the hospice people they brought a hospital bed and plastic sheets and adult diapers . . . and bottles of pills and waste disposal bags and other things you need to die at home"), she notes in a prominently placed acknowledgment that "Every dying person and every dying person's family should always have such thoughtful, loving care."[74]

Yet when hospice houses patients in its own facilities—often buildings or wings of buildings architecturally indistinguishable from nursing homes—even this commendable institution offers a way to sequester the dying, to "hide the unseemly invalid whom the world [can no longer] endure." As Moller notes, both the concept of such a structure and the service it offers are "consistent with the modern societal and medical tendency toward specialization" since, like the hospital, the nursing home, or the "assisted living" center, the hospice "is a highly specialized institution, which caters to needs of a highly specific population, namely, terminally ill patients." Thus its "treatment objective" is the "normalization of life" and, more specifically, the construction of a space in which "the extraordinary and the horrible have become reduced to the ordinary and the 'natural'" so that cries of "anguish are channeled into silent whispers of acceptance."[75]

"Death with Dignity" is the motto of hospice's proponents along with Kübler-Ross's followers (as well as, more ironically, the members of the Hemlock Society). But even if Vivian hadn't been forced to bear the indignities of medicine, in what sense of the word "dignity" could her death from a wasting, often excruciatingly painful disease have been considered "dignified"? Like birth, death is surely by its nature undignified in the dictionary senses of the word that define "dignity" as a quality of "poise and self-respect, stateliness and formality in manner and appearance." How can one ensure "death with dignity"? Sherwin Nuland reports asking a friend who had survived the deaths of several lovers from AIDS, and the response he records is enlightening precisely because it questions the very concept of "dignity" in the context of terminal illness: "Dignity is something, said John, that the survivors snatch—it is in their minds that it exists, if it exists at all."[76]

Perhaps for the dying, though, or at least for some of the dying, there are ways of meeting death with indignation—or at least of challenging the indignity of death itself—that more accurately represent the self's protest against imminent annihilation. "Do not go gentle into that good night," admonished Dylan Thomas in a famous villanelle addressed to his dying father, for "Old age should burn and rave at close of day"—should not, in other words, accept death "with dignity" but instead should "Rage, rage against the dying of the light." Indeed, as Moller argues, the admonition to die "with dignity" often functions as a way of "suppressing and containing the tribulations of dying in a fashion that minimally disturbs and threatens the world of the living," while Thomas is willing to disrupt not just the prescribed resignation of the patient nearing death but also the acquiescence of the survivor by imploring his father to "Curse, bless, me now with your fierce tears."[77]

But if many of the alternatives to medicalized hospital death are management strategies for the containment of rage and fear that aren't all that different from the many other depersonalizing techniques of the hospital itself, what hope is there for Edson's Vivian Bearing—and for the rest of us, who must sooner or later confront the unbearable temporality that means the "whole earth," as T. S. Eliot put it, is in both the physical and the metaphysical sense "our hospital"? Would the intervention of a hospital chaplain—priest, minister, or rabbi—have fortified her and "dignified" her death? That in her academic career she has focused primarily on Donne's *Holy Sonnets* suggests, at least on the surface, that this twentieth-century intellectual has a mind that can in several senses of the word comprehend death in a theological framework. But in fact no man or woman "of the cloth" appears in the course of *Wit*, and in their various ways Ariès and Nuland point ruefully to this clerical absence.

Writing in the 1970s, Ariès struck a doleful note: "Gone are the days of the solemn procession of the *Corpus Christi*. . . . Gone, long gone, the days when this procession was welcomed sadly by the dying man and his entourage."[78] Decades later Nuland reported that his own hospital has abandoned the custom of automatically summoning a priest when a Catholic's name is on "the Danger List," because "the appearance in his room of someone with a clerical collar" is too "often a person's first intimation that his life is waning." The skeptical "mythology of modern death," these writers imply, has transformed the chaplain from a source of comfort to an omen of impending annihilation. And in the not-so-brave new world from which such traditions have vanished, Vivian's lecture on Donne's Holy Sonnet 5 ("If poysonous mineralls"), dramatized in a flashback halfway through *Wit*, takes on special significance: "We want to . . . remind [the speaker of the poem] of the assurance of salvation. But it is too late. The poetic encounter is over. We are left to our own consciences. Have we outwitted Donne? Or have we been outwitted?"[79]

"All that nonsense that's written about stages of dying, as if there were complete transitions—rooms that you enter, walk through, then leave behind for good. What rot. The anger, the shock, the unbelievableness, the grief—they are part of each day." The speaker here is "Gordon Stuart," a young man dying of cancer whose story the psychiatrist and anthropologist Arthur Kleinman includes in his illuminating book *The Illness Narratives*. "Who says you work your way eventually to acceptance—I don't accept it!" adds this patient, whose indignation and skepticism mirror Vivian Bearing's attitude toward her imminent death. Like Vivian, Gordon finds no solace in traditional religion, wondering, instead, if death "perhaps is the meaning of life."

Unlike Vivian, however, Gordon is helped in his dying by an attentive physician whom Kleinman calls Hadley Eliot. "Gordon died a good death," this doctor tells Kleinman, because although he was "was no less angry, not accepting at the end," he "kept his sense of irony" and "seemed to grow into whom he wanted to be." As for Hadley Eliot, he ultimately functions, Klein-man suggests, neither as priest nor as physician but rather as a compassion-ate comrade. Comments Kleinman, the "remarkable quality" of the interaction between Gordon Stuart and Hadley Eliot is "the participants' struggle to maintain authenticity, to avoid sentimentalizing or in other ways rendering inauthentic a relationship centered on the most existential of problems." For although the doctor "has no answers" to his patient's ques-tions, what he provides "is intense listening," a kind of "empathic witness-ing [that] is a moral act, not a technical procedure."[80]

In the case of Vivian Bearing, no such empathic witness emerges onstage to listen intensely and attentively to the dying woman's own voice. Nor can the audience, passively watching in the dark, offer the empathy—the active "feeling *with*"—that might offer significant acknowledgment of the patient's experience. In fact, as Edson's play moves toward its protago-nist's death, only Vivian's nurse, Susie, and her onetime dissertation direc-tor, a retired professor who's now a grandmother, tender her anything resembling human warmth. Although their ministrations effectively infan-tilize her, perhaps, Edson hints, the little childlike comforts both women offer represent the only plausible kinds of deathbed rituals that remain to the sufferer sequestered in the inhospitable hospital and isolated from empathic witnessing.

Significantly, in both their kindness and their minimalism these ges-tures recall the small but redemptive acts of compassion offered to Tolstoy's howling Ivan Ilyich by his servant Gerasim, who holds the dying man's aching legs on his shoulders because Ivan Ilyich "thought that in that posi-tion he did not feel any pain at all," and by Ivan's schoolboy son, who kisses the sufferer's hand toward the end as he screams in despair.[81] First, in the middle of what any scholar of early modern literature would define as the dark night of the soul, Susie brings Vivian a Popsicle, a last cold, sweet sacramental meal, because the "epithelial cells in [her] GI tract have been killed by the chemo." Then, as the Donne scholar lies dying, soothed by nothing more transcendent than morphine, E. M. Ashford, her former teacher, reads her the allegorically resonant children's tale of *The Runaway*

Bunny, who struggles to leave the mother—here evoking "Mother Earth"—from whom he cannot ever escape, and the poignant little story constitutes the liturgy of a kind of last rites:

> *"If you become a fisherman," said the little bunny, "I will be a bird and fly away from you."*
> *"If you become a bird and fly away from me," said his mother, "I will be a tree that you come home to."*

Finally, therefore, Vivian returns to her beginnings as her end—symbolizing the death of us all—opens and unfolds, in Sylvia Plath's words, "like a black tree, blackly."[82] Behind and around her there are the useless noises of the "code team." Behind those noises there are only the clickings and hissings of ineffectual machinery: the recordings of the EKG and the other monitors that are merely "the dust jacket . . . the white piece of paper that bears the little black marks." At this point, Edson's script calls for the actress playing the part of Vivian to divest herself of her two hospital gowns so that, at the moment when her "character" dies, the performer too is "*naked and beautiful, reaching for the light*"—as the stage lights go out.

Is this highly theatrical gesture intended to remind us of the strippings that hospitals require? Or is it meant to evoke the ultimate stripping of death, its redaction of the nakedness in which we were born—and to suggest as well that as the soul journeys toward "the light," it too is "naked and beautiful"? Though each of these interpretations is equally reasonable, what the audience actually sees is the real body of the real actress, "naked and beautiful," human, vulnerable, and exposed. Perhaps, in an age when illness and death are dominated by the role and rule of the technologized hospital rather than by theologies whose tenets we doubt, this moment of fleshly reality is all many of us can believe in. The familiar beauty of the dying animal, terminating. Its nakedness, hopelessly transient, despite the elaborate interventions of the mind and its machines.

A Day in the Death of . . .

CHRONOLOGY NO. 1: RECORDING DEATH

1963. Again and again the president's young wife, pink-suited and smart, crawls toward the back of the open limousine. Again and again the president crumples.

1997. Again and again the blond princess leaves the hotel to wait for her car. Over and over again, just a few minutes later, swerving cars catapult through the tunnel.

2001. Again and again the plane dips low, curves slightly up, seems to be taking aim, and plunges into the tower.

Someone keeps saying, "Shit, oh, shit," over and over again.

"Oh my God, oh my God," moan countless other barely visible observers.

Now here's a voice surrounded by crackling and buzzing, a voice on a cell phone: "We're alive in here."

Another voice: "I love you. I just want to tell you I love you." Over and over again: *I just want to tell you I love you.*

And again and again, human bodies looking "like rag dolls" dive toward the pavement from one hundred stories up.

"This is the most horrifying thing I've ever experienced," a bystander tells a reporter. "Look; oh my God, look; there's a person falling. I can't watch. Don't watch."[1]

Yet the camera watches: the still cameras, the movie cameras, the video cameras. And the mikes pick up the screams, the roar of the explosions, the "sharp crack" before the imminent crash.

One journalist later describes that crash as sounding, "oddly, like a waterfall, thousands of panes of glass shattering [and then] a slow, building rumble like rolling thunder."[2] Even before his similes appear in print, millions of people all over the world will have heard at least a simulacrum of the crash for themselves.

That afternoon the owner of a downtown photo store confides that "people rushed in to buy disposable cameras." "*Some didn't wait for their change, just ran out. Some were screaming.*"[3] Screaming and taking pictures. Witnessing death. Recording it.

CHRONOLOGY NO. 2: DEATH WATCHING

1976. The mind and body of a man named Frank Tugend decay and die on the pages of a photojournal produced by his grandsons Mark Jury and Dan Jury [figs 7. and 8]. A backward glance to 1954 offers an image of Frank—"Gramp"—as a cheerful youngish man in a visored cap, holding his plump-cheeked baby grandson, Dan. But 1974 yields a picture of the barely grown-up Dan, blond hair in a Prince Valiant pageboy, carrying his nearly skeletal, diapered grandpa, still Frank Tugend, but oh, how changed. In another photo a long-haired youthful person, maybe Dan, wipes Gramp's bottom; in another the old man sits naked on the toilet lovingly attended by

7. Mark Jury and Dan Jury: *Gramp Holding Dan* (1954).

8. Mark Jury and Dan Jury: *Dan Holding Gramp* (1974).

someone indeterminate, and in yet another Nana, Gramp's distressed wife, holds up his soiled underpants as she remarks "to no one in particular, 'Gosh, it's an awful ordeal.' "[4]

Unmistakably "an awful ordeal"—and its lineaments are exposed, preserved, continually presented and represented by the peering eye of the camera.

From the eighties onward—not in any one year but increasingly, as the decade dissolves into the nineties—AIDS patients wither and die in the chill light of the "camera lucida." Emaciated, young men named Tom Moran and Joey Brandon gaze obliquely out of the frames in which each has been, it seems, permanently "captured" by the photographer Nicholas Nixon. Their eyes are focused on something that isn't the viewer and isn't Nixon. As we watch *them*, they watch this something that's coming toward them, stripping them moment by moment of everything that isn't *it* [fig. 9].[5]

Comments one critic, the "imperative to visualize, confirm, and fix

9. Nicholas Nixon: *Tom Moran* (1987).

AIDS on the body solves the 'problem' of how to know the disease," for a certification of "knowledge" can "be produced visually, and knowledge of HIV infection and AIDS is produced, in many ways invented, by the photograph."[6]

But inside the ice of their frames, Tom Moran and Joey Brandon know little of this knowledge that their skeletal selves constitute. Instead they stare, unceasingly, into a corner that implies a different knowledge. And George Garrett, whom Nixon photographed even closer to death, gazes toward an IV pole and a hospital trash can, as he lies pinioned by illness in the dead center of a bleak black-and-white design.

1993. Herb Goldberg is dying of metastatic cancer, and his son Jim, a professional photographer, has decided to "document my father's death." "As an artist," he explains in an interview, "it made no sense for me to look at somebody else's death when my father's life and death were events I had to come to terms with."[7]

Here is Herb being bathed by his nurse, Fran, and here he is in an unnervingly blurry close-up, as someone spoon-feeds him Jell-O, and here he is—again, always again—on December 25, 1993, mouth open as he exhales his last breath, and someone's wristwatch, nearer the lens than the dead man's face, tells us that it's precisely 7:41 A.M.

1995. Morrie Schwartz, a septuagenarian sociology professor stricken with Lou Gehrig's disease, appears on *Nightline* in a series of conversations with Ted Koppel. The sick man's "ebullient spirit and positive attitude were so life-affirming," the show's producer later remembers, "that 'Lessons on Living' became the only logical title for the series."[8] Indeed, when Schwartz's former student, sportswriter Mitch Albom, sees the program, he gets back in touch with his old professor and writes *Tuesdays with Morrie*, a set of conversations on life and death and dying destined to top the *New York Times* best seller list for two years running.

But even while both *Nightline* and *Tuesdays with Morrie* record and celebrate Schwartz's affirmative vision, they trace his literally unnerving decline.

"So how do you know things are going downhill?" Koppel asks. And Albom, recalling this episode, observes that as Morrie speaks, "it became obvious. He was not waving his hands to make a point as freely as he had in their first conversation. He had trouble pronouncing certain words. . . . In a few more months, he might no longer speak at all." Nor is the dying man "upbeat" about his deterioration. There are "days when I am depressed," he confesses. "Let me not deceive you. I see certain things going and I feel a sense of dread. What am I going to do without my hands? What happens when I can't speak?"[9]

2000. Dr. Bill Bartholome is dying of esophageal cancer. Bill Moyers is interviewing him for PBS as part of a series called *On Our Own Terms*, devoted to end-of-life issues. Later in the series Kitty Rayl, a patient with terminal uterine cancer, will be videotaped as she discusses choosing to die.[10]

"I think we need to think of death as sugar, as something that gives life that pizzazz," Bartholome tells Moyers.

But then, over and over again, on VCRs and computer screens, listeners can hear him whispering a different comment in a voice wounded by cancer's assault on his esophagus. You wonder, he confides, "How do you actually *get* dead, how do you actually experience *that* in your body and in your daily life?" and he admits it's hard, hard to "brush your teeth, take a shower" when "you're locked in the trajectory of dying . . . that changes everything."

"I want every day that I can get," murmurs Kitty Rayl, but "I don't want to be out of control," a "vegetable." She too can be repeatedly heard confessing her feelings on-screen and online.

In a shaking voice, Bartholome's wife, Pam Roffol Dobies, tells Bill Moyers how she spoke to her dying, apparently comatose husband, over and over again telling him that she loved him, and then "I just sat there for a couple minutes, and he said, 'Love you, love *you*,'" she exclaims in wonderment. "Two hours later he died," she adds, "but he stayed with me through the whole thing, came back from wherever to say it one last time, I love you."

We can hear Pam Roffol Dobies recounting this story over and over again, online and on-screen.

2002. Laura Rothenberg, a twenty-one-year-old undergraduate at Brown who is dying of cystic fibrosis, records a diary she entitles "My So-Called Lungs," which is broadcast on NPR's *All Things Considered* as part of a continuing series called "Radio Diaries." "The voice on the tape is so close," marvels a *New York Times* reporter, that "it is as if Laura Rothenberg were on the pillow next to her listener, whispering into the person's ear."

In a husky voice "punctuated with little coughs," Laura confides that most of her friends who also suffered from this disease "aren't around anymore": "Gina died when we were 13, Damien died that year. He was 17. . . . My friend, Sophie, died when she was in 11th grade. . . . And my friend Marcy died this past summer."

2003. After Laura herself succumbs, her diary of her final months is published posthumously, under the title *Breathing for a Living.*[11]

2005. The New York Times Magazine features an essay titled "Will We Ever Arrive at the Good Death?" with illustrations by Nicholas Nixon, the photographer who had earlier produced controversial portraits of people dying from AIDS, among them Joey Brandon and Tom Moran. Now working on a more general study of terminal illness, Nixon here pictures in graphic—almost terrifying—detail the final ends of Robert Arnold, a statistician, and Suzanne Richardson, a former dean of students at Harvard Law School.

CHRONOLOGY NO. 3: HOME MOVIES

In the forties, my father, like many other dads, buys a sixteen-millimeter movie camera with which he begins to record my childhood. In the serene gaze of the camera, I romp on the beach, walk to church with grandparents, and dance with cousins in a little garden.

In the fifties, as I grow into my teens, my parents and I now and then watch those "old" home movies, marveling, I suppose, at the differentness and yet the *presentness* of the *temps perdu* they capture and reiterate. No madeleines necessary, thank you!

In the sixties, when our three children are little, my husband buys an eight-millimeter movie camera, on which he begins to record their doings—romping on beaches, frolicking on hillsides, taking walks with me and their grandmother.

In the seventies, a decade after my father's death, my mother relinquishes a projector, a movie screen, and a stack of the sixteen-millimeter films to my husband and me. She doesn't know how to use the projector, she explains, so we'll now be custodians of these relics.

In the eighties, with the advent of a new technology, my husband has my mother's sixteen-millimeter films and our eight-millimeter films transferred to videotape. He and I and our three children watch them from time to time as the kids grow up. I think looking at the family videos seems to all of us like going to a strange party at which we encounter guests from the past, guests who are and aren't ourselves but who, in any case, still *are.*

At the end of the eighties one of my husband's cousins comes to visit us in California. A lifelong fan of Elliot's jokes, she persuades her husband to make a thirty-minute video of several of his almost-as-good-as-standup-comic routines. And in 1991, a week after my husband's death, she mails us this video, entitled *Elliot 1988*, with a note of sympathy in which she comments that perhaps it will comfort us to see him sometimes on our VCR.

Throughout the nineties my three grown children and I watch *Elliot*

1988 now and then when we're all together. Of course we also watch videos of my children growing up, in which younger avatars of me and my husband and our parents also appear. On these occasions it's again as if we were attending a strange party, to which the dead have been invited. The dead who are still, in Alan Shapiro's fine phrase, "alive and busy," if only on-screen.[12]

CHRONOLOGY NO. 4: FLASHBULB MEMORIES

1944. Majdanek, the concentration camp near Lublin, has been liberated by the Russian Army, and in October the Western press begins to publish "recycled Sovfoto images." As tales of the tormented dead start to proliferate in newspapers and magazines, reporters bear witness to atrocity while apologizing for subjecting their readers to revelations that constitute, in the words of one journalist, "the most horrific story I shall ever have to write."[13]

But for many people photographs are the most "horrific" items in the swelling tide of what comes to be called Holocaust testimony. "It is not the custom of the *Illustrated London News* to publish photographs of atrocities," remarks one editor, but because some readers may think the "reports of [German] crimes exaggerated [we] consider it necessary to present them, by means of the accompanying photographs, with irrefutable proof," although he assures the squeamish that "even these pictures are carefully selected from a number [that] are too horrible to reproduce."[14]

Compared with the photos that will be widely disseminated in another year, these "carefully selected" images are mild. In the words of historian Barbie Zelizer, they tend "to be cleansed of human bodies," emphasizing, instead of the dead, the "gas cells, hanging ropes, furnaces . . . cans of Zyklon B . . . mounds of shoes," all signs of murders whose victims are still largely invisible even to wartime photojournalists.[15]

1945. American forces enter "the camps of the western front": Buchenwald, Bergen-Belsen, Dachau. The press comes with them. What soldiers, reporters, and photographers find is (in the words of the Holocaust scholar Saul Friedlander) "at the limits of representation." Nevertheless, as reporters testify to what they've seen, photographers train their lenses on the dying and the dead.

"I saw these dead. . . . I saw the living beside these dead. . . . I saw children walking about in this hell," declares William Frye in the *Boston Globe*.

Describing "39 Carloads of Bodies on Track at Dachau," Howard Cowan notes in the *Washington Post* that German civilians passed the bodies "with no more than curious glances"; and children "pedaled past the bodies on bicycles," with "looted clothing hung from their handlebars."[16]

Now some of the most distinguished wartime photographers start to produce unprecedented images of atrocity. Margaret Bourke-White takes a famous picture of dozens of bodies stacked in a wagon—a sort of dumpster—that's simply captioned "Corpses of civilians killed at Buchenwald, April–May 1945." In a shocking "atrocity spread" that runs in the May 7 issue of *Life* that year, this photo appears with a confessional comment by Bourke-White herself: "The sights I have just seen are so unbelievable *that I don't think I'll believe them myself until I've seen the photographs*" [emphasis added]."[17]

(My parents, longtime subscribers to *Life*, like so many other Americans, carefully excise the May 7, 1945, "atrocity spread" because they believe, like countless other parents, that their child is too young to confront such evidence of brutality. But perhaps because they consider these photos "historic," they store the clippings on the top shelf of the hall closet, where unbeknownst to them I'll find the pictures—and they'll indeed terrify me—in a few years.)

("One's first encounter with the photographic inventory of ultimate horror is a kind of revelation, the prototypically modern revelation, a negative epiphany," Susan Sontag writes three decades later, adding that for her such a revelation was triggered by "photographs of Bergen-Belsen and Dachau which I came across by chance in a bookstore in Santa Monica in July 1945. Nothing I have seen—in photographs or in real life—ever cut me as sharply, deeply, instantaneously. Indeed, it seems plausible to me to divide my life into two parts, before I saw those photographs [I was twelve] and after. . . . When I looked at those photographs, something broke."[18])

(According to one historian of film, "Jean-Luc Godard has said that cinema was invented to film the concentration camps."[19])

George Rodger, another *Life* photographer, "force[s] himself to take photos and to his horror" is soon so "inspired by the grotesque spectacle" that he starts "to shoot frantically, 'subconsciously arranging groups and bodies on the ground into artistic compositions in his viewfinder.'"[20] One of *his* most famous pictures is indeed a beautifully composed depiction of a little boy, eyes averted, walking along a road beside which dozens of dead bodies have been flung down like ninepins by a bowling ball [fig. 10]. Years later a historian of photography comments that this "definitive image from the concentration camps [is] impossible to paraphrase," adding that confronted with this horror, "we can only note details: the park-like presence of the trees, the strolling child, the piles of dead bodies laid out on the right, for example."[21]

10. George Rodger: *Bergen-Belsen Concentration Camp* (April 1945).

Inevitably, many photographers soon realize that even while masses of corpses make one kind of point about the scale of atrocity, tightly focused pictures of the individual dead make another, equally crucial kind of statement. One such photo appears in the pages of the New York newspaper *PM* as well as in a *London Daily Mail* roundup of *The Horrors of Nazi Concentration Camps Revealed for All Time in the Most Terrible Photographs Ever Published*. It is a portrait of two beautiful, apparently serene dead children, lying side by side near another, blanketed body, as if Hansel and Gretel had somehow wandered into Bergen-Belsen. Sometime later an image that has been cut from this poignant "composition" appears in print: the gaunt corpse of the children's mother, now "depicted alone and without the blanket [and] revealed to be nude and beautiful, her long curly hair spread across her shoulders."[22]

Of course professional photographers aren't the only ones taking pictures. Many of the "liberators" share Bourke-White's feeling that they won't believe the sights they've seen until they "see the photographs." As Barbie Zelizer later comments, "The photos' resonance was so great that liberators of the camps developed their own practices involving them. Often preferring the group's visual memory over their own, individual liberators treated the photos with marked deference."[23] "Flashbulb memory," Zelizer notes, is what these photos constitute: glossy epiphanies reflecting "the extent to which humanity had sunk during World War II." And she cites one young German-born writer's comment: "Black and white images were my most prevailing memory of the Holocaust. The first Jews I met were documented on photographs. . . . On these photographs, the Jewish people were dying time and again—eternal victims."[24]

"An event known through photographs certainly becomes more real than it would have been if one had never seen the photographs," Susan Sontag writes in 1977, adding, "Think of the Vietnam War."[25]

1968. Think of the Vietnam War. On a "bright clear warm day" in March of this year, nearly a decade before Sontag's groundbreaking study of photography appears in print, Sergeant Ron Haeberle, part of a two-man journalism team from the Thirty-First Public Information Detachment, hitches a helicopter ride with eighty men of "Company C (First Battalion, 20th Infantry, 11th Light Infantry Brigade)" from their "base camp at Landing Zone Dottie" to the village of My Lai. There, according to the record of a subsequent investigation, he uses government-owned "color film to record scenes of atrocities" and later remarks to his team partner that he wonders "what the press would do with photos like that."[26]

1969. Once the story breaks, the press of course buys the film from Haeberle, and in its December 5 issue, *Life* publishes an "atrocity spread" reminiscent of the piece the magazine ran on May 7, 1945, only this time the atrocity has not only been recorded by an American photographer but perpetrated by American soldiers. Second only to Hung Cong ("Nick") Ut's famous *Accidental Napalm Attack*, in which five Vietnamese children, with a naked little girl at the center of the group, run screaming from an American assault, Haeberle's images of My Lai become instant "flashbulb memories" of this war in Indochina.

"Guys were about to shoot these people," Haeberle comments to *Life* about the picture entitled *People About to Be Shot*. "I yelled, 'Hold it,' and shot my picture. As I walked away, I heard M16s open up. From the corner of my eye I saw bodies falling, but I didn't turn to look" [fig. 11].[27]

1972. Jeffrey Silverthorne, a young photographer, begins *Morgue Work,*

11. Ron Haeberle: *People About to Be Shot* (1968).

a series of portraits of the dead, which includes the now-famous *Woman Who Died in Her Sleep*, an image of a lovely nude young woman bisected and then in effect *re*sected by the coarse stitches with which pathologists sew up a cadaver following autopsy.[28]

1981. Joel-Peter Witkin, a sometime poet studying for an MFA in photography at the University of New Mexico, produces an image entitled *Hermes*, in which, as critic Peter Schwenger later explains, the "baby Dionysus becomes a dead fetus, suggesting a parallel to nineteenth-century photographs showing grieving parents holding a dead infant."

1984. Witkin creates *Harvest*, a work the same critic describes as "simultaneously corpse and homage to Arcimboldo," the sixteenth-century artist who constructed parodic human heads out of fruits and vegetables.[29]

1987. Robert Morris produces *Untitled*, a sort of eroticized reimagining of the dead mother from Bergen-Belsen whose (at first blanketed, then uncovered) body was found beside her two beautiful dead children. In this "renovated form," Barbie Zelizer later remarks, "the woman look[s] as if she [has] innocently fallen asleep under neon and strobe lights."[30]

1994. Witkin creates *Glassman,* one of his best-known works, an image of a cadaver from the Mexico City morgue that the artist himself describes as having "gone through a kind of transfiguration . . . on the autopsy table" and looking, now, "like a Saint Sebastian."[31]

1997. In an essay entitled "Dead Stuff," the writer E. Annie Proulx observes: "Since the 1970s there has been an explosion of photographic interest in images of death and the grotesque, with scores of books and exhibitions of work in the so-called 'post-mortem' genre.' "[32]

1998. The CBS newsmagazine *60 Minutes* airs a story that shows Dr. Jack Kevorkian "administering a lethal injection to Thomas Youk, a 52-year-old Michigan man suffering from Lou Gehrig's disease." A PBS commentator notes that although "the broadcast of the tape, including the actual moment of death, has already provoked sharp debate over the journalistic and medical ethics involved," it "also proved a ratings success for CBS."[33]

2000. Peter Schwenger expands on Proulx's point about photographs of death. *Morgue Work, Hermes, Harvest,* and *Untitled,* he writes, "participate in a new version of the photography of corpses" in which the dead are photographed "for artistic purposes rather than as memoirs or documentation."[34]

2001. Featuring graphic images of dead bodies in a mortician's workroom, HBO's television hit *Six Feet Under,* "one of the most acclaimed shows of the 2001 season," proclaims that its episodes take "a darkly comic look at the Fishers, a dysfunctional family who own and operate an independent funeral home in Los Angeles."[35]

2002. On February 22, American officials in Karachi receive a video confirming the death of abducted *Wall Street Journal* reporter Daniel Pearl. According to CNN, a "spokesman for the Home Government Department of the province of Sindh" notes that the tape "contain[s] scenes showing Mr. Daniel Pearl in captivity and scenes of his murder by the kidnappers." Entitled *The Slaughter of the Spy-Journalist, the Jew Daniel Pearl,* the video eventually leaks onto the Internet through a Jihadist site.[36]

2002. The April 29 issue of *Time* reports on how "Images of Death" have become "Must-See TV" in the Middle East, where "silently rolling footage reveals [Palestinian] corpses in every conceivable state."[37]

2002. Professional photographer Thomas Condon is jailed in Cincinnati for taking pictures of corpses in the local morgue as part of "an artistic series intended to portray the cycle of life and death." The judge in the case comments that he sees "no redeeming value in the photographs," which he considers "disrespectful and really the worst invasion of privacy."[38]

2004. In January a soldier stationed in Iraq reports to his superiors that he has discovered digital images of detainee abuse at Abu Ghraib prison. After an investigation, Major General Antonio Taguba concludes that American soldiers stationed at the prison committed "egregious acts and grave breaches of international law." On April 29 the television newsmagazine *60 Minutes II* shows some of the photos, including pictures of naked prisoners cowering before snarling guard dogs and at least one image of a dead man packed in ice, an inmate who is said to have gotten "too stressed out" and died.

Comments critic Sarah Boxer in the *New York Times*, if the Abu Ghraib photos have a "precedent in the world of photography, it is not the photographs of heaps of bodies left by the Nazis, but rather, appalling though it might sound, tourist snapshots." A few days later, also writing for the *Times*, photography theorist Susan Sontag adds that these photographs are comparable to "some of the photographs of black victims of lynching taken between the 1880s and 1930s, which show Americans grinning beneath the naked mutilated body of a black man or woman hanging behind them from a tree."[39]

2004. In early May, Iraqi militants film the beheading of American hostage Nicholas Berg, and the video immediately runs on the Arab news network Al Jazeera.

2004. On August 1, a *New York Times* writer, Jacques Steinberg, observes that kidnappings like those of Pearl and Berg "are becoming a tactic of choice in the Middle East, and nearly every group that has recently captured a foreigner in Iraq has produced an accompanying video. Presumably filmed by the perpetrators themselves, the tapes often follow a theatrical ritual announcing the abduction: A list of demands is outlined. Deadlines are set. Hostages plead for their lives. In several grotesque instances, the hostages are killed." But this proliferation of videos poses difficult problems for news organizations, adds Steinberg. If they play the videos, will they be complicit in the filming and display of atrocities? If they don't play the videos, will they be shirking their responsibility to report the news?[40] While professional journalists debate the issue, most of the videos, including those of Pearl and Berg, circulate freely on the Internet.

THE CELLULOID AFTERLIFE

By the mid-nineteenth century the pioneering experiments conducted by such technicians of the visual as Joseph Nicéphore Niepce and Louis

Jacques Mandé Daguerre had evolved from crude heliographs and daguerreotypes to the detailed representations of real-life images that came to be called photographs. What one early theorist of the subject defined as "the pencil of nature" by which light rays pass through a lens to inscribe given figures on a "plate" or "film" made it possible for a range of artists to record people and settings as they perceived or (in many cases) "composed" them. From Mathew Brady in America to Lewis Carroll and Julia Margaret Cameron in England, photographers scrutinized scenes from the American Civil War to Victorian garden parties, from the Wild West to the upper-class English nursery and "captured" them with what seemed to be unprecedented realism.

Mathew Brady's Lincoln and Whitman, Étienne Carjat's Baudelaire, Lewis Carroll's Alice Liddell, Paul Nadar's Sarah Bernhardt, and Julia Margaret Cameron's beautiful pre-Raphaelite ladies—all manifest an uncanny *presence*, indeed a present*ness*, as we gaze at their portraits. Do their pictures tell us that they *were* here or that they *are* here? The line between *were* and *are* begins to blur if we stare back hard enough as Baudelaire stares fiercely toward *us* or if we follow the meditative gazes of Lincoln and Whitman toward a world just outside the camera's range into which they seem, still, eerily to peer as they "sit" for the camera. To quote a remark that Ansel Adams made in 1974 about the subjects of pictures taken by the early-twentieth-century photographer Jacob Riis, "These people live again in print as intensely as when their images were captured on the old dry plates of sixty years ago. . . . I am walking in their alleys, standing in their rooms and sheds and workshops, looking in and out of their windows. *And they in turn seem to be aware of me* [emphasis added]."[41]

Now, much more than a century later, as we inch into a new millennium, haven't we become accustomed to the "reality" of such printed images? As they've entered history, my dead grandparents, my dead parents, and my dead husband all have assumed places in the celluloid afterlife the camera bestows—places alongside, as it were, the disembodied yet weirdly authentic figures of Lincoln and Whitman, Baudelaire and Bernhardt and Jacob Riis's subjects. Because I'm seeing them as they somehow "truly" looked, don't *all* these people from the past have a persuasiveness that, say, Socrates and Shakespeare, Elizabeth I and Napoleon Bonaparte lack? To be sure, I suppose it should go without saying that I "believe" in the poets, philosophers, queens, and generals of the past, or at least I believe in their *words* and (at least some of) what I've been taught about their deeds. But the knowledge of the actual physical *being* that these figures had, even when it's asserted by the most scrupulously detailed sculptures and paintings, isn't in any way comparable to the sense of plausible livingness that photographs give me, or at least *seem* to give me.

And on film or video? Doesn't Charlie Chaplin still seem to live, along with Humphrey Bogart, Franklin Delano Roosevelt, John Fitzgerald Kennedy, Princess Diana—and my husband, and my mother? Here's Kennedy again in the open car in Dallas, his head exploded by an epochal bullet. Yet here he is again too, youthful and exuberant, waving to the crowd, and reiterating one or another famous speech as his chic wife in her pillbox hat gazes at him adoringly. And here's my husband, telling for maybe the hundredth time that joke about Goldberg and Rabinowitz on the Grand Concourse.

Even more remarkably, perhaps, the dead can now still seem to live not in reiterations of familiar scenes and often told jokes but in new scenes in which their ghostly images will do different things from the things they did when they were actually alive. In August 2004 the *New York Times* reported that "computer technology has resurrected Sir Laurence Olivier, who died in 1989," that indeed a "combination of manipulated archival film footage and fresh soundtrack dialogue will give Olivier a role—speaking lines he never spoke and making gestures he never made—in a new movie."[42]

DEATH AND THE CAMERA

In 1972, in his widely circulated *Ways of Seeing*, a kind of Marxist "how to look at paintings, photos, and other graphic images" for the visually and theoretically naive, the British writer John Berger remarked that the "invention of the camera changed the way men saw." A year earlier, the photographer Diane Arbus—a practitioner rather than a theorist—had already meditated quite specifically on the evidentiary stillness of photographs, commenting that "they are the proof that something was there and no longer is. Like a stain." And five years later, in her groundbreaking *On Photography*, Susan Sontag elaborated on this notion, observing that perhaps for the first time in history photographs constitute a visual genre capable of offering "experience captured"; in fact she flatly stated, "Photographs furnish *evidence* [emphasis added]."[43]

Four years later still, the French theorist Roland Barthes speculated even more fully on the wide-ranging implications of the camera's work. "Perhaps we have an invincible resistance to believing in the past," Barthes muses in *Camera Lucida*. Yet the photograph, "for the first time, puts an end to this resistance; henceforth the past is as certain as the present, what we see on paper is as certain as what we touch. *It is the advent of the Photograph [that] divides the history of the world* [emphasis added]."[44]

What does that cleft in history mean to those who mourn or, more generally, to all who must confront the "mythology of modern death"? Has photography changed our consciousness of mortality itself? More specifically, how have the camera and its constellation of related technologies shaped our attitudes toward death, the dying, and the dead? To evoke Marshall McLuhan's famous phrase, do these media constitute a message of some sort?

If they do, it's a contradictory message. On the one hand, in the midst of what is supposedly a "death-denying" culture, such technologies of representation as photography, film, audio, and video continually bear witness to the deaths we are said to deny. On the other hand, these same technologies represent the dead to us as "alive and busy"—and seeming, *as it were*, still to be here among us. The camera watches the dying and watches over the dead. The black box of the flight recorder reiterates the pilot's last words. The video resurrects the dead president and the dead father. The tape recorder, the answering machine, the sound track—all preserve the voices, songs, and stories of people who've vanished.[45]

In Latin and Italian, the word *camera* means "room" (from that source come the French *chambre* and the English "chamber"), and historians of photography note that the specialized room called a camera obscura, whose principles Leonardo da Vinci, among others, clearly defined, was the precursor of the apparatus known as a camera lucida, itself an ancestor of today's Kodak, Leica, or digital Olympus. But now, whether one imagines the technological machine that ultimately came into being in the mid-nineteenth century as obscura or lucida, black box or room of light, it's figuratively a strange chamber in which what is (or was) life (or death) is preserved with effects that have even confounded such sophisticated thinkers as Sontag and Barthes. For although both theorists comment on what seems to be the uncanny livingness with which the camera invests its objects, both, in what is apparently a peculiar paradox, associate the photograph with death.

Noting, for instance, that to "photograph people is to violate them, by seeing them as they never see themselves," Sontag declares that "just as the camera is a sublimation of the gun, to photograph someone is a sublimated murder." Photography, she adds, "is an elegiac art [and] [a]ll photographs are *memento mori*," for to "take a photograph is to participate in another person's [mortality]" since "precisely by slicing out this moment and freezing it, all photographs testify to time's relentless melt." Thus, even while photographs "furnish evidence" of life by capturing experience, these same photographs testify to the imminence of death by preserving life's experience *when it has already passed*. Similarly, even while photographs perpetuate life by bearing witness to the presence of someone's body, these same photographs enact the separation of mind or self and body that is emblematic of death by defamiliarizing—in effect stealing—their subjects' sense of their own physical presence ("seeing [people] as they never see themselves").[46]

Barthes makes this point even more powerfully. On the one hand, he observes, "by attesting that the object has been real, the photograph surreptitiously induces belief that it is alive, because of that delusion which makes us attribute to Reality an absolutely superior, somehow eternal value." On the other hand, however, "by shifting this reality to the past ('this-has-been'), the photograph suggests that it is already dead." By extension, moreover, Barthes says that despite certain generic differences, films and audio recordings have the same oddly paradoxical effects. "I can never see or see again in a film certain actors whom I know to be dead without a kind of melancholy," he comments, adding that this is "the melancholy of Photography itself (I experience this same emotion listening to the recorded voices of dead singers)." Differently put, "Photography has something to do with resurrection," yet at the same time there is a sense in which as the object of the camera's gaze becomes "Total-Image," s/he is in effect "embalmed" in the past, "which is to say, Death in person."[47]

But if we attribute a paradoxical death-in-life (along with a posthumous life-in-death) to photographs of living subjects—even living subjects who are "locked" in what Bill Bartholome calls "the trajectory of dying"—how are we to think about photographs of the dead who are represented as *really* dead?

In the early years of its history, photography became a mortuary genre, supplementing and eventually replacing the death mask as a final representational token of a beloved body before burial or cremation could efface once-familiar lineaments. As Annie Proulx points out, the apparently morbid "morgue work" of such artists as Silverthorne and Witkin has precedent in the keepsake photographs produced in the nineteenth century, "when death was intimate and people both died and were prepared for burial at home." In France *le dernier portrait* was de rigueur for celebrities, with notables from Victor Hugo to Marcel Proust "sitting" (or, more accurately, lying) for final pictures. But bourgeois families too, on both sides of the Atlantic, eagerly demanded such keepsakes of deceased loved ones. And though the custom of photographing the dead may be said to have itself died out within the first few decades of the twentieth century, Proulx's description of a particularly "striking" work that appeared in a history of American fashion is telling in its evocation of a composition that might just as well have been produced by, say, Witkin: "A boy in a sailor suit sits on porch stairs surrounded by a large, carefully arranged display of expensive toys; only the telltale set of the face, the heavy eyes and stiffened left foot show he is not alive. It is at once a memorial photograph and a statement of social position." If photographs of the living come paradoxically to represent that which is "already dead" or even "Death in person," what meanings collect around the depictions of this dead "boy in a sailor suit" and of Witkin's *Glassman* (or indeed of the two dead children and their dead mother photographed in Buchenwald)?[48]

Quoting Barthes on the ambiguities of the photographic image, Peter Schwenger argues that whereas Barthes asserts that the photograph of a living person "implies that it is alive, even if that life is always in the past tense and thus already dead," when "the image is that of a corpse, the photograph 'becomes horrible' . . . largely because of its undecidability; it is 'the living image of a dead thing.' "[49] Yet Schwenger's point might be pressed even further, for what is frequently most compelling about these "living images" of "dead things" is precisely their life*likeness* rather than their deathliness. Indeed, this paradoxical lifelikeness is a quality often singled out by commentators on such photographs. As Proulx notes of the "boy in a sailor suit," "Only the telltale set of the face, the heavy eyes and stiffened left foot show he is not alive." Declared Witkin, as he described photographing *Glassman*: "I spent an hour and a half with him, and after that, [his fingers seemed to have] grown 50 percent. . . . It was as if they were reaching for eternity."[50] And Zelizer, we should recall, observed that in Robert Morris's *Untitled* the dead mother from Buchenwald looks "as if she [has] innocently fallen asleep under neon and strobe lights."

If photographic portraits of the living constitute reminders that all life is shadowed by death and become therefore tokens of death-in-life, photographic portraits of the dead seem to tell us not that the dead are inanimate objects but rather that they're somehow alive *inside death*, as if the lens of the camera could look through the weight and coldness of the unliving body and with its "pencil of nature" trace the shape of a self still inhabiting what watchers by the actual corpse know to be motionless and stony. On the one hand, then, we respond with horror not so much to the "undecidability" of the "morgue work" image as to what we consciously realize is its absolute deadness; on the other hand, we also respond with grief and sorrow to the pathos of what we perceive as the image's livingness, a life-in-death different from, but related to, the death-in-life that photography bestows on the living.

To note that photographic portraits of what we might call dead souls have a curious life isn't of course to deny that camera images of the dead en masse (bodies stacked in boxcars or flung in ditches, heaps of bones in makeshift ossuaries) evoke the horrifying *thingness* of the dead. Nor is it to deny that representations of even a single effaced body—on a slab in a dissecting room, for example, with features veiled as they often are for medical students and pathologists—also represent what was once a person as now, in death, mere matter. It *is*, however, to insist on the confusions between life and death with which photography haunts us, complicates grieving, and derides our strategies for denying our own mortality and that of those we love.

SEEING AND BELIEVING

Many of these comments about the technologies of representation, including even those of such subtle analysts as Barthes and Sontag, seem to presuppose that such "media" are in fact honest, if not always honorable. I, at least, have been writing as if I really believed (as basically I do) not only the witnessings of American liberators who photographed the bodies of Holocaust victims but also, say, Ron Haeberle's account of what he saw and "shot" in My Lai as well as (rather more provisionally) Joel-Peter Witkin's description of how he photographed *Glassman*. From the recent theoretical perspective called postmodern, however, the productions of film and video are almost always suspect. Scenes can be faked, and indeed they are now as they were even in the nineteenth century. (Wasn't the "boy in a sailor suit" the star of a faked narrative? And doesn't *Glassman* also tell a made-up story?) Videos can be doctored—and certainly are, especially in a digital age, as the "resurrection" of Sir Laurence Olivier demonstrates. Moreover, even the most "honest" and "honorable" documentary photograph is taken from a specific perspective and is therefore inevitably biased, as current analysts of the genre continually remind us.

Yet of course, when film theorists stress the artifice of the camera's "gaze" or commentators on still photography emphasize the potential fakery of the photograph, that's surely because the *illusion* of reality produced by this technology is so extraordinarily powerful. Thus, when it first became possible to look at images that seemed to certify themselves as veritable documents of material existence, viewers of photography—and later film—began to experience a new kind of representational practice that brought the dead into the space of the living and the living into the orbit of the dead.

To be sure, there's a long history of *looking* at disease and decay, death and dying. From bloodthirsty "games" to grisly beheadings, from monitory images of death and the maiden to those ultimate representations of agony the Crucifixion, the Pietà, and the entombment of Christ, Western culture has gazed with fascination and terror at the emblems of mortality. And the very term "death*watch*" incorporates looking (and being looked *at*) into the very heart of the process of dying. Modern *looking* at what we now call the end of life, however, is radically different from most traditional ways of *regarding* death, dying, and the dead.

Such looking in the past was usually, after all, both looking *at* and looking *for*: looking at the dying body in order to look for an essence or soul that would expire into transcendence and looking at the dead body for a soul that could withstand the disintegration of its material "home." Such looking, in other words, was thought to be moral and monitory. In the revulsion from pain and decay that constitutes *timor mortis*, taught the Church fathers (as did the Buddha and the Hindu sages), we learn how the flesh and its desires are essentially corrupt, and thus we come to place our faith in what is *not* material, what can escape the filth of death.

Neither modern nor postmodern looking, however, imagines any such redemption. On the contrary, modern looking is only looking *at*, rarely looking *for*. Modern looking stares at death and dying to confirm the seemingly bizarre (because unpalatable, even inconceivable) "truth" that death is truly the *end*—the purpose as well as the termination—of life.[51] As representative "modern" viewers, for example, we're shocked and distressed when Holocaust victims like the Buchenwald mother and children or the murdered villagers of My Lai seem somehow to be alive in the midst of their deaths since we imagine such apparent "life" as merely a mystifying but not particularly redemptive immanence in the corporeal.

Equally troublesome, from a suspicious "post"-modern perspective we might be inclined to inquire into the provenance of a photograph—for instance, whether the picture was designed "to record, to mock, to remember, to exploit." Did it depict "a freak incident" or an event "representative of a larger pattern of violence?" In any case, whether or not a film or photo was designed to exploit, might it ultimately have appealed to prurient rather than sympathetic feelings? The memoirist and critic Ruth Kluger, a Holocaust survivor, remarks on "photos as an instrument of sublimated voyeurism, the victims helpless objects of the camera," adding that the British "made a documentary film about a liberated camp showing naked young women taking showers, "and speculating that perhaps such a film was merely a thin" veil for visual exploitation?"[52]

With Barbie Zelizer we might worry too that photography "may function most directly to achieve what it ought to have stifled—atrocity's normalization," since images of horror may make us "voyeurs of the suffering of others, tourists amidst their landscapes of anguish." Perhaps even more troublesome, adds Zelizer, "Some critics [now] argue that 'seeing and believing have come unglued' in the contemporary age," since not only academic theorists but even "much of the public" understands that "alternatives to photographic truth [can be] facilitated by retouching, cropping, montage, setup, and collage."[53]

As documentation of "real" life and death, photography has in a comparatively short time traveled a long route, evolving from what Barthes called a "certificate of presence," a guarantor of reality, to a potential tool of voyeuristic sensationalism.[54] What social and cultural forces have helped shape that journey? And how have the changing roles of photography not only reflected but also themselves helped shape the ways in which many artists imagine the complex intertwinings of life and death, mourning and memory?

MORTALITY ON DISPLAY

The mortuary photographs so popular throughout the second half of the nineteenth century were sometimes of course accompanied by photographs of death scenes, and both genres obviously had counterparts in the graphic and plastic arts. Paintings of notable figures on their deathbeds, of fallen soldiers dying on fields of battle, and of beautiful women breathing their last, along with death masks and sculptures of the dead and dying, are ubiquitous in the great museums of the West. Arguably, moreover, both the daguerreotype of the dead and the photograph of the death scene originated as copies of such works, simply employing the newly developed technology of the camera to bring a more scrupulous realism to the representation. As has often been noted, too, the Victorian death scene was in a sense soft-edged, even bathetic, and the same might be said of most nineteenth-century photographs of the dying and the "departed."[55]

Just as the pose of the "boy in a sailor suit" was meant to emphasize its subject's privileged life and angelic innocence, the studied serenity and decorous sorrow of, say, Henry Peach Robinson's famous photograph entitled *Fading Away* reflected, in the words of one commentator, "the Victorian penchant for the sentimental and melancholic." Even so, despite the decorum of its images, *Fading Away* evoked considerable protest when it was (at first) considered an authentic documentation of a death scene and believed therefore to constitute "a photographic intrusion into private family space." Only when Robinson's work was revealed to be a posed imitation of a death scene did it become "acceptable to the public"—and then precisely because it was "a fabrication, not . . . a literal image" [fig. 12].[56]

Perhaps the rise of what I've called military and political technologies of death along with the concurrent development of what I've defined as medical technologies of dying facilitated documentary photography's increasing movement away from a mimesis of painterly techniques and toward an ever more powerful assertion of the camera's special verisimilitude. Certainly both the American Civil War and the First World War in Europe yielded what were for their time shocking images of dead or dying combatants. Mathew Brady's *Dead in the Hole*, for instance, suggests that the photographer had almost scandalously peered into an open grave to capture the scat-

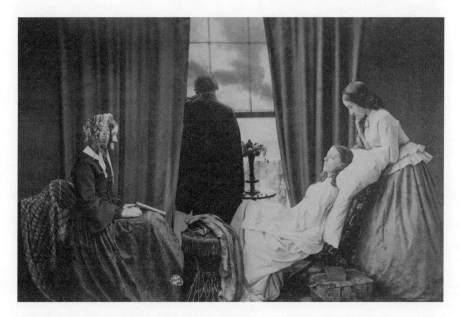

12. Henry Peach Robinson: *Fading Away* (1858).

tered remains of what were once living soldiers. Similarly, the so-called Great War yielded quite a few grisly photographs of soldiers who, like Brady's subjects, were "dead in the hole" or "on the wire" [fig. 13].[57] It wasn't, however, until it became possible in the mid-thirties to transmit photographic images by telegraph so that they could travel "as quickly as words" that newspaper and magazine editors could demand a photographic "realism" that is "hard, cold, exact, detached, and sometimes cruel." Such a technology was then available, as Zelizer shows, to capture the most horrifying event of the century, an event that was itself a product of advanced technology and intricate bureaucracy: the mass slaughter of civilians in Nazi death camps.[58]

Just as the technologies of death that facilitated genocide demanded from liberators and other observers the kind of scrupulous witnessing pro-

13. Mathew Brady: *Dead in the Hole* (c. 1861–65).

vided by photography, so the medical technologies developed to aid the sick and dying, as well as related technologies intended for forensic or other autopsies, often required the camera's techniques for recording both the "normal" and the pathological. That such techniques could also be brought to bear on sensational, supposedly medical or medicalized spectacles of death was probably inevitable. By the end of the very century that gave us photography, for instance, in the city where the genre's technology was pioneered by Daguerre, the voyeuristic inspection of anonymous dead bodies became a crowd-pleasing diversion, one that gave rise to widespread dissemination of photographs of the dead that were quite different from memorial images like "boy in a sailor suit."

At the Paris Morgue, "corpses were displayed behind a large glass window" for the delectation of (sometimes) thousands of people a day, who could "freely pass" through the premises "seven days a week, from dawn to dusk." Ostensibly this arrangement, which now seems so peculiar, was made for a utilitarian purpose: to facilitate the identification of anonymous bodies that had been found in the Seine or elsewhere—perhaps suicides, perhaps the victims of crimes—and even to assist in determining the cause(s) of death. Declared Dr. J. C. Gavinzel in 1882, in his *Étude sur la morgue au point de vue administratif et médical*: "Sympathetic reader! When you go past this somber building [the morgue] no longer shiver . . . enter boldly, and if any object strikes you or jogs your memory, go to the registrar, make a declaration." But few of those who frequented this building, which often seemed more circuslike than "somber," had come in search of a lost loved one or to do their civic duty and identify a body. On the contrary, most people in the milling crowds had evidently come for the excitement of the "spectacle" (a word that in French means "show" or "performance" as well as "sight"). The place "even merited a stop on the Thomas Cook tour of the city" since as its director explained, it was "much more fascinating than even a wax museum because the people displayed are real flesh and blood."[59]

Indeed, in just a few days at the beginning of August 1886, according to one historian, as many as 150,000 people filed past the body of a four-year-old girl found in a stairwell on the rue du Vert-Bois. Known as *l'enfant du Vert-Bois*, this tiny unknown heroine of *le mystère de la rue du Vert-Bois* was strapped to a red velvet chair in much the same way that the "boy in a sailor suit" was propped on a staircase, and in addition to the morgue exhibit itself a photograph of the pitiful tableau (as of many other comparable morgue exhibits) was prominently displayed in newspapers.[60] And despite pious rhetoric about *l'enfant*, neither religiosity nor science seem to have played much part in the public enthusiasm.

As should be clear from the circumstances surrounding, on the one hand, the production of Paris Morgue photographs and comparable clinical camera studies of the dying or the dead and, on the other hand, such war scenes as *Dead in the Hole* or *Dead on the Wire*, photography of the dying and the dead became increasingly secular as the uses and strategies of the camera moved away from the spiritualized models that had governed so many Victorian representations of life's end. Just as poets and painters working within the Christian tradition had for centuries imagined dying as the "expiration" of a soul that could transcend the flesh, so nineteenth-century photographers often figured death as a beautiful sleep presaging eternal redemption, with immortality implicit even in the material remains that signify mortality.[61] But just as poets and painters became increasingly skeptical about the long-standing assumption that death is an expiration rather than a termination, so photographers increasingly focused on the pain and pathos, the materiality and even filth of mortality.

To inquire which genre "influenced" which would very likely be to enter into hopeless chicken vs. egg circularity. For if photographers had once tried to represent the dead and the dying in "poetic" works that looked like paintings, twentieth-century painters and poets often sought to rival the camera's potential for dedicating itself to a "hard, cold, exact," mode of "realism" in their representations of death.[62] Zelizer notes that after World War II, atrocity photos "turned up as reality markers" in other genres. Artists, for instance, "began to use photos of the dead as visual cues. Pablo Picasso's *The Charnel House* was based on atrocity photos, and Rico Lebrun gave his versions of photographed corpses explicit captions like *Buchenwald Cart, Buchenwald Pit,* and *Dachau Chamber.*"[63] More recently, the painter Gerhard Richter has frequently deployed photographic images in such works as *October 18, 1977,* a series of paintings focusing on the lives and, especially, the deaths of the Baader-Meinhof gang. That Richter is a product of the postwar German culture whose leaders had been forced to look again and again at photographs of the stacks of cadavers that were the Nazis' handiwork makes his patent obsession with photography particularly telling; perhaps not surprisingly, he keeps as a sort of source book an enormous archive—an *Atlas*— of mostly photographic images.[64]

But even before pictures of the Nazi death camps had horrified the world, modernists working in a range of genres had begun to deploy the documentary realism that was to mark the atrocity photos coming out of the Second World War. With its vision of absolute termination, for instance, William Carlos Williams's "Death" could easily be describing a photograph of an exhibit in the Paris Morgue. That Williams was both a practicing physician and a friend of the photographer Alfred Stieglitz may or may not have shaped his conscious intentions in this clinical meditation on an "old bastard" who's become "a godforsaken curio / without / any breath in it." Nor would Wallace Stevens's longtime friendship with Williams necessarily have shaped his portrait in "The Emperor of Ice-Cream" of a dead woman whose body the poet might almost be preparing to photograph, shrouded in a sheet from which "her horny feet protrude . . . To show how cold she is, and dumb." Yet both poems reflect very much the same imperative to expose the utter materiality of death and the dead that marks *Dead in the Hole*, *Dead on the Wire*, and the Paris Morgue photographs and would soon infuse the images to emerge from the Holocaust and, later, Vietnam.[65]

Taken together, were photographs, poems, and paintings of this sort reactions against, on the one hand, the soft-edged sentimentality with which nineteenth-century culture had regarded and represented what Ariès has called the "beautiful death" and, on the other hand, rebellions against what Ariès considers a general twentieth-century tendency to deny or repress death? Arguing that the twentieth century's medicalization of death completed "the psychological mechanism that . . . eliminated [death's] character of public ceremony, and made it a private act," the French historian drew on a groundbreaking essay by British sociologist Geoffrey Gorer, who claimed in "The Pornography of Death" (1955) that by the mid-twentieth century death had become as unmentionable as sex had been in the Victorian era.[66] But how can we reconcile the escalating proliferation of images of *ugly* death with an imperative to conceal or repress the factuality of mortality? How, in other words, reconcile death denial with death display?

To be sure, we might conjecture that both Ariès and Gorer were at least in part wrong. How, after all, could a society that had dwelled so intimately with front-page atrocity photos possibly evade its knowledge of death? Yet to deny what Ernest Becker has called "the denial of death" would itself be to repress an important fact both about human "nature" and about secular Western culture's deepest terrors and defenses. At the same time, however, we might hypothesize that our contemporary death denial isn't just an inevitable human fear but is at least in part a specific function of the raw materiality of the proliferating images of death to which, starting with the First World War and escalating with the Holocaust, the citizens of the twentieth century and beyond have been subjected.

Historians have frequently noted, for instance, that in the post-Holocaust fifties and sixties, following a cascade of horrifying visual evidence of death and destruction, a resonant silence swallowed up the subject of the Holocaust itself, to be followed, in the last third of the twentieth century, by a newly fervent cascade of evidence *and* analysis. Similarly, in a more general sense, modern efforts to sequester the "evidence" of mortality that is the aging/dying body have been followed (or in some cases contrapuntally accompanied) by impassioned "outings" of death and its "symptoms," mutinous revelations ranging from documentaries like the Jurys' *Gramp* to the AIDS photos of the eighties and the often rebelliously grotesque "morgue work" of such photographers as Silverthorne and Witkin. And inevitably, perhaps, these defiant representations of death and dying were accompanied by gentler displays of mortality. Some of these are as innovative as they are affirmative. For instance, *The Last Year* and *Surrounded by Family and Friends*, fabric artist Deidre Scherer's beautiful sequence of stitched deathbed portraits, transform photographic images into richly textured works that, as one critic puts it, combine "craft and fine art in a kind of artistic guerrilla warfare to change people's notions about aging and dying, and, therefore, about living" [fig. 14]. Other efforts of this sort are more commercial, more clearly and perhaps problematically intended for popular consumption. Just as the Holocaust had its heartwarming *Schindler's List*, so what has come to be called the "dying process" at the "end of life" had its *Tuesdays with Morrie*, its *On Our Own Terms*, and its *Barbarian Invasions*.[67]

Whether defiant or conciliatory, however, such documentations of death and dying functioned for modern and postmodern artists as "reality markers" or even, for some poets (for example, Williams and Stevens), as what we might call reality *models*.

Let the lamp affix its beam. The fierce imperative with which Stevens concludes "The Emperor of Ice-Cream" might be a motto for all.

HAUNTING PHOTOGRAPHS

But if photographs of the bodies of the dead or dying frequently work as reality markers or models for a range of artists, it's perhaps even more often on photographs of the (once) living that writers—poets, novelists, and perhaps especially memoirists—brood. Much of the time, it turns out, we

14. Deidre Scherer: *Bigger Than Just Each Other* (2001).

writers aren't just haunted by memories of the dead; as if that weren't bad enough, we're haunted by photographs of the dead, which seem to take the place of ghosts in a culture that no longer believes in what Wallace Stevens rather scornfully called "spirits lingering."[68]

Roland Barthes's *Camera Lucida*, for instance, may at first appear to be "merely" a treatise on photography, but at the center of the book, framed yet never obliterated by the apparatus of theory, there's a meditation on the photograph of a little girl that's also an elegiac memoir of this particular little girl—the author's mother, as she once was. Moreover, if photographs are in any case our modern "ghosts," this photograph is unusually ghostly, since Barthes ensures that although it's the pivot of his book, it's visible to no one but him.

Barthes invests the scene in which he recounts his discovery of what will become a kind of epiphany in black and white with almost gothic tension: "There I was, alone in the apartment where she had died, looking at these pictures of my mother, one by one, under the lamp, gradually moving back in time with her, looking for the truth of the face I had loved. And I found it." Once he finds the photograph, moreover, he devotes several paragraphs of tantalizing, virtually novelistic description and narration to it, explaining: "The photograph was very old [and] just managed to show two children standing together . . . in a glassed-in conservatory, what was called a Winter Garden in those days. My mother was five at the time (1898), her brother seven. . . . I studied the little girl and at last rediscovered my mother [whose image revealed] a sovereign *innocence* [as well as] the kindness which had formed her being immediately and forever, without her having inherited it from anyone."

This photograph, Barthes adds, is crucial in a Proustian way to his mourning. "[M]y grief wanted a just image," he explains, observing that "the Winter Garden Photograph was indeed essential" because "it achieved for me, utopically, *the impossible science of the unique being.*" Yet essential as this image is, Barthes quickly produces a parenthetical proviso: "(I cannot reproduce the Winter Garden Photograph. It exists only for me. For you, it would be nothing but an indifferent picture, one of the thousand manifestations of the 'ordinary.')"[69]

"It exists only for me": Barthes's assertion is, to begin with, open to question, since he after all never knew his mother when she was (as he believes) the little girl in the Winter Garden Photograph. Although he tells us that during her last illness his dead mother had (metaphorically) "become my little girl," in fact the only "*unique being*" she has in this photo of a (real) little girl is as an image or ghost, in whose verisimilitude he believes though he has no direct evidence to support his conjecture. Thus "the just image" that his grief desires is paradoxical, an image of an absence—as a ghost is.

At the same time, because we might suppose, despite Barthes's disclaimers, that this picture would appear as one of the many illustrations in *Camera Lucida*, its very absence, along with its portentously capitalized title, may be what gives it such an uncanny presence throughout his text. In the Winter Garden of memory—objectified here as the poignant sepia space of an enduring never-neverland—the dead mother, who had in her last days "become my little girl," waits with "sovereign *innocence*" for her life (and death) to happen.

She is "sovereign" because, though Barthes might not explain his language this way, he makes it clear throughout his mournful eulogy for his mother that while innocence is sovereign over *her*, she is sovereign of his heart, having added to her abstract maternal goodness the "grace of being an individual soul." But innocence is hers not just in her purity, the way she's untainted and, insists her son, can't be tainted by life, but also because she's innocently free of the knowledge of her life *and* inexorable death, whose date the son meditating on her photograph now knows all too well, and knows with a knowledge that we readers cannot share. For to us, it would be "nothing but an indifferent" date of an *un*different death, one of those "thousand manifestations of the 'ordinary'" that include the countless passages ordained by mortality.

Remember the ghost of Hamlet's father, a spectral image that repeatedly reappears ("Look where it comes again"), seeming to be a perfectly accurate representation of the man "it" had been ("In the same figure like the King that's dead"), yet will "unfold itself" only to Hamlet the son. Just as the Winter Garden Photograph really exists only for Barthes, so the ghost "exists only" for Hamlet, who must question it just the way Barthes, in his moving contemplation of the photograph, interrogates the spectral image of his dead mother.

Yet even while Barthes would rightly have us believe that those who are outsiders to a specific life and death cannot recognize the unique "truth" of an unknown person's *being* in an image like this one of his mother, there are surely many Winter Garden Photographs that function for readers as well as writers to summarize a "sovereign *innocence*" whose bittersweet paper immortality evokes precisely the fleshly mortality that photography transcends.

Think of the famous image of teenage Anne Frank, eager and awkwardly beautiful, smiling on the cover of her internationally best-selling (for many decades) *Diary of a Young Girl*.

Think of the blurrily grave portraits of (the long-dead mother) Anja, (the long-dead older brother) Richieu, and (the now-dead father) Vladek that suddenly disrupt Art Spiegelman's sardonic cartoon iconography in

Maus I and *II*. Each is inserted into the text at a key point: Anja in *Maus I*, when the narrator is reproducing the early strip, "Prisoner on the Hell Planet," in which he depicts the story of her suicide; Richieu as part of his dedication of *Maus II* to this brother an aunt poisoned in childhood to save him from Auschwitz, as well as to Nadja, his new daughter; and Vladek on the next to the last page of *Maus II*, where the author reveals its urgent testimonial meaning for him—and for his readers.

"I passed once a photo place what had a *camp* uniform—a new and clean one—to make *souvenir* photos . . ." begins Vladek, adding: "Anja kept this picture always. I have it still *now* in my desk! *Huh?* Where do you go?"

"I *need* that photo in my book," replies Art, who then exclaims, "Incredible!" as he stares at the photo.

A paradoxical "evidentiary" photo—faked in a studio with an ersatz, "new and clean" camp uniform—but nonetheless necessary to make the "incredible" credible.[70]

And think of the elegant, golden-haired little boy dressed as an eighteenth-century page, who leans toward us from the cover of W. G. Sebald's *Austerlitz*, a representation, as we learn nearly two-thirds of the way through the book, of the protagonist, "*Jacquot Austerlitz, paze ruzove kralovny,*" Austerlitz "himself," in February 1939, dressed as a page for a masked ball in honor of the "Rose Queen" of Prague, a self buried and nearly forgotten until this phantom image surfaces, with its familiar yet foreign-sounding caption, "*paze ruzove kralovny*" ("page of the Rose Queen").[71]

Anne Frank, Anja, Richieu, Vladek, "Austerlitz"—these photographs are all specters like the one Barthes withholds, but we understand at once because of our familiarity with their genre that they are the dead who still live with a life-in-death that's both polar opposite and function of the death-in-life the camera bestowed on them.

Surfacing, disappearing, and resurfacing in our lives and thoughts, these paper surrogates of the (once but now no longer) living represent simultaneous certifications and annihilations of mortality, just as ghosts would. Like ghosts, the subjects of these elegiac photographs once lived as flesh and blood. And like ghosts, the subjects of these photographs now inhabit bodies that are (as we imagine ghosts "bodies" to be) shadows of their once-"real" bodies, occupying a realm that Barthes calls "flat Death."[72]

Memoirists, who are nearly as often poets and novelists as they are writers of nonfictional narratives, display these ghosts for their own contemplation as well as for ours. Often they are both objects of analysis and reality markers. Spiegelman's family photographs certainly function in both ways. And Sebald enriches his memoiristic, quasi-Proustian novels with uncaptioned, sometimes blurry, and often cryptic photographs of places, people, and things whose mysterious resonance seeps strangely into the surrounding prose, illuminating episodes in the straightforward manner we might expect from "illustrations" but also, at the same time, giving what seems to be perhaps fiction, perhaps memoir, an uncanny verisimilitude.

But, as Barthes does too, Sebald deploys photographs not just to contemplate each in itself and to mark or question the "reality" it represents but also to meditate on the intertwined topics of death, memory, and photography. Early in the book, the narrator of *Austerlitz* tells us that his eponymous protagonist, an architectural historian, regularly takes photographs of the sites he studies and that he has entrusted to the narrator "many hundreds of pictures, most of them unsorted . . . after we met again in the winter of 1996." And long before the photo of little Jacquot Austerlitz as a page of the Rose Queen surfaces amid a cascade of lost and found stories, bric-a-brac of the past, "images from a faded world," it has become clear that in the minds of author, narrator, *and* protagonist the dead, memories, and photographs are not only related but in a deep sense equivalent.

Austerlitz discloses, for instance, that as a child in Wales, where he was sent to escape the Nazis, he had obsessively studied a photograph album that contained the only pictures kept by the austere Calvinist couple who adopted him—pictures of the village of Llanwyddyn that was "drowned when the dam [of the Vyrnwy reservoir] was finished in the autumn of 1888." "Sometimes," he remarks, "I even imagined that I had seen one or other of the people from the photographs in the album walking down the road in Bala, or out in the fields, particularly around noon on hot summer days, when there was no one else about and the air flickered hazily." Thus he's drawn to "Evan the cobbler . . . who had a reputation for seeing ghosts" and who tells him "tales of the dead who had been struck down by fate untimely, who knew they had been cheated of what was due to them and tried to return to life." As Evan (and Austerlitz) characterize them, these figures do indeed resemble photographs because "[a]t first glance they seemed to be normal people, but when you looked more closely their faces would blur or flicker slightly at the edges."

Nearly two hundred pages and many years later, when the picture of the small, solemn Jacquot appears, Vera, his old nurse, begins speaking to the

now-grown Jacquot "of the mysterious quality peculiar to such photographs when they surface from oblivion": "One has the impression, she
said, of something stirring in them, as if one caught small sighs of despair
[or] as if the pictures had a memory of their own and remembered us."
Thus just as the dead are (like) photographs, so photographs are (like) the
dead, inhabitants of a realm of memory that is just barely (or perhaps just
barely *not)* retrievable and therefore ghosts with claims of their own on us,
since they feel they have been "cheated of what was due to them."

   Adieu, adieu, adieu. Remember me, groans Hamlet's father as he fades
"on the crowing of the cock." But photography would have weirdly preserved him, disembodied though he is, from such dissolution. He'd be
there, somewhere, though maybe only in the fraying corner of a photo in a
dusty album or secreted, somehow, in one frame of a film or video.

   Austerlitz later spends hours in the Imperial War Museum, studying a
film of Theresienstadt—that "Potemkin village . . . sham Eldorado"—as he
searches for an image of his mother, Agata, later to be found in yet another
photograph in yet another archive. And this research ultimately reminds
him of an Alain Resnais film "entitled *Toute la mémoire du monde,*" which
has gradually "assumed ever more monstrous and fantastic dimensions in
my imagination."[73]

   But doesn't Resnais's collection of moving images sound very like that
huge compendium of stills the *Atlas,* kept by Sebald's countryman Gerhard
Richter, as well as like Sebald's own omniverously photophilic work?
Richter's enterprise has been described by a recent critic as one among a
number of projects undertaken by "European artists from the early to mid
1960s whose formal procedures of accumulating found or intentionally
produced photographs . . . have remained enigmatic," though this commentator does venture that "photographs by their sheer accumulation attempt
to banish . . . the collection of death" whereas "in reality [they] have succumbed to it."[74] Yet perhaps the "enigma" of these projects resides precisely
in their authors' inability to distinguish between "banishing" death and
"succumbing" to it. We can't banish death through photography, as Barthes
reminds us, but the ones we mourn haven't really succumbed to it either so
long as they are part of *toute la mémoire du monde*—the world's unending
accumulation of haunting images.

   Inevitably such icons of memory figure in works that are more obviously autobiographical than Sebald's postmodern Proustian novel. In passages that the critic Nancy K. Miller, herself a memoirist, highlights in

Bequest and Betrayal: Memoirs of a Parent's Death, both the French theorist Simone de Beauvoir and the American novelist Philip Roth focus on
photographs at key moments. And in both cases, the photos in effect
become the people whose images they were, specters to interrogate, like
Hamlet's father.

As she comes to the end of *A Very Easy Death*, her account of her
mother's final illness, Beauvoir writes that there "are photographs of both
of us, taken at about the same time: I am eighteen, she is nearly forty. Today
I could almost be her mother and the grandmother of that sad-eyed girl. I
am so sorry for them—for me because I am so young and I understand
nothing; for her because her future is closed and she has never understood
anything. But I would not know how to advise them." Roth too, concluding
Patrimony, his narrative of his father's last years, turns to the photograph
that's the frontispiece of his book, nostalgically celebrating this "fifty-two-
year-old snapshot" of himself, his older brother, and his youthful father
("We are four, nine, and thirty-six") even while he laments the impossibility of uniting "the robust solidity of the man in the picture with the
strickenness [of the dying man] on the sofa." Yet juxtaposing these sights,
he confides, "I could even believe (or make myself believe) that our lives
only seemed to have filtered through time, that everything was actually happening simultaneously, that I was as much [a child] with him towering over
me as [an adult] with him all but broken at my feet."[75]

Time and its collapse, death and its dizzying denial as well as its fearful
display—these are themes that ache in both Beauvoir's and Roth's sentences. Thus the writer's identification with the photograph that is and is
not the lost parent raises unnerving questions not only about the boundaries between self and (ancestral) other but also about what Sebald
describes as the blur or flicker that separates us from the dead, in whose
funerals, as Beauvoir notes, we attend a facsimile, like a photograph, of our
own obsequies, "taking part in the dress rehearsal for our own burial." And
as if, in a way, photographing these photographs, Miller-as-critic also
becomes Miller-as-memoirist, interpolating into the pages of her book her
own loved, puzzled-over photographs, photographs of herself and her
father, herself and her sister, herself and her mother, including (as in *Camera Lucida*) one of her and her mother that she does not show: "a color
photograph that captures the state of the war between my mother and me
in the mid-sixties. . . . We are alone, fixed in our struggle. [But my] father
likes this picture, which he had enlarged from a color slide and framed."[76]

"We *are* alone." "We *are* four, nine, and thirty-six." "I *am* eighteen, she *is* nearly forty." The narrative present tense into which one naturally falls when describing photographs helps illuminate the aura of perpetual pre-sentness that surrounds these ghostly presences. Inevitably poets, especially those who mourn, muse on this aura, and their grief is paradoxically both healed and exacerbated by it. For precisely what the photograph offers in its lifelikeness—a guarantee that here, just *here*, is the beloved's actual shadow—it withholds in the two-dimensionality through which it reminds us that this is, as Barthes put it, "flat Death."

Paul Monette, for instance, confesses in "Half Life," one of the fierce "eighteen elegies for Rog" in *Love Alone*:

> *I blow up pictures*
> *to 5 by 7 and stare in your eyes and you're*
> *all there more finely boned more grown than I*
> *and always looking at me the cavorting dunce*
> *of the Nikon wild as a tourist with ten minutes*
> *left in Rome*

But now, with Rog hopelessly gone, "life's mostly snapshots"—which is to say, life itself has *become* "flat Death" because the poet's own third dimension, his solidity, has drained away along with his lover's fleshly reality. At the same time, however, the guarantee that such a reality at least *has been* can be found not just in the trivial "snapshots" taken by "the cavorting dunce / of the Nikon" but in the serendipitous "wedding portrait" that Monette describes as "paydirt" found when he was "combing the attic for anything extra / missed or missing evidence of us."

A hitherto undeveloped print taken on a vacation in Tuscany, the picture shows the couple side by side—photographed this time by Brother John, an ancient monk from an even more ancient Benedictine abbey through which he was guiding them—and the writer stresses its sacramental quality by, in a sense, framing his book with it: it appears on the cover, and its provenance is described in "Brother of the Mount of Olives," the concluding elegy. For ultimately, its representation of love *together* rather than the "love alone" that is all Monette has left constitutes the proof of a historical reality that's the bare minimum the elegist seeks. What remains, the poet seems to wonder, after the "remains" have been buried?

the way we laughed the glint in our eyes
as we played our Italian for four hands but my sole
evidence is this sudden noon photograph
the two of us arm in arm in the cloister . . .
[we look] unbelievably young our half smiles precisely
the same. . . .

"Precisely / the same": Monette's enjambments and unpunctuated lines make for telling ambiguities throughout *Love Alone*. Here the double meaning is especially clear. When Rog was alive, the lovers were "precisely / the same"—two halves of a single self—but here, in the photograph, they remain "precisely / the same" as they were, hauntingly so. As if echoing Barthes, in *Borrowed Time: An AIDS Memoir* and a companion volume to *Love Alone*, Monette, a collector of vintage photographs as well as an inveterate amateur cameraman, points out that the portrait photograph displays the "body as memorial, locked in time," simultaneously preserved and inaccessible.[77]

But if some poets long for a loved body whose contours photography so uncannily yet deceptively embalms, others are tormented by exactly the persistence of the image that keeps a dreaded original alive. Perhaps the most famous photograph in contemporary poetry is the picture of Otto Plath that his daughter Sylvia vilifies in "Daddy," a shadow of a professor who stands "at the blackboard" with a "cleft in [his] chin instead of [his] foot." In black and white at the blackboard, "daddy" seems to survive and thrive! Even when his daughter insists that she's "finally through," can we really believe her? As she no doubt did, we suspect the photograph is as immortal as "a devil," and certainly Ted Hughes thought it was.

Years after his first wife's suicide, in one of his *Birthday Letters* to her, Hughes too addressed "A Picture of Otto." "You stand there at the blackboard," he begins, picking up at once one of the key themes of "Daddy": the grotesque persistence of the father's image. Then, also echoing Plath's fusion of himself and Otto, he concedes that he too has become part of the photograph, as if he'd stepped into the realm of perpetual celluloid where the father rules. "Your ghost," Hughes ruefully admits, will be "inseparable from my shadow / As long as your daughter's words can stir a candle."

"They are always with us, the thin people," wrote Plath in an early poem about the dead—the starved, the victims, the scapegoats of Holocaust after Holocaust—adding, incisively, that they are:

Meager of dimension as the gray people

On a movie-screen. They
Are unreal, we say:

It was only in a movie, it was only
In a war making evil headlines when we

Were small that they famished and
Grew so lean. . . .

But as in "Daddy," she intuits here the terrible persistence of the denizens of "flat Death": "their talent to persevere / In thinness" and the menace of their "thin silence."[78]

Yet such two-dimensional people can have voices too, as we know from movie screens and videos. In his prayerful "Fragment," C. K. Williams broods on a video that becomes a perpetual record of dying and therefore a memento mori for self as well as for other:

This time the hold up man didn't know a video-sound camera hidden up in
*   a corner*
was recording what was before it or more likely he didn't care, opening up
*   with his pistol,*
not saying a word, on the clerk you see blurredly falling and you hear—
*   I keep hearing—*
crying, "God! God!" in that voice I was always afraid existed within us,
*   the voice that knows*
beyond illusion the irrevocability of death. . . .[79]

They are always with us, the thin people—alive in their deaths, already dying in their lives, speaking to us with the voice we never want to hear in our own throats but always know we must, someday, hear, the voice that's part of an ongoing "dress rehearsal for our own burial." Probably, then, our engagement with the remarkably new—only century-and-a-half-old—technologies of preservation that have increasingly captured *toute la mémoire du monde* must necessarily be as ambivalent as those of Barthes, Sebald, and all the others. Even as we shrink from the unending factuality of death and dying, the clerk "blurredly falling," the menace of "thin silence" or the equivalent menace of the shriek of fear, we long to see the living, to resurrect the couple radiant in the monastery, the selves we had that were "struck down by fate untimely."

And so the way Paul Monette studies his snapshots of Rog as if he could resurrect him from these, we too, my children and I—on special holidays or maybe my husband's birthday—gather to watch the video where their father still tells his stories of those mythic characters Rabinowitz and Goldberg. My children bring new friends to see *Elliot 1988* and I bring mine, David, who joins our circle of fleshly and ghostly jokesters with kindness and interest. Together we lean forward in our chairs, laughing through our sorrow, and watch what seems like the eternal return of a particular shadow on the screen.

As if we too can say, with Marcellus and Barnardo, *Look where it comes again, / In the same figure like the King that's dead.*

Millennial Mourning

A PRAYER FLAG

Although Zack (Zhe) Zeng was born in faraway Guangzhou, I first encountered his image at an artist's colony in the south of France, where I saw it on what seemed to be a Tibetan prayer flag fluttering on a clothesline at the edge of a nearby terrace.

"It *is* a sort of postmodern prayer flag," my host told me, explaining that one of the resident artists was producing a series of such banners. A minute later he brought me a blue-green square of cotton that I still have. It bears the image of a youthful Asian man with bushy dark hair, thick eyebrows, and a pleasant half smile. Above and below the image is printed (with some letters and numbers obscured):

Any inform . . .
Wengee Pou . . .
917-885-79 . . .
Weight
145 lbs.
Eyes
Brown
Hair,
Short, Black
A Mole at
left eye
Zack (Zhe) Zeng
9/30/1972

The telephone number beginning with "917" has a black square around it, and to the left of the young man's image are faintly scribbled another phone number ("HOME") and an address.

This "prayer flag" replicates, of course, one of the countless, desperate flyers begging for "Any information" that sprang up in lower Manhattan after the bombing of the World Trade Center. Its original was posted by one of Zack (Zhe) Zeng's friends or colleagues—or maybe by his girlfriend ("Wengee Pou . . ."?). Then, along with a number of other flyers, it was photographed by the artist who decided to imprint flaglike squares of colored cloth with such cries for help [fig. 15].

Zack Zeng, who emigrated to the United States at the age of fifteen and earned an MBA from the University of Rochester in 1998, didn't live to see his twenty-ninth birthday. But his face and name and the particularity of his death are flung far and wide, even onto a clothesline in Provence and draped near the desk where I sit at my computer, researching the story of his short life.

I can read quite a few details of that life on the Internet. Zeng's University of Rochester alumni magazine is online, carrying an obituary for him and another classmate who was also killed on 9/11. And in one of those *New*

15. Zack (Zhe) Zeng (2001).

York Times "Portraits of Grief" that pioneered an innovative style of eulogizing suited to the new modes of mourning that the millennium's most startling early catastrophe engendered, a reporter writes:

> *Zhe Zeng was safe. The first plane struck the north tower as he was leaving the Brooklyn Bridge subway stop, and he could have stayed in his Barclay Street office, blocks away from the carnage, at the Bank of New York where he was project manager for American depositary receipts.*
>
> *But Mr. Zeng, 29, who was known as Zack, was also a certified emergency medical technician, and after stopping by his office for some supplies, he plunged into the maelstrom of dust and ash. A news video broadcast later that day showed him working, still in his business suit, over a prostrate form. But he has not been seen since.*
>
> *"It didn't surprise anybody who knew him," said Peggy Farrell, his supervisor. "He was a completely selfless person."*[1]

Even before Zeng's story ran in the *Times*, however, it had appeared in a number of Asian-American and Chinese-language venues. A Web site called TANG BEN'S FORUM noted that though the young man's heroism had not yet been "covered by mainstream media," it was already online in Chinese and added some details about his life and death that the *Times* omitted.[2] And a few months after Zeng was featured in "Portraits of Grief," tributes began to appear in a "Guest Book" at Legacy.com, a Web site devoted to memorializing the victims of the 9/11 attack on the World Trade Center:

> *For those of us who wished to help that day but had not the courage, I wish to thank Mr. Zeng for his sacrifice.*
>
> *January 3, 2002*

> *MAY THE YOUNG HEROIC SOUL OF ZHE ZACK ZENG AND THE SOULS OF ALL THE FAITHFULLY DEPARTED THROUGH THE MERCY OF GOD REST IN PEACE AMEN.*
>
> *May 28, 2002*

The Tibetan word for "prayer flag," I've learned, is *Lung ta*, which means "wind horse." According to one source, these banners, inscribed with blessings and wishes, "are traditionally hung atop mountain summits, outside temples, at crossroads, holy sites, or anywhere open to catch the wind and carry the prayers off." If the terrace in Provence was one such site, the Internet would seem to have become a comparable crossroads, where visitors plant little banners of grief in the hope that something, somehow, may "carry the prayers off."

MOURNING BECOMES ELECTRONIC

As Gertrude Stein might put it, mourning is mourning is mourning. Mourning is weeping at loss and lack and absence. But now, on the cusp of a new millennium, we shape our mourning *differently* from the way, say, our nineteenth-century precursors did. For one thing, the "mythology of modern death," inflected by new technologies associated with death and dying, has presented us with transformed visions of mortality and therefore new approaches to the experience of bereavement. At the same time, hitherto unimaginable technologies of mourning have begun to alter our procedures for grieving.[3] If the techniques of memory and preservation represented by film and video represent one such technology, the invisible but everywhere-and-nowhere realm of cyberspace on which I've been researching the brief, brave life of Zack (Zhe) Zeng represents another. For in fact, nearly a decade before Legacy.com began memorializing victims of 9/11, the grandly named World Wide Web offered mourners some ten "virtual cemeteries" in which they could figuratively erect "monuments" commemorating lost loved ones.

Ranging from the VIRTUAL MEMORIAL GARDEN which contains, by one researcher's count, more than "1,500 memorials to people and over 1,000 memorials to pets," to the VIRTUAL PET CEMETERY, DEARLY DEPARTED, the GARDEN OF REMEMBRANCE, and the CYBER CEMETERY, many of these sites are available free of charge to the bereaved, and a number of them include entries that are quite engaging and often moving. Just as a number of "visitors" want to address words of sympathy and admiration to the lost Zack Zeng in the Legacy.com "Guest Book," many mourners write what I've called "e-mail to the dead" as part of their cyberspace memorials to loved ones. Here are a few such missives:

Kathryn Gibb Dessereau
25 Dec 1923–7 Jan 1995

Gram, you were the best! Not a day goes by that I don't think of you. You lived your life your way. You are a great grandmother now and I wish Steven and Casey could have known [you].

Love, Val

Jennifer Lorraine Gibbons
1963–1993

Jenny, your stern gaze impressed me when I first saw you in the Weekly World News article, "Genius Twins Won't Speak." Below you was the mournful but guarded face of your sister June. . . . As you lay dying before June's eyes, what did you give her to take on her solitary journey? . . .

Honorable Lady Fantaye Nekere
Date of birth: December 25, 1908
Place of birth: Addis Abeba [sic], Ethiopia
Date of death: July 4, 1950
Place of death: Addis Abeba, Ethiopia
Place of burial: St. George Cemetery, Addis Abeba, Ethiopia

Brilliant feminist when almost none existed. . . . This cemetery site is dedicated to your memory.

Your loving son.
Professor Dr. Ashenafi Kebede
USA

Andrew Kevan Shreeves
Name at birth: Andrew Kevan Shreeves
Date of birth: 11.7.75
Place of birth: Wellington, New Zealand
Date of death: 27.10.95
Place of death: Waihi, New Zealand
Place of burial: Waihi Cemetery, Bay Of Plenty, New Zealand

I do not know why you committed suicide Andrew, you took the answer to that question to the grave. I do know that I love you and miss you little brother. I wish I could turn back the clock and change things but I cant [sic]. . . .

Love Karen[4]

Nor do the words of mourners go unnoticed by other wanderers in cyberspace. Many apparently casual readers of the memorials posted in the GARDEN OF REMEMBRANCE, the WORLD WIDE CEMETERY, and other elegiac sites add their own tributes (sometimes called flowers) to the "monuments" they encounter. Some are addressed to individuals. The mother of a baby named Jessica, who was born with a tumor of the spinal cord and died at two and a half months in 1981, composed a memorial to her infant daughter in the middle nineties ("She died in my arms [but] [i]f she had to die, I'm so glad that I was there! [and] I still think about her a lot"), eliciting sympathy from a range of electronic bystanders. "I have a daughter called Jessica and shed [a] tear for you," wrote a man in England. "You have left an impact in my heart," admitted an American woman, and a Canadian man, similarly, wanted to express "deep sympathy at the loss of your precious daughter."[5]

What drives these rapidly multiplying throngs of internet users to tour virtual cemeteries and leave virtual flowers for people who are really—not virtually—dead? Perhaps, along with compassion, many writers are motivated by loneliness, curiosity, and even (or perhaps especially) that fluttering, shadowy fear of mortality we always try but sometimes fail to hide from ourselves; taken together, these feelings infuse the entries of visitors to the GARDEN OF REMEMBRANCE and all those other imaginary graveyards.[6]

But such feelings only partly explain the proliferation of virtual memorial flowers. To understand the phenomenon further, we probably need to think in more detail about how a number of Western cultures have been inclined to treat not only death but also bereavement throughout most of the last century. For never before, as Philippe Ariès has argued, have the twin human necessities of dying and mourning been construed as so scandalous. On the one hand, as we've seen, the twentieth century's medicalization of death "eliminated [death's] character of public ceremony, and made it a private act," and on the other hand, associated with this privatization of death was the "second great milestone in the contemporary history of death": the "rejection and elimination of mourning."[7]

In fact, just as we've relegated the dying to social margins (hospitals, nursing homes, hospices), so too we've sequestered death's twins—grief and mourning—because they all too often constitute unnerving, in some cases, indeed, embarrassing reminders of the death whose ugly materiality we not only want to hide but also seek to flee. When bereavement is itself nearly as problematic as death, however, it's no wonder that sufferers feel freest to air their feelings of loss when they're most alone—at the glimmering computer screen. And it shouldn't surprise us either if words of consolation are easiest to utter when they're articulated in silence, on a keyboard.

THE EMBARRASSMENT OF THE COMFORTER

Grief and mourning as embarrassing reminders of death? How strange to think of embarrassment—with all its connotations of shame, humiliation, social discomfort—as a sensation associated with bereavement. Yet the word "embarrassing" crops up over and over again in memoirs of twentieth-century mourning, starting with *A Grief Observed*, the classic journal the British writer C. S. Lewis produced as he was struggling to cope with the death in 1960 of Helen Joy Davidman, the passionately loved woman whom he'd married in 1956.

Beginning with a confession that he couldn't even mention his sorrow at losing "H.," as he called her in print, to her children from an earlier marriage ("The moment I try, there appears on their faces neither grief, nor love, nor fear, nor pity, but the most fatal of all non-conductors, embarrassment. They look as if I were committing an indecency"), Lewis mused that perhaps this was merely because "[i]t's the way boys are," then went on to speculate that perhaps "the boys [are] right" and even his personal "jottings morbid." For after all, he ultimately conceded, it wasn't "only the boys" whom his grief offended. On the contrary, his very presence seemed almost universally troublesome. "An odd byproduct of my loss," he confided, "is that I'm aware of being an embarrassment to everyone I meet," observing that wherever he went he could sense that those who approached him were uncomfortably "trying to make up their minds whether they'll 'say something about it' or not." Perhaps, he half-seriously speculated, the bereaved "ought to be isolated in special settlements like lepers."[8]

But why would the grieving C. S. Lewis, an eminent author and professor, be an embarrassment to anyone? Have we been culturally conditioned to avert our gaze or *blush* at mourning because, as Ariès claims, we're determined to deny or at least marginalize death? Earlier, in discussing the anxiety that so often shrouds contemporary approaches to death and dying, I quoted David Moller's report of a conversation with a representative of the American Cancer Society who insisted that his organization didn't " 'want to be associated with a book on death. We want to emphasize the positive aspects of cancer only.' "[9] In the same vein, an article that appeared in the late nineties in *Lingua Franca*, a journal of academic life, sought to deflate the supposed sentimentality associated with tearful bereavement by quoting a hard-nosed researcher who reported that "grief-stricken individuals who express intense negative emotions when discussing their loss appear to do worse in the long term, while so-called repressors recover more successfully." Indeed an "odd mourning mini-mall" visited by the author of this story was said to feature "books like *Why Are the Casseroles Always Tuna? A Loving Look at the Lighter Side of Grief.*"[10] Ought we to isolate the sorrowful bereaved "like lepers," then, because we want to be upbeat, to walk smiling into what we long to imagine as the friendly skies of the future? Is it mainly our communal commitment to what used to be called "the power of positive thinking" that conditions the peculiar embarrassment with which we confront bereavement?

No doubt this is a significant part of the truth, just as it's partly true that people visit virtual cemeteries because many Web surfers are lonely or bored. Yet the striking embarrassment about death, dying, and grieving that's explicit in Lewis's journal of bereavement and implicit in the American Cancer Society's anxiety appears so often in the testimonials of mourners that other forces too must surely be at work. Indeed, shortly after Lewis published *A Grief Observed* in 1961, the British anthropologist Geoffrey Gorer produced a groundbreaking examination of such forces. As much of a classic in its way as Lewis's slim volume, Gorer's *Death, Grief, and Mourning in Contemporary Britain* glosses precisely the discomfort with which Lewis regards his own grief.

"At present," declares Gorer, expanding on an insight he outlined in his earlier "The Pornography of Death" (1955), "death and mourning are treated with much the same prudery as sexual impulses were a century ago." Noting that he considers this observation applicable to "all English-speaking countries with a Protestant tradition," he elaborates his point, adding that just as it was once assumed "good women" had "no sexual impulses" and "good men" could "keep theirs under complete control," so today

> it would seem to be believed, quite sincerely, that sensible, rational men and women can keep their mourning under complete control by strength of will or character so that it need be given no public expression, and indulged, if at all, in private, as furtively as if it were an analogue of masturbation. The gratitude with which a number of my informants thanked me for talking to them without embarrassment about their grief . . . *must I think, be similar to the gratitude felt a couple of generations earlier by people when their sexual secrets could finally be discussed without prudery or condemnation [emphasis added].*[11]

Throughout *Death, Grief, and Mourning* Gorer records the comments of one subject after another who bears witness to such embarrassment. An "antique dealer in the South-West" whose father has recently died confides, for instance, that "[p]eople are a little embarrassed to talk about these things, even if they feel quite sorry," while a "recently widowed woman from the South-East" claims that her friends and neighbors "probably felt a little bit embarrassed. . . . I think people tend to be embarrassed if you speak to them." Similarly, a "professional man in the South-West who had lost his 15-year-old boy in a tragic accident" remarks that though the "whole office staff was very, very good," they "were embarrassed in trying to offer sympathy."

More dramatically, in an autobiographical introduction to his book, Gorer remembers that when, after his brother's death in 1961, he'd refused a few invitations to parties with the explanation that he was in mourning, his would-be hosts had reacted "with shocked embarrassment, as if I had voiced some appalling obscenity," perhaps because "they were frightened lest I give way to my grief, and involve them in a distasteful upsurge of emotion." Such reactions, he adds, in a passage that echoes one of Lewis's comments in *A Grief Observed*, would surely explain why his sister-in-law was avoided by friends who "treated her, she said, as though she were a leper." In fact, only "if she acted as though nothing of consequence had happened was she again socially acceptable."[12]

Grief as leprosy, compassion as embarrassing: following Gorer, the German sociologist Norbert Elias commented in *The Loneliness of the Dying* (1986) on "a peculiar embarrassment felt by the living in the presence of dying people" (and by implication in the presence of the bereaved), noting that bystanders "often do not know what to say" because nowadays many "feel uneasy" using traditional phrases of comfort, which "seem shallow and worn-out." More recently Zygmunt Bauman has elaborated on these points in *Mortality, Immortality, and Other Life Strategies* (1992), observing that because for "a few centuries now, death [has] stopped being the *entry* into another phase of being" and been "reduced," instead, "to an *exit* pure and simple," it "has no meaning that can be expressed in the only vocabulary we are trained and allowed to use: the vocabulary geared [to] the collective and public denial or concealment of [death itself]." In our thoroughly secular and science-oriented society, he explains: "We may offer the dying only the language of survival; but this is precisely the one language which cannot grasp the condition from which they [unlike us] can hide no more."[13]

The "leprosy" of grief and the embarrassment of compassion, then, are in the views of these thinkers functions of the death denial that is itself precisely a function of death anxiety. More specifically, as Bauman argues, the "language of survival" that shapes our ordinary way of offering comfort is "an *instrumental* language, meant to serve and guide instrumental *action* . . . a language of *means* and ends"—that is to say, a language of therapy, advice, and admonition, the language of self-help books and "second opinions."[14] But what "second opinion" can follow the grave pronouncement of death? And what admonition to action can be offered either the dying or the grieving?

In an era when "expiration" has been reconfigured as "termination," embarrassed, even dumbfounded responses to mortal pain are probably inevitable. Although Gorer reported in the mid-twentieth century, for instance, that "religion impinges on more British people in early bereavement than on any other occasion in their lives," he also noted that few of his respondents believed in the traditional consolations of religion—the "hope and belief that one's loved ones are in bliss."[15] And of course, when what we assume we "know" is tainted with sheer dread as if with some polluting chemical, we don't want to know what we know yet can't say: the unspeakable.

Perhaps it isn't quite so obvious, though, that the unspeakable is etymologically almost coextensive with the embarrassing. But according to the *American Heritage Dictionary*, our word "embarrassment" is derived from the "French *embarrasser*, to encumber, hamper" and the Italian "*imbarrare*, to block, bar." To be "embarrassed" means to be hindered "with obstacles or difficulties; impede[d]." At least in one sense, then, to be "embarrassed" is to be locked up in a silenced self, a self that can't and perhaps doesn't want to escape the prison of muteness if such an escape means having to confront the literal impossibility of speech about the unspeakable.

For what, after all, can one say about one's friend's or neighbor's or relative's dead loved one if there's no comfort to offer beyond words that now feel "stale" or, worse, *false*? We suppose we ought to murmur, as our ancestors presumably did, "So-and-so is in the arms of God" or "the bosom of Christ," but as Lewis also remarks, most highly educated people simply can't conceive of such a transfiguration. Confessing his own doubts about an afterlife, even the usually devout Lewis, author of such Christian classics as *The Screwtape Letters* and the *Narnia* series, wonders: "Can I honestly say that I believe [H.] now is anything?" and adds: "The vast majority of the people I meet, say, at work, would certainly think she is not. Though naturally they wouldn't press the point on me. Not just now anyway." Not wanting to "press the point," though, that "vast majority" are embarrassed, impeded in their speech, leaving Lewis to muse that he might as well be isolated in a leper colony.[16]

One of Gorer's happier mourners (if one can apply a positive adjective to a person in the throes of sorrow) was a widow who did find comfort in traditional religion, cheerfully explaining to the anthropologist that her husband's cremation was "a marvelous service [and the vicar] read some marvelous passages to me." But then, she noted self-deprecatingly, she was exceptional: "I'm *peculiar*, I believe in the New Testament [emphasis added]."[17]

Yet ironically the belief in the New Testament that inspired such brilliant fantasies as *The Lion, the Witch, and the Wardrobe* and *The Voyage of the* Dawn Treader, failed to comfort their author in the initial extremity of his bereavement. "Only a real risk tests the reality of a belief," Lewis admitted in *A Grief Observed*, adding: "Apparently the faith—I thought it faith—which enables me to pray for the other dead has seemed strong only because I have never really cared, not desperately, whether they existed or not. Yet I thought I did." To be sure, he continued, "Kind people have said to me, 'She is with God.' " Yet he himself, so famously Christian, was nonetheless unconsoled, mourning that in her death his wife had become "like God, incomprehensible and unimaginable."[18]

Was Lewis's faith, then, itself a fantasy, like his vision of Narnia, and was the God who seemed "unimaginable" to him in the turmoil of grief as much a fairy-tale creature as the "Great Lion, Aslan," who sings Narnia into existence during a "stately prowl"? "Childhood is the kingdom where nobody dies," Edna St. Vincent Millay once wrote, hinting that in a way death itself is a secret that "grown-ups" know, perhaps *the* secret that in fact divides grown-ups from children:

> To be grown up is to sit at the table with people who have died,
>   who neither listen nor speak;
> Who do not drink their tea, though they always said
> Tea was such a comfort.

But as such a secret, death is a truth children wouldn't and shouldn't want to hear: neither the children of "H." nor Lewis's child-self.[19]

"For Their Own Good," a dazzling riff by the *New Yorker* cartoonist Roz Chast on the determination of some contemporary parents to maintain death as a "grown-up" secret, comments hilariously on the denial that marks our cultural mourning practices and at the same time analyzes the procedures through which "grown-up" secrecy is preserved. Though her images are charming, Chast's text alone makes her point quite devastatingly:

> It isn't that difficult to shield children from death. "Mommy? Where's Grandpa?" With a little ingenuity, you can keep them in the dark for 15,

*16 years—or even more. . . . Let's say he or she gets curious about cemeter-
ies: "It's a STONE STORE." Pet death? Watch and learn: "What's wrong
with Fifi?" "Quick! Look over there." Do the old switcheroo—"What?
Where? I don't see anything"—and it's like nothing ever happened. [A new
cat is substituted for Fifi.] "Fifi had brown stripes." "No, she didn't." Why
not keep it on a "need to know" basis? After all—who needs to know?
"Grandpa is in the Belgian Congo."*[20]

Are we embarrassed by grief because we don't want to tell the "secret" that
we're surrounded by people who "neither listen nor speak," don't even want
to tell our children that the family cat is mortal? Perhaps, then, such secretive-
ness further explains our hesitancy around the bereaved. Circumlocution is
the rhetorical mode through which we refer to secrets: we talk *around* them
in coded language, with meaningful looks, shrugs, sighs. And it's one way in
which many people in our culture deal with death and the dead.

When more than four decades ago (around the time Gorer was
researching his book) my husband and I came home from Germany in a
military plane that bore, along with us and a number of other army families, the tiny white coffin of our premature baby, our families met us at an
air base in New Jersey. They embraced us gravely, dabbing at their eyes with
Kleenex. "I'm so sorry you had *that trouble over there,*" murmured my husband's favorite uncle, hugging me as the little white box was unloaded from
the aircraft.

Nor did late-twentieth-century would-be comforters, plunged into
confusion by the pain of the bereaved, cease responding to grief with circumlocution, clumsiness, or just plain silence. "What is it about death that
makes people go loony?" a puzzled survivor wrote to the advice columnist
Miss Manners in 1997. "Since my companion of 30 years died unexpectedly [I have] learned that when someone dies, those still living often
abandon their manners. When I called a dear friend from the hospital
emergency room after having just learned there was no hope, his response
was 'I don't feel so good myself; I think I'm coming down with a cold.' Five
days after my beloved died . . . friends began telling me, 'The sooner you
let go, the better.' "[21] Even more recently, in *Losing Malcolm: A Mother's
Journey through Grief,* Carol Henderson offers an astute narrative of an
excruciating voyage through mourning. One notable feature of her
account, along with her precise observations of her own and her husband's efforts to deal with their sorrow, is her record of the inappropriate
responses with which her grief was greeted by a number of embarrassed

bystanders, in particular those who were themselves still (as she puts it) "innocent" of loss.[22]

When she came home from the hospital after her baby's death, Henderson reports, one neighbor "looked up from his lawnmower and then quickly looked down again. I knew he didn't want to talk to me, that he'd already heard the story from his wife, a nurse at the hospital—and the whole thing scared him." Other associates were less subtle. In the "bereavement group" that she eventually joined, the writer and her friends who were also mourning lost babies traded tales of what can at best be called thoughtlessness: grim anecdotes about, for instance, the "childless bachelor" who told Henderson that "losing a child 'seems momentous at the time, but it's really like having one of your kids stay back a year in school. It's not a big deal, ultimately,'" or the friend who responded to a sorrowful confidence (after his death "Malcolm's crying still woke me up at night") with evident surprise: " 'You mean you're still thinking about that?' As if," comments Henderson dryly, "the possibility that I would still be thinking about my dead son three months after he died was totally preposterous."[23]

Such memories, I can ruefully testify, are ineradicable. Was it really more than forty years ago that my husband and I sat at his parents' dinner table when my mother-in-law suddenly asked me how I'd feel if my sister-in-law gave her new son the same name we'd chosen for our little boy, now maybe three months dead? It would really be a tribute, said my mother-in-law, and of course, as Jewish custom has it, it would. After all, she added, "it isn't as though that baby was ever really a *baby*!"

I think I gazed off into the distance, embarrassed—not by what I considered my mother-in-law's failure of imagination but by the anger that was starting to give me heartburn. What I didn't take into account was precisely my mother-in-law's own horror and, yes, her consequent mute embarrassment at our child's death, an embarrassment so grave that in order to cope with loss, she had to convert a real (dead) baby into a nonbaby.

Even while it wounds the mourner, the embarrassment of the comforter is a sign of a wound for which neither mourner nor comforter has proper language.

In the end my sister-in-law didn't use the name whose association with such wounding was so painful. Then, strange as it may seem, I was embarrassed not by anger but by feelings of guilt. Why would I be so childish as to keep another couple from giving their baby whatever name they chose?

My very grief was a source of shame. In fact, I came to believe, the embarrassment and humiliation that I'd thought others were directing toward me were really centered in *me. I*, the mourner, the site of sorrow, *I* was the disgrace. Others were embarrassed because I was an embarrassment! And indeed, if we press further into the entanglements of grief and shame, mourning and embarrassment that so complicate our confrontations with modern death, I suspect we'll discover that at least in our age and culture, it's ultimately the mourner who is embarrassed by her own suffering, encumbered with a weight of woe that fences her around with shame and blocks or mutes her speech.

THE SHAME OF THE MOURNER

Soon after speculating that perhaps "the bereaved ought to be isolated in special settlements like lepers," Lewis confides his belief that to some friends "I'm worse than an embarrassment. I am a death's head." Though he goes on to offer a rational explanation of this view ("Whenever I meet a happily married pair I can feel them both thinking, 'One or other of us must some day be as he is now'"), the aura of anxiety and humiliation surrounding his confrontation with bereavement suggests that his self-definition as "a death's head," a polluting presence, is a feeling that Freud would call "over-determined."[24]

On the simplest level, of course, it's easy enough to see why someone would suppose that if he causes embarrassment in others, he must himself be doing something embarrassing. In his bereavement Lewis evidently imagines that he must appear exactly as grief-stricken as he feels, and perhaps indeed he does. Not only is he in secret the author of "morbid jottings," but he *looks* like the morbid author of such jottings. Perhaps then, it's because he's morbid—a "death's head"—that he ought to be isolated like a "leper." For what if his morbidity isn't just contaminating but contagious? Might one "catch" despair from a mourner as one would catch tuberculosis from a consumptive?

The idea that grief might be catching is on its face frivolous, yet we should note the assumptions that underlie it. From Freud onward, countless psychiatrists and mental health "counselors" have defined the feelings and behaviors associated with mourning as potentially, if not actually, unhealthy. "I know of only one functional psychiatric disorder whose cause is known, whose features are distinctive and whose course is usually predictable. And that is grief," wrote the British psychiatrist Colin Murray Parkes in 1972.[25] And although Parkes might not consider himself a strict Freudian, his definition of grief as a "psychiatric disorder" echoes the Viennese psychoanalyst's discussion of "successful" versus "unresolved" mourning in his classic "Mourning and Melancholia" (1917).

In this influential essay, Freud identifies "the absorbing work of mourning" as not only a task of great magnitude which requires the griever continually to bear witness as "[r]eality passes its verdict—that the object no longer exists—upon each single one of the memories and hopes through which the libido was attached to the lost object" but also a perilous enterprise, threatening the unsuccessful mourner—perhaps the one who cannot disentangle himself from his "morbid jottings"—with the permanent illness of "melancholia."[26] Successful (that is, healthy or good) mourning, in other words, is mourning that ceases to mourn, ceases to cling to grief, as opposed to unhealthy (bad) mourning, which preys on its own misery. Following Freud's essay, a range of other theorists similarly deployed a rhetoric of wellness and illness in analyzing what later came to be called the stages of grief.

In 1940, for instance, Melanie Klein published *Mourning and Its Relation to Manic-Depressive States*, a book that was nearly as influential as Freud's essay. Here she states flatly: "In normal mourning early *psychotic* anxieties are reactivated. The mourner is in fact *ill*, but because this state of mind is common and seems so natural to us, we do not call mourning an illness [emphasis added]." Not much later, in 1944, Eric Lindemann produced a short paper, tellingly entitled "Symptomatology and Management of Acute Grief," in which even while asserting that "acute grief" is "normal," he described a "syndrome" of "somatic distress" along with a range of other sensations and behaviors ("preoccupation with the image of the deceased . . . guilt . . . hostile reactions and . . . loss of patterns of conduct") that he regarded as "*pathognomic* of grief [emphasis added]." He adds that "a sixth characteristic, shown by patients who border on pathological reactions[,] . . . is the appearance of traits of the deceased in the behavior of the bereaved." And even such a staunch defender of traditional grief rituals as Gorer, with his intense dislike of the twentieth-century treatment of mourning as a "reprehensible bad habit," agreed in 1965 that certain modes of extended mourning are problematic, calling "unlimited mourning" a sort of psychological "mummification" and noting that in recent British history the "most notorious exemplar" of this phenomenon was the grief-stricken Queen Victoria, "who not only preserved every object as [her beloved consort] Prince Albert had arranged them, but continued the daily ritual of having his clothes laid out and his shaving water brought."[27]

Of course theorists from Freud to Klein, Lindemann, Gorer, and Parkes were hardly the first commentators to observe that mourning might so feed on its own excess that it would metamorphose into melancholia. What Gorer sardonically describes as "mummification" afflicts a range of Shakespearean characters, from the gloomily paralyzed Hamlet, whose grief at his father's murder turns into what we might now define as a "clinical" depression, to *Twelfth Night*'s moping Olivia, who reacts to the death of a brother by resolving to immure herself in her private apartments for seven years and, "like a cloistress," "veiled walk / And water once a day her chamber round / With eye-offending brine." Comparatively new, however, is the notion that grief itself can be considered, if not actually a pathology, sufficiently *like* a pathology to elicit medical analyses.

Yet from the point of view of the bereaved, who must now consider herself a sufferer from at least the threat of illness, Freud's distinction between healthy mourning and unhealthy melancholia implies that one might need to be cured of grief as one would be cured of a disease and even, indeed, that one might become hypochondriacal about one's sorrow at radical loss. For what if, after all, one isn't doing one's "grief-work" properly? What if one's sorrow doesn't just *feel* but *is* pathological? Without in any way denying the legitimacy of psychiatric or sociological research into the thoughts and acts of mourners, it's easy to see that the medicalization of grief associated with such research is likely to produce a new kind of self-consciousness in those who are bereaved. To what's surely a traditional, essentially moral (and cross-cultural) question—am I doing the right things to honor the memory of the dead?—twentieth-century Western society has added another, distinctively clinical anxiety: Am I *recovering* from the *illness* of grief at the proper rate?

Given that every healthy mourner is potentially an unhealthy melancholic, then, it oughtn't to be surprising that those who are bereaved feel embarrassment, anxiety, even shame. If so magisterial an intellectual as C. S. Lewis feared his jottings were "morbid" and regarded himself as "a death's head," how much more tumultuous might be the feelings of thinkers less self-possessed and less (ultimately) anchored in Christian faith? Surrounded by comforters constrained by the embarrassment widespread social anxieties foster, the mourner who is in the grip of overwhelming emotions feels herself to be an excrescence on the body of her community.

That neither the mourner herself nor her comforters are able to draw upon any culturally agreed-upon procedures for grieving intensifies her embarrassment even while it may further shape her shame. Even after the AIDS pandemic and the catastrophe of 9/11 forced countless contemporaries to confront the not so "positive aspects" of death and dying, the social bewilderment fostered by changing mythologies of extinction continued to inflect a number of sometimes contradictory modes of encountering loss. Grief "therapy," most of it designed to ensure that the bereaved will healthily "recover," is now so widely practiced that although its efficacy is dubious, it's become a lucrative industry, as the physician-writer Jerome Groopman has shown. More radical "spiritualist" counseling is prescribed by Elisabeth Kübler-Ross and her followers, who seek to cheer mourners by arguing that the dead are really alive and well. Dying "can be the most wonderful experience of your life," claims Kübler-Ross, because "[d]eath is simply [a] transition to a higher state of consciousness where you continue to perceive, to understand, to laugh, and to be able to grow."[28]

Predicated on either the tenets of grief therapy or those of spiritualist counseling, peculiarly cheerful do-it-yourself memorial services focus on "celebrations of the life" of the "departed" rather than the pain that his departure caused, while "New Age" activities, from channeling to past life therapy, retool Victorian spiritualism with twenty-first-century technology. Among the thousands of Web sites devoted to these activities, for instance, www.pastlifetherapy.org welcomes internet surfers interested in hypnotherapy with a glamorous home page titled PHOENIX RISING, while www.channel ing.net offers "Spiritual Connection: a Path to Love and Light," proudly noting at one point that "this page has been visited by 315,794 souls since August 1998."

Even stranger strategies for handling grief draw on more radical technologies and practices. In 2001 the *New York Times* reported on the plan of a set of grief-stricken parents to clone their dead ten-month-old baby boy with the help of a "science-loving, alien-fixated sect called the Raelians," who describe themselves online as "the world's largest Atheist, non-profit UFO related organization." In 2002 the *Washington Post* described the project of a Chicago company called LifeGem, which has undertaken to transform "the ashes of your loved one" into "a synthetic diamond." In the view of this company, diamonds, not tears, are a mourner's best friend. After all, as *Post* reporter Libby Copeland put it, "Your loved one was precious," and so is a diamond; "your loved one was beautiful," and so is a diamond; and best of all, a diamond "is forever" so that as a "metaphor, the dead-person-turned-diamond is breathtakingly neat." And in 2004 *New York Times* reporter Craig S. Smith, covering France, bemusedly recounted the wedding of one Christelle Demichel, thirty-four, to her dead fiancé, noting that since 1959 it's been possible "to marry the dearly departed in France" and that hundreds of "would-be widows and widowers have applied for postmortem matrimony since then," presumably just for sentimental reasons since "to avoid abuses, the 1959 law bars such spouses from any inheritance as a result of their weddings."[29]

From real-life therapy to online spiritualism, genetic experimentation, gemstone manufacturing, and posthumous wedlock, this confusing plethora of prescriptions and procedures for mourning supports the view of the sociologist David Moller that the absence of communal "rituals for grieving is reflective of a society that seeks to disengage [pain] from the fabric of everyday social activity." But in such a context, even the so-called stages of dying and grieving become not confrontations of the scandal society would rather avoid but strategies for crisis management, all ultimately serving, as one observer puts it, "a behavior control function for the busy American death professional." Similarly, as Moller notes, the "trivialization of bereavement and pathologizing of mourning curtail" public expression of grief-related suffering" in order to preserve "the public sanctity of [a] pleasure and entertainment ethos." On the mourner herself, however, such maneuvers are bound to leave a mark. If, on the one hand, she doesn't know what to do to "get through" her grief, she is at the least embarrassingly ignorant, perhaps really a fool. If, on the other hand, she can't do what she believes she ought to do—that is, if she hasn't "gotten over it yet," hasn't "moved on" to the "right stage"—then she's shamefully sick, even perhaps monstrous.[30]

A fool or a monster? My husband's uncle may have been tongue-tied and my mother-in-law clumsy, but at twenty-one, just after my baby died, I myself had no idea how to signify my grief for my lost child. I felt foolish when I tried to formulate my feelings about the name I felt ought to belong to him and him alone because he was the baby who had *that* name in our family. I felt monstrous precisely because I feared that my possessiveness about his name was selfish and wrong. And even while brooding on the feelings of foolishness and monstrosity that I was then unable to articulate, I felt that what had happened to me was calamitous because unnatural.

The sorrow of the bereft mother whose infant has died at or near birth is of course particularly horrifying. The replacement of life in bloom or ripeness by the hopeless eventlessness of death is terrible enough, but when life at the start of a story is supplanted by the death which should come only at, and as, an end to a narrative, then reason quails, stymied by what appears to be a desperate oxymoron—death in the place of birth. Childhood may not be, as Millay said, the kingdom where nobody dies, but it's supposed to be, among other things because the mother is supposed to keep it so. Thus, besides feeling foolish and monstrous, I think I feared that I was guilty. Like the suffering animal about whom Browning's Childe Roland remarks that he "must be wicked to deserve such pain," I had somehow done something undefined but nevertheless opprobrious, for which I was being punished.

To be sure, as Elias comments, the "association of the fear of death with guilt-feelings is already to be found in ancient myths"—for example, in the story of Adam and Eve, condemned to mortality for their disobedience. But as Lindemann notes in his 1944 discussion of acute grief, guilt is frequently intertwined with bereavement too. Often, for example, the "bereaved searches the time before the death for evidence of failure to do right by the lost one. He accuses himself of negligence and exaggerates minor omissions." When a pregnancy has gone awry, however, issuing either in prematurity or in a child (like Henderson's baby) born with what doctors call a "deficit," then the mother inevitably wonders if the calamity is a sign of something she *did* that was wrong or if, just as troubling, it's a sign of something she *is* that's wrong, an emblem of an infirmity inherent in her being.[31]

Perhaps not just because childhood is supposed to be the kingdom where nobody dies but also for these last reasons, women whose babies do die often represent what's most terrible, and therefore (in our culture) embarrassing, about bereavement. *Loss*, the bereft mother fears, *makes me into a leper. My loss is shameful so inevitably others feel it may be polluting.*

Carol Henderson is as scrupulous in recording such feelings about her own grief as she is in transcribing the sometimes bizarre comments of onlookers. Summarizing her anxieties to her bereavement group, she wonders aloud: "Did you ever feel like your grief was so enormous [that] you just wanted to disappear . . . ?" But she confesses that even before baby Malcolm died, she had felt sensations of shame as she entered the phase of what's now called "anticipatory" grieving. She'd forced herself to stay cheerful when some workmen were renovating her house as she cared for her sick infant, explaining that she was "trying to pretend everything was fine" as she had done "around the nurses and the doctors" while wondering: "Why the hell did I care so much what the workmen thought of me or my circumstances?" Confiding that she feared "being the subject of people's sympathy [as though she were] some lowly creature . . . a powerless victim of circumstance," she concludes: "Ours was potentially a pitiful scenario and I felt exposed, weak, vulnerable. But I wasn't about to show my feelings."[32]

"Exposed, weak, vulnerable": Henderson later remembers wanting to hide and shrewdly comments that in the past the mourner's veils—the widow's "weeds"—were barriers against the world. "In the bygone days," she remarks, "a person in mourning wore black and was probably treated with deference; people were careful what they said in the presence of the bereaved. . . . Some women even wore black veils. I understood why. I longed for one, a *tangible buffer* against the bustling world around me [emphasis added]."[33]

The shame of the mourner is Job's shame, the shame that wants to hide itself deep in the clefts of the earth, the shame of the one who fears he has been singled out for suffering because he is unworthy of happiness.

Nor is the bereft parent the only mourner who experiences such abjection. As a widow afflicted with what therapists today call "unanticipated" grief, I felt a sorrow that was shadowed by shame, a grief darkened by guilt. I've noted earlier that even as I began drafting the memoir of my husband's calamitous postoperative death—"writing wrong" in an effort to *right* wrong—I was haunted by the fear that *I* was somehow responsible for what had happened, *I* had encouraged the man I loved to make bad medical choices, *I* hadn't (in a thousand ways I could barely conceive) been sufficiently vigilant. And hadn't my husband himself, when first diagnosed with prostate cancer, wondered if he'd done something wrong? Commenting on the way "mortality [has] been deconstructed into diverse events of private death, each with its own *avoidable* cause," Bauman argues that in our time death has come "perilously close to [being] declared a personal guilt" and cites a comment made by sociologist Robert Fulton in 1965: "We are beginning to react to death as we would to a communicable disease. . . . Death is coming to be seen as the consequence of personal neglect or untoward accident."[34]

But surely the wife of the dead man is at least as guilty of "personal neglect" as he himself. If his death was *avoidable*, I must be guilty of failing to help him avoid it. And beyond comparatively rational anxieties, there was a deeper, barely definable shame or anxiety, an oppressive sense that something secretly wrong in *me* had finally been exposed. At last, I feared, everyone could see what I'd always known in some part of myself but cleverly hidden from the world: that I was by nature and destiny unlucky, pitiable, a *loser*! Just as Henderson, watching over her dying baby in grief and terror, nevertheless felt *herself* to be a "lowly creature," a "powerless victim of circumstance," so even as I mourned my husband's untimely death, I felt stigmatized by the tragedy that had befallen *me*.

For weeks, in fact, I hid in my house, though I wouldn't have used the word "hiding" to describe what I was doing. I simply couldn't bear to appear in public, couldn't enter (even) a supermarket or drugstore, so "exposed, weak, vulnerable" did I feel.

In Indian tradition, widows constitute almost a caste in themselves—barred from festive occasions, destined to wear unadorned white and subsist on a punitively austere diet—because they are thought to have helped bring about their husbands' deaths through their own bad karma. With the rare exception of the wife who chooses immolation on her husband's funeral pyre, the widow cannot exculpate herself. The husband's death betokens the wife's inauspiciousness, an indefinable taintedness that clings to her like a bad odor.

In the West, as Lynn Caine pointed out decades ago in her best-selling *Widow*, grieving wives "have to face up to the fact that they have what Robert Fulton calls a 'spoiled identity' " because they " 'are stigmatized by the death of the ones they loved,' " even though we don't explain our stigmatizing of the mourner—our embarrassment at her loss—through theories of evil karma. But arguably, in a culture where loss itself is an embarrassment, every mourner has in some sense a "spoiled identity." Caine comments on the pathos of her meeting with a little "well-dressed, somehow birdlike" woman who introduced herself as "Mrs. Wendell Willkie." (Her politician husband "had died years before. But he was still providing her identity!") Yet equally poignant is the insistence of grieving mothers that they can continue to maintain their identities as the "moms" of their dead babies: "I am Jessica's mom," "I am Malcolm's mom," "I am *still* Claire's mom."[35]

Half selves, the bereft mother no longer a mother, the grieving wife no longer a wife, we have yet another reason for the wish to hide: torn apart, we need a darkness in which to reconstitute ourselves however we can. Gorer describes with a certain wistfulness his mother's "full panoply of widow's weeds and unrelieved black, a crepe veil shrouding her (when it was not lifted) so that she was visibly withdrawn from the world." Though at least one contemporary commentator has accused him of "nostalgia," I can imagine, with Henderson, the relief provided by such a custom, along with the convenience of slowly signaling one's ultimate survival of loss through "the shortening and abandoning of the veil, the addition of a touch of white at the proper calendrical moments," and so on.[36]

After all, yet another reason for wanting to hide—maybe *the* reason for *needing* to hide in a society that dislikes "unseemly displays of emotion"—is the behavior that often accompanies the shock of loss, the guilt of bereavement, the shame of survival. "Out of nowhere I heard a woman screaming," writes Henderson. "Something terrible was happening. Several seconds—maybe it was minutes—passed before I realized the shrieks were coming from my mouth. . . . The dam of numb denial had broken. My shrill cries echoed sharply off the cold brick walls. . . . Suddenly, I seemed to leave my body and look down at myself from somewhere high above me. I saw an unkempt woman, raging like Rochester's crazy wife." Caine too describes such an episode, though one over whose timing she has slightly more control: "It was after six and the building was practically empty. I called the elevator. Pushed the button for the top floor. And I started screaming. Long wailing screams. No words. Like an animal. I pushed the hold button and kept on screaming. It seemed like hours, but it was more like a minute."[37]

In Robert Pope's striking *Family*, the powerful contrast between the darkly contained, impassive figures of the human mourners—holding themselves "together" as their culture prompts them to do—and the blackly howling figure of the dog in the foreground graphically expresses Caine's point [fig. 16]. Just as her screams of grief made her feel *like* "an animal," so, here, the animal howls, on behalf of the reserved and silent family. "The dog is the key to the image," explained Pope.

16. Robert Pope: *Family* (1991).

Just as we no longer "go into mourning," so we no longer keen; we have no oral modes of lamentation. My own mother's Sicilian shrieks of grief for my father had, remember, embarrassed and frightened me. How could I myself have uttered such sounds? Yet inevitably I did, on several occasions. For as Toni Morrison writes in *Sula*, there "must be rage" in the presence of death. "The body must move and throw itself about, the eyes must roll, the hands should have no peace, and the throat should release all the yearning, despair and outrage that accompanies the stupidity of loss." But although such behavior is considered proper in many cultures, most American and British mourners struggle to repress it; in our society, such loss of control is often seen as a source of shame beyond even the guilt of survival. Indeed, as Henderson's and Caine's similes imply, it can seem like a sign of *sub*humanity—bestiality or madness. No wonder the mourner needs to hide. Where Sicilian or Greek lamenters and Celtic keeners place themselves in conspicuous, public positions, beside the coffin, at the center of the wake or funeral procession, we modern screamers automatically try to hide: Caine in an elevator, Henderson near a brick wall, I (at least once) in a closet.[38]

The shame of the mourner is a shame that wants to hide itself deep in the clefts of the earth because it is the shame of the one who cannot bear the suffering for which she has been singled out, the one whose unseemly screams *identify* her as guilty and shameful.

And "morbid jottings" too, as C. S. Lewis knew, can be very much like screams. Thus even Lewis, the great writer of Christian texts and counselor of weak unbelievers, *even Lewis* wanted to hide. He published *A Grief Observed* pseudonymously, under the self-protective name of N. W. Clerk.

MOURNING AS MALARKEY

Given that death is, in Bauman's words, the "most exceptionless of *norms of human existence*"—given, in other words, that everyone sooner or later has to die—it may seem odd that mourners should experience a shame not only inspiring them to want to hide but also requiring extended analysis. If everyone eventually has to die, then surely almost everyone will have to mourn! Yet as if to complete our medicalization of mourning and marginalization of "ugly" death, we do our best to conceal from ourselves the evidence of mortality constituted by the bodies of the dead. Echoing Ariès, Elias notes: "Never before in the history of humanity have the dying been removed so hygienically behind the scenes of social life," and—in a parallel move—"never before have human corpses been expedited so odorlessly and with such technical perfection from the deathbed to the grave."[39]

On the face of it, indeed, the savage social criticism dramatized in Evelyn Waugh's 1948 novel *The Loved One* and Jessica Mitford's 1963 best seller *The American Way of Death*, along with its 1998 sequel, *The American Way of Death Revisited*, seems like an elaboration of Elias's second point, for Waugh's fiction and Mitford's muckrakers focus on what both writers see as the grotesque "technical perfection" with which the modern American "funeral industry" conveys human corpses (as well as the corpses of pets) from the deathbed to the grave. In this respect, in fact, Mitford's acclaimed studies are basically revisionary supplements that add real names and places, facts and figures, to Waugh's devastating satire.

In 1947, hoping to sell the film rights to *Brideshead Revisited*, Waugh journeyed to California for the first time. There he became fascinated by Forest Lawn, which he instantly spotted as "wonderful literary raw material." He outlined his view of the cemetery, shaped by what he defined as an "old-fashioned" (conservative, Catholic) theology, in a talk for BBC Radio that might just as easily have been a description of *The Loved One*'s Whispering Glades. Noting that embalming "is so widely practiced in California that many believe it to be a legal obligation," he went on to describe what he considered some of the salient features of Forest Lawn:

> *Behind the largest wrought-iron gates in the world lie three hundred acres of parkland judiciously planted with evergreen, for no plant that sheds its leaf has a place there.*
>
> *The visitor is soothed by countless radios concealed about the vegetation which perpetually discourse the Hindu Love-Song and other popular melodies, and the amplified twittering of caged birds.*
>
> *We are very far here from the traditional conception of the adult soul naked at the judgement-seat and a body turning to corruption. In Forest Lawn, as the Builder claims, these older values are reversed. The body does not decay; it lives on, more chic in death than ever before, in an indestructible class A steel and concrete shelf. The soul goes straight from the Slumber Room to Paradise, where it enjoys an endless infancy. That, I think, is the Message.*[40]

"No plant that sheds its leaf has a place there." Forest Lawn's sham evergreen facade, as well as its other instances of cultural and biological artifice ("the Hindu Love-Song [and] the amplified twittering of caged birds") were especially repellent to Waugh not just because they represented the sentimentality and vulgarity of the place's quintessentially American "Builder" but, more to the point, because they were manifestations of what he found most damnable about the cemetery: its foundation in the practice of embalming, the notion that the body *can* somehow "liv[e] on, more chic in death than ever before." For Waugh, indeed, as for Mitford after him, the "American way of death" would seem to have been an offense against life itself since it was based on a profound refusal to accept the material death that is inextricably part of fleshly life—based, that is, on an insistence that the body "does not [read, *need not*] decay."[41]

That the body might not only be made to "live on" through embalming but even made, through cosmetology, to live on "more chic in death than ever before" was equally repellent to Waugh, as, later, to Mitford. For if to em*balm* is to deny death by (literally) perfuming (em*balming*) decay with sweet unguents, to decorate the face of the dead with makeup is (literally) to *make up* a new, unreal version of reality. Both embalming and cosmetology, after all, are procedures through which the dead are brought to masquerade as living; through these procedures the "modern" technologist with the scientific-sounding name "mortician" helps deny death by forcing it to imitate or impersonate life.

But to deny death in this way, Waugh and Mitford both imply, is to hide it, not as Victorian mourners hid their grief in "unrelieved black" but in a manner that either absurdly refuses or weirdly falsifies grief itself. Indeed, from any rational perspective, both also suggest, such an effort at hiding death is literally (because etymologically) "grotesque." Not only does our word "grotesque" mean "characterized by ludicrous or incongruous distortion," but it's derived from the Italian *grottesca* (signifying "of a grotto"), which in its turn is derived (via the Latin word *crypta*) from the Greek *kruptein*, meaning "to hide." And what, as both writers imply, is more grotesque than a dead body that impersonates a living man or woman, a cemetery that imitates a pleasure park, a chapel of the dead that masquerades as a "slumber room"?

As if to emphasize the distortions of reality that are the rule in Whispering Glades, Waugh populates his American graveyard with figures who allegorize the grotesque. Two of the most prominent are the novel's naive heroine, Aimée Thanatogenos, and her oleaginous suitor, Mr. Joyboy. Aimée is a "junior cosmetician" who was named in honor of the popular radio evangelist Aimée Semple MacPherson and whose art has been bizarrely inspired by her study of the corpse (and corpus) of the best-selling poet Sophie Dalmeyer Krump. Equally bizarre, Mr. Joyboy is the chief embalmer, who moves among his adoring assistants "like an art-master among his students" and whose conversation sounds "as though there were an amplifier concealed somewhere within him and his speech came from some distant and august studio."[42]

The connection of these two with what we now call the "media" is of course crucial. As Waugh repeatedly demonstrates, Whispering Glades (like its original, Forest Lawn) is really an outpost of Hollywood, although where the "solid-seeming streets and squares" of "the Megalopolitan Studios" are no more than "plaster facades," the cemetery's imitation chapels, cottages, and castles are "three-dimensional and permanent," even if "as everywhere in Whispering Glades, failing credulity [has to be] fortified by the painted word":

> This perfect replica of an old English Manor, a notice said, like all the buildings of Whispering Glades, is constructed throughout of Grade A steel and concrete with foundations extending into solid rock. It is certified proof against fire earthquake and   Their name liveth for evermore who record it in Whispering Glades.
>
> At the blank patch a signwriter was [replacing] the words "high explosive" [with the words] "nuclear fission."[43]

"Liveth for evermore"? The urgent, arrogant denial of death articulated throughout Whispering Glades in "Grade A steel and concrete" and written, as well, in the fluids of the embalmer and the cosmetologist is echoed in the language that insists on the authenticity and longevity of replicas. Assertions of invulnerability are crossed out and revised, just the way dead lips are made to smile and dead bodies to assume appropriate "poses." Even the novel's protagonist, the ambitious young English poet Dennis Barlow, is infected by the lies that inhabit this anti-Edenic garden built by the "Dreamer" who was its founder. In his efforts to woo the seductive Aimee Thanatogenos, Dennis plies her with poems cribbed from a veritable anthology of English verse, all masquerading as his own original work.

Despite his lamentable proclivity for falsehood, however, Dennis is virtually a Candide in his exploration of the American ways of death on display at Whispering Glades. Waugh records with some glee the poet's search for "suitable clothes" in which to attire his friend Sir Francis Hinsley, who has just hanged himself in despair after being fired by the Megalopolitan studios. Explaining that "a casket-suit does not have to be designed for hard wear," an efficient "mortuary hostess" shows Dennis a garment that is "the apotheosis of the 'dickey' "; though it looks "like a suit of clothes," it's "open down the back," with faux cuffs, collar, and waistcoat. At Whispering Glades, even what appears to be clothing is only "in appearance like a suit of clothes," and its very trickery, reveals the hostess, is an "idea [that] came from the quick-change artists in vaudeville."[44]

But if the "casket-suit" provided by Whispering Glades is as comic as a vaudeville turn, the effects of the embalming procedures and cosmetological operations performed on Sir Francis are positively gruesome—or perhaps, more accurately, gruesomely positive. In particular, "the face which inclined its blind eyes toward him" was "a painted and smirking obscene travesty by comparison with which the devil-mask Dennis had found in the noose was a . . . thing an uncle might don at a Christmas party." Shocked by this alien object, Dennis wanders off to a replica of Yeats's "Lake Isle of Innisfree," where he's actually inspired to pen a poem of his own, albeit one haunted by rhythms "from the anthologies," in which he laments the dead Francis Hinsley, first "hung / With red protruding eye-balls and black protruding tongue," now "pickled in formaldehyde and painted like a whore, / Shrimp-pink incorruptible, not lost nor gone before."[45]

Describing a "Loved One . . . who was found drowned" and not at all "presentable," the "mortuary hostess" offering Dennis a "casket-suit" has suddenly and "disconcertingly [lapsed] from the high diction" of euphemism universally employed at Whispering Glades to declare: "They fixed that stiff . . . so he looked like it was his wedding day. The boys up there surely know their job." But as the young poet's encounter with his patron's cadaver demonstrates, the "job" the embalmers and cosmetologists "surely know" travesties the onetime life of the body much as their euphemistic language betrays the truth of death.[46]

Although Jessica Mitford's *The American Way of Death* was intended primarily as an exposé of the cynicism and greed motivating the "funeral industry" in the United States, this book also dealt with the grotesque modes of death denial that shaped and were shaped by embalming, cosmetology, and euphemism. And exactly fifty years after Waugh had published *The Loved One*, Mitford was still returning obsessively to the same themes, in an "updated" version of the work, whose title, *The American Way of Death Revisited*, implies a subtle homage to the author of *Brideshead Revisited*. Reviewing the original version of what he called "Miss Mitford's jolly book," Waugh claimed to "sniff" in it "a resentment that anyone at all (except presumably writers) should make money out of anything," for although he conceded that the "presence of death makes the activities of undertakers more laughable," he believed that Mitford would "have the same scorn for hatters or restaurateurs."[47] But in fact, like Waugh himself, Mitford seems on the surface to have been at least as troubled by death and its denial as by death and the dollars to be wrung from it.

Early in *Revisited*, for instance, she describes in some detail "the live demonstration by Dina Ousley, luscious blond president of Dinair Airbrush Systems, of her maquillage as applied to corpses," noting that "Ms. Ousley thinks there would be much less demand for direct cremation" (a bane of what, Mitford gleefully notes, is now called the "death care" business) "'if 'people didn't look so dead—if they looked more alive.'" Hence the author reports that an "appreciative audience" gathers around as Ousley (who also sells her products to stage and screen performers) "deftly" sprays "the face of Max Carroll, owner of a Stockton funeral parlor, standing in (or rather lying in) for the cadaver." Ousley claims, adds Mitford, that she's had "a wonderful success on the [I]nternet," selling "to mortuaries from Ireland to Argentina," because her "Glamour Kit" is "the ultimate *camouflage* [emphasis added]."[48]

But if cosmetology involves a form of "camouflage," embalming, despite its promise of preservation, is also little more than a disguise. Although "a body can be preserved for a very long time indeed," Mitford observes, such a body doesn't "look very pretty," tending instead "to resemble old shoe leather." Thus, explaining that the sort of "dilute" embalming fluid used in most American mortuaries is designed to preserve no more than appearances, she quotes a telling passage from a standard textbook, *The Principles and Practices of Embalming*, which decrees that "to us the creation and maintenance of a lifelike naturalness is [*sic*] the major objective, and post-burial preservation is incidental."[49]

Just as offensive an instrument of camouflage as the embalmer's needle or the cosmetologist's brush, though, is the euphemist's pen (or, less euphemistically, his keyboard). Indeed, from Mitford's highly literary perspective, as from Waugh's, euphemism might be said to subsume all the other modes of death denial prevalent in America's Forest Lawns and Whispering Glades. One of her discussions is therefore devoted to the manual for salespeople in which one "death care" corporation lays out linguistic do's and don't's, warning: "CERTAIN WORDS AND PHRASES long associated with cemeteries sometimes increase sales resistance because they suggest images of a negative, morbid, and depressing nature." A "partial list of SCI's deathless words," according to Mitford, would include:

Casket Coach	not	Hearse
Display Area	not	Casket Room
Interment Space	not	Grave
Opening Interment Space	not	Digging Grave

In the end, adds the author, ironically: "The gravedigger has a problem. He may not fill the grave with Dirt, he must fill it with Earth. His task will be preceded not by a Funeral, but by a Memorial Service. The decedent was not Sick, he was Ill. And he didn't Die, he Passed On. His remains were not Embalmed, they were Prepared. There were no Mourners present for the Service, only Relatives and Friends."[50]

Both Waugh and Mitford are so sardonic in their representation of twentieth-century American modes of mourning and memorializing the dead that one inevitably wonders with what mythologies of (modern) death they might replace the Forest Lawns of California and the Whispering Glades of, say, the Midwest. Waugh's theology is of course clear enough. As a Catholic, he was committed to "the traditional conception of the adult soul naked at the judgement-seat" and the concomitant notion of the material "body turning to corruption." Yet such orthodoxy would seem to have no significant future in "Megalopolitan" Los Angeles. In this dystopia, doomed by her name, if not her job, the gentle Aimée falls victim to the drunken advice proffered by one "Guru Brahmin," a columnist impersonated by the alcoholic "Mr. Slump," who casually tells her to "go take a high jump." That she instead kills herself with a lethal injection of cyanide in Mr. Joyboy's embalming room is perhaps more appropriate to the themes Waugh pursues throughout *The Loved One*, but that she ever might have had a significant alternative to the belief system in which she's trapped is out of the question. By the end of the book Dennis Barlow, now openly a surrogate for the novelist himself, has begun planning "an opus on the subject" of Whispering Glades, but as he blithely assures Aimée, if she should ever "come to read it," she wouldn't understand "a word of it," or indeed of the "old-fashioned" assumptions about living and dying that inform its *saeva indignatio* toward the American way of death.[51]

As a bracingly atheistical former Communist, however, Mitford espoused no views as regressive as Waugh's Catholicism. On the contrary, the poet-essayist Thomas Lynch reported after interviewing her two surviving children that "Decca, being a Communist, did not believe in 'that pie in the sky when you die thing.'" But how, then, would she propose that we handle death and dying? Although at one point in *Revisited* Mitford herself nostalgically celebrates the fact that in "the English countryside, the style and conduct of funerals are . . . pretty much unchanged from time immemorial," a little further research reveals her as stereotypically stiff-upper-lip old school English in her attitudes—not, in fact, unlike Gorer's painfully embarrassed subjects.[52]

To be sure, by establishing "English Country Funerals" as a standard against which she measures American ways of death, Mitford implicitly concedes that for some mourners at least, there's a need for communal grieving and public memorializing. However, her ideal service for the dead (the funeral "of a retired farm foreman who bred his own Shire horses") sounds like an event in a Merchant-Ivory film, to which the local squire might come out of a sense of obligation to his "people," rather than a ritual occasion at which a muckraking radical would feel at home. A friend of Mitford's evidently described this ceremony in a letter to the author, noting that the "tiny church was packed," the coffin was carried through the snow by "a dray drawn by a Shire," and the "farm men lined up outside the church and made an arch of pitchforks when the coffin was carried out." Conceding that she was moved "to tears," Mitford's friend added that "a village funeral is a killer, far worse than a big London affair."[53]

Of course Mitford knew perfectly well that even if such a funeral was a consummation devoutly to be wished, it was a most unlikely one. Thus, denouncing the "big London affair" as well as its commercialized American cousins, she chose to preach the virtues of cremation, a method of body disposal that ordinarily precludes embalming and cosmetology, while nevertheless, in the modern way, "expedit[ing] the dead] odorlessly," and with "technical perfection from the deathbed to the grave" or urn. Cremation, she writes in the 1963 edition of *The American Way of Death*, offers "a simple, tidy solution to the disposal of the dead. . . . It is applauded by rationalists, people concerned with sanitation, land conservation and population statistics, and by those who would like to see an end to all the *malarkey* that surrounds the usual kind of funeral [emphasis added]."[54] And though many pages of *Revisited* are devoted to the strategies through which today's entrepreneurs of "death care" manage, nonetheless, to extract money from grieving families (for fancy urns and "cremation containers," niches in columbaria, even in some cases cosmetology in preparation for preincineration "viewing"), she herself chose to be cremated.

In fact, before she died, Mitford arranged with customary flamboyance that following her cremation her research assistant, Karen Leonard, would send the letter below to a funeral industry representative. Somewhat surprisingly the text of the missive appears on a disconcertingly elaborate JES-SICA MITFORD MEMORIAL (WEB)SITE. Some key passages:

> *As you have probably read in* The New York Times *today, Ms. Mitford has "passed away". Prior to her death, she and I discussed her final arrangements. I think you would be delighted to know that you were in her thoughts. . . .*
>
> *Ms. Mitford feels that you should pay the bill. In her own words "after all, look at all the fame I've brought them!"*
>
> *Enclosed you will find the statement of funeral goods and services selected. I'm sure you will appreciate her frugality. I think you will particularly like the price of $15.45 for the cremation container.*[55]

Addressed to an executive of SCI, a major player in contemporary American "death care," this letter is charmingly insouciant and particularly comical in its concluding quotation of "the price of $15.45 for the cremation container," especially considering that as Leonard goes on to say, "While looking through SCI's price lists . . . we couldn't find a cremation container for under a couple of hundred!" Certainly Mitford herself would seem, at least in her own death, to have brought to an end "the malarkey that surrounds the usual kind of funeral."

Did she end the malarkey, though? And is ceremonial mourning, despite the bad rap its more grotesque American manifestations get in *The Loved One* and in both Mitford volumes on the subject, anything more than mere malarkey?

Thomas Lynch's interview with Mitford's two surviving children suggests that this author's definition of mourning as malarkey may have itself been a kind of defense mechanism designed to help her cope with personal loss. Indeed, if Lynch's interpretation of Mitford's life is correct, then we might read both *The American Way of Death* and *Revisited* as extended evasions of grief, for certainly bereavement is a key subtext of both works.

Himself a funeral director as well as a writer, Lynch has professional reasons for seeking to undermine Mitford's attacks on his business, although he argues that her work had a significant impact "on the customs and culture of funeral practices in this country" and praises the author herself as "nothing if not a wit."[56] But the facts he discussed with her oldest daughter, Constancia Romilly, and youngest son, Benjamin Treuhaft, are indisputable even if susceptible to a range of interpretations. Yet Mitford herself rarely mentioned them, nor are they included in the biographical material that appears on the JESSICA MITFORD MEMORIAL SITE.

In the late thirties, married to her cousin Esmond Romilly, Mitford had a baby daughter, Julia, who died of measles. In 1941, Esmond was shot down in an air battle over Britain. In 1954, after she'd married the American lawyer Bob Treuhaft, her son Nicholas, ten, was "killed when a bus hit him on his bicycle half a block from their home in Oakland." And though her memorial site does devote a few sentences to her grief for Esmond (testifies a friend, Virginia Durr: "She used to wake up at night and I would hear her weeping"), her two dead children might as well never have existed.[57]

Writes Lynch: after Nicky's death, " 'We went dysfunctional,' the siblings both say now. . . . We never talked about it again. It was as if Nicky was eradicated from the family,' " for, given Mitford's atheism and her dislike of psychotherapy, there was "no god to get mad at and no doctor to talk to," so that "we did our best but we didn't do very well." Significantly, the first version of *The American Way of Death*—with its theme of mourning as malarkey—was begun not long after Nicky was killed, in the "mid-to-late 1950s," ostensibly because in Mitford's words, "my husband, Bob Treuhaft, got fired up on the subject of the funeral industry."[58] But for Mitford, mourning had very likely metamorphosed from malarkey to muckraking because like so many of the English subjects Gorer was interviewing in this period, she considered the public expression of grief a kind of behavior that ought to be "indulged, if at all, in private, as furtively as if it were an analogue of masturbation." As her friend Virginia Durr put it, despite her radical politics and her inclination to make "a joke of everything," "Decca" could "be terribly arrogant and upper class," and though she was "a very feeling person," she kept her emotions "under very tight control, I must say."

Making "a joke of everything" is also of course a way of repressing—or at least keeping "under very tight control"—that which is embarrassing or, worse, painful, frightening, even horrifying. Given their common dislike of falsehood, neither Waugh nor Mitford wished to evade death's often grisly physical reality. Waugh's Dennis is haunted by an image of the hanged Sir Francis, "the sack of body suspended and the face above it with eyes red and horribly starting from their sockets." And Mitford, interviewing a professor of pathology, dwells at some length on his descriptions of the depredations wrought by the "putrefactive bacteria" that inhabit corpses. Eventually, though, both writers found ways to transform horror into humor, Waugh through Dennis's parodic jingle about dead Sir Francis Hinsley and Mitford through a ludicrous anecdote about the way the body of Queen

Elizabeth I, lying unburied in a "sealed, lead-lined coffin . . . for an uncon-scionable thirty-four days before interment," finally "burst with such a crack that it splitted the wood, lead and cerecloth."[59]

Arguably, then, both Mitford and Waugh struggled in their macabre comedies to cope with the "ugly and dirty" secrets of death and grief. Para-doxically, we might even speculate that these writers who so loathed the grotesque deceptions represented by the death-denying practices of embalming, cosmetology, and euphemism were themselves hiding not just their horror of death but also their embarrassment at what they considered unseemly modes of mourning by transforming "vulgar" expressions of grief into comic spectacle. But that besides satirizing the lugubrious masquer-ades on show throughout America's Forest Lawns and Whispering Glades both writers tended rather xenophobically to associate such shams with racial, class, or ethnic others may also have been an inevitable consequence of the "terribly arrogant and upper class" Englishness that inspired them to emphasize stiff-upper-lip control over what Gorer saw as the "distasteful upsurge of emotion" his English friends, too, sought to avoid.

Plainly seeking a laugh, Waugh has a boatman ferrying Dennis Barlow to Whispering Glades' imitation "Lake Isle of Innisfree" tell the young Eng-lish poet that it's not the Irish but "mostly the good-style Jews we get here. They appreciate the privacy. It's the water you see keeps out the animals." And as part of her tirade against embalming, Mitford declares that the prac-tice of preserving, decorating and displaying dead bodies "has its origin in antiquity—but not in Judaeo-Christian antiquity. This incongruous behav-ior towards the human dead originated with the pagan Egyptians."[60] That an "English Country Funeral" might not seem as "natural" to people from non–Anglo-Saxon cultural backgrounds as it did to her evidently never occurred to Mitford, just as it evidently never occurred to Waugh (who ded-icated The Loved One to Decca Mitford's older sister Nancy) that a vision of "the adult soul naked at the judgement-seat" might not constitute every-one's "traditional conception" of the afterlife.

What in the world would these two upper-crust English writers have thought of a recent Washington Post story reporting that "the dead are immigrating" because Asian-Americans in great numbers are bringing their ancestors' ashes to the United States, whose "wide-open fields" seem to them "perfect for honoring the dead with prodigious grave sites designed with the principles of feng shui for the free flow of energy"? Are Chinese burial customs also "malarkey"?[61] And the ritual cremations of Indian tra-dition? And the "Towers of Silence" on which the Parsis, following the rules of Zoroaster, expose the bodies of their dead to the appetites of vultures in order to avoid "the smallest possibility of polluting the earth, or contaminating a single living being dwelling thereon"?[62]

To be sure, despite the embarrassment and insularity with which Waugh and Mitford reacted to grief, both authors shed a scalding light on the most manipulative practices of the twentieth-century American "death care" industry. But as observers from Gorer to Bauman have argued, *all* mourning isn't altogether malarkey. In fact, as the late *Newsweek* columnist Meg Greenfield once noted, "crows have funerals, or something akin to funerals, for other crows," and elephants too have been observed to grieve almost ceremonially for their dead.[63] But of course even more than most animals— more than most because we're *talking* animals—we humans need to mourn, to grieve, to weep communally. We need "malarkey": not the lies of Whispering Glades, not the simulacra of "life" that trick us into overlooking death's reality, but frank words that speak the sorrow of the dying and those who survive them.[64]

After Jessica Mitford died, as it happens, more than six hundred mourners gathered to memorialize her in San Francisco. According to one newspaper account, a "glistening funeral hearse . . . held photos and memorabilia from her long career" and not far away, in an acknowledgment of her "standing joke that she wanted an elaborate funeral with 'six black horses with plumes,'" stood "six black horses with plumes, pulling another hearse, followed by a 12-piece brass band."[65]

As her daughter Constancia told Thomas Lynch, mourning is what survivors need to do: "The person who dies doesn't get to say anything about their funeral. . . . No matter how many books they might have written about it. The funeral is for the people who are left behind."[66]

RITUAL OFFERINGS

Recollecting the spirit in which she designed the Vietnam Wall, arguably the most successful war memorial produced in the twentieth century, architect Maya Lin remembered feeling that "as a culture we were extremely youth oriented and not willing or able to accept death or dying as a part of life," and thus the "rites of mourning . . . have been suppressed in our modern times." But how do we mourn, how *can* we mourn when even those who don't fear that mourning is malarkey may find themselves, along with writers from C. S. Lewis to Lynn Caine and Carol Henderson, embarrassed by grief or shamed by loss?[67]

On the one hand, considering the many cultural valedictions forbidding mourning that we're all likely to encounter, the question is unsettling. On the other hand, considering that even the skeptical author of *The American Way of Death* ended up with a highly visible, carefully structured memorial service, it's almost unnecessary. For like Decca Mitford's family or like the crowds of visitors to Lin's Vietnam Veterans Memorial, most "people who are left behind" do, with increasing unself-consciousness, find ways to grieve, even in an era marked by the apparent "rejection and elimination of mourning" that Ariès considered a "milestone in the contemporary history of death." In fact, some of our millennial modes of mourning are as defiant of social euphemisms about death and grief as Waugh and Mitford could want, even while in some cases these relatively new mourning customs flout precisely the traditional decorum of the "old-fashioned" services to which both writers were nostalgically attached.

What Walt Whitman called "the tolling tolling bells' perpetual clang" was heard worldwide in September 1997, for instance, as the funeral cortège of Diana, princess of Wales, passed through the flower-banked streets of London. A few weeks later, describing what he scornfully called "the kitsch of the Diana shrines," Adam Gopnik exclaimed in a *New Yorker* essay entitled "Crazy Piety" that "for two weeks good gray London took on the look of Lourdes or Fatima, with vast heaps of floral bouquets and honey-colored Teddy bears and hand-scrawled messages that seemed less like funeral tributes than like the contents of some vast piñata, filled with party favors, that someone had broken above" the city.[68]

As countless other visitors to London in that period of apparently unlikely, even bizarre ritual mourning testified, some ten to fifteen thousand tons of flowers and countless stuffed animals were only the most familiar of the "funeral tributes" that appeared, memorializing Diana, outside Kensington Palace and throughout the public parks of London. The much-described " 'grave-gifts' of toys, tokens, letters, poems, photographs, votive candles [and even] playing cards," one friend told me, were supplemented by bottles of wine leaning against the trunks of trees, while here and there offerings of foods lay beside them or festooned the branches.[69] Aerial photos showed that the "field" of flowers extended at least several acres beyond the fence surrounding the dead princess's official residence, but, said my friend, few pictures could capture the eeriness of the groves of "tributary" trees in, say, Kensington Gardens.

Indeed, as most of the millions who watched will also recall, the princess's funeral ceremony was marked by a similarly odd concatenation of the traditional and the trivial, craziness and piety, sentimentality and solemnity. Anglican ritual and Elton John, the grave words of the King James Bible and the warble of the American Bible Belt echoed through Westminster Abbey like radio frequencies colliding in the stratosphere. "Brightness falls from the air / Queens have died young and fair," lamented Thomas Nashe in the 1590s, and "Goodbye England's rose. . . . This torch we'll always carry / For our nation's golden child," crooned Elton John, recycling not Nashe's poem but his own slightly earlier tribute to another queen who died young and fair, Marilyn Monroe, as he produced what was to become one of the greatest hits of the decade. Well, conceded Gopnik, in the excesses of the princess's funeral, which was "in many ways a triumph of the popular, intuitive version of the Old Religion [i.e., Roman Catholicism] it was possible to discern a glimmer of religious feeling, of a very traditional kind."[70] But in one sense, anyway, the funeral itself was almost as *un*traditional as the vaguely pagan "spontaneous shrines" that sprang up throughout London (and ultimately in many other parts of the world) soon after the news of Diana's fatal car crash had been broadcast. For like the stacks of flowers, banks of votive candles, and other tokens of mourning, the service in Westminster Abbey was shaped by what some commentators came to consider at best a kind of vulgar *popular* pressure and at worst "mass hysteria"—shaped, that is, from "below" rather than, like most royal obsequies, by hierarchical fiat from "above."[71]

To be sure, as the former wife of the crown prince of England, Diana was so closely associated with the monarchy that her death might seem to have functioned, straightforwardly enough, the way the deaths of rulers almost always and everywhere have: as a "symbolic paradigm of our own deaths and the meaning of death itself." And indeed in a sense it did, but far more subversively than the usual royal demise. For as a range of cultural commentators theorizing what one critic rather pretentiously calls "the Diana events" have pointed out, Diana was from the perspective of "ordinary" onlookers around the world a glamorous transgressor who became the object of "many *transferred feelings*" precisely because of the problems that put her in ill favor with the autocratic queen, her former mother-in-law and the grandmother of her two sons.[72]

Comments the critic Diana Taylor, the wayward princess's "vulnerability, unhappiness and physical distress only contributed to her popularity, for, as someone noted, the unhappier she was, the better she looked."[73] More seriously, though, because media representations cast Diana as a compassionate hospital visitor and a committed crusader against land mines, as a charismatic rebel against Buckingham Palace's icy mores and a betrayed wife, as a victim of bulimia and a jet-setting playgirl, as a widely admired mother and a social martyr, she became a different kind of representative royal—became in fact the fairy-tale young queen of hearts whom Tony Blair was astutely to label "the People's Princess."

Because of this multifaceted glamour, "Diana, or the Diana figure, was," as sociologist Richard Johnson puts it, available to a huge public, which "made her a rich resource for the cultural and psychic work of others." Thus, as many observers remarked, her death provided a "theatrical opportunity through which the unspeakable losses felt in the exigencies of everyday life could be 'acted out,' " so that mourning Diana was a way of "mourning multiple possibilities as well as multiple losses." Johnson notes, for example, that his own experience grieving the 1992 death of his wife "made me sympathetic to 'mourning Diana,' especially to its 'madness' or excess, more sympathetic, perhaps, than many 'intellectual' contemporaries," and he adds that many people told interviewers "how they had cried for Diana, but also at the same time for some other loss, unmourned at the time."[74] I too remember watching with sorrowful fascination not just as the mass grieving reenacted my own sorrows but also as "ordinary" women and men in the streets of London confided their feelings to strangers with microphones, betraying deeper emotions of which they were perhaps only half aware.

"I didn't cry like this when me own mum died," said one young woman, looking wistful, as though she'd have liked to at the time but hadn't dared.

Might those unwept tears have provided some of the sheer energy of the grief that piled flowers and stuffed animals next to the fences around Buckingham Palace, draped wreaths and poems over the shrubbery of Kensington Gardens? What another commentator calls the royal family's "'old somber stiff-upper-lip' culture of grief"—a culture of which Decca Mitford's aristocratic "tight control" was another manifestation—"came to be widely viewed as yet another symptom of the ways in which the royals were out of touch with many of their subjects, whose 'expressive grief' demanded signs . . . of feeling."[75] But the wellsprings of mourning had always been there, in other classes and races, even if they'd been repressed by those aspiring to social advancement. Now, with Diana's death, the sorrow exploded, showering "good gray London" with what Gopnik likened to "the contents of some vast piñata."

It was arguably this explosion of ritual offerings that brought with it the demand, from "below," for a different kind of royal funeral. When the queen refused to allow Diana's body in any of the royal palaces and when at first she omitted to fly the Union Jack at half-mast, the "non-royals wouldn't have it, not for 'their' princess." In Diana Taylor's succinct summary, it was "the Queen's turn to undergo public shaming. . . . 'Show Us You Care,' demanded *The Express;* 'Your People are Suffering: SPEAK TO US MA'AM,' *The Mirror* shouted from the stands. 'Let the Flag Fly at Half Mast,' the *Daily Mail* insisted, giving the Queen her own little lesson in protocol."[76]

The ritual offerings and revisionary funeral service that followed the death of Diana weren't, of course, unprecedented. What anthropologists call spontaneous shrines have been springing up on both sides of the Atlantic at the scenes of accidental or violent death for decades now. Some observers in England trace them to "Gypsy or tinker" customs, others remark on "the influence of Mediterranean wayside shrines seen on holidays abroad," and still others connect them with "spiritual rituals garnered from 'New Age' practices."[77] But whatever their origin, they're familiar to most of us. They appear locally, at the sites of car crashes and "drive-by shootings"; nationally, at the scenes of major public catastrophes (the Oklahoma City bombing, the shootings at Columbine High School); and internationally, in the vicinity of similar communal calamities—the Hillsborough football stadium disaster near Liverpool, the Lockerbie plane crash, the Dunblane shooting. As anthropologist Sylvia Grider has pointed out, they also mark "celebrity burial sites": "Elvis Presley's Graceland; the grave of Jim Morrison in Paris; and throughout Corpus Christi, Texas, the home of slain Tejano music star Selena."[78]

Most dramatically, however, a multitude of such spontaneous shrines proliferated after September 11, 2001. And more than the tributes that followed the death of Diana, these extraordinary collages of sorrow revealed the new ways in which we display our grief in an age that is at best ambivalent toward the procedures of mourning. For the 9/11 shrines are even more representative of the strategies through which we cope with loss than the Diana tributes. As a fairy-tale princess whose royal charisma made her death into a "symbolic paradigm," Diana was after all a special kind of cult figure who was in a sense sacramentalized by her celebrity—not unlike such other objects of cult veneration as, say, Elvis Presley, Jim Morrison, and Selena. (Notes the critic Diana Taylor slyly: "Sightings [of Diana] have already been reported.")[79] But unlike these celebrities, the 9/11 victims weren't our sacred surrogates or symbolic paradigms. On the contrary, like the office workers of Oklahoma City or the schoolchildren of Dunblane, those who died in the World Trade Center were just like *us;* metaphorically, indeed, they *were* us, a point that reminded many of us just how lucky we were not to be *them*.

Nor were the "shrines" to these victims of terror intended, at first, as sites of sorrow; to begin with, as we all know, the pictures and notices that eventually came to form the core of countless assemblages that developed into shrines were urgently functional, without any connection to grief or prayer. The picture of Zack (Zhe) Zeng fated to appear on a prayer flag in the south of France was originally part of one such collection of images.

> *Any inform . . .*
> *Wengee Pou . . .*
> *917-885-79 . . .*

As the flyer bearing Zeng's likeness flapped in the breeze, however—as its corners shredded and no one phoned the young man's mother to tell her, *Yes, he's here with me now*, its nature and purpose changed. Now the poster asking for "Any inform" was no longer a call to action; instead, it had become an object of contemplation and commemoration, a testimonial to someone who *had been* rather than an attempt to get in touch with someone who might *still be*.

The experience recounted by Michael Bronski, a writer for the *Boston Phoenix*, recapitulates this metamorphosis from the practical to the commemorative. Just a month after the twin towers collapsed, Bronski described how in "an impulse half journalistic, half sociological," he'd tried to "take in as many 'missing' posters as I could." But, he confessed, the "effort lasted for just over two city blocks because gazing at each name and face quickly became unbearable. The photographs were of people at parties, at dinners, in the office. They were smiling, looking silly or playful. It was excruciating to read their ages, their years of birth, their nicknames, which floors they worked on." No longer serving the purpose for which they had been constructed, the "missing" posters had become "a form of public keening," Bronski decided, or perhaps, in the words of Sylvia Grider, a "vast archive of grief." Ultimately, as Grider notes, the now-famous wall of missing persons' photographs at the Armory became the "most dramatic shrine" precisely because it proffered such a "vast archive." Thus, as "more and more photographs accumulated," the aggregate "became a pilgrimage site for those who wanted to see the spontaneous picture gallery firsthand, maybe out of curiosity but perhaps more as a means of connecting somehow with those previously anonymous faces."[80]

"The sheer numbers, the repetition," comments Bronski, "and my attempt to remember the details—who was holding the black-and-white cat? who was waving into the camera at a birthday party? who looked drunk at an after-work party?—drove home the awful personalness of the event."

And isn't it the *"awful* personalness" or—maybe—*awesome* personalness that moves us most when we view the spontaneous shrines flung up in memory of the 9/11 victims or any of the countless other "ordinary" people for whom we individually or communally mourn? To be sure, as several observers have noted, the increasingly widespread appearance of such evanescent monuments to the dead means that their structure has lately become somewhat stylized. Notes one commentator: "the media coverage now regularly given to [the shrines] is perhaps beginning to give them a conventionality that makes the descriptive term 'spontaneous' less appropriate.' "[81] Nonetheless even what might be considered "conventional" about these memorials differs strikingly from traditional modes of commemoration.

First, these apparently improvisational shrines are personal, whether awfully or awesomely so, and as such they're particularized testimonials, ways of bearing witness to individual lives. Often structured (like most of the 9/11 shrines) around a photographic portrait or even a collage of snapshots, they also include personal items—religious tokens, letters to the dead or missing person, poems, toys and trinkets that belonged, or might have belonged, to the dead [fig. 17].

Second, no doubt because they're so deeply personal, the shrines don't just summarize grief (as traditional monuments do) in a single "classic" symbolic image—an angel, say, or a pietà. Rather, in actually re-*viewing* key moments (photographs, objects) from individual lives, they reenact what Freud considered the very process of mourning itself, albeit in static collages of sorrow. For on the one hand, the task of assembling tokens and images associated with the dead and, on the other hand, the act of viewing and meditating on the final assemblage allow—in fact force—the griever both to bear witness to and to come to terms with loss as, in Freud's words, "Reality passes its verdict—that the object no longer exists—upon each single one of the memories and hopes through which the libido was attached to the lost object." *Remember that this* was *someone you loved,* says the aggregate of images that is the shrine, *and know that now the one you loved no longer* is. For to mourn is to acknowledge the realness of the past even as reality "passes its verdict" on the absolute severance of that past from the present.

Finally, precisely because each shrine celebrates a particular individual rather than either a representative person (a ruler, a celebrity) or an undifferentiated mass of persons (a battalion, a community), these countless transient memorials attest, in their very transience and multiplicity, to what numerous commentators have begun to call the "democratization of death" in an age when even if we're embarrassed by grief or define certain "old-fashioned" performances of piety as "malarkey," most of us still feel the need to find modes of mourning that we experience as honest, honorable, and authentic.[82]

The apparently spontaneous or seemingly "makeshift" quality of these shrines implies, of course, that those who build them, whether separately or together, aren't necessarily conscious that they're searching for ways to grieve. Unlike the Victorian funeral, the requiem mass, the Irish wake, the Greek lament, these strategies for mourning aren't predetermined or patterned, even if they're a "form of public keening." Instead they *happen* over time, as tokens of memory accrete and find appropriate places in a complex whole. Thus the various tokens of love and loss that collect here and there on or near the graves in some cemeteries might also be said to constitute improvisational shrines of a sort.

Over the years since my husband died, I've become an amateur connoisseur of the material tributes that constitute a crucial part of what might be called "cemetery culture." At the Sunset View Cemetery in El Cerrito, where my husband is buried, these tokens of sorrow change with the seasons. Obviously, most are simply floral offerings, with potted plants allowed only

17. Martha Cooper: *Gloves*, *Guitar*, and *Gennie*, from *Missing* (2001).

on certain stated holidays, but sometimes too they're balloons, flags, toys. During Christmas week, the time I find most astonishing, they're often miniature Christmas trees, some actually bearing ornaments and tinsel, others decked with tiny gift packages.

Not far from my husband's grave a little girl named Katie is buried. Her parents and grandparents regularly leave her "gifts": an Easter bunny in the spring, a miniature tree in December, a balloon on her birthday.

"Kitsch"? "Malarkey"? Coincidentally, the picture of Decca Mitford that appears on the back jacket of *The American Way of Death Revisited* was taken just outside the crematorium at Sunset View. I suppose those are the words the "Queen of the Muckrakers" would have used if she'd ever bothered to notice the ritual offerings scattered on that California hillside.

MONUMENTAL PARTICULARITIES

The transformation in memorial customs demonstrated by the "public keening" of the 9/11 shrines—along with earlier the semiroyal, semipop funeral service for the princess Elton John called "England's rose"—wasn't as sudden as it might have seemed. In fact, a number of historians and social scientists trace the collapse of the kinds of traditions for which Waugh (and even at times Mitford) arguably yearned to the period between 1914 and 1918, when the First World War confronted the Western world with an overwhelming mass of deaths representing the loss of virtually an entire generation of young men.

In a 1915 meditation on the war, Freud himself observed that in this period of communal trauma, "We are unable to maintain our former attitude towards death, and have not yet found a new one." More recently the historian David Cannadine, commenting specifically on British bereavement customs, declared: "Mourning succumbed [by 1917–1918] before the vast numbers of the dead," because Victorian conventions now appeared "insufficient" and even the Church "seemed unable to cope when confronted with so much mortality and grief." Indeed, noted Cannadine, "how could one realistically continue to believe in the resurrection of the body" promised by the traditional Anglican funeral service "when all that was left might be a few rat-bitten pieces of rotting flesh?" Along the same lines, Geoffrey Gorer associated the disappearance of "widow's weeds" with the massive annihilation of soldiers at the front. "The holocaust of young men had created such an army of widows," he noted, that "it was no longer socially realistic for them all to act as though their emotional and sexual life were over for good, which was the underlying message of the ritual mourning. And with the underlying message, the ritual too went into the discard."[83]

As "weeds" of ritual were stripped from daily life and words of reassurance excised from liturgical ceremony, however, monuments decorated with sacred or heroic figures symbolically memorializing the huge mass of the dead began to seem increasingly irrelevant. The so-called Great War was anything but morally great, and it was as violently antiheroic as it was profanely irreligious. Though both sides frequently invoked a deity, the idea of divine "intentions" came to seem absurd to the men in the trenches. Wrote the British poet J. C. Squire:

> *God heard the embattled nations sing and shout:*
> *"Gott strafe England"—"God save the King"—*
> *"God this"—"God that"—and "God the other thing."*
> *"My God," said God, "I've got my work cut out."*[84]

But because even in hierarchical and (formerly) hieratic Britain the war leveled custom and ceremony, it fostered a democratization of death in the very design of the once-celebratory military memorial. Thus this conflict's representative monuments ushered in new styles of architectural mourning that we have with us still: abstract structures that are simply lists of (the masses of) names of the fallen—accumulations of the *particular* unmarked by any efforts at sentimentality about sacrifice or glorification of country. Probably the two most famous works of this sort are Sir Edwin Lutyens's Monument to the Missing of the Somme, at Thiepval in northern France, and Maya Lin's Vietnam Veterans Memorial, in Washington, D.C. The first was completed in 1932, the second fifty years later in 1982, and in a sense they enclose the heart of the twentieth century in walls constituted out of the names of the dead, with, in between them, a host of other, similar memorials, the most important of them those that list the unending series of names of Holocaust victims.[85]

Before the First World War, Lutyens was noted as an architect of imperialism. In the service of the British raj, he designed the capital city of Delhi, where the most prominent of his buildings was the grandiose viceroy's palace known as Rashtrapati Bhawan (now the official residence of India's president), begun in 1913. Yet the years between 1914 and 1918 radically altered his ambitions as a designer, for as the historian Jay Winter has noted, his monument at Thiepval is "an extraordinary statement in abstract language about mass death and the impossibility of triumphalism." Explains

Winter, in this work the architect "diminished the arch of triumph of Roman or French art . . . literally to the vanishing point." Indeed, brooding over a cemetery devoted to British and French war dead, the building is a strange one, a series of dark brick, funereal- (rather than imperial-) looking arches flanking a central vault that is architecturally a kind of vacancy. One critic has characterized the monument as a "silent scream," but it might also be considered a meditation on emptiness [fig. 18].[86]

As an architect Maya Lin never made the sort of volte-face that marked Lutyens's career. She was only twenty-one and still an undergraduate at Yale when her design for the Vietnam Veterans Memorial won a nationwide competition. But she had in fact studied and learned from Lutyens's work, and in the new, distinctively twentieth-century tradition he'd pioneered she created a memorial that was even more simplified, indeed abstract, in its sculpting of stone, one that, as Winter comments, offers no "hint of a celebration or affirmation of patriotism . . . or the dignity of dying for a just cause."[87]

There are certainly major differences between the structures of the two works, notably a difference that may mark the increasing dispiritedness of the century itself. Where despite its untriumphal arches, Lutyens's monu-

18. Joanna Legg: *Lutyens's Monument to the Missing of the Somme*, Thiepval, France (n.d.).

ment, like most of its historic predecessors, still goes *up*, albeit up into emptiness, Lin's memorial goes *down*, descending gradually but inexorably into a cleft cut right into the mall at the heart of (still) imperial Washington. To be sure, as the visitor descends the path that parallels the wall, and as the numbers of war dead rise, the black stone of the monument grows almost uncannily higher and higher. Nevertheless, the structure itself is "essentially," as Louis Menand puts it, a "gravestone in a park" whose downward positioning in cleft earth suggests a "scar, the memory of a wound"— in Lin's own words, an "initial violence and pain that in time [has] heal[ed]." Yet at the same time Lin's memorial is also a *wall*, as its popular name (not the Vietnam Veterans Memorial, as it's officially titled, but the Vietnam Wall) reminds us: a polished black wall, a redaction of the traditional *wailing* wall, holding back tons of dirt and mirroring its observers and their world on its darkly gleaming surface.[88]

Yet although the one ascends into emptiness and the other descends into darkness, neither the monument at Thiepval nor the apparently "abstract" and "simplified" Vietnam memorial is vacant or empty. On the contrary, both are linked by the vast burden they bear: the burden of thousands and thousands of the names of the dead. The resonance of those names is what the designers of both structures seem to have understood perhaps best of all, at any rate at least as well as they understood the modern metaphysic of emptiness that their structures can also be said to illustrate.

The Monument to the Missing of the Somme at Thiepval is inscribed with the names of 73,000 men, lost in the savage Battle of the Somme, whose bodies were never found. The Vietnam Veterans Memorial is inscribed with the names of more than 57,661 Americans killed in the dragged-out, dolorous war in Indochina. And it is ultimately the particularity of these names, ineradicably graven on stone, that endows both monuments with their sorrowful resonance, making each feel not only like the sort of "archive of grief" that the armory wall became after 9/11 but even like a physical embodiment of memory itself.[89]

Entering the diminished, no longer triumphal arches at Thiepval, you find yourself in the hollowness of what was once imperial space, surrounded by the proliferating names of those sacrificed to the militaristic will to conquer. Tracing the trajectory of the Vietnam Wall, you go down into the grave of the imperial impulse—the will to conquer and colonize others—and find there, again, floating in darkness, the names of those who died as part of what was yet another exercise in the futility of military command.

That in both cases the names are set in metaphorically fitting sites, of course, gives the blur of what seem to be indefinitely multiplying letters extra, ghostly power. At Thiepval, you stand exposed to the wind and weather of northern France, in a hollow, chilly space where the names of the dead endlessly swarm, and gaze out at ranks of graves, each with its identical marker. Walking beside the Vietnam Wall, you seem, in Menand's words, to "look into the underground, where the dead are buried, and you see, behind their names, the ghost of your face."[90] Around and behind you too, you see the faces of your fellow citizens and the cloud shadows of the American capital, with its other, deliberately grander memorials—the Washington Monument, the Lincoln Memorial. And over and above those structures, so suddenly insubstantial in the mirror of stone, you see passing planes, emblems of civilian or military might, reflected—also bodiless as cloud shadows—in the same glossy blackness where the names of the dead are clustered [fig. 19].

But it's the names that ultimately constitute the particulars of grief, reminders of the specifics we need to mourn. For in each of our lives, after all, it's a name—chosen *for* or perhaps now and then *by* us—that symbolizes the particularity of our selfhood, the formula that summons each of us

19. Leah Asofsky: *Maya Lin's Vietnam Veterans Memorial*, Washington, D.C. (2005).

forth. *What are you going to call her?* we ask about a newborn baby. *What's his name?* we wonder about someone to whom we want to be introduced. It's the name that distinguishes the person and the name that evokes him. Think of the solemn incantation of names on ceremonial occasions: the roll call at any important assembly, the announcements of the names of the graduates at commencement rituals. And think of the names on tombstones that testify *Here was a living person who is now no longer living*.

Even during someone's lifetime, the French theorist Jacques Derrida has argued, mourning is inextricably entwined with naming. Writes Derrida, "in calling or naming someone while he is alive, we know that his name can survive him and *already survives him*" since during his life "the name begins . . . to get along without him, [thereby] speaking and bearing his death each time it is pronounced."[91]

But names are therefore also—to risk an oxymoron—the most abstract of particulars. Even while my name bespeaks *me* and the circumstantiality of my life, it can be entirely detached from me and my circumstances, as Derrida observes. Perhaps for this reason, the purity of the lists of names that are, in a way, the building blocks of Thiepval and the Vietnam Wall demands to be supplemented by specifics. Thus, from the AIDS Memorial Quilt, undertaken by the tellingly titled NAMES project, to the VIRTUAL MEMORIAL GARDEN to the *New York Times'* obituary series entitled "Portraits of Grief," some of the most dramatic millennial mourning practices have expanded on the democratizing of death represented by Thiepval and the Vietnam Wall by enriching and complicating the particularities that surround the names of specific individuals among the hosts of the dead.[92]

The quilt does this by sewing the names of AIDS victims, together with inventive, passionate images intended to represent the details of lost lives, into what almost seems like a massive collage of diverse "spontaneous shrines," which together make up a gigantic allusion to quotidian domesticity. Though it's modeled on both friendship quilts (also known as autograph quilts, in which each swatch is devoted to a "stitched proper name") and so-called crazy quilts (in which unrelated, individual stories are "told within frames"), the AIDS quilt is actually, as commentator Richard Mohr observes, "a pieced, nonquilted appliqué coverlet." Yet as Mohr goes on to note, this ersatz quilt's accumulation of "lightning-quick, single-frame narratives" ultimately offers "snapshots of the soul as posed in memory," so that embroidered into each panel, the "unique depicted name" becomes "in its decor the very vehicle of its person's story." And as the panels accumulate, stitched together by the common

AIDS death that brought each individual's life/story to an end, the work in its entirety does become the assemblage of unified differentnesses that we call a quilt.[93]

Finally, then, if the wall memorializes those who died in Vietnam by mourning the black wall of silence into which all alike have been assumed, the quilt commemorates the AIDS dead by grieving for the blanket of deathly stillness into which each vivid individual has been fastened forever. But even more than the wall subverts the monolithic abstraction of traditional monuments through its accretion of particular names, the quilt subverts monumentality itself. For where conventional monuments to the dead are hard—usually, indeed, cold and stony—the quilt-as-monument is soft, and generically it evokes a household object that is intended to warm, comfort, and protect [fig. 20]. Yet as a "friendship" quilt this antimonument is nevertheless a traditional token of remembrance; as a textile scholar and artist reminded me recently, the individual squares of such a quilt were fre-

20. Louis Gubb: *Man Sitting Beside AIDS Quilt*, Durban, South Africa (2000).

quently "signed" and pieced together by members of a sewing circle who wished to offer a token of their love to one of their number who was departing on a long journey, in most cases never to return.[94]

Both the *New York Times*' "Portraits of Grief" and Web remembrances are in their ways as antimonumental, particularized, and democratic as the AIDS quilt, for both—figuratively—embroider or embellish the names of "ordinary" dead individuals with at least miniature narratives of their lives, and in doing so, they subvert traditional hierarchies of grief. As related in the *Times*, the stories of Zack (Zhe) Zeng and thousands of other 9/11 victims repudiate the traditional genre of obituary, with its eulogies to the rich and famous, by dwelling rapidly and informally, but with poetic succinctness, on the personal specifics that marked the lives of common people, whose names would very likely never have appeared in print had they not died so catastrophically. Similarly, the brief introductions to, say, the Lady Fantaye Nekere, Jennifer Lorraine Gibbons, and Andrew Kevan Shreeves that appear online give at least a "local habitation" to the names of the dead they commemorate, most of whom were neither celebrities nor in any other way publicly memorable.[95]

And now some funerals and at least one cemetery have developed technologies that allow the dead to tell their own tales. One wonders whether even Evelyn Waugh could have imagined the online site of HOLLYWOOD FOREVER, though the real, rather than virtual, site of the cemetery suspiciously evokes his Whispering Glades. Both on and off-line, however, this "burial" ground features a "Library of Lives" that includes videos of the departed relating the stories of their lives along with advice to future generations. At the "real" Hollywood Forever, in fact, you can simply touch one of the video stations scattered around the memorial park and then the dead will appear on-screen and speak to you. Wandering among the graves, you may also find headstones with photographs of the occupants of the graves they mark engraved directly in the rock.

The traditional "form of the funeral seemed broken," confided Tyler Cassidy, one of the cemetery owners, in an interview with radio commentator Ira Glass, whose *This American Life* featured a story about the funeral videos Cassidy makes. But "being broken [the form] was much more powerful"—and powerful, very likely, because it had cracked open to admit all kinds of heretofore illegitimate modes of memory, including the voices of the dead themselves.

Some of the videos he encountered as he strolled through the "real" Hollywood Forever, confessed Ira Glass, who may well have arrived on the scene with the sardonic expectations of an Evelyn Waugh, are "impossibly sad."[96]

But maybe we need the sorrow such portraits of the dead really as well as virtually evoke and enact because otherwise we'd be just too embarrassed to grieve in public. Maybe, as we're catapulted forward into the brave new world of a new millennium, we'll come to understand that mourning has become electronic or taken shape as ritual offerings and lists of names engraved in stone because the impulse to grieve has been rechanneled in ways earlier theorists of funeral customs, from Freud and Gorer to Ariès and Mitford, could never have anticipated.

How strange and strangely moving it is, though, to browse through some of the flowers "left at the cemetery gate" for people "interred" in the WORLD WIDE CEMETERY.

> **jp.lelievre** (jp.lelievre@wanadoo.fr)
> 01 April, 1999
> un fiore per tutti quei ragazzi a cui l'AIDS ha portato
> via per sempre il sorriso nella speranza che presto lo
> si possa guarire monica

> **ilya@pop.mftcomp.ru**
> 05 March, 1999
> I am sending these flowers from Russia for all peo-
> ple this cemetery. I am loving their. Jane

> **Gian Paolo Coppola** (gpcoppola@dimensione.com)
> 7 March, 1998
> I surfed into this site just for a curiosity, but now I
> feel a great commotion. I remember all my deads,
> and I ask my grandpas and granma to watch over
> me. If you can, read "I sepolcri", by the Italian poet
> Ugo Foscolo.

> **Matthias Zimmermann**
> (Matthias.Zimmermann@siemens.at)
> 6 March, 1998
> Eine neue Form des Gedenkens—mögen sie in
> Frieden ruhen. May they rest in peace.
> Greetings from Austria

T. Reznor@netcom.ca
19 October, 1997
May we always keep in our hearts the fate of our
loved ones.
Flowers from Hamilton Ontario

Vanina Grisel Cisneros (vcisneros@way.com.ar)
08 October, 1997
Saludos desde Argentina.

scoop@sonic.net
Sat, 07 Dec 1996
This site is strangely moving . . . that one of the
unanticipated uses for electronic communications
has turned out to be a digital columbarium is, to
me, quintessentially human.

Georg R Douglas (george@ismennt.is)
Mon, 16 Oct 95
Rest in Peace. Greetings from Iceland.

PART THREE

The Handbook of Heartbreak: Contemporary Elegy and Lamentation

This is the mythology of modern death
And these, in their mufflings, monsters of elegy,
Of their own marvel made, of pity made.

—WALLACE STEVENS,
"THE OWL IN THE SARCOPHAGUS"

On the Beach with Sylvia Plath

BERCK-PLAGE

S eptember 24, 2002. Hot equinoctial sun, a chill wind from the north, and a cloudless sky over Picardy, where we sit in a nearly empty café on the seafront, at Berck-Plage. David and I have come here to see what Sylvia Plath might have been seeing when she began the poem she named after this place, for increasingly it seems to me that the ambitious seven-part sequence she entitled "Berck-Plage" offers crucial, if disquieting, insights not just into its author's life and her often death-drenched work but more generally into our contemporary poetry of mourning.

Berck-Plage is a rather worn-looking little town set on the edge of la Manche, the channel that divides Britain from the Continent. Our old Michelin for the *Nord de la France, Champagne, Ardennes* describes it as "*une station à la fois balnéaire, familiale et médicale climatique*"—a bathing resort, a family vacation spot, and a medical haven. But right now, though the sun's so fierce on this out-of-season Tuesday, the seaside is deserted, as if bathers, families, patients all had fled inland for the French *rentrée*, a communal back-to-school week in which the whole nation participates.

Sylvia Plath and Ted Hughes came to this town at a very different time of year. In June 1961, the young parents of one child with another on the way, they were taking a fortnight's holiday in France while Sylvia's mother, Aurelia, baby-sat little Frieda back in London. After an ill-starred five-night stay with their friends Bill and Dido Merwin in the Dordogne, they must have traveled north by northwest as they made their way back to England.[1] Berck-Plage may have been their last stopover before they got on the ferry at Calais, and they probably chose the spot because it was cheaper than the ritzier Le Touquet-Paris-Plage a few kilometers up the coast. By the early sixties Hughes and Plath were already literary luminaries, recording for the BBC and publishing widely; as the poet Peter Porter put it not so long ago, they then "appeared in poetic assemblies with almost Charles and Di radiance, the youthful princelings of romantic promise."[2] But they had to scrimp like any other not very well-off young couple.

The sea that David and I gaze at today from our perch on the sun-struck concrete beachfront promenade is flat and vast in all directions, for as Plath notes in her poem, the beach is huge—"*se prolonge durant une douzaine de kilomètres*," according to Michelin—so that a "sandy damper" does indeed stretch "for miles." Right now, though, despite steady sun, the wind's so strong that hardly anyone has ventured out onto the enormous glaring plain of that "sandy damper." Only a middle-aged couple in heavy sweaters walk a tiny dog who looks as though the blasts might blow him away any minute, while a younger couple, struggling to shield a small baby, huddle next to the boarded-up bathhouses, and—rather bizarrely—a man in swim trunks tries to sunbathe in the dubious shelter of a few buildings Plath described as "concrete bunkers," which house a cluster of ice-cream stands, all shut down because the season's over.

Even along the seaside Esplanade Parmentier most of the cafés and souvenir shops are closed, though a few lingering tourists—ourselves among them—sip coffee among the folded umbrellas on the terraces, and a couple of the wheelchairs that betoken the town's status as a *station médicale* proceed along the front at a stately pace.

The wheelchairs remind me that the indomitable French editor Jean-Dominique Bauby, so severely paralyzed by a stroke that in his "locked-in" state he could communicate only by blinking his left eyelid, wrote his moving memoir *The Diving Bell and the Butterfly* when he was being cared for in the Naval Hospital at Berck in 1996, the last year of his life. The frontispiece of the book shows him "tethered to an inclined board" and propped in a wheelchair, overlooking the *plage* we're staring at right now. At one point in this memoir Bauby counts himself, as Plath might have, among the "ravens of doom" that "spoil the view," as "rigid and mute, we make our way through a group of more fortunate patients." At another point he describes an excursion to the beach with his ex-wife and their two young children, noting that the "hospital chimes . . . assume funereal tones as the time for farewells draws near," and as wind "begins to whip up the sand," the "tide has gone out so far that swimmers look like tiny dots on the horizon."[3]

Of course, though wheelchairs, crutches, and canes still proliferate along the promenade, much has no doubt changed in Berck-Plage since

Plath and Hughes strolled here in 1961. But much is surely still the same, not just the sandy damper, the concrete bunkers, the hospitals, and the tubular steel wheelchairs glittering in the sun but, in particular, what I suspect must be another distinction of the place: the rickety little wooden *cabines* in a rainbow of pastels that serve as private bathhouses, tilting crazily as they sink into the drifting sand, which right now hisses in the wind as layers and layers of fine, gritty grains are driven, low to the ground, along the shore. As images of mortal frailty teetering in the sands of time, these peculiar structures seem singularly appropriate in such a medicalized setting. Plath's "Berck-Plage" is too strange and original to mention them, but maybe they haunted her and her text anyway, as they seem to haunt the beach.

It was probably hot and calm when the couple visited this multipurpose resort. Certainly Plath's poem tells us that the sun was shining and it was warm enough for ice-cream (some people are eating "colored sherbets"), bright enough for sunburn (the sherbet eaters have "scorched hands"), a good day for swimming and loafing (there are women in the dunes wearing bikinis), either a holiday or a weekend (children are playing on the beach), and relatively windless (the air is "still"). Yet here, on a sunny beach, among frolicking vacationers, she was prompted to begin a poem whose ultimate configuration suggests to me that she is perhaps *the* poet of modern death.

"BERCK-PLAGE"

To begin with, what might have been a carefree vacation spot was from the start blighted for Plath by the ubiquitous medicalization of the place, which, as Hughes later remembered, "was one of her nightmares stepped into the real world." Thus with extraordinary power she represented even the most innocent aspects of a holiday by the sea as either sick or sickening. Note, in the passages below from the first two sections of the poem, that the sea is an "abeyance," the heat of the sun is a "poultice," the colors of the sherbets are "electrifying" (never a cheery qualifier for a onetime sufferer from shock treatment), sunburned hands are "scorched," voices are "shrunk" and "crutchless," a priest has a "dead foot," and a pool is "sick with what it has swallowed."

(1)

This is the sea, then, this great abeyance.
How the sun's poultice draws on my inflammation.

Electrifyingly-colored sherbets, scooped from the freeze
By pale girls, travel the air in scorched hands.

Why is it so quiet, what are they hiding?
I have two legs, and I move smilingly.

A sandy damper kills the vibrations;
It stretches for miles, the shrunk voices

Waving and crutchless, half their old size. . . .

(2)

This black boot has no mercy for anybody.
Why should it, it is the hearse of a dead foot,

The high, dead, toeless foot of this priest
Who plumbs the well of his book. . . .

Obscene bikinis hide in the dunes. . . .

While a green pool opens its eye,
Sick with what it has swallowed—

Limbs, images, shrieks. Behind the concrete bunkers
Two lovers unstick themselves. . . .

And the onlooker, trembling,
Drawn like a long material

Through a still virulence,
And a weed, hairy as privates.[4]

Given this portrayal of a diseased geography, I guess it isn't surprising that I still remember the curiously chilling combination of bafflement and envy with which I read "Berck-Plage" when it first came out in a magazine. I was both puzzled and piqued by what I understood was far beyond my writerly (and even readerly) grasp, a presiding tension that gave shape, depth, and mystery to the poem, a tension between formal precision, on the one hand, and on the other, almost mystically daring metaphorical leaps. But I was also unnerved. Nor was my reaction all that unusual. The critic Al Alvarez, a friend to whom Plath read "Berck-Plage" aloud in September 1962, "sitting cross-legged on the uncomfortable floor" of his studio, reported later that he'd "had a vague impression of something injurious and faintly obscene." A more recent student of the work goes so far as to declare that it "contains 126 lines of seemingly unmitigated malaise."[5]

Although such words as "injurious," "obscene," and "malaise" are hyperbolic, they're attempts to get at what is certainly disconcerting in this poem. Plath's "shrunk voices / Waving and crutchless" are succeeded by a first glimpse of the black-booted priest who seems so ominous that a group of fishermen—"mackerel-gatherers"—"wall up their backs against him." And the mackerel gatherers themselves are so subtly sinister, "handling the black and green lozenges like the parts of a body," that they too troubled me when I first read the piece, especially because I didn't understand why and how they mattered in this gravely elegiac work. I was inexplicably sickened too by the riddle of the passing priest, with his "high, dead, toeless foot," by the "obscene bikinis" and the furtive lovers who weirdly "unstick themselves" behind those "concrete bunkers," by the plight of the "onlooker, trembling," who is drawn "like a long material // Through a still virulence," and by the "weed, hairy as privates" that this cryptic observer confronts.

As for the old man who is dying in section 3 of the sequence, then is dead in section 4, those prophetic anxieties that, like most aspiring poets, I carefully cultivated, made his meaning all too clear to me.

(3)
. . . On a striped mattress in one room

An old man is vanishing.
There is no help in his weeping wife.

Where are the eye-stones, yellow and valuable,
And the tongue, sapphire of ash.

(4)
A wedding-cake face in a paper frill.
How superior he is now.

It is like possessing a saint. . . .

The bed is rolled from the wall.

This is what it is to be complete. It is horrible.
Is he wearing pajamas or an evening suit

Under the glued sheet from which his powdery beak
Rises so whitely unbuffeted?

They propped his jaw with a book until it stiffened.

The poet's observations—of, say, the partly shrouded dead man's "wedding-cake face in a paper frill," of his surreal lost "eye-stones, yellow and valuable," and of his useless "tongue, sapphire of ash," along with his grimly propped jaw—were frighteningly ruthless.

I came across "Berck-Plage" in the early sixties—maybe after Plath's death, maybe not—but I'd been following her career with fascination for nearly a decade, ever since I was transfixed by a disturbing story she published in the girls' magazine *Seventeen*, when she must have been little more than that age herself and I was still in my "preteens." An aspiring poet myself, I'd been disappointed for a while by the decorum of Plath's poems, few of which seemed to have the strange intensity of that story in *Seventeen*, which had been appropriately entitled "Den of Lions." But of course, most of the Plath verses I'd been reading had been the relatively careful texts of her first collection, *The Colossus*, rather than the great *Ariel* poems, which I was just beginning to discover when I stumbled on "Berck-Plage." Looking back now on those astonishing reading experiences, I realize how lucky it was for me that I *could* "stumble" on the *Ariel* poems.[6]

In the early sixties Plath's vehement last words swam randomly, haphazardly into my ken, and even when, later, I began seeking them out, knowing she had lost her life (although not quite how or why) and eager to see what she had left behind, I remained for quite a while an innocent, if no longer a random, reader. None of her poems had yet been privileged over any other; she was not yet the figure of melodrama who became notorious as the "poetess" of "Daddy." Rather, she was someone from a college cohort half a decade ahead of my own who had suddenly written a number of unfathomably compelling poems that kept emerging along with odd, unverifiable rumors about the circumstances of her death.

Compelling, compulsive, almost *compulsory* reading. That was the point about the poems themselves. Whatever their author's story—and no one I knew could explain it to me, at least for a while—there were the poems. Scorching the page with a kind of fatality. Hissing through the page. Weird. I had never seen anything like them, nor have I since.

"Berck-Plage" wasn't, to be sure, the most searing of Plath's late works. (Even all those years ago I'd have reserved that adjective for the notorious "Daddy"and "Lady Lazarus" as well as "Fever 103," "Getting There," "Stings," and a few others.) But its metaphoric leaps had a disciplined dazzle that I sensed was rooted in something hectic, something that in lesser hands would be out of control. At the same time, control was manifest in the poem's surprisingly dispassionate tone, despite its speaker's sometimes almost paranoid edginess ("Why is it so quiet, what are they hiding? . . . These children are after something, with hooks and cries"). Indeed, studying the piece today, I begin to suspect that what I'm calling control is the flip side of a kind of madness, a narrative estrangement that makes it possible for Plath the artist to fashion disturbing material into an elegy that is both deeply moving and deeply skeptical.

For "Berck-Plage" is of course an elegy, perhaps the finest one this often indefatigable mourner ever produced, though the gravity of its lamentation has been overlooked in favor of the more conventionally confessional "family elegies" the writer addressed to her father.[7] Its comparative neglect is particularly odd in view of its ambition: with the exception of "Poem for a Birthday" (more a suite than a sequence) and "Three Women" (a radio play), "Berck-Plage" is the longest and most complex of the texts included in Plath's Collected Poems. Its seven sections—each arranged in nine fluid couplets—are as technically accomplished as they are meticulously observant. And in its articulation of a nihilistic vision that dominated much verse in English after, say, Eliot's Four Quartets and Robert Lowell's "Quaker Graveyard at Nantucket," this restrained and elliptical seaside poem offers an extraordinarily useful model of the poetry of lamentation that was produced in the second half of the twentieth century.

Like so many strong elegies, "Berck-Plage" juxtaposes the world of the desirous flesh—what Yeats called "those dying generations at their song"— with the timor mortis that the very processes of generation beget. Carnal appetites flourish on Plath's beach, bordered by the sea, that "great abeyance" of the solid, but so does fear, in the person of the deathly Father, a priest who no doubt "plumbs the well of his book" to uncover the truth of ashes to ashes, dust to dust. For on this "sandy damper" that stretches for miles, the earth is depicted as (what at least part of the plage literally still is) the ground of a hospital where the "onlooker, trembling," observes the hosts of material *things*, the quotidian objects in which we put our trust when we put our trust in human life.

"On the balconies of the hotel," Plath writes, "things are glittering. / Things, things—":

Tubular steel wheelchairs, aluminum crutches.
Such salt-sweetness. Why should I walk

Beyond the breakwater, spotty with barnacles?
I am not a nurse, white and attendant,

I am not a smile.
These children are after something, with hooks and cries,

And my heart too small to bandage their terrible faults.
This is the side of a man: his red ribs,

The nerves bursting like trees, and this is the surgeon:
One mirrory eye—

A facet of knowledge.
On a striped mattress in one room

An old man is vanishing.

Wheelchairs, crutches, even a surgeon with a clinical "mirrory eye": all have been assembled to stave off death, but nonetheless a representative old man is "vanishing."

This old man's death, nearly halfway through the seven-part poem, sets off the work's remaining (and its major) action: the laying out of his body ("They propped his jaw with a book until it stiffened / And folded his hands, that were shaking: goodbye, goodbye"); the problematic condolences of mourners ("It is a blessing, it is a blessing") as they confront the "long coffin of soap-colored oak . . . and the raw date / Engraving itself in silver with marvelous calm"; the rituals of wake and funeral ("the pallors gather— // The pallors of hands and neighborly faces, . . . while the hills roll the notes of the dead bell"); and the final resolution of burial, attended by the poem's speaker, "dark-suited and still, a member of the party."

"A member of the party": that Plath was actually one of the mourners who followed the coffin of her octogenarian neighbor Percy Key to its "stopping place" in Devonshire testifies to the craft with which she fashioned this apparently seamless work. For the old man who is said to "vanish" at the center of "Berck-Plage" (and presumably therefore at or near the "real" Berck-Plage) did not actually expire anywhere near the beach in northern France where the poem's conflicted protagonist moves "smilingly."

When I first read "Berck-Plage," I understood as little about someone in Devon named Percy Key as I did about the town of Berck, on the shore of Picardy. As I'm sure many other readers do, I assumed that the episode the poem represents was a single coherent event that took place at a seaside hospital in France or Belgium. Nor did I learn the work's sources until decades later, when one of Ted Hughes's endnotes in Plath's *Collected Poems* explained that "Berck-Plage" is a beach "which SP visited in June 1961" and where "there was a large hospital for mutilated war veterans and accident victims—who took their exercise along the sands." Added Hughes: the "funeral in the poem is that of Percy Key . . . who died in June 1962, exactly a year after her visit to Berck-Plage."[8] Later still, I discovered in our old Green Michelin what might explain the importunate children with "hooks and cries": that Berck, with its "*immense plage de sable fin, très sûre*"—its huge firm sandy beach—is "*mondialement connu pour le traitement des malades osseuse, specialement chez les enfants*," but that "*ces affections, y compris la tuberculose osseuse, ne sont pas contagieuses, aussi les malades peuvent-ils mener une vie sociale normale*."[9] Though the town is world-famous for treating childhood maladies that include tuberculosis of the bone, the diseases of its young patients aren't contagious, so they're free to romp on the shore.

According to one scholar who's worked with the manuscripts of "Berck-Plage," a "fragmentary rough draft" begins with an image of the sun, "silent and violent," laying "its bright poultices on the promenade"; this may well have been a jotting on or near the beach at Berck. Eventually these sketches of the local scene mingled observations *balnéaire* ("Electrifyingly colored sherbets" floating above the long "sandy damper"), *familiale* (bikinis, children, "white sea-crockery"), and *médicale* (the sun's "poultice," wheelchairs, crutches, "a green pool . . . Sick with what it has swallowed," and a priest whose black boot "is the hearse of a dead foot").[10] But the work's genius is evident in the skill with which Plath brought such notations to bear on the elegiac tradition in which she undertook to compose a work memorializing the death of her octogenarian neighbor Percy Key. For as in T. S. Eliot's "East Coker," where the "whole earth is our hospital," the sanitaria at Berck-Plage become monitory establishments, with each crutch and wheelchair a memento mori meant to warn all alike—sick or well, consumers of sherbets or wearers of obscene bikinis—that priestly death comes always closer with his "black boot [that] has no mercy for anybody." Unlike Eliot, however, Plath imagined no Christlike "wounded surgeon" capable of plying the redemptive "steel" that might cure the disease of mortality.

Inevitably, Hughes understood that Berck-Plage constituted one of Plath's "nightmares stepped into the real world" because hospitals and ill-nesses had long had special metaphysical as well as physical resonance for her. Her own, unpriestly father's "dead foot," destroyed by gangrene that developed from long-untreated diabetes, killed him when she was only eight, and she herself was institutionalized with multiple physical injuries as well as a mental breakdown at the time of the suicide attempt she fictionalized in *The Bell Jar*.[11] Thus the turn in "Berck-Plage" from beach scene to death scene is unobtrusively accomplished in section 3 through the poet's intense focus on "nightmare" associations with medical images. First her gaze is fixed on prosthetic "Things, things—"; then she moves to thoughts of her own inadequacy in the face of mutilated children "with hooks and cries"—her "heart too small to bandage their terrible faults"—and then she swivels to examine "the side of a man: his red ribs" and the surgeon who's tending—also inadequately—the opened body. That opened body (once the object of surgery, now in the last stages of an illness surgery couldn't cure) implicitly belongs to the old man "vanishing" on a "striped mattress in one room." He seems to be dying in a chamber of the hotel where the speaker is staying or in one of the nearby hospitals, but in fact his death is based on an event that actually took place in the parlor of a cottage in Devon.

Plath had met Percy Key and his wife, Rose, in August 1961, on the day she and Hughes moved to Court Green, the old manor house in North Taw-ton, Devonshire, that they bought soon after returning from their vacation in France. A retired London pub keeper who seemed to her "about 20 years older" than his wife, he was "very tall, spare, almost cadaverous," and it quickly became clear that he was suffering from some sort of chest ailment. By the following February he was in hospital for a series of lung surgeries, and in "Among the Narcissi" Plath portrayed him recovering from one of these on a breezy early-spring hillside where the flowers are "vivid as ban-dages" and "the octogenarian . . . is quite blue" because "the terrible wind tries his breathing."

Then, on April 17, 1962, Percy suffered multiple strokes in one day. At this point he became a subject of Plath's continued clinical (though not unsympathetic) surveillance.[12] Her journal entry for that date records: "A terrible thumping on our door about 2 o'clock. . . . Rose's hysterical voice 'Ted, Ted, come quick, I think Percy's had a stroke.' . . . I thought I would stay and wait, and then something in me said, *now, you must see this, you have never seen a stroke or a dead person*. So I went. Percy was in his chair in front of the television set, twitching in a fearsome way, utterly gone off [emphasis added]." By early June Plath noted that "Percy Key is dying. That is the verdict." On July 2 she told her journal that "Percy Key is dead" and "I have written a long poem 'Berck-Plage' about it. Very moved. Several terrible glimpses."

Those "glimpses"—still unflinchingly clinical yet sorrowful and shocked—came as the result of another deliberate, no doubt writerly choice: "*I decided to see him, I must see him* [emphasis added]." They're worth quoting here at some length because they include a great deal that she incorporated into her poem, merging them with the details of her holiday visit to France the previous summer. The emphases below are mine, intended to stress key details that went into "Berck-Plage" in one form or another.

The livingroom was full, still, hot with some awful translation taking place. Percy lay back on a heap of white pillows in his striped pajamas, *his face already passed from humanity*. . . . His eyes showed through partly open lids like dissolved soaps or a clotted pus. . . . *The end, even of so marginal a man, a horror.*

Went down after his death, the next day, the 27th. Ted had been down in the morning, said Percy was still on the bed . . . his jaw bound and a book . . . *propping it till it stiffened properly. . . . He lay . . . in a long* coffin of orangey soap-colored oak *with silver handles, the lid propped against the wall at his head with a silver scroll: Percy Key, Died June 25, 1962.* The raw date a shock. . . . *A sheet covered the coffin. Rose lifted it.* A pale white beaked face, as of paper, rose under the veil that covered the hole cut in the glued white cloth cover. . . . *They have no hearse, they have only* a cart.

Friday, the day of the funeral. . . . Ted & I, dressed in hot blacks, passed the church, saw the bowler-hatted men coming out of the gate with a high, spider-wheeled black cart. . . . *We strolled round the church in the bright heat,* the pollarded green limes like green balls, the fat hills red, just ploughed. . . . *We went in.* Heard priest meeting corpse at gate, incantating, *coming close. Hair-raising. We stood.* The flowery casket, nodding and flirting its petals, led up the aisle. . . . *I hardly heard a word of the service, Mr. Lane [the rector] for once* quenched by the grandeur of ceremony, a vessel, *as it should be.*

Then we followed the funeral party. . . . *up the hill to the cemetery.* . . . *Ted motioned me to look* at the slow uplifted faces of children in the primary school yard . . . *utterly without grief, only bland curiosity, turning after us. We got out at the cemetery gate, the day blazing.* . . . Six bowler hats of the bearers left at the first yew bushes in the grass. *The coffin on boards, words said, ashes to ashes—that is what remained, not glory, not heaven.* The amazingly narrow coffin lowered into the narrow red earth opening, left. . . . *An unfinished feeling. Is he to be left up there uncovered, all alone?*[13]

That Plath is forcing herself to attend to every detail of Percy's death and burial ("something in me said, *now, you must see this*") despite being so horrified by what she's seeing that at one point she's "seized by dry retching" no doubt gives "Berck-Plage" some of its unnerving quality, even perhaps the disturbing tone that Alvarez defined as "injurious and faintly obscene." At the same time, even before the introduction of a terminally ill patient the sheer *strangeness* of the beach at Berck—both its foreignness and its uncanny juxtapositions of jovial holiday making and sorrowful cure taking —fosters the tone of solemn estrangement that governs the sequence from the start. Certainly such distancing is apropos, like muffled drums, in the presence of death, but this beautifully crafted elegy has, throughout, a firmness of defamiliarization that seems singularly suited to the "*immense plage de sable fin, très sûre*" on which it is so dramatically set.

The aesthetic processes that shape such defamiliarization are, moreover, as nightmarish as Plath's worst medical dreams might have foretold. On the one hand, as priestly death stalks the living, people are disassembled into surreal fragments of themselves, with the "toeless foot" of doom drawing ever nearer to the "shrunk voices" of the bathers and to the "confectioner's sugar" of breasts and hips hidden in the dunes, while the "green pool," sick from swallowing "limbs, images, shrieks," and the "weed, hairy as privates," prefigure the "red ribs" and "mirrory" surgical eye that will soon appear, along with the "eye-stones" and tongue of the dead man, the pallid "hands and neighborly faces" of mourners, and the crusted "blood of limb stumps" evoked by the red earth of the graveyard. On the other hand, as the living disintegrate into body parts, inhuman objects ("Things, things") take on a bizarrely autonomous existence: "Electrifyingly-colored sherbets . . . travel the air in scorched hands" as if of their own volition; "washed sheets fly in the sun"; the "raw date" of the old man's death engraves "itself with marvelous calm." Finally, indeed, the thoughts of his widow are "Blunt practical boats // Full of dresses and hats and china and married daughters," as if there were no distinction between people and possessions, and the "actions" of the dead man have solidified "like livingroom furniture, like a decor," while the trees with serene composure "march to church."[14]

Such processes of estrangement set the scene for the climactic funeral and burial passages of "Berck-Plage," two episodes (6 and 7) set inland in Devon, far from the medicalized beach in Picardy, which nonetheless appear to have evolved as astonishingly out of the poet's encounter with the "great abeyance" of the sea on a foreign shore as out of the journal entries I just quoted:

(6)
. . . *The voice of the priest in thin air*
Meets the corpse at the gate,

Addressing it, while the hills roll the notes of the dead bell;
A glitter of wheat and crude earth.

What is the name of that color?—
Old blood of caked walls the sun heals,

Old blood of limb stumps, burnt hearts.
The widow with her black pocketbook and three daughters,

Necessary among the flowers,
Enfolds her face like fine linen,

Not to be spread again. . . .
And the bride flowers expend a freshness,

And the soul is a bride
In a still place, and the groom is red and forgetful, he is featureless.

(7)

. . . I am dark-suited and still, a member of the party,
Gliding up in low gear behind the cart.

And the priest is a vessel,
A tarred fabric, sorry and dull,

Following the coffin on its flowery cart like a beautiful woman,
A crest of breasts, eyelids and lips

Storming the hilltop.
Then, from the barred yard, the children

Smell the melt of shoe-blacking,
Their faces turning, wordless and slow,

Their eyes opening
On a wonderful thing—

Six round black hats in the grass and a lozenge of wood,
And a naked mouth, red and awkward.

For a minute the sky pours into the hole like plasma.
There is no hope, it is given up.

It's hard, now, to ignore every aspect of the moment when the "naked mouth" of earth opens, "red and awkward," to swallow the coffin of the dead man who turns out to have been Percy Key but obviously signifies Everyman. I don't think I noticed, though, when I was first seized by the austere ferocity of this elegy, how carefully—how theologically!—Plath prepares for such a denouement, from the very beginning of the work dressing death in the black cassock of a priest and juxtaposing his affectation of piety with the cryptic ritual of the mackerel gatherers, who "wall up their backs against him" to handle "the black and green lozenges [of fish] like the parts of a body." But if only unconsciously I must have been gripped by the fatality with which the sacramental "lozenges" of dead mackerel dissolve into the defamiliarized "lozenge of wood" in which the body parts of the dead man have been secreted. And I must have in some part of myself grasped the bitter allusion to the traditionally hopeful trope of the soul as a bride of Christ in Plath's image of the soul as a bride whose groom is no Redeemer but, rather, "red and forgetful"—indeed a "featureless" mass of dirt. Finally I must have at least intuited the skepticism that shaped the transformation of priestly death (from the poem's beginning) into (at the end) a hopeless human cleric who is merely a "tarred fabric, sorry"—in several senses—and "dull," though he dutifully presides over the ceremonial futility with which the "coffin on its flowery cart like a beautiful woman, / A crest of breasts, eyelids and lips" (echoing the obscenely titillating breasts and hips of section 2) storms the hilltop graveyard.

I'm sure, though, that I didn't quite appreciate the brilliance with which Plath assigns the poem's final vision to a group of children in a "barred yard," children who in their representation of mortal innocence and fleshly entrapment surely share with the children in section 3 the "terrible faults" the speaker cannot "bandage." From their (ironically) naive perspective, the last communion in which the earth must swallow a eucharistic "lozenge of wood" is a "wonderful thing." But the speaker knows better. Though "the sky pours into the hole" in the graveyard as plasma might be desperately poured into a fatal wound, she concludes, "there is no hope, it is given up."

Here "it" has of course multivalent references. Most obviously "it" is the lozenge / coffin that must be "given up" to the voracious earth mouth. But "it" is also hope for some ritual of redemption from the "sorry and dull" human priest. And "it" is even the sky, which only pours *like* plasma but can neither resuscitate the dead one nor offer him and his mourners the promise of a heavenly home. To the question Plath had posed in her journal, as she recorded her "unfinished feeling" after the graveside ceremony for Percy Key— "Is he to be left up there uncovered, all alone?"—the answer this passage offers is *yes, he is.* Oh, of course he'll be covered with earth, but no ceremony else will clothe his termination with anything resembling celestial radiance.

Whether sacrifice or surrender, says this classic mid-century elegy, giving up is what one does in the face of death. In *Four Quartets* Eliot assuages his terror of going "into the dark" of "the silent funeral" by telling his soul to "be still, and let the dark come upon you / Which shall be the darkness of God," and in "The Quaker Graveyard at Nantucket" Lowell comforts himself with the assurance that "The Lord survives the rainbow of His will."[15] But like so many of her contemporaries and descendants Plath merely concludes that the circumstances of defeat must be scrupulously recorded and set against the oncoming priest of the grave. The living must "wall up their backs against" his "black cassock" as the mackerel gatherers do, even if the details out of which they build their defenses are as nauseating as the "Limbs, images, shrieks" that have sickened the green pool among the dunes. In this respect, I think even my earliest readings of "Berck-Plage" prepared me for much of what I've come to believe about late-twentieth-century public as well as private procedures for mourning and perhaps, more generally, laid the foundations for my thoughts about the theological "damper" on which our aesthetic locates itself. Certainly those readings have prepared me to regard Plath herself as our most highly sensitized and representative poet not, as is often asserted, of suicidal "extremism" but rather of later-twentieth-century mourning.

To be sure, the skeptical resignation with which Plath gives "it" (the coffin, hope, the sky) up at the end of her desolate elegy wasn't without precedent, even before the twentieth century dawned with "the growing gloom" that Thomas Hardy depicted in "The Darkling Thrush," his bleak greeting to New Year's Day 1900. In 1851, for instance—over a century before Plath and Hughes visited Berck-Plage—Matthew Arnold recorded the "melancholy, long, withdrawing roar" of the "Sea of Faith" in "Dover Beach." But the channel dividing Berck-Plage from Dover Beach is even more historical than geographical. On "the French coast the light / Gleams and is gone," mourned Arnold, but he insisted that "the cliffs of England stand, / Glimmering and vast, out in the tranquil bay" and imagined that there might still after all be something substantive to fight about, even if the battle was joined by "ignorant armies" that clash by night. For Plath, though, the sea that primordially "crystallized" body parts, limbs, images, shrieks, simply "Creeps away, many-snaked, with a long hiss of distress." I suspect it was that devastating and devastated hiss of distress I found so eerily compelling in "Berck-Plage" almost four decades ago.[16]

Now, certainly, that long hiss of distress, permeating so much of Plath's work, means to me that among the countless modern poets who have found themselves stationed beside death's door, this nearly legendary young woman has a special status. For perhaps more than anyone else—more even than her much-admired Wallace Stevens himself—she really did articulate not just the vision but the "*mythology* of modern death" that Stevens tentatively proposed. And it was a mythology whose fathomless points of origin and destination were in what Arnold called "the unplumbed, salt, estranging sea."[17]

THIS IS THE SEA, THEN, THIS GREAT ABEYANCE

If Sylvia Plath was as distant from Arnold as Berck-Plage was from Dover Beach, her defamiliarized elegy signals its own estrangement from both traditional elegy and conventional discourse with its very first line: "This is the sea, then, this great abeyance." The formal poem of mourning often begins with flowers and almost always with some sign of feeling. "Yet once more O ye laurels / And once more ye myrtles brown . . . I come to pluck your berries harsh and crude," begins Milton's "Lycidas." "I weep for Adonais— he is dead!" cries Shelley as he launches into "Adonais." "When lilacs last in the dooryard bloom'd," declares Whitman in the first (and title) line of his elegy for President Lincoln, "I mourn'd, and yet shall mourn." The oddly restrained, apparently naive definitional structure of the sentence with which Plath opens her poem—"This is the sea, then" (as if she'd never seen such a phenomenon before)—certainly doesn't introduce this work as a poem of bereavement and sorrow.

Odder still is her metaphor for the sea on which she gazes. A great *abeyance*? My dictionary gives the meaning of the (here) peculiar word "abeyance" as "1. The condition of being temporarily set aside; suspension . . ." and "2. *Law* A condition of undetermined ownership, as of an estate that has not yet been assigned." It adds further, about the word's etymology, that it is "Anglo-Norman, variant of Old French *abeance*, desire, from *abaer*, to gape at: . . . *see* BAY^2."[18] And as we know, Plath, a thesaurus addict who once called herself "Roget's trollop," was fascinated by etymologies. As her husband commented in a note on *Ariel* that he wrote after her death, her words "are all deeply related within any poem, acknowledging each other and calling to each other in deep harmonic designs," as if governed by a "musical almost mathematical hidden law."[19]

Ordinarily, of course, we do use the word "abeyance" to suggest a pause or remission, as in a disease. In this sense, the "great abeyance" of the sea on which the poet gazes as she strolls the promenade at Berck-Plage may suggest an abeyance or remission in the disease of mortality represented by the instances of illness all around her. In another sense, however, what would it mean to think of the sea as a gape, a gap, or an absence—a setting aside or stopping—of the land itself, along with the human life it nurtures? Certainly to one who's lived inland, the sea might at first seem like just such an absence or *stopping* of land. Or like, perhaps more accurately, a gaping wound—an abyss, a death—in the real human world of "Things, things": a wound whose nullity no plasma of dailiness can fill, a wound whose cure has been "given up."

Or perhaps, from the perspective of a bleak imagination, the "abeyance" of the sea might even suggest, as it does in a well-known poem by Marianne Moore, "A Grave." "Man looking into the sea," declares Moore, "it is human nature to stand in the middle of a thing, / but you cannot stand in the middle of this; / the sea has nothing to give but a well excavated grave." And Moore, whom Plath described as "someone's fairy godmother incognito" when she met her in 1955, had long been among the poets the young writer most admired.[20]

Yet Plath spent early and (she claimed) idyllic years by the sea, as she recalled in the lovely memoir "Ocean-1212-W." "My childhood landscape was not land but the end of the land—the cold, salt, running hills of the Atlantic," she wrote here, adding that "I sometimes think my vision of the sea is the clearest thing I own." And the sea's gifts, she noted, were many, for it "spoke of miracles and distances," tossing up bits of china and glass and "purple 'lucky stones.' " "Sea-crockery," gems, sailboats, chowders, even a washed-up monkey statue, she tells us, were oceanically bestowed on her, as if sea life and land life were in some way continuous; indeed she remembers her childhood Atlantic as having had "running *hills*."[21]

This sea the poet-to-be loved was the same sea once celebrated by Matthew Arnold, though she tells us it wasn't his elegiac "Dover Beach" but his differently sorrowful "Forsaken Merman" from which her mother read her passages that signaled "a new way of being happy." Among the lines Plath recalls from this haunting tale in verse of a mer*male* whose human bride has abandoned his underwater habitat for the solidity of the shore, she singles out some that describe "Sand-strewn caverns, cool and deep, / Where the winds are all asleep [and] the sea snakes coil and twine / Dry their mail and bask in the brine."[22] The sea snakes from Arnold's subaqueous pastoral will reappear, far less idyllically, in the last line of section 1 of "Berck-Plage," where the receding sea is "many-snaked" and seems to emit "a long hiss of distress."

For as the poet herself observes, even while the sea whose breath enfolded her childhood appeared to have a glamorous livingness ("Was it some huge, radiant animal?"), she was early alert to its alienness. Its mystifying susurrations suggested that the "Something . . . breathing" was "larger, farther, more serious, more weary" than her child self or her own mother. And by the end of her essay she admits that her primary vision of a magical sea—serenely peopled and beneficent of "lucky stones"—had "*stiffen*[ed]" and become "inaccessible, obsolet." When "My father died, we moved inland."

"My father died, we moved inland": for this famously father-haunted poet the comma splice that joins those two clauses is significant, suggesting that the death of the father and the sealing off of a life-giving *animal* sea are conjoined events. The dead father, Plath's grammar implies, begot a dead sea or perhaps, as in some earlier Plath poems, sank into such a sea, like the forsaken merman of Arnold's poem, whose calling is never heeded by the mortal "loved one" who's cast him aside for a life on land. How "cruel is she!" broods Arnold's salt-water soliloquist. "She left lonely forever / The kings of the sea." Figuratively, this plaint might be construed as the reproach of a dead man, a voice of the Arnoldian "buried life" of the past clamoring to be heard by the present and reminding us that, as Nigel Barley puts it, in most cultures the dead are imagined to "feel desperate grief and loneliness"—perhaps because we, the living, fear that we've abandoned them to the "other world" as the merman's wife has abandoned him.

Did Plath believe that, like the merman's "loved one," she'd left "lonely forever" an underwater king of the sea? Certainly, as she noted in her journals, she felt the kind of unjustified guilt about her father's demise that suggests she thought she'd somehow betrayed him, leaving him to grief and loneliness rather than the other way around. "It was my love that did us both to death," she insists in "Electra on Azalea Path." And in a later piece, titled simply "A Life," she envisions "a drowned man, complaining of the great cold, / [Who] crawls up out of the sea," as if about to utter Arnoldian reproaches.

That drowned/dead/abandoned man appears far more dauntingly in the relatively early "Full Fathom Five," a poem whose title Plath once considered using for the collection that eventually became *The Colossus*. But here the young writer depicts an opulently transformed sea-god–father as barely accessible ("you surface seldom") and mythically vast: "Miles long // Extend the radial sheaves / Of your spread hair." Yet though this paternal figure is scary and icy (he floats "near / As keeled ice-mountains // Of the north, to be steered clear / Of, not fathomed"), the poet is hopeful about his potential for her art, noting in one journal entry that as a title "Full Fathom Five" is "richly" significant because it "has the background of *The Tempest*" along with "the association of the sea, which is a central metaphor for my childhood [to] the father image," evoking both "my own father" and "the buried male muse and god-creator risen to be my mate in Ted."[23] And although Plath doesn't mention Arnold's poem here, such a sea-father–god again suggests the "Forsaken Merman," plaintively calling a landlocked mortal beloved.

Gradually, however, Plath's dead "sea-father" appears to have split into, on the one hand, an underwater absence or abeyance and, on the other hand, the stony landlocked ruin she confronts in "The Colossus" and even in the "cramped necropolis" and "speckled stone askew" of her father's grave "on Azalea Path." Gradually, too, the sea itself suffered a "sea-change" from the "something rich and strange" that it had been during her early childhood and into which it had at first seemed to transform the dead father: a change into a "something" that she describes in the late "Sheep in Fog" as "starless and fatherless," a "dark water" of annihilation.

Chronicling Plath's poetic evolution, Ted Hughes noted that not long after the couple's visit to Berck-Plage "the voice of *Ariel*" was coming into being. In "the poems of September, October, and November of 1961," he asserts, we "see her new self confronting—to begin with—*the sea. Not just the sea off Finisterre and off Hartland, but the Bay of the Dead, and 'nothing, nothing but a great space'*—which becomes the surgeon's 2 A.M. ward of mutilations [and then] her own moon-faced sarcophagus, her mirror clouding over, the moon in its most sinister aspect, and the yews—'blackness and silence' [emphasis added]."[24] The series to which Hughes refers here starts in late September 1961, with "Blackberrying" and "Finisterre," then moves through "The Surgeon at 2 A.M.," "Last Words," and "The Moon and the Yew Tree." It's a group of poems marked by mortal dread and desolation, most notably the poet's claim in "The Moon and the Yew Tree" that the moon "drags the sea after it like a dark crime; it is quiet / With the O-gape of complete despair [emphasis mine]" and her transcription of "the message of the yew tree" as "blackness—blackness and silence." But initially such hopelessness rises like a mist from the portrayals of the sea in "Blackberrying" and "Finisterre," two poems whose nihilistic vision of the poet's once-beloved ocean is of a piece with the suggestion in "Berck-Plage" that the sea is an "abeyance" of all that is familiar, an abeyance like death itself.

As Hughes indicates in an endnote, these works are in a sense companion pieces, with "Blackberrying" set in an English "cliff cove looking out on to the Atlantic" and "Finisterre" at the "westernmost tip of Brittany: the same outlook as 'Blackberrying' but a different country." But on a first reading the two poems may seem as far apart in mood as in geography, for where "Finisterre" frankly meditates on death, "Blackberrying" begins by describing an exuberant landscape ripe with berries, among meadows that glow "as if lit from within." Soon, though, it becomes clear that the "blue-red juices" and "blood sisterhood" of the berries, hung among a path "going down in hooks" to the sea, are almost allegorically deceptive.

> *I come to one bush of berries so ripe it is a bush of flies. . . .*
> *The honey-feast of the berries has stunned them; they believe in heaven.*
> *One more hook, and the berries and bushes end.*

As in some medieval *paysage moralisé*, the "hooks" of desire snare mortals—humans and flies alike—into believing that the sensual pleasures incarnated in the "honey-feast" of ripeness will go on forever; gorging on all they desire, duped and doped, the flies "believe in heaven."

"Overhead," however, the local crows known as choughs fly "in black, cacophonous flocks" and "Theirs is the only voice, protesting, protesting"; from above, presumably, they can see where the path is leading, as its hooks lure the traveler

> To the hills' northern face, and the face is orange rock
> That looks out on nothing, nothing *but a great space*
> *Of white and pewter lights, and a din like silversmiths*
> *Beating and beating at an intractable metal [emphasis added].*

Here the abeyance that is "nothing, nothing but a great space" becomes also frighteningly loud and—significantly—"intractable," meaning that it's both "Difficult to mold or manipulate" *and* "Difficult to alleviate, remedy, or cure," as in "*intractable pain.*"[25]

That this irremediable "nothing, nothing" is the great space or "abeyance" not just of the sea but of death becomes clear in "Finisterre," in which the "land's end" of the title is compared with "the last fingers" of the world, "Cramped on nothing." The sea here, the poet tells us, has "no bottom, or anything on the other side of it," though the cliffs that border it "are edged with trefoils, stars and bells / Such as fingers might embroider, close to death, / Almost too small for the mists to bother with." As for the mists themselves, they too

> . . . are part of the ancient paraphernalia—
> Souls, rolled in the doom-noise of the sea. . . .
> They go up without hope, like sighs.
> I walk among them, and they stuff my mouth with cotton.
> When they free me, I am beaded with tears.

That Plath completed this poem nearly a month before composing the more theatrically morbid "Moon and the Yew Tree" must have seemed at the least ominous to Hughes, her regular first reader. Certainly it isn't surprising that he described the entire group to which it belonged as "the most chilling pieces she had written up to this time."

Intensifying the chill of fear that haloes these works is surely their confrontation of a theological hopelessness that's notably modern: a definition of death as blank, black termination and thus of the consolations of the church—the "ancient paraphernalia" of religion—as what Philip Larkin was over a decade later to call "a vast, moth-eaten musical brocade."[26] Plath's confrontation of that paraphernalia is particularly sardonic in "Finisterre," where she describes the statue of Notre-Dames-des-Naufrages that still stands at Raz Point, in the Breton department of *Finistère*:

> *Our Lady of the Shipwrecked is striding toward the horizon,*
> *Her marble skirts blown back in two pink wings.*
> *A marble sailor kneels at her foot distractedly, and at his foot*
> *A peasant woman in black*
> *Is praying to the monument of the sailor praying.*

No more than a pointlessly pious mimesis of a mimesis, the peasant woman's prayer is directed to statuary that hears and sees nothing, though the female figure dominating the scene seems to be "striding toward the horizon." But "Our Lady of the Shipwrecked," the poet tells us, doesn't "hear what the sailor or the peasant is saying." Impervious to prayer, she is "in love with the beautiful formlessness of the sea."

In fact, the statue of Notre-Dame-des-Naufrages that still stands at Point du Raz in Brittany is significantly different from the figure that Plath describes in this poem. Rather than gazing out to sea as the poet asserts, the Madonna is looking benevolently down at both the desperately prayerful sailor and the marble baby in her arms (whose presence Plath suppresses)— and the holy child, for his part, is also gazing beneficently at the worshipper. Plath thus strikingly revises the conventional piety of the French tableau, which, as its engraved pedestal notes, was dedicated by the Church with great ceremony in 1904. From her skeptical perspective, this representation of a female divinity who is supposedly a life-giving mother goddess, her "lips sweet with divinity," is devoted to neither heavenly nor earthly life but, instead, to the alluring abeyance of death itself, the salt-water grave in which, as Moore put it, "dropped things are bound to sink— / in which if they turn and twist, it is neither with volition nor consciousness."[27]

Finally, in "The Moon and the Yew Tree," Plath amplifies her points about traditional religious beliefs, the church, the Madonna, and the yew tree emblematic both of death and of the lost "you/yew" who was the poet's father.[28] Here the moon that "drags the sea after it like a dark crime" and is "quiet / With the O-gape of complete despair" refutes by its simple presence the efforts of the church bells to "startle the sky" with their "Eight great tongues affirming the Resurrection." For the long-lived, poisonous yew "points up" to a savagely natural ("bald and wild") moon who "is my mother" and "is not sweet like Mary."

To be sure, the poet admits that she would "like to believe in tenderness," especially in the possibility that the "face of the effigy, gentled by candles," might single her out with "its mild eyes." But the very word "effigy," evoking both a statue of the dead and the poet's view of the marble Madonna in "Finisterre," illuminates what Plath does, apprehensively, believe. For she's "fallen a long way" from the hope for redemption guarded within the archaic structure of the church that's separated from her house "by a row of headstones"—by, that is, the stony reality of death itself. There, in the consecrated interior, saints float over "cold pews" and are "stiff with holiness," rigidified with a piety that's as stylized as that of the marble sailor frozen in his distracted pose. But "the light of the mind" by which this writer judges her surroundings guides her to a conclusion from which, throughout the rest of her life and work, she will not swerve.

"Bald and wild," the moon-as-"mother" is no Madonna; she can't even be mythologized as the White Goddess whose cult Robert Graves made famous and in whose mysteries Hughes had instructed Plath. Like the sea whose deadly tides she governs, she's "intractable" to human wishes, blank, indifferent. Even the attribution of a gender to "her" is provisional, for "she" is, after all, "it" earlier in the poem. Thus, although the yew tree that grows from the bodies of the dead points in "her" direction, "she" isn't even its message. For, declares Plath, "the message of the yew tree" is *only* "blackness—blackness and silence."

NOBODADDY

Sylvia Plath isn't usually treated as a theological thinker. Although Ted Hughes long ago counseled Judith Kroll to investigate his deceased wife's interest in *The White Goddess,* and although Tim Kendall's recent study of the poet's work has a good chapter titled "Piranha Religion: Plath's Theology," neither really examines the evolution of her (anti)system of (dis)beliefs in journals and poems. Kroll shows how Graves's pagan revivalism brought the young writer what Yeats once described as "metaphors for poetry," and Kendall is illuminating on her attitudes toward organized religions. But to the extent that both address the nihilism underlying the "O-gape" of the moon and the abeyance/gape of the sea, they approach it psychoanalytically, as part of what so many readers of Plath have considered the private mythology of death and rebirth most famously dramatized in "Lady Lazarus."[29]

But even as a child Plath had the kind of highly developed God-consciousness that one might expect from a precocious student. "I'll never speak to God again," she declared as a grief-stricken eight-year-old on the day her father died, or so her mother was later to testify.[30] Indeed, although Plath was raised as a Unitarian (with various Catholic or lapsed Catholic relatives), she was consistent in defining herself as what a friend of mine once called a "believing atheist." Nevertheless, like many bright adolescents, she frequently brooded on the existence or nonexistence of God, on the existence or nonexistence of a spiritual afterlife, and on the question of human destiny. But in her late teens, she confided to her journal what became her indelible belief system. "I don't believe there is life after death in the literal sense," she declared. "I don't believe my individual ego or spirit is unique and important enough to wake up after burial and soar to bliss and pink clouds in heaven. If we leave the body behind as we must, we are nothing." More specifically she added: "I think I will be snuffed out. Black is sleep; black is a fainting spell; and black is death, with no light, no waking."[31]

The relentless honesty that later forced Plath to confront the volcanic feelings underlying such poems as "Daddy," "Medusa," "Lesbos," and "Burning the Letters" left her with no defenses against her own lack of faith. The consolations of philosophies that envision the soul's merging with the cosmos or its regeneration in nature—ideas propounded by, say, a Whitmanian transcendentalism or a Lawrentian pantheism—seem to have been as unavailable to her as they were to Sartre and Camus, the two existentialist thinkers in whose views her generation of student intellectuals was most immersed. "(Oh, the grimness of atheism!)" she exclaimed parenthetically in one early journal entry, and in another she drove herself to face the *timor mortis* formulated by Beckett's Lucky when he hints that "a personal God quaquaquaqua with white beard" only signifies "the earth abode of stones in the great cold."[32] "Now, you begin to get scared," she warned herself. "You don't believe in God, or a life-after-death, so you can't hope for sugar plums when your non-existent soul rises. . . . Cats have nine lives, the saying goes. You have one; and somewhere along the thin, tenuous thread of your existence there is . . . the stopped heartbeat that spells the end of this particular individual which is spelled 'I' and 'You' and 'Sylvia.' "[33]

Of course, like many other nonbelievers, Plath struggled against the "grimness of atheism," flirting with what felt like comforting possibilities: Christian Science, Catholicism. And like many other literary intellectuals, she resolved to study the Bible for its "symbolic meaning, even though the belief in a moral God-structured universe [was] not there [in her mind]. Live As If it were? A great device." The "risen Christ," she added, is "a parable of human renewal and nothing of immortality."[34] Yet neither symbolic readings of Scripture nor parables of "human renewal" assuaged a fear that, like Beckett's unfortunate Lucky, Plath couldn't *not* face. "The horror," she wrote when she was a graduate student at Cambridge, is "the sudden folding up and away of the phenomenal world, leaving nothing. Just rags . . . no space and no time: the whistling breath of eternity, not of god, but of the denying devil."[35]

With this metaphysical horror was mingled the more physical horror of death dreams that afflicted the poet throughout her life. In one, she found herself walking along a corridor filled with dead and decaying bodies, a dream from which she "woke screaming [at] the horror of the deformed and *dead, alive as we are,* and I among them, in the filth and swarming corruption of the flesh [emphasis added]."[36] The terrible notion that the dead might somehow be "alive as we are," suffering in what this poet was to call in "Lady Lazarus" the "flesh the grave cave ate," is a common fantasy. But in Plath's case it took on a resonance even more terrifying than the emotion it elicits in most mourners. For as she came to understand, the God to whom she resolved "never" to speak again when her father died had Himself died into the grave of the dead father, where the two merged and became one fearsome dead God, a God very like the sinister Father God whom William Blake—ironically fusing "Nobody" and "Daddy"—labeled "Nobodaddy."

For Plath, to be a "believing atheist" was to believe in God's absence as if it were a presence, immanent in all things as the divine supposedly is. Asked in a late interview about writers who were important to her, she responded that she'd begun "to look to Blake, for example," and at least one critic has detected the influence of his "Marriage of Heaven and Hell" in "Lady Lazarus," while the poet herself commented on his significance in "Death & Co.," where his death mask actually appears in the text.[37] But the opening lines of Blake's "To Nobodaddy" summarize a great deal about the antideific deity who looms not just behind the familiar, familial patriarch usually identified with Plath's "Daddy" but also within the "blackness and silence" that she sees as ultimately engulfing the whole phenomenal world.

Why art thou silent & invisible
Father of Jealousy
Why dost thou hide thyself in clouds
From every searching Eye

Why darkness & obscurity
In all thy words & laws. . . .[38]

Like the dead father Plath tries to resurrect in "The Colossus," like the daddy from whom she seeks to disentangle herself in "Daddy," and perhaps above all like the God in whom she didn't believe, Nobodaddy is a "denying devil" and thus an "abeyance"—a "blackness and silence"—in the world of the living. And it's his (anti)religion that the sinister priest of "Berck-Plage" serves in the role of Father Death, stalking the living with his dark glasses, his black cassock, and his merciless black boot, which "is the hearse of a dead foot."

Of course it's clear that the infamous daddy of "Daddy" isn't only a Blakeian "Nobodaddy." That scary "man in black with a Meinkampf look" has autobiographical, political, and sociocultural origins, not just in the poet's own dead German-born father and the black-jacketed husband from whom she was angrily estranged but also in the Nazi figure of the Führer (the "father" of his people), in the technocratic engines of power that drive "Daddy"'s "roller / Of wars, wars, wars" and in the hierarchical structure of patriarchy itself. Thus this Nobodaddy is the God of Hiroshima, whose "ash" circles the globe (in "Fever 103") as well as the God of "Dachau, Auschwitz, Belsen" (in "Daddy"). And like a predatory Frankenstein, he is the God of the scientists who invented not just the "mercuric / Atoms that cripple" (in "Nick and the Candlestick") but also the injurious drug thalidomide (in the poem of that name) as well as the ovens, glowing "like heavens," that have already, unnervingly, "*emptied* one man into space" (emphasis added; in "Mary's Song").

One of the comments that Plath wrote for the BBC when she was preparing to read "Daddy" on the air, however, suggests a special link between a personal father and a theological "Nobodaddy." "Here is a poem spoken by a girl with an Electra complex," noted Plath, explaining: "Her father died while she thought he was God." And indeed the poet's own father *did* die "while she thought he was God"—became helplessly ill and died while his child might still have attributed at least semidivine powers to him. But if the father-as-"God" couldn't save himself and was instead both fallible and hopelessly mortal, then the God who let the father die—even perhaps killed him—wasn't only a *bad* God ("I'll never speak to God again") but a *dead* God, just as the father was a dead God, a nonexistent God of "blackness and silence," a Nobodaddy. In this way, a childhood loss to which the precocious eight-year-old Sylvia Plath reacted with theologically tinged intensity helped transform the child into the adult poet "Sylvia Plath," whose vision of the void represented by "Nobodaddy" was, as Freud might put it, "over-determined." For even while it was a vision weighted down by public feelings of metaphysical loss and political revulsion that she shared with many other writers of her generation, it was also a vision thickened and darkened by private grief.

Against both public loss and private grief, Plath set a series of performative poems in which she sometimes sought to resurrect "Nobodaddy" and sometimes to resurrect her lost, believing self. In "The Colossus," for instance, she describes trying to piece together the shards of an enormous collapsed statue: both the dead father and the dead God with whom he's merged. And her use of the colossus as a metaphor for the dead is uncannily astute, for as the classicist Jean Pierre Vernant has pointed out in his *Myth and Thought among the Greeks*, in the ancient world the term "colossos" didn't primarily "refer to effigies of gigantic, 'colossal' dimensions as it later came to do." Rather, the "colossos" was a roughly hewn slab of stone that "took the place of the dead man," embodying "in permanent form . . . the life that is opposed to that of living men as the world of night is opposed to the world of light." In fact, Vernant claims, the primordial "colossos is not an image; it is a 'double,' as the dead man himself is a double of the living man," and this stony double often stands in some isolated place "so wild that it is said to belong to the powers of the underworld."[39]

Whether or not Plath (who wrote a college thesis on the double in Dostoyevsky) knew of this ancient Greek practice, her shattered effigy of a god/father is certainly a colossus in Vernant's sense besides being "colossal" in the usual sense that alludes to a monument both gigantic and deific, like, for instance, the famous Colossus of Rhodes, a huge statue of the god Helios that was one of the seven wonders of the antique world. Thus this poet's insolent address to the fragments of "fluted bones and acanthine hair . . . littered" in "their old anarchy to the horizon-line" implies that she means her title in both senses (colossus as effigy of the dead, colossus as effigy of the divine) even while she confesses that any effort at communication with such a Nobodaddy is actually sens*eless*. "Perhaps you consider yourself an oracle," she mockingly taunts the broken statue, yet "Thirty years now I have labored / To dredge the silt from your throat" and "I am none the wiser."

Though its meanings and intentions are quite serious, however, "The Colossus" is also a comic poem, with its depiction of a dead father/god whose indecipherable "speech," such as it is ("Mule-bray, pig-grunt and bawdy cackles"), is "worse than a barnyard" and of a daughterly acolyte who has to clean his dismembered ruins "with gluepots and pails of Lysol." Similarly, both "Daddy" and "Lady Lazarus," the two works for which Plath is probably most famous, are also comic performances, vaudeville turns designed to trivialize the dead father/god who is, in both, the speaker's invisible antagonist. On the one hand, just as deliberately as "The Colossus" strove to re*member* a shattered deity, these poems strive to resurrect an autonomous self for their speaker, a self that's confidently skeptical and therefore free from dependence on the Nobodaddy who is in any case either absent or malevolent. On the other hand, the "dancing and stamping" nursery rhymes into which the poet immediately plunges in both works ("You do not do, you do not do / Any more black shoe" in "Daddy" and "I have done it again. / One year in every ten" in "Lady Lazarus") make her burlesque plans clear from the start.[40]

For if God the Father is as dead as her human father, the poet implies, maybe there's nothing to do but mock Him (the God) along with him the (father). Thus one of Plath's biographers reports that the poet performed "Daddy" for a friend so comically that both women collapsed in gales of laughter.[41] Blitzed by historical catastrophe, the theology in both works is formulated with impudent defiance, as if one of Nobodaddy's enraged children were acting on a dare. "Panzer-man, panzer-man, O You— // Not God but a swastika / So black no sky could squeak through," this speaker jeers at the "Daddy" whom she'd once imagined as God but now sees as merely an effigy, "marble-heavy, a *bag* full of God [emphasis added]"; and "Herr God, Herr Lucifer / Beware / Beware," she shrieks in "Lady Lazarus." Identifying with the Jews victimized by the Holocaust, Plath here even puts aside her own late, intermittent anti-Semitism and her ferocious jealousy of her estranged husband's half-Jewish mistress to imagine a speaker willing to bet recklessly on an impossible triumph at the very edge of existence, the way some doomed Jews did in Warsaw and Auschwitz, Treblinka and Bergen-Belsen.[42]

Yet even these assured little monodramas in which the speaker becomes a metaphysical stand-up comic were written, so Plath explained in a letter to a friend, in "God's intestine"—written, that is, by a poet who felt herself being inexorably digested by the blackness and silence of Nobodaddy. In the last analysis, then, their fierce religious play collapses into the grotesque harlequinade of Beckett's Lucky, chained to the cesspool mastery of Pozzo and mouthing parodic platitudes about "a personal God quaquaquaqua with white beard" while shrinking from his dread of "the earth abode of stones." The comic premise of "Lady Lazarus," after all—"I am only thirty. / And like the cat I have nine times to die"—is one that Sylvia Plath had long since ruefully dismissed: "Cats have nine lives, the saying goes. You have one; and somewhere along the thin, tenuous thread of your existence there is the black knot, the blood clot, the stopped heartbeat." And the final, presumably triumphant line of "Daddy"—"Daddy, daddy, you bastard, I'm through"—punningly undercuts itself. For the poet's last word on the subject of the "bag full of God" to whom she's been so long enthralled could mean either "through with *you*" or "*through* myself" (finished, over and "done for"). Through with the being of "this particular individual . . . spelled 'I' and 'You' and 'Sylvia.'"

IT IS GIVEN UP

Ultimately, Plath's great sequence of poems on beekeeping—beginning with "The Bee Meeting" and moving through "Stings" to "Wintering"—may have represented the limit of the self-creation this poet could imagine in the face of Nobodaddy's all-effacing absence. Here, implicitly punning on "bee-ing" and "being," she imagined a queenly self escaping from "the mausoleum, the wax house" of what she saw as colossally empty theological and social structures betokening a universe of death. But as the lonely *annus mirabilis* in which Plath composed the *Ariel* poems wore on, the strain of maintaining an aesthetic of defiance took its toll. By the time she left Devon to move to London with her children in December 1962, the exhilarated rebellion that had animated the verse she'd produced earlier in the autumn—poems ranging from "A Birthday Present" to "Childless Woman"—had begun to falter.

And Nobodaddy, who'd been briefly tamed or at least trivialized when he was reduced to an old shoe, a bag full of God, a parodic Nazi, a sideshow villain, had swelled again to blot out the stars. In "Lyonesse," he's become "the *big* God" who "lazily closed one eye" and let the inhabitants of the legendarily drowned land of Lyonesse, a Celtic kingdom in Cornwall, "slip // Over the English cliff." In "Getting There," the poem's speaker is dragged through Europe's history of "wars, wars, wars" in boxcars powered by the "terrible brains / Of Krupp," the munitions manufacturer, only to step "from the black car of Lethe" into the deadliness of a "you" who is clearly the same indifferent "big God." And the mind—or, more accurately, the mindlessness—of that God shapes the "black amnesias of heaven" soaring above the "night dances" of Plath's baby son in the poem so named: tiny, beautiful gestures that are "warm and human"—and doomed. For as the poet complains in "Brasilia," this amnesiac God in whose "intestine" she's writing her poems is no more or less than a voracious black hole, a "You who eat[s] // People like light rays."

At last, in "Death & Co.," Plath's speaker reports a visit from two of Nobodaddy's emissaries, one who wears Blake's death mask and is savagely honest, letting her know that she is "red meat," and the other who is his snakily seductive partner, "Masturbating a glitter." Together they seem to seal her fate, for although she swears, "I do not stir," she hears "The dead bell, / The dead bell" and knows that "Somebody's done for." That somebody, by implication, is the "particular individual . . . spelled 'I' and 'You' and 'Sylvia,' " an identity from which she has already begun to imagine detaching herself.

As Ted Hughes was among the first to note, then, Plath's style and attitude changed significantly in the poems she wrote following "Sheep in Fog," which was begun on December 2, 1962.[43] In the increasingly fatalistic works that she produced in January 1963 after a poetic silence that lasted through most of December 1962, the nihilism toward which the graveyard led in "The Moon and the Yew Tree" has already invaded the human body, in "The Munich Mannequins" becoming a part of the womb where "the yew trees blow like hydras," blooming with death rather than life, and in "Totem" transforming "people that were important" into no more than "round eyes . . . teeth . . . grimaces / On a stick that rattles and clicks."

Nor does the skeletal stick of "Totem" merely inhabit human flesh; in the end, so this poem argues, it is a tool wielded by Nobodaddy in his guise of a figure whom Plath, an inveterate student of mythology, would have associated with Anansi the Spider, a West African trickster and intermediary of the sky god often associated with Ashanti death rituals.[44]

I am mad, calls the spider, waving its many arms.

And in truth it is terrible,
Multiplied in the eyes of the flies.

They buzz like blue children
In nets of the infinite,

Roped in at the end by the one
Death with its many sticks.

The flies here recall the deluded insects of "Blackberrying," believing in the "honey-feast" of heaven but doomed, instead, to a bitter end of blackness and silence. And the many-legged (many-sticked) spider god of death that ropes them in may seem at first glamorously "mad" ("Masturbating a glitter") as it waves "its many arms" like Shiva, the dancing Hindu avatar of destruction. But ultimately it's merely "mad" in the sense of absurd—a lunatic emblem of a universe in which, as in the earlier, unnerving "Insomniac," even the stars are no more than "peepholes" letting in a "bonewhite light, like death, behind all things."[45]

And for the poet herself, in this last month of her life, the metaphor of the roped-in fly, caught in a net of the infinite, replaces the figure of the queen bee, unleashed and soaring above the mausoleum of the old hive. In a reading of "The Colossus," Jahan Ramazani has noted that although early in the poem Plath mocks the dead father/god's "vast incoherence," by the end of the work "she seems to have been sucked into his enormous bulk," and of course that's true.[46] Yet at least the author of "The Colossus" *could* mock her antagonist. By January 1962, however, her personal and philosophical intuition of a suction drawing her into absolute blackness and silence had become no laughing matter.

Two days after composing "Totem," Plath returned to the image of the hopeless and foolish fly, in "Mystic," a strikingly irreligious meditation on organized religion.

The air is a mill of hooks—
Questions without answer,
Glittering and drunk as flies . . .

she begins, then propounds a pained question to which, given the system of beliefs she's developed throughout her career, the answer—if there is one—can only be itself painful. "*Once one has seen God, what is the remedy?* [emphasis added]." Evoking the illness of mortality that the poet earlier encountered in "Berck-Plage," the word "remedy" suggests that any vision of the awful "big God" who is Nobodaddy must be a vision of what is poisonous (as a yew tree), deadly (as a spider), and malevolent (as Father Death). Nor can such a bleak vision be treated with spurious medications like the "pill of the Communion tablet" and "the bright pieces / Of Christ in the

faces of rodents. . . .Whose hopes are so low they are comfortable." Consequently, among the handful of poems that Plath wrote following "Mystic"
in the last two weeks of her life, there are several that dwell with entranced
urgency on illness and injury. "Contusion" and "Edge," both marked by the
estranged language that gives "Berck-Plage" so much power, are the most
notable of these.

In "Contusion" (which rhymes evocatively with "conclusion"), a bruise
or "contusion" ("Color floods to the spot, dull purple") recalls, first, "the
doom-noise of the sea" in which "souls" were "rolled" in "Finisterre" ("In a
pit of rock / The sea sucks obsessively"), and then the doomed flies of
"Blackberrying," "Totem," and "Mystic":

> *The size of a fly,*
> *The doom mark*
> *Crawls down the wall.*

And the appearance of this final, emblematic fly evokes the terror of human
destiny as formulated by Gloucester in *King Lear*: "As flies to wanton boys
are we to the gods, / They kill us for their sport." For a mortal fate has been
sealed, though there is in fact no person in the poem—neither an "I" nor a
"she"—nor even (as in "Death & Co.") a "somebody" who's "done for."

> The *heart shuts,*
> The *sea slides back,*
> The *mirrors are sheeted [emphasis added].*

At last, in "Edge," the "self-elegy" Plath wrote shortly before her suicide,
the poet enacts a separation of soul and body in which, dispassionately
describing a Medea-like mother whose immolation of herself and her children gives the "illusion of a Greek necessity," she offers a revision of the traditional mourning poem that's even more disturbing than "Berck-Plage." To
be sure, as Ramazani points out, by representing a version of her dead self
"as a flower" who has folded her children "back into her body as petals / Of
a rose close when the garden // Stiffens," Plath "again returns to the reper-
toire of the elegy," but this time deploying the flower imagery that marked,
say, the writings of Milton and Whitman, in order to figure herself "among
the elegized dead who live on in the flowers of poetry." Yet even such a subtle image of "living on" is subverted both by the nihilism of the poem's

simultaneously suicidal and infanticidal premise and by the speaker's almost zombielike detachment from this radically depleted imagining of her own destiny.

Equally terrible is the vision of the moon's vision with which Plath finally brings her poem, along with her poetic career, to a close:

> *The moon has nothing to be sad about,*
> *Staring from her hood of bone.*
>
> *She is used to this sort of thing.*
> *Her blacks crackle and drag.*

As in "The Moon and the Yew Tree," the moon is here once again presiding over a message of blackness. Yet what had earlier been the moon's passive and impassive silence has now become an actively malevolent "crackling." For like the "mad" spider in "Totem," the moon here is a figure of death searching for victims. Simultaneously in an armor or "hood of bone" and dwelling in a (neighbor) "hood of bone," "she" crackles as if with lightning and drags for victims with "nets of the infinite." And as in "Berck-Plage" there is indeed a very special "nothing to be sad about": the nothing that is the great abeyance of the sea and the nothing that is the big dead God to whom all must ultimately surrender.

SYLVIA PLATH AND "SYLVIA PLATH"

All the works on which I've been meditating here are of course *poems,* which is to say they are in some sense *fictions.* Thus, although they're plainly what the critic Judith Kroll called "Chapters in a Mythology," they needn't necessarily predict any particular life course or, more specifically, any pull toward death. What they do show, however, is that Plath's career as a poet, an elegist, and a metaphysician was shaped by the same tide of existential despair that has engulfed many other late-twentieth-century elegies, although it sounds with an unusually "long hiss of distress" in "Berck-Plage." Trying to find something to set against the "great abeyance" of the sea and with which to defy the grim figure of Father Death, whose "black boot has no mercy for anybody," this artist positions gestures of defiance and "Things, things—"—"dresses and hats and china" and beehives and flowers—in their proper poetic places. Yet in the end, as she's forced to concede, the "lozenge" of wood that is the coffin of the dead man is and must be "given up" to the earth that will eat it as Nobodaddy eats light rays. And the project of defiance, too, must be given up.

Nonetheless, just as there is Berck-Plage and there is "Berck-Plage," so there was Sylvia Plath and there is "Sylvia Plath." And just as in Berck-Plage Plath unerringly chose the right beach to metamorphose into "Berck-Plage," so she unerringly singled out the personal details that transformed her from the complex and variegated person who was Sylvia Plath to a more simplified version of the self as "Sylvia Plath." By all accounts, Sylvia Plath was a brilliant, extremely intense, astonishingly accomplished young woman. Whether her composition of often disturbingly nihilistic verse might have precipitated her suicide, however, and, if so, through what psychological mechanisms this could have happened must always be a matter for conjecture. Yet within the first years after her death Sylvia Plath began to be mythologized by others as a "Sylvia Plath" whom her own poems hadn't necessarily chosen to represent. Her onetime verse-writing teacher Robert Lowell characterized her as "hardly a person at all [but instead] one of those super-real, hypnotic, great classical heroines," and her literary friend Al Alvarez described her as having the "pale face . . . gaunt figure [and] curiously desolate, rapt air [of a] priestess emptied out by the rites of her cult."[47]

Much of the notoriety Plath posthumously achieved was clearly a consequence of her suicide, her youth, and her embattled relationship with the estranged husband who survived her to function as a villain in a story whose contours will perhaps never be entirely understood. Hughes's subsequent fame, his accession to the pomp and circumstance of England's poet laureateship, his widely publicized affairs, and the theatrical death of the woman for whom he left Plath (Assia Guttman gassed herself *and* her child) added a further and more lurid glow to the outline of what came to be called "the Plath myth." Lately, indeed, these soap opera elements of the myth have given rise to several novels and a film along with numerous biographical studies not just of the author's life and work but of the myth itself. "Sylvia Plath haunts our culture," begins Jacqueline Rose's book on Plath as eerie revenant, and the critic adds that "Plath herself has . . . become a figure for death, Death in the shape of a woman, femininity as deadly," so that the "spectre of psychic life rises up in her person as a monumental affront for which she is punished."[48]

Yet need we assume that the legend of "Sylvia Plath" is integrally related to the dismal fate of the talented "real-life" Sylvia Plath? Sylvia Plath died with her head in an oven after (perhaps) being dosed with an antidepressant to which she was allergic, in the midst of a "snow blitz" in London and at the end of a weekend when (according to one informant) she may have had an unsatisfactory meeting with her husband so that (according to another) she wept inconsolably in his car as he was driving her back to her apartment on the evening before she killed herself. But suppose Sylvia Plath hadn't taken her own life. Suppose she'd survived and moved, say, to Mexico, where she might even now be drafting new and brilliant poems in a Oaxacan villa. Wouldn't "Berck-Plage," like so many other works she authored, still "haunt" our culture? Yet they'd have been written by a "Sylvia Plath" very different from the "gaunt," death-dedicated "priestess" of Alvarez's imaginings or the "super-real, hypnotic" heroine Lowell portrayed.[49]

"How your bad dreams possess and endow me," cries the tormented tree that is the speaker of Plath's "Elm," a poem that, along with "The Moon and the Yew Tree," is one of two arboreal works Hughes considered central to his wife's aesthetic self-creation. Indeed, *our* cultural bad dreams—our dread of termination, our Holocaust technologies of killing, our medicalized technologies of dying, our inescapable photos of the dead—possessed "Sylvia Plath" and endowed her with an extraordinarily compelling poetic voice in which she lamented wounds, darknesses, and absences that we all feel or fear. Perhaps what Jacqueline Rose defines as the "spectre of psychic life [rising] up in [Plath's] person" began to seem to some observers like "a monumental affront" for which the poet should be punished precisely because this very young but very accomplished woman boldly took on the arduous task of speaking to, and for, a death-denying society—and speaking as if with what Shelley called "the mantle of a prophecy."

In a late interview Plath declared:

The issues of our time which preoccupy me at the moment are the incalculable genetic effects of fallout and a documentary article on the terrifying, mad, omnipotent marriage of big business and the military in America. . . . Does this influence the kind of poetry I write? Yes, but in a sidelong fashion. I am not gifted with the tongue of Jeremiah, though I may be sleepless enough before my vision of the apocalypse. My poems do not turn out to be about Hiroshima, but about a child forming itself finger by finger in the dark. They are not about the terrors of mass extinction but about the bleakness of the moon over a yew tree in a neighboring graveyard.[50]

Yet in fact her poems *do* "turn out to be about Hiroshima" and "the terrors of mass extinction" even while they're also about "a child forming itself fin-

ger by finger in the dark" and "the bleakness of the moon over a yew tree."
Beyond specific mentions of what Edith Wyschogrod calls the twentieth
century's "death-events," Hiroshima and Auschwitz among them, Plath's
"vision of the apocalypse" summarized much that terrified most of her contemporaries and continues to terrify her descendants in an age that's as anxious as it is skeptical.

More specifically, some of the verse meditations this troubled young
mother-poet set in the border zones between life and death—seaside works
from "Finisterre" to "Berck-Plage" along with more openly apocalyptic
visions like "Fever 103," "Mary's Song,"and "Edge"—dramatize the nightmares haunting the cold war culture of the 1950s that shaped her sensibility. Much of what obsessed Plath, for instance, is enacted in Stanley
Kramer's *On the Beach*, an end-of-the-world film about nuclear holocaust
(based on a best seller by Nevil Shute) whose ominous music won an Academy Award in 1959. Here, with most of the globe annihilated, the only
remaining survivors of a catastrophic war are the inhabitants of Australia,
but they too are merely waiting for the end of humanity, as a radioactive
cloud draws nearer to their continent. They prepare for catastrophe by
stockpiling suicide pills to administer to their children and then themselves,
as the "mass extinction" becomes reality. Whether or not Plath saw Kramer's
movie (or read Shute's novel), its apocalyptic "terrors" are surely among the
social pressures that shaped her imaginings of doom.

"Red was your colour . . . red / Was what you wrapped around you. /
Blood red . . . for warming the dead?" So begins the last poem of Ted
Hughes's *Birthday Letters* to the dead Sylvia Plath. "But," he concludes, "the
jewel you lost was blue."[51] The jewel was blue? Hughes explains: "Blue was
wings. . . . Blue was your kindly spirit." But he may have also meant that, as
he knew better than most, the young woman who was to become "Sylvia
Plath" had early lost the sense of magical safety that most children experience as, in Freud's words, a feeling of "oceanic oneness" with a sheltering
parent. The blue jewel of the nurturing sea that she describes so vividly in
"Ocean 1212-W" as a "huge, radiant animal" bestowing "purple 'lucky'
stones" had, she tells us, "stiffened" and receded when "My father died, we
moved inland." Instead, that dead sea became a great abeyance, a starless
and fatherless dark water. And as Sylvia Plath turned herself into "Sylvia
Plath" in the course of her mourning for the lost blue jewel, this preco-
ciously "believing atheist" became, first, Elektra, then electrifying, as she
dramatized the bad dreams that possess us all. For in one way or another
many of us have lost that blue jewel.

Now too, because so many readers sense the resonance with which the bad dreams of "Sylvia Plath" reiterate our own just as her loss replicates ours, her mourning has become electronic. Google now lists "343,000 English pages for Sylvia Plath," including (at present count) more than thirty Web sites entirely devoted to her work. At one of those sites, as I musingly calculated their numbers, I found a photo of a page from the young poet's copy of Walt Whitman's *Leaves of Grass*. Here, in her determined, blocky handwriting, she's commenting on one of the most famous lines about death and mourning that her magisterial precursor uttered in "Song of Myself." "All goes onward and outward, nothing collapses," Whitman affirms. "And to die is different from what anyone supposed, and luckier."

"Optimist!" remarks Plath, on the margin of the page.

"The suicide sprawls on the bloody floor of the bedroom," writes Whitman. "I witness the corpse with its dabbled hair," he continues, "I note where the pistol has fallen."

Plath underlines "witness" and "note." Then adds, "but doesn't <u>understand</u>" at the end of the passage.[52]

Like the channel that divides Berck-Plage from Dover Beach, Plath's sense of the gap between Whitman's mysteriously confident witnessing and her own certainty of death's *un*luckiness dramatizes the gulf between nineteenth-century views of how death should at least *seem* to the hopeful believer and twentieth-century visions of "modern death."

Was the Nineteenth Century Different, and Luckier?

THE DEATH BOOK STUFF

What *did* Whitman mean when he argued that "to die is different from what anyone supposed, and luckier"? Was he just a nineteenth-century acolyte of what our own era was to call the power of positive thinking, as Sylvia Plath's marginal exclamation ("Optimist!") implied? Decades ago, after I had finished my dissertation, I planned a project in literary criticism that was intended to address this question: a study of the ways nineteenth- and twentieth-century poets imagined and reimagined death. At one point I was going to quote Wallace Stevens's great antitheological poem "Sunday Morning" and call this treatise "'The Mother of Beauty': Romantic and Post-Romantic Metaphors of Death," and at another point—in an homage to the line from Whitman that so bemused Plath—I decided to title it " 'Different, and Luckier': Romantic and Post-Romantic . . . etc."

I applied for fellowships to research the book, earned a summer stipend, and eventually taught a course whose syllabus was based on my work-in-progress. But within a few years history intervened, in the form of the second wave of feminism, utterly changing my critical focus. Without a backward glance, I put aside " 'Different, and Luckier' " to set out on an entirely new enterprise.

But why was my projected exploration of "Romantic and Post-Romantic Metaphors of Death" so easily relegated to the back of a file cabinet? When a few months ago I unearthed my old notes —a bulging folder with "Death Book Stuff" scribbled across the top—I reread the "Description of Proposed Study" that I'd drafted for various funding agencies. It began by defining "a modern tradition of death poetry in which death, in a number of significantly a-Christian ways, is consistently defined as 'the mother of beauty'" and went on to argue that the development of life's end into a "complex poetic metaphor" really originated in the early nineteenth century, with the Romantic poets Keats and Shelley, themselves both fated to die young. For tubercular John Keats, I noted, death seemed at least some of the time to be "life's high meed": a reward but perhaps also, punning on "mead," a source of ecstatic intoxication. And for his contemporary Percy Bysshe Shelley, death was a weird goal, a mystical end in itself. "Die, / If thou wouldst be with that which thou dost seek!" Shelley advised readers of "Adonais," his elegy for Keats. Death continued to radiate a mysterious glamour for later-nineteenth-century writers too, I added, especially for Walt Whitman, who defined it as a "delicious word" that clarified life itself and insisted that "to die is different from what anyone supposed, and luckier."

Several years elapsed between the time when I outlined these plans and the moment when I abandoned the project. In the spring semester of one of those years I taught a course actually named "Different, and Luckier." And that course did indeed constitute a learning experience.

What I learned was that my argument didn't work—at least not for me and not the way I'd shaped it. It probably didn't work for my students either, though they were more inclined to blame themselves than me, their supposed "teacher," for their failures to "get" what I was saying.

"Different, and luckier"? The more we meditated on Whitman's "delicious word, *death*," and the ways in which, I averred, it "clarified life itself," the more we got entangled in our own, and Whitman's, mystical vocabulary. Was this death from the *inside*, as it's experienced by the dying one at a—at *the*—agonistic moment of extremity, or death from the *outside*, as its preternatural serenity appears to a desirous observer? And the perspectives of other poets we discussed turned out to be equally confusing. We considered, for instance, the aesthetic pleasures presumably proffered by "horrible but voluptuous" images of disintegration, from Keats's fatally seductive "belle dame sans merci" who has "death pale" kings and princes "in thrall" to the scarily persuasive business partners who star in Sylvia Plath's "Death & Co."—a lineup of lyrics that might be said to glamorize dying by making it sound as luxurious as an expensive perfume. But while these decadent images of dying were more persuasive, because more sinister, than the abstract notion of a consummation that was enigmatically "different, and

luckier," they didn't have more than a surface meaning for any of us, probably because we all were too young and cheerful to grasp the lure of the
suicidal.

I was on safer philosophical ground when we turned, next, to death as a
"mother of beauty" because "she" fosters what I defined as "that frisson of
awareness which is an acknowledgment of mortal beauty." Here we examined the fairly standard idea that the imminence of death makes beauty
beautiful or happiness happy precisely because we humans understand that
the term of our delights is by nature limited. As I guided my students
through Keats's "Ode on a Grecian Urn" or Stevens's "Sunday Morning,"
emphasizing the ways these great poems critique the idea of eternal joy as
not only impossible but icy (in Keats) or boring (in Stevens), we encountered arguments that made logical sense to everyone in the room.

Yes, the figures on Keats's urn were frozen forever. His courting swain,
endlessly approaching the maiden whose lips were his "goal," could never
die. But at the same time, he could never attain his desire; as Keats almost
tauntingly declared, "Bold lover, never, never canst thou kiss." And yes,
Stevens concedes that his poem's protagonist feels the "need of some imperishable bliss." But the paradise he depicts in his poem is a heaven of tedium,
a perpetual life that's so static it's a form of eternal death: "Is there no *change
of death* in paradise? / Does ripe fruit never fall? Or do the boughs / Hang
always heavy in that perfect sky . . . ? [emphasis added]."

Yet I suspect no one present for our stimulating metaphysical discussions came away feeling "different" and "luckier" about our mortality. How
many of us would have concluded, "Thank God I can die—since it means I
can also kiss" or "Thank heaven I don't have to go to *that* heaven"? We
sensed (though we never said) that there was a kind of casuistry in our—or
rather, to be honest, in *my*—approach to this material. I had left out something important, something central.

I had left out dread and suffering, grief and sorrow.

Why did my lesson plans, lectures, and grant applications repress mortal suffering? In part, I guess, I was too fascinated by the positive glow that
surrounded Stevens's "mother of beauty" and Whitman's "different, and
luckier" to wonder what anxieties these phrases concealed. Or perhaps I was
enthralled by Stevens's and Whitman's words precisely because I needed
their evident certainties to assuage my own fears and sorrows. For after all,
even then I had suffered losses—mourned the deaths of my firstborn child,
of my still-youthful father, and my much-loved grandparents. Maybe I
wanted to comfort myself with this book that was going to be titled, with

such vigorous assurance, either "The Mother of Beauty" or "Different, and Luckier."

Yet when my students and I tried to disentangle those cryptically affirmative locutions, we found ourselves going in circles, deciphering one riddle with another: "[T]he mother of beauty" *means* "different, and luckier"—or maybe vice versa, "different, and luckier" means "the mother of beauty."

Toward the end of the class, oddly enough, our discussions were often dominated by one member of the group, a young man who'd worked summers as a paramedic, riding along on ambulances to respond to 911 calls. He'd witnessed a number of deaths, he told us, and we listened eagerly to his real-life stories of life's real end. By this time I knew the course hadn't yielded me any of the insights I sought, but I consoled myself with the consideration that at least I'd introduced my students to some of the greatest poems of the nineteenth and twentieth centuries. As for our absorption in the young man's anecdotes, I think I considered it a sign that we really didn't have much else to say about "Romantic and Post-Romantic Metaphors of Death" rather than what it really was: a clue to what was wrong with my approach to these metaphors.

For ultimately, "Different, and Luckier," both class and book, were projects about how death was *okay*, yet somehow in the course of our investigation the subject itself began to seem *not so okay*. Rooted in what appeared to be Whitman's mystical optimism, my project evaded pain. In a curious way, I was reenacting not just the cultural sequestration of the dying that sociologists and historians have lately studied but also our modern tendency to deny or marginalize grief and mourning. Had the great poets of the last two hundred years done that too?

"NOT POETRY"

The "great" poets: if one of my mistakes had been to misread the pain implicit in some of the "metaphors of death" I proposed to analyze, another may have been to suppose that the visions dramatized in the works of poets we now consider "great" necessarily represented widely held views. I seem in those days to have been very sure that what I described as "the increasingly scientific and post- (or a-) Christian eighteenth century" had given rise to a period in which traditional religious consolations had become "gradually unavailable" so that "Romantic and post-Romantic poets" had been forced to "reconcile themselves" to mortality "through distinctly a-Christian strategies." But the relations between the poet and the age are of course more complex than I'd been willing to concede.

True, Friedrich Nietzsche notoriously claimed in 1882 that the "death of God," a consequence of the mounting skepticism of the era, had left mankind "straying, as through an infinite nothing."[1] Yet most rank-and-file citizens of the nineteenth century wouldn't have felt themselves to be wandering through nothingness. On the contrary, throughout the century Nietzschean nihilism was counterpointed by religious commitments ranging from orthodox Catholicism or Anglicanism to more esoteric spiritualist and "theosophical" movements, just as the "believing atheism" that led so many twentieth-century intellectuals to subscribe to the existentialism propounded by Sartre and Camus has often been paralleled in our own era by a range of born-again theologies.

Nonetheless, even if I didn't grasp the intricacy of the philosophical drama underlying Whitman's "to die is different from what anyone supposed, and luckier," I wasn't wrong to see the line as central to an understanding of the ways poets have formulated visions of mortality in the course of the last two hundred years. In fact Whitman's mystical confidence may have masked anxieties that I didn't detect, conflicts that also swirled behind a number of the other writings I'd planned to study. Thus, as I look back on the confusions that beset me as I tried to organize classroom discussions of poems whose apparent resolutions of the enigma of mortality became themselves increasingly puzzling to me and my students, I realize that I should have studied the problems the poems posed rather than the solutions they seemingly offered. I might also have made greater headway in defining those problems if I'd focused more intensively not just on Whitman's tantalizingly cryptic phrase but also on the even more frankly riddling definitions of death and dying embedded in the poems of his great American contemporary Emily Dickinson.

Now, given the prevalence of such riddling in the works of both these writers, it's increasingly clear to me that, more than any other nineteenth-century verses, the poems of Whitman and Dickinson embody our literary culture's passage from a traditional Christian theology of "expiration" to a modern, post-Christian (anti)theology of "termination." But it's equally clear that these poems record such a passage not because they summarize widespread views of death and dying but because they test and contest such views.

Like Dickinson, Whitman was hardly a traditional Christian, and his and Dickinson's revisionary theologies were among the factors that made this pair of pioneering poets "different," if not "luckier," while pointing the way to what Stevens was to call the "mythology of modern death." For the majority views of death and dying against which Whitman's and Dickinson's visions have to be set were better expressed by the sentimental "poetess" Lydia Sigourney, also known as the "Sweet Singer of Hartford," than by either the man sometimes described as the "Good Gray Poet of Camden" or the woman sometimes labeled the "Myth of Amherst." The author of over twenty best-selling collections of verse, Mrs. Sigourney, as she was usually called, painted uplifting pictures of a heavenly afterlife in such poems as those she included in *The Weeping Willow* (1847), a book of consolatory verse dedicated to her patron, "Daniel Wadsworth, Esq.," whom she sententiously described as "The Friend Of All Who Mourn."

Both in Britain and America, poetry like Mrs. Sigourney's, which today's scholars appropriately define as "mortuary verse," was far more representative of popular beliefs than anything Whitman or Dickinson ever produced. "The Orphan's Second Birthday" offers a good example of the ways in which Sigourney could pull out all the emotional stops in depicting the celestial destiny of a charming, dead, parentless child. As the "orphan with her fairy tread / So full of merry glee" looks forward to a "birthday feast" with a "sweet group of infant friends," she exultingly claps "her tiny hands" and "wear[s] her mother's smile." But lo!, when the longed-for day arrives, the "change, how great!" For the "banquet" that the little girl now attends is "not here" but "above, / At the Redeemer's feet," where the "cherub" is in her "parents' arms" and "every bliss [is now] complete."[2]

In *Huckleberry Finn*, Mark Twain caricatured such sugary authoresses as Mrs. Sigourney in the figure of the lugubrious Emmeline Grangerford, a girl poet who, explains Huck, "could rattle off poetry like nothing" because she "warn't particular; she could write about anything you choose to give her to write about just so it was sadful. Every time a man died, or a woman died, or a child died, she would be on hand with her 'tribute' before he was cold. . . . The neighbors said it was the doctor first, then Emmeline, then the undertaker."[3] But "The Orphan's Second Birthday" came closer to expressing a common sensibility than Twain's satire did. Studying letters to the editor that appeared in a nineteenth-century children's magazine titled *Robert Merry's Museum*, one historian summarizes the religious "themes" that probably dominated most people's thoughts about death and that certainly underlie Sigourney's poem: "that heaven is our true home; that life is brief, but even a brief life is not pointless; that God sometimes takes the very young to protect them from life; and that, given life's briefness, one must be prepared to die at any time."[4]

Nor were such notions foreign to some of the nineteenth-century British poets whose works, unlike Sigourney's, are still taught in university classrooms: Alfred Lord Tennyson, for instance, who was England's poet laureate for much of the period, and Robert Browning, whose verse was not only widely read but also widely considered both obscure and elite. Although neither produced such syrupy memorials as "The Orphan's Second Birthday," both published poems based on traditional visions of a beatific afterlife. By Tennyson's own request, all collections of his work still conclude with his late (though not last) poem "Crossing the Bar," a straightforward utterance of faith in which he prays, "[May] there be no moaning of the bar, / When I put out to sea"—no sad sound of the ocean beating on a sand bar at the mouth of a harbor—because "I hope to see my Pilot face to face / When I have crossed the bar." And in "Prospice" Browning devoutly anticipated a postmortem reunion with his beloved dead wife, the poet Elizabeth Barrett. When the "black minute" of dying is "at end," he swears, "O thou soul of my soul! I shall clasp thee again, / And with God be the rest!"[5]

In fact, from the perspective of readers who admired the writings not just of Mrs. Sigourney but also of such poets as Tennyson and Browning, the works of Walt Whitman and Emily Dickinson appeared so strange that some commentators thought them *not* "poetry" at all, for the radical ideas of these artists were reflected in radical aesthetic strategies, unusual modes of versification as well as peculiar metaphors. To be sure, Ralph Waldo Emerson had hailed Whitman "at the start of a great career," but even as late as 1891, not long before Whitman's death, for every adulatory Emerson there were "many fairly educated people who," in the words of a *New York Times* editorial, "do not find Whitman's writing *poetry* at all [emphasis added]." Similarly, although the idiosyncratic verses Dickinson often included in letters were treasured by many recipients and even passed down from generation to generation, this reclusive writer came to be called the Myth of Amherst not because she was a brilliantly innovative poet but because she was an eccentric spinster who spoke bizarrely, rarely appeared in public, and from 1860 on dressed entirely in white.

Reviewers of the first (1855) edition of Whitman's *Leaves of Grass* claimed to be repelled by both what they saw as the book's antipoetic style and what they considered its antigenteel substance, denouncing it as a "gathering of muck" and "the rotten garbage of licentious thoughts." But even as Whitman earned praise in some quarters, later critics emphasized the supposedly nonpoetic quality of his style. " '*Leaves of Grass*,' in many parts, is the most amorphous agglomeration of unpoetic words ever shoveled together," wrote one outraged reader in 1901, while another declared that Whitman "could not use the instruments that had sufficed for Homer, Shakespeare, and Tennyson," and the writer of an 1897 *Introduction to American Literature* insisted that he could "scarcely [be] regarded as a poet at all."[6]

As for Dickinson, who barely published in her own lifetime, she was perhaps even more underrated than Whitman by the few men of letters to whom she showed her poems. Thomas Wentworth Higginson, the editor of the *Atlantic*, from whom she asked advice early in her career, assumed from the start that she didn't write what *he* would call poetry. The man who asserted, "It is no discredit to Walt Whitman that he wrote 'Leaves of Grass,' only that he did not burn it afterwards," urged Dickinson to relinquish what she defined as "the Bells whose jingling cooled [her] Tramp"—her distinctively inventive meters. Although he regarded her as a kind of untutored genius, Higginson never abandoned his notion that Dickinson's poetry was "uncontrolled." Even after he joined Mabel Loomis Todd in producing the first (posthumous) edition of Dickinson's verse, he had doubts about her "unconventional utterance[s]."[7] Nor were his misgivings unique. Mrs. Todd also confessed herself "exasperated" by Dickinson's "carelessness of form," and the poet's other literary friends concurred. Dr. Josiah Holland, the physician who founded *Scribner's Magazine*, thought Dickinson's poems "not poetry." And like some of Whitman's reviewers, many readers of Dickinson's first volumes concurred with the doctor's diagnosis: again and again, critics insisted that hers was "bad poetry . . . divorced from meaning, from music, from grammar, from rhyme," that "her style is clumsy, her language is poor; her technique is appalling."[8]

Ironically, however, it can be argued that the deviation of these two artists from nineteenth-century norms explains the influence both were to have on their descendants. Alike in their disaffection from much of the poetry written by their English-speaking contemporaries, the two were also alike in their dependence on odd modes of literary skill, peculiar wellsprings of inspiration. Was it precisely because of their alienation from the mainstream not just of nineteenth-century poetry but of nineteenth-century thought that both these writers were also alike in their revisionary meditations on the implications of what Whitman called "the low and delicious word *death*"? If so, their inspired "metaphors of death" may have had more complex meanings about their century, and our own, than I understood when, as a know-it-all junior professor, I began trying to draft a book called "Different, and Luckier."

WHITMAN—AND MOTHER DEATH AND FATHER EARTH

"A child said *What is the grass?* fetching it to me with full hands." So begins section 6 of Whitman's magisterial fifty-two-section "Song of Myself," the work that was throughout his career the linchpin of the ever-expanding, fluently evolving book of verse that—always under the same title, *Leaves of Grass*—he published and republished from 1855 to 1891. The poet's answer to the child's question begins with professions of uncertainty ("How could I answer the child? I do not know what it is any more than he") but moves steadily toward assertions of mystical certitude, starting with *guess*'s, *seem*'s, *may be*'s and *wish*'s and ending with unqualified declarative assurances. I have emphasized the relevant verbs in the passages below.

> I guess *[the grass] must be the flag of my disposition, out of hopeful green stuff woven.*
>
> Or I guess *it is the handkerchief of the Lord. . . .*
>
> And now it seems to me *the beautiful uncut hair of graves.*
>
> *Tenderly will I use you curling grass,*
> It may be *you transpire from the breasts of young men . . .*
> It may be *you are from old people. . . .*
>
> *This grass* is *very dark to be from the white heads of old mothers,*
> *Darker than the colorless beards of old men,*
> *Dark to come from under the faint red roofs of mouths.*
>
> O I perceive *after all so many uttering tongues,*
> And I perceive *they do not come from the roofs of mouths for nothing.*
>
> I wish *I could translate the hints about the dead young men and women. . . .*
>
> *What do you think has become of the young and old men?*
> *And what do you think has become of the women and children?*
>
> *They* are *alive and well somewhere,*
> *The smallest sprout shows there* is *really no death. . . .*

All goes *onward and outward, nothing collapses,*
And to die is *different from what any one supposed, and luckier.*[9]

Increasingly visionary, Whitman's stream of answers to the naive yet crucial query *"What is the grass?"* clearly draws upon the biblical "For all flesh is as grass, and all the glory of man as the flower of grass. The grass withereth, and the flower thereof falleth away: But the word of the Lord endureth for ever," a text that Johannes Brahms set to music not many years later in his *German Requiem*. But where both Brahms and the Bible offer spiritual transcendence as consolation for mourners, stressing that salvation will come to those who are "born again not of corruptible seed, but of incorruptible, by the word of God, which liveth and abideth for ever," Whitman plants his hopes in a mystical materialism. For it is the flesh-as-grass that itself utters cryptic promises and ineffable hints of immortality both to the poet and to the audience that is always present in his imagination.[10]

The striking passage where Whitman seems to plunge underground, below even the roots of the grass, toward the eerily sprouting bodies of the dead, marks his turn from *guess*'s and *may be*'s to a sibylline grasp of the dynamics of cosmic recycling. After commenting, "This grass is very dark to be from the white heads of old mothers" and "the colorless beards of old men," the poet observes that this grass is even dark "to come from under the faint red roofs of mouths"—and then, with apparent inevitability, concludes that the grass is "so many uttering *tongues*," which "do not come from the roofs of mouths for nothing." The promise of redemption that the Bible defines as "the word of God" (and that in Christian rhetoric is personified by the "Word made Flesh" in the body of Christ) here becomes, instead, the word *of* flesh and, more generally, the speech or utterance of the surging world of biological matter. For indeed, as Whitman's overarching metaphor of grass suggests, the leaves of grass that give every otherwise different edition of his book its unvarying title aren't merely botanical phenomena. Besides being "leaves" as in "the exfoliations of a plant," they're also "leaves" as in "the pages of a book," "leaves" as in the "casual compositions" of a printer, and "leaves" as in "the leavings of departed travelers." And on these richly ambiguous leaves, the poet also suggests, *something* or *someone*—some source of mysterious strength, along with the prophetically empowered poet himself—has inscribed secret meanings, just as the ancient Sibyl of Cumae once lettered enigmatic leaves for priestly interpreters to decipher.[11]

Whitman's literarily recycled *Leaves of Grass*, then, don't just stand for biologically recycled flesh; they're also sibylline—oracular—leaves. But in the context of the biblical certainty that flesh is transient like the grass so that only the spirit endures and has mystic significance, it's surely heretical to insist that on the contrary, only the flesh endures and is inscribed with "different, and luckier" meanings. No wonder Whitman's work seemed like a "gathering of muck" that was "not poetry" in an age dominated by the theologically hopeful verses of poets from the Sigourney of "The Orphan's Second Birthday" to the Tennyson of "Crossing the Bar." Meditating on the passage I've just discussed, a reviewer writing for the *Washington Daily National Intelligencer* in 1856 was scornful. He agreed that "Holy Writ informs us that 'all flesh is grass'" but then attempted a reductio ad absurdum of Whitman's ideas, noting that as "quaint old Sir Thomas Browne" had argued, this is literally as well as metaphorically the case: "[A]ll the adipose matter deposited in the human body from roast beef and mutton is, after all, [merely] grass taking upon itself a coat of flesh," so that "the most carnivorous gastronome, no less than the most immaculate vegetarian, is nothing but grass at the last chemical analysis." Thus, he scathingly suggested, "a handful of grass fetched by a child to Walter [sic] Whitman inspires him with mysterious thoughts which he vainly essays to grasp" and "intrusive questionings which he vainly endeavors to answer."[12]

But was Whitman really inspired by a contemplation of the relationship between human "adipose matter" and the grass on which cattle graze? From our current perspective, such a notion misses the point. For at least the last hundred years "mysterious thoughts" and "intrusive questionings" have marked most confrontations with mortality. Yet although Whitman's persistence in adhering to his title dramatizes the depth of his commitment to a mystical materialism, the riddling vagueness with which he answered his own perfectly good (and not at all "intrusive") questions similarly hints at the intensity of his own confusion. Given the embattled philosophical position in which he must have found himself, it's perhaps not surprising that from time to time he produced poems that depend on buried references to traditional genres and conventional uses of what a student of mine once called the "resurrection trope"—the metaphor of rebirth based on Christ's return from the dead.

Tellingly, along with the schoolroom favorite "O Captain! My Captain!," Whitman's most frequently read and taught poem is "When Lilacs Last in the Dooryard Bloom'd." Both are works mourning the death of Abraham Lincoln, but whereas the first is a rousing, uncharacteristically rhymed

WAS THE NINETEENTH CENTURY DIFFERENT?

lament ("O Captain! my Captain! our fearful trip is done / The ship has weather'd every rack, the prize we sought is won"), the second is a majestic elegy in sonorous free verse. Indeed "Lilacs" may at first appear as different from the pastoral elegies produced by, say, Milton ("Lycidas") and Shelley ("Adonais") as section 6 of "Song of Myself" ("A child said *What is the grass?*") is from the Bible's "For all flesh is as grass." Nevertheless, it features a number of elements reminiscent of these traditional elegies.

To begin with, there's something reassuringly familiar about the poem's ritualized invocations—

> *O powerful western fallen star!*
> *O shades of night—O moody, tearful night!*
> *O great star disappear'd—O the black murk that hides the star!*

—along with its symbolic "trinity sure" of flower-bird-star, representing three aspects of nature that simultaneously grieve with the speaker and promise the redemption of "ever-returning spring." There's reassurance, too, not just in the poem's reiterated references to the regenerative powers of the earth but in the poet's allusive evocations of the Egyptian Book of the Dead, the comradeship of fathers and sons, and the "wondrous chant" of brother poets, all of which offer him and his audience the comfort of an affiliation with long cultural traditions.

For as a number of commentators have remarked, although Whitman's art is certainly innovative in "Lilacs," he's also tracing the time-hallowed contours of the pastoral elegy throughout the work. Indeed, from his opening lament for the "powerful western fallen star" that symbolizes the assassinated Lincoln and his first complaint against the "harsh surrounding cloud that will not free my soul" to his ceremonial offering of lilacs to the journeying coffin, his identification of himself as priestly spokesman for "my cities," his visionary reconciliation with the armies of the dead, and his final perception of the fallen president as a star—a comrade "with silver face in the night"—Whitman might almost be rewriting Shelley's "Adonais," with its movement from mourning for the fallen "star" of Keats ("Thou wert the morning star among the living") to joy that "the soul of Adonais, like a star, / Beacons from the abode where the Eternal are."

At the same time, even while the structure of "Lilacs" allows Whitman to gain poetic strength from the tradition of the pastoral elegy and the long history of the "resurrection trope," the poem's imagery of death itself is as riddling and *un*traditional as the poet's earlier characterization of mortality as "different" but "luckier" had been. Throughout Western history, death has usually been personified as a sinister male figure: a skeletal rider on a pale horse, a hooded scythe-wielding shadow, a demonic stalker. But in "Lilacs" death is personified as the life-giving, supposedly nurturing and selfless *female* figure most venerated by the nineteenth century: a "dark *mother* always gliding near with soft feet," a "strong deliveress." And in celebrating the approach of this "lovely and soothing" divinity, Whitman produces an incantation that may have been even more baffling to his contemporaries than his sibylline assertion that "All goes onward and outward, nothing collapses, / And to die is different from what anyone supposed, and luckier":

> *Have none chanted for thee a chant of fullest welcome?*
> *Then I chant it for thee, I glorify thee above all. . . .*
> *Approach strong deliveress,*
> *When it is so, when thou hast taken them I joyously sing the dead,*
> *Lost in the loving floating ocean of thee,*
> *Laved in the flood of thy bliss O death.*

Does the poet here "protest too much"? My students and I never considered such a possibility when I taught my ill-fated course on "Romantic and Post-Romantic Metaphors of Death," but I now think we should have. Etymologically, as I ought to have remembered, the word "mother" derives from the Latin *mater*, out of which the word "matter" also evolved. But if mother/*mater* and *mater*/matter are one (or at least two in one), then the idea of Mother Death hints at the insentience of inert matter. And the *mer* or sea (of life and death) out of which living matter evolved promises in the end to engulf human consciousness in the oblivion to which Marianne Moore alluded when in "A Grave" she confronted "that ocean in which dropped things are bound to sink— / in which if they turn and twist, it is neither with volition nor consciousness." Thus, even while Whitman praises this "strong deliveress," Mother Death threatens to become not the recycling redeemer for whom the poet-prophet of mystical materialism has yearned but a merciless terminator of flesh-as-grass, a female Grim Reaper, who may at any moment "deliver" the mystic himself to nothingness.

In another of his most famous poems, "Out of the Cradle Endlessly Rocking," written nearly a decade before "Lilacs," Whitman actually surfaced some of these anxieties, associating death with a female figure, but this time with the "*savage*" or "*fierce* old mother" (emphases mine) who is the sea. As a boy, the poet discloses here, he wandered on the shores of "Paumonok" (now Long Island), struggling to decipher the "drown'd secret hissing" of this oceanic mother's primordial language-below language. And as he bonded with the sorrow of a male mockingbird singing what the poet considers a "carol" of grief for his lost mate—

O past! O happy life! O songs of joy! . . .
Loved! loved! loved! loved! loved!
But my mate no more, no more with me!
We two together no more. . . .

—a "key" word that is the counterpart of *"loved"* emerged from the waves:

. . . the low and delicious word death,
And again death, death, death, death . . .
Creeping steadily up to my ears and laving me softly all over,
Death, death, death, death, death.

Reiterated as often as *"loved"* and thus love's shadowy double, the word *"death"* represents what the boy who is the poet-to-be must comprehend if he is to become a "solitary singer" speaking to and for his New World community. But the word is both bewilderingly and scarily resonant. Is the word *"death"* what Whitman calls a key because the poet believes that he alone understands that "to die is different from what anyone supposed, and luckier"? Is *"death"* a key because Whitman wants to console readers (and himself) by demonstrating that life and death are merely aspects of each other in the endlessly rocking cradle of nature? Or because the "solitary singer" must transcend death (even if it's "different," and "luckier") in order to become powerful and priestly? Or, more unnervingly, because it would be death to merge with the materiality of the mother, the chaos of the deep? All these possibilities may be equally valid, a point that I now think suggests not just the richness of Whitman's associations with death but also the depth of the confusion and dread that undermine his apparently confident assertions of death's luckiness, delicacy, and deliciousness. This ambivalence toward mortality—a conflict that my old "Death Book Stuff" failed to recognize in this poet—becomes very clear in his bleak "As I Ebb'd with the Ocean of Life," which functions as a dark companion piece to "Out of the Cradle."

Here, as Whitman once again walks the shores of Paumonok, he begins to fear that like the sea wrack around him, "I too but signify at the utmost a little wash'd-up drift," so that he suddenly scorns himself and his art ' ("before all my arrogant poems the real Me stands yet . . . untold"). Indeed the proud translator, who once mediated the mystic language of bird and sea, unexpectedly confesses a defeat that appears to be absolute:

> *I perceive I have not really understood anything, not a single object, and*
> *that no man ever can,*
> *Nature here in sight of the sea [takes] advantage of me to dart upon me*
> *and sting me,*
> *Because I have dared to open my mouth to sing at all.*

What follows this confession is such a despairing vision of personal extinction that it's hard to connect it with the same man who composed the assured and optimistic "A child said *What is the grass?* . . ." Gazing at the debris on the beach, Whitman describes it as constituted of

> *Me and mine, loose windrows, little corpses,*
> *Froth, snowy white, and bubbles,*
> *(See from my dead lips the ooze exuding at last,*
> *See the prismatic colors glistening and rolling,)*
> *Tufts of straw, sands, fragments,*
> *Buoy'd hither from many moods. . . .*

From a nineteenth-century perspective, this passage was so frighteningly graphic that the poet-editor James Russell Lowell insisted on excising the parenthetical "See from my dead lips. . . . See the prismatic colors. . . ." from the text he published in the *Atlantic Monthly*.

Still, extinguished though he is—a drift on the shore, one of a gathering of "loose windrows, little corpses"—Whitman nevertheless still imagines his "musing, pondering" endurance. At the end of the poem he's still *there*, commenting on his own abjection. And the strategy through which he moves from the nihilism of an imaginary death scene to the imagining of a qualified survival dramatizes yet again the covert search for strength that this writer also enacted in "Lilacs." In section 3 of "As I Ebb'd," Whitman turns from self and sea, poet son and Mother Death, to an entirely different figure: a metaphorical father. Significantly, however, he imagines this father not as a transcendent spirit but as the land itself upon which he lies and for which he speaks. It's as if, at least in some part of himself, the poet feels that only Father Earth can protect him against Mother Death.

Of course, just the way the personification of death as a mother is far less usual than the representation of "him" as a (male) Grim Reaper, so the personification of earth as a father is strange in a culture where the bounty of the seasons is usually offered metaphorically by Mother Earth or Mother Nature. Thus, when Whitman flings himself on the solidity of paternal Paumonok, he seems to be actually clinging to the substance of life—the *ground* of his being—as well as to the paternal tradition embodied in his native land itself, in the hope of salvation from a mortal threat he never explicitly defines: the threat posed by the watery womb-tomb of Mother Death.

> *I throw myself upon your breast my father,*
> *I cling to you so that you cannot unloose me,*
> *I hold you firm till you answer me something.*

Yet despite the poet's demands that Father Earth tell him *something*— even something minimal—about his own fate and, by extension, the fate of all mortal souls, he's left in ignorance. Enigmatic as the earlier assertion that death is "different" and "luckier" but far grimmer than that passage, the last three lines of "As I Ebb'd" portray the poet as one among a "we" who are abased before a cryptic "you up there." A coldly indifferent, godly being? A survivor? A divine reader? Whoever this "you" is, he (she?) dispassionately surveys the wreckage of those doomed to extinction—a "we" from which Whitman can't here separate himself:

> *We, capricious, brought hither we know not whence, spread out before you,*
> *You up there walking or sitting,*
> *Whoever you are, we too lie in drifts at your feet [emphasis added].*

As for the poet himself, his contemplation of the random desolation that lies in "drifts" on the beach hardly suggests a notion of mortal fate as "different, and luckier" than the end promised by, say, Nietzsche in a world where "God is dead." But perhaps for Whitman the concept of extinction as "lucky" may itself have been a defense against mounting anxieties about a terrifying, recurrent vision of "the ooze" or breath of life "exuding at last," like a few final, stammered words, from his own dead lips.

DICKINSON—AND DEATH AND THE MAIDEN

If Whitman's apparent optimism concealed grimmer visions than the author of "Song of Myself" was usually willing to admit, Dickinson's elliptical, often fragmentary-seeming and highly condensed verses were extraordinarily candid in their confrontation of the terror this supposedly pious New England "lady" associated with—in her ironic words—the "Cordiality of Death— / Who drills his Welcome in—." A Dickinson elegy probably composed a few years before Whitman wrote "Lilacs" and more than a decade after Mrs. Sigourney drafted "The Orphan's Second Birthday" is almost astonishing not just in its refusal of Sigourney's consolatory platitudes but in its avoidance of even the subtle aesthetic strategies through which Whitman confronts and confounds grief. Equally shocking is the poem's characterization of the dead person as not a "he" or a "she" but merely an "it," a *thing*:

> *"I want"—it pleaded—All its life—*
> *I want—was chief it said*
> *When Skill entreated it—the last—*
> *And when so newly dead—*
>
> *I could not deem it late—to hear*
> *That single—steadfast sigh—*
> *The lips had placed as with a "Please"*
> *Toward Eternity— [J 731/ F 851]*[13]

Reducing the subject of elegy from a "lustrous" star (or a guest at a celestial banquet) to a mere yearning object, an "it" whose "wants" are both hopeless desires and helpless lacks, Dickinson allows herself no role as priestly interpreter or prophetic mediator. Rather, she is herself little more than an ear that hears and records the "single—steadfast sigh" of the dead, a sigh uncannily prolonged toward an "Eternity" neither obscurely blissful (like Whitman's) nor redemptively radiant (like Sigourney's).

Nor does Dickinson enrich this scene of mourning—if her flat account of "its" demise can be called mourning—with references to communal grief. Her brief encounter with "its" assimilation into "Eternity" occurs in a setting of absence, blankness; the little the poet speaks about death as an event is spoken nowhere and for nobody, in an atmosphere of unadorned skepticism that she was more sardonically to elaborate a year later in a piece in which both the citizen of the graveyard and the soul in eternity are presented as equally alien:

> *The Owner of this House*
> *A Stranger He must be—*

Eternity's Acquaintances
Are mostly so—to me. [J 892/F 1069]

Uttered with Yankee taciturnity, these lines bring to a close an estranged description of a New England cemetery, which, comments the speaker dispassionately, "seems a curious Town— / Some Houses very old, / Some— newly raised this Afternoon."

But Dickinson's visions of death and dying aren't always quite so understated as those she formulated in " 'I want'—it pleaded—All its life—" and "The Owner of this House." Quite often she gazes at mortality, especially at her own, with dread, much as Whitman did in "As I Ebb'd." Then, with bravura self-reflexiveness, she gazes at her dread itself with further dread. In her early twenties she wrote a letter to her orphaned friend Jane Humphrey that reveals the almost masochistic circularity of this process. Musing here on the possibility that "if God choose," he "could take my father, too, and my dear [sister] Vinnie, and put them in his sky to live with him forever," she goes on to imagine herself also dead, "with my eyes shut, and a little white gown on, and a snow-drop on my breast; and I fancied I heard the neighbors stealing in so softly to look down in my face—so fast asleep—so still." Then, "Oh Jennie, will you and I really become like this," she wondered disingenuously, adding an apologetic afterthought: "Don't mind Darling, I'm a naughty, bad girl to say sad things, and make you cry."[14]

Older, dropping her pose of playfully naughty child, Dickinson produced poem after poem in which, gazing with dread at death and dread, she argues that "The Truth, is Bald, and Cold—" for "Looking at Death, is Dying—." To be sure, she suggests in the poem below that there's a self-wounding pleasure in such dire looking, but clearly this pleasure arises primarily from relief at knowing the worst. "Looking at Death," she declares:

. . . is Dying—
Just let go the Breath—
And not the pillow at your Cheek
So Slumbereth—

Others, Can wrestle—
Yours, is done—
And so of Woe, bleak dreaded—come,
It sets the Fright at liberty—

And Terror's free—
Gay, Ghastly, Holiday! [J 281/ F327]

But if the spectacle of liberated terror sometimes feels to Dickinson like a ghastly holiday, there are other times when to scrutinize is purely to agonize. Whether the looking at dying happens in a sickroom or under a naked sky, what was in the nineteenth century very frequently called the "death-watch" meant a consciousness of struggle, as the word "wrestle," a locution of which Dickinson was fond, implies both in the poem above and the one below:

Two swimmers wrestled on the spar—
Until the morning sun—
When One—turned smiling to the land—
Oh God! the Other One!

The stray ships—passing—
Spied a face—
Upon the waters borne—
With eyes in death—still begging raised—
And hands—beseeching—thrown! [J 201/ F227]

This poem might of course be read as a Christian allegory, with the swimmer who turns smiling to land one of the "saved" on his way to heaven and the drowned beseeching swimmer a damned soul. But whether death is a metaphor for hell or hell a metaphor for death, Dickinson's *look* at mortal struggle is unnerving here. For in this poem, as in some of her other works, the agony of the death"watch" is multiplied as in a hall of mirrors: while the speaker of the poem looks at both the drowning swimmer and the "stray ships," and the sailors on the ships look at the drowning swimmer, the swimmer in his death agony looks at death, with eyes "still begging raised—."

Inevitably, such multiplied looking suggests uncertainty, as though death and dying were so mysteriously complex that they must be examined from as many different perspectives as possible. But in particular the look *of,* and *at,* the dying person fascinates this poet, who was frank in admitting both her fascination and the mystery that fueled it:

I've seen a Dying Eye
Run round and round a Room—

In search of Something—as it seemed—
Then Cloudier become—
And then—obscure with Fog—
And then—be soldered down
Without disclosing what it be
'Twere blessed to have seen— [J 547/F 648; emphases added]

What might it have been "blessed" to see? An earthly beloved or a heavenly one? Dickinson's religious beliefs have been much investigated and much disputed, including the doubts she expressed about Christian visions of an afterlife when, for instance—with or without irony—she asked a clerical friend, "Is immortality true?" But ultimately she herself was recalcitrant about offering more than riddling "disclosures" of what she believed it would be blessed to see.

To be sure, this often brilliantly ironic woman was quite capable of what may well have been exercises both in writing and in faith. One of her most frequently anthologized poems, "I never saw a Moor," plays with precisely the idea of seeing and not seeing, in order to assert a standard contemporary belief in the unseen. Just as she never personally visited "a Moor" or encountered "the Sea" yet knows that both really exist, so, Dickinson notes, in a clever argument from analogy:

I never spoke with God
Nor visited in Heaven—
Yet certain am I of the spot
As if the Checks were given— [J 1052/F 800]

At the same time, however, she was capable of such a dry observation as

That it will never come again
Is what makes life so sweet.
Believing what we don't believe
Does not exhilarate. [J 1741/F 1761]

For whatever afterlife is to come, the poet adds here, is "at best / An ablative estate"—a state of "ablation" or (as one dictionary puts it) of "excision or amputation"—that "instigates an appetite / Precisely opposite." In other words, as Stevens was to put it, "Death is the mother of beauty" because it makes us appreciate *this* world.

On the one hand, therefore, Dickinson was unlike Mrs. Sigourney, who consistently articulated pious Christian views, and on the other hand, she was unlike Whitman, who was steadfast in exploring both the best and worst implications of his own mystical materialism. Rather, at one point or another Dickinson seems to have adopted a range of very different religious and antireligious positions. But that she could so vigorously toy with theology reinforces in itself arguments that she was deeply skeptical, as much about Christianity as about any form of atheism. Although her thinking, as some scholars have shown, had been shaped by "a sentimental religious culture," she repudiated most of her society's platitudes and once remarked that "sermons on unbelief ever did attract me."[15] "God is a distant—stately Lover," she notes teasingly in one poem:

> Woos, as He states us—by his Son—
> Verily, a Vicarious Courtship—
> "Miles", and "Priscilla", were such an One—
>
> But, lest the Soul—like fair "Priscilla"
> Choose the Envoy—and spurn the Groom—
> Vouches, with hyperbolic archness—
> "Miles", and "John Alden" were Synonym—[J 357/F 615]

The comedy here is at the least anti-Trinitarian, but such unseemly joshing with "God" becomes even more radical when the poet declares:

> God is indeed a jealous God—
> He cannot bear to see
> That we had rather not with Him
> But with each other play. [J 1719/F 1752]

That she understands the historical context out of which such skepticism arose becomes clear in the distinction she draws, below, between visions of the afterlife "then" and "now":

> Those—dying then,
> Knew where they went—
> They went to God's Right Hand—
> That Hand is amputated now
> And God cannot be found— . . . [J 1551/F 1581; emphases added][16]

Given the crises of belief Dickinson explores in so many poems, it's not surprising that she often sought to look not just from the outside but from the inside at what is by definition the indescribable experience of dying and that in poems presumably spoken from beyond the grave she described the indescribable with virtuoso anxiety. One of the best-known and most stunning of these works is "I heard a Fly buzz when I died," a poem whose syntax seems so straightforward that the piece is frequently taught to schoolchildren, but whose enigmatic preoccupation with a "mere" fly makes it as hard to decipher as it is to forget:

> I heard a Fly buzz—when I died—
> The stillness in the Room
> Was like the Stillness in the Air—
> Between the Heaves of Storm—
>
> The Eyes around—had wrung them dry—
> And Breaths were gathering firm
> For that last Onset—when the King
> Be witnessed—in the Room—
>
> I willed my Keepsakes—Signed away
> What portion of me be
> Assignable—and then it was
> There interposed a Fly—
>
> With Blue—uncertain stumbling Buzz—
> Between the light—and me—
> And then the Windows failed—and then
> I could not see to see—[J 465/F 591]

The deathwatch scene here is a classic one that was quite familiar in the nineteenth century, when people were still likely to expire at home, in their own beds, surrounded—if theirs was to be what Philippe Ariès calls a "good" or "beautiful" death—by family and friends. At this point the weeping onlookers have composed themselves in preparation for the inevitable, while the sufferer has made her last wishes known (willed "Keepsakes," "Signed away" the properties of her material self) so that all are reverently awaiting the arrival of "the King."

But who is this "King," and what does the uncertain, stumbling, buzzing

interposition of a "Fly" have to do with him? Ordinarily, in the religious culture out of which Dickinson's poems arose even though they sometimes
contest its pieties, we'd associate such a majestic personage with God. And
in this setting it would certainly make sense to believe that the poet has
imagined God regally arriving to scoop up and judge the soul as it passes
through the veil that separates this world from what the nineteenth century
often called "the other side." Moreover, if the "King" is God, then "witnessing" his presence in the room would be a ceremonial act of piety since the
word "witness" is itself an evangelical term.

That Dickinson disliked evangelism, however, and as a girl had rejected
evangelical proseletyzings at her school, suggests that the word "witnessed"
is itself ambiguous. For such a skeptical thinker, Christian "witnessing" was
problematic, especially when the coming of physical death was about to be
clinically witnessed—i.e., observed—during the deathwatch. If we read the
poem literally, then, the "King" in fact equals death "himself," who is, in this
interpretation, the king or ruler of life. Yet when the "King"—whether God
the Father or King/Father Death—is expected to appear, the speaker instead
encounters a "Fly."

Can the "Fly" then *equal* the "King"? If so, does the Fly-as-King signify
God the King or *Death* the King—or both (which would add up to a dark
image of God)? And if the Fly isn't identical with the King but is just "His"
herald, what then? Some analysts have considered this cryptic insect's
"Blue—uncertain stumbling Buzz" a metaphor for the speaker's struggling
last breaths—her death "rattle." Some have thought the Fly itself a symbol
of the "Blue—uncertain stumbling" soul as, expiring, it escapes from the
body, leaving the eyes of the flesh unable to "see [physically how] to see
[spiritually]." And some have even commented on the factual precision of
the poem, which accurately transcribes the deathbed truth that the sense of
hearing, as nurses often explain to relatives of the dying, is "the last to go";
even when you can't "see to see" you can hear, say, a fly's buzzing.[17]

Given these many alternative interpretive possibilities, we obviously
can't locate a definitive plotline in this poem. What we can note, however,
is that when Dickinson, perhaps masochistically, identifies in fantasy with
the dying object of the deathwatch, she herself watches, with terrified
irony, the juxtaposition of King and Fly as the eyes of the dying, like the
windows in the poem, "fail" and life stumbles away into an indeterminate
blindness. And such a juxtaposition inevitably recalls Gloucester's horrified "As flies to wanton boys are we to the gods, / They kill us for their
sport," a line from Shakespeare that Dickinson certainly knew, even while

it anticipates Sylvia Plath's obsessive use of the fly as an emblem of human vulnerability.

If, then, Whitman's unnerving vision of himself with the final "ooze" of life trickling from his dead lips suggests that nineteenth-century imaginings of death and dying weren't always so much "different, and luckier" than we might have supposed, Dickinson's scary triangulation of Death/God, Fly, and mortal soul supports that point. Lydia Sigourney may have expected celestial banquets, but the two American contemporaries who were to be most influential in later years were intermittently haunted by more dismal thoughts. In Dickinson's case, indeed, these thoughts were made resonant by her frequent gendering of death as a predatory male—the Grim Reaper of cultural myth represented not just as a faceless "King" but as a sinister lover, a courteous cold gentleman come acalling. Such a figure is the (anti)hero of another one of her most famous poems, "Because I could not stop for Death," but he also appears in quite a few other verses, as "a supple suitor," a sinister charioteer, or a sepulchral mate.[18] Wherever this phantom wooer intrudes, however, his lineaments are shaped by an allegorical confrontation that had long haunted the Western imagination: the meeting of Death and the Maiden, with its eerie merging of death and sexuality, Thanatos and Eros.

A European iconographic tradition that explores the implications of such a meeting between eternal oblivion and feminine pulchritude goes back at least to the Renaissance, an era in which artists produced numerous images of Death, embodied in a grisly corpse or a leering skeleton, accosting a shapely, scantily clad or entirely nude young woman, presumably to remind her (and any onlookers, both inside and outside the picture) that earthly beauty must fade and decay. But the nineteenth-century work that most vividly draws on this tradition is one of the most popular German lieder ever composed: Schubert's 1817 setting of "Der Tod und das Mädchen," a poem by the German Romantic writer Matthias Claudius. This work, which Dickinson may well have known, is itself almost as terse as some of her own verses, and like "Because I could not stop for Death," it enacts an uncanny drama of Death and sexuality [fig. 21].[19]

A dialogue usually performed by a single soprano who impersonates both "voices," the song opens with the shrill, panicky cry of the Maiden, set against a hectic musical accompaniment: "Pass by, oh! pass by, / You savage skeleton! / I am still young, go, my dear, / And do not touch me." Then, in a disturbingly hymnlike melody infused with eroticism, Death seductively replies: "Give me your hand, you fair and tender creature: / I am a friend and do not come to punish. / Be of good cheer! I am not savage, / Gently you will sleep in my arms." Death's courtship, the words and melody imply, may be sinister, but it is suavely, even sexily sinister, proffering a perverse hymn to the beauty of the woman whom the skeletal wooer implacably desires. And what makes "his" wooing curiously plausible is the half-conscious complicity of the Maiden in death's scheme. For the words of terror that the "fair and tender creature" utters as the song begins include one phrase that does not "fit" with her exclamations of revulsion. "Pass by, oh! pass by, / You savage skeleton! / I am still young, go, *my dear*, / And do not touch me." Go, my dear! In the German this phrase is even stronger: "*Geh,*

21. Hans Baldung Grien:
Death and the Maiden (1517).

Lieber!" Go, love or loved one! Even as she struggles to repudiate the advances of this "savage skeleton," the maiden fantasizes yielding to his wiles.

Did Dickinson not only dread death and dread her dread of death but also, at the same time, fear *wanting* death? Certainly the constellation of anxieties around the erotic encounter of Death and the Maiden suggests that she may be using this centuries-old theme to explore a troublesome aspect of her preoccupation with her own demise. "Because I could not stop for Death" (J 712/F 479) elaborates the tale of the phantom wooer and the fainting female, exposing both the eroticism of the morbid and the morbidity of the erotic while, as one critic has pointed out, conflating the plot of the kinds of seduction-and-betrayal novels so popular in the nineteenth century with the evangelical imperative to prepare for a holy dying that was also prevalent throughout the period.

At least on the surface the poem's tone is gently ironic:

> *Because I could not stop for Death—*
> *He kindly stopped for me—*
> *The Carriage held but just Ourselves—*
> *And Immortality.*

Certainly Death's "kindness," as portrayed by Dickinson, matches the beguiling tone of Schubert's singing skeleton. And after all, Dickinson's Death has provided in the genteelest way a horse-drawn carriage and a theoretically consoling third inhabitant of that vehicle: "Immortality." Yet as this suitor and his awestruck lady journey onward, her sense of his intentions—indeed her sense of the ending toward which his intentions inexorably lead—becomes increasingly fearful. For once the speaker has obligingly "put away / My labor and my leisure too, / For His Civility—," she discovers that she's passed (and "passed away" from) crucial symbols of the human, indeed the terrestrial world: "the School, where Children strove / At Recess—in the Ring—," the "Fields of Gazing Grain—," and even "the Setting Sun—."

> *Or rather—He [the Sun] passed Us—*
> *The Dews drew quivering and chill—*
> *For only Gossamer, my Gown—*
> *My Tippet—only Tulle—*

"He passed *Us*": it's one thing to have passed the school where children strove—to have passed, that is, the labors of humanity—yet another thing to have passed the natural cycles of growing grain that "gaze" (perhaps hungrily) at the life-giving sun, and still another thing indeed to have *been passed* by "the setting Sun" in a moment of cosmic abandonment. It's even worse to have become aware of one's near nakedness in such a situation. As the chill dews penetrate the lady's frail garments of "gossamer" and "tulle"—perhaps bridal clothes or nightclothes but also garments symbolizing the fragility of the flesh—so death and the knowledge of death will unspeakably penetrate her body and mind in a simultaneously physical and metaphysical deflowering. Thus the longest interval is inevitably that of the swept-away speaker's central epiphany:

Since then—'tis Centuries—and yet
Feels shorter than the Day
I first surmised the Horses' Heads
Were toward Eternity—

"Centuries" feel shorter than the day she "first," in a moment of supreme helplessness, understood that this seduction must issue in betrayal, the day she "first surmised the Horses' Heads / Were toward Eternity—"

Of course, as Dickinson surely realized, many of her readers no doubt believed that the "Eternity" toward which Death's carriage aims was a positive goal, given the Christian rhetoric of the soul's "eternal life" after death, the wedding imagery of garments made from "Gossamer" and "Tulle," and the long-standing concept of Christ the Bridegroom that permeates Catholic and Protestant theology. Yet this "Eternity" isn't identical with the "Immortality" here personified as just another passenger in a vehicle that finally pauses before a grave: "a House that seemed / A Swelling of the Ground," with a "Cornice—in the Ground" too. On the contrary, the poet hints, with a shudder of horror, that Death has lured the unsuspecting Maiden into his chariot so that he can keep her eternally in his underground prison, along with whatever "Immortality" she might have fancied would be her everlasting companion. Note, after all, that Dickinson uncharacteristically rhymes "Ground" with "Ground" in her next-to-last quatrain, as if to italicize the subterranean fate to which Death is here, as in several Renaissance illustrations of the theme, leading the Maiden.

It's arguable, then, that in "Because I could not stop for Death," as in her other poems about Death as a phantom wooer, Dickinson transforms the traditional image of Christ the Bridegroom coupling with the Soul into the more fearful iconography of Death and the Maiden so that she can tell a horrified story of death's obliterating "love" for the human body in order to question the ecstatic conventions of a culture that would transform a funeral into a wedding. Her tale would be echoed by a number of descendants, notably Sylvia Plath and Joyce Carol Oates. Plath revived its plot in the terrified cadences of "Death & Co." ("Two, of course there are two"—are they Death and Immortality?) and "Berck-Plage" ("The soul is a *bride* in a still place / And the groom is *featureless*, he is red and forgetful [emphases added]"). More recently its scary contours have been explored in sensation fictions ranging from Patricia Highsmith's *The Talented Mr. Ripley* and Judith Rossner's *Looking for Mr. Goodbar* to Joyce Carol Oates's classic account of the confrontation between a terrified teenager and a mysterious rapist-murderer in the short story "Where Are You Going, Where Have You Been?," a work originally entitled "Death and the Maiden."

But obviously, if we compare Whitman's ambivalent obsession with *Mother* Death to Dickinson's ambivalent terror of Death the *Lover*, we have to think about the different ways in which nineteenth-century America's most richly influential male and female poets en*gendered* visions of death and dying, a difference I didn't consider when I was first planning "Different, and Luckier: Romantic and Post-Romantic Metaphors of Death" in the early seventies. For it's surely meaningful that both these radically innovative poets often depicted dying as an encounter with a magically powerful member of the opposite sex. Perhaps it's equally meaningful, though, that Whitman's imaginings were frequently different—and luckier—than Dickinson's. Death as a "strong deliveress" certainly seems like a more welcome figure than Death as a Lord of the Flies or a skeletal suitor. And even when Whitman feared that the "fierce old mother" might annihilate him, leaving his remains in "drifts" at the feet of heaven, he appeared able to defend himself against "her" onslaughts through a symbolic embrace of the solidity of Father Earth, in whose customs and traditions he could imagine *grounding* himself. What comfort was left to Dickinson, though, when she couldn't "see to see" anything except a "Swelling of the Ground"?

GRAVE, TOMB, AND BATTLE CORPSES

Emily Dickinson died on May 15, 1886, and on May 19 her "dainty, white casket" was carried into the library of the Dickinson family house, known as the Homestead, where she had sequestered herself for many years. It was a beautiful spring day, with, according to Higginson, who journeyed to Amherst to pay his last respects, "an atmosphere of its own, fine & strange. . . . The grass of the lawn full of buttercups violet & wild geranium; in [the] house a handful of pansies & another of lilies of the valley on [the] piano."[20]

In a redaction of the scene the young poet had imagined when she fantasized to Jane Humphrey how it would be if she were dead, "with my eyes shut, and a little white gown on, and a snow-drop on my breast," Dickinson was attired in a new white gown, with violets "at her neck" and two heliotropes in her hand. The funeral service itself was simple and private, with several local clergymen reading from scripture or reciting prayers, and Higginson reading Emily Brontë's "No coward soul is mine," one of the American poet's favorite verses. "I will read a poem," he is reported to have said, that "our friend who has just now put on Immortality, and who seemed scarce ever to have taken it off, used to read to her sister." Later he noted that he thought Dickinson "looked transformed from her actual years, fifty-five, to thirty," observing that she had "not a gray hair or wrinkle, & perfect peace on the beautiful brow," and another mourner added that she seemed to have "a very spirituelle face."

"The brief service concluded," the poet was carried across the fields to the family grave. "Six stalwart men," wrote one observer, "lifted her on their shoulders and bore her—into the street? Ah no! That would have been a way almost as strange and unknown for her, to pass, as is to us today that upon which she has entered, while we stand without, as yet unbidden to follow." The poet's funeral cortège, like her life, would be hidden; the "Cemetery lay three fields away, and the bars being lowered between—the light little burden led the way through meadows *filled* with buttercups and daisies."[21] And in keeping with the simplicity of the proceedings, Dickinson's grave was at first little more than a "Swelling of the Ground," identifiable only by a small marker indicating it as part of the family plot. A few years later, however, after a collection of her verses had finally been published and she'd gained fame, her sister, Vinnie, arranged for a larger headstone to be erected, on which were engraved the two words "Called Back," two of the four words that made up a note to her cousins constituting Dickinson's last letter to the world: "Little Cousins, Called Back!" [fig. 22].

Coming from this often ironic poet's pen, the phrase had a certain ambiguity since it alluded to a popular gothic thriller about murder, amnesia, and madness that one Hugh Conway had published in England in 1883.[22] But as it appears on her grave, it was meant to suggest (and has usually been assumed to mean) that, as in a verse by Mrs. Sigourney, Dickinson

22. Dietrich Christian Lammerts: *Emily Dickinson's Grave* (2002).

had been "called back" to the heavenly home whence she came. Despite the iconoclasm that marked so much of her work, the "sentimental religious culture" of nineteenth-century America took this often skeptical thinker back into its velvety bosom.

Whitman's death was different from Dickinson's, and perhaps luckier too, since he not only had seen many publications of his work but had also lived considerably longer. The author of *Leaves of Grass* died in his seventies, surrounded by disciples who immediately arranged for the painter Thomas Eakins to make a death mask while they were efficiently taking possession of his papers and packing them "into barrels" for future biographers. By contrast with Dickinson's quiet obsequies in Amherst, Massachusetts, Whitman's funeral in Camden, New Jersey, was a massive affair, with a local newspaper even describing it as "a red letter day in the annals of the town." As part of the proceedings, a notorious agnostic, Colonel Robert Ingersoll, remarked that "death is less terrible than it was before. Thousands and millions will walk into the dark valley of the shadow, holding Walt Whitman by the hand." Perhaps fittingly, the service also included readings from "Confucius, Buddha, Plato, the Koran, the Bible, and *Leaves of Grass.*" Later, one William Sloane Kennedy, a journalist and devoted acolyte of the poet's, testified that he felt he'd just witnessed "the entombment of Christ."[23]

And Whitman's *was* an entombment, rather than a mere burial. For despite his youthful celebration of the cosmic recycling that results when "curling grass [transpires] from the breasts of young men" and his assertion at the end of "Song of Myself" that "I bequeath myself to the dirt to grow from the grass I love," Whitman chose in advance *not* to enter the bare earth. Two years before he died he contracted with a firm of "monumental manufacturers" to build a large tomb in the form of a "plain massive stone temple" hewn from unpolished granite [fig. 23]. He designed this structure himself, with William Blake's symbolic etching "Death's Door" as a model [fig. 24], and he regularly journeyed to the Harleigh Cemetery, near his home in Camden, to check on its progress as it was being built. As described by one of his biographers, this mausoleum was practically Egyptian in its weight, mass, and sumptuousness; some "of the blocks weighed eight or ten tons," and "the roof was a foot and a half thick," while the vault "was faced with marble and tile and contained eight burial spaces" for members of Whitman's family. In "a lasting assertion of self," however, the poet "merged their identities into his," since "the pediment . . . bore only one name, 'Walt Whitman,' carved in high relief."[24] For such a design to have come from the proponent of mystical materialism who wrote "Song of Myself," "Out of the

23. Dietrich Christian Lammerts: *Walt Whitman's Tomb* (2002).

24. Louis Schiavonetti, after William Blake: "Death's Door" (1808); illustration for Robert Blair, *The Grave* (1st pub. 1743).

Cradle," and "Lilacs" was odd indeed. But perhaps it was less strange as a product of the sensibility that transcribed the anxieties of "As I Ebb'd."

In Whitman's life those anxieties about the wrecks and drifts—the literal *carnage*—of the mortal world had been reinforced by his experiences during the Civil War. Between 1862 and 1865, he volunteered on the battlefields as a "wound-dresser" and hospital visitor, a traumatic yet, he declared, gratifying occupation that brought him into close physical contact with countless injured and dying young men whose shattered bodies he cherished and mourned. In the sections of *Leaves of Grass* titled "Drum Taps" and "Memories of President Lincoln" he transformed the sights he had seen into passages marked by eloquent mysticism. In a beautiful sketch entitled "A Sight in Camp in the Daybreak Gray and Dim," he gazed at three dead figures lying outside a hospital tent: an "elderly man so gaunt and grim," a "sweet boy with cheeks yet blooming," and a third with a "face nor child nor old" that seemed to him "the face of the Christ himself, / Dead and divine and brother of all, and here again he lies." And in "Lilacs," he testified:

> I saw battle-corpses, myriads of them,
> And the white skeletons of young men, I saw them,
> I saw the debris and debris of all the slain soldiers of the war,
> But I saw they were not as was thought,
> They themselves were fully at rest, they suffer'd not. . . .

But in "The Wound-Dresser" Whitman was more specific about the horrifying scenes he'd witnessed—"the perforated shoulder, the foot with the bullet-wound"—confessing that though "I dress with impassive hand," there was "deep in my breast a fire, a burning flame." In *Specimen Days*, a prose work drawn from his journals, he was even franker in confiding his anguish at what the title of one chapter called "The Real War [That] Will Never Get in the Books." "The dead in this war," he wrote in a chapter that was unusually fragmentary and distraught,

> there they lie, strewing the fields and woods and valleys and battle-fields of the south . . . the varieties of the strayed dead, (the estimate of the War department is 25,000 national soldiers kill'd in battle and never buried at all, 5,000 drown'd—15,000 inhumed by strangers, or on the march in haste, in hitherto unfound localities—2,000 graves cover'd by sand and mud by Mississippi freshets, 3,000 carried away by caving-in of banks, &c.,)—Gettysburgh, the West, Southwest—Vicksburgh—Chattanooga—

*the trenches of Petersburgh—the numberless battles, camps, hospitals
everywhere . . . and blackest and loathesomest of all, the dead and living
burial-pits, the prison-pens of Andersonville, Salisbury, Belle-Isle, &c., (not
Dante's pictured hell and all its woes, its degradations, filthy torments,
excell'd those prisons)—the dead, the dead, the dead . . . somewhere they
crawl'd to die, alone, in bushes, low gullies, or on the sides of hills—(there,
in secluded spots, their skeletons, bleach'd bones, tufts of hair, buttons, fragments of clothing, are occasionally found yet)—our young men once so
handsome and so joyous, taken from us—*[25]

Surely this passage helps explain Whitman's late-life drive to construct for
himself a burial place sealed in granite, as far as possible from the "filthy
torments" of Mother Death. At the same time, the traumatized witnessing
that he recorded here constitutes a crucial rehearsal of the elegiac mode that
was to dominate much of the twentieth century's poetry of mourning.

Emily Dickinson's pastoral, posthumous journey across the fields bor-
dering the Homestead to the Amherst town cemetery wasn't in any obvious
sense governed by wartime trauma, though Higginson, the most distinguished speaker at her service, had certainly been a Union hero. But the
reclusive Myth of Amherst had, in her fashion, been deeply affected by the
conflict whose carnage left so many dead. As several recent scholars have
demonstrated, "the national political and moral crisis . . . severely challenged her faith," leaving her wondering how God's supposedly "providen-
tial justice" could allow such overwhelming human suffering.[26]

When Frazer Stearns, the cherished son of Amherst College's president,
was killed in battle—his "big heart," Dickinson wrote to Frances and Louise
Norcross, "shot away by a 'minie ball' "—the poet concluded her letter to
these "little cousins" with the only consolatory advice she could muster, a
distinctly nonevangelical exhortation that might as well have come from
Kierkegaard: "Let us love better, child, it's *most that's left to do* [emphasis
added]." And when another local son had died a few months earlier, "from
a wound at Annapolis," she'd lamented in the same mode to Louise Norcross: "Poor little widow's boy, riding to-night in the mad wind, back to the
village burying-ground where he never dreamed of sleeping! Ah! The
dreamless sleep!"[27]

Did dying somehow seem "different, and luckier" in the nineteenth century? Now, as I review some of the materials I'd planned to use in studying
"Romantic and Post-Romantic Metaphors of Death," I'm not as sure as I
once was that the period really helped shape a tradition of death poetry in

which death is consistently defined as "the mother of beauty," although I do think the era was one in which an anxious modern tradition of death poetry did begin to form, despite the pious certainties of Lydia Sigourney and Alfred Lord Tennyson. But that tradition was far more heavily inflected by both skepticism and trauma than I'd wanted to admit in those days. Another of Dickinson's letters to Louise Norcross summarizes the nervous questioning that underlies so much of her poetry—and Whitman's, and ours. "I wish 'twas plainer, Loo, the anguish in this world. I wish one could be sure the suffering had a loving side."[28]

13

"Rats' Alley" and the Death of Pastoral

THE ARMY OF THE DEAD

When Whitman lamented "the dead, the dead, the dead" of the Civil War who crawled "somewhere . . . to die, alone, in bushes, low gullies, or on the sides of hills," his elegiac words prophesied the deaths of equally overwhelming wars to come within the next century, deaths whose grisly relics ("bleach'd bones, tufts of hair, buttons") he might also have been enumerating. By the turn of the century, for instance, some twenty-two thousand British troops had been killed in the Boer War along with over five thousand Boer combatants, and twenty-eight thousand Boer civilians (mainly women and children) as well as fourteen thousand South African natives had died in concentration camps established by the British, among the first such camps ever to be founded.[1] Back in England, the poet-novelist Thomas Hardy offered in "Drummer Hodge" a wartime elegy whose emphasis on the details of hasty military burial might have been drawn from Whitman's notebooks even while its ironic detachment prefigured the mode in which so many poets of the Great War worked just fifteen years later.

"They *throw in* Drummer Hodge," wrote Hardy, "to rest / *Uncoffined—just as found* [emphases added]." Nor, he noted in a poignantly understated stanza, would this boy (for "drummers" were always adolescents) have been able to comprehend the alien landscape into which he was destined to merge:

Young Hodge the Drummer never knew—
Fresh from his Wessex home—
The meaning of the broad Karoo,

The Bush, the dusty loam,
And why uprose to nightly view
Strange stars amid the gloam.[2]

But even the popular poet Robert W. Service, a Canadian born in England, found it hard to celebrate the vexed triumph that produced so many corpses. In his uncharacteristically gloomy "The March of the Dead," Service envisioned a moment of imperial glory ("everyone was shouting for the Soldiers of the Queen") that is shadowed by the appearance of an "Army of the Dead," "uncoffined" like Hardy's Drummer Hodge but also horrifyingly resurrected in all their wounded physicality:

They were coming, they were coming, gaunt and ghastly, sad and slow;
They were coming, all the crimson wrecks of pride;
With faces seared, and cheeks red smeared, and haunting eyes of woe,
And clotted holes the khaki couldn't hide. . . .
They were come, were come to mock us, in the first flush of our peace.[3]

In 1746 William Collins had eulogized the supposedly happy warriors who defended their country against interlopers, admiring the noble "sleep" of "the brave who sink to rest / By all their country's wishes blest!" and stressing the ghostly virtues that, as it were, glossed over the actual "clotted holes" made by bullets and bayonets. "By fairy hands their knell is rung," Collins wrote of the heroic military dead, and "By forms unseen their dirge is sung."[4] But by the beginning of the twentieth century both the aesthetic and the metaphysical assumptions that marked such patriotic abstractions were as riddled with holes as the cadavers churned out by the American Civil War, the Anglo-Boer War, and—soon—the Great War in Europe. Indeed, just as traditional Christianity seemed increasingly like a "moth-eaten, musical brocade," so the war elegy itself, with its quasi-Christian promises of national rebirth and renewal, had become a tired genre, whose intransigently dead subjects were coming "to mock us" in the "first flush of our peace."

Even in the muddy trenches of the First World War, of course, a number of combatants struggled to uphold the ideals of wartime valor and sacrificial death that infused Collins's ode. For such writers, a model of patriotic self-immolation was outlined in Rupert Brooke's widely read "The Soldier," with its nearly ecstatic imagining of the personal body fused into the public body of the state: "If I should die, think only this of me: / That there's some corner of a foreign field / That is forever England."[5] But by the war's end a number of ambitious soldier-poets had agreed on the literary implications of the wounds the conflict had opened in both aesthetics and theology. In 1917, Wilfred Owen, along with Siegfried Sassoon, Robert Graves, and—later—David Jones, the most distinguished of the combatant-poets, summarized an increasingly typical modern bitterness toward Victorian idealizations of death and dying in a letter he sent to his mother from Craiglockhart, a mental hospital for shell shock victims.[6]

Musing on the vision of redemption Tennyson had confidently expressed in "Crossing the Bar" ("I hope to see my Pilot face to face / When I have crossed the bar"), Owen set his own daily wartime confrontations with the haunting physicality of "the dead, the dead, the dead" against what seemed to him the nineteenth-century laureate's all too easy metaphor of a divine sandbar between the harbor of earth and the sea of heaven's bliss. Was Tennyson, he wondered, "ever frozen alive, with dead men for comforters? Did he hear the moaning at the bar, not at twilight and the evening bell only, but at dawn, noon, and night . . . always the close moaning of the Bar; the thunder, the hissing, and the whining of the Bar?"[7] Solid and sinister, Owens's "Bar" was the war itself—the thunder of its guns, the hissing of its gas, the whining of its descending shells—and its gruesome reality, as he argued in poem after poem, could be neither justified nor sentimentalized.

Paradoxically, though, it was the noncombatant American Wallace Stevens who made the most ambitious efforts to analyze the war's meaning for traditional poetic mourning and, more generally, for traditional cultural modes of mourning. In "The Owl in the Sarcophagus," an elegy that he composed not long after the end of World War II, Stevens announced a new poetics of grief even as he predicted the disintegration of the very genre in which he was writing. Here he frankly declared that what he called his "inventions of farewell" were rooted in a set of fresh assumptions about both death and grief:

> This is the mythology of modern death
> And these, in their mufflings, monsters of elegy,
> Of their own marvel made, of pity made.[8]

Defining his own efforts at memorializing the dead as "monstrous," Stevens was calling attention to a genre disfigured by a traumatized modernity. But the death he lamented in "Owl" was by no means the first event to evoke this poet's thoughts on procedures for mourning. Stevens's views on both the modernity of death and the monstrosity of the (modern) elegy can be traced back to a poem first published in a World War I sequence entitled "Lettres d'un Soldat" (1917–1918).

One of Stevens's most frequently anthologized texts, "The Death of a Soldier" formulates a view of bereavement in which time-honored funerary customs have been annihilated as definitively as the combatant who is the subject of the piece.

> *Life contracts and death is expected,*
> *As in a season of autumn,*
> *The soldier falls.*
>
> *He does not become a three-days personage,*
> *Imposing his separation,*
> *Calling for pomp.*
>
> *Death is absolute and without memorial,*
> *As in a season of autumn,*
> *When the wind stops,*
>
> *When the wind stops and, over the heavens,*
> *The clouds go, nevertheless,*
> *In their direction*

Prefiguring the conditions of all "modern death," the soldier's demise in this work "is absolute and without memorial" or at least without the kind of memorial associated with the "three-days personage" of long-established ceremonial lament. Nor do "the heavens" of traditional Christianity show the slightest concern; their high, indifferent clouds sail on unperturbed. After *this* first (modern) death, as Stevens was later to suggest in "The Owl in the Sarcophagus," there will be *every* other.[9]

Emphasizing death's historical particularity, the sequence in which "The Death of a Soldier" first appeared drew on details in letters from the front written between August 1914 and April 1915 by the French painter Eugène Emmanuel Lermercier, who was killed in combat in 1915. And documenting the literary changes that followed upon history's reshapings of death, the sequence concludes with a vision of wartime death that prescribes the "monsters of elegy" Stevens and his contemporaries were beginning to produce. Like all the other poems in the series, this piece (XIII) is prefaced by a quotation from Lermercier's letters home, in this case the bleakest of the passages Stevens excerpts:

> *Rien de nouveau sur notre hauteur que l'on continue d'organiser. . . . De temps à autre la pioche rencontre un pauvre mort que la guerre tourmente jusque dans la terre.*

> ["Nothing new from our hilltop which we continue to organize. . . . From time to time the pickaxe hits a wretched corpse that the war torments even in the ground."][10]

But rather than brood on the morbid reality implicit in Lemercier's words about the "wretched corpse" *re*tormented even in death, Stevens uses his verse variation on the theme announced in the French prose to decree a poetics of grief appropriate to modern death.

Traditionally, Stevens observes, death was personified as a reaper "with sickle and stone" or as a rider gesturing "grandiose things in the air, / Seen by a muse." Now, though, the poet considers these "Symbols of sentiment" outworn images. Instead, he urges that "Men of the line"—by implication both soldiers (men of the *front* line) and poets (men of the *poetic* line)—should

> *Take this new phrase*
> *Of the* truth *of Death*—
> *Death, that will never be satisfied,*
> *Digs up the earth when want returns.* [emphasis added][11]

Like Owen, in other words, Stevens insists that the sordid reality of death in the Great War revises literary as well as literal relationships to dying, death, and the dead. In fact, just as for Owen the traumatized *modernity* of "modern death" resides in the gulf between the poetic "Bar" imagined by Tennyson and the bodily *War* experienced by Owen ("frozen alive, with dead men for comforters"), so for Stevens, death's modernity is dramatized by the continuum along which death as a pale rider on a pale horse "gesturing grandiose things in the air" dissolves into a "symbol of sentiment" that must be replaced by a new phrase—and a new phase—of voracity. Thus for both these otherwise very different artists the war that was supposed to end all wars has become as crucial a turning point in the history of both death and elegy as it is in the history of warfare. In fact, as we can see after the passage of nearly a century, rather than being a war that ended all wars, it was a war that ended most established elegiac traditions along with long-standing traditions of mourning and memorializing.

WHAT WAS "PASTORAL"?

So-called pastoral elegies have long dominated our culture's poetry of grief. In one of the paradoxes of literary tradition, the poets who authored these highly polished, classic works of mourning "spoke" as if they were untutored shepherds of ancient Arcady, grieving for the deaths of fellow shepherds. The word "pastoral" derives from *pastor*, the Latin word for "shepherd," but it also connotes a life that's "charmingly simple" and can in addition refer to clergymen, who are often called pastors in a metaphor that defines a priest or vicar as "shepherd" of the congregation that constitutes his "flock."[12] Embedded in the label "pastoral elegy," therefore, are at least three assumptions about death and grief that the Great War was to annihilate: first, the notion that the mourner inhabits a peaceful, even idealized ("pastoral") landscape; second, the idea that the mourner has some control over his environment (he's a *pastor* or shepherd, after all, not a *sheep*); and third, the view that the natural cycles of seasonal renewal shaping the shepherd's calendar are emblematic of the spiritual resurrection promised by the *pastoral* letters of Christian theology.

Focusing on the function of pastoral elegy, the scholar Peter Sacks has shown that many of the characteristics of the conventional elegiac "plot"— for instance, its bucolic context, its references to dying and rising vegetation gods (Adonis, Osiris), its reiterations of questions and curses, its enumerations of mourners, and finally its "movement from grief to consolation" symbolized through "traditional images of resurrection"—are as driven by the psychological needs of the mourning process that Freud described as they are strategies for achieving aesthetic closure.[13] By the end of the Great War, however, when what seem like determinedly antipastoral elegies began to replace the pastoral poem of lamentation, the literature of mourning had suffered a grave blow. For because the struggle that killed more than eight million combatants seemed to have closed the gates of a heaven into which the soul could "expire," that conflict also sounded the death knell of the consoling and cathartic elegy.[14]

Arguing against this view, the historian Jay Winter has claimed that the war's catastrophic annihilation of almost an entire generation of young men actually regenerated a "complex traditional vocabulary of mourning, derived from classical, romantic, or religious forms," which "flourished, largely because it helped mediate bereavement."[15] For most commentators, however, the conflict represents an especially terrifying instance of "future shock," an "apocalypse that [led] the way" toward the often nihilistic aesthetic that shattered the assumptions of the traditional elegy. For even while the war poets did indeed yearn for the symbolic resurrection promised by time-honored forms of lamentation, the rats' alley in which history had trapped them looked more like a blind alley leading to the dead end of termination than a stairway to heaven. Thus those elements of the pastoral elegy embodying a redemptive drama appear to have been as definitively obliterated by the war as were the bodies of countless mortally wounded combatants.[16]

Yes, certain of the stylistic mannerisms Sacks identifies—reiterations of questions and curses, for instance, along with the all too plausible enumeration of mourners—do endure in the postwar period's "monsters of elegy." And many observers have noted the desperation with which the many communities of the bereaved struggled to mediate grief through an almost feverish revival of old myths and pieties. While some combatants claimed that they had seen heavenly messengers, with the most famous of these being the "Angel of Mons" who supposedly led the British to victory during a 1914 battle in Belgium, grieving parents and bereft widows on the home front frequently tried to communicate with their dead sons and husbands through the intervention of spiritualists.[17] But the comforting literary materials out of which, say, "Lycidas" and "Adonais" were made—a "pastoral" context, allusions to dying and rising vegetation gods, a "movement from grief to consolation" fostered by "traditional images of resurrection"—had been exploded in the mud of No Man's Land. Finally, therefore, the war tore such a hole in history that the generic form as well as the consolatory function of pastoral elegy was permanently defiled for combatants and noncombatants alike.

THE POETRY IS IN THE PITY

The very word "pastoral" takes on an ironic cast in relation to the cities of death that marked the wasteland of No Man's Land, as do the phrases "vegetation god" and "resurrection." As, in the words of the combatant-poet Richard Aldington, "an infernal cemetery" filled with "smashed bodies and human remains," the landscape of the war was barely a *land*scape in the ordinary sense of the word, but rather a gigantic charnel house. Wrote the

English memoirist Vera Brittain when the clothes of her dead fiancé were returned from the front, "the mud of France" that stained them seemed "saturated with dead bodies"; what once might have been fertile earth was now a horrifying pollutant. Indeed, to the extent that life could be discerned in the deathscape of No Man's Land, it was a deadly life, a life that was paradoxically *anti*life.[18]

For the earth that ought to have been (as in pastoral) a consoling home for the living and a regenerative grave for the dead had become instead a grave for the living, who were buried alive in trenches and ditches, and a home for the dead, who were often strewn unburied among the living. Testified the British novelist Ford Maddox Ford as he remembered overlooking the fields along the Somme: "In the territory beneath the eye, or hidden by folds in the ground, there must have been—on the two sides—a million men, moving one against the other [in] a Hell of fear that surely cannot have had a parallel in this world. It was an extraordinary feeling to have in a wide landscape." And a German memoirist noted: "I can still find no word nor image to express the awfulness of that waste. . . . A desert is always a desert, but a desert which tells you all the time that it used not to be a desert is appalling. That is the tale which is told by the dumb, black stumps of the shattered trees which still stick up where there used to be villages. [They] stand there like corpses upright. Not a blade of green anywhere round."[19]

Perhaps the most ferocious summary of this transformation of land to limbo—or, worse, earth to hell—appears in one of Wilfred Owen's bitterest letters home, written on January 19, 1917. "They want to call No Man's Land 'England,'" the young soldier-poet scoffed, "because we keep supremacy there." But No Man's Land

> is like the eternal place of gnashing of teeth: the Slough of Despond could be contained in one of its crater-holes; the fires of Sodom and Gomorrah could not light a candle to it—to find the way to Babylon the Fallen.
>
> It is pock-marked like a body of foulest disease and its odour is the breath of cancer.
>
> I have not seen any dead. I have done worse. In the dank air I have perceived it, and in the darkness, felt. Those "Somme Pictures" [by the establishment "war artist" Muirhead Bone] are the laughing stock of the army. . . .[20]

Owen's comment on "those 'Somme Pictures'" refers to Bone's bizarrely bucolic landscapes titled *Battle of the Somme*, renditions of the battlefield in France that Ford had described, on which sixty thousand British soldiers were killed in a single day. What outraged Owen was that Bone (whose name is morbidly comic here) made only one concession to the reality of modern warfare: a string of barbed wire in the foreground—backed up by lines of healthy-looking trees in a field where no trees could have survived.[21]

Death's ubiquity and the consequent transformation of a once restorative natural world into a debilitatingly unnatural realm also became a central subject in David Jones's innovative part-prose part-verse war narrative entitled *In Parenthesis*. Tracing the experience of his protagonist, John Ball, as this archetypal infantryman journeys with his company from home to front, Jones describes the group's first entry into the hellish "city" of the trenches as an encounter with death and decay in which soldiers who seem like the living dead—"Lazarus figures"—loom out of a land of shadows, bearing the remains of a comrade who is now no more than "a bundle-thing": "Appear more Lazarus figures, where water gleamed between dilapidated breastworks, blue slime coated, ladling with wooden ladles; rising, bending, at their trench dredging. They speak low. Cold gurgling followed their labours. They lift things, and a bundle-thing out; its shapelessness sags. From this muck-raking are singular stenches, long decay leavened."[22]

As for the trenches themselves, Jones describes them as gravelike pits, filled with "icily discomforting" mud and punctuated by the "squeaking, bead-eyed hastening, many footed hurrying" of the rats that were as omnipresent throughout the war as death itself. His verse depiction of night in No Man's Land emphasizes not just the inhumanity of a land where no men should live but also the grotesque inhospitality of a rats' alley in which "carrying parties" of soldiers are paralleled and parodied by "carrying-parties" of rodents:

> *You can hear the silence of it:*
> *you can hear the rat of no-man's-land*
> *rut-out intricacies . . .*
> *You can hear his carrying-parties rustle our corruptions through the*
> *night-weeds—contest the choicest morsels in his tiny conduits, bead-eyed*
> *feast on us. . . .*
> *When it's all quiet you can hear them:*
> *scrut scrut scrut. . . .*[23]

Nor do the only apparently triumphant rats themselves fare much better than men in this antipastoral deathscape, for amid the "untidied squalor" the soldiers see "swollen rat-body turned-turtle to the clear morning."

In such an antipastoral deathscape, even life that was neither the imper-
iled life of comrades nor the threatening life of enemies appears ironic,
maybe deadly, while what might in traditional pastoral elegy have por-
tended rebirth instead signals dissolution. As the poet-critic Jon Silkin has
pointed out, for instance, in Siegfried Sassoon's "Counter-Attack," "Nature
has certainly been transformed," but in a way that is hardly affirmative.
Beginning "the place was rotten with dead," Sassoon goes on to describe
how "green clumsy legs / High-booted, sprawled and groveled . . . face
downward, in the sucking mud," and then remarks ironically, "the rain
began,—the jolly old rain!" Here the adjective " 'Green' suggests gangrene,"
not the green of nature, while the "jolly old rain" that ought to "set up"
nature's restorative potency merely portends further disintegration.[24]

Similarly, Robert Graves's "A Dead Boche" depicts the hideousness with
which the body of a German soldier, "propped against a shattered trunk" in
Mametz Wood, is assimilated into a corrosive rather than regenerative
earth: "[H]e scowled and stunk / With clothes and face a sodden green."
And Graves outlines his own understanding of the literary conventions his
poem flouts in a prefatory explanation of the lesson to be learned from the
appalling figure of the "dead Boche":

> To you who'd read my songs of War
>   And only hear of blood and fame,
> I'll say (you've heard it said before)
>   "War's Hell!" and if you doubt the same,
> To-day I found in Mametz Wood
> A certain cure for lust of blood.

That some readers hoping to "hear of blood and fame" from the young poet
were indeed sickened, even scandalized by his description of the German
corpse simply proved his point.[25]

Two of Isaac Rosenberg's most caustic poems—"Break of Day in the
Trenches" and "Returning, We Hear the Larks"—make the same kind of
somber sport with images that tradition defines as regenerative but that
turn out to be as degenerative as Sassoon's green that dissolves into gangrene or Graves's "sodden green" of fleshly corruption. In the first, the dawn
that should bring renewal brings the poet only the company of a "queer sardonic rat" with disturbingly "cosmopolitan sympathies," while in the second, the "unseen larks . . . showering" music on the combatants' "upturned
list'ning faces" mean to the poet that "Death could drop from the dark / As

easily as song" and, worse, that the natural world out of which such apparently innocent song arises isn't a nurturing Mother Nature but instead a sort of oblivious femme fatale, with beauties like "a girl's dark hair for she dreams no ruin lies there." As Herbert Asquith, the son of Britain's prime minister, noted in "After the Salvo," "Up and down, up and down, / They go, the gray rat, and the brown," and the "temple of the gossamer" woven by spiders inscrutably endures while "Man's house is crushed."[26]

That Rosenberg was aware of his deviations from a tradition of pastoral affirmation is clear from his choices of form (in the first poem, an aubade) and symbol (in the second, Shelleyan larks). But Owen, whose excoriation of Tennyson's "Crossing the Bar" might serve as a manifesto for all these writers, is even more explicit about his quarrel with literary precursors. His "À Terre," for example, spoken by a combatant survivor who describes himself as "blind, and three parts shell," takes on "Adonais" directly:

> "I shall be one with nature, herb, and stone,"
> Shelley would tell me. Shelley would be stunned:
> The dullest Tommy hugs that fancy now.
> "Pushing up daisies" is their creed, you know.[27]

In fact the combatants' living burial has so defamiliarized the natural world that nature and a denatured charnel house of nothingness become one in many of their poems. In such a state of alienation, even the body of a comrade becomes, as in Jones's poem, "a bundle-*thing*" or, as in one of Ivor Gurney's poems, a "red wet / *Thing* I must somehow forget" (emphases added).[28]

From some religious perspectives the charnel house of the front might at first seem like the setting for a medieval dance of the dead. Like citizens of the plague years, the soldiers of World War I inhabited a realm in which, says Guy Chapman, the dead "remained a long time without burial, for who was going to risk lives for such a task? The weather was no longer hot, and the dead would keep. They lay out there at the side of the track in the drizzle, yellow or grey or blue with blood dried black on their skin and clothes; sometimes a shell would hasten the indignity of slow decomposition. They were certainly not worth another life."[29] But unlike victims of the Black Plague, these dead men hadn't been killed by what might be construed as the will of God but rather by the will of man. Casualties of technology, moreover, they became even in death grotesque tools of technology; as one historian notes, "New trenches might be dug through them; parapets might be made of them."[30]

That such technology ultimately took on a ghastly life of its own also has religious implications, as the journalist Donovan Webster emphasizes in *Aftermath: The Remnants of War*. Interviewing a few of the professional *démineurs* who to this day spend one week of every month out at sea detonating some of the countless unexploded shells with which the French countryside is still littered, Webster reports a theologically resonant conversation with René Teller, head of the technical center in charge of such operations. Asked, "What was the worst weapon of the war?," Teller gestures toward a (poison gas) shell and a shrapnel bomb, commenting that "with these two weapons, whole armies could be killed without their opponents ever seeing them. When the power to destroy faceless men came into our hands, men learned that God can abandon them. With these weapons, a religion without God had arrived."[31]

Because the will of man could replace with such demonic inventiveness what medieval divines defined as the will of God, poets often directed as much invective against religious sermons of consolation as against literary traditions of redemption. From the perspective of disillusioned combatants (and some of their survivors), the windy spokesmen of the established Church emitted a gas nearly as toxic as the substance more hideously encountered on the battlefield. Sassoon's acerbic "They," for example, achieves an almost postmodern level of black comedy in its assault on empty platitudes:

> The Bishop tells us: "When the boys come back
> They will not be the same; for they'll have fought
> In a just cause: they lead the last attack
> On Anti-Christ; their comrades' blood has bought
> New right to breed an honorable race,
> They have challenged Death and dared him face to face."
>
> "We're none of us the same!" the boys reply.
> "For George lost both his legs; and Bill's stone blind;
> Poor Jim's shot through the lungs and like to die;
> And Bert's gone syphilitic; you'll not find
> A chap who's served that hasn't found some *change*."
> And the Bishop said: "The Ways of God are strange!"

Remembering the ferocious Battle of the Somme, in which the British suffered sixty thousand casualties (including twenty thousand deaths) in a single day, one soldier commented: "From that moment, all my religion died. All my teaching and beliefs in God had left me, never to return."[32]

Summarizing comparable disillusionment, Wilfred Owen begins his "Anthem for Doomed Youth" with the antielegiac question "What passing-bells for those who die as cattle?," declaring the bankruptcy of both religion *and* genre as sources of comfort. Neither church bells nor the bells of verse can toll appropriate dirges for young men led like beasts to slaughter. Nor can the elegist assume his traditional role either as *pastor*/shepherd guarding his flock or as *pastor*/preacher promising resurrection. He himself, after all, has become just another sheep in a dumb and doomed flock. For even "Poetry" in the grandest sense seemed contaminated to Owen, though he was an ambitious young writer who had begun his career by modeling his art on the verse of the Romantic poet John Keats. "Above all," he declared in the wartime manifesto that eventually became a preface to his slender posthumous collection,

> *I am not concerned with Poetry.*
> *My subject is War, and the pity of War.*
> *The Poetry is in the pity.*
> Yet these elegies are to this generation in no sense consolatory
> [emphasis added].

Rawly factual in subject though artfully crafted in style, Owen's antipastoral elegies are "in no sense consolatory" precisely because the poetry is in the "pity" that can't be healed or abolished, just as the sermons of Sassoon's Bishop are "in no sense consolatory" because the ways of the "God" of war are too "strange" for comprehension. And to Hamlet's mordant question—arguably the central question of the griever—"What ceremony else?," Owen replies, in effect, that only an act of witnessing, of attesting to the antipastoral reality of the scenes of death and dying, can constitute a properly elegiac tribute to the slaughtered multitudes. Although tradition prescribes ritual measures, the only "passing-bells for those who die as cattle" are "the monstrous anger of the guns" and "the stuttering rifles' rapid rattle." No visions of transcendence, Owen argues, can redeem the mud "saturated with dead bodies." Testimony—the telling and sometimes nearly obsessive *re*telling of the *details* of the event—is the only available tribute to the war's inescapable factuality.[33]

It was through a range of testimonial gestures, therefore, that combatant-poets reshaped the traditional pastoral elegy into the skeptical poetry of mourning with which we are familiar today. Their strategies of witnessing crafted a genre that is for the most part resolutely antipastoral in its meticulous attention to the mechanisms of "modern death": death conceived as a bleak termination of life rather than an expiration into a blessed hereafter. In fact, the first of the powerfully influential testimonial strategies through which writers from Sassoon, Owen, and Rosenberg to Graves and Jones frequently sought to acknowledge and articulate grief was an explicit confrontation of the scene of dying. The second was an equally frank preoccupation with the actual body or bodies of the dead. The third was an almost psychoanalytic review and retelling of the events that led to the scene of dying and the corporeality of death. Taken together, these three modes of testifying to the particulars of loss inevitably tilted the war elegy, and its countless peacetime descendants, toward a conclusion emphasizing resignation rather than redemption, stoic acquiescence rather than prayerful hope.

If we turn once more to Felman and Laub's study of Holocaust testimony as "a crucial mode of our relation to events of our times" because it is the fragmentary product of a mind "overwhelmed by . . . events in excess of our frames of reference," the writings of combatant-poets can be understood as efforts to make sense of battlegrounds shockingly unlike the heroic battlefields of glory the young men of 1914 had been led to expect. That, as Felman also notes, to testify is "to accomplish a *speech act*, rather than simply formulate a statement" further illuminates the crucial role of First World War elegies as both missives and missiles, angry dispatches sent from the agonized front to what soldiers perceived as a complacent home front. Finally, if we define this wartime testimony as, in Felman's words, a kind of "*action*" with an "*impact* that dynamically explodes any conceptual reifications," it becomes clear that a testimonial urgency underlies the many elegies whose transgressions of expected forms shatter the pieties of traditional mourning while also disrupting literary convention.[34] For ultimately testimony to the shell shock of the First World War fostered just the literary shock of the new that in so many ways exploded those "conceptual reifications" assumed by the historically consolatory genre of the elegy.

As we've seen in Part Two of this volume, as early as 1915 Sigmund Freud was remarking that in the shadow of the Great War the "civilized cosmopolitan" finds himself "helpless in a world grown strange to him—his all-embracing patrimony disintegrated." His words shrewdly predicted the vast cultural change soon to be known as modernism even while they reflected the terrible gulf that had opened not just between nations but also between the front and the home front. For as the psychoanalyst added while he lamented the shattering of an international order whose stability had once offered "unhindered" travel within the "wider fatherland" of Western culture, a "distinction should be made between two groups—those who themselves risk their lives in battle, and those who have stayed at home and have only to wait for the loss of one of their dear ones."[35]

For those shocked by the shells of the battlefield, the ignorance of those at home was almost equally shocking; to those who had quailed at the horror of a new order of industrialized violence, those who still thought themselves safely embedded in a pastoral world appeared smug and stupid. At times, in fact, to judge from the anticivilian rhetoric of Sassoon and Owen, the ignorance of citizens at home seemed more culpable than the assaults of the enemy. In any case, civilian unawareness was experienced by most soldier-poets as neither innocence nor indifference, and it made the bearing of witness to dreadful particulars especially crucial (and cruel).

Paradoxically, however, concerned noncombatants also understood themselves to be utterly dependent on the testimony of combatant-witnesses for meaningful information not just about the individual fates of friends and relatives at the front but also, more generally, about the fatality that had befallen a world slowly growing as strange to those at home as it already was to those in the trenches. It's telling, in this regard, that Wallace Stevens—thousands of miles from the war and its various fronts—carefully bases "Lettres d'un Soldat" on Lermercier's testimony about modern death in battle. If the soldier-witness assaults what he considers civilian complacency with grim battlefield evidence, the noncombatant, guiltily internalizing the combatant's accusations, also internalizes soldierly testimony and transforms it into a revisionary act of witnessing that allows him to testify *as if* he had shared the soldier's trench.

At the same time, among soldier-poets the need to testify was uniquely exacerbated by equally overwhelming feelings of guilt and fears of complicity, for even while the combatants were victims, mourners, and witnesses of the charnel house created by the "monstrous anger of the guns," they were also dealers of death. As the historian David Cannadine puts it, these "soldiers themselves had been the agents of death, killing . . . in a manner which would be unimaginable in civvy street. Shock, guilt, anguish, grief, remorse: these were only some of the emotions which such an experience left behind."[36] The paradoxical status of the mourner as *himself a murderer* thus gives special anguish to some of the antipastoral elegies that evolved out of World War I.

Nor were noncombatants exempt from such emotions. Obviously the gulf that separates deed from word yawns between the literal and the symbolic wielders of a bayonet, yet just as obviously the civilian, safe on the home front, must suffer a grievous case of survivor's guilt. Rudyard Kipling, whose seventeen-year-old son John was killed at the front within a month of his arrival there, summarized such guilt in one of his tersely bitter "Epitaphs of the War," in which a dead soldier-speaker reproachfully urges, "If any question why we died, / Tell them, because our fathers lied."[37] For the No Man's Land that stretched between allies and enemies, along with a metaphorically comparable No Man's Land that stretched between front and home front, dramatically manifested the rending of the basic ancestral bonds that had traditionally shaped what Freud called "the wider fatherland" in which educated European men had hitherto moved unhindered.

At the same time, the torn-up terrain of No Man's Land came to represent the fragmentation, if not the outright destruction, of the inspiring ceremonies of mourning epitomized by the pastoral elegy. "We cannot maintain our former attitude towards death," wrote Freud in his 1915 meditation on the war, "and have not yet discovered a new one." Notes a more recent observer, commenting on twentieth-century changes in British bereavement customs, "Mourning succumbed [by 1917–1918] before the vast numbers of the dead," for how, after all, "could one realistically continue to believe in the resurrection of the body when all that was left might be a few rat-bitten pieces of rotting flesh?"[38]

As for the soul, an eerie dislocation of the dead was the only comfort promised by the turn toward spiritualism that some have interpreted as a striving toward a surrogate religion in the war and interwar years.[39] Far from "the solemn troops and sweet societies" among whom Milton imagined Edward King as having taken his rightful place, and distant too from the firmament in which Shelley portrays the soul of Adonais beaconing "like a star," the unquiet ghosts of the Society for Psychical Research seem to have been conceived as inhabitants of a void as unsponsored as No Man's Land itself, from whose dismal reaches they were struggling to communicate in cries and whispers conveyed through half-conscious mediums. Most established religions thus astutely defined such imaginings of the afterlife as blasphemous, and few elegists, wishfully pastoral or wistfully antipastoral, would have disagreed.

DOWN SOME PROFOUND DULL TUNNEL

Three of the most brilliant elegiac texts to emerge from the Great War—two by combatant-poets and one by a noncombatant—dramatize the complex ways this catastrophic conflict revised cultural imaginings of "modern death" along with the aesthetic responses to such imaginings embodied in "monsters of elegy." Wilfred Owen's "Strange Meeting," T. S. Eliot's *The Waste Land*, and David Jones's *In Parenthesis* are superficially very different, but all three are as haunted by the pastoral elegy as they are by death and the dead; all are strikingly antipastoral in their representation of landscapes that have become uncanny (*unheimlich*) cities of death; all, like the testimonies of which Felman writes, appear to be the fragmentary products of minds struggling to comprehend "events in excess of our frames of reference"; and all are impelled by a testimonial urgency.

One of Owen's two or three best-known poems, "Strange Meeting" is set in a "profound dull tunnel, long since scooped" out of an inhospitable earth "saturated with dead bodies," a space whose contours suggest not only the subterranean passages that linked the trenches but also the halls of hell. In this place, as in a nightmarish parody of the orderly underground where Dante and his poetic guide, Virgil, encountered so many monitory figures of the dead, the poet-speaker testifies that he finds himself face-to-face with a brotherly double who turns out to be an unnervingly eloquent ghost:

> It seemed that out of battle I escaped
> Down some profound dull tunnel, long since scooped
> Through granites which titanic wars had groined.
> Yet also there encumbered sleepers groaned,
> Too fast in thought or death to be bestirred.
> Then, as I probed them, one sprang up, and stared
> With piteous recognition in fixed eyes,
> Living distressful hands as if to bless.
> And by his smile, I knew that sullen hall,
> By his dead smile I knew we stood in Hell.
> With a thousand pains that vision's face was grained;
> Yet no blood reached there from the upper ground,
> And no guns thumped, or down the flues made moan.
> "Strange friend," I said, "here is no cause to mourn."
> "None," said that other, "save the undone years,
> The hopelessness. Whatever hope is yours,
> Was my life also. . . ."

But after further confirmations of all the tormented dead man and the poet had in common, the poem draws to an end with a stunning enactment of both the wartime disintegration of male bonding and the plight of the mourner/murderer, for the ghost reveals that "I am the enemy you killed, my friend." As in many other twentieth-century elegies, the poet has already brooded on the projects of the life that his own complicity has cut short ("Whatever hope is yours, / Was my life also," discloses the ghost), but now Owen broods on the scene of dying, as the dead man recounts the event from *his* perspective: "*[S]o you frowned / Yesterday* [emphasis added] through me as you jabbed and killed. / I parried; but my hands were loath and cold."[40]

From a literary-historical perspective, "Strange Meeting" doesn't just meet up with Dante per se but also with several other poets, notably the author's mentor, Siegfried Sassoon, whose "The Rear-Guard" depicts a soldier "Groping along" a similar "tunnel, step by step," until he stumbles over a "soft unanswering heap," a corpse whose "eyes yet wore / Agony dying hard ten days before."[41] But the "profound dull tunnel" of "Strange Meeting" is also plagued by the ghost of pastoral elegy, a genre into whose aesthetic space it cannot fit. If Milton had imagined *himself* visiting "the bottom of the monstrous world" and there encountering the drowned body of Edward King, the original of his "Lycidas," would he have produced this hallucinatory lament, with its portentous rhymes ("hall" leads to "Hell," "moan" to "mourn," "friend" to "frowned")? Worse still, if instead of ritually wondering "[W]here were ye, nymphs, when the remorseless deep / Closed o'er the head of your loved Lycidas?" Milton had believed *himself* to be the agent of remorseless fate, what strategies of consolation could he have devised?[42] Does the trauma of Owen's guilt foster both the urgency of his need to testify and his poem's uncertain grasp of an intolerable reality ("It *seemed* that out of battle I escaped [emphasis added]")? And does the grimness of his witnessing account too for his text's fragmentation, a state in which "the mind . . . has not settled into understanding" because perhaps it cannot?

The inconclusive ending of "Strange Meeting"—"Let us sleep now. . . ." —was a tentative resolution, penciled in by the poet in his last draft manuscript of the work. But it is also a notable example of the rhetorical device known as *aposiopesis*, which my dictionary defines as a "sudden breaking off of a thought in the middle of a sentence, as though the speaker were unwilling or unable to continue." Here, as even in more definitive poetic closures, the morning of resurrected pastoral imagination eludes Owen, as it has eluded most writers following the Great War and its discontents. The poet-mourner of "Lycidas" can plan a journey to "fresh fields and pastures new" after he has gained confidence in his dead friend's redemption, but such a vision of starting afresh eludes Owen. "Let us sleep now" (already a provisional, last-minute thought) is the only hope that can replace "Whatever hope" was the dead man's or the poet's in "Strange Meeting."

I THINK WE ARE IN RATS' ALLEY /
WHERE THE DEAD MEN LOST THEIR BONES

It's hardly necessary to show that a comparable hopelessness haunts Eliot's *The Waste Land*, given the poem's tone, its title, and its fame as *the* literary model of modernist nihilism. Nevertheless, to this day many readers are surprised to learn that the author of this supposedly "impersonal" cultural document once insisted that he considered the piece "only the relief of a personal and wholly insignificant grouse against life."[43] What can the magisterial poet-critic-editor have meant by such a remark? On the surface, surely, it would seem that an impersonal cultural document would be quite the opposite of a personal grouse! Nonetheless, the categories "cultural document" and "personal grouse" aren't necessarily incompatible. Indeed to the question "when is a personal grouse a cultural document?" we might reply, "when it is a poem elegizing the death of a beloved friend in a war that traumatized an entire culture."

That *The Waste Land* is not only elegiac in manner but at least in part an elegy for a specific person has already been argued by a number of critics, most of whom draw on an episode in Eliot's youth that was first examined in 1952 by John Peter, a Canadian scholar whose essay on the subject was quickly suppressed by the poet's solicitors. When Eliot was studying philosophy in Paris in 1911, Peter wrote, young Tom formed an intense relationship with a French medical student named Jean Verdenal. Some four years later, on May 2, 1915, Verdenal was killed in action at Gallipoli. And it was to "Jean Verdenal / 1889–1915" that the 1917 *Prufrock and Other Observations*, the 1920 *Ara Vos Prec*, and the 1925 *Poems: 1909–1925* were dedicated, with the addition in 1925 of the identifying tag "*mort aux Dardanelles*" and a wistfully loving epigraph from Canto 21 of *The Purgatorio* that declares: "Now you are able to comprehend the quantity of love that warms me toward you, / When I forget our emptiness / Treating shades as if they were solid." And it seems likely that Eliot was thinking of Verdenal as well as of his own unhappy marriage when he remarked that his ostensibly impersonal document was really only the product of "a personal . . . grouse against life."

By the time he published *The Waste Land* in 1922, the poet must have reconciled himself to Verdenal's death. Yet Peter claimed that the poem's central but repressed theme is its author's grief for a cherished male friend whom we now know to have been Verdenal.[44] And though Eliot scholars remained skeptical about this thesis for many years, by now—following the publication not only of the work's original draft manuscript but also of the writer's early letters—many would concede that Verdenal's death inspired a major crisis in the writer of *The Waste Land*. Understanding the young Frenchman to have been "mixed with the mud of Gallipoli," the poet plunged his imagination into the muck of a "rats' alley" where "the dead men lost their bones," a wasteland at whose center his dead friend was buried.[45]

But if it's read as a dirge for Verdenal, *The Waste Land* becomes an antipastoral elegy that both continues and disrupts the tradition of a man mourning for a man that extends from the Greek lyric poets to Milton, Shelley, and Whitman, a tradition that's also radically mutilated in Owen's "Strange Meeting." Indeed, read as a comment on literary history, Eliot's *Waste Land* seems like a symbolic version of No Man's Land itself, a ravaged terrain littered with the shards of the English elegy. Here, haunted not so much by the ghost as by the literal body of a dead comrade ("Those are pearls that were his eyes") whose friendship had given meaning to his own identity, Eliot becomes a witness to the woes of a world shattered by the war's shattered armies of the night.

At the same time, because he's a mourner driven by the need for consolation that impels the speakers of the traditional elegies whose outlines his poem explodes, the poet of the *The Waste Land* ironically evokes many conventional features of the pastoral elegy: the disturbing discrepancy between, on the one hand, nature's endurance as manifested in the returning spring and, on the other hand, his own sense of mortal loss ("April is the cruelest month"); a consciousness that he speaks for, even while he is somehow set apart from, a community of mourners ("crowds of people walking round in a ring"); a feeling that the world that has survived his friend is itself debilitated by loss ("I had not thought death had undone so many"); a vision of the dead man journeying deeper into death ("He passed the stages of his age and youth / Entering the whirlpool"); a warning that such a fate is universal ("Consider Phlebas, who was once handsome and tall as you"); and an effort to confound death either by imagining resurrection ("a damp gust / Bringing rain") or by redefining the terror of mortality ("Shantih Shantih Shantih").[46]

But because Eliot has lost his friend to an unprecedentedly calamitous war and finds himself in a postwar deathscape where the "all-embracing patrimony [of Western culture is] disintegrated," he has only fragments of the pastoral elegy to shore against his ruin. Thus the muses, nymphs, envoys of nature, and spectral visitors who appear in most elegies to guide the sufferer toward consolation are here even more deformed than the dead double Owen encounters in the dull tunnel of *his* elegy. "Lycidas"'s "sisters of the sacred well" and "Adonais"'s Urania become the parodic Madame Sosostris, the sinister Belladonna, and the vulgar Lil while Milton's and Shelley's nymphs metamorphose into the nymphs who have "now departed" with or without "the loitering heirs of city directors," into the bored typist, into the betrayed Thames daughters, and into the intransigently common "Mrs. Porter and her daughter," antiheroines of a bawdy ballad sung by Australian troops at Gallipoli, where Verdenal died. Whitman's bird victoriously singing "death's outlet song" becomes not just the hallucinatory "water-dripping" hermit thrush but also the raped nightingale who says "jug jug" only to "dirty ears." And Whitman's comforting "Dark mother always gliding near with soft feet" dissolves first into a disembodied "Murmur of maternal lamentation" and then into a ghastly woman prefiguring death, who draws "her long black hair out tight."

As for the dead friend himself, the name the poet bestows on him, *Phlebas*, has neither the Theocritan resonance of *Lycidas* nor the theological overtones of *Adonais* despite the subtle ways in which Eliot's poem evokes such classic pastoral elegies as "Lycidas," "Adonais," and "Thyrsis." Rather, as one Eliot scholar has pointed out, the Greek word *phlebas* means both "vein" and "phallus," suggesting that the loss of this man makes the speaker feel as though he has lost his own phallus, the emblem of manhood.[47] Unlike Lycidas and Adonais, therefore, both of whom are compared to dying and rising gods, Verdenal/Phlebas has problematic mythic as well as linguistic associations. And even if this drowned comrade momentarily evokes a hopeful image of "sea-change" drawn from *The Tempest* ("Those are pearls which were his eyes"), such a vision is merely, says the poem, a "Shakespeherian rag"—a meaningless scrap of cloth, a bit of vulgar song, or no more than a deceitful joke. For as a drowned Phoenician, Eliot's Phlebas is a phoenix that will not rise again.

Finally, even the godlike voice of thunder that emerges from the text to instruct and console at *The Waste Land*'s close is problematic. Speaking from another culture, neither the classical nor the Christian West, this voice elicits the thought that "London Bridge is falling down" even while it reminds the speaker of what has been (in the original manuscript, "we brother ... my friend, my friend ... / The awful daring of a moment's sur-

render") and that what has been will not be again (in the original manuscript, "friend, my friend I have heard the key / Turn in the door, once and
once only") and forces him to admit his present desolation (in the original
manuscript, "You over on the shore [There I leave you / Clasping empty
hands]").[48] Eliot critics have divided into two schools on the issue of
whether or not the poem's conclusion implies redemption either for the
speaker or for the wasteland of his bereaved consciousness. But whatever
the "real" truth may be, their quarrels stress again the equivocation that
marks this exploded elegy.

But if *The Waste Land* responds to the trauma of the war by fragmenting the pastoral elegy, it also retains within the text significant traces of what
we might consider the deadly shell that shocked its author. Although the
poem is usually seen as marked by the war in only the general way in which
most postwar art was affected by a pervasive cultural disillusionment,
Eliot's "impersonal" document is imprinted with wistful memories of Verdenal, with haunting references to Gallipoli, and with allusions to the
details of the battlefield, whose most gruesome particularities had been
widely reported by the time the author began to write his poem. Of course,
as is the case with any great work, the imagery of *The Waste Land* has multiple sources and references, but even just a quick look at the text yields
striking evocations of personal pain.

Verdenal: in the "cruelest month" of April the poet's friendship with
this simpatico young Frenchman, a lover of Wagner and Laforgue, seems
to have truly flowered, as is evident from a letter of Eliot's to a cousin,
from Verdenal's letters to Eliot, and from Eliot's single published reference
to his Paris *ami*, apart from the dedications of early volumes. In a jubilant
letter of April 26, 1911, Eliot wrote that "Paris has burst out . . . into full
spring: and it is such a revelation that I feel that I ought to make it
known," adding: "M. Verdenal was in the garden [and] I threw a lump of
sugar at him." On April 22, 1912, a year later, Verdenal wrote Eliot in Cambridge to tell him: "*Vous me fûtes particulièrement évoque par le contact de
ce paysage senti ensemble*," that Eliot was particularly evoked for him by the
verdant landscape that they had admired, appreciated, *felt* together ("*senti
ensemble*"). (In a previous letter he quoted a passage from André Gide's
Paludes [1895] filled with yearning to return to "that place I know, where
in darkened . . . water, the *leaves* of bygone years are still steeping and soft-
ening—the leaves of *adorable springtimes*").[49] Finally, decades later, in *April*
1934, Eliot wrote in the *Criterion*, in a rare personal moment, about his
own bittersweet memory of "a sentimental sunset [and] a friend coming

across the Luxembourg gardens in the late afternoon, waving a branch of lilac, a friend who was later (so far as I could find out) to be mixed with the mud of Gallipoli."⁵⁰

Gallipoli: in *April* 1915 the British army sailed for the Dardanelles, with a French division attached. The British intended to pass through the strait into the Sea of Marmara and on to Constantinople while the French "made a diversion on the Asiatic shore." In fact, from the long perspective of cultural history, the British were sailing to Byzantium (or at least trying to) while the French were attempting to land not far from the fabled ruins of Troy. And as the historical writer James Morris reminds us, any man of letters would have known that. The Dardanelles, notes Morris, were so central to a classical education "that every educated man knew of the myths and dramas that surrounded them. . . . [N]earby stood Troy itself, and all around lay the islands of the ancients." Thus "everything about Gallipoli conspired to haunt [men] with this sense of tragic nobility."⁵¹

At the same time, even while Gallipoli was as haunted by the ghosts of literary tradition as Eliot's text itself, it was a land as desiccated as the wasteland of the poet's nightmare. As one commentator has noted, had "he set out specifically to describe a Gallipoli dugout, Eliot could scarcely have chosen better words than 'mudcracked houses' from which 'red sullen faces sneer and snarl,'" while his fearful observation that "There is not even silence in the mountains / But dry sterile thunder without rain" proves to have been an all too accurate conjecture in the context of the ceaseless artillery barrages mounted by the Turks, whom the British and French were never able to dislodge from the highlands.⁵² That this deathscape, rimmed by "Dead mountain mouth of carious teeth that cannot spit," was as regularly disfigured by drought as by the ceaseless thunder of the guns, moreover, is mentioned in the testimony of countless journalists and combatants.⁵³ The poet John Masefield, who turned military historian in order to bear witness in his *Gallipoli* (1916) to the narrative that Eliot too is in some sense reconstructing, makes this point perhaps most dramatically:

> *The flowers which had been so gay with beauty in the Helles fields in* April *[emphasis mine] soon wilted to stalks. The great slope of Cape Helles took on a savage and African look of desolation. The air quivered over the cracking land. . . . Men in Gallipoli in the summer of 1915 learned to curse the sun as an enemy more cruel than the Turk. With the sun and the plague of flies came the torment of thirst, one of the greatest torments which life has the power to inflict. . . . Possibly to most of the many thousands who were*

*in the Peninsula last summer, the real enemies were not the Turks but the
sun in Heaven, shaking "the pestilence of his light," and thirst that with-
ered the heart and cracked the tongue.*[54]

And on this historically resonant yet ultimately "savage" and "desolate"
peninsula, this "arid rocky" finger of Europe reaching toward Asia, Verdenal
was cited for his heroism on *April* 30, 1915, when "scarcely recovered from
pleurisy [he] did not hesitate to spend much of the night in the water up to
his waist helping to evacuate the wounded by sea."[55] And in this liminal
place between land and sea, rock and shadow, the young French doctor was
killed in action, again tending the wounded, two days later.

Details of Verdenal's death, and of the battlefield on which he died, may
have at first been difficult to obtain, but as Eliot admitted in his comment
in the *Criterion*, the poet sought to find out as much as he could. Much of
what he understood to have happened was surely gleaned from information
that gradually emerged about combat conditions. He would very likely have
read Masefield's book—a narrative by a literary colleague, after all—and he
would have learned from other accounts too. Learned, for instance, that on
the Gallipoli peninsula the "labyrinths of trenches" had sardonic names like
"Dublin Castle, Half Moon Street" or (I'd add) "rats' alley."[56] That the
Anzacs sang bawdily about Mrs. Porter and her daughter. That the dead
men lost their bones because they so often went unburied. That queer sardonic rats were everywhere. That the jolly old rain gave no relief. And later,
long after the war, that on the Gallipoli peninsula and elsewhere the (re)
"Burial of the Dead," those never properly buried and those only (as it were)
temporarily buried, became a significant issue, with, as the historian Jay
Winter reminds us, in the early twenties hundreds of thousands of dead soldiers' being dug up (like the corpse in *The Waste Land*) and posthumously
"demobbed"—that is, sent home for reburial.[57]

Was the Dog that's "friend to man" no Dog Star but the blasphemously
canine God of Henri Barbusse's wartime battlefield dispatches, in which the
editors who prepared the French novelist's material for periodical publication cautiously substituted *Nom d'un* Chien for *Nom de Dieu* before the
reports later appeared as the devastating memoir *Le Feu* ("Under Fire")?[58]
And was the need to testify beyond the boundaries of what Felman calls
"conceptual reifications" manifested in the urgent stammerings of *The
Waste Land*?

Certainly that mystifying text's obsession with an only partly buried
corpse, with the rats' alley in which that body was lost, and with the details

of its death opened the way into the monstrous elegies of modernity, even if the poem's author yearned to resanctify the traditions of the past. That Eliot himself understood the implications of all this, despite the repressions that were to mark his later career, is made clear by his insistence to Ezra Pound that the original Conrad epigraph (from *Heart of Darkness*) was, to understate the case, "somewhat elucidative," for it focused—as do so many modern monsters of elegy—on testimony about the moment of death rather than on the dawning of an afterlife:

> *Did he live his life again in every detail of desire, temptation and surrender during that supreme moment of complete knowledge? He cried in a whisper at some image, some vision—he cried out twice, a cry that was no more than a breath—*
> "The horror, the horror!"[59]

THE MAN WHO DOES NOT KNOW THIS
HAS NOT UNDERSTOOD ANYTHING

By the mid-thirties a young Welsh-English Catholic convert named David Jones had long read and admired the poem that became known as Eliot's modernist masterpiece. And in many ways Jones's *In Parenthesis* was modeled on *The Waste Land*, to which the writer frankly alluded in admitting that his goal was to convey "the war landscape," showing how "the day by day in the Waste Land, the sudden violences and the long stillnesses . . . profoundly affected the imaginations of those who suffered it." An allusive, fragmented narrative to which Jones appended some thirty pages of sometimes formidably learned, sometimes casually chatty endnotes, *In Parenthesis* is as experimental in structure and style as Eliot's poem, and perhaps even more generically transgressive, since it boldly blurs prose and verse as it recounts the wartime experiences of its hero, John Ball. Nor did Eliot himself fail to grasp the connection. In his capacity as an editor at Faber & Faber, he enthusiastically accepted the book, noting in a later preface, "I am proud to share the responsibility for [its] first publication," and confiding, "On reading the book in typescript I was deeply moved. I then regarded it, and I still regard it, as a work of genius."

More specifically, the author of *The Waste Land* observed in Jones's writing "some affinity with that of James Joyce . . . and with the later work of Ezra Pound, *and with my own* [emphasis added]," though he disingenuously claimed that "any possible influence seems to me slight and of no importance" because after all the "lives of all of us were altered by [the] War, but David Jones is the only one to have fought in it." In fact, however, Jones's account of the war was marked by the same radical revisions of elegiac tradition and the same testimonial urgency that characterize Eliot's poem along with the earlier writings of such combatant-poets as Owen and Sassoon.

"These fragments I have shored against my ruins," declares the distraught speaker of *The Waste Land* toward the end of that shattered and shattering elegy, referring to the dismembered quotations that shape and shadow his personal "grouse," and Jones employed a similar strategy. In the words of Paul Fussell, an important commentator on the literature of the Great War, *In Parenthesis* is "strenuously allusive," associating "the events of front-line fighting not only with Arthurian legend but with Welsh and English folklore, Old Testament history, Roman Catholic liturgy," and a range of other historical scripts.[60] Even while it's allusive, however, *In Parenthesis* is passionately testimonial; only the work's protagonist survives to utter this book-length elegy for his doomed company, and his broken shards of memory bear witness to "the day by day in the Waste Land" in a struggle to come to terms with "some things I saw, felt, & was part of"—"things, which, at the time of suffering, the flesh was too weak to appraise."[61]

About *In Parenthesis* (as about *The Waste Land*) it's been argued that its author's decision to parallel the poem's nihilistic depictions of World War I combatants trapped in the trenches of "rats' alley" with "Arthurian legend" as well as "Welsh and English folklore [and] Old Testament history" implies an intention to discover redemptive significance in a war that has no such meaning. Fussell, for example, declares that Jones has set himself the task of "re-attaching traditional meanings to the unprecedented actualities of the war" and concludes that the book "is a deeply conservative work which uses the past not . . . to shame the present, but really to ennoble it." But in fact, by Jones's own account and as the reader experiences it, *In Parenthesis* offers the same disillusioned view of the gap between past and present, between idealized "fields of glory" and the gory No Man's Land of industrialized modern warfare, that impelled Owen's and Eliot's antipastoral and "in no sense consolatory" elegies.

In an explanatory Preface to his book Jones writes:

> *It is not easy in considering a trench-mortar barrage to give praise for the action proper to chemicals—full though it may be of beauty. We feel a*

rubicon has been passed between striking with a hand weapon as men used to do and loosing poison from the sky as we do ourselves. We doubt the decency of our own inventions, and are certainly in terror of their possibilities. *That our culture has accelerated every line of advance into the territory of physical science is well appreciated—but not so well understood are the unforeseen, subsidiary effects of this achievement [emphasis added].*[62]

And that he believes some of the "unforeseen, subsidiary effects" of military advances "into the territory of physical science" are specifically literary is evident in the comment with which he expands on the passage above: "Some of us ask ourselves if Mr. X adjusting his box-respirator [gas mask] can be equated with what the poet envisaged, in 'I saw young Harry with his beaver on.' . . . For the old authors there appears to have been no such dilemma. . . . For us it is different. There is no need to labour the point, nor enquire into the causes here. I only wish to record that for me such a dilemma exists, and that I have been particularly conscious of it during the making of this writing."

"*I saw young Harry with his beaver on*": Jones is quoting a celebrated speech from *Henry IV, Part I* in which Sir Richard Vernon responds to Hotspur's query about the young prince ("Where is . . . / The nimble-footed madcap Prince of Wales / And his comrades, that daff'd the world aside, / And bid it pass?") with a glowing description of the nearly supernatural and certainly heroic army led by the onetime "madcap":

> —*All furnish'd, all in arms . . .*
> *As full of spirit as the month of May,*
> *And gorgeous as the sun at midsummer;*
> *Wanton as youthful goats, wild as young bulls.*
> *I saw young Harry, with his beaver on,*
> *His cuisses on his thighs, gallantly arm'd*
> *Rise from the ground like feather'd Mercury,*
> *And vaulted with such ease into his seat,*
> *As if an angel dropp'd down from the clouds,*
> *To turn and wind a fiery Pegasus*
> *And witch the world with noble horsemanship.*[63]

In its "richness and profusion of images," this passage from Shakespeare seemed to Edmund Burke, the eighteenth-century literary theorist, a key example of the "*Magnificence*" that he considered "a source of the sublime." And there can be little doubt that David Jones regarded it as an instance of an idealizing "richness"no longer available to a poet who wished to describe an army. For if his hypothetical "Mr. X adjusting his box-respirator" could never be compared to "feather'd Mercury," Mr. X's World War I companions—Private John Ball, Mr. Jenkins, and the others who plod anxiously among the "chemical-corrupted once-bodies" that stud the muddy trenches of *In Parenthesis*—are hardly "gorgeous as the sun at midsummer; / Wanton as youthful goats, wild as young bulls." The loss of what was historically called "the Sublime," with its "profusion" of simultaneously pastoral and mythical imagery, was surely what Jones considered one of the "subsidiary effects" of "our culture['s] accelerated . . . line of advance into the territory of physical science."

In fact, as if to counter Burke's (and Shakespeare's) "sublime" with a profusion of nihilistic images, Jones concludes Part II of his protagonist's journey into battle with a dense Joycean riff on the descent of a single shell that's fired on the company as John Ball stands "alone on the stones, his mess-tin spilled at his feet":

> *Out of the vortex, rifling the air it came—bright, brass-shod, Pandoran; with all-filling screaming the howling crescendo's up-piling snapt. The universal world, breath held, one half second, a bludgeoned stillness. Then the pent violence released a consummation of all burstings out; all sudden up-rendings and rivings-through—all taking-out of vents—all barrier-breaking—all unmaking. Pernitric begetting—the dissolving and splitting of solid things. In which unearthing aftermath, John Ball picked up his mess-tin and hurried within; ashen, huddled, waited in the dismal straw. Behind "E" Battery, fifty yards down the road, a great many mangolds, uprooted, pulped, congealed with chemical earth, spattered and made slippery the rigid boards leading to the emplacement. The sap of vegetables slobbered the spotless breech-block of No. 3 gun.*[64]

Yes, there's a mythical reference here, but note that it's to the sinister myth of Pandora, who opened the box that released ills on the world. There's a pastoral reference too, but note that it's *anti*pastoral. "A great many mangolds" are "uprooted, pulped, congealed with chemical earth" by the descending shell, and the "sap of vegetables" has "slobbered" the hitherto "spotless breech-block of No. 3 gun." What Jones calls the "unmaking" of a once-chivalric and pastoral world is his theme here, as it is throughout *In Parenthesis.*

But maybe the most moving and (at least on the surface) traditionally elegiac pages of this unnerving book of "unmaking" appear at the very end of the text. As the wounded John Ball crawls toward safety, he passes the dead men of his company, lying not far from the Germans who had killed or been killed by them, all embedded in a verdant landscape. To Ball's delirious gaze, it seems that the "Queen of the Woods has cut bright boughs of various flowering" and bestowed them upon the bodies of his companions and their opponents:

> Some she gives white berries
> > some she gives brown
> Emil has a curious crown it's
> > made of golden saxifrage.
> Fatty wears sweet-briar,
> he will reign with her for a thousand years.
> For Balder she reaches high to fetch his.
> Ulrich smiles for his myrtle wand.
> That swine Lillywhite has daisies to his chain—you'd hardly credit it.
> She plaits torques of equal splendor for Mr. Jenkins & Billy Crower.[65]

"In another writer," comments Fussell, this passage "might be highly ironic, but here it's not, for Jones wants it to be true."[66]

Whether or not Jones wants the passage to be true, however, it's surely ironic because in context it's the hallucination of a wounded soldier, a hallucination behind which lies a vision of the real: a host of men who have died (in Whitman's words) "alone, in bushes, low gullies, or on the sides of hills" and who are now (in Owen's sardonic phrase) "pushing up daisies" as the "dullest Tommy" liked to "fancy." Nor can these dead men ever be assimilated into a single classical figure of the kind that Milton created in "Lycidas" and Shelley in "Adonais." Instead, the only survivor of the mechanized maelstrom that destroyed them names them individually, in the *new* mode of mourning fostered by "modern death": Emil, Fatty, Balder, Ulrich, Lillywhite, Mr. Jenkins, Billy Crower.[67]

And as a symbolic comment on the "subsidiary effects" of "physical science," John Ball's final gesture is telling. As he prepares to lie still and wait for the "stret-cher bear-errs!," Jones's protagonist decides to leave his rifle, with its "dark barrel . . . under the oak"—

leave it—under the oak.
Leave it for a Cook's tourist to the Devastated Areas and crawl
as far as you can and wait for the bearers.[68]

What was once the garden of pastoral will now be permanently disfigured by the machine that destroyed both pastoral and (traditional) elegy. Those

25. David Jones: frontispiece of *In Parenthesis* (1937).

generations of readers and writers who inherit a postwar culture in which their "all-embracing patrimony" has "disintegrated"—literal and figurative "Cook's tourist[s]" of the "Devastated Areas" of history—will have to confront a token of the war's despoilment.

Ironically too, the last words of Jones's book, drawn from the *Chanson de Roland*, insist not on the truth of chivalric romance but rather on the necessity of bearing witness to the experience of unmaking that has been the subject of the whole work. "The geste says this *and the man who was on*

26. David Jones: endpaper of *In Parenthesis* (1937).

the field . . . and who wrote the book . . . the man who does not know this has not understood anything [emphasis added]."⁶⁹ What the "geste" (romance) says has been both supplemented and superseded by the testimony of "the man who was on the field" and wrote the book in all its grim detail.⁷⁰ In the end it's such crucially modern testimony to the specifics of war and death that differentiates *In Parenthesis*, along with *The Waste Land* and the poems of Owen, from traditional elegy, on the one hand, and, on the other hand, from idealizing visions of heroic warriors—for instance, "young Harry with his beaver on."

Besides being a poet, Jones was a graphic artist, and he flanked his prose-verse narrative with two extraordinary drawings. The book's frontispiece is literally crammed with particulars of the war, so much so that Fussell faults it for being "too crowded with everything [Jones] can recall as relevant: a dead body, wire-pickets, rats, barbed wire, a tunic, a steel helmet, an ammunition belt, sandbags, blasted trees, mules, carrying-parties, bull-beef tins, shattered houses, chicken-wire netting, and an entrenching tool. Too much."⁷¹ But "too much" is precisely the point the poet-artist made with this testimonial collage of images. The war was *too much*: it offered an accretion of experiences that, as Felman puts it, "overwhelmed." In such a setting, the poetry could *only* be "in the pity" generated by a cascade of shocks [figs. 25 and 26].

When we juxtapose the endpaper Jones appended to *In Parenthesis* with the work's frontispiece, it becomes clear, too, that from his view, as from Owen's, the antipastoral poetry of industrialized warfare could be "in no sense consolatory." On the last page of his book, the artist placed a drawing of a young animal, a scapegoat who also looks suspiciously like a divine lamb, skewered by a bayonet and tangled in barbed wire. Behind the creature rise the twisted trunks of the dead trees of No Man's Land. The pastoral world is here as dead as the sacrificial beast. And clearly there are no traditional "passing bells" for this victim of the Great War or for any of the others who died "as cattle." Only, from now on, "monsters of elegy."

14

Monsters of Elegy

July 2003. It's a steamy afternoon in Kyoto, but I've escaped from the sweltering temple gardens we visited this morning into an icily air-conditioned lecture hall at one of the city's universities. Too icy, it feels at the moment, though only a few hours ago, trudging through humid glades, I'd have welcomed this chill. Right now, though, I fear I myself may be responsible for the coolness in the room. I've just delivered a version of "Different, and Luckier?," my thoughts on Whitman, Dickinson, and the history of the elegy, and my audience gazes at me in what looks depressingly like discomfort.

The professor who's chairing the meeting rises to thank me but almost immediately confesses that she found the bleakness of the talk "somewhat horrifying." Diminutive and elegantly suited, she seems embarrassed but perseveres, adding that "my question would be, my question *is*, What consolation do Whitman and Dickinson have to offer us? Is there no consolation?"

I stand to respond. Consolations in the face of skepticism and dread, death and grief? I muse on all this yet again, trying to find something "consoling." But the inconsolability of these poets was part of my point, I apologetically explain, and wasn't that why they weren't after all quite so popular among their contemporaries?

Sinking back into my chair, I think of Ryoan-ji, the great temple we visited two days ago, with its renowned "dry garden," known as a "garden of emptiness." A little sea of white pebbles neatly raked around fifteen rocks of various sizes. A tatami-matted viewing platform where visitors sit to meditate on what Wallace Stevens, in another context, called the "Nothing that is not there and the nothing that is."[1]

"Perceive the blankness. / Listen to the voice of the silence," says the narrator of a film entitled *MA: Space/Time in the Garden of Ryoan-Ji.*[2]

The day we saw that garden a fierce sun struck the sea of pebbles with such force that it seemed to radiate from them rather than pour into them, as if their mimesis of emptiness had evolved into a glare of pure blankness. Why would people who commune with such a space need consolation from Whitman and Dickinson? But I realize that I know next to nothing of Zen, and certainly I understand nothing of the "Nothing that is *not* there," the fullness such emptiness is said to bring to the adept.

Even so, however, I suspect my bewilderment in the face of wishes for consolation is somewhat representative. My thinking about Whitman and Dickinson has after all been shaped by a series of twentieth-century British and American poets who were mostly skeptical and therefore inconsolable mourners.

LET THE LAMP AFFIX ITS BEAM

In 1915, as the Great War unfolded its shadows over Europe, the British little magazine the *Egoist* published a surprisingly cheerful letter from an American correspondent, William Carlos Williams. In New York that spring, wrote the young doctor, "one was feeling a strange quickening of artistic life," adding that perhaps the preoccupation of Paris and London with "cruder affairs" had allowed America to take over "those spiritual controls for which no one had any time in the war-swept countries" so that here "was a chance to assert oneself magnificently." Like his friend Ezra Pound, Williams was enamored of the key modernist imperative to "Make it new," and in this respect, he insisted, America had now "triumphed!"[3]

American poets weren't, of course, unconcerned with the battles raging across Europe. Although one commentator argues that Williams's failure to discuss the war in *Others* "was an omission like living on a rock in the Atlantic and never mentioning the Atlantic," the doctor-poet claimed that he'd have enlisted if he hadn't been needed at home, both to treat the sick in Rutherford and to care for his own extended family, but in any case his medical practice brought him close to some of the realities of the conflict.[4] Other American poets, however, were more intimately involved, in either life or art or both. As we've already seen, Wallace Stevens critiqued the traditional elegy in poems based on the letters of a soldier killed at the front. Similarly, Pound's "Hugh Selwyn Mauberley" elegized his close friend Henri Gaudier-Brzeska, another French painter killed in the war, and extended its lamentation to the fate of the countless other combatants who had also died "non 'dulce' non 'et decor'" but rather "eye-deep in hell." And not long after these poems by Stevens and Pound appeared, T. S. Eliot published *The Waste Land*, with its elaborate, if elliptical, grief for Jean Verdenal, "*mort à Dardanelles.*" That the young Frenchmen whose lost lives these last three Americans lamented were killed in the spring of 1915, just when Williams was proclaiming a "quickening of artistic life" in New York, gives a bitter edge to his exuberance.[5]

In any case the "new" that Williams wanted to make was in its way as unconsoling as Wilfred Owen's "in no sense consolatory" elegies. On the one hand, this physician-poet was a warmhearted artist who celebrated the dance of desire in, for example, "Brueghel's great picture, The Kermess," but on the other hand, as we saw in noting his vision of death as "termination," he often cast a cold eye on life and death, as in his clinically precise description (in "Death") of a rigor mortis that lets a cadaver lie "like an acrobat" with "his head on / one chair and his / feet on another." Asked in late life "what had been the strongest influence on his writing, Williams said medical case histories." And in the early volume of experimental prose and verse he entitled *Spring and All*, he had hinted at this point, insisting that the "imagination uses the phraseology of science" and "is radio-active in all that can be touched by action." That he also, early and late, summarized his aesthetic credo in the often quoted line "No ideas but in *things* [emphasis added]" underscores the empirical bias that shaped his art.[6]

In practice as well as in theory, the daily standoff with death that is a doctor's lot intensified Williams's impatience with received European traditions of the "poetical." T. S. Eliot's allusively learned "Love Song of J. Alfred Prufrock" enraged him because he felt its author "had rejected America and I refused to be rejected," and he defined that apotheosis of cosmopolitanism *The Waste Land* as "the great catastrophe to our letters." Against what he considered such refinements of stale traditions as well as against the airy abstractions he disliked, Williams set the physician's belief in the primary facticity of the human body. "When we think of the body as the sole source of all our good the return of an attenuated or spent 'culture' to that ground can never after be seen as anything but a saving gesture," he declared in a review of a popular medical treatise, insisting that the body "stands guard not only over our comings and goings, but over our wits also." For this reason, he explained, he was satisfied "to live by the practice of medicine, which combines the best features of both science and philosophy with that imponderable and enlightening element, disease." At the same time, tellingly, he compared his wish to have "more money for *literary* experiments" with the needs of "Pasteur, when he was young." Dr. Williams knew, in other words, that he wasn't only a medical scientist in his role as physician; as a writer, too, he was a clinician.[7]

If the body is "the sole source of all our good," however, both "our good" and the physician who is its guardian are vulnerable to "that imponderable and enlightening element, disease," whose onslaughts promote the daily familiarity with the corruptions of the flesh that soldier-poets learned in the trenches of the Great War. The celebrant of the primacy of the body must bear witness to the details of its decline. One of the young doctor's favorite "new" poems was Carl Sandburg's "Cool Tombs," which, with its straightforward American cadences, its colloquial specifics, and its nihilistic chill, he considered "a splendid thing":

> *When Abraham Lincoln was shoveled into the tombs, he forgot the copperheads and the assassin . . . in the dust in the cool tombs.*

> *And Ulysses Grant lost all thought of con men and Wall Street, cash and collateral turned ashes . . . in the dust, in the cool tombs.*

Thus, while combatants like Owen, Sassoon, and Jones bore witness to the particulars of decay on which such noncombatants as Eliot and Stevens also brooded, Williams as physician-poet offered comparable testimony to the details of disease that propelled all human bodies into "cool tombs." "Instead of breaking the back of a willing phrase," he admonishes himself in *Kora in Hell*, a book of prose poems that he defined as "improvisations," "why not try to . . . approach death at a walk, take in all the scenery." But in this collection, which he also described as "death's canticle," his approaches to the dying and the dead are various, with some taken "at a walk" and others harshly impetuous, as if assaulted in a race.[8]

Emphasizing this author's role as clinician, one of the "improvisations" in *Kora* sounds suspiciously like chart notes on a hopeless patient: "Jacob Louslinger, white haired, stinking, dirty bearded, cross eyed, stammer tongued, broken voiced, bent backed, ball kneed, cave bellied, mucous faced—deathling,—found lying in the weeds 'up there by the cemetery.' " And not long after this we encounter a case history of one woman's struggle with death: "You speak of the enormity of her disease, of her poverty. . . . You speak of the helpless waiting, waiting till the thing squeeze her windpipe shut. . . . You speak of her man's callous stinginess. Yes, my God, how

can he refuse to buy milk when it's alone milk that she can swallow now? ...
You speak of so many things, you blame me for my indifference. Well, this
is you see my sister and death, great death is robbing her of life. It dwarfs
most things." In both these exemplary texts the doctor seems to be approaching death "at a walk," slowly revealing its encroachments, its depredations
and robberies.[9]

But because, as Williams understatedly puts it, death "dwarfs most
things," the physician's slow-stepping walk toward loss becomes at times a
dance of death, a fevered tarantella of ironic and inconsolable mourning:

> *Nothing is any pleasure but misery and brokenness. THIS is the only up-
> cadence. This is where the secret rolls over and opens its eyes. . . . The com-
> plaints of an old man dying piecemeal are starling chirrups. Coughs go
> singing on springtime paths across a field; corruption picks strawberries
> and slow warping of the mind, blacking the deadly walls. . . . The moaning
> and dull sobbing of infants sets blood tingling and eyes ablaze to listen. . . .
> Dance! Sing! . . . An old woman has infected her blossomy grand-daughter
> with a blood illness that every two weeks drives the mother into songs of
> agony, the pad-footed mirage of creeping death for music. . . . Here is danc-
> ing! The mind in tatters. . . . Ay de mi, Juana la Loca, reina de Espana, esa
> esta tu canta, reina mia!*

The "up-cadence" of mourning here is ironic because why and how can the
celebrant of the "sole good" of the body find pleasure in "misery and brokenness"? At the same time, paradoxically, this tarantella of mourning is
inconsolable because the celebrant of the "sole good" of the body can in the
end find *no* pleasure but "misery and brokenness." And Juana la Loca, the
mad queen of Spain, leaps onto the scene because this legendary widow
revealed both her madness and her inconsolable grief by carrying everywhere with her the ultimate memento mori, the body of her dead husband,
for she "would not be parted from his coffin."[10]

That Williams's medical training did little to inure him to "misery and
brokenness" is plain enough in the passages above, as in many other passages from his prose and verse. Although his work as a physician endowed
him with the observational skills that give his writing what is often a clinical particularity, he appears never to have gained the glaze of indifference
with which many doctors protect themselves during encounters with a
patient's pain. "Death is difficult for the senses to alight on," Williams confessed in a story that begins with an account of a death from influenza:

There is no help from familiarity with the location. There is a cold body to be put away but what is that? The life has gone out of it and death has come into it. Whither? Whence? The sense has no footspace.

After twelve days struggling with a girl to keep life in her, losing, winning, it is not easy to give her up. One has studied her inch by inch *[and now she] lies gasping her last: eyes rolled up till only the whites show, lids half open, mouth agape, skin a cold bluish white, pasty, hard to the touch—as the body temperature drops the tissues congeal. One is definitely beaten [emphasis added].*[11]

An empathetic participant ("One is definitely beaten") as well as a meticulous observer ("one has studied her inch by inch"), he was also a bewildered bystander to meaninglessness ("Whither? Whence? The sense has no footspace").

Given such principled bewilderment, Williams evidently never believed that his stance as witness to "misery and brokenness" offered him any metaphysical privilege. Even while he mused on the role of poetry in American culture, he sometimes saw the imminence and ubiquity of death as a reproach to his aesthetic meditations. In *Spring and All* he placed an angry self-rebuke just after a discussion of the "nature of the difference between what is termed prose on the one hand and verse on the other":

Somebody dies every four minutes
in New York State—

To hell with you and your poetry—
You will rot and be blown
through the next solar system
with the rest of the gases—

What the hell do you know about it?[12]

Perhaps it's appropriate, then, that it wasn't Williams himself but his friend Wallace Stevens who not only theorized "modern death" and its "mythologies" but also provided what might be the best general description of Williams's working methods. In his early and at least on the surface deliberately anticlinical "The Emperor of Ice-Cream," Stevens produced what seem like playful instructions for a woman's obsequies. Beginning with a series of amusingly lush imperatives ("Call the roller of big cigars, / The muscular one, and bid him whip / In kitchen cups concupiscent curds"), he outlines in the first stanza a procedure based on a combination of pleasure and practicality ("Let the wenches dawdle in such dress / As they are used to wear, and let the boys / Bring flowers in last month's newspapers"). These injunctions lead to a more comprehensive command: "Let be be finale of seem"—in other words, regard the *appearance* of being as the only reality, for there is no (divine) being that transcends the state this poet elsewhere called "mere being." Thus the assumptions underlying all these commands shape this poem's title and its refrain: "The only emperor is the emperor of ice-cream." That is, there is no ruling principle of existence beyond the chill finality of death (ice) and the sensuous delight of life (cream).[13]

More specifically, however, the second stanza of Stevens's poem incorporates instructions for both funeral and inquest, reversing the usual order:

> *Take from the dresser of deal,*
> *Lacking the three glass knobs, that sheet*
> *On which she embroidered fantails once*
> *And spread it to cover her face.*
> *If her horny feet protrude, they come*
> *To show how cold she is, and dumb.*
> *Let the lamp affix its beam.*
> *The only emperor is the emperor of ice-cream.*

As the dead woman's mourners assemble what imperfect materials they can from the meager specifics with which what Stevens calls "life's destitution" has endowed them, they obliterate the individuality of the woman who has died, covering her face with a winding sheet on which she once sewed the particulars of her life. Only "her horny feet"—the calloused, desirous feet on which she once walked through the world—"protrude" from the winding sheet, and they do so not to affirm her history but to prove her death. It is on the irrevocable factuality of this death that the "lamp" of the observer, like the unflinching gaze of the clinician, must "affix its beam." For if the "only emperor is the emperor of ice-cream," if there is no truth beyond the materialities of death and pleasure, the funeral must itself be conducted with an eye to and on these bare facts, which have to be studied "inch by inch." Like the strong lamp of the physician in the autopsy room, the lamp of the mourner, and especially of the poet, must "affix its beam" on the cold, dumb physicality of death and the dead.

Yet while Stevens summarized the elegiac imperative as a command to conduct an "in no sense consolatory" inquest into death, he frankly admitted the fictive or abstract nature of his own elegiac projects. An elegant poetic philosophe who continually reminded himself of "life's destitution," "of mere being," of the icy intransigence of mortality, he struggled to rationalize dread and grief, as we've seen, by postulating that "death is the mother of beauty." At the same time, however, as in "The Owl in the Sarcophagus" he mourned his friend Henry Church, he groped for consolation while defining the figures of peace, sleep, and memory who populated his "inventions of farewell" with the phrase that gives this chapter its title. As part of "the mythology of modern death," he said, such made-up lyric constructs were "in their mufflings, monsters of elegy, / Of their own marvel made, of pity made." In other words, Stevens's "monsters of elegy"—strange figures created by "a desire that is the will, / Even of death"—were ways for the mind to mediate the reality at which the poet must gaze when the lamp affixes its beam on the horny feet of the dead.

Thus although Stevens theorized the necessity for a stern inquest into death, it was Williams who pioneered the *practice* of the grief poem as unconsoling inquest or case history, a testimonial mode that, along with the testimonial mode of so many World War I poets, was to mark most of the "in no sense consolatory" verse laments produced by his contemporaries and descendants. Where Stevens insisted that the mind wants comfort as does "a child that sings itself to sleep . . . among the creatures that it makes," Williams really did affix the beam of a clinician's lamp on the "cold bluish white" skin of physical death, reminding himself with the ferocity of Juana la Loca that "Somebody dies every four minutes / in New York State. . . . To hell with you and your poetry—" And in the early poem entitled "Tract" he produced a far more detailed model for a funeral than Stevens's "Emperor of Ice-Cream" while urging his "townspeople" to "sit openly . . . to grief."[14] In doing so, he outlined "monsters of elegy" notably different from those Stevens was to name in "The Owl in the Sarcophagus."

For while Stevens's consoling fictions were "monsters" in the dictionary sense of "imaginary or legendary creatures," I'm using his phrase to characterize the rather different "monsters of elegy" heralded by Williams's "Tract," creatures more like those to which we usually refer when we use the word "monsters." These monsters, in their dictionary definition, are creatures "having a strange or frightening appearance" or even organisms "having structural defects or deformities." Thus as "monsters of elegy" they are grief poems that seem deformed in relation to literary tradition because they swerve strangely, even frighteningly from the historically redemptive structures usually offered by the English-language elegy. Often they scare us or sicken us, as if—to go back to the improvisations of *Kora in Hell*—they are dances of "the mind in tatters." For they arise out of a clear-eyed acceptance of what the contemporary poet Alan Shapiro calls "an aesthetics of inadequacy," a recognition that since even the most passionately elegiac poem "can't raise the dead, everything else is a piss-poor substitute." Thus, like my hostess in Kyoto, we often find these characteristically modern laments more than a little "horrifying" because they force us to ask, "Is there no consolation?"[15]

HOW TO PERFORM A FUNERAL

Williams's vocation as *physician*-poet manifested itself plainly in "Tract," for this set of funeral instructions that the New Jersey general practitioner addressed to his fellow citizens in 1916 sounds much like the prescription an impatient doctor might dictate at a communal bedside. The poet begins by praising his interlocutors for their native shrewdness, their American "ground sense":

> *I will teach you my townspeople*
> *how to perform a funeral*
> *for you have it over a troop*
> *of artists—*
> *unless one should scour the world—*
> *you have the ground sense necessary.*

But then, in a series of roughly phrased yet urgent imperatives, the young doctor outlines the elegiac practice he considers appropriate to a world of "misery and brokenness" in which even the medical expert is inevitably "beaten" by death. The piece was probably composed before Stevens wrote "The Emperor of Ice-Cream," yet it implicitly assumes the clinical confrontation with mortality that Stevens demands in urging the lamp of consciousness to "affix its beam" on the dead. Indeed, if Stevens's poem refuses to shrink from "life's destitution" even while celebrating the not very consoling pleasures of symbolic or literal "ice-cream," Williams's piece goes further in prescribing the painful necessity of yielding to grief's destitution—the necessity, as it were, of inconsolability and consequently an aesthetics of inadequacy like the one Shapiro describes.

"The hearse leads," Williams notes, stipulating the hierarchical order of a traditional funeral procession in which mourners follow the vehicle that bears the body of the dead to its final home. Though this proviso seems at first to be a concession both to convention and to the tautological fact that the survivors constitute those who live—and thus should ride or walk—*after* the dead person, even here the physician-poet is offering his patients a bitter pill: the hearse "leads" mourners down the road of life because death is after all the only ineluctable fact beside birth, the hearse the vehicle toward which, and ultimately in which, all journey. As Stevens put it in his shuddering wartime discussion of "the truth of Death," "Death, that will never be satisfied, / Digs up the earth when want returns."

More radically, following the resonant comment that the hearse "leads," Williams systematically dismantles or revises all the trappings of the elaborate late-Victorian (and early-twentieth-century) funeral. Instead of the usual funereal conveyance, he tells his audience to choose a hearse that's "weathered—like a farm wagon—," its only decoration "gilt wheels . . . or no wheels at all: / a rough dray to drag over the ground." Nor should this vehicle feature any other ostentatious, and pointless, luxuries like glass, flowers, plushy upholstery:

> *Knock the glass out!*
> *My God—glass, my townspeople!*
> *For what purpose? . . .*
> *To keep the rain and snow from him?*
> *He will have a heavier rain soon:*
> *pebbles and dirt and what not.*
> *Let there be no glass—*
> *and no upholstery, phew!*
> *And no little brass rollers*
> *and small easy wheels on the bottom—*
> *my townspeople what are you thinking of?*

As for other decorations, beyond the transient glint of "gilt wheels" (the gilt "applied fresh at small expense"), the doctor demands "no wreaths" but instead a "common memento" (something the dead man "prized and is known by: / his old clothes—a few books perhaps"). And over the deliberate antipageantry of this revisionary ceremony no self-important "driver" should preside. "Take off the silk hat!" Williams insists, and, he adds, "bring [the driver] down!"

Low and inconspicuous! I'd not have him ride
on the wagon at all—damn him—
the undertaker's understrapper!
Let him hold the reins
and walk at the side
and inconspicuously too!

Similarly, the mourners should walk "behind—as they do in France, / seventh class, or if you ride / Hell take curtains!" For in the presence of death, all should

Go with some show
of inconvenience; sit openly—
to the weather as to grief.
Or do you think you can shut grief in?
What—from us? We who have perhaps
nothing to lose?

Noting that "the American 'funeral director' enjoyed a rapid ascent toward professional status between the 1880s and the First World War," Jahan Ramazani has argued that in both "Tract" and "The Emperor of Ice-Cream," the "poet becomes a kind of 'funeral director,' instructing and admonishing auditors on how to mourn the dead" even while he "also competes with his more powerful rival" by producing "parodically hortatory" poems.[16] At the same time, however, in these works both Williams and Stevens—but especially the former—compose aesthetic manifestos that prescribe distinctively modern procedures for confronting death. In an era when (both poets believe) dying must be understood as a purely biological system of termination rather than a potentially redemptive process of spiritual expiration, the soothing platitudes mouthed by "funeral directors" ring false because they are at best fake ("hot house flowers"), and at worst stale padding ("upholstery—phew!") meant to soften but unable to controvert "the truth of Death." Rather than conspire with the lies of "funeral directors" by becoming "the undertaker's understrapper" or lackey, the contemporary elegist must "sit openly— / to the weather as to grief."

So sweeping, indeed, are Williams's instructions to his townspeople that they can be read not only as a manifesto dictating "how to perform a funeral" or compose an elegy but also, more generally, as a set of guidelines for how to write any kind of poem at all. "See! The hearse leads": not form but function, the purpose or goal of the writing, should "lead" the way into a poem. And the "hearse" shouldn't be "polished" but "weathered," perhaps with a little "gilt": the poet should avoid superficial decoration; her subject should have the authenticity of "ground sense" lightened, perhaps, by the fleeting decoration of fancy, but never the tedious polish deployed by "a troop / of artists." "Knock the glass out . . . and no upholstery": again, no artifice, no fakery, should come between the writer and the point of his writing. "No wreaths please. . . . Some common memento is better": there should be no lies, no abstractions, "no ideas but in things," and those things should bear witness to the particulars of daily life. "Let [the driver] hold the reins / and walk at the side": the poet should move through and with his poem, humbling himself to its exigencies rather than magisterially ruling it from "up there" in a "silk hat." Finally, all should "sit openly— / to the weather as to grief"; the poet and her audience should let feeling prevail, should fully mourn and rage, because, after all, you can*not* "shut grief" or the weather of any other feeling "in."

Even the title of Williams's poem, "Tract"—meaning "an expanse of land or water" as well as "a leaflet or pamphlet containing a declaration or appeal, especially one put out by a religious or political group"—implies that the doctor who is authoring the work wishes to lay down large principles suitable to the "*ground* sense" of his "townspeople," those who inhabit the same tract of land on which he both literally and figuratively dwells. But that the poet chose to delineate such major principles as part of a prescription for proper (modern, American) *mourning* suggests the centrality of "modern death" to all the projects of poetry in a world where, increasingly, there are "no ideas but in things"—a world, that is, whose materiality inescapably contains and constrains its reality. Moreover, because he eschewed, on the one hand, what he considered the worn-out comforts offered by no longer redemptive elegiac traditions and, on the other hand, what he thought of as the hollow promises of no longer redemptive religious visions, Williams probably taught more young poets "how to perform a funeral"—and compose a poem—than any of his contemporaries did. He was right, in other words, when he insisted that T. S. Eliot, the most celebrated Anglo-American poet of the modernist era, "was looking backward; I was looking forward." For while Eliot's work is still much admired, his "classicist, royalist, Anglo-Catholic" worldview seems retrograde now, whereas countless elegists in America and Britain have carried the principles of Williams's "Tract" forward into the twenty-first century.

DOCUMENTING DEATH

Although redemptive visions of "expiration" mostly expired in the rats' alleys where the bodies of dead good soldiers festered throughout the First World War, major works by both Eliot and Stevens show the extent to which early-twentieth-century "inventions of farewell" were still haunted by the shards of a classical poetics of grief at least in part because a number of modernists still yearned for a consoling tradition with which their individual talents might affiliate. The lilacs bred in the dead land of Eliot's lament for Jean Verdenal evoke the lilacs blooming in the dooryard of Walt Whitman's great elegy for Abraham Lincoln, flowers that in turn recall the laurel and myrtle of Milton's pastoral "Lycidas," while even Stevens, the archtheorist of modern death's finality, rarely "let the lamp affix its beam" quite as sharply as he might have. The dark companions he encounters in "The Owl in the Sarcophagus," for instance, resemble the comrades who sustain Whitman through the elegiac ceremonies of "Lilacs," as well as the mourners who move through "Lycidas" and "Adonais." Similarly, his apparently resolute repudiation of an afterlife in "Sunday Morning" assembles traditional emblems of consolation (a rising sun, a regenerative natural world of deer, birds, and berries) while hinting at a view of death-as-expiration through a vision of men evaporating like dew.[17]

For many poets, then, the gates of a heaven into which the soul could "expire" stood ajar until the various holocausts of the mid-century seared their way into the cultural unconscious. But by the time millions of human bodies had been unceremoniously reduced to rubble, to ash, to chemical fumes, there was almost no literary ceremony else beyond the stripped-down ritual Williams prescribes in "Tract." The human form scorched onto stone, whether by incineration or radiation, is no longer what Blake called "the human form divine"—nor, for that matter, is the cadaver dissected in the autopsy room—and none of the traditional consolations of the elegy seem able to counter loss. As Sylvia Plath put it, recording her "terror / Of being wheeled off under crosses and a rain of pietàs," "Cold blanks approach us: / They move in a hurry."[18] Thus, even when the elements of pastoral elegy appear allusively in recent laments for the dead, they've usually been modified by the unconsoling view of death-as-termination that explicitly or implicitly reduces historically soothing concepts to ashen outlines of what they had been.

As I've noted throughout this book, by the mid-century such a mythology of modern death-as-termination seems to have elicited not just the kind of high-cultural gloom that Beckett formulates but also popular con-

fusion and distress. Geoffrey Gorer's discussion of the social embarrassment bred by what he called "The Pornography of Death" dates from 1955,
while Jessica Mitford's muckracking *The American Way of Death*, based on
a set of assumptions symptomatic of just the anxieties about mourning that
Gorer examined, appeared just a few years later. What "handbook of heartbreak" could guide sufferers through bereavement in the face of new vari-
eties of emptiness? We may have read somewhere that, as Meg Greenfield
put it, "crows have funerals, or something akin to funerals, for other crows,"
but what do those big black birds *do* on such occasions? The phenomenon
sociologists call normlessness had become the funereal norm.[19]

At the same time, as I've also noted, unfilled needs for ceremonial grief
had by mid-century been given special poignancy by technological innovations that transformed the relationship of mourners to history and memory—namely, the development of films and videos that allow the bereaved
to see and hear images of the dead as if they were still among the living. But
even while such ghostly presences were unprecedented, they were (and are)
especially unnerving in a cultural context in which death is a scandal to be
avoided or denied and grief an embarrassment to be deplored or derided.
Can the dead be in and of history and memory if we can still see them and
hear them? Since we don't want to mourn anyway, how do we mourn them
when they seem still to be here? Equally to the point, how can we bear witness to the absolute fact that they are *not* here?

Perhaps it's no wonder that even before the AIDS pandemic, followed by
the catastrophe of 9/11, forced death and dying out of the closet, the social
bewilderment fostered by changing mythologies of extinction issued in a
number of sometimes contradictory modes of encountering loss, ranging
from "death counseling" to "past life therapy." Death-as-termination and
deathly termination as scandal, the dead apparently alive and well on
screens and tapes, grief-as-illness and illness as culpable: taken together,
these phenomena would seem to have stifled any drive to construct poetic
inventions of farewell. Yet contemporary verse resists the repression of
death as determinedly as the great modernists resisted the repression of sex.
Indeed, in reaction against both the cultural evasions that constrain
mourning and the technological innovations that delude the bereaved with
images of the dead alive and well in a celluloid universe, recent writers have
insisted on constructing a defiant poetics of grief that insists on meticulously documenting loss and sorrow.

Echoing Williams's "Tract," this poetics of grief begins with both unbelief and disbelief—*unbelief* in traditional sources of consolation; *disbelief* in

the shattering reality of the individual death itself—and then strives to come to terms with the dead one's termination through individual elaborations of the same three aesthetic imperatives that shaped the "in no sense consolatory" elegies produced by so many poets during and after the First World War. As in those works, these imperatives certainly don't function like what Elizabeth Kübler-Ross defined as stages of dying (and others have called stages of grief), but sometimes they follow each other in a single poem for obvious narrative reasons.

First, contemporary elegists often focus, to begin with, on the actual scene of dying, which in this revisionary mode of lamentation is rendered with exacting, often excruciating attention.

Second, the "monsters of elegy" these writers produce frequently feature, as well, a preoccupation with the actual body of the dead one, as if it were necessary, in an era haunted by the two-dimensional ghosts of film and video, to assert the stony solidity of the deceased.

Third, the authors of such elegies frequently recount in detail the private as well as public histories of the lives of the dead they elegize, along with their own participation in those histories, as if to ensure, on the one hand, that significant personal events did come to pass and, on the other hand, that such events have passed *away* with the "passing" of the dead. Often, indeed, these recollections of things past function figuratively like the "common memento" that Williams counseled his townspeople to substitute for flowers on the hearse.

Finally, to these shaping elegiac imperatives, poets from the mid-century on have often added a fourth strategy for poetic closure: a resignation to loss that sometimes involves a deliberately fantastic resolution and sometimes merely a stoic acquiescence in the inevitable.[20]

Unlike the traditional procedures through which, as Peter Sacks showed, the pastoral elegist generally shaped his poem of grief (the invocation of eternal muses, the evocation of a stable community, the pastoral context itself with its implicit "movement from grief to consolation" symbolized through "images of resurrection"), these mid- and late-twentieth-century strategies are lonely and usually empirical or eccentric. If the poets who deploy them allude to the historical consolations of elegy, they often do so parodically, even bitterly, as Alan Shapiro does in his powerful "The Accident," in which he invokes and berates precursors from Whitman and Dickinson to Stevens while describing the abjection of his dying brother's body as it falls from a nurse's grasp, stripped of a hospital gown:

beloved singers, tricksters

of solace, if
you had known this, seen

this . . .
you would have offered him

no sumptuous
destitution, no fire-

fangled feathers,
or blab about death as being

luckier than one
supposes. You would have bowed

your heads, you would
have silently slipped back

into the shadows
out of which you surged forth,

singing to me.

The strategies with which Shapiro and others seek to confront and confound "tricksters // of solace" can be summarized in four words: *listening*
(*to*, for instance, "last words" or *for* last breaths); *looking* (at the dying or the
dead); *remembering* (the life of the dead); and occasionally, but not always,
imagining (the fate of the dead). In deploying these often clinical techniques
for confronting loss, contemporary poets produce monsters of elegy that
are in effect photographic studies of the stripped bodies of the dead and of
death, while also functioning as studies of the poet's own grief—documentaries of inconsolable mourning and melancholia.[21]

DEATH STUDIES

In 1959 two admirers of William Carlos Williams mourned important
losses in volumes that, each in its own way, smashed the glass and ripped

up the upholstery of elegiac tradition just as the New Jersey physician-poet had told his "townspeople" to do in "Tract." Both Robert Lowell and Allen Ginsberg had come to know Williams in the 1940s, Lowell after publishing a glowing review of the first book of Williams's long, ambitious *Paterson* and Ginsberg after introducing himself to the older poet in letters that were eventually to be incorporated into the fifth book of *Paterson*. Writing in the *Sewanee Review* in 1947, Lowell, already a widely praised poet himself, had declared: "I can think of no book published in 1946 that is as important [as *Paterson*], or of any living English or American poet who has written anything better." A few years later Ginsberg, who had actually grown up in the working-class town of Paterson, New Jersey, that Williams (a resident of Rutherford) was mythologizing in his effort at an American epic, introduced himself in a fan letter as "an unknown young poet" who "has inherited your experience in this struggle to . . . know his own world-city."[22]

For his part, Williams responded with praise for both the younger men. Though he'd initially found Lowell's work "turgid" and "dull," he began to appreciate the skill with which the Bostonian used American place-names in the 1946 collection *Lord Weary's Castle*. As for Ginsberg, Williams developed a long-standing affection for this literary son of Paterson (the town) who was to become a figurative son of *Paterson* (the poem). Eventually, indeed, Williams produced introductions to several of the aspiring poet's works, notably a preface to *Howl*, which he defined as "an arresting poem" whose author "sees through and all around the horrors he partakes of in the very intimate details of his poem."[23]

Williams's warmth wasn't misdirected, for by the end of the 1950s it was obvious that both younger poets had learned key lessons from the art of the older man they so much esteemed, in particular from what Kenneth Burke was to call the "physicality imposed upon [Williams's] poetry by the nature of his work as a physician." In a further twist, Lowell, the older and more established of the two, later noted that he'd also been instructed by Ginsberg's aesthetic, explaining that in 1957, "giving readings on the West Coast," he found himself in "the era and setting of Allen Ginsberg," beside whose frank and unbound poems his own "seemed like prehistoric monsters dragged down into the bog and death by their ponderous armor [so that when] I returned to my home, I began writing lines in a new style."[24] But once Lowell began writing in this "new style," the poems of mourning that both he and Ginsberg produced in 1959 were themselves to have an extraordinary impact on the contemporary English-language elegy.

These works appeared in two influential volumes—Lowell's *Life Studies* and Ginsberg's *Kaddish*—but though Lowell's title intimates that the author will be offering studies of living bodies like the portraits of live human models that graphic artists produce in their ateliers and Ginsberg's title defines a traditional Jewish prayer for the dead, both writers assembled groups of poems that might more readily be labeled "death studies." For Lowell's book focused not on the living but on the dead and scrutinized not just the lives of the dead but their deaths, while Ginsberg's, despite its ceremonial elements, was more like a case history than an extended prayer.[25]

Even the subjects that Lowell and Ginsberg lamented that year in two of the most famous poems they published—respectively, "Sailing Home from Rapallo" and "Kaddish," the title piece of the volume of the same name—were historically unusual, for both poets elegized their mothers in these works whereas the tradition studied by Peter Sacks and others is founded on a man's mourning for a *man*, and often a man who is a brother poet.[26] Arguably it's because the bonds between male intellectual comrades are abstractions marking intellectual and spiritual connections that they lend themselves to the highly stylized genre in which Milton mourned "Lycidas" and Shelley lamented "Adonais." By comparison, the mother-child link, like the umbilical cord itself, is a primary, physical connection. In mourning the mother, therefore, a (male or female) poet inevitably mourns a material loss, the actual decay of the flesh out of which his or her own flesh was made. For this reason, it was especially appropriate that Lowell's and Ginsberg's innovative elegies announced the inception of a genre rooted in a view of death as a condition affording neither wish nor hope but constituted instead simply as and by its inexorably brutal materiality.

Death-as-termination, after all, begins and ends with the metamorphosis of a living body into a dead one. Thus, after groping to understand the last days of his mother's life ("Your nurse could only speak Italian, / but after twenty minutes I could imagine your final week"), Robert Lowell focuses "Sailing Home from Rapallo" on dead flesh. "When I embarked from Italy with my Mother's body," the poet opens, and as the ocean liner carrying mother and son voyages figuratively as well as literally away from the summery "*Golfo di Genova* [that is] breaking into fiery flower," the speaker is possessed by thoughts of the coffin that betokens his absent mother's dead presence, just below his living one, brooding that "Mother traveled first-class in the hold" in a "*Risorgimento* black and gold casket" that was "like Napoleon's at the *Invalides*."[27]

Lowell as elegist is troubled, too, by the fact that even as the passengers on his luxury liner are "tanning . . . in deck-chairs," the family cemetery toward which he is journeying with his mother lies "Dour and dark against the blinding snowdrifts, / its black brook and fir trunks . . . smooth as masts" of a kind very different from the masts on the pleasure boat he rides. Worst of all, as his thoughts once more revert to the maternal body in its pretentious coffin whose "grandiloquent lettering" ironically misspells "*Lowell*" as "*LOVEL*," the poet can no longer evade his knowledge of the casket's unnerving contents: "The corpse / was wrapped like *panetone* in Italian tinfoil—" shrouded, as utterly inert and material as a loaf of raisin-studded holiday bread, in the shiny wrapping bakers and grocers use to preserve their products.

Disturbing though it is, "Sailing Home from Rapallo" is quite short, at least in comparison to Ginsberg's expansive "Kaddish." Yet Lowell's relatively brief "study" of maternal dying and death has something like the weight and feel of "Kaddish" because it's part of a longer series of poems constituting a single family album at the heart of which the poet has pasted this especially riveting image of his mother's body. Framed by snapshots of "Uncle Devereux Winslow," of "Great Aunt Sarah," of "Grandfather [waving] his stick / like a policeman," of "Grandmother, like a Mohammedan [wearing] her thick / lavender mourning and touring veil," and of "Father," who was "once successful enough to be lost / in the mob of ruling-class Bostonians," "Mother" only just survives the "abrupt and unprotesting" death of "Father." In other photographic death studies, we're told that "afraid / of living alone till eighty," she "mooned in a window, / as if she had stayed on a train / one stop past her destination," that her "master-bedroom / looked away from the ocean," and that her "nuptial bed / was as big as a bathroom." The protagonist of a poetic series in which there are "no ideas but in things," "Mother" *is* her possessions: her master bedroom, her "silver hot water bottle / monogrammed like a hip flask," her "Italian china fruity / with bunches and berries," her "nuptial bed," the forlorn window in which she "moon[s]," and finally her "*Risorgimento* black and gold casket" as well as, more terribly, the "Italian tinfoil" that wraps her corpse. Nor can the poet ever evade his bothersome recognition that both the life and the death of this inexorably material "Mother" are constituted by and through these objects. When she and the rest of the family constellated around her have disappeared, so has all the "town-house furniture" of the past, which in itself always "had an on tiptoe air / of waiting for the mover / on the heels of the undertaker."[28]

Where Lowell enumerates and, as it were, catalogs grief through photographic inventories of what Plath was to call "things, things," Allen Ginsberg begins his "Kaddish" for his mother with what seems like a more spiritual recognition that as person and body Naomi Ginsberg is "gone without corsets & eyes," gone without both the "stays" of flesh and the physical eyes through which an *im*material self once looked out at the world. He begins his lament too with a reference to a crucial earlier elegy, noting that his preparation for the act of mourning he's undertaking has included "reading the Kaddish aloud, listening to Ray Charles blues," and reading "Adonais' last triumphant stanzas aloud." But as his poem builds through catalogs of memory, vision, revulsion and desire, Ginsberg expands his knowledge of the body of his mother's death into a penultimate incantation that ultimately marks his elegy as a kind of anti-"Adonais" because, unlike Shelley's neo-Platonic masterpiece, it incorporates a litany of sheer factuality at least as disturbing as Lowell's accumulated snapshots of family furnishings. Indeed, with what was at the time he composed "Kaddish" a degree of candor even more shocking than Lowell's stunning vision of his mother's corpse as "*panettone*," the young writer whose "Howl" had already horrified many critics prepared for the litany of lamentations that make up section IV of his poem with a series of flashbacks in section II, recounting crucial moments in the life of his mother's body.[29]

If Ginsberg had outraged prudish readers with some of the confessions he incorporated into "Howl," he scandalized many more with a few of the memories he jammed into section II of "Kaddish." Here, in a densely detailed narrative sequence, he traces his mother's descent into madness, her incarcerations in various mental hospitals, and her final lobotomized years in an "Asylum [that] spreads out giant wings above the path to a minute black hole—the door—entrance thru crotch," and he renders his account extraordinarily vivid by recording clinical views of the maternal body that violently defy not just major elegiac but also major cultural taboos.[30] These views include, most notably, a scatological glimpse of his mother in the bathroom, "croaking up her soul—convulsions and red vomit coming out of her mouth—diarrhea water exploding from her behind—on all fours in front of the toilet . . . the tile floor smeared with her black feces," as well as what some considered an even more lurid vision of a

*time I thought she was trying to make me come lay her—flirting
to herself at sink—lay back on huge bed that filled most of the
room, dress up round her hips, big slash of hair, scars of*

operations, pancreas, belly wounds, abortions, appendix,
stitching of incisions pulling down in the fat like hideous thick
zippers—ragged long lips between her legs.

In a gesture that emphasizes the crucial—and sensational—nature of
the memory that has surfaced here, the poet follows this last, especially
shocking passage with the poem's only direct quotation from the actual
Kaddish that is the traditional Hebrew prayer for the dead. Yet the lines
Ginsberg quotes—

Yisborach, v'histabach, v'yispoar, v'yisroman, v'yisnaseh, v'yishador,
v'yishalleh, v'yishallol, sh'meh d'kudsho, b'rich hu.
[Blessed, praised, glorified, exalted, extolled, honored, elevated and
lauded be the Name of the holy one, Blessed is he.]

—are in themselves crucial, for juxtaposed with the horrifying materiality of the moment they follow, they suggest a profound ambiguity in the
poet's attitude toward the maternal flesh he is elegizing. On the one
hand, they imply his need to redeem both himself and his mother from
a humiliating consciousness of what in the same passage he calls "the
Monster of the Beginning Womb." On the other hand, they imply his
need to bless and praise *even* (or perhaps especially) the absolute fleshli-
ness of that "Monster of the Beginning Womb." The world of the flesh
may be a terrifying "asylum" into which we gain entrance through "a
minute black hole," an "entrance through crotch," yet what's sometimes
called the "temple" of the body is also a holy asylum because it's the only
sanctuary we have.

The two concluding sections of "Kaddish" (IV and V) reinforce the
ambiguity revealed by the juxtaposition of the apparently degraded materiality of maternal flesh with the ritualized, yearningly spiritual language of
the Kaddish. For in section IV of his poem Ginsberg indicates his continually broadening awareness that his mother is truly "gone" through a series
of meditations on the literal and figurative parts of her body organized by
the poetic move that the French call a *blazon*, a term derived from heraldry
but referring in a literary context to the practice of Renaissance love poets,
many of whom celebrated the manifold beauties of their beloved ladies by
proclaiming the splendor of individual features (for instance, shining eyes,
rosy lips, snowy bosom).[31] But precisely because he evokes this courtly tradition, the American poet's incantatory enumerations of Naomi Ginsberg's

body parts are both bitterly and poignantly ironic, performing a ghastly autopsy on the dead woman's self and life:

> *O mother*
> *farewell . . .*
> *with six dark hairs on the wen of your breast . . .*
> *farewell*
> *with your sagging belly . . .*
> *with your mouth of bad short stories . . .*
> *with your arms of fat Paterson porches . . .*
> *with your chin of Trotsky and the Spanish War*
> *with your voice singing for the decaying overbroken workers*
> *with your nose of bad lay with your nose of the smell of the pickles of*
>   *Newark . . .*
> *with your eyes strapped down on the operating table*
> *with your eyes with the pancreas removed . . .*
> *with your eyes alone*
> *with your eyes*
> *with your eyes*
> *with your Death full of Flowers*

But "your Death full of Flowers"? Strangely, in this relentlessly clinical context, the phrase hints at classic pastoral redemption, and perhaps an allusion to such redemption is what Ginsberg intended. Yet the phrase also refers back to another key moment in "Kaddish": another moment, in fact, of powerful juxtaposition. For as the poet draws to the end of his mother's history in section III, remembering her in her last lobotomized years— "One hand stiff . . . the hand dipping downwards to death"—he retrieves another memory that seems to have been preserved in a photograph "from 1920 in Camp Nicht-Gedeiget" (Camp "Don't Worry"). Here is his mother's sane, laughing, Madonna-like youthful self, and here is the flowering— blooming yet transient—body whose beauties he can unequivocally praise:

> *O Russian faced, woman on the grass, your long black hair is crowned with flowers, the mandolin is on your knees—*
> *Communist beauty, sit here married in the summer among daisies, promised happiness at hand—*
> *holy mother, now you smile on your love, your world is born anew, children run naked in the field spotted with dandelions, . . .*

But of course, though Naomi Ginsberg is "here" in this photograph, she is also *not* here, for as Susan Sontag puts it, "precisely by slicing out this moment and freezing it, all photographs testify to time's relentless melt."[32] At the same time, however, in her death the Naomi Ginsberg who *was* here can return, superimposed, as it were, on the final, deformed Naomi Ginsberg her son so traumatically discovered among "the vast lawns of madtown on Long Island."

Perhaps it's this saving superimposition of Ginsberg's mother's earlier, "holy mother" self on her later, disastrous incarnation that makes it possible for the writer to imagine her ignominious death as also a "Death full of Flowers." Certainly the poetic inquest that he conducts in the course of his litany of *blazons* issues in ambiguous visions of a kind of blessedness that is both reassuring and terrifying, for in section V, gazing at his mother's grave, the elegist imagines her—and himself after her—knitted into the physical substance of cosmic mystery, over which an enigmatic "Lord" presides, attended by crows who shriek perhaps elegiacally, perhaps unintelligibly:

> *Caw caw caw crows shriek in the white sun over grave stones in Long Island*
> *Lord Lord Lord Naomi underneath this grass my halflife and my own as*
>   *hers . . .*
> *Lord Lord great Eye that stares on All and moves in a black cloud*
> *caw caw strange cry of Beings flung up into sky over the waving trees . . .*
> *Lord Lord Lord caw caw caw Lord Lord Lord caw caw caw Lord*

Alternating the Hebraic certainty of an uppercase rabbinical invocation ("Lord Lord Lord") with the biological opacity of a lowercase crows' cry ("caw caw caw"), the poet buries his mother in the only sacred tomb this most mystical of contemporary elegists can imagine: "underneath this grass" above which some kind of "Lord" "moves in a black cloud" in the midst of a funeral enacted by shrieking crows.

LISTENING, LOOKING

The extraordinary frankness that marks much late twentieth-century elegiac, verse is, of course, overdetermined. To begin with, both Lowell and Ginsberg were central to the earliest definition of what has come to be called "confessional poetry"; in a review of *Life Studies*, M. L. Rosenthal, the critic who coined the phrase, remarked that the "use of poetry for the most naked kind of confession grows apace in our day."[33] But soon Ginsberg—along with

Berryman, Snodgrass, Plath, Sexton, and others—came to be associated with this mode of writing in which by relating ("confessing") traumatic details of personal history, the poet appears to guarantee the individual authenticity of experiences that gradually accumulate universal meanings. More generally, however, Williams's dictum that there should be "No ideas / but in things" governs a genre of verse focusing on quotidian existence in which most contemporary poets have worked at one time or another.

Nevertheless, it's remarkable how obsessively recent elegists bear witness to the particulars of death and grief, as if to defy, on the one hand, celluloid illusions that the dead are alive and, on the other hand, social valedictions forbidding mourning. Willfully, often horrifyingly scandalous, our contemporary monsters of elegy emerge from the Intensive Care unit, the mortuary, and the crematorium to insist that the dead one has in fact died, and this is how it happened, and where it happened, and why it happened. The death scene is, of course, a staple of tragedy, opera, sentimental fiction, murder mystery, and *verismo* cinema. In addition, such nineteenth-century sentimental poets as Lydia Sigourney and Felicia Hemans offered numerous visions of angelically dying children and saintly maidens pointing toward the heavens while the more innovative Whitman and Dickinson dwelt on crucial deathbed details: the "blue uncertain stumbling buzz" of a mysterious fly, the "ooze exuding at last" from the poet's own dead lips. But fully rendered, meticulously factual death scenes comparable to Flaubert's dispassionate scrutiny of Emma Bovary's end or Tolstoy's of Ivan Ilyich's are relatively new to poetry. Yet these are the episodes that poets from Williams to Lowell, Ginsberg, Thom Gunn, Sharon Olds, and Alan Shapiro either struggle to imagine or claim to have witnessed.

Just as Williams's "Tract" functioned as a manifesto for a new elegiac movement, his "The Last Words of My English Grandmother" constitutes a model for a twentieth-century version of the old deathwatch. Drafted in 1920, the poem critiques the highflown deathbed arias idealized by Victorian culture through both its realistically grimy setting and its apparently literal transcription of ordinary speech. Deliberately anti-"poetic," the piece introduces both the grandmother and the space she inhabits with details as clinical as those in "Kaddish":

> *There were some dirty plates*
> *and a glass of milk*
> *beside her on a small table*
> *near the rank, disheveled bed—*

Wrinkled and nearly blind
she lay and snored
rousing with anger in her tones
to cry for food,

Gimme something to eat—
They're starving me—
I'm all right I won't go
to the hospital. No, no, no

Then the raging old lady is ensconced in an ambulance, where she utters "last words" that, as the poet records them, are poignant precisely because they're the opposite of theatrical. On the way to the hospital, writes Williams,

we passed a long row
of elms. She looked at them
a while out of
the ambulance window and said,

What are all those
fuzzy-looking things out there?
Trees? Well, I'm tired
of them and rolled her head away.[34]

A comparable understatement marks Robert Frost's startling account in "Out, Out—" of the death of a teenage boy whose hand has been amputated in an accident with a buzz saw:

The boy's first outcry was a rueful laugh,
As he swung toward them holding up the hand
Half in appeal, but half as if to keep
The life from spilling. Then the boy saw all—
Since he was old enough to know, big boy
Doing a man's work, though a child at heart—
He saw all spoiled. "Don't let him cut my hand off—
The doctor, when he comes. Don't let him, sister!"
So. But the hand was gone already.
The doctor put him in the dark of ether.
He lay and puffed his lips out with his breath.

And then—the watcher at his pulse took fright.
No one believed. They listened at his heart.
Little—less—nothing!—and that ended it.
No more to build on there. And they, since they
Were not the one dead, turned to their affairs.

Similarly, although Lowell never specifically explores the pain of his mother's death (disclosing only that "after twenty minutes" with an Italian-speaking nurse "I could *imagine* your final week"), he recounts his father's "abrupt and unprotesting" demise with terse informality: "After a morning of anxious, repetitive smiling, / his last words to Mother were: / 'I feel awful.'"[35]

More recent poets—among them Gunn, Olds, Donald Hall, and Alan Shapiro—brood more explicitly on the physical horrors of the death scenes their art refuses to repress. Poem after poem in Gunn's searing *The Man with Night Sweats* narrates the stages of what his bravura "Lament" calls "the difficult enterprise" of a friend's dying, from the "small but clustering duties of the sick" to the spinal tap, the "hard headache," and the final shot of morphine ("Nothing was said, everything understood, / At least by us") that dispatches the patient. Published in the same decade, Olds's *The Father* just as unblinkingly records details of a parent's terminal disintegration: the "bright glass of / spit on the table" by his hospital bed, "the call button pinned to the sheet / like a pacifier," the "tiny snowflakes . . . on the cotton" gown that covers his wasted body, all bearing witness to the factuality of death-as-termination by speaking what is all too often culturally unspeakable, as if to document mortality itself. And Hall's *Without* recounts even more disturbingly vivid particulars as the poet traces the terminal months of his wife, Jane Kenyon. In "Last Days," for instance, he notes graphic details of the dying woman's decline with the impassivity of someone so grief-stricken he would himself collapse without the discipline of the bedside diary he has undertaken to keep:

> *Incontinent three nights*
> *before she died, Jane needed lifting*
> *onto the commode. . . .*
> *Leaving his place beside her,*
> *where her eyes stared, he told her,*
> *"I'll put these letters*
> *in the box." She had not spoken*
> *for three hours, and now Jane said*
> *her last words: "O.K."*

> *At eight that night,*
>   *her eyes open as they stayed*
> *until she died, brain-stem breathing*
>   *started. . . .*
>   *A sharp, almost sweet*
> *smell began to rise from her open mouth.*
>   *He watched her chest go still.*
> *With his thumb he closed her round brown eyes.*[36]

Most recently, Shapiro's *Song and Dance* examines the particulars of his brother's death from a brain tumor in much the way that his earlier prose memoir, *The Vigil,* had recorded the details of his sister's death from breast cancer. Indeed, in their unflinching examination of particularity, the poems of *Song and Dance* are as much interrogations as they are investigations, for more frankly than most of the other writers who scrutinize the pain of the deathwatch, Shapiro admits to being confounded by what he must confront and record. In "The Big Screen," for instance, he formulates a set of questions that brilliantly summarize the bafflement of a bystander who forces himself to listen to a ceaseless deathbed "moaning" that eerily echoes the incessant deathbed screaming of Tolstoy's Ivan Ilyich:

> *What did it mean, the moaning? Or could you even*
> *call it a moan, what bore no trace of a voice*
>   *we could recognize as his?*
> *Was there even a his by then? Or was it only*
> *a sound, mere sound of the body becoming a thing,*
>   *a spasm, a mere electrical event?*

Willfully naive, these questions that hopelessly seek to extract a meaning from terminal moaning prefigure the supposedly larger questions in the book's next poem, explicitly entitled "Three Questions"; "What was it like to see him die?"; "Was he ready to die?"; "Was he at peace?"—the standard and somewhat sanctimonious queries that outsiders offer, as tokens of sympathy, to survivors. But where Tolstoy was able to project his own vision of redemption into his account of Ivan Ilyich's death so that ultimately the howl of the dying man is replaced by a redemptive vision of light (facilitating the conclusion "yes, he was at peace when he died"), Shapiro's resigned contemporary skepticism prevents what he would clearly consider presumptuous views of the sufferer's subjectivity. To the "Three Questions" so many would have him answer, he can only reply that he heard the "sound of the body becoming a thing," the sound of consciousness terminating. Yet it is this sound that his poems are driven to reconstruct, just as Hall, Olds, and Gunn are driven to bear witness to specifics that signal the extinction of loved ones.[37]

Even when poets can't testify firsthand about a scene of dying, many strive to reconstruct the physical minutiae of the event. John Berryman, for example, seeks to cope with Delmore Schwartz's death through repeated, inconclusive, but increasingly frantic speculations: "What final thought / solaced his fall to the hotel carpet, if any," "He fell on the floor / outside a cheap hotel-room," "at 4 a.m. on the wrong floor too // fighting for air." More assured of a narrative, Ruth Stone confronts her husband's suicide by moving from the known to the inexplicable:

> The gendarme came
> to tell me you had hung yourself
> on the door of a rented room
> like an overcoat
> like a bathrobe
> hung from a hook;
> when they forced the door open
> your feet pushed against the floor.
> Inside your skull
> there was no room for us,
> your circuits forgot me.

Just as horrifyingly but more elliptically, Frank Bidart hypothesizes a tale of ghastly discovery in the command with which he concludes "The Sacrifice," his elegy for "Miss Mary Kenwood; who, without / help, placed her head in a plastic bag, // then locked herself / in a refrigerator":

> When Judas writes the history of solitude,
> let him record
>
> that to the friend who opened
> the refrigerator, it seemed
>
> death fought; before giving in.[38]

If the death scenes produced by contemporary poets are surprisingly candid in facing mortality, however, many are equaled in frankness by verse in which the materiality of the dead body is itself the subject of meditation. Again, Williams is paradigmatic here. Lowell's mother's corpse "wrapped . . . in Italian tinfoil," and Ginsberg's mother's splayed "eyes with the pancreas removed" can be traced back to the savage truthfulness of Williams's early "Death," with its delineation of the rigor mortis of a man who has become "nothing at all." But even earlier D. H. Lawrence's "The Bride" had provided a model for Williams, with its image of the poet's dead mother looking "like a girl to-night," though "she is old" and "The plaits that lie along her pillow" are "threaded with filigree silver, / And uncanny cold."[39]

Recent poets, however, write even more forthrightly about the factuality of what Sharon Olds calls "the mortal one" embedded in dead flesh. In their caustic delineation of common funeral practices, indeed, some might well have been tutored by Jessica Mitford at her most acerbic. "Flowers like a gangster's funeral; / Eyeshadow like a whore," writes W. D. Snodgrass of his dead sister in "Viewing the Body," adding: "They all say isn't she beautiful. / She, who never wore // Lipstick or such a dress." And Mark Doty, elegizing a transvestite friend who "died in a paper tiara," remembers a moment at the wake when "the tension broke" after "someone guessed // the casket [was] closed because he was *in there in a big wig / and heels.*"[40]

At the same time, by dwelling with virtually necrophiliac intensity on what funeral directors call "the remains" of dead loved ones, some poets enact their love for those they have lost while others protest the horror of what Berryman describes as Delmore Schwartz's "terrible end, out of which grows . . . an unshaven, disheveled *corpse.*" In the latter mode, Thom Gunn's "The Beautician" limns the loving care with which a woman whose job is hair care attends to the remains of an old friend whose body has been "dumped . . . all awry" in the morgue. As if to refute Mitford's scorn for those who would beautify a cadaver, the poet notes: "She gave her task a concentrated mind," because she found in it

> . . . *some thin satisfaction*
> *That she could use her tenderness as skill*
> *To make her poor dead friend's hair beautiful*
> *—As if she shaped an epitaph by her action,*
> *She thought—being a beautician after all.*

Even more extravagantly, those mourning a lost beloved dwell with special, often erotic intensity on the materiality of the dead spouse, with some
also performing the little tasks of grooming that Gunn's poem describes.
Paul Monette's *Love Alone: Eighteen Elegies for Rog* includes a memory of
the poet's last moments with his lover's body: "for hours at the end," Monette confides in an address to his partner, who died of AIDS,

> *I kissed your temple stroked*
> *your hair and sniffed it it smelled so clean we'd*
> *washed it Saturday night when the fever broke . . . oh why*
> *don't all these kisses rouse you I won't won't*
> *say it all I will say is goodnight patting*
> *a few last strands in place you're covered now*
> *my darling*

Similarly, the elegies for Raymond Carver that Tess Gallagher collects in
Moon Crossing Bridge record her loving attention to "the powerful raft" of
her husband's body:

> *Since his feet were still there and my hands*
> *I rubbed them with oil*
> *because it is hard to imagine at first*
> *that the dead don't enjoy those same things they did when alive.*

The same erotic intensity often infuses Ruth Stone's thoughts about inter-
acting with the dead. As we've seen, in "Habit" she confesses to her long-
dead husband, "Every day I dig you up / And wipe off the rime / And *look*
at you [emphasis added]," and in "Becoming You" she even daydreams
about devouring him, as if ingestion could facilitate resurrection ("taking
my time / I come on digesting you"). The need of the bereaved for corporeal consolation is so urgent as to be almost monstrous, these poems tell us,
for grief's desire is insatiable. "It is your skeleton I crave," Stone eventually
confides.[41]

Finally, however, a number of poets are open in their analyses of the
purely physical processes through which the material of living bodies
decomposes. In an early draft of *The Waste Land* T. S. Eliot experimented
with such a vision of disintegration, parodying Shakespeare in an anti-
Semitic and perhaps anti-"Shakespeherian rag":

Full fathom five your Bleistein lies
Under the flatfish and the squids.

Graves' Disease in a dead jew's/man's eyes!
Where the crabs have ~~nibb~~ eat the lids. . . .

That is lace that was his nose

Roll/stir him gently side to side
See the lips unfold unfold[42]

But more recent writers consider with less disgust—and often with wistful love—the body's reduction to elemental matter, with many meditating on the metamorphosis of flesh to bone and ash. Tess Gallagher dwells with mystical intensity on the Japanese custom of "picking bones" after "cremation of the loved one," while Thom Gunn proffers a ceremonial benediction to his friend's ashes, intoning, "may rain leach discontents / From your dust, wash what remains // Deeper into damper ground." More extravagantly, Tony Harrison fantasizes on the fate of his father's body in the oven of the crematorium to which it was consigned, and his fantasy, as he remarks, is especially apropos because the dead man was a baker.

When the chilled dough of his flesh went in an oven
not unlike those he fueled all his life,
I thought of his cataracts ablaze with Heaven. . . .
I thought how his cold tongue burst into flame
but only literally, which makes me sorry,
sorry for his sake there's no Heaven to reach. . . .
The baker's man that no one will see rise
and England made to feel like some dull oaf
is smoke, enough to sting one person's eyes
and ash (not unlike flour) for one small loaf.[43]

And in "His Ashes," Sharon Olds defines what is for all these poets a kind of ontology. Opening her father's urn and gazing at its contents, she seems to be staring at the very center of material reality:

there it was, the actual matter of his being: . . .
was that a bone of his wrist, was that from the

elegant knee he bent, was that
his jaw, was that from his skull that at birth was
flexible yet—I looked at him,
bone and the ash it lay in, silvery
white as the shimmering coils of dust
the earth leaves behind it as it rolls, you can
hear its heavy roaring as it rolls away.[44]

There it was and there it *is*, these poets imply: "the actual matter" of all "being" and all beings, the physical stuff that we are and were, ashes to ashes, dust to dust, "the shimmering coils," the "heavy roaring" that "rolls away." Nor, since "there's no Heaven to reach," do these writers envision any fiery particles like the "soul of Adonais" beaconing and beckoning "from the abode where the Eternal are" as the soul of Keats supposedly did in Shelley's great but now unimaginable elegy.

REMEMBERING

The trauma of such concrete encounters with mortality is so intense that the mind of the mourner tends to seek stability in recollections of things past, telling the tale of experience with the lost one over and over, as if to guarantee its reality. After skeptically musing in his late poem "The Rock" on the apparent unreality of the past ("The meeting at noon at the edge of the field seems like // An invention"), Stevens recovered confidence in the substance of memory by asserting that the "blooming and the musk / Were being alive . . . a *particular* of being, that gross universe" (emphasis added). In affirming this creed, he articulated not only a founding assumption of what was to become the confessional strain in contemporary verse but also an important procedure for grieving on which contemporary elegists rely over and over again.

That a review of the particulars of being is especially necessary to the bereaved was of course part of Freud's creed too; in "Mourning and Melancholia" he argues that "healthy" mourning requires a "testing of reality" to prove that "the loved object no longer exists" so that the libido can be "withdrawn from its attachments to this object . . . bit by bit."[46] But whether or not contemporary English-speaking writers are mindful of Freud's counsel, in the wake of Lowell's *Life Studies* and Ginsberg's *Kaddish* detailed reminiscences have become such staples of contemporary verse that it would be difficult to summarize the multifarious techniques of recollection poets, memoirists, and novelists now employ. As Freud implies, though, for the mourner the processes of memory are intensified and obsessively reiterated. "As if needles were stuck / in the pleasure zones of our brains, / we repeated everything / over and over and over," Ruth Stone remembers about the early days of her marriage, and as she grieves following her husband's suicide, a needle seems to be stuck in the pain zone of her heart, repeating the steps to calamity over and over. In a different vein, Tess Gallagher confesses in "Crazy Menu" to compulsively using up all the household products her husband left behind, as if in that way she could incorporate the very stuff of their life together:

> Last of his toothpaste, last of his Wheat Chex, last
> of his 5-Quick-Cinnamon-Rolls-With-Icing, his
> Pop Secret Microwave Pop-
> corn, his Deluxe Fudge Brownie Mix next to my
> Casbah Nutted Pilaf on the sparser
> shelf. I'm using it all up. Chanting: he'd-want-me-
> to-he'd-want-me-to.[47]

More generally, as in both *Kaddish* and *Life Studies*, grieving poets often seek to objectify the histories of their lives with those who have died by examining the sequences of *things* out of which those lives were shaped. Elaborating on Williams's famous dictum "No ideas but in things," many indeed suggest that most memories *are* in things and are, as it were, *spoken* by things. In "A Woman Mourned by Daughters," Adrienne Rich makes this point explicitly. As she and her sister confront the loss of their mother, they find themselves literally surrounded by their past lives with her, which take material shape like what Sylvia Plath called in "Berck-Plage" "a decor." For though the dying woman had dwindled until she was "a straw blown on the bed / crisp as a dead insect," Rich, her poet-daughter, declares: "You breathe upon us now / through solid assertions / of yourself: teaspoons, goblets, / seas of carpet."[48]

A range of other poets similarly remember their dead chiefly in and through the things that function as "solid assertions" of a vanished selfhood. Elaine Feinstein, for instance, begins an elegy simply entitled "Dad" by confronting the literal as well as figurative pressures of sorrow and memory:

> Your old hat hurts me, and those black
> fat raisins you liked to press into

my palm from your soft heavy hand.
  I see you staggering back up the path
with sacks of potatoes from some local farm,
  fresh eggs, flowers.

Tony Harrison remembers his father through details too, noting, for instance, that in his last years "His home address was inked inside his cap / and on every piece of paper that he carried," and Seamus Heaney has such a vivid memory of regularly peeling potatoes with his mother after Sunday mass that

  while the parish priest at her bedside
Went hammer and tongs at the prayers for the dying
And some were responding and some crying
I remembered her head bent towards my head,
Her breath in mine, our fluent dipping knives—
Never closer the whole rest of our lives.[49]

Inventorying the possessions of the dead as if to claim that, as Lowell implies in *Life Studies*, those who have "passed away" from the material world can be known only by the material goods they left behind, late-twentieth-century poets assemble list after list of the things that metonymically stand in for those who have died. The very stuff of domesticity—for instance, clothing on which the dead have left their imprint, like Feinstein's father's hat—frequently forms the basic substance of memory. Maxine Kumin meditates on the blue jacket she has inherited from her friend Anne Sexton ("In the left pocket, a hole. / In the right, a parking ticket"), noting: "My skin presses your old outline. / It is hot and dry inside." Similarly, Richard Garcia takes stock of his mother's clothes as part of a fantasy about resurrecting "Mi Máma, the Playgirl"—"She wore black dresses. Her closet was lined with identical pairs of black shoes"—while Marilyn Hacker describes browsing among "Fall Sale bargains" in Macy's, "(where forty-five years / past, qualified by her new M.A. / in Chemistry, [her mother had] sold Fine Lingerie)," when she's overwhelmed by her intuitive knowledge that her hospitalized mother has "finally" died of heart failure. And in a wrenching elegy for a dead child, Paula Meehan confides:

  I chose your grave clothes with care,
  your favorite stripey shirt,

your blue cotton trousers.
They smelt of woodsmoke, of October,

your own smell there too.
I chose a gansy of handspun wool,

warm and fleecy for you. It is
so cold down in the dark.[50]

But if clothing recalls "your old outline" or "your own smell," the food or flavors the dead loved, prepared, or shared—or indeed the "bread of life" the body itself incarnates—signifies, as in Tess Gallagher's "Crazy Menu," the bittersweet tastes of the past. Wendy Barker depicts her family's sorrow at her father's death through a rueful meditation on "the dividing of spoils. / He would have said it like that, with a grin," noting, for instance:

My son keeps his last four rolls
of Stick-O-Pep lifesavers, says he will
keep them unopened in memory of Grandfather,
maybe once a year peel back the foil
and suck just one, for good luck.

As Douglas Dunn laments his wife's death, he explains that the "recipes she used . . . each kitchen-spotted page, / Each stain, each note in her neat hand" can "spin" him into grief. Donald Hall strains to envision Jane Kenyon's return from the dead with a quotidian image of "our circular driveway . . . bags of groceries upright / in the back of [her] Saab." And Sharon Olds, recounting a visit to her father's grave after he's been dead a year, confesses: "When I kissed his stone it was not enough," so that she licked it, and then "my tongue went dry a moment" as "I ate his dust, I tasted my dirt host."[51]

Like other writers who both celebrate and lament the transience of the fleshly world ruled by the "emperor of ice-cream," these poets are of course indebted to Proust's famous five-volume-long meditation on the taste of the madeleine out of which all his remembrances of things past ultimately bloomed. But, too, they owe their literal and figurative incorporation of food into art to William Carlos Williams's early riff on what is supposedly a late-night note to his wife. "This Is Just to Say" (whose title and first line are one and the same) presents itself as a scribble that apologizes for having "eaten / the plums / that were in / the icebox," adding, as if in a variation on Stevens's "ice-cream":

> *Forgive me*
> *they were delicious*
> *so sweet*
> *and so cold*

And the past too, these poets suggest—the personal past that shaped those sensual memories that guarantee, if anything does, the authenticity of both the dead and the living who mourn them—*was* (at its best) "delicious," once "so sweet" and now "so cold."[52]

IMAGINING

Yet what imaginings can comfort those who elegize the absolute evanescence of what *was*? In an age where few poets hope for transfiguration through the "dear might of him that walks the waves," visions of redemption are at best fanciful, at bottom skeptical or nihilistic. Many poets, like most other mourners, reproach the dead for their absence and absentmindedness, their stonyheartedness. "See what you miss by being dead?" exclaims Ruth Stone after telling the story of a hilarious encounter with a landlord. Some, like Marilyn Hacker, rail "Against Elegies," protesting the need for such a genre. Some, like Donald Hall and Ted Hughes, hope against hope for knowledge of an afterlife, exclaiming to the dead beloved (with Hall), "You know now whether the soul survives death. / Or you don't," or else asking (with Hughes): "What can I tell you that you do not know / Of the life after death?"[53]

Others, in tentative fantasies of a hereafter, imagine the dead spinning away or watching the living with indifference. "The soul's like all matter," Louise Gluck reasons; why would it "stay faithful to its one form, / when it could be free?" More comically, Thom Gunn proposes that at least for a time the dead

> *watch friend and relative*
> *And life here as they think it is*
> *—In black and white, repetitive*
> *As situation comedies.*

And in a fairy-tale rendering of a domesticated heaven, Seamus Heaney imagines his dead mother arriving in a celestial replica of her childhood dwelling: "Number 5, New Row, Land of the Dead, / Where grandfather is rising from his place . . . To welcome a bewildered homing daughter . . . And they sit down in the shining room together."[54]

Perhaps most grandly, in the late elegiac fantasy entitled "White Shroud" Allen Ginsberg revises the "Kaddish" of his youth to imagine a reconciliation with his dead mother that happens through a dream. As if to emphasize its visionary status, this poem opens with an epigraph that sets the unreal scene with Blakean panache:

> I am summoned from my bed
> To the Great City of the Dead
> Where I have no house or home
> But in dreams may sometime roam
> Looking for my ancient room
> A feeling in my heart of doom,
> Where Grandmother aged lies
> In her couch of later days
> And my mother saner than I
> Laughs and cries She's still alive.

Then follows the poem proper, in which the speaker finds himself "again in the Great Eastern Metropolis / wandering under Elevated Transport's iron struts." Here, among the "many windowed apartments" that crowd the "Bronx road-way," he finds his grandmother alive in an "open Chamber" and himself "vigorous Middle aged," so that he immediately declares "what / relief, the family together again, first time in decades!"[55]

But strangest of all, as the poet revisits characters from his earlier writings, he encounters a "shopping-bag lady [who] live[s]in the side alley on a mattress" and looks "desolate, white haired, but strong enough to cook and stare." Slowly he recognizes that she is his mother, "Naomi, habiting / this old city-edge corner," and though she insists that "I'm a great woman, I came here / by myself, I wanted to live," he understands his own deep wish to "live" (read "die"?) *with* her: "Has she an extra room? I noticed her cave / adjoined an apartment door. . . . I could live here, worst comes to worst, best place I'll find:

Those years unsettled—were over now, here I could live
forever, here have a home, with Naomi, at long last,
at long long last, my search was ended in this pleasant way.

How many of us have encountered the dead "in this pleasant way" in dreams? Ginsberg brings his poem to a close with a return "from the Land of the Dead to living Poesy" in which he inscribes his "tale of long lost joy, to have seen my mother again!" And his vision of conciliation undertaken in those alleys of desire that crisscross the unconscious is no doubt as familiar to readers from experience as from readings in Freudian theory. Yet can even the most profoundly desired conciliation count as consolation? Could I— *should* I—have broached such dream resolutions to my hostess in Kyoto? For after all, when Whitman, who was along with Blake and Williams one of the saints of Ginsberg's imagination, pronounced that death was "different, and luckier," might he have merely meant that the imminence of extinction forces us to reimagine the best of the past, "the family together again," our search for love and meaning "ended in this pleasant way"?

But didn't Whitman bring his family "together again" only when he assembled them under the great granite roof of his tomb in Camden, New Jersey, not all that far from where Ginsberg grew up?

IS THERE NO CONSOLATION?

The encounter at the heart of "White Shroud" was in several senses a dream. By comparison, most waking efforts at ceremonial benediction seem futile, at least unless it's understood that the Benedictus the living offer the dead is really not for the dead but for the living. Little traditional consolation— not even Whitman's mystical hope—is available to writers shaped by a mythology of modern death-as-termination. "And what of the dead?" asks Anne Sexton, a lapsed Catholic:

> *They are more like stone*
> *than the sea would be if it stopped. They refuse*
> *to be blessed, throat, eye, and knucklebone.*

In the end that we conceive at this turn of the century, most poets are comforted simply by the tautology that what goes on goes on: Sharon Olds listens to the roaring of the earth as it rolls away; Brenda Hillman admires "the shine off the back of a very large beetle" on the grave of a woman she'd loved, an insect that persists in symbolically "lifting its legs as high as it can—"[56]

That this bleakness often shapes great poetry may be a consolation to literary critics, but it doesn't placate those poets who, in the disconsolate mode of much contemporary elegy, contemplate the deaths of those they love as well as their own promised ends. Writes W. S. Merwin of his poet friends, in a twentieth-century revision of William Dunbar's powerful fifteenth-century "Lament for the Makers:" "one by one they have all gone / out of the time and language we / had in common," for their literary art didn't save them; "the best words did not keep them from / leaving themselves finally." Now, as he ages, he too finds himself facing the same departure, for "this day is going from me." *Poeisis*—by definition the art of making— "never promised anything / but the true sound of brevity / that will go on after me."[57] In the same vein, Ginsberg links a meditation on his own mortality with a speculation on the fate of a poet friend. Confessing in "Mescaline," a purportedly drug-induced poem produced in the same era as "Kaddish," that "I want to know what happens after I rot," he turns anxiously to William Carlos Williams, his aging literary father. What was Williams "thinking in Paterson" as he neared death, Ginsberg wonders, adding plaintively:

> Williams, what is death?
> Do you face the great question now each moment. . . .
> Are you prepared to be reborn
> to give release to this world to enter a heaven
> [or to] see a lifetime—all eternity—gone over
> into naught, a trick question proposed by the moon to the
> answerless earth.

Throughout the twentieth century and on into the twenty-first, most poets in America and Britain have sought to give voice to the voiceless bewilderment of "the answerless earth." In doing so, they've chiefly memorialized only what memory offers, sparse representations of the things and doings of this world. Lowell, Ginsberg's counterpart in pioneering modern poetic mourning, ends the "Epilogue" to his last book, *Day by Day*, with the minimalist credo on which many of our "monsters of elegy" have been based:

> We are poor passing facts,
> warned by that to give

> *each figure in the photograph*
> *his living name.*[58]

And though I was still dazed from the luminous emptiness of Ryoan-ji, I might have outlined this aesthetic to my Kyoto audience and found a sympathetic response.

But the voice of my interlocutor in that lecture hall was clear and chill. "What consolation do Whitman and Dickinson have to offer us? Is there no consolation?" What ceremony else was there as those poets neared the turn from the nineteenth century to the twentieth? And what ceremony is there for us at this turn of the twenty-first century? Will a vision of the ongoing earth or of "the shine off the back of a very large beetle" suffice? Surely, despite material continuities, there's no denying the sorrow mourners feel as they enter into full consciousness of what does *not* go on.

I could, I suppose, have speculated that Whitman and Dickinson console us with the mere *endurance* of their poems and of the empowered voices that continue to speak to us as if alive in marks on a page. Whitman suggested to his readers, we should recall, that he himself was (re)incarnated in his texts—"Who touches this [poem] touches a man"—while Dickinson imagined her verses dwelling "in ceaseless rosemary," the herb of remembrance. But I suspect that our twentieth- and twenty-first-century elegists are too skeptical about the abyss of the future to trust in the endurance of their own ways and words.[59]

Yet perhaps if contemporary elegists don't find consolation in contemplating the potential for greatness and endurance inherent in their own poems of mourning, there's solace for them as well as their readers in the arduously visionary acts of *making* from which elegies arise, and consolation too in the process of reimagining the particular lives of the dead that such makings honor. At a conference on the elegy some years ago, the poet-critic Douglas Dunn, the author of a number of moving elegies following the death of his young wife, mused that a "transfiguration of the commonplace" was the most "redemptive" poetic possibility he could propose. His argument emphasized the foundation of our recent poetry of mourning in the particular, the ordinary, the common *place* of the material world in which we mortals dwell, while also stressing the metamorphic power of the human imagination. Through *poesis*—the acts and arts of making that empower the elegist's evocations of the dead—the poet as both a private griever (an individual facing a grave loss) and a public scribe (a writer setting down words that others will read) converts the particularities of a completed life into elements radiant with new meaning.

As a public scribe too, the poet often speaks to, of, and for the overarching community of state and nation in an attempt to remedy the ills that led to what is frequently characterized as needless or wrongful death. As I noted in my discussion of "writing wrong" and as Gail Holst-Warhaft has meticulously demonstrated in *The Cue for Passion*, the burden of elegy frequently presents itself as a moral or political obligation to lament and correct a skewed social order. Thus, in the contemporary AIDS elegy, for instance, as in a number of comparable works energized by genocide and war, the only consolation the mourner can find in a confrontation of loss is not a vision of celestial resurrection but a dream of societal redemption. It is as if for writers of such poems of mourning, the Miltonic diatribe against "Blind mouths! that scarce themselves know how to hold / A sheep-hook"— together with a hope of changing the systems that spawn such evils—comes at the end of the text, replacing the image of Lycidas "mounted high / through the dear might of him that walked the waves," rather than functioning as a impassioned digression in medias res. If the dead can't be cured or restored, such poets aspire to heal the social wound that killed them, singly or communally.[60]

Although it may seem "monstrous" in relation to elegiac tradition, the reshaped contemporary elegy is thus, on the one hand, a poignant literary version of a personal "spontaneous shrine," with its assemblage of snapshots, candles, and tributary gifts, and, on the other hand, a literary panel in the vast public memorial wall or quilt that we dedicate to the history of those who have gone before us and the hopes of those who will come after us. And if the elegist's words are in every sense "true"—right, just, and harmonious—they endow us with what we trust will persist along with the shine of the beetle's back and the rolling of the earth: the grievous yet inspired and sometimes transformative "sound of brevity" that, as Merwin writes, we humans make "out of the time and language"—the place—"we had in common."[61]

Apocalypse Now (and Then)

Y2K

We expected crashes, yes. Widespread computer crashes, we were told, might mark the much-hyped millennial moment. These in turn would cause all kinds of other crashes and collapses, given the highly networked technology on which more than half the world so heavily depends. People were advised to store bottled water and to have supplies of canned goods on hand, as well as manual (rather than electrical) can openers. Homeowners should know how to shut off gas and water mains.

The preparations of some families for New Year's Eve 1999–2000 were weighty and serious; the stockpiles of supplies recommended by various "authorities" were eerily reminiscent of the necessities with which, in the 1950s, citizens were told to furnish their fallout shelters. Admonished one Web site, the "basics" (beside manual can openers) "include extra toilet paper," a Swiss army knife ("always a handy item"), and Dr. Bronner's liquid castile soap, which can be used as body soap, shampoo, and dish soap—and, "in a pinch, as toothpaste."

And indeed, once the pantries and cellars of America had been properly fitted out, some anticipations of the millennium must have taken on the curious coziness that used to mark glossy magazine photos of the well-provisioned fallout shelter. If only by flashlight, the champagne would still be drunk—though finished rather quickly, before the fridge lost its cool—and the glasses would be rinsed in bottled water and Dr. Bronner's soap.[1]

How humdrum our anxieties were, compared with those of the impassioned poets—Yeats, Lawrence, Auden, and so many others—who prophesied and fulminated earlier in the twentieth century! Inevitably, these writers argued, death and maybe rebirth, or at any rate some sort of transformation, would be implicit in the creaking of the great wheel of history as it made its turn from the fatigue and clutter of A.D. 1999 to the unfilled openness of A.D. 2000. While we worried about our computers, our closest literary forebears fantasized rough beasts and second comings, deaths of "the old gang," doves descending and swans arising. Arguably, their apocalyptic imaginings loomed as grandly over ours as, say, Stravinsky towers over MTV, Virginia Woolf over Fay Weldon.[2]

Of course, in the last decades of the twentieth century countless futurologists, theosophists, astrologists, pentecostalists, and any number of other old-school and New Age prophets did pursue apocalyptic visions. From Ruth Montgomery, an erstwhile journalist who asserted in her *Herald of the New Age* that in the summer of 1999 the earth would " 'flip' on to its side, with the result that the poles will shift to South America and the Pacific respectively," to the British esotericist Benjamin Creme, who claimed that the Himalayan master "Lord Maitreya" had descended from his mountain fastness to inaugurate the Age of Aquarius predicted by Madame Blavatsky in the nineteenth century, acolytes of pop apocalypse arose to predict either the beginning of the end or the end of the beginning or both. Extraterrestrials would soon arrive to redeem us, said some, while others declared that a host of quasi-angelic ETs would sweep the best of us off to the stars so that at least a few humans could survive the earthquakes and tidal waves generated by the wild careenings of the North and South Poles.[3]

Preaching the fundamentalist doctrine of the "Rapture," Hal Lindsey, author of the best-selling *The Late Great Planet Earth*, insisted: "Without benefit of science, space suits, or interplanetary rockets, there will be those who will be transported [at the now-imminent Last Judgment] into a glorious place more beautiful, more awesome, than we can possibly comprehend," and more concretely, the "pastor of the new First Church of Elvis, Presbyterian" predicted that "Elvis will make his second coming at the end of the millennium." Indeed a few of these ambitious apocalyptists—perhaps they should be called popalyptists—even defined our quotidian technological tools as instruments of revelation. While, as we've seen, American spiritualist James Van Praagh claimed that ghosts were using television and computer screens to communicate news from the spirit realm, Marina Tsvygun, a Ukrainian writer, "issued a warning to the world about Satan's subversion of the world's economic system through the use of bar codes."[4]

Surrounded by video visionaries and struggling with the fantasies of powerful precursors, while ordinary citizens were preoccupied with the fate of their computers, our serious seers were, not surprisingly, contorted with skepticism and irony. We have "already passed [the apocalypse] unawares," lamented the French social theorist Jean Baudrillard, "and now find ourselves in the situation of . . . already being in the hereafter, that is, without horizon and without hope." Whether or not one commentator was right in arguing that precisely because we are "paralyzed by irony," we "collude with the cruder endtime scenarios of our period," it was clear that many intellectuals wondered how anyone could produce texts of "apocalypse now" that might even remotely compete with modernist imaginings of "apocalypse then."[5]

What serious thinkers could have imagined that a band of Saudi terrorists would initiate a terrifying drama that might almost have been drawn from the pages of William Butler Yeats, enacting a version of the millennial crisis he outlined in "The Second Coming"?

Brooding on the catastrophes of the early twentieth century, the Irish poet pronounced the end of the cycle of Western civilization that began with the birth of Christ: "Things fall apart, the center cannot hold; / Mere anarchy is loosed upon the world, / The blood-dimmed tide is loosed." We've journeyed far from our cultural origins, Yeats meant to say; the "center" represented by Christianity's cradle in Bethlehem no longer unites us. But, he added ominously, as we spin away from each other and from the beliefs that once held us together, something new—and terrible—is about to arrive. "Surely some revelation is at hand," he prophesied, "Surely the Second Coming is at hand." Then he transcribed an unnerving millennial vision—"somewhere in sands of the desert / A shape with lion body and the head of a man"—a sphinx—"Is moving its slow thighs,"—adding: "And what rough beast, its hour come round at last, / Slouches towards Bethlehem to be born?"

Even though the messianic fanatics who crashed planes into the World Trade Center were neither rough beasts nor sphinxes, the extremity of their act exploded the millennial fizzle of Y2K into the apocalyptic conflagration of 9/11. In its way too, it might even have been thought to dramatize the brutal outcome of Zeus's rape of Leda in another of Yeats's millennial visions—"Leda and the Swan"—where airborne violence engenders a "burning roof and tower." But which of us, "paralyzed by irony," would have imagined that Yeats's melodramatic premonitions might come true? Perhaps not even Yeats himself! For indeed few would have taken Yeats's anxieties literally, though his poetic nightmares, transcribed in the early twentieth century, come closer to the contours of what was to be the "real" millennial moment than any of the dire predictions about Y2K.[6]

"What was Y2K again?" inquired a friend when I told him I've lately been contemplating that phenomenon. But it's hard to imagine that anyone, even a decade from now, will ask, "What was 9/11?" For 9/11, the shattering event that marked the first year of what some consider the "true" millennium, was of course the millennial—indeed the *apocalyptic*—moment, at least in America and probably throughout most of the industrialized West.

THE UNSPEAKABLE EMERGENCY

In September 2000 the movie review Web site known as "rotten tomatoes.com" updated its review of *Towering Inferno*, a 1974 disaster movie starring Steve McQueen and Paul Newman. "Should you be one of the few who hasn't seen the film then here's the plot: Paul Newman builds a stupidly high skyscraper, lots of rich people go into it and it catches fire so they have to escape. Perhaps what is so remarkable about this film is that it sustains a running time of 159 minutes despite such a flimsy premise."[7]

A year later, in September 2001, *Towering Inferno* was one of the films invoked by stunned observers trying to make sense of the kamikaze attacks that demolished the World Trade Center, destroyed part of the Pentagon, and killed more than three thousand people. As the critic Claire Kahane has noted, newscasters were only a few of the onlookers who kept on invoking "the virtual reality of Hollywood," with some likening the scene before them to *Towering Inferno*, others mentioning *Independence Day*, and, as Kahane puts it, even "King Kong scrambling up the Empire State Building after having devastated midtown Manhattan [entering] the chain of association," so that the actual disaster " took on an uncanny ambiguity," for was this apparently real event truly "real" if one had already seen it at the movies? Wasn't it just another titillating instance of torture-by-celluloid?[8]

Yet it was after all the gigantic and spectacular reality of the disaster that was incomprehensible, requiring one simile after another ("it's like a movie"; "it's like *Towering Inferno*") to elicit from witnesses a formulation of its parameters. The attack on the twin towers constituted a real-life, real-time emergency of such massive proportions that no emergency services—not the fire fighters, not the police—could save its thousands of victims; many, instead, became victims themselves. And the event provoked a linguistic emergency too, which helps explain the allusions to so many film scenarios. Those on the scene as well as those before millions of TV screens struggled to find words for the unspeakable sights they were viewing, sights that violated ordinary epistemological categories: airplanes neither taking off nor landing but with apparent calm flying (really) into buildings; bodies (really) falling from the sky; towering tons of concrete, steel, and granite suddenly (really) imploding, collapsing, in seconds, in the biblical "blinking of an eye."

As I write, we're still inhabiting the state of emergency precipitated when these real crashes came: not the crashing of computers but the crashing of planes and towers. And did the terrorists, plotting in pizza parlors and flight schools, deliberately choose to loose the "blood-dimmed tide" of their rage on a date whose numbers signify "emergency" everywhere in America? Or did their master—whoever controlled the trajectory of doom they carried in their heads—sardonically activate these human bombs at a time that meant the urgency of *911* would inevitably blur into the fatality of *9/11*?

Putting aside questions about the terrorists' choice of date, most of us would agree that what *emerged* on that September morning in New York was precisely the millennial towering inferno which late twentieth-century intellectuals had failed to imagine, even though so many of their precursors had brooded on it or something like it. Hollywood had imagined it, yes, but what a "flimsy premise" it seemed—an idea, in fact, to be classed with rants about the "Rapture," the Age of Aquarius, and the second coming of Elvis. And is it because the enormous spectacle of death produced on 9/11 *was* raised on what seems like a flimsy premise that the ultimate character of the emergency itself continues to be in some sense unspeakable?

For some time I've collected works by a range of writers—poets and journalists, novelists and theorists—responding to what might be called the 911 of 9/11, for surely such prose and poetry illuminate the ways we think about "death's door" at this twenty-first-century moment. But it's striking how problematic most of these texts are: some are overwritten; others are banal, many are clumsy or melodramatic. Quite a few, in other words— even those by accomplished authors—are embarrassingly awkward. Poets in particular seem to have been at a loss for words with which to capture the magnitude of the disaster.

To be sure, shortly after 9/11/01 countless commentators preached the efficacy of verse, as if meter and metaphor might have medicinal powers to heal the unhealable wound. Confided the poet and memoirist Mary Karr in the *New York Times*, the "events of Sept. 11 nailed home many of my basic convictions, including the notion that lyric poetry dispenses more relief— if not actual salvation—during catastrophic times than perhaps any art form." And another poet, Samuel Hazo, insisted that the event "was not something that could be readily translated into prose or mere talk. . . . The only language was poetry or silence."[9]

Yet whether they expressed helpless empathy for the victims or helpless vengefulness toward the villains, most writers who essayed comments in verse seemed as incapable of effectively articulating sorrow and wrath as they were powerless to assist or attack. "How does it feel to be exploded into human flesh confetti?" wondered a writer calling herself Antler, who produced a poem entitled "Skyscraper Apocalypse," adding, for emphasis, "How does it feel to be crushed, squashed, / decapitated, dismembered, disemboweled?" And in a piece titled "10:45 A.M. Sept. 11/WTC," Mark Kuhar simply asked (over and over again, in a poem that goes on for twenty-one mostly unvarying lines):

> *whywhywhy . . . . whywhywhy*
> *whywhywhy . . . . whywhywhy*
> *whywhywhy . . . . whywhywhy*

Moreover, if others spoke their horror in somewhat less sputtering phrases, their efforts appeared equally inadequate to the occasion. Proclaimed Emily Borenstein:

> *Our feelings are carried,*
> *bleeding and raw*
> *on gurneys through the streets*
> *of Manhattan.*

Similarly, Richard Foerster declared that "already I bear the raised, raw / welt, the thrust fiery brand of grief hard / upon the brain." As for fantasies of vengeance, they too were hard to formulate. Dan Giancola may have meant to be ironic when he confessed that he imagined "the hijackers gut-stuck, / pitched in a sty where swine / gobble their entrails," but his language too appeared "gut-stuck," or at least tongue-tied.[10]

Nor were more measured verse commentaries notably successful. Some attempts at meditation came off as platitudinous, like Fred Chappell's

> *Let us, in this time of bitterest lament,*
> *Go awhile apart and meditate*
> *And reverently attend the ancestral choir*
> *Of prophets, sages, founders of the state.*

Others, like Lucille Clifton's "thunder and lightning and our world / is another place," just restated the obvious. And of course there were (as always) aesthetic entrepreneurs whose efforts to transform the event into a marketable commodity paralleled the grander-scale projects of media moguls who churned out souvenirs that ranged from patriotic bumper stickers to coffee table picture albums. One contribution to a 9/11 anthology, for instance, consisted of the prospectus for an avant-garde performance piece ("PHOENIX RISING promises to be improvisatory, incantatory, soul searching and passionate") complete with an e-mail contact address for those interested in "future bookings."[11]

In fact the most poignant poems immediately elicited by the calamity of 9/11 were works that either, on the one hand, reassembled the factual minutiae of the event, or, on the other hand, commented on the difficulty of any commentary at all—commented, that is, on the unspeakability of the emergency. Two recent American poets laureate—Robert Pinsky and Billy Collins—chose the first strategy. In "Newspaper," Pinsky alluded only obliquely to 9/11 as one calamity among the heaped-up disasters of history. "The craving for some redemption is like a thirst," he wrote, adding that "It's in us as we open the morning paper," then briefly noted one item in the news one issue of that paper brought: "It says the smoke / Was mostly not paper or flesh. First white, the drywall, / Then darker pulverized steel and granite and marble, / And then, long-smoldering toxic plastic and fiber."[12]

More overtly addressing the most excruciating details of the catastrophe, the impersonally multiplying lists of the dead, Collins was nevertheless just as understated in his approach, simply reiterating names in an elegiac poem quietly entitled "The Names":

> Yesterday, I lay awake in the palm of the night.
> A soft rain stole in, unhelped by any breeze,
> And when I saw the silver glaze on the windows,
> I started with A, with Ackerman, as it happened,
> Then Baxter and Calabro,
> Davis and Eberling, names falling into place
> As droplets fell through the dark.[13]

Even more low-key than Collins's piece was a poem by W. S. Merwin, who chose the second strategy, that of silence, in a moving acknowledgment of speechlessness entitled "To the Words (9/17/01)." "When it happens you are not there," he began, as he addressed the particles of language that sometimes seem so easy to find yet in moments of crisis become inaccessible: "you beyond numbers / beyond recollection / passed on from breath to breath." And though his poem concludes as a prayer, it doesn't issue in the access of verbal inspiration that it gravely seeks:

> *you that were*
> *formed to begin with . . .*
> *to say what could not be said*
>
> *ancient precious*
> *and helpless ones*
>
> *say it*

Despite its muted eloquence, one senses that even this soft-spoken poem was torn from a man who felt impelled to say some minimal something in a situation where nothing would really do, at least not yet and maybe not for quite some time.[14]

Two other artists, a novelist and a composer, made statements that illuminate the air of reluctance shadowing many of the most thoughtful responses to the "real" millennial trauma. Wrote Don DeLillo: "First the planes struck the towers. After a time it became possible for us to absorb this, barely. But when the towers fell. When the rolling smoke began moving downward, floor to floor. This was so vast and terrible that it was outside imagining even as it happened. *We could not catch up with it* [emphasis added]." And surely what one commentator called DeLillo's "stammering syntax" suggests the shock of a cultural crisis about whose contours witnesses can only "testify" in the sense defined by Felman and Laub—can only, that is, produce a recalcitrant speech-act as part of a struggle to come to terms with, and find terms for, an event "in excess" of any "frames of reference" that prosperous citizens of the twenty-first century could locate outside the movies.

Yet if DeLillo's language at least came close to speaking the unspeakability of the emergency that the industrial West confronted on 9/11/01, the radical and, to a number of commentators, scandalous words of the avant-garde German composer Karlheinz Stockhausen may have come closer still. In a radio interview just a few days after the planes crashed into the twin towers, Stockhausen declared, in what became a much-reviled comment, that the terrorist action was itself "the greatest work of art for the whole cosmos."[15]

Did the composer mean to congratulate the hijackers? Although he quickly disclaimed any such intentions, insisting that he was "speaking of the darkest side of human creativity, not necessarily about art as such," Stockhausen was rebuked by countless critics who assumed that he intended to express admiration. Yet if one reads his remark dispassionately, taking his own disclaimer at face value, it isn't so hard to see what he meant.

What poem after all could rival or replicate the spectacularly horrifying images offered by the event itself? To be sure, Yeats had come close to outlining it in "The Second Coming" and "Leda and the Swan," and so had Hollywood movies from *King Kong* to *Towering Inferno*. But the literalization of such fantasies constituted a rending of ordinary reality far more theatrically terrifying than anything Yeats or Hollywood—or for that matter Dante or Wagner—could have produced. The actions of the terrorists, Stockhausen implied, weren't just transgressive because they were criminal; they were transgressive because they crossed—they *transgressed*—the crucial border between fantasy and reality that makes art possible.

Dante imagined the Inferno and even imagined placing some of his real-life Florentine contemporaries in the hell his mind constructed, but he didn't actually build a physical place called "hell." Wagner imagined a conflagration consuming Valhalla in *Götterdämmerung*, the "Twilight of the Gods," but he didn't set the walls of his own world on fire. And even experimental twentieth-century artists at their most radical were only knocking at tiny doors between the imagined and the real when they tested the boundaries between fantasy and physicality in projects like those of, say, Andres Serrano (who in 1989 really submerged a crucifix in a glass of urine to create his controversial *Piss Christ*) or Christo and Jeanne-Claude (who in 1994 actually wrapped the Reichstag in "100,000 square meters of thick woven polypropylene fabric with an aluminum surface").[16]

But the nineteen hijackers of 9/11 created a cultural and epistemological emergency as well as an actual cataclysm when they chose to mount an attack on America's global dominance by immolating thousands in a display of destruction that actualized what ought by rights (or so observers assumed) to have been illusory. Commenting on Stockhausen's "provocative statement" about the attack as an "ultimate work of art," the Slovenian philosopher and psychoanalyst Slavoj Zizek perhaps almost as scandalously remarked that "with regard to Hollywood catastrophe movies" this event was "like snuff pornography versus ordinary sadomasochistic porno movies." Indeed, he continued, "we can perceive the collapse of the WTC towers as the climactic conclusion of twentieth-century art's 'passion for the

Real'—the 'terrorists' themselves did not do it primarily to provoke real material damage, but *for the spectacular effect of it* [*sic*].'"

As a comment on popular culture, Zizek's reference to a twentieth-century "passion for the Real" is astute, but as a summary of the emergency generated by 9/11 it's perhaps misleading. For what after all is "the Real"? Zizek goes on to argue that the "authentic twentieth-century passion for penetrating the Real Thing (ultimately, the destructive Void) through the cobweb of semblances which constitutes our reality [ordinarily] culminates in the thrill of the Real as the ultimate 'effect,' sought after from digitalized special effects, through reality TV [and] up to snuff movies . . . which deliver the 'real thing' [and are therefore] perhaps the ultimate truth of Virtual Reality." Yet there's a disturbing ambiguity here precisely because "the thrill of the Real" for which we have been taught to yearn is the thrill (as the philosopher himself notes) of the *Virtual* Real. What about the *Real* Real, though—which is to say, "the destructive Void" itself?[17]

The phenomenon with which the inhabitants of New York City lived for months after 9/11—inhaling it, ingesting it, their eyes smarting with it, their throats raw with it—was the appalling *pall* of the Real, a smoke that signaled the ancient but nevertheless true cliché of "ashes to ashes, dust to dust." The death that had first seemed like "only" a "spectacle" settled into the air of the city, and as it did so, its presence unsettled the thoughts of those who had to live with it until they could somehow banish it from consciousness.

But it was hard to banish this emergent death from the minds of the living. The apparently virtual spectacle that left a real scar in the shape of a gigantic pit at what came to be called Ground Zero was (to understate the case) a problem because it was no TV fantasy, no Hollywood blockbuster. Was it, as some right-wing fundamentalists actually think, a prefiguring of apocalypse, when the walls of reality will fall down, the spirit will quail, and the "destructive Void" will definitively manifest itself? And if this heavy smog of human flesh and of "long-smoldering toxic plastic and fiber" was a prequel, what could the sequel be?[18]

APO-KALYPSO

To imagine apocalypse is to imagine the death of everything—and then, perhaps, to imagine a rebirth or birth of the new. Etymologically the word "apocalypse" is derived from the Greek *apo-kalypso*, meaning "to unveil; thus to reveal, to disclose," which, as the theologian Catherine Keller observes, "[p]rebiblically . . . connotes the marital stripping of the veiled virgin."[19] Such a rending of the veil between us and the naked truth of history—in particular of what might be considered the generative truths of death and (re)birth—is a project that has preoccupied priests and prophets in every age and culture, with eschatological visions of "last things" more often than not succeeded by hopeful fantasies of rehabilitated *first* things. In the Book of Revelation, for instance, after countless torments have been inflicted on the wicked by various angelic horsemen, supernatural beasts, and finally the "KING OF KINGS, AND LORD OF LORDS" Himself (out of whose mouth "goeth a sharp sword that with it he should smite the nations"), the "holy city, new Jerusalem, [comes] down from God out of heaven, prepared *as a bride adorned for her husband* [emphasis added]."

The unveiling of universal annihilation, in other words, is to be followed by the revelation of a marriage between God and the cleansed world whose consummation will produce "a new heaven, and a new earth." Thus those who die in the doomsday slaughter, or anyway the righteous who die in that debacle, can expect to live again in a regenerated space where the tree of life is nourished by "a pure river of water of life" that proceeds "out of the throne of God and of the Lamb."[20] For just as the apocalyptic "marital stripping of the veiled virgin" leads to her symbolic impregnation with the fruit of the womb that is the new, so in a theological best-case scenario the mass deaths of universal apocalypse quite literally issue in mystical renewals and rebirths. In this respect the structure of apocalyptic thinking parallels the structure of the classic Western pastoral elegy, in which, just as the fertility of spring succeeds the barrenness of winter, so the elegist renews his own powers with thoughts of the sacramental restoration and spiritual transformation of the beloved dead. Indeed, many apocalyptic fantasies could also be defined as *collective* elegies that retrace on a larger scale the pastoral elegy's movement from mourning to reconciliation and renewal.

Well into the twentieth century, even among the often skeptical modernists, the lineaments of such a hopeful apocalyptic plot continued to fascinate a number of writers. In particular, such an imaginative structure haunted both Yeats and Lawrence so persistently that it became a central theme in prose texts the two produced almost simultaneously in the 1920s and in a number of poems associated with those texts. In a sense, in fact, Yeats's *A Vision* and Lawrence's *Apocalypse* have the same name since both titles stress revelation, but in any case the two books have much the same goal: the stripping of veils from the primal scenes and secrets out of which time itself, as we humans experience it, is over and over again constituted. Of the two authors, Yeats was more famously an adept of the hermetic wisdom he called "mummy truths," yet Lawrence was also widely read in mystical lore. Indeed both writers could no doubt have taught a thing or two to the late twentieth century's New Age popalyptists. But what most interestingly links these two visionary artists is their yearning sexualization of the apocalyptic moment, a nostalgic strategy that evokes the etymology of *apo-kalyptos*: the unveiling of the bride who is in a sense a kind of angel of history.

To be sure, the symbolic bride imagined by Yeats and Lawrence is largely oblivious of her power even though she is so potent that she gives birth to a new history. Lawrence introduced her in *Apocalypse*, a commentary on the Book of Revelation that was also a meditation on history. Quoting from Revelation 12:1–7, he declares that the following passage, which he defines as a "pagan birth-myth," is "really the pivot of the Apocalypse":

> *And there appeared a great wonder in heaven; a woman clothed with the sun, and the moon under her feet, and upon her head a crown of twelve stars: and she being with child cried, travailing in birth, and pained to be delivered.*

> *And there appeared another wonder in heaven; and behold a great red dragon . . . and the dragon stood before the woman . . . [and] she brought forth a man child . . . [and] there was war in heaven.*

"This wonder-woman clothed in the sun and standing upon the crescent of the moon," Lawrence continues, is "splendidly suggestive of the great goddess of the east, the great mother" who looms so "far back in history" to the days of matriarchy that it is very likely "the existing Apocalypse" was founded on "a book of her 'mystery'" coupled with the mystery of that "other wonder," the "Dragon." And if the mother goddess's mystery is that of the womb, the dragon's is that of the phallus, for coiling "within us potent and waiting, like a serpent," the dragon "is "the great vivifier, the great enhancer of the whole universe."[21]

That the confrontation between wonder-woman and wonder-dragon is basically a primal scene is implicit in both Lawrence's own narrative and the episode from Revelation that he excerpts, in which the mystical mother travails while the "great red dragon" "stands" before her. And that this primal scene of generation, *degeneration*, and ultimately *regeneration* moves history itself is a point the author explicitly stresses. "The long green dragon with which we are so familiar on Chinese things is the dragon in his good aspect of life-bringer, life-giver, life-maker, vivifier," Lawrence comments, while "the red dragon is the great 'potency' of the cosmos in its hostile and destructive activity." Moreover, the green dragon "becomes with time the red dragon. . . . The god of the beginning of an era is the evil principle at the end of that era. For time still moves in cycles [and the] good potency of the beginning of the Christian era is now the evil potency of the end."[22]

Whether or not Lawrence meant to echo Yeats's "The Second Coming," the Yeatsian parallels in this cyclical view of history are striking.[23] Striking too is the parallel between, on the one hand, Lawrence's version of the confrontation between mystical mother and phallic dragon and, on the other hand, the primal scene between Zeus and Leda that Yeats summarizes in "Leda and the Swan" and includes in *A Vision* as one among a long set of events that the poet considered symbolic turning points in history, in particular the recurrent annunciations defined in the chapter of *A Vision* titled "Dove or Swan?" Lawrence's own verse underscores these parallels, for although Yeats's "Leda and the Swan" is perhaps *the* anthology piece through which this myth is transmitted to contemporary readers, Lawrence too produced a series of Leda poems, along with an erotic painting that became a scandalous cause célèbre.

In meditating on the apocalyptic potential in the coupling of a brutal god—a (superhuman) god incarnated in a (subhuman) creature—with a human female, both poets were working with an iconographic tradition that was particularly absorbing to artists during the last fin de siècle. But as Yeats and Lawrence indicated, both were conscious of their departures from a genre that by the time they embarked on their verses had become more decadent than reverent. Recalling that he had been asked by "the editor of a political review" to produce a poem on current events, Yeats reported: "I thought, 'Nothing is now possible but some movement from above preceded by some violent annunciation.' My fancy began to play with Leda and the Swan for metaphor . . . but as I wrote, bird and lady took such possession of the scene that all politics went out of it." Similarly, Lawrence began his series with a brief truculent poem entitled "Religion," arguing for the authoritative structures of patriarchal religion ("Life is nothing without religion / and religion nothing without the father of all things / stooping over his bride"). But the way they had for Yeats, "bird and lady" quickly "took possession of the scene," as the poet became enthralled by his own gaze at an apocalyptic sexual encounter.[24]

That like Yeats, Lawrence associated his vision of "the father of all things / stooping over his bride" with the possibility of a postapocalyptic new earth becomes clear in "The Spiral Flame," the last poem of his Leda/swan series, in which he not only assimilates the swan's potency into all (human) men but also implies a linguistic connection between the encounter of wonder-dragon with wonder-woman and that of "bird and lady." Stressing a key word he uses in *Apocalypse* to characterize the potency of the (good) dragon—"the life-bringer" or "*vivifier* [emphasis added]"—he declares here that the traditional Christian God, along with His Graeco-Roman precursors, is dead, but that a humanized godly energy "is a vivifier" that promises renewal: there is "a swan-like flame that curls round the centre of space," and "the same flame that fills us with life, it will dance and burn the house down, / all the fittings and elaborate furnishings."[25]

Perhaps it was because of such meditations on the sexualized renewal associated with apocalypse that in "Bavarian Gentians," one of the strongest of Lawrence's *Last Poems*, this writer sees an episode of apocalyptic (re)generation as a source of personal as well as cultural hope. Mortally ill with tuberculosis, Lawrence was able to confront death's door with a certain serenity because in this poem he imagined guiding himself with the "blue, forked torch" of a Bavarian gentian, oxymoronically described as a "torch-flower of the blue-smoking darkness," into the underworld, where Pluto, the death-god, enfolds as his bride the wonder-woman here named Persephone (though she might as well be called Leda). Then, in one draft of "Bavarian Gentians," Lawrence is transfixed by the illumination that "torches of darkness" shed on this primal scene while in another he imagines himself more intimately involved in the episode—a "wedding guest / at the marriage of the living dark"—and truly, therefore, a member of the wedding that brings the renewal of spring to a wintry world.

Where is this marriage performed if not in the bulb of the gentian that is the core or heart of its new life, out of which fresh roots must descend in the underground awakening and a fresh stem be born in a renewed journey toward light and sight? Wrote the dying Lawrence, in a first, penciled version of the poem, "it is dark / and the door is open / to the depths," adding

> *and all the dead*
> *and all the dark great ones of the underworld . . .*
> *are gathering to a wedding in the [winter] dark*
> *down the dark blue path*[26]

And in "The Ship of Death," another poem he wrote as he lay dying, Lawrence identified not just with a member of the wedding "in the [winter] dark" but with the seed or soul that is the product of that mystical union, a spirit that journeys toward rebirth at a crack of dawn that signals delivery into a renovated history.

Such a birth of the new was an apocalyptic event that preoccupied more than a few other modernists, including T. S. Eliot (whose wise men in "The Journey of the Magi" were transformed by their "cold coming" toward a "Birth" that signified their own death), Wallace Stevens (who dreamed in "Sunday Morning" that "our blood, commingling, virginal, / With heaven" might bring "requital to desire"), and H.D. (who fantasized in *Helen in Egypt* about the birth of a semidivine child to Achilles, son of the "sea-mother" Thetis, and Helen, daughter of Leda and the swan). And at least one of the modernists' mid-century heirs, Dylan Thomas, seems to have tried to maintain the fundamental hopefulness of that tradition in several of his most famous elegiac poems. Written following the World War II German "fire raids" during the 1942 blitz on London, Thomas's "A Refusal to Mourn the Death, by Fire, of a Child in London" and his "Ceremony after a Fire Raid" respond to catastrophic events analogous to the terrorist assault that produced the "burning roof and tower[s]" of the World Trade Center. Of these two poems, "A Refusal to Mourn" is shorter, more straightforward, and more successful in its assertion that there is no need to grieve for the "majesty and burning of the child's death" because she has entered a pastoral and apocalyptic system in which she will be reborn in "the synagogue of the ear of corn":

> Deep with the first dead lies London's daughter,
> Robed in the long friends,
> The grains beyond age, the dark veins of her mother,
> Secret by the unmourning water
> Of the riding Thames.
> After the first death there is no other.[27]

By comparison, the lengthier, more ambitious "Ceremony" is both bombastic and confusing, even though over the years it's been used as a text in choral works by various composers. As in "A Refusal to Mourn," Thomas links the wartime immolation of a child, in this case a newborn infant with "its kneading mouth / Charred on the black breast of the grave," to biblical promises of redemption. But though his poem ends with an invocation to the "masses of the infant-bearing sea," urging them to "Erupt" and "utter forever / Glory glory glory" in the "sundering ultimate kingdom of genesis'

thunder," it isn't clear how this is to happen. Indeed even one of the composers who set the words to music confessed that the poem "took my breath
away" because he was "entranced" by Thomas's language, *where the sound
of a word is often more important than the typical meaning of the word itself*
[emphasis added]." Which is to say, "the sundering ultimate kingdom of
genesis' thunder" doesn't signify a whole lot, even to someone who has
spent a good deal of professional time with it.[28]

And how much, after all, does "A Refusal to Mourn" mean to contemporary readers? More important, are its certainties as certain as they seem?
"After the first death there is no other" was a much-quoted line in Thomas's
lifetime, when he was a sort of rock star on the poetry circuit. But though
he usually pronounced these words with preacherly conviction, and their
proximity to "the long friends"—especially the annually resurrected "grains
beyond age"—is heartening, they grow increasingly ambiguous with
rereading. Is there "no other" death after the "first" one because there is only
(spiritual) *life* after the first (physical) death? Is there "no other" death after
the "first" one because the first wartime death is so horrendous that it
doesn't matter whether anyone else dies? (Try telling that to the mother of
the baby killed in the fire raid!) Or is there "no other" death after the "first"
one because there is *no other life* from which to die after that death? (And
unlike Lazarus, the London child will only once have had to endure the misery of dying?)

The indeterminacy of Thomas's apparently affirmative pronouncement
reminds us that in the face of real-life, real-time apocalypse—what we
might rightly call "apocalypse *now*"—we're mostly at a loss for words that
would help us formulate loss itself. Perhaps merely *imagining* the apocalyptic moment enables the seer to envision annihilation accompanied by
redemption and rebirth, whereas actually *experiencing* a revelation of what
Zizek calls "the destructive Void" as it erupts "through the cobweb of semblances which constitutes our reality" leaves us stunned, dumb, defenseless.

Before the emergency of 9/11, most contemporary writers, along with
other intellectuals, were in any case at sea on the "horizonless" waters of
postmodernity, a state that left us far closer to that bleak *premodernist*
Thomas Hardy than to such visionary modernists as Yeats and Eliot. In his
nihilistic "The Darkling Thrush," drafted on December 31, 1900, Hardy
entered the twentieth century gazing at a landcape that seemed "the Century's corpse outleant," a field in which the "ancient pulse of germ and birth
/ Was shrunken hard and dry." Ironically noting the "happy good night air"
of an aged thrush, the poet wondered if there "trembled" through that song

some "blessed Hope, whereof he knew / And I was unaware." If we change the rhetoric a little here—make it rather more parodic, more affectlessly aware of the quotidian banality shaping what Hardy elsewhere called "life's little ironies"—how easily such estrangement from "blessed Hope" might speak for an age in which the Madonna who was once a mother goddess had become a media queen named "Madonna"-in-quotation-marks, while Leda-and-the-swan had devolved into parts of a costume once worn to a Hollywood party by yet another media queen, Marlene Dietrich.[29]

For after all, as it's hardly necessary to note, modernist predictions of apocalypse had *already* come true by mid-century—true in the firestorms of the Second World War in Europe that inspired Thomas's ambiguities but also true in the fiery furnaces of Auschwitz and Dachau, and true too in the holocausts of Hiroshima and Nagasaki. And the multiplying deaths of all those cataclysms together were followed, for decades, by silence and denial; what had happened was not only horrible to contemplate but impossible to formulate. If there was an angel, an icon of the sacred, who presided over this history, such a figure certainly did not descend "from God out of heaven, prepared as a bride" offering renewal. Rather, this angel of history was the avatar of accumulated despair whom the cultural critic and theorist Walter Benjamin described in an excruciating little allegory based on an image in a painting by Paul Klee (*Angelus Novus*).

Lately, this passage from Benjamin's "Theses on the Philosophy of History" has been often and justly evoked as an image of contemporary powerlessness beneath the burden of proliferating calamities known as "history." Unlike the bride or "nymph" of *apokalyptos*/apocalypse, Benjamin's version of Klee's angel is male, and he has his face "turned toward the past":

> [But where] we perceive a chain of events, he sees one single catastrophe which keeps piling wreckage upon wreckage and hurls it in front of his feet. The angel would like to stay, awaken the dead, and make whole what has been smashed. But a storm is blowing from Paradise; it has got caught in his wings with such violence that the angel can no longer close them.
>
> This storm irresistibly propels him into the future to which his back is turned, while the pile of debris before him grows skyward. This storm is what we call progress.[30]

As a figure of historical knowledge, therefore, this backward-facing angel is hopeless and helpless, virtually paralyzed, yet all too conscious not only of his own powerlessness but also of all that has (inexorably) happened and is happening.

Nor can he speak of what he has seen and what he continues to see, for what he sees, over and over again, is the seemingly interminable reiteration of a nil—a "destructive Void" or "hole in the Real"—that, following 9/11, came to be called Ground Zero.

GROUND ZERO

The phrase "ground zero" wasn't, of course, coined to describe the yawning pit left by the collapse of the twin towers. Rather, as dictionary definitions stress, it originally referred to the "site directly below, directly above, or at the point of detonation of a nuclear weapon." Thus, as the critic Richard Stamelman reminds us, in "its original designation as a place of complete and devastating destruction and injury, 'ground zero' was site-specific, and that site was atomic and Japanese"; indeed in some sense the phrase came to represent what was also called the atomic age. Inevitably, therefore, our use of the phrase "ground zero" to describe the destruction of the World Trade Center evokes, "either consciously or unconsciously, those wastelands of total ruination that newsreels and photographs of Hiroshima (and Nagasaki, three days later) have embedded in our visual memories" so that, as Stamelman goes on to observe, the "image of the earlier disaster lies behind the later event like a ghostly, tragic presence." Appropriately, indeed, Stamelman uses Benjamin's allegory of the angel of history to illuminate the weight of association that burdens us. "In Benjamin's terms," he comments, "the wreckage of one catastrophe has yet again been piled atop that of another. The ruins of the two events lie fused together, their fragments intermingled in the same debris field of history."[31]

At the same time, though, the phrase "ground zero" has a resonance that goes beyond the accretions of historical meaning provided by the violent events in Hiroshima, Nagasaki, and New York with which it's been specifically linked. For the words "ground zero" literally signify a fundamental emptiness, a core of nothingness, a grounding in a (or *the*) void. Thus if "ground zero" opens a door into the nihilism of a death that leads to the nowhere of extinction rather than the somewhere of an apocalyptic rebirth, we shouldn't be surprised that it also evacuates coherent speech, at least temporarily. For in its way "ground zero" summarizes the apocalypse that the twentieth century most dreaded, the one so many thinkers awaited, if not in fear and trembling, at least with averted eyes.

Archibald MacLeish dramatized this revelation of ultimate emptiness in a widely anthologized sonnet entitled "The End of the World," in which what he depicted as the trivial carnival caperings of modern life are suddenly and finally interrupted by an apocalypse that is the very opposite of the transformative event envisioned by St. John:

> Quite unexpectedly, as Vasserot
> The armless ambidextrian was lighting
> A match between his great and second toe,
> And Ralph the lion was engaged in biting
> The neck of Madame Sossman while the drum
> Pointed, and Teeny was about to cough
> In waltz-time swinging Jocko by the thumb—
> Quite unexpectedly the top blew off:
>
> And there, there overhead, there, there hung over
> Those thousands of white faces, those dazed eyes,
> There in the starless dark the poise, the hover,
> There with vast wings across the canceled skies,
> There in the sudden blackness the black pall
> Of nothing, nothing, nothing—nothing at all.

But Ernest Hemingway too, among many other modernists, articulated this belief in the "black pall" or "ground zero" of emptiness, outlining its parodic creed from the perspective of a café waiter in "A Clean, Well-Lighted Place" who muses that his sense of the terrible hollowness of things wasn't a feeling of "fear or dread." Rather, "It was a nothing that he knew too well. It was all a nothing and a man was a nothing too. . . . Some lived in it and never felt it but he knew it all was nada y pues nada y nada y pues nada. Our nada who art in nada, nada be thy name thy kingdom nada thy will be nada in nada as it is in nada. . . . Hail nothing full of nothing, nothing is with thee." That both "The End of the World" and "A Clean, Well-Lighted Place" were written in 1926, in the same post–World War I decade when Yeats and Lawrence were contemplating more hopeful versions of the Book of Revelation, suggests the density of the philosophical darkness against which A Vision and Apocalypse struggled to set fantasies of rebirth.[32]

But what Jean Paul Sartre was going to call la nausée, the illness triggered by the nothingness that haunts being, would intensify in the course of

the next few decades. Although Benjamin's parable tells us that his helplessly staring angel is gazing at all history in the form of "one single catastrophe which keeps piling wreckage upon wreckage," the violence and
velocity with which such wreckage accumulates appear to have escalated
exponentially in the twentieth century, so much so that the traumas confronting countless real, human onlookers became increasingly unspeakable.

In a lecture series on "Air War and Literature" that he delivered in
Zurich before his death, W. G. Sebald mused on the vast silence with which
most Germans responded to the "devastation suffered by the cities of Germany in the last years of the Second World War"—a silence, ironically
enough, analogous to the silence which long surrounded the terrible facts
of the European Holocaust. Declared Sebald, even the so-called "literature
of the ruins" produced by some postwar German writers "proves on closer
inspection to be an instrument already tuned to individual and collective
amnesia . . . a means of obscuring a world that could no longer be presented
in comprehensible terms." And where eyewitnesses to, say, the firebombing
of Dresden or Hamburg did describe their experiences, he added, they "often
resorted" to clichés whose function must have been to "neutralize experiences beyond our ability to comprehend," for the "death by fire within a few
hours of an entire city" inevitably caused "paralysis of the capacity to think
and feel in those who have succeeded in escaping."

Writing more than half a century after these events, Sebald himself
undertook to find unflinching words with which to describe what happened in the early morning of July 27, 1943, when "ten thousand tons of
high explosive and incendiary bombs were dropped on the densely populated residential area of [Hamburg] east of the Elbe," creating a "firestorm
of an intensity that no one would ever before have thought possible":

> The fire, now rising two thousand meters into the sky, snatched oxygen
> to itself so violently that the air currents reached hurricane force, resonat-
> ing like mighty organs with all their stops pulled out at once. The fire
> burned like this for three hours. At its height, the storm lifted gables and
> roofs from buildings, flung rafters and entire advertising billboards through
> air, tore trees from the ground and drove human beings before it like living
> torches. [The flames] rolled like a tidal wave through the streets. . . .The
> water in some of the canals was ablaze. The glass in the tram car windows
> melted; stocks of sugar boiled in the bakery cellars. . . . No one knows for
> certain how many lost their lives that night, or how many went mad before
> they died.[33]

How uncannily the astonishment voiced in Sebald's description of this firestorm "no one would ever before have thought possible" anticipates the rhetoric of amazement with which DeLillo describes the collapse of the World Trade Center as an unspeakable event that was "outside imagining" yet "real, punishingly so": "But when the towers fell. When the rolling smoke began moving downward, floor to floor. This was so vast and terrible that it was outside imagining even as it happened. We could not catch up with it. But it was real, punishingly so, an expression of the physics of structural limits and a *void in one's soul*, and there was the huge antenna falling out of the sky, straight down, blunt end first, like an arrow moving backwards in time [emphasis added]." Adds DeLillo, the "writer wants to understand what this day has done to us," yet in "its desertion of every basis for comparison, the event asserts its singularity. There is something empty in the sky."[34]

"Is this the promised end? Or image of that horror?" One feels that as both Sebald and DeLillo contemplated the "something empty in the sky" laid bare by the catastrophes of history, they were left with little more than the questions that Kent and Edgar, dumbfounded onlookers to the denouement of *King Lear*, utter in bewilderment as the aged father prays in vain to revive his definitively dead daughter Cordelia.

But it was Cordelia herself, after all, who introduced the theme of nothing and nothingness that permeates what may be Shakespeare's most nihilistic tragedy. Asked to "Speak," she replies that she can say "Nothing," and her father's dire warning to her—"Nothing will come of nothing: speak again"—proves grimly prophetic.[35]

Yet as the alternately awkward and halting responses to the emergency of 9/11 indicate, there comes a time when only silence can speak the truth, as we wait for the "ancient precious / and helpless" words to "say it." Commenting on the "silence fuming at the century's door" that hung over ground zero, the poet Gail Griffin noted that "From here we walk with smoke in our throats," and added what may be the two most crucial questions we can ask: "What story begins here? / What book follows Revelation?"[36]

CLOSURE?

On 9/11/01—a sunny morning in New York, a misty afternoon in Paris, a rainy night in Tokyo—a vast population all around the world stared in disbelief at death's door, which took the form of a glimmering TV screen that swung wide to reveal—what?—"a hole in the Real"? "the destructive Void"? "the black pall / Of nothing, nothing, nothing—nothing at all?"

We wanted the door to close. How we wanted the door to close! We wanted what has come to be called "closure," a term on which mental health professionals frequently pontificate.

"Closure" is what mourners are said to seek, what the ill or dying are thought to need, what victims of crimes and other ugly plots are supposed to require. And we're counseled that "closure" can be achieved through certain actions, sometimes actions undertaken by others in behalf of the wronged and wounded, sometimes undertaken by the bereaved and wronged in their own behalf.

The attorney general claimed to believe that the execution of Timothy McVeigh would bring "closure" to survivors of the Oklahoma City bombings. The president declared that the victims of the attacks on the World Trade Center and the Pentagon might gain "closure"—or at least some comfort—when American planes bombed the caves of the terrorists "back into the Stone Age," or when our troops "took out" Saddam Hussein. Indeed, because a number of fundamentalist apocalypticists associated Baghdad with the ancient Babylon that Revelation defines as the ultimate symbol of evil—and juxtaposed Saddam with Nebuchadnezzar, the ruler of that place—some implied that the "end-time scenario" of 9/11 had to be replaced by a more "redemptive" end-time scenario: "Babylon's prophesied destruction" might come about through the American assault on Iraq! In all these cases, politicians and preachers alike were proposing *public* methods, albeit disconcerting ones, through which they thought it would be possible to achieve group as well as individual "closure."[37]

Others who are more moderate in their strategies nevertheless also believe in "closure," which, they suggest, can be achieved through proper mourning procedures as well as through the development of positive attitudes toward the future. Some grief counselors, perhaps drawing on Freud's "Mourning and Melancholia," prescribe processes that sound almost like group therapy sessions for the living and the dead together, with the living advised to summon up the dead in their wholeness so that they can both forgive and release them while learning to endure life without them. Some mourners, perhaps following such advice, "internalize" the dead, along with the needs and causes the dead might represent, and find "closure" or at least a kind of relief, in speaking *for* those they loved who can no longer speak for themselves. And such methods for gaining "closure" are basically *private* ones, although it might be argued that they often serve collective purposes.

All these various kinds of "closure"—and more—were of course attempted following 9/11. The most immediate signs of public as well as private grief may have been the countless spontaneous shrines that appeared around New York City in the days after the attack, with candles and flowers and teddy bears, a flood of compassionate tokens that even outdid the extraordinary tide of similar memorials that marked the death of Princess Diana. And both within these shrines and in the pages of journals and books that reported on their presence, there were photographs, which seem to have been taken, in response to communal astonishment, to provide perpetual and definitive proof that both the event of 9/11 itself and the "ground zero" it uncovered were really *real*.

Then, almost immediately, there were the reimagined obituaries—the relatively new mode of journalistically eulogizing the dead—that the editors of the *New York Times* called "Portraits of Grief." Each of these was, in essence, a way of transcribing the emblems of individuality that decorated so many spontaneous shrines, and each was dedicated not just to private but to public "closure," or anyway *relief*. If we remember him—how he loved baseball and was a doting father and baked his own pizza on Friday nights—maybe we'll bring some part of him back and appease his ghost, which wishes to be remembered. If we remember *her*—her aspirations, her recipes, her hobbies and blessings—won't we bring some part of her back while appeasing her ghost, which longs to forget the ground zero of death?

DeLillo wrote with a certain bemusement about the "artifacts on display" in the "improvised memorials," observing that they "represent the confluence of a number of cultural tides, patriotic and multidevotional and retro hippy." Yes, and twenty-first century. For though the usual official services took place in the Washington Cathedral and Westminster Abbey and other great spaces of public worship around the world, it was these "improvised memorials," these spontaneous shrines to personhood rather than to godhood, that really spoke for the needs of a cultural sensibility that no longer unites to find consolation in traditional religious structures.

And did we—they—*anyone* achieve some kind of "closure"? To be sure, as time passed, the event and its shock waves passed too. Grieving widows became advocates for the families of survivors while working to aid investigations of the underlying causes that made "9/11" possible. Other mourners sought to work more generally for "homeland security." Politicians began to turn the wound to their own uses, scapegoating both persons and nations that looked like "terrorists," a term that itself expanded to include people who seemed *other* or *different* in ineffably sinister ways.

But obviously, no matter how we struggle to achieve "closure," death's door didn't close, can't and won't close. Indeed, the truism that death's door is always open has been the argument of this book. Although the Church once closed or at least glamorized that portal, it's now almost always at least ajar. And so we surround it with, as DeLillo put it, the "aromas of candle-wax, roses and bus fumes" as we stare, often transfixed, into emptiness.

Even the winning design for a major memorial to be constructed at the site where the twin towers once stood emphasizes the absence and blank-ness that we now associate with life's end [fig. 27]. Write Michael Arad and Peter Walker, the landscape architects whose design won a contest in which 5, 201 competing plans were entered, "This memorial proposes a space that

27. Michael Arad and Peter Walker: Aerial View of *Reflecting Absence*, design for World Trade Center Memorial (2004).

resonates with the feelings of loss and absence that were generated by the destruction of the World Trade Center. . . . It is located in a field of trees that is interrupted by two large voids containing recessed pools. The pools and the ramps that surround them encompass the footprints of the twin towers. A cascade of water that describes the perimeter of each square feeds the pools with a continuous stream. They are large voids, open and visible reminders of the absence."[38]

Can we say that to stare into these voids is also, at the same time, to stare into some sort of meaning? When light hits the "recessed pools" that are also "large voids," what will the grieving bystander see beyond her own reflection?

The painting by René Magritte that I've used as the frontispiece of this volume offers a glimpse into a glimmering pool or sea of light that suggests a vision not unlike the one that Walker and Arad seem to be delineating. I'm not the first to use Magritte's image to represent a project on modern attitudes toward death, dying, and mourning, so I feel some confidence that my "reading" of the painting will be shared by others.

A door. A sturdily built, ordinary-looking door that's a door into a sea of emptiness—or is it light—or is it sky? A door into indeterminacy. A cloud. A cloud on both sides. A cloud going through the door, but in which direction, in or out? And a golden solid, or is it a beach, a landfall, a kind of Japanese dry garden, into and out of which the door opens, never closes, just opens and opens, with a few tufts of grass on one side—the "wrong" (or is it the "right"?) side.

Would Walt Whitman have thought this door a lucky one, as in "Death is different from what anyone supposed, and luckier"?

Is this the beach on which Sylvia Plath brooded?

Enigmatically, Magritte entitled his painting La Victoire.

And is the victory a triumph of emptiness or a triumph of those who stand on its threshhold? Surely, as we peer through Magritte's frame into a radiant sea of emptiness that streams into infinite distances, we fill it, or allow it to fill itself, with the images and ideas that our own minds provide, depending on where and how we stand.

But even to focus on such a mysterious blank is a struggle. So perhaps Magritte meant to tell us that looking, just *looking*, at this perpetually open door is in itself a victory.

ENDNOTES

Throughout this text, standard titles of collected or selected works will be abbreviated as follows:

Complete (or Collected) Poems: CP
Complete Poems and Prose: CPP
Selected Poems: SP
Selected Letters: SL
Complete Plays: PLAYS
Complete (or Collected) Letters: CL
Leaves of Grass: LG
Complete (or Collected) Short Stories: CSS

Unless otherwise noted, all dictionary references are to the *American Heritage Dictionary,* 4th edition.

PREFACE: A MATTER OF LIFE AND DEATH

1. Bataille, p. xxxii.
2. "A Valediction Forbidding Mourning," Donne, pp. 44–45.
3. Lewis, *A Grief Observed,* pp. 12–13.
4. For books by these authors, see the bibliography, p. 525. The field of death studies has also of course produced professional journals (e.g., *Omega: The Journal of Death and Dying*), at least one book series (the Springer Series on Death and Dying), and a number of Web sites, including www.thanatology .org.
5. "Rolling thunder": see Cronin.

CHAPTER 1: DEATH OPENS

1. On "All Souls' Day" and "double sight," see Durdin-Robertson.
2. Barley, p. 87.
3. Schnell, "A Lament," p. 9.
4. Croce, pp. 22–24, quoted in R. Harrison, p. 55; D. Collins, p. 55. On the wish "to die with our dead," Harrison also offers a more general speculation, remarking that the "obligation conveyed by grief is that of self-mortalization. To mortalize oneself means to learn how to live as a dying creature or better, to learn how

to make of one's mortality the foundation of one's relations to those who live on, no less than to those who have passed away" (p. 71).

5. See Austin.

6. Gonzalez-Crussi, pp. 68–70, passim, and on Aztec custom, pp. 46–52, especially p. 45 on the goddesses who represent creation and destruction: "Coatlicue, meaning 'she of the skirt of serpents,' Cihuacoatl, or 'woman of the viper,' and Tlazolteotl, or 'goddess of filth.'" For comparable "festivals of the dead" in Japan and Corsica, see Ozeki, "A Vacation with Ghosts": "during Obon the spirits of the dead walked among us and the living raised red lanterns to guide them"; and Sebald, *Campo Santo*: "Remembrance of the dead never really came to an end. Every year on All Souls' Day a table was especially laid for them in Corsican houses, or at least a few cakes were put out on the windowsill ... since it was thought that they visited in the middle of the night to take a morsel of food" (p. 29).

7. See the *Catholic Encyclopedia*.

8. Lawrence, *Letters*, vol. I: 1901–13, p. 199.

9. Plath, "Little Fugue," *CP*, p. 188.

10. See "When Lilacs Last in the Dooryard Bloom'd," *LG*, p. 335.

11. Baudrillard, p. 141; and for Baudrillard the "primitive" also sees the converse as true, blurring the distinction even further: "the double is the familiar living figure of the dead." See also Freud's comment that "it was beside the dead body of someone he loved that [man] invented spirits" ("Thoughts for the Times") and Redfield's comment that in the *Iliad*, "Between death and burning, the dead is in a liminal condition. . . . He is decaying, yet he is clung to; his mourners thus enter the liminal realm with him [and] share his death" (p. 181).

12. As if echoing and revising Baudrillard, R. Harrison notes, "In its perfect likeness of the person who has passed away, the corpse withholds a presence at the same time as it renders present an absence," and thus "there is nothing more dynamic than a corpse" (pp. 92–93). In contrast, consider Kristeva's claim that the "corpse, seen without God and outside of science[,] is the utmost of abjection" and this is, according to Schwenger, because it is "the body become wholly waste, wholly associated with the vulnerability and decay of its coherence"; see Kristeva, p. 4, and Schwenger, p. 399.

13. "The Bride," Lawrence, *CP*, p. 101. In the short story "Odour of Chrysanthemums" the stripped corpse of a young miner, "lying in the naive dignity of death," leaves his mother and wife "arrested in fear and respect," while in *Sons and Lovers*, Gertrude Morel, the protagonist's mother (based on Lawrence's own mother), appears "like a girl asleep and dreaming of her love": Lawrence, *CSS*, p. 299; *Sons and Lovers*, p. 399.

14. Barley, p. 30.

15. Sebald, *Austerlitz*, p. 54.

16. Yeats, *CP*, p. 331.

17. Lawrence, *CP*, pp. 232–33.

18. Gonzalez-Crussi, p. 70–71.

19. Stanley and Simon, p. A-7.

20. Henderson, p. 65.

21. "How you call to me": see Hardy, "The Voice," *CP*, p. 346; on Emma's "great going," see "The Going," *CP*, pp. 338–39; on talking with "Shades," see "I Have Lived with Shades," *CP*, pp. 184–85; on relativity and the dead, see Hardy, *Life and Work*, p. 417. I am grateful to Marit J. MacArthur for directing me to Hardy's comment about Einstein's theory of relativity.

22. *Hamlet*, I, 4: 68–70; Plath, *CP*, pp. 222–24. For an unusually fine discussion of Hamlet's interaction with his father's ghost, see Greenblatt. For a more general discussion not only of *Hamlet* but of ritual mourning as the basis of tragedy, see S. Cole: "The grave is the birthplace of tragic drama and ghosts are its pro-creators. For tragedy is the performance of [a kind of] ambivalence which ghosts emblematize . . . the revenant [whom we fear also represents] what we desire—the extending of life beyond the moment of death" (p. 9).

23. Hardy, *CP*, p. 349.

24. Lawrence, *Sons and Lovers*, p. 420.

25. Lawrence, *CP*, pp. 108–09.

26. Ibid., pp. 114–15.

27. Ibid., p. 134.

28. Ibid., p. 134.

29. Hardy, *CP*, pp. 345–46.

30. Rossetti, "The Blessed Damozel," p. 234. On "The Raven," see Caine, p. 284. For an ambitious overview of prosopopoeia as a strategy for giving voice to the dead, see Fuss, pp. 1–30; noting that by "corpse poem I mean poetry not about the dead but spoken by the dead," Fuss claims, "I have uncovered not a single poem in which a poet ventriloquizes the voice of a deceased parent, child, sibling, lover, or friend," a claim that, curiously, overlooks such works of prosopopoeia as Hardy's "Haunter" and Rossetti's "Blessed Damozel."

31. The hot darkness "down there" that Beloved describes is also often understood to refer to the hold of a slave ship packed with the traders' sick and dying booty, but the ambiguity of her account is telling. This revenant has, after all, literally risen from a grave marked by the single word "Beloved" and only figuratively from the slave ship in which her agony was originally conceived.

32. Freud, "Mourning and Melancholia," pp. 165–66.

33. Lawrence, "Everlasting Flowers: For a Dead Mother," *CP*, p. 227.

34. Song of Songs 8:6–7. For this translation, see *New American Bible*, p. 678.

35. Henderson, p. 189.

36. Barley, p. 31.

CHAPTER 2: WIDOW

1. *Henry V*, II, iv, 15–17.

2. Sandra Gilbert, "After a Death," *Kissing the Bread*, p. 301. The evasiveness of this poem's title recently struck me ("After *a* Death") as if for me my father's death was somehow no more special than any other demise.

3. Plath, *CP,* pp. 164–65.

4. Ibid., pp. 172–73.

5. Barley, p. 31.

6. Perhaps, Plath implies, *all* death is a form of the limbo that Coleridge described in a poem of that name, a chilly realm that "frightens Ghosts, as here Ghosts frighten men." (See "Limbo" [1817], pp. 429–31). At the same time, in a passage that may have haunted Plath as she drafted her eerie lines about the soul of the dead man, Coleridge offers a more positive vision of the gaze toward emptiness, describing the invisible "moonlight on the dial of the day" as something that is like a blind "Old Man with a steady look sublime" whose "eyeless face [is] all eye" as "He seems to gaze at that which seems to gaze on him!"

7. For "feme covert," see Blackstone, p. 442.

8. W. C. Williams, *CP,* vol. 1, p. 171.

9. Narasimhan, pp. 36, 40.

10. Harlan, p. 85.

11. Ibid., p. 81.

12. Cited and discussed in Figueira, p. 64.

13. Holst-Warhaft, *Dangerous Voices,* pp. 1–2. For my argument on the engendering of ceremonial elegy, see chapter 12 ("Was the Nineteenth Century Different, and Luckier?") of this volume along with Sandra Gilbert, "American Sexual Poetics," pp. 143–48. For a different view of "death, sexuality, and the changing shapes of elegy," see Zeiger, passim.

14. Lewis, *A Grief Observed,* pp. 1, 38.

15. See Gewanter; this illuminating essay also shows how thoroughly absorbed the poet was in a dialogue with his dead wife's journals, both a "diabolical," angry diary, entitled "What I Think of My Husband," and a more "breathless and sentimental memoir," entitled "Some Recollections" (pp. 193–94 and passim.)

16. Beckett, *Krapp's Last Tape,* p. 18.

17. Holst-Warhaft, *Dangerous Voices,* p. 46.

18. Holst-Warhaft is here drawing on work done by anthropologists Anna Caraveli-Chaves and Nadia Seremetakis, who have studied women's laments on the Greek island of Mani (pp. 45–46). Later, in a discussion of "The Ritual Nature of Ancient Lament," she notes that evidence for "the differing behaviour of men and women during the *prosthesis* [wake] and at the tomb comes from a limited but persuasive combination of archaeological and literary sources. In vase paintings, men are rarely depicted close to the body, but appear in formal procession with right arms raised in a conventional gesture of mourning. Around the bier of the dead man, whose head is clasped by the chief mourner, the women stand, their arms raised, sometimes beating their heads, or pulling out their hair in what [one analyst] refers to as 'wild ecstasy.'" For another analysis of such ritual lamentation, see R. Harrison's discussion of Ernesto de Martino's *Morte e pianto rituale* (Turin: Bollati Boringhieri, 1975), pp. 56–65.

19. Holst-Warhaft, *Dangerous Voices,* p. 47.

20. Ibid., pp. 7–8; I give the poem in the translation that Holst-Warhaft uses (by Eilis Dillon) because it's much the strongest version I've encountered.
21. Gallagher, p. 5.
22. Stone, *Cheap*, p. 14.
23. See Praz, pp. 123–24, 178, n. 80. In some circumstances, the grief-stricken widow can also become a vengeful figure; in the Russian-Chechen conflict, "women known as 'black widows'" became suicide bombers in order to avenge "the deaths of husbands, brothers or sons"; see Myers, p. 1.
24. Wilde, p. 36.
25. Kingston, p. 122.
26. Stevens, *CPP*, pp. 431–32.
27. Lowell, *SP*, pp. 17–18.

Chapter 3: Yahrzeit

1. For Jewish mourning customs and ceremonies, see Kurlander. For a good discussion of comparable mourning rituals in other cultures and their relationship to tragedy, see S. Cole, pp. 9–28.
2. Jewish mourning: see Louchheim.
3. Lawrence, *CP*, pp. 716–20. For an overview of funeral customs, see Barley, and for a diverting account of funeral foods and feasts for the living as well as the dead, see Rogak.
4. That the anniversary of a death or loss is widely considered significant comes into focus in Maya Lin's discussion of her fight to order the names of the Vietnam dead chronologically (by death or "missing" date) rather than alphabetically; Lin notes her conviction that "the time in which an individual was noted as missing was the emotionally compelling time for family members"; see Lin, p. 4, section 13.
5. Lawrence, *CP*, pp. 280–81.
6. *The American Heritage Dictionary* gives these two definitions of "epitaph": "1. An inscription on a tombstone or monument in memory of the one or ones buried there. 2. A brief literary piece summarizing or epitomizing a deceased person." It adds that "tomb" is derived from the Indo-European *dhemb*, meaning (as *ghrebh* does) "to bury." For a useful discussion of "the connection between the epitaph and writing in general" as well as a survey of epitaphic writing and its Romantic associations, see Fry, pp. 413–34. For a useful, historical "archaeology" of gravestones and the mourning practices they embody, see Tarlow.
7. Hallam, Tennyson's closest friend at Cambridge and the fiancé of the poet's sister Emily, died in Vienna on September 15, 1833, at the age of twenty-two. Of *In Memoriam*, Tennyson was to explain that the "sections were written at many different places, and as the phases of our intercourse came to my memory and suggested them. I did not write them with any view of weaving them into a whole, or for publication, until I found that I had written so many. . . . After the Death of A. H. H., the divisions of the poem are made by First Xmas Eve (Sec-

tion XXVIII.), Second Xmas (LXXVIII.), Third Xmas Eve (CV. And CV. Etc)." (Quoted in H. Tennyson, vol. 1, pp. 304–05.)

8. A. Tennyson, *Poems,* p. 239 ("Behind the veil"), pp. 243–44 ("When on my bed"). For a comparably moving and eerie transcription of an epitaphic vision, see Hardy's late, beautiful "Lying Awake," which concludes with a similar vision of dawn over markings of death, in this case multiple gravestones: "You, Morningtide Star, now are steady-eyed, over the east, / I know it as if I saw you; / You, Beeches, engrave on the sky your thin twigs, even the least; / Had I paper and pencil I'd draw you. // You, Meadow, are white with your counterpane cover of dew, / I see it as if I were there; / You, Churchyard, are lightening faint from the shade of the yew, / The names creeping out everywhere."

9. H. Tennyson, vol. 1, p. 305.

10. A. Tennyson, *Poems,* p. 289.

11. Tennyson himself pointed out to his longtime friend John Knowles that *In Memoriam* "begins with a funeral and ends with a marriage—begins with death and ends with promise of a new life" (Knowles, p. 164).

12. Even the verb "rocks" in the phrase "The blind wall rocks" seems for a moment ambiguous; on first reading, it's not quite clear that "rocks" is a verb rather than a noun describing the substance ("rocks") of which the "blind wall" is made. In that case, the "blind wall" wouldn't be rocking like a cradle, it would be a modifier of the noun "rocks," reinforcing the inaccessibility of the dead in a kind of redundant heaping up of words for imperviousness.

13. Frost, p. 221.

14. On the historic terror of living burial, a terror that became especially intense during the nineteenth century, see Bondeson. In a curious way, the so-called locked-in syndrome suffered by some victims of strokes and other brain injuries also dramatizes this terror; see, for instance, Bauby's classic account of his experience. In the eighteenth and nineteenth centuries, a slew of books and pamphlets fostered the fear of "premature interment." See, for instance, William Hawes, *Address on Premature Death and Premature Interment* (1777); Joseph Taylor, *The Danger of Premature Interment* (1816), Walter Whiter, *Treatise on the Disorder of Death* (1817); and John Snart, *Thesaurus of Horror; or, The Charnel House Explored* (1817). I am grateful to Kerry Hanlon for pointing me toward much of this material. Her 2004 University of California at Davis dissertation, "Antigone's Wake," offers a fine survey of the theme of living burial.

15. Hardy, *CP,* pp. 341, 42.

16. "Full fathom five": *The Tempest,* I, ii, 329–34; "Ah, cannot . . .": Millay, p. 290.

17. Brontë, *Gondal's Queen,* p. 126.

18. Eliot, "Burnt Norton," *Four Quartets,* p. 13; Wright, pp. 282–84.

19. Donald Hall, pp. 53, 55, 76.

20. Ibid., pp. 54, 74, 77.

21. Ibid., p. 61.

22. Ibid., p. 62.

23. Shelley, p. 550; Yeats, *CP,* pp. 325–28; Gay, "My Own Epitaph," p. 253; "Master Elginbrod," quoted by Mitford, *American Way of Death Revisited,* p. 138. The notes of irony, even comedy, struck by Gay and "Master Elginbrod" reappear on the twenty-first-century Internet in the Web site designed by one Lance Hardie, who claims to be the "creator of *Plan Your Epitaph Day,*" which "occurs every year on November 2 to coincide with the *Day of the Dead*" and is devoted to the proposition that a "*forgettable gravestone is a fate worse than death,*" so you shouldn't "give up your power over the most important words of your life. Take control: it's *your* life, it's *your* death, it's *your* stone—*YOU* say something!" (Emphases Hardie's; see Hardie).

24. Dyer, in Washington, p. 101.

25. Olds, pp. 54–55.

26. Hughes, *Moortown,* p. 159.

CHAPTER 4: E-MAIL TO THE DEAD

1. Sandra Gilbert, *Kissing the Bread,* p. 59.

2. Kipling, *Selected Stories,* p. 145.

3. Kipling, *Verse,* p. 560

4. Stevens, *CPP,* pp. 445–47; Donald Hall, pp. 63–64.

5. A. Tennyson, *Poetry,* p. 214.

6. Ibid., pp. 215–16.

7. "Death's Door": Gunn, pp. 82–83; "Freedom of Speech": Hughes, *Birthday Letters,* p. 192.

8. Yeats, *Plays,* pp. 433.

9. See Poe, p. 414. In one of the author's most famous passages, the narrator of this tale describes Ligeia's horrifying resurrection: "[T]he thing that was enshrouded advanced boldly and palpably into the middle of the apartment. . . . Shrinking from my touch, she let fall from her head, unloosened, the ghastly cerements which had confined it, and there streamed forth, into the rushing atmosphere of the chamber, huge masses of long and disheveled hair; it was blacker than the raven wings of the midnight! And now slowly opened the eyes of the figure which stood before me. 'Here then, at least,' I shrieked aloud, 'can I never—can I never be mistaken—these are the full, and the black, and the wild eyes—of my lost love—of the lady—of the LADY LIGEIA.'"

10. Brontë, *Wuthering Heights,* p. 27

11. Keats, p. 365; Whitman, p. 194.

12. See R. Gilbert, "From Anxiety to Power," a far more nuanced and detailed reading of the work than I am offering here.

13. Doyle., p. 54.

14. Ibid., pp. 84, 91, 93, 95–96.

15. Ibid., pp. 71, 96. In the Bible, declared Doyle, "which is the foundation of our present religious thought, we have bound together the living and the dead, and the dead has tainted the living. A mummy and an angel are in most unnatural

partnership. There can be no clear thinking, and no logical teaching until the old dispensation has been placed on the shelf of the scholar, and removed from the desk of the teacher. [The Bible] is indeed a wonderful book [but] it has no connection with modern conceptions of religion" (p. 16).

16. See the Society for Psychical Research Web site. Former presidents, the Web page boasts, prove the "interdisciplinary nature of [the society's] subject matter," for they include philosophers (Henri Bergson), psychologists (William James), physicists (Sir William Crookes), a physiologist and Nobel laureate (Charles Richet), a classicist (Gilbert Murray), and even a prime minister of England (A. J. Balfour). To be sure, the spiritualist enterprise has also continued to be of great interest in popular culture, not only through the writings of, say, the telegenic spiritualist James Van Praagh but also in more informal circles. Not long ago an "Elvis Séance" was posted on the Internet; it purported to record the responses of "Elvis Presley *Himself*" to a set of questions posed on a homemade Ouija board; see Miles.

17. See Sampson, pp. 46–47; and MacMillan and Brown, pp. 122–25, passim.

18. The American novelist Elizabeth Stuart Phelps had explored that realm in *The Gates Ajar, or, Our Loved Ones in Heaven* (1868), and the British poet Elizabeth Barrett Browning had regularly attended séances, though her husband, Robert, scorned them, satirizing the celebrated Victorian practitioner D. D. Home in his scathing "Mr. Sludge the Medium" (1864).

19. Yeats, *CP*, p. 22.

20. Plath, *CP*, p. 279.

21. On Hughes, see Faas, pp. 214–15; *Sandover:* see Merrill; on modernism and spiritualism more generally, see Sword, passim.

22. Among supportive scientists, Doyle listed "Flammarion and Lombroso, Charles Richet and Russel Wallace, Willie Reichel, Myers, Zollner, James, Lodge, and Crooks" (p. 52). In addition, declaring, "I have never in my thirty years of experience known one single scientific man who went thoroughly into this matter and did not end by accepting the Spiritual solution" (pp. 52–54), he pronounced himself scandalized by the skepticism of such unbelievers as Faraday, Darwin, Huxley, and Spencer: "Faraday declared that in approaching a new subject, one should make up one's mind *a priori* as to what is possible and what is not! Huxley said that the messages, *even if true,* 'interested him no more than the gossip of curates in a cathedral city.' Darwin said: 'God help us if we are to believe such things.' Herbert Spencer declared against it, but had no time to go into it" (pp. 36–37).

23. Ibid., p. 77. "Ectoplasm," Doyle noted, seemed "to possess an inherent quality of shaping itself into parts of the whole of a body, beginning in a putty-like mould and ending in a resemblance to perfect human members" (p. 77), and as for "spirit photography," the "fact that the photograph does not correspond in many cases with any which existed in life, must surely silence the scoffer, though there is a class of bigoted sceptic who would still be sneering if an Archangel alighted in Trafalgar Square" (p. 79). A little more than a decade later, however,

in *Regurgitation and the Duncan Mediumship* (London, 1931), Harry Price, himself a magician and spiritualist, exposed the phenomenon of "ectoplasm" as fraudulent, explaining that many mediums were concealing painted strips of cheesecloth in their mouths or noses and "regurgitating" them during séances. Others who sought to expose the tricks of spiritualists included, perhaps most famously, the conjurer Harry Houdini along with his contemporary John Nevil Maskelyne. Nonetheless, to this day the American Society for Psychical Research maintains a file of "spirit photographs" in its New York City library.

24. Kipling, *Traffics and Discoveries*, p. 233; for the parallels between spiritualism and electronic communication more generally, see Sconce.

25. Kipling, *Traffics and Discoveries*, pp. 239, 226.

26. Donald Hall, p. 77.

27. Ibid., p. 50.

28. Byatt, p. 233. Perhaps worst of all, the bereft Emily senses that in writing *In Memoriam* her brother had somehow usurped both her love and her grief: he "had taken Arthur and bound him to himself, blood to blood and bone to bone, leaving no room for her" (pp. 232, 234). "*In Memoriam* . . .was, she knew and said often, the greatest poem of their time. And yet, she thought in her bursts of private savagery, it aimed a burning dart at her very heart, it strove to annihilate her, and she *felt* the pain of it, and could not speak of that pain to a soul" (p. 233).

29. Ibid., pp. 232, 203, 206, 218.

30. Ibid., pp. 201, 249–50.

31. Ibid., pp. 274, 283.

CHAPTER 5: WRITING WRONG

1. Stone, *Second-Hand Coat*, p. 85.

2. For my efforts at answers to these questions, see the version of this chapter that was published as "Writing/Righting Wrong" in Sharpe. On "broken stories" of medical mistakes, see also Berlinger, passim.

3. E. Gilbert, pp. 121–23.

4. J. Milton, "Lycidas," p. 291.

5. Shelley, p. 432.

6. E. B. Browning, vol. 3, p. 341.

7. Sandra Gilbert, *Wrongful Death*, p. 341. For an incisive discussion of mourning, rage, and "the political uses of grief," see Holst-Warhaft, *Cue for Passion*.

8. Feldman, "The Shape of Mourning," quoted in R. Harrison, pp. 178–79.

9. R. Browning, pp. 616–17.

10. "Art is a lie": quoted in Barr, p. 270. "[A] great Hole in the Heart": see Defoe, p. 99.

11. Pinsky, pp. 34, 36.

12. Benjamin, p. 94.

13. Certeau, p. 46.

14. Felman and Laub, p. 5.
15. Plath, *CP,* pp. 187–89.

CHAPTER 6: EXPIRATION/TERMINATION

1. For Stevens's alleged deathbed conversion, see Brazeau, pp. 294–97. For Pascal's wager, see Pascal, pp. 200–205:

   "God is, or He is not." But to which side shall we incline? Reason can decide nothing here. There is an infinite chaos which separated us. A game is being played at the extremity of this infinite distance where heads or tails will turn up. . . . Which will you choose then? Let us see. Since you must choose, let us see which interests you least. You have two things to lose, the true and the good; and two things to stake, your reason and your will, your knowledge and your happiness; and your nature has two things to shun, error and misery. Your reason is no more shocked in choosing one rather than the other, since you must of necessity choose. . . . But your happiness? Let us weigh the gain and the loss in wagering that God is. . . . If you gain, you gain all; if you lose, you lose nothing. Wager, then, without hesitation that He is.

2. For further discussion of "Madame La Fleurie," see chapter 2, "Widow," of this book.
3. W. C. Williams, *CP,* vol. 1, pp. 346–48.
4. See, e.g., "Cortège for Rosenblum" and "The Worms at Heaven's Gate," in Stevens, *CPP,* pp. 63–64, 40.
5. See Stevens, "The Owl in the Sarcophagus," VI, "This is the mythology of modern death / And these, in their mufflings, monsters of elegy," in Stevens, *CPP,* p. 374. The emphasis on the word "modern" is here added by me. For particularly interesting comments on this poem, see Bloom, *Wallace Stevens,* pp. 281–92.
6. See Certeau, cited in chapter 5 of this volume: "Discourse about the past has the status of being the discourse of the dead."
7. "Cancer Society": Moller, *Confronting Death,* p. vii; "twentieth-century" death as "unmentionable": Alvarez, p. 71, fn.
8. Larkin, "Aubade," *CP,* pp. 208–09; see also (among others) "The Old Fools": "At death, you break up: the bits that were you / Start speeding away from each other for ever / With no one to see" (p. 196). For a comparable formulation from a poet of Larkin's generation, see William Empson's sardonic "Ignorance of Death," in Empson, pp. 29–30: "I feel very blank upon this topic, / and think that though important . . . It is one that most people should be prepared to be blank upon."
9. For more about this scene, see Sandra Gilbert, *Wrongful Death,* pp. 279–309.
10. Larkin, *Further Requirements,* pp. 332–33.
11. "I that in health was and gladness / Am troubled now with great sickness, / And enfeebled with infirmity: / The fear of death dismays me." Dunbar, "Lament for the Makaris" pp. 98–101; Nashe, Ferguson, et al., pp. 254–55; first published in Nashe, *Summers Last Will and Testament* (1600).

12. *Hamlet*, III, 1, 79–80. The Talmud: Quoted in Bloom, *Kabbalah and Criticism*, p. 51; La Rochefoucauld, Maxim 26, pp. 10–11. For further commentary on the Talmudic passage, see Rotman, pp. 72–73, and on La Rochefoucauld, see Ricks, p. 20.

13. Ariès "familiar simplicity," p. 18; the "transition from the Last Judgment to the decisive moment of personal death," p. 112; "continued existence . . . Pauline Christianity," p. 95. Of course, even during the nineteenth-century era when in Britain and America Victorian piety shaped the so-called good death, Nietzsche was speculating on "the death of God" (*Thus Spake Zarathustra*, 1883–1885) and the British essayist Joseph Jacobs published an influential essay on "The Dying of Death" in which he declared that "Death as a motive is moribund" because the "flames of Hell are sinking low, and even Heaven has but poor attractions for the modern man" (p. 264).

14. Nagel, p. 1 fn. For another formulation of this point, by a contemporary journalist, see Henig: "The scariest part about dying, at least to me, is how it ends: with the immutable fact of no longer existing."

15. Huizinga, p. 147.

16. Alvarez, p. 237.

17. Ludolph of Saxony, *Vita Christi*, Part II, ch. 69. I am grateful to C. Abbott Conway for information about this text, which he has transcribed and translated from Ludolphus de Saxonia, *Vita Domini Nostri Iesu Christi* (ed. Jodocus Badius Ascensius. Lyons: Bouillon, 1519). The Latin text, in which Ludolph was himself quoting from a sermon by Leo the Great, more literally translates to

> For the LORD's Resurrection was not the ending, but the changing of the flesh, and His substance was not destroyed by His increase of power. The quality altered, but the nature did not cease to exist: the body was made impassible, which it had been possible to crucify: it was made incorruptible, though it had been possible to wound it. And properly is Christ's flesh said not to be known in that state in which it had been known, because nothing remained possible in it, nothing weak, so that it was both the same in essence and not the same in glory. . . . For that most magnificent body was endued so greatly with the keen, lively, and immortal glory of brilliance so that it might be more resplendent than the sun, displaying a beauty paradigmatic of [that] of the rising human bodies of whom the Saviour himself spoke.

18. When in "Adonais" Shelley calls upon the "breath whose might [he has] invoked in song," he is referring to his evocation of the "correspondent breeze" of inspiration in his shamanistic and revolutionary "Ode to the West Wind"; on this trope for inspiration, see the essay of that title in Abrams, pp. 25–43.

19. Sacks, p. 2. As Sacks argues, consolation, catharsis, and closure are one and the same in the poetics of grief that shapes the traditional elegy. In addition, gathering much previous scholarship on the features of pastoral elegy, Sacks offers a masterful quasi-Freudian analysis of its "use of pastoral contextualization, [of the] myth of the vegetation deity . . . of repetition and refrains, [of] reiterated questions, . . . of vengeful anger or cursing, [of a] procession of mourners, [of

a] movement from grief to consolation, and [of] traditional images of resurrection."

20. Ibid., pp. 2–3. Sacks draws on the work of Alexiou, whose *Ritual Lament* explores this history. But Sacks himself adds that the "funerary function of the flute . . . is widespread, appearing also, for example, in the beliefs and practices of Brazilian Indians" (p. 331).

21. "Whatever Is": Alexander Pope, "An Essay on Man," Epistle I, l.194, p. 15; Russell, pp. 66–67. The complete passage—even more nihilistic in its entirety—reads:

> *That Man is the product of causes which had no prevision of the end they were achieving; that his origin, his growth, his hopes and fears, his loves and his beliefs, are but the outcome of accidental collocations of atoms; that no fire, no heroism, no intensity of thought and feeling, can preserve an individual life beyond the grave; that all the labours of the ages, all the devotion, all the inspiration, all the noonday brightness of human genius, are destined to extinction in the vast death of the solar system, and that the whole temple of Man's achievement must inevitably be buried beneath the debris of a universe in ruins—all these things, if not quite beyond dispute, are yet so nearly certain, that no philosophy which rejects them can hope to stand. Only within the scaffolding of these truths, only on the firm foundation of unyielding despair, can the soul's habitation henceforth be safely built.*

Choron's comparable generalization is based, to begin with, on a discussion of Nietzsche, whose "torment and despair," he argues, are now "known to multitudes. In the innermost recesses of their hearts they know or at least suspect what Zarathustra openly confessed: 'Human life is frightful and still without meaning' ": Choron, pp. 205–06. For more specialized discussions of such thinking, see Demske, and see Agamben, *Language and Death*. For a succinct meditation on the scientific assumptions that underlie these philosophical views, in particular Freud's grim notion that "Life is a tension which seeks to extinguish itself, to 'cancel itself out,' " see Phillips.

22. Becker and Monod are quoted in Roszak, pp. 81–83; Weinberg, pp. 143–44. As early as 1818, however, in *The World as Will and Representation*, Arthur Schopenhauer had definitively formulated a nihilistic philosophy, asserting: "Every breath we draw wards off the death that constantly impinges on us. . . . Ultimately, death must triumph, for by birth it has already become our lot and it plays with its prey only for a short while before swallowing it up. However, we continue our life with great interest and much solicitude as long as possible, just as we blow out a soap-bubble as long and as large as possible, although with the perfect certainty that it will burst" (Schopenhauer, p. 311). I am grateful to Irvin Yalom for calling attention to this passage. For a more recent formulation of scientific atheism, see also, e.g., Dawkins.

23. Beckett, *Waiting for Godot*, p. 58.

24. 1997 *Time*/CNN: see Van Biema, 71–78, passim; Moyers: see "Bill Moyers on Health and the Global Environment"; Lewis, *A Grief Observed*, p. 24. Earlier in

the century the revisionary theologians Paul Tillich and Reinhold Niebuhr had formulated a Christianity in which God/Christ was immanent rather than transcendent, and traditional notions of an "afterlife" had to be reimagined accordingly. As Van Biema notes, even the Catholic Church shelters skeptics. In a recent memoir the theologian Karen Armstrong, a former nun, reports writing an essay in her convent days on "the historicity of the Resurrection" and when she confided her doubts about the factuality of the event to her Mother Superior, the older woman responded, "No, Sister . . . it isn't true. But please don't tell the others"; (see Winner on Armstrong). But for a comparatively recent sociological perspective on these matters, see Wuthnow, passim, whose overview of American spirituality should remind us that there is a significant gap between the skepticism of an educated elite and the belief professed by a majority of U. S. citizens. That there is also such a gap between most Americans and most citizens of "old" Europe has also lately become a journalistic truism.

25. On the afterlife, see Sweeney, p. 124; for "Unarius" and "Coltrane," see Niebuhr, pp. 66–72. On freezing, see the Cryonics Institute Web page with its assurances that "Your Last Best Chance for Life—and Your Family's" lies in its "cryonic suspension services," which are initiated as "soon as possible after legal death, [when] a member patient is prepared and cooled to a temperature where physical decay essentially stops, and is then maintained indefinitely in cryostasis. When and if future medical technology allows, our member patients hope to be healed and revived, and awaken to extended life in youthful good health." Robert C. W. Ettinger, the founder of the organization, also offers here "A Brief History and Overview." See also Ellin for a discussion of the "Timeship" (a site for storage of "cryopreserved" bodies) being designed by the architect Stephen Valentine, and online see *Timeship.*

26. G. Johnson, p. 18.

27. Updike, pp. 71–72; G. Stein, p. 250; Hemingway, p. 379.

28. Nuland, pp. 10, xvi–xvii.

29. Tolstoy, pp. 151, 159.

30. See Scarry on pain as "pre-linguistic," esp. pp. 3–11.

31. Seale, pp. 211, 18–19, 149. Seale also observes: "In particularly debilitating diseases shame at this failure [of the body to sustain its cultural identity] all too easily surfaces since barriers of privacy may be broken in the invasions of intimacy necessary to maintain a leaking decaying body, which mirrors a disintegrating sense of self whose boundaries are increasingly beyond control" (p. 149).

32. Merleau-Ponty, passim; Yeats, "Sailing to Byzantium," *CP,* p. 193; "Death," *CP,* p. 234.

33. Heidegger, "Man dies constantly": *Being and Time,* p. 294; "Only man dies": *Poetry, Language, and Thought,* p. 178. Blanchot, "Literature and the Right to Death," p. 55. For Heidegger, see also R. Harrison, esp. pp. 90–92.

34. Crace, pp. 12, 210; Seltzer, p. 16.

35. Aquinas, *Summa Theologica,* pp. 686–87; Descartes, cited in Coetzee, *Lives of Animals,* p. 33.

36. Coetzee, *Disgrace*, pp. 143, 219.

37. On Pullman, see Lyall, p. 26; for Beau, see Doty, *Atlantis*, p. 63.

38. Dickey, pp. 60–61; Steiner, quoted by Nemerov, p. 191. I am grateful to Roger Gilbert for calling this passage from Steiner to my attention.

CHAPTER 7: TECHNOLOGIES OF DEATH

1. Replansky, pp. 31–32.

2. Heyen, "Blue," *Erika*, pp. 69–70.

3. Wyschogrod, p.1.

4. Norris, p. 2. Noting that "World War I is conservatively estimated to have produced 10 million dead and 20 million wounded," Norris quotes Fussell (*Norton Book of Modern War*, pp. 307–08) on the mass slaughters of World War II: "Killed and wounded were over 78 million people, more of them civilians than soldiers," including six million Jews, one million in the siege of Leningrad, seventy thousand at Hiroshima, thirty-five thousand at Nagasaki, and "the same at Dresden." As for the period after that war, she adds, Ehrenreich "reports an estimated 22 million dead from the 160 wars that have been fought since the end of World War II" (*Blood Rites*, p. 226). About Hiroshima, one of the most singularly dramatic "death events" of the century, Lifton has written, in a statement that parallels Wyschogrod's remarks, that "our perceptions of Hiroshima are the beginnings of new dimensions of thought about death and life" (*Death in Life*, p. 14; quoted in Norris, pp. 29–30).

5. Weinberg, pp. 143–44.

6. Beckett, *Waiting for Godot*, p. 58; on infanticide as an act of kindness, see Todorov, p. 72; on the fate of "the little tyke," Todorov quotes Lengyel, p. 100.

7. On "the combination of the death-world and the technological world as a philosophy of war," Norris quotes Jeffords's analysis of the way "U.S. engagement in the Persian Gulf War moved warfare in the post–Cold War era into a distinctively different and more terrifying phase" (Norris, p. 3, citing Jeffords), but such a combination seems to me to have characterized the twentieth century generally, from the Great War onward.

8. For the conversion of human hair into "industrial felt and thread," see Müller, p. 65; "respected citizen," p. 4.

9. Levi, *Survival in Auschwitz*, p. 29.

10. Agamben, *Homo Sacer*, p. 166.

11. "Life unworthy . . .": ibid., p. 136.

12. Ibid., p. 114.

13. Ibid., pp. 159, 166.

14. Ibid., p. 166.

15. Conrad, pp. 50–51.

16. A "mundane extension": Feingold, pp. 399–400; "Buchenwald was of our West as much as Detroit's River Rouge—we cannot deny Buchenwald as a casual aberration of a Western world essentially sane": Stillman and Pfaff, pp. 30–31; both

quoted in Bauman, *Modernity and the Holocaust,* pp. 8–9, as part of a carefully rea-
soned argument that "every 'ingredient' of the Holocaust . . . was 'normal' not in
the sense of the familiar . . . but in the sense of being fully in keeping with everything we know about our civilization" since in "the Final Solution, the industrial
potential and technological know-how boasted by our civilization has scaled new
heights in coping successfully with a task of unprecedented magnitude."

17. "Rare, yet significant": Bauman, *Modernity,* p. 12; "technological achievement":
ibid., p. 13, quoting C. Browning, p. 148.

18. Müller, p. 40.

19. Bauman, *Modernity,* p. 17.

20. Levi, *Survival,* pp. 26–27.

21. Beauvoir, "Introduction" to *Shoah,* pp. vii–viii, in Lanzmann; Plath, "Getting
There," in *CP,* pp. 247–49.

22. See Kyle, *Spectacles of Death,* passim. See also Kyle, review of Potter and Mattingly, *Life, Death, and Entertainment*: "Bloodshed and death were found
mostly at mass slaughters in beast hunts and staged executions"; "man into a
corpse" (pp. 2, 40). For a slightly different view of the long history of fascination with the "force" that turns a man into a "thing," see Weil: "The true hero,
the true subject matter . . . of the *Iliad* is force. The force that men wield, the
force that subdues men, in the face of which human flesh shrinks back. . . .
Force is that which makes a thing of whoever submits to it" (p. 45). Of course
Weil's essay is as much a meditation on the military force dominating Europe
in the thirties and forties as it is an analysis of the dynamics of force in Homeric Greece.

23. Quoted on the Gravensteen Castle (Ghent, Belgium) Web site. This tourist also
confessed to being especially "sobered" by his "realization that much of the torture meted out was meted out on fellow Christians just because their beliefs
were different from those of other Christians."

24. Kyle, *Spectacles,* p. 53; see also Kyle, review of Potter and Mattingly: such ordeals
were "exhibitions of the imperial government's monopolization of force . . . reassuring acts of social vengeance against persons who had offended societal norms."

25. Fritsch, p. 7. Among many other comments on the possibility or impossibility of
"closure," see this transcript of a report by CNN anchor Bill Hemmer, who covered the execution in Terre Haute, Indiana. Focusing on "a woman named Peggy
Broxterman" whose older son was killed in the Oklahoma City bombing, Hemmer notes: "Through all the sadness and the tears and the pain that we heard
today, Peggy had a smile. It struck me as she told me live on CNN that from the
first day she felt Timothy McVeigh should die, and today she said her wish and
her dream came true."(See Hemmer.) For a sardonic comment on such closure
and the "white noise of an all-American circus" surrounding it, see F. Rich.

26. Agamben, *Homo Sacer,* pp. 154–58. In a further discussion of this issue, Agamben notes that "in the 1920s, [for example,] 800 people held in United States
prisons were infected with malaria plasmodia in an attempt to find an antidote

to paludism [and] . . . [o]utside the United States, the first experiments with cultures of the beriberi bacillus were conducted by R. P. Strong in Manila on persons sentenced to death (the records of the experiment do not mention whether participation in the experiment was voluntary)" (pp. 156–57).

27. Ariès, pp. 29–31, 64. Ariès notes that many people actually lived in the cemetery and "were utterly oblivious to the sight of burial or to the proximity of the large common graves, which were left uncovered until they were full," and adds that the cemetery also "served as a forum, public square, and mall, where all members of the parish could stroll, socialize, and assemble," citing the view of Auguste Bernard, "an expert on [medieval] burial fees," that the cemetery was "'the noisiest, busiest, most boisterous, and most commercial place in the rural or urban community [p. 64].'"

28. See *New Cassell's German Dictionary.*

29. On the names of trenches, see J. Morris, p. 193; for Rutter's poem, see Stephen, pp. 92–93 (from "The Song of Tiadatha"); for the "saturated" landscape, see Leed, p. 20.

30. "Trenches rise up": quoted in Leed, p. 21; "Sodom and Gomorrah . . .": see Owen, January 19, 1917, *Letters;* for Kipling and the travel agent, see Eksteins in Mackaman and Mays, pp. 161–60. As many historians have noted, the Great War had marked not only "the arrival of mass culture, mass politics and mass society" but also the definitive disintegration of the pastoral mode, along with the redemptive visions of resurrection and regeneration that pastoral had traditionally made possible. Neither Lycidas nor Adonais could be reborn in the *city* of death, nor could poets imagine fruitful journeys to "fresh fields and pastures new." (See chapter 13, "'Rats' Alley' and the Death of Pastoral," of this volume.)

31. See N. Frye, p. 150.

32. "Reflections upon War and Death," *Character and Culture,* pp. 109, 113, 124; "MCMXIV," in Larkin, pp. 127–28.

33. "The Painter of Modern Life," in Baudelaire, pp. 9, 11, 13.

34. Nor was it possible for the citizen of this city to consider himself in a Baudelairean sense "away from home" yet "everywhere at home." Rather, as the distinction between front and home front implies, one could never be at home even in what one Canadian balladeer called one's "little wet home in the trench" at the front even while, dislodged from the now radically defamiliarized home front, one could no longer feel at home there either. See Stephen, "Canadian Song," by "Anonymous," p. 107. The whole poem reads:

> There's a little wet home in the trench,
> That the rain storms continually drench,
> A dead cow close by, with her hooves in the sky,
> And she gives off a beautiful stench.
>
> Underneath us, in place of a floor
> Is a mess of cold mud and some straw,

> *And the Jack Johnsons roar as they speed through the air*
> *O'er my little wet home in the trench.*

35. Mackaman and Mays, "Introduction," p. xviii.
36. Cannadine, p. 204. "The heads": Richards, p. 199, quoted in Hynes, *Soldiers' Tale*, p. 69.
37. Jünger, p. 23, quoted in Hynes, *Soldiers' Tale*, p. 67; Eliot, *The Waste Land*, p. 145.
38. Léger, p. 70.
39. Owen, *CP*, p. 55.
40. Cruttwell, pp. 153–54, quoted in Hynes, *Soldiers' Tale*, p. 56.
41. Brittain, p. 423.
42. Müller, pp. 60–61.
43. Steiner, *Bluebeard's Castle*, pp. 53–54.
44. Whether intentionally or not, the following description of "the hell of Auschwitz" evokes traditional Western nightmares of hell, as it has been imagined from Dante onward: "Corpses were strewn all over the road; bodies were hanging from the barbed-wire fence; the sound of shots rang in the air continuously. Blazing flames shot into the sky; a giant smoke cloud ascended above them. Starving, emaciated human skeletons stumbled toward us, uttering incoherent sounds. They fell down right in front of our eyes, and lay there gasping out their last breath" (J. Newman, p. 18; quoted in Des Pres, p. 77). On Auschwitz as anti-city, see Cantor's fine discussion of Alain Resnais's assertion in *Night and Fog* (1955) that the SS "managed to reconstitute the semblance of a real city": "The ordinary becomes horrible—the tracks from our city of the living lead to the camp. The horrible becomes ordinary. The camp becomes a city. Not our city? Perhaps, but not, anymore, *not* our city, either" (p. 27).
45. Levi, *Drowned*, pp. 113–14.
46. Todorov, pp. 160–61. Todorov adds that the "same effect was achieved by forcing the camp inmates to live in their own filth or by subjecting them to a starvation diet that turned them into scavengers, ready to swallow just about anything they found. 'They were no longer men,' [observed one Nazi witness]. 'They'd turned into beasts who thought only about eating.'"
47. Todorov, p. 185, quoting Frank, p. 12.
48. See Wallace.
49. Levi notes that "the Lager's German was a language apart . . . a variant, particularly barbarized, of what a German Jewish philologist, Klemperer, had called *Lingua Tertii Imperii*, the language of the Third Reich, actually proposing for it the acronym LTI with an ironic analogy to the hundred other acronyms (NSDAP, SS, SA, SD, KZ, RKPA, WVHA, RSHA, BDM, etc.) dear to the Germany of that time." He adds: "About LTI, and its Italian equivalent, much has already been written, also by linguists. It is an obvious observation that where violence is inflicted on man, it is also inflicted on language" (*Drowned*, p. 97). In this connection, Todorov remarks that a "secret memorandum" about

"modifications to be made to the trucks that would serve as mobile gas chambers at Chelmno is particularly chilling. The human beings marked for death are always referred to as 'the cargo' or 'the items,' or they are not called anything at all, as in 'ninety-seven thousand have been dealt with'" (p. 161); "in *Shoah*": Lanzmann, p. 13, quoted in Todorov, p. 161.

50. Levi, *Drowned*, p. 91. Levi notes that when "a young *kapo* referred to his charges as men rather than *Häftlinge*, he was corrected" (p. 92).

51. On "excremental assault," see Des Pres, pp. 53, 55; "urine and excreta": Des Pres is quoting Weiss, p. 211.

52. Müller, pp. 46–47. See also Lifton, who notes in *The Nazi Doctors*: "Since the SS stole the meat used to produce the culture media, the chief SS physician found it very simple to replace it with human flesh" (p. 289).

53. Levi, *Drowned*, pp. 155–56.

54. See Todorov, p. 162: "This is the way Himmler justified the gas chambers to [Rudolf] Höss; there were too many people to kill simply by shooting them, he said, and 'if we take the women and children into account, this method would be too painful for the SS.'" Such dehumanization, Todorov notes, is even essential to Höss's own view of the death factory: "Having succeeded in depersonalizing his victims, Höss regards his work at Auschwitz as a technocrat might his own: all that interests Höss is how his factory is performing. He never wonders about the final product. [Though his writing exudes anti-Semitism, he insists that he wants] 'to emphasize the fact that I personally have never felt hatred toward the Jews' (p. 174). As Arthur Seyss-Inquart points out, the 'work of death' is particularly successful when it is done without hatred. Höss sees to it that his factory functions smoothly, that there are no hitches, that the various raw materials (poison, human beings, combustibles) arrive in synchrony" (p. 172).

55. Des Pres, pp. 156–57. As if to emphasize both the absurdity of Auschwitz and the confusion of categories out of which such absurdity often arose, Des Pres quotes the testimony of one prisoner, who worked in the depository where "the belongings of millions of victims—money and foodstuffs . . . and all kinds of clothing—were gathered and packed for shipment back to the Reich," that "We used the bank notes as toilet paper."

56. Von Alphen quotes the testimony of a Dutch SS volunteer about his experiences at the Russian front: "[Y]ou had to go forward! You had to seek cover in the mud filled with cadavers! . . . Sometimes you pulled a couple of dead bodies together to make a shelter out of them. You pulled three or four of them together. Yourself behind them. That is totally normal at the front" (p. 56); this is von Alphen's translation of Sleutelaar, p. 63.

57. See Felman and Laub, p. 5.

58. Des Pres, p. 35; Todorov, p. 264.

59. Revelation, I, 14, 18; VII, 14–16; IX, 1.

60. Celan, p. 31.

61. See Holst-Warhaft, "Deathfugue," pp. 1, 4–5

62. Felman and Laub, p. 2; Norris, p. 31.

63. Adorno, "Cultural Criticism," p. 34, and *Negative Dialectics,* pp. 362–63. Adorno also commented that although "I do not want to soften my statement that it is barbaric to continue to write poetry after Auschwitz," it "is the situation of literature itself and not simply one's relation to it that is paradoxical. The abundance of real suffering permits no forgetting. . . . But that suffering . . . also demands the continued existence of the very art it forbids" ("Engagement," pp. 87–88).

64. I. Smith reviews *Prometheus,* a feature film made by Harrison in 1998, noting that in "a direct challenge to Adorno's statement, Tony Harrison's first feature sets out to prove that 'after Auschwitz there is only poetry'"; see also Rowland, p. 253, 300n., and Hejinian, p. 320. For a scrupulously argued, book-length discussion of English-language "poetry after Auschwitz," see Gubar, *Poetry after Auschwitz.* On Adorno's assertion, Gubar also cites counterarguments by C. K. Williams, Adrienne Rich, Charles Bernstein, and Joseph Brodsky, among others; see pp. 10–13. On problematic second generation "testimony" about the Shoah, see also Hoffman.

65. Scholes, p. 7.

66. Von Alphen, p. 50.

67. Hartman, in Friedlander, pp. 326–27.

68. Adorno, "Engagement," vol. 2, p. 88; quoted in von Alphen, p. 18. As Holst-Warhaft shrewdly notes, it is "not surprising that it should be the non-survivor who insists on the impossibility of the task of bearing witness, either in factual accounts or in works of art. Problematic and painful as it was, the survivors of the camps felt the task to be a necessity. Through the literature on the Holocaust runs the constant reiteration of the need to remember, to bear witness, not to allow such suffering to be forgotten" (*Cue for Passion,* p. 181).

69. Delbo, pp. 32–33.

CHAPTER 8: TECHNOLOGIES OF DYING

1. Haskell, pp. 149–59.

2. Murray, pp. ix–xi.

3. Waring, "Euthanasia," in Davis and Schaefer, p. 205. For another slant on the "hospital spaceship," see the comment of a physician quoted by Bosk, p. 171: "What you have to do is this, Bosk. When you get up in the morning [to go to the hospital], pretend your car is a spaceship. Tell yourself you are going to visit another planet. You say, 'On that planet terrible things happen, but they don't happen on my planet. They only happen on that planet I take my spaceship to each morning.'"

4. Ariès, p. 584. Ariès elaborates: The "dying man is given food and water intravenously, thus sparing him the discomfort of thirst. A tube runs from his mouth to a pump that drains his mucus and prevents him from choking. Doctors and nurses administer sedatives, whose effects they can control and whose

doses they can vary. All this is well known today and explains the pitiful and henceforth classic image of the dying man with tubes all over his body."

5. Kaufman, "In the Shadow," p. 75. Kaufman adds that some ethnographers "have shown how death is controlled depending on ideologies of particular medical specialties, the organizational features of technology-intensive settings, and power relations and communication strategies among physicians, nurses, and families. In the ICU setting, especially . . . death is challenged, postponed, and, finally, medically controlled." For further discussion of this, see also Kaufman, . . . *And a Time to Die*, passim.

6. Ibid.

7. Haskell, p. 170. Since "Auschwitz" has become a trope for extremity, the Auschwitz metaphor is perhaps as frequently used by observers of patients as by patients themselves. Kaufman, for instance, notes that nurses described one "extremely malnourished" elderly patient as looking as though "she arrived from Auschwitz" ("Intensive Care," p. 718).

8. Nuland, p. 254. Nuland notes that perhaps because of its seemingly magical power to penetrate and analyze while also distancing, the stethoscope remains to this day "visible evidence of status" for doctors: "One need only spend a few hours on rounds with young resident physicians to observe the several roles played by this dangling evidence of authority and detachment." On the evolution of such medical power and "objectivity," see also Foucault, passim, and for a more detailed discussion of the history of the stethoscope, see Blaufox; ironically, Blaufox sees the stethoscope as symbolizing an old-fashioned kind of medical practice, noting that although it has "greatly facilitated physical diagnosis, it is being put aside by [higher-tech] devices which obviate the basic skills of history-taking, observation and examination" (quoted in Langone).

9. Cooper, pp. 1, 3. However, "Nearly five months after becoming the first person kept alive by a fully implantable artificial heart, Robert Tools died just before 1 P.M. [on November 30, 2001] at Jewish Hospital," in Louisville, Kentucky (see Gil).

10. For further information on the history of the iron lung as well as patients' comments, see the VIRTUAL MUSEUM OF THE IRON LUNG Web site. I am particularly grateful to Chana Bloch and to my daughter, Susanna Gilbert, a scholar of medicine and literature, for introducing me to O'Brien's life and work; see Susanna Gilbert, " 'I Scream the Body Electric.' "

11. "Terminally ill": Mark O'Brien, "A Quack Remedy" ; "labor like a stevedore": O'Brien, "Breathing," *Man*, p. 33. O'Brien considered the Death with Dignity movement a "quack remedy" and passionately defined Kevorkian as "a killer on the loose." See O'Brien, "A High Quad." In response to Kevorkian's assertion that his "critics [should] consider the quality of life of a high quad who's dependent on a ventilator," O'Brien passionately declared, "I am such a high quad, high quad being medical jargon for a person who has suffered an injury high up on the spinal cord. As a high quad, I cannot move my arms or legs, hands or feet [and] need a ventilator, that is, a respirator, to help me breathe. [Yet] I ask you to consider the quality of my life," and he went on to say that he

lived "in a pleasant new apartment," was a practicing journalist and published poet, and had "tons of books, an alarming collection of cassettes and CDs, a girlfriend, a web site, a documentary film about me and a proclamation from the city of Berkeley declaring Mark O'Brien day."

12. Bauby, p. 12. All of Bauby's interactions with visitors were conducted through an arduous alphabetic mode of communication in which an interlocutor would read off the letters of the alphabet in the order of their frequency in French "until with a blink of my eye, I stop you at the letter to be noted. The maneuver is repeated for the letters that follow, so that fairly soon you have a whole word, and then fragments of more or less intelligible sentences" (p. 20).

13. Ibid., pp. 32, 97.

14. Ibid., p. 12.

15. See Kaufman, "Narrative," pp. 354, 351.

16. Lynn et al., p. 104. The authors add that if such patient preferences are "informed and deeply committed," then "public policy will have to come to terms with the expenses and suffering that will be engendered by honoring these wishes," but if "preferences for aggressive care . . . arise from a misunderstanding . . . then improving decision-making might be a high priority."

17. Carver, p.122. Murray, p. 274; he is citing SUPPORT, "A Controlled Trial," pp. 1591–98.

18. According to the IMPLANTABLE ARTIFICIAL HEART PROJECT Web site, maintained by the University of Louisville Medical Center, this surgery was "the first of its kind in the world. The experimental procedure is the result of 20-plus years of product research and development by Danvers, Mass.–based ABIOMED, INC., and a three-year partnership with the University of Louisville and Jewish Hospital, where pre-clinical in-vivo device research was performed."

19. Stolberg.

20. Cf. Foucault.

21. On defibrillators, see Kolata, pp. A-1–A-16. Kolata describes a case in which the patient's "heart disease was so advanced" that his defibrillator "was going off six times a day or more, with a jolt that felt like a boxer's punch to the chest." On the problems of the AbioCor, see Stolberg and "Artificial Heart Pioneer Passes Away," CURRENT SCIENCE AND TECHNOLOGY CENTER Web site.

22. On the problematics of the "cyborg," see Susanna Gilbert, pp. 196–200; she is commenting on Haraway's celebration of the utopian "world without gender" that might be attained through reconstituting the human being as "a hybrid of machine and organism" (Haraway, p. 150). On this same issue, Agamben comments: "The hospital room in which the neomort, the overcomatose person, and the *faux vivant* waver between life and death delimits a space of exception in which a purely bare life, entirely controlled by man and his technology, appears for the first time [for] the comatose person has been defined as an intermediary being between man and an animal" (*Homo Sacer*, pp. 164–65).

23. Bauby, p. 9.

24. Yeats, *CP*, pp. 193–94.

25. Szasz, p. 70.

26. On Yeats's late-life affairs, his sexual anxieties, and the Steinach operation, see Maddox, pp. 277–302. Significantly, the emperor in Hans Christian Andersen's famous tale ultimately learns that just as a flesh-and-blood limb is superior to a prosthesis, the flesh-and-blood woodland nightingale is superior to the bejeweled artificial bird with which his courtiers have convinced him to replace it.

27. Gunn, "Lament," pp. 61–64, "Still Life," p. 66. There's much more that could be said about this richly allusive poem, of course. Echoing the theme announced by the title—still life—the word "astonished," for instance, incorporates "stone," while, in the homoerotic context Gunn establishes, the image of the "tube his mouth enclosed" evokes a grim fellatio with the phallus of death it(him)self.

28. "Paralytic," in Plath, *CP*, pp. 217–18.

29. "The world occur[s]": see Plath, "Little Fugue," *CP*, pp. 187–89 ("I was seven, I knew nothing. / The world occurred").

30. Ibid., pp. 266–67. In the light of the poem's ambivalence toward life (support), it's obviously significant that Plath wrote "Paralytic" on January 29, 1963, just two weeks before she took her own life on February 11. That may not really be, as the old saying has it, "another story" if life support became in her own mind a metaphor for life itself.

31. Murray, p. 14.

32. Price, pp. 12–13.

33. Gunther, p. 28. On the depersonalizing and demeaning aspects of "the vast mechanism of a modern hospital," see Carey's disturbing study of the "degrading shift from person to patient" experienced by so many who are hospitalized. For other relevant articles in this *New York Times* series entitled "Being a Patient," see Gross, "Alone"; J. Hoffman; and Kolata, "Sick and Scared."

34. Harmon, p. 24.

35. Heinemann, in Schoenberg, p. 22. To be sure, from the medieval infirmary for the impoverished ill to such historically unnerving institutions as Bedlam and Salpetrière, institutions designed to treat the indigent or the insane could hardly be defined as "comfortable."

36. Moller, *On Death*, p. 50; Moller here also quotes Mechanic, pp. 170–71. See also Pope, passim, and on Pope see T. Murray, passim. See also www.robert pope foundation.org/gallery.cfm?id=40.

37. According to the *OED*, our word "hospital" meaning an "institution or establishment for the care of the sick or wounded, or of those who require medical treatment" dates back to the fifteenth and sixteenth centuries.

38. Plath, "Tulips," *CP*, pp. 160–62; Eliot, *CPP*, p. 128. Arguably, Eliot was quite consciously following Christian tradition in his use of the word "hospital" here; cf. Browne, II, XI: "For the world, I count it not an Inne, but an Hospitall, and a place, not to live, but to die in," and also Flavel, p. 217: " Jesus Christ is the

only physician for sick souls. The world is a great hospital, full of sick and dying souls, all wounded by one and the same mortal weapon, sin."

39. See Freud, "The 'Uncanny,' " *CP*, vol. 4, pp. 368–407. The long linguistic meditation on the words *heimlich* and *unheimlich* that constitutes the first part of this famous paper is particularly useful in this connection. Arguing that the "uncanny," or *unheimlich*, is associated with the return of the repressed and thus, as David Morris puts it, "derives its terror not from something externally alien or unknown but—on the contrary—from something strangely familiar which defeats our efforts to separate ourselves from it," Freud investigates a series of etymologies and definitions in order to demonstrate that "*heimlich* is a word the meaning of which develops in the direction of ambivalence, until it finally coincides with its opposite, *unheimlich*" (pp. 299–319).

40. Kaufman, . . . *And a Time*, pp. 85–86.

41. Von Trier.

42. Nuland, p. 255; Ariès, pp. 569–71. Kaufman gives different figures from Nuland's for hospital deaths: while noting that patterns and statistics "vary considerably across the nation," she cites a 1997 Institute of Medicine report indicating that "62 percent of deaths occurred in hospitals; 17 percent in nursing homes" and a "2004 report [indicating] that 41 percent of Americans died in hospitals in 1998" (. . . *And a Time*, p. 338). Interestingly, Ariès's comments about the "unseemly" dying patient are echoed by the quote from the informant Kaufman cited earlier, who declared that "You're not supposed . . . to see bodily fluids" and was disturbed by "unsettling debris."

43. Roth, pp. 172–73. In fact the memoirist discloses that he did "clean up [the] shit" but confesses that he decided "once is enough," and adds, "addressing myself mentally to the sleeping brain squeezed in by the cartilaginous tumor; if I have to do this every day, I may not wind up feeling quite so thrilled."

44. N. Miller, p. 30.

45. Moller, *On Death*, pp. 49–50. For other sociological analyses of the "management" of "the dying trajectory," see the pioneering works of Glaser and Strauss.

46. Kayser-Jones et al., pp. 76–84. On nursing homes, see also Stephenson, pp. 62–68.

47. Kayser-Jones, pp. 79, 80.

48. Ibid., p. 79. "[A]ll day and all night": Kayser-Jones, personal conversation with this author.

49. On, for instance, chemotherapy and certain other medical treatments as "torture," see Franks, pp. 173–74; "going to Hiroshima": see R. Price, p. 50.

50. G. Rose, p. 81.

51. Mary Duffy: Carey; R. Price, p. 13.

52. Plath, "Lady Lazarus," *CP*, pp. 244–47. For a searching discussion of Plath's reimaginings of doctors, see Susanna Gilbert, " 'some god got hold of me': The Medicalization of Sylvia Plath," in Susanna Gilbert, especially "Herr Doktor, Herr Enemy/Herr God, Herr Lucifer," pp. 152–64.

53. At least one Nazi physician who escaped the military tribunals has also long cut

a grim swath in the popular imagination: Josef Mengele, Auschwitz's "Angel of Death," who oversaw countless "selections" while also "collecting" twins and "individuals with any other physical abnormalities: midgets, dwarfs, hunchbacks" for cruel experiments. In addressing "Herr Doktor . . . Herr Enemy," Plath is at least on a primary level alluding to such a figure of notoriety, just as when she refers in the same poem to "a Nazi lampshade," she's thinking of Ilse Koch, the "Bitch of Buchenwald," who "collected the skins of inmates, both dead and alive, if they had a tattoo she liked" and turned them "into book covers, gloves, lampshades and other sorts of furniture."

54. Bauby, pp. 53–54. "I finally discovered why he had put a six-month seal on my eyes," the author adds; "the lid was no longer fulfilling its function as a protective cover, and I ran the risk of an ulcerated cornea" (p. 54).

55. Price, pp. 40–41, 145; Pope, op. cit.

56. Moller, *On Death,* pp. 49–59: Moller cites P. Berger et al. For a good overview of the hospital as a bureaucracy, see Stephenson, pp. 48–62.

57. On the trauma of the medical student's first dissection of a cadaver, see S. Harrison; for a more detailed history of the use of the cadaver in medical training, see both Richardson and Roach.

58. Nuland, pp. 3, 7–8.

59. Ibid., p. 257.

60. Moller, *On Death,* p. 62. Moller also flatly states "that I observed no instances whereby physicians offered comfort to family members, and in *every* case where conversation drifted towards death and dying, the idea of death was couched in a technical emphasis and language" (p. 61). He adds that this "'death work' which typifies the modern urban medical center has remained notably consistent over the years. It is in this way that, despite the extraordinary influx of books . . . and media coverage of death and dying, the American approach to death remains moored within a framework of technological and bureaucratic control" (p. 63).

61. Ibid., p. 50; on the doctor's anxiety and consequent detachment, see also Stephenson, pp. 103–09.

62. Moller, *On Death,* p. 93.

63. Nuland, pp. 207–13, passim. Interestingly, later in this passage Nuland replaces the military metaphor with a conceit that likens cancer cells to sexual troublemakers: "The bastard offspring of their hyperactive (albeit asexual) 'fornicating' are without the resources to do anything but cause trouble and burden the hardworking community around them."

64. Shapiro, *Vigil,* pp. 53–54; for a more recent, equally poignant formulation of this point, see Brody, "A Doctor's Duty," p. D-7, which prints a letter that a grieving husband wrote to his deceased wife's oncologist, protesting the doctor's absence and apparent indifference in her last days.

65. Bauman, *Mortality, Immortality,* p. 137; Fulton, "Introduction," p. 4.

66. In addition to Groddeck, see Reich and Siegel. For a more nuanced discussion of these ideas, see Groopman, *Anatomy of Hope.*

67. Sontag, *Illness as Metaphor,* pp. 51, 52, 57; G. Rose, pp. 77–78. To be sure, nineteenth-century medical thinkers often engaged in similarly aetiological fantasies. When the famous nutritionist and health advocate Sylvester Graham (father of the graham cracker) "died in 1851 at the not-quite-ripe age of 57," his doctor, "a partisan of cold baths and plain water . . . attributed [his] death to 'warm baths' and the consumption of . . . mineral water." Similarly, "posters were put up during cholera epidemics blaming sloth, vice and bad habits for the disease"; see Angier.

68. Auden, *English Auden,* pp. 217–18. In writing "Miss Gee," Auden was almost certainly influenced by Groddeck, whose *Book of the It* he much admired at this point in his career: see Izzo, *Auden Encyclopedia,* p. 104, and *W. H. Auden: A Legacy,* p. 137.

69. Edson, pp. 32–33, 53.

70. Moller, *On Death,* pp. 58–59. On the prevalence of "shortcomings in communications" and "frequency of aggressive treatment" that almost lead to Vivian's subjection to a code despite her DNR (do not resuscitate) order, see "A Controlled Trial" (note 17 of this chapter).

71. See Saunders and Bain; Kübler-Ross, *On Death and Dying*; and de Hennezel; on hospice as an institution, see also, e.g., Stephenson, pp. 68–74.

72. See Humphry and, for Kevorkian's "Mercitron," see FANS OF FIEGER Web site. Arguing against Kevorkian's practices, O'Brien asserts: "His main interest, nay, his obsession is killing disabled people or people who say they are disabled. This mostly cashes out to mean depressed middle-aged women" ("A High Quad"). On Kevorkian too, see Mairs, also commenting from a disabled perspective; noting that the disabled are often "characterized as drains upon resources," Mairs observes that one of Kevorkian's "clients" was "told repeatedly by her husband that she was a vampire sucking his blood" (p. 144). Physician-assisted suicide is a topic on which scores of books and articles, pro and con, have been written; for a good online overview of the subject, with numerous useful links, see DOCTOR ASSISTED SUICIDE: A GUIDE TO WEBSITES AND THEIR LITERATURE; helpful books reviewing the issue from an American perspective include: Magnusson; Field and Cassel; Moreno; Jamison; National Council on Disability; Snyder and Kaplan; and Foley and Hendin. For a poignant and often paradoxically witty account of the way physician-assisted suicide is practiced in the Netherlands, see Keizer. For information about NOT DEAD YET, see its Web site.

73. "Plastic bag": Humphry, p. 92; as part of this discussion Humphry permits himself a few pleasantries—viz. "One member recently asked me how she could inflate the bag! I told her that it's deflation that's needed!" and "Should you use a clear plastic bag or an opaque one? That's a matter of taste." "The dying transition": see Kübler-Ross, *On Death and Dying,* pp. 118–20.

74. Brown, p. 75, and acknowledgment, n.p. Moller, *On Death,* p. 51.

75. See Moller, *On Death,* p. 51. Going beyond the points Moller makes here, a recent *New York Times Magazine* article notes that "Hospice today is . . . different from its grass-roots origins" as an "antiestablishment . . . movement advo-

cating a gentle death as an alternative to the medicalized death many people had come to dread." It has become increasingly technologized and "institutional-ized" (there are "hospice patients on ventilators, hospice patients with feeding tubes . . . hospice patients who panic when they can't breathe and call 911") perhaps in part because our contemporary "death-denying culture has led to a system of care for the terminally ill that allows us to indulge the fantasy that dying is somehow optional" (Henig: 28–29).

76. Nuland, p. 195; adds "John," as Nuland reports his words: "Those of us left behind search for dignity in order not to think ill of ourselves. . . . [M]y own experience is that the only means we have of knowing if we have helped some-one to a better death is whether or not we feel regret, or whether there is any-thing we feel sorry about or have left undone." O'Brien, explaining his opposition to Oregon's physician-assisted suicide movement, makes a compa-rable comment on this subject: "Instead of investing in respectful care of the dying and independent living for the disabled, society is now being encouraged to consider the quack remedy of Death with Dignity. In response, I quote dis-abled writer Cheryl Marie Wade: 'I don't want to hear about death with dignity until we are all allowed life with dignity' " ("A Quack Remedy"). For another disabled writer's responses to the assisted suicide movement and its "remedy of Death with Dignity," see Mairs.

77. Moller, *On Death*, pp. 51, 23, 102; Thomas, p. 128. In "different ways," Moller adds (in *On Death*), "the social and personal dying-with-dignity mandate and technological management facilitate the social isolation of the dying patient." In particular, "personal dying-with-dignity places the burden of successful and appropriate death squarely on the shoulders of the individual" (p. 102). Fur-thermore, notes the sociologist with considerable bitterness, the "primary interactional significance of social dying-with-dignity is the facilitation of medical work for physicians and nurses. Dying patients achieve the social dimension of dying-with-dignity when they adapt their behavior and expres-sions to fit the requirements of the process of medicalized death. . . . The per-sonal dimension of dying-with-dignity becomes an issue for patient management when the private factors of a patient's inability to successfully cope with dying rage into the public arena and jeopardize the behavioral tran-quillity of social dying-with-dignity" (p. 86). On this, see also Zaroff, who claims that Ivan Ilyich, "dying slowly, makes life miserable—complaining, crit-icizing, screaming—for his family until the last day, when he realizes that they love him. He then understands what he *owes his wife and children: a good death* [emphasis added]. In the end he dies quietly, blissfully, a good death for him and his family." This radical misreading of Tolstoy's proto-existentialist (and deeply moralizing) vision depressingly dramatizes the social imperative of "death-with-dignity" as "an issue for patient management."

78. Ariès, p. 563; the historian adds:

> It is clear that the clergy finally had had enough of administering to cadav-ers, that they finally refused to lend themselves to this farce, even if it was

> inspired by love. Their rebellion partly explains why, after Vatican II, the Church changed the traditional name of Extreme Unction to the "anointing of the sick," and not always the terminally sick. Today it is sometimes distributed in church to old people who are not sick at all. The sacrament has been detached from death, for which it is no longer the immediate preparation. In this the Church is not merely recalling the obligation to be fully conscious when one receives the unction. It is implicitly admitting its own absence at the moment of death, the lack of necessity for "calling the priest."

79. Edson, p. 50.
80. Kleinman, pp. 146–49, 153–54.
81. Tolstoy, pp. 142, 160. Interestingly, the acts of kindness performed by Gerasim and Susie parallel the willingness of the servant, Anna, in Bergman's *Cries and Whispers*, to comfort Agnes in her death when the dead woman's own sisters, Karin and Maria, have shrunk from her cadaver in disgust and fear.
82. Plath, "Little Fugue," *CP*, pp. 187–89. Curiously, the ministrations of the two women who visit Vivian when she's dying anticipate a pilot program of *doulas* (the term is drawn from an Arabic word for midwife or birth companion but here refers to friendly visitors or companions for the dying) that was recently established in New York City. See Kleinfeld, pp. 1, 20–21, a story that examines in depth the "I-thou" relationship between Bill Keating, a retired lawyer, and Lew Grossman, a retired elevator operator dying at a geriatric center in Washington Heights. Keating "broke the ice" with Grossman "by taking [him] lox and cream cheese, big-band recordings and other treats," notes the *Times* reporter. In both cases, *small* kindnesses, from Susie's gift of a Popsicle to Keating's gift of lox and cream cheese, or from Ashford's reading of a nursery story to Keating's "big-band recordings," affirm and honor the humanity of the dying.

CHAPTER 9: A DAY IN THE DEATH OF . . .

1. See Cronin, "A Black Cloud. A Shower of Glass. A Glimpse of Hell. Run!": "This is the most horrifying thing," Jim Zamparelli, "standing near Stuyvesant High School."
2. Ibid., David Rohde, a *Times* reporter, "outside the World Trade Center when the collapse started."
3. Ibid., Malkie Zadai, "owner of Ben-Ness Photos on University Place."
4. See Mark and Dan Jury. For introducing me to their work, I'm indebted to Bertman, whose *Facing Death* surveys visual representations of death and dying.
5. See Nicholas and Bebe Nixon, *People with AIDS*; for further discussion of these photographs, see Tanner, pp. 135–59.
6. Gagnon, pp. 61, cited in Tanner, fn. 6, p. 139.
7. For Goldberg's photographs and comments, see Andre, Brookman, and Livingston, pp. 24–51.
8. See D. Morris, ABCNews.com.

9. Albom, pp. 69–70.

10. All quotes from *On Our Own Terms* appear as audio extracts on the program's PBS Web site.

11. See D. Smith, p. B1; Harvey, pp. 24–31; and Rothenberg, passim. Other notable recent first-person journals of death and dying include Brodky and Broyard. There are many third-person memoirs produced by mourners, including such best sellers as L. Caine's *Widow* and Eggers's *Heartbreaking Work* . . . , both of which precede narratives of grief and survival with descriptions of the deaths of loved ones; Eggers in particular offers unnerving, clinically detailed accounts of the deaths of both his parents (pp. 1–45). More recently, the *San Francisco Chronicle* has run a seven-part series titled "Alicia's Story," in which Alicia Parlette, a twenty-three-year-old copy editor, stricken with an incurable cancer, recounts her struggle to survive; see Parlette. For a Web site with interviews and photos that accompany the series, see www.sfgate.com/alicia. For Nixon's photographs of Arnold and Richardson, see Henig.

12. See Shapiro, *The Dead Alive and Busy*.

13. Winterton, p. 4, quoted in Zelizer, p. 51; for more about coverage of Majdanek, see Zelizer, pp. 49–61; I have made extensive use of Zelizer's invaluable work throughout my discussion of Holocaust photography. For a sophisticated discussion of Holocaust photography from a different angle, see Gubar, "About Pictures out of Focus," *Poetry after Auschwitz*, pp. 99–144.

14. "The Most Terrible Example of Organized Cruelty in the History of Civilization," *Illustrated London News*, October 14, 1944, quoted in Zelizer, p. 57.

15. Zelizer, p. 57.

16. Friedlander, p. 3; W. Frye, pp. 1, 3, and Cowan, p. 2, both quoted in Zelizer, p. 67.

17. Zelizer points out that this comment by Bourke-White is relatively unusual for the period, since ordinarily reporters would produce the writing, photographers the pictures; see Zelizer, p. 198.

18. Sontag, *On Photography*, pp. 19–20.

19. Warren, p. 9.

20. Quoted in Zelizer, p. 88; Zelizer adds that the "revelation—that he was 'treating this pitiful human flotsam as if it were some gigantic still life'—so disgusted and appalled him that he promised himself 'never again to photograph a war.'"

21. Clarke, p. 158. For a nuanced discussion of the moral ambiguities associated with the aesthetic of photographs of atrocity, Sontag's *Regarding the Pain of Others* is invaluable, as is her more recent "Regarding the Torture of Others."

22. See Zelizer, pp. 115–16; for the picture of the children, she cites Furst, p. 12, and Hibbs, p. 20; the mother's image evidently appeared in *Lest We Forget*, p. 73.

23. Zelizer, p. 147; she adds: "One soldier recalled how his commander had chased the company out of the camp at Nordhausen because of typhoid yet afterward 'went back and took a whole series of pictures. He gave each one of us a set. I have them home yet. Every once in a while if you want to refresh your memory, you take those out and look at 'em.'"

24. "Flashbulb memory": Zelizer, p. 155; "The first Jews I met": Krondorfer, p. 276, quoted in Zelizer, p. 159.

25. Sontag, *On Photography*, p. 20; "for a counter-example," Sontag continues, tellingly, "think of the Gulag Archipelago, of which we have no photographs."

26. For the story of the My Lai investigation, see Valentine, and (among other Web sites) Douglas Linder's MY LAI COURTS-MARTIAL Web site.

27. About another photo, this time one in which the subjects have already been shot, Haeberle notes dispassionately: "When these two boys were shot at, the older one fell on the little one, as if to protect him. Then the guys finished them off." And off yet a third—the one perhaps most comparable to Holocaust images of piled-up corpses inside or outside the death camps—he explains that he "found these bodies on a road leading from the village." He adds: "Most were women and babies. It looked as if they tried to get away."

28. See Silverthorne.

29. Both these images are reproduced in Schwenger, pp. 403, 406. In *Harvest*, Schwenger remarks, the "corpse's face hovers between the unconsciousness of the dead and a certain conscious pose, displaying the line of the profile, elegant and spare."

30. Zelizer, p. 179.

31. Sand, "Interview." In 1996 this photograph was featured in a Witkin retrospective at the Guggenheim Museum, New York.

32. Proulx, pp. 30–35.

33. See "Death Watch," PBS Online.

34. Schwenger, p. 397. More recently, in "What Remains," her "show of the dead," the well-known photographer Sally Mann offers portraits of "her decaying greyhound, Eva," of battlefields at Antietam, and "putrefying corpses lying . . . at a facility for studying human decomposition." Says Mann: "I want people to have to accept the existence of beauty where they would never expect to find it. In death" (Mann, online). But, complains *New York Times* critic Sarah Boxer, the "most morbid pictures contain two kinds of violation . . . the violation of the privacy and the decency of the dead [and] the dreadful things Ms. Mann has done to the surfaces of her photographs [to make them] look burned, torn or spotted" ("Slogging").

35. See the SIX FEET UNDER Web site.

36. On the death of Daniel Pearl, see Levy as well as El-Ghobashy and Hutchinson, p. A-8.

37. Moaveni, p. 40.

38. See Kenzer, pp. A-1, 21.

39. Boxer, "Humiliating Photographs"; Sontag, "Regarding the Torture."

40. Steinberg, p. 4-1: "If [news organizations] broadcast such images, even in part, they run the risk of goading future kidnappers with the implicit promise that their actions, too, will be screened before a wide audience, striking fear in the enemy and possibly gaining them leverage." Yet at the same time "any news organization that spikes such footage leaves itself open to criticism that it is

violating a basic tenet of journalism, namely that it should report what it knows and show what it has seen."

41. Adams, cited in Sontag, *On Photography*, p. 202.

42. Klawans.

43. J. Berger, p. 18; Arbus, p. 226: Arbus was writing to Davis Pratt, then the curator of the Fogg Museum, and added, as she continued musing on photographs, that "the stillness of them is boggling. You can turn away but when you come back they'll still be there looking at at you." Sontag, *On Photography*, pp. 3–5.

44. Barthes, pp. 87–89.

45. For a meditation on these issues from a slightly different perspective, see R. Harrison, p. 148, emphasizing the photograph's continuity with earlier modes of representation—for instance, its "essential links to its ancestral origins in the death mask, if only because it allows a person's likeness to survive his or her demise." For Harrison, a "cleft" in history comes with "the invention of . . . voice-recording technologies [that allowed] the dead . . . to speak posthumously in their own phonetic voices for the first time" (p. 151). In an interesting note, he cites Thomas Alva Edison's view that one of the key uses for his phonograph was to record "the last words of dying persons" along with the view of the German inventor Alfred Parzer-Mühlbacher that because of such technology, "[c]herished loved ones . . . who have long since passed away will years later talk to us again with the same vividness and warmth [and we will also] hear the speech of those who lived countless years before us . . . whose names were only handed down by history" (pp. 180–81).

46. Sontag, *On Photography*, pp. 14–15.

47. Barthes, pp. 78–79, 82.

48. On deathbed photographs (as well as death masks and deathbed paintings) in France, see Héran, passim, and Proulx, p. 30. To be sure, the tradition of funerary likenesses also includes tomb sculptures and coffin decorations, some of which can be traced back at least to ancient Egypt and Rome. For such portraits, see, for instance, Doxiadis as well as Walker. Of Doxiadis's book, *Publishers Weekly* commented that "staring at us with intense, disturbing gazes, these men and women speak to us as if from the other world, transcending mortality and death"; see *Publishers Weekly*, vol. 242, no. 48 (November 27, 1995), p. 60.

49. Schwenger, p. 396

50. Sand, interview with Witkin.

51. For a brilliant and wide-ranging discussion of the "inconceivability" of death, see Bauman, "Living with Death," *Mortality, Immortality*, pp. 12–50, passim, but especially, e.g., pp. 12–13—"Death is the ultimate defeat of reason, since reason cannot 'think' death"—and p. 13, quoting Edgar Morin, "the idea of death 'is the hollowest of the hollow ideas,' since its content 'is unthinkable, inexplicable, a conceptual *je ne sais quoi*'" (Bauman cites Morin, pp. 29–30).

52. "To record, to mock . . .": S. Milton, cited in Zelizer, pp. 45, 250. The whole passage Zelizer cites is of interest: "Who had taken a given photograph and under what circumstances? Was it a neutral passerby, a Nazi who photographed and

then killed his or her victim, a resistance fighter or, later, a liberator? And for what purpose had he or she taken the image? Was it to record, to mock, to remember, to exploit?" See also S. Milton, "The Camera as Weapon." Kluger, p. 159; on the same page, noting that many "people [among those liberated] died because they couldn't digest the heavy food that was indiscriminately shoved at them," Kluger also remarks that the "liberators had been better at taking horrifying pictures of the living skeletons than at rescuing them."

53. "Atrocity's normalization": Zelizer, p. 212; "unglued": Zelizer, p. 215. Postmodern looking isn't just "suspicious" because it asks cui bono, therefore, but also because seeing and believing have come "unglued." In this regard, postmodern looking seeks confirmation of *un*reality—artifice, parody, manipulation—rather than reality. Postmodern looking is even capable—as in the grotesquely macabre *Pulp Fiction* or the funereal comedy *Six Feet Under*—of contempt for the materiality in which it nevertheless solely believes. When someone's brains are spattered all over a getaway car in *Pulp Fiction*, for instance, audiences may respond with nervous laughter at least in part because of a sickened belief that such squashed meat constitutes all there is of the character who was just killed, but at the same time audiences may respond with relieved laughter because they recognize that such "squashed meat" is merely a *simulation* "of all there is."

54. See Barthes, pp. 87–89, where he not only asserts that a photograph is a "certificate of presence" but adds: "Photography never lies."

55. On the Victorian death scene as well as Victorian paintings of the dying and the dead, see Christ, pp. 133–51, passim, and, more generally, Stewart, pp. 8, 142, 99–198, passim. For more about nineteenth-century mortuary photography, see Burns.

56. On "Fading Away," see Clarke, p. 44. Robinson himself was quite frank about the artifice of this photograph, and, ironically, some of his comments on artifice in photography, though based on a sentimental Victorian aesthetic of the "beautiful," anticipate contemporary postmodern skepticism toward photography's potential to manipulate and in a sense "revise" reality. In "Pictorial Effect in Photography" (1867), he declared that any "dodge, trick and conjuration of any kind is open to the photographer's use. . . . It is his imperative duty to avoid the mean, the base and the ugly, and to aim to elevate his subject . . . and to correct the unpicturesque. . . . A great deal can be done and very beautiful pictures made, by a mixture of the real and the artificial in a picture" (p. 78).

57. A number of Great War images illustrate the kinds of points made by such poets as Sassoon, Rosenberg, and Gurney: see chapters 7 and 13 of this book. "We set to work to bury people," remembers one Great War combatant in a passage quoted on the Great War Web site, adding: "We pushed them into the sides of the trenches but bits of them kept getting uncovered and sticking out, like people in a badly made bed [and the] bottom of the trench was springy like a mattress because of all the bodies underneath." See also Blythe, p. 40.

58. See Zelizer, pp. 17, 20.

59. For a detailed discussion of the Paris Morgue and of its relationship to photography, see Schwartz, pp. 45–88; Schwartz cites Dr. Gavinzel ("Study of the Morgue from an Administrative and Medical Point of View") on p. 62, fn. 70. Émile Zola's *Thérèse Raquin* (1867) contains several scenes set in the Paris Morgue, where Zola's hero is simultaneously "nauseated by a sickly smell, the smell of washed flesh [so that] chill shivers ran over his skin" and "spell-bound" by the "brutal display of naked bodies" laid out on stone slabs. Comments Zola, "The Morgue is within the reach of every purse. . . . Some connoisseurs make a special detour so as not to miss one of these displays of death, and when the slabs are bare people go out muttering, feeling let down and swindled" (pp. 106–10). I'm grateful to Frank Gonzalez-Crussi for directing me both to Schwartz's book and Zola's novel.

60. For *l'enfant du Vert-Bois*, see Schwartz, pp. 76–78.

61. For more about nineteenth-century mortuary photography, see Burns.

62. The aesthetic of "hard, cold, exact, detached, and sometimes cruel" "realism" has of course numerous sources in early twentieth-century thought. See, for example, Marinetti's "Futurist Manifesto": "[T]he world's magnificence has been enriched by a new beauty; the beauty of speed. . . . We will sing of the multicolored, polyphonic tides of revolution in the modern capitals . . . of the vibrant nightly fervor of arsenals and shipyards blazing with violent electric moon" etc. (Marinetti, pp. 41–42).

63. Zelizer, p. 147; Zelizer goes on to note here that "Early fictional representations of the camps wove in visual scenes that had been already etched in memory by the press," citing John Hersey's *The Wall* (1950) and Anatoli Kuznetsov's *Babi Yar: A Document in the Form of a Novel* (1970).

64. Particularly interesting in this regard is the insistence of a number of contemporary critics that Richter bases paintings "on portrait, newspaper, and police photographs [in order to call] into doubt the inherent truthfulness of a supposedly documentary medium, especially insofar as it purported to accurately record history in all its elusive and conflicted detail": *Gerhard Richter Forty Years of Painting, February 14–May 21, 2002, The Museum of Modern Art*, n.p.; it's also interesting that there's no attribution of authorship on this exhibition "program," though presumably it was written by Robert Storr, the curator of the exhibition.

65. Williams, "Death," *CP*, vol. 1, pp. 346–48; Stevens, *CPP*, p.50.

66. Ariès, p. 573; Gorer, pp. 165–75.

67. See Scherer. For "a kind of artistic guerrilla warfare," see Ewald.

68. See Stevens, "Sunday Morning": "She hears, upon that water without sound, / A voice that cries, 'The tomb in Palestine / Is not the porch of spirits lingering. / It is the grave of Jesus, where he lay.'"

69. Barthes's major discussions of the Winter Garden Photograph appear on pp. 67–73.

70. Spiegelman: Anja, I, 100; Richieu, II, 5; Vladek, II, 135. For an interesting extended discussion of these photographs, see Liss, pp. 54–68.

71. Sebald, *Austerlitz*, p. 183. More recently, in *Saturday*, Ian McEwan's protagonist, Henry Perowne, speculates on the innocence (or, more crudely, the *ignorance*) of figures in photographs. Meditating on a picture of his parents, taken just after his own birth, he notes that his mother is "pretty in a white summer dress" and his father—"smoking a cigarette"—is tall, with an "untroubled" grin. "It's always useful to have solid proof that the old have had their go at being young," Perowne thinks, then goes on to muse that "there is also an element of derision in photography. The couple appear vulnerable, easily mocked for appearing not to know that their youth is merely an episode, or that the tasty smoulder-ing item in Jack's right hand will contribute—Henry's theory—later that same year to his sudden death" (p.161).

72. Barthes, p. 92.

73. Sebald, "hundreds of photos": p. 7; "faded world": p. 127; "photo album/tales of the dead": pp. 53–54; "something stirring": p. 182; Theresienstadt, pp. 245–47; "*Toute la mémoire*": p. 261.

74. Buchloh, p. 11.

75. Beauvoir, p. 103; Roth, pp. 230–31; for Miller's discussion of these passages, see N. Miller, pp. 43–49.

76. Beauvoir, pp. 99–100; N. Miller, pp. 44–45.

77. Monette, *Love Alone*, pp. 16–17, 64, 62; *Borrowed Time*, p. 16.

78. Plath, *CP*: "Daddy," pp. 223–24; "The Thin People," p. 64. Hughes, *Birthday Letters*: "Picture of Otto," p. 193.

79. C. K. Williams, p. 8.

Chapter 10: Millennial Mourning

1. Profile published in the *New York Times* on October 3, 2001. I am grateful to Garrett Stewart for connecting me with Zack Zeng.

2. "Details": for example, "While at Stuyvesant High [he] was always willing to help the other students specially in math. He is so well liked such that the land-lord where his family lived even lowered the rent in order to lighten his family's burden"; see Tangben.

3. For a more general formulation of this point, see R. Harrison, p. 124: "[T]he cultural rules of passage [that govern mourning] are themselves historical, hence they too pass away in time, to be replaced by others."

4. For "Nekere" and "Shreaves," see the WORLD WIDE CEMETERY online.

5. For "Jessica Renee Carr," see the WORLD WIDE CEMETERY.

6. For interesting investigations of Web memorials, including analyses of those who "post" such virtual monuments and those whom they mourn, see Roberts, pp. 337–58, and Roberts and Vidal, pp. 521–45.

7. Ariès, p. 575.

8. Lewis, *A Grief Observed*, pp. 8–11.

9. Quoted in Moller, *Confronting Death*, p. vii.

10. Nussbaum, pp. 49, 50.

11. Gorer: "English-speaking," p. 113; "under control," p. 111. For "The Pornography of Death," see *Encounter* (October 1955), and also Appendix 4 of *Death, Grief*. Nor did things radically change in the course of the century. Not long ago, for instance, the influential British stage director Peter Hall told a BBC interviewer that while he can be as sexually frank as he pleases in the productions he stages, audiences just won't "tolerate" too many references to death.

12. Gorer, pp. 58–59, 14–15; in his own case, Gorer adds his opinion that if he'd responded to invitations by explaining "that the invitation clashed with some esoteric debauchery I had arranged, I would have had understanding and jocular encouragement."

13. Elias, pp. 23–24; Bauman, *Mortality, Immortality*, p. 130.

14. Bauman, *Mortality, Immortality*, p. 130: adds Bauman: "Certainty of death incapacitates; uncertainty of outcome boosts energy and spurs into action. In the language of survival, practical concerns with specific dangers to life elbow out the metaphysical concern with death as the inescapable ending to existence. Keeping fit, taking exercise, 'balancing the diet' . . . are all feasible tasks . . . that redefine the unmanageable problem (or, rather, non-problem) of death (which one can do nothing about) as a series of utterly manageable problems (which one can do something about . . .)." At the same time, looking at the "unmanageable problem" of death from the perspective of an "undertaker," the poet–essayist–funeral director Thomas Lynch comments: "We are embarrassed by [our dead] in the way that we are embarrassed by a toilet that overflows the night that company comes. It is an emergency. We call the plumber"—i.e., the undertaker, who relieves us of the "unmanageable problem" (*Undertaking*, p. 33).

15. According to Gorer (writing in the 1960s), a "quarter of the [British] population states firmly that they do not believe in a future life, and the same number is uncertain; of the remainder some 15 per cent say that they believe in a future life but have little idea what it will be like; and the rest voice a series of unorthodox beliefs, with no overt religious content" (p. 33). In this respect, of course, the British are very different from Americans, a majority of whom profess belief in an afterlife. Nevertheless, contemporary American belief-systems are often tenuous, with even some major theologians suggesting that the concept of heaven is surrounded by "a wall of popular skepticism." (See chapter 6, pp. 121–24 of this volume.)

16. Lewis, *A Grief*, p. 24.

17. Gorer, p. 42.

18. Lewis, *A Grief*, pp. 25–27.

19. Lewis, *The Lion, the Witch and the Wardrobe*; Millay, pp. 286–87.

20. Chast: 106.

21. "Miss Manners," *San Francisco Chronicle*, October 10, 1997.

22. Henderson recounts telling a young mother, "trim and carefully made up," from whom she's buying a house, "My first baby died," and instantly notes that "her mouth formed into a tight, frightened little circle." Henderson comments,

a "year earlier, I too would have been paralyzed if someone had dropped that on me–their dead baby. . . . Back then, I knew nothing about illness, tragedy, and death. I would have been horrified, repelled. I could see the abhorrence—and the fear—in her eyes. They were the eyes of an innocence. Dot [a friend from Henderson's bereavement group who had lost her own baby] was right. You could tell immediately the people who had lost someone, the folks who understood in their hearts about grief. Dot had baby Carolyn to thank for turning her into a person who knew, a person who always now reached out to others who were grieving. Carolyn had taken away her fear of death, she said, and had given her the gift of empathy" (pp. 192–93).

23. Ibid., pp. 172, 187.

24. Lewis, *A Grief*, p. 11.

25. Parkes, p. 20.

26. More specifically, according to Freud, the task of mourning entails a "testing of reality," which, "having shown that the loved object no longer exists, requires forthwith that all the libido shall be withdrawn from its attachments to this object," a job that is done "bit by bit, under great expense of time and cathectic energy" (*General Psychological Theory*, pp. 165–67).

27. Klein (quoted in Gorer, p. 121); Lindemann (quoted in Gorer, pp. 123–24); Gorer, p. 79. Gorer implies that those who have lost spouses are the most frequent sufferers from "mummification," suggesting that Lewis might have feared himself to be in danger of such a fate; like Queen Victoria, "mummified" widows and widowers preserve their "grief for the lost husband or wife by keeping the house and every object in it precisely as he or she had left it, as though it were a shrine which would at any moment be reanimated [p. 79]."

28. On the problematics of mainstream grief therapy and counseling, see Groopman, "The Grief Industry," pp. 30–36, and Brody, "Often, Time Beats Therapy." As for Kübler-Ross, though she's best known for *On Death and Dying* (1970), she later turned to spiritualist mysticism in such books as *On Life after Death* and *The Tunnel and the Light*, works in which she elaborates her consoling visions of the afterlife. (See also www.elisabethkublerross.com.)

29. On cloning, see Talbot; on "LifeGem," see Copeland; on marriage, see C. Smith.

30. "Rituals for grieving": Moller, *Confronting Death*, p. 134; "behavior control": Rosenbaum, pp. 32–42; "trivialization": Moller, *Confronting Death*, p. 134. Notes Rosenbaum: "dividing dying into stages was a stroke of genius. Kübler-Ross brought forth her five stages at just about the time when people were dividing life into 'passages,' stages, predictable crises. Getting dying properly staged would bring every last second of existence under the reign of reason." Similarly, Moller criticizes Kübler-Ross for having established "an Imperial Journey of Dying that monolithically defines a good death as one grounded in peaceful, tranquil acceptance" so as to create "*a more cooperative patient*" (p. 51). Arguably, discussions of the stages of grief might serve comparable purposes for mourners, rendering them more malleable and less embarrassing.

31. Elias, p. 10; Elias adds that the "feeling, too, that death is a punishment imposed

... by a father or mother figure, or that after death they will be punished by the great father for their sins, has [long] played a ... part in the human fear of death" (pp. 10–11). Lindemann: quoted in Gorer, p. 123. On pregnancy gone awry, see B. Johnson, p. 705: "*any* death of a child is [often] perceived as a crime committed by the mother, something [she] ought by definition to be able to prevent."

32. Henderson, pp. 184 ("so enormous"); pp. 40–41 ("exposed, weak").

33. Ibid., pp. 144–45.

34. Bauman, *Mortality, Immortality,* p. 137; Fulton, p. 4.

35. "Spoiled identity": see Caine, p. 176, and also Caine, pp. 147–49, for an expansion of this point, drawing on Konrad Lorenz's description of the "lonely goose": "From the moment a goose realizes that the partner is missing, it loses all courage [and] rapidly sinks to the lowest step in the ranking order." Caine also cites Helena Lopata, who argues that the "ten million widows of the United States, despite their numbers, 'share the characteristics of other minority groups that are targets of discrimination' because they are 'women in a male-dominated society' who are 'without mates in a social network of couples.'" For "Jessica's mom," see online memorial of Jessica Renee Carr, this chapter, pp. 246–47; "Malcolm's mom," see Henderson; "Claire's mom," see Schnell.

36. Gorer, pp. 4–5; on the "nostalgias of Gorer and Ariès," see Ramazani, p. 372, fn. 48. Citing Tolchin, Ramazani argues that "the Victorian overritualization and the modern suppression of mourning result in similar problems. Victorian mourning rituals did not merely release grief but sometimes ... 'prolonged' and 'blocked' it: since Victorian culture proscribed public expression of negative feelings toward the dead, 'conflicts were driven underground, thus setting the scene for lifelong chronic grief'" (cf. Tolchin, p. xxii).

37. Henderson, pp. 71–72; Caine, p. 116.

38. Morrison, *Sula,* p. 107. On Greek women's public lamentation, see Holst-Warhaft, *Dangerous Voices,* passim. On Irish keening, see Bourke, p. 287. Bourke notes that although "keening" "in English suggests a high-pitched, inarticulate moaning ... the Irish word *caoineadh,* from which it derives, signifies ... a highly articulate tradition of women's oral poetry," and adds that "texts of *caoineadh* ... embody a disciplined and powerful expression" of grief. For a comment on the shame attached to such practices in contemporary America and Britain, however, see Metcalf and Huntington, p. 207: "[D]isplays of emotion [after death] are kept to a minimum, and those who, it is feared, will 'break down' in public are avoided. Such intense embarrassment surrounds loss of control that widows or widowers will often stay away from the funeral rather than risk it."

39. Bauman, *Mortality, Immortality,* p. 130; Elias, p. 23.

40. Waugh, BBC radio talk, at AN EVELYN WAUGH WEB SITE.

41. To be sure, as a Catholic Waugh did indeed believe in a spiritual afterlife beginning with "the traditional conception of the adult soul naked at the judgement seat," but this wasn't a belief he could reconcile with the "endless infancy" presumed by the American "paradise."

42. Waugh, pp. 71, 80, 55. Explaining to Dennis Barlow that Krump is "in Poets' Corner now," Aimée naively tells him that she "took the chance to study" the lineaments of this ersatz poet because she "had very marked Soul. You might say I learned Soul from studying Sophie Dalmeyer Krump" (p. 71).

43. Ibid., p. 35.

44. Ibid., p. 41.

45. Ibid., pp. 61, 69.

46. Ibid., p. 40.

47. Cited in Lynch, *Bodies in Motion*, p. 131.

48. Mitford, *Revisited*, pp. 9–10.

49. Ibid., pp. 54–55.

50. Ibid., pp. 193–94.

51. Waugh, pp. 115, 117.

52. Lynch, *Bodies*, p. 128; Mitford, *Revisited*, p. 234. ("Decca" was Jessica Mitford's widely used nickname.)

53. Ibid., p. 235.

54. Mitford, *American Way*, p. 161.

55. Leonard, letter to Robert Waltrip.

56. Lynch, *Bodies*, p. 133. Lynch argues further that the decline of small, family-owned mortuaries, like his own, and their replacement by "corporate giants" able to practice "economies of scale," can be traced to Mitford's complaints about funeral costs: "she fails to notice that cremation, pre-need and cost cutting were notions the marketplace learned from her. Ever ready to trade custom for convenience, to discount meaning for cost efficiency, she fails to recognize her own hand in shaping the future of a 'death-care' marketplace that has been 'Mitfordized'" (pp. 132–33).

57. "Killed when a bus": ibid., pp. 127–28; for Mitford, see Elliot and McCreery. Lynch does quote Mitford's comment that "the day after the baby was buried we left for Corsica [where] we lived for three months in the welcome unreality of a foreign town, shielded by distance from the sympathy of friends"—and shielded too, perhaps, from the embarrassment of comforters, the shame of mourning (Lynch, *Bodies*, p. 131).

58. Lynch, *Bodies*, pp. 127–28.

59. Waugh, pp. 39, 69; Mitford, *Revisited*, pp. 58, 144.

60. Waugh, p. 67; Mitford, *Revisited*, p. 142.

61. Fears, p. 7.

62. See Tappan, pp. 234–44 (quoting "The Indian History Source-Book: Sir Monier Monier-Williams, 'The Towers of Silence, 1870'"), in which a native informant explains that "God, indeed, sends the vultures, and . . . these birds do their appointed work much more expeditiously than millions of insects would do, if we committed our bodies to the ground. . . . Here in these five Towers rest the bones of all the Parsis that have lived in Bombay for the last two hundred years. We form a united body in life, and we are united in death."

63. See Greenfield, passim.

64. On contemporary confusion about funerals and mourning, see Stephenson, especially "The Ritual-less Society and the Death of Ceremony," pp. 212–13. For a more sardonic account of changing customs, see the undertaker-poet Lynch, who explains in "Socko Finish" that at today's "funeral home the hot topics (forgive me) are cremation and designer funerals. Members of my parents' generation, in their 70's now, are behaving as their boomer children once did—fast and mobile. . . . They do not want to be 'grounded' to the graves they bought when people stayed put and always came home. Their ashes are Fed-Exed around the hemisphere in little packages, roughly the weight of a bowling ball [but] their sons and daughters, in receipt of these tiny reminders are beginning to wonder: Is that all there is?" ("Socko," p. 36).

65. Burress.

66. Lynch, *Bodies*, p. 126.

67. Lin, p. 4, section 9.

68. Gopnik, p. 36.

69. "Tons of flowers" and "grave-gifts": see Greenhalgh, p. 42. Greenhalgh notes that flowers "form the most traditional and conventional feature of funerals and death commemoration in Western culture [but in Britain they] largely disappeared from religion after the Reformation, returning only in the mid nineteenth century as part of what has been called the cult of mourning" (p. 42).

70. Gopnik. As witty a writer in his way as Waugh and Mitford, Gopnik also notes here, somewhat crossly, that poor Mother Teresa was the "Groucho Marx of grief [since] Groucho, as nobody any longer remembers, died three days after Elvis."

71. On "mass hysteria," see Walkerdine, who also notes that although at first the so-called chattering classes of intellectuals and journalists thought the reaction to Diana's death was mass hysteria, "the tide against mass hysteria began to turn when television commentators spoke to the crowds leaving flowers and queuing to sign books of condolence to discover that they were not mindless zombies but actually could make coherent, even rational, arguments about the importance of the princess and the importance of their presence and mourning" (p. 99).

72. Greenhalgh, p. 46, quotes Metcalf and Huntington (p.134 ff) on the royal death as "a symbolic paradigm." On "the Diana events," see Kear and Steinberg, "Ghost Writing," p. 4 (a sample passage: "The complex intersections of globality and locality figured the Diana events as forms of post-colonial cultural renewal as well as nostalgic imperialistic return. For example, a globalizing media made claims of national and global unification even as the imagined 'community of mourning' produced exclusionary closures and disunities"). On "*transferred feelings*," see R. Johnson, p. 31.

73. Taylor, p. 205.

74. R. Johnson, pp. 18, 24, 31; "a theatrical opportunity," Kear and Steinberg, p. 7.

75. Greenhalgh, p. 47.

76. Taylor, pp. 200–201.

77. See Greenhalgh, p. 43, Walkerdine, p. 100, and Gross, passim.

78. On spontaneous shrines, see Grider, passim.

79. Taylor, p. 205.

80. Bronski: "The thousands of 'missing' posters in Lower Manhattan are a form of public keening not seen in this country since the AIDS quilt." See also "Missing: Streetscape of a City in Mourning," an exhibit mounted by the New-York Historical Society in collaboration with City Lore: The New York Center for Urban Folk Culture; the homepage for this exhibit notes that in "striking images, in items left at Union Square, and in personal memorials and shrines from all five boroughs, the streetscape of public grief that followed September 11th was unprecedented in American history in its dispersion across the greater New York area."

81. Greenhalgh, p. 43.

82. On the "democratization of death," see, e.g., Bronski, passim, as well as "The Democratization of Death," in the *Chronicle of Higher Education*.

83. Cannadine, p. 218; Gorer, p. 6. Gorer adds that there was also "almost certainly, a question of public morale; one should not show the face of grief to the boys home on leave from the trenches."

84. Hibberd and Onions, p. 115.

85. The poignant Children's Memorial at Yad Vashem, in Jerusalem, is a particularly powerful instance of this memorial strategy; as the visitor moves through darkness in a labyrinth of mirrors among which candles seem to float in nothingness, a disembodied voice recites, endlessly, the names, ages, and homelands of children killed or lost in the Holocaust.

86. Winter, pp. 107–08, 105; "silent scream": Scully, p. 28. For an overview of memorials, monuments, cemeteries, and mourning practices associated with the British war dead in the twentieth century, see Tarlow, pp. 147–70.

87. On Lin and Lutyens, see Tatum, pp. 10–16; "no hint": Winter, pp. 104–05.

88. Menand: 58; Lin, p. 4, section 10. For a participant's history of the conception and construction of the Vietnam Wall and the controversy surrounding its design, see Scruggs and Swerdlow, and for interesting discussions of the wall and other similar monuments, see Laqueur et al., *Grounds for Remembering*.

89. Noting the "irresistible need many visitors [to the Vietnam Veterans Memorial] feel to touch a chiseled name, kiss it, talk to it, offer it flowers or gifts, leave it notes or letters," R. Harrison remarks that such gestures are "evidence enough of the dead's privative presence in the stone—a presence at once given and denied" (p. 137), like, I would add, the presence/absence of the dead in our memories.

90. Menand, p. 62.

91. Derrida, p. 49.

92. In a discussion of the difference between the Vietnam Wall and the AIDS quilt, Mohr notes that the dead named on the wall "are not even shades of themselves but are reduced merely to that about them which was most public and ultimately arbitrary, given by others. . . . A name here serves not as a sign of distinctiveness or uniqueness but as a mere place holder. Uniqueness is set aside for the sake of the representation of the massiveness of death" (p. 114). See also Hawkins, p. 760:

"As with the Vietnam Veterans Memorial, the names themselves are the memorial." Yet even while I agree with the notion that the names of the dead are "public and ultimately arbitrary" and that they are at least metaphorically the material out of which Thiepval, the wall, and the quilt are constructed, I would still claim that they are *particular* in their abstraction; the accumulation of names in which all these memorials are founded renders these monuments notably different from such memorials as the Tomb of the Unknowns (and nameless) in Arlington, Virginia, or for that matter Lutyens's Cenotaph in London (dedicated simply to the unnamed "Glorious Dead"). In this connection, see also Holst-Warhaft's comment that as memorials "designed to keep the memory of each . . . person alive" neither the wall nor the quilt "is monumental in the sense of the First World War memorials that towered above the landscape" but both must be "read from close hand" (*Cue for Passion*, p. 185).

93. Mohr notes that the quilt isn't technically a "real" quilt because "it has no filling or even a backing, no lamination and none of the painstakingly detailed stitchery that makes quilts quilts" (p. 107).

94. I thank the textile scholar and artist Virginia Davis for this perspective on the friendship quilt; on the likeness of the individual panels in the AIDS quilt to "spontaneous shrines," see Mohr's account of the project's inception on a night in San Francisco in 1985, when mourners on an annual candlelight march in memory of George Moscone and Harvey Milk "covered the walls of San Francisco's old Federal Building with placards bearing the names of people who had died of AIDS" (p. 107). Hawkins points out that "Unlike stone, with its illusion of an eternal witness, cloth fades and frays with time; its fragility, its constant need for mending, tell the real truth about 'material' life" (p. 765), and adds that the quilt "has taken a female art form and opened it up to men" (p. 767).

95. To be sure, some commentators have considered the *Times'* "Portraits of Grief" too relentlessly (and perhaps propagandistically) upbeat. See, for instance, Simpson: "[T]he stories were almost all versions of the same story: happy people, fulfilled in their jobs, fountains of love and charity. . . . Everyone, under the roofs of the Twin Towers, was happy and getting happier. . . . The effect [was] one of sameness, of a very limited range of differences." But to read the "Portraits" this way is to overlook their revision of the traditional obituary through an innovative use of quotidian details as well as their striking particularizing of the individual lives of those who died in a mass catastrophe.

96. See Salamon, p. B-36, as well as Glass, THIS AMERICAN LIFE online, and HOLLY WOODFOREVER.COM. on the Forever Network.

CHAPTER 11: ON THE BEACH WITH SYLVIA PLATH

1. For the couple's vacation with the Merwins at their farmhouse in the Dordogne, see Stevenson, pp. 215–17, 336–42.

2. Porter, "Poetic Justice" (Monday, July 30, 2001), online at www.theage.com .au/entertainment/2001/07/30/FFX3ZSW4RPC.html.

3. Bauby, pp. 32, 74.

4. "Berck-Plage" appears in Plath, *CP*, pp. 196–201.

5. Alvarez, p. 31; Folsom, p. 1. Folsom goes on to argue that the "poison" of Plath's "festering memory" of her father's death "distorts her vision of the scene" and "must be drawn out by the poultice of the poem's making, and be replaced by healthy tissue" (p. 3).

6. Plath was just enough ahead of me—four or five years older, I gathered—that I could be secretly competitive without being as overwhelmingly daunted by her achievements as I would be by those of an exact contemporary. That I too had been guest managing editor of *Mademoiselle* (albeit four years after she was) during the triumphant "prize" month she later so devastatingly portrayed in *The Bell Jar*—that I'd indeed worked closely with Cyrilly Abels, the very Jay Cee of that novel—cemented what I considered an obscure bond between my own quotidian domesticity and the more glamorous life of this author strolling a European beach of which I'd never heard. (For more about this, see my " 'Fine White Flying Myth.' ")

7. For a fine discussion of the "American family elegy" see Ramazani.

8. Hughes, note to "Berck-Plage," Plath, *CP*, p. 293; he offered the same explanation in C. Newman, pp. 187–95.

9. *Michelin*, p. 57. Interestingly, the *Michelin Guide* goes on to note that this "*centre de cure*" which in 1980 consisted of six establishments with three thousand beds among them "*est né du dévouement d'une humble femme, Marianne Brillard, dite Marianne 'toute seule' parce qu'elle avait perdu son mari et ses quatre enfants, qui recevait, vers 1850, les petits soffreteux, malingres ou scrofuleux*" (p. 57). The benevolence and devotion of the long-suffering Marianne contrasts dramatically with the insistence of Plath's speaker that "I am not a nurse, white and attendant" as well as with her assertion that her own "heart [is] too small to bandage [the] terrible faults" of the children who seem to be following her "with hooks and cries." Considering Plath's skills as a researcher, it's perfectly possible that she'd read about the famous Marianne in a guide to the town or even in an earlier edition of the *Michelin*. At the same time, Bauby notes: "After devoting itself to the care of young victims of a tuberculosis epidemic after the Second World War, Berck gradually shifted its focus away from children" (p. 31).

10. See Folsom, who discusses variant drafts but doesn't indicate whether the Berck-Plage passages were begun earlier than (or separately from) the Percy Key material.

11. Among Plath's hospital poems, see "Morning in the Hospital Solarium," "Three Voices," "Tulips," "In Plaster," "The Surgeon at 2 A.M.," and "Paralytic." She also fictionalized medical scenes in such prose writings as "Johnny Panic and the Bible of Dreams" and "The Daughters of Blossom Street." For an extended discussion of Plath's representations of medicine, see Susanna Gilbert, "Some God Got Hold of Me."

12. Kendall notes that Plath had been "charting the gradual decline of her neighbor,

Percy Key, for several months" and adds that "Percy's fate colored—or cor-
rupted—Plath's imaginative life during these months: not only her notebooks,
but also 'Among the Narcissi' and 'Berck-Plage', are heavily preoccupied with his
deteriorating health and approaching death. This ever-present intimation of
mortality also inspires 'Apprehensions,' a meditation on dying and the fear of
death, in which the speaker confesses to 'a terror / Of being wheeled off under
crosses and a rain of pietàs,' 'The Rabbit-Catcher' and 'Event' . . . [works whose]
concerns inspire and become part of a more general malaise: as Plath reports,
'Everybody, it seems, is going or dying in this cold mean spring' " (p. 97).

13. For Plath's comments on the Keys, see her *Journals*, especially pp. 664, 668–73.
14. Arguably the reification of the dead man's body parts as jewels ("eye-stones, yellow and valuable," a "tongue, sapphire of ash") echoes the transformation of
death into treasure so famously described in *The Tempest*'s "Full fathom five," a
Shakespeare song (and play) that haunted Plath: "Nothing of him that doth
fade, / But doth suffer a sea-change / Into something rich and strange." For a discussion of Plath's own poem called "Full Fathom Five," see this chapter, p. 313.
15. Eliot, "East Coker," *Four Quartets*, p. 27; Lowell, "Quaker Graveyard," *SP*, p. 10.
16. Hardy, *CP*, p. 150; Arnold, pp. 165–67.
17. Arnold, "To Marguerite—Continued," pp. 111–12.
18. The full text of this definition adds that *abaer* derives from "a-, at (from Latin
ad–. . .) + baer, *to gape*." Readers who intrepidly go to bay2 will discover that
it refers primarily to an architectural "bay," from (again) "Old French *baee*, an
opening, from *baer*, to gape."
19. Plath, *Journals*, p. 207; and ("Roget's strumpet") p. 212; Hughes, "Sylvia Plath:
Ariel," *Winter Pollen*, p. 161.
20. Plath referred to Moore in her journals as among "the ageing giantesses &
poetic godmothers" (p. 360). For "incognito," see *Letters Home*, p. 168.
21. See Plath, "Ocean 1212-W," *Johnny Panic*, pp. 109–16.
22. Arnold, "The Forsaken Merman," p. 186.
23. Plath, *Journals* (August 1957–October 1958), p. 381. In addition, Plath felt that
the sea was a metaphor for her poems and for "the artist's subconscious" while
the father image / male muse / Ted also suggested "the sea-father Neptune—
and the pearls and coral highly-wrought to art: pearls sea-changed from the
ubiquitous grit of sorrow and dull routine." More forebodingly, however, she
closed this upbeat entry with a quotation from Joyce's Anna Livia Plurabelle (in
Finnegans Wake): " 'It's old and old it's sad and old it's sad and weary I go back
to you my cold father, my cold mad father, my cold mad feary father. . . .' so
Joyce says, so the river flows to the paternal source of godhead."
24. Hughes, "Sylvia Plath and Her Journals," *Winter Pollen*, p. 186.
25. See *American Heritage Dictionary of the English Language*.
26. Larkin, pp. 208–09; for a discussion of this poem, see chapter 10 of this volume.
27. For a description of this statue, see the *Michelin Guide to Brittany*, p. 185. The
guide also notes that the "Raz du Sein or tide race" that the statue overlooks is
a phenomenon about which "an old saying has it [that] 'no one passes [it] with-

out fear or sorrow.'" For a brief but incisive discussion of Moore's "A Grave," see R. Harrison, pp. 5–8.

28. For a fine discussion of the psychological and textual connections between Plath's imaginings of her father and the "yew hedge of orders" she describes in "Little Fugue," see Kendall, pp. 75–77, especially his analysis of successive drafts of the poem based on the idea that "the yew 'stops' the mouths of the dead even while acting as a 'go-between.' " Adds Kendall: "Graves's *The White Goddess* reports the legend to which the draft undoubtedly alludes: 'In Brittany it is said that church-yard yews will spread a root to the mouth of each corpse.' "

29. Cf. Kroll, passim, and Kendall, pp. 111–28.

30. A. Plath, Introduction to *Letters*, p. 25.

31. Plath, *Journals*, pp. 44–45 (July 1950–1953). Interestingly, when this already quite ambitious young poet adduced examples of annihilation, she thought about the deaths of famous writers, noting that "Sinclair Lewis died [and] is now slowly decomposing in his tomb. The spark went out; the hand that wrote, the optical and auditory nerves that recorded, the brain folds that recreated—all are limp, flaccid, rotting now. Edna St. Vincent Millay is dead—and she will never push the dirt from her tomb and see the apple-scented rain in slanting silver lines, never." For the useful phrase "believing atheist," I am indebted to Marlene Griffith.

32. Beckett, *Waiting*, p. 29.

33. Plath, *Journals*, p. 63.

34. Ibid., pp. 120, 412, 462, 475. At one point, working as a mother's helper for a family of Christian Scientists, Plath engages in a long meditation on their creed, then turns to "hide irreverent laughter" when one of the children, "constipated, gets a lesson instead of a laxative." At another point she reports feeling "a sudden ridiculous desire this morning to investigate the Catholic Church," but then has to admit, "I would need a Jesuit to argue me [into believing]."

35. Ibid., p. 204 (November 1955–April 1956).

36. Ibid., p. 459 (December 1958–November 1959).

37. See Plath, *CP*, p. 294, which quotes her comment, intended to accompany a BBC reading of "Death & Co.," that one of the death figures she represents here has "the marmoreal coldness of Blake's death mask."

38. Blake, p. 144. The note on the etymology of "Nobodaddy" is by Alicia Ostriker, the editor of this Blake edition.

39. "The Representation of the Invisible and the Psychological Category of the Double: The Colossos": In Vernant, pp. 305–07, and passim. Plath clearly couldn't have known about Vernant's work at the time she wrote "The Colossus" but he may have been drawing upon sources with which she was familiar. Bronfen also cites Vernant in a reading of "The Colossus" in which she argues that although the poet's "incessant mourning produces not just a fragmentary but also an inanimate representation of the father, this stony frame also proves to be a viable shelter from the contingencies of worldly existence" (i.e., "Nights, I squat in the cornucopia / Of your left ear, out of the wind"); see Bronfen, pp. 80–81.

40. Blake also used "Nobodaddy" for comic purposes, though "To Nobodaddy" is

deeply serious. In the doggerel verse of "When Klopstock England defied," Blake turned his diabolical antideity into a buffoon: "When Klopstock England defied, / Uprose terrible Blake in his pride / For old Nobodaddy aloft / Farted and belch'd and cough'd," etc. See "Notebook Poems, c. 1800–1806," in Blake, p. 488.

41. Kendall, p. 153, quoting Stevenson, p. 277.

42. See Kendall, pp. 111–12, for a good discussion of Plath's occasional "troubling and as yet unremarked references to Jewishness" and the "undercurrent of anti-Semitism [revealing that her] growing sense of affinity with Holocaust victims, already the subject of considerable controversy, is even more problematic than has been suggested." In several character sketches and late letters (one contemporaneous with "Daddy"), Kendall notes, Plath uses the derogatory word "Jewy." And although Kendall doesn't mention this, that Assia Guttman, the "other" for whom her husband had left her, was half Jewish is relevant here too. In this context indeed, the famous assertion in "Daddy" that "I may be a bit of a Jew" can be read as a competitive boast. For further, and different, discussions of Plath's Holocaust imagery, however, see (among many others) Steiner, "In Extremis," and Gubar, "Prosopopoeia and Holocaust Poetry," pp. 112–28.

43. "Sheep in Fog" was completed on January 28, 1963, and in an incisive analysis of the drafts, Hughes uses its variants to illustrate key changes in Plath's style and outlook. See Hughes, "Sylvia Plath: The Evolution of 'Sheep in Fog,'" *Winter Pollen*, pp. 191–211.

44. For Plath's readings of West African tales and legends, see Kroll, pp. 89–91, 96–97, 103, 238–41.

45. For a fuller discussion of stars in "Insomniac" and "Crossing the Water," see Kendall, pp. 82–83.

46. Ramazani, pp. 282–83.

47. Lowell, Foreword to *Ariel*, p. vii; Alvarez, p. 46.

48. See J. Rose, pp. 1–3.

49. For a perhaps not entirely reliable account of Plath's final weekend in London, see Becker. On Plath's depression, see also Middlebrook, pp. 206–11. For another perspective on Plath's death, see Fainlight, the poet-friend to whom Plath dedicated "Elm"; Fainlight confesses in a memoir of their friendship that she was "haunted" for months, wondering whether she might have "saved Sylvia" if circumstances had been different.

50. Plath, "Context," *Johnny Panic*, p. 82.

51. Hughes, "Red," *Birthday Letters*, pp. 197–98.

52. See Plath's comment in her copy of *Leaves of Grass* online: "Plath on Whitman."

CHAPTER 12: WAS THE NINETEENTH CENTURY DIFFERENT, AND LUCKIER?

1. In Nietzsche's *The Gay Science,* the "madman" who is a prophet of atheism and nihilism declares that we humans have "killed" God with what is essentially our scientific relativism and wonders, "What were we doing when we unchained this earth from its sun? Whither is it moving now? Whither are we

moving? Away from all suns? . . . Are we not straying, as through an infinite nothing? Do we not feel the breath of empty space? Has it not become colder? Is not night continually closing in on us? Do we not need to light lanterns in the morning? Do we hear nothing as yet of the noise of the gravediggers who are burying God? Do we smell nothing as yet of the divine decomposition? Gods, too, decompose. God is dead. God remains dead. And we have killed him" (pp. 181–82).

2. Sigourney, p. 12, dedicated "To Daniel Wadsworth, Esq., The Friend Of All Who Mourn." In its entirety, stanza two of this mawkish poem reads:

> *The birthday came! The change, how great!*
>   *Fast fell the mourner's tear,*
> *The gourd had wither'd in a night,*
>   *The banquet was not here;*
> *No! no! the banquet was above,*
>   *At the Redeemer's feet,*
> *The cherub in its parents' arms,*
>   *And every bliss complete.*

3. Twain, p. 121.

4. See Pflieger.

5. A. Tennyson, "Crossing the Bar," *Poems*, p. 523; R. Browning, "Prospice," pp. 296–97.

6. The authors of several other turn-of-the-century academic texts called his "lines . . . the very drybones of prose" and described *Leaves of Grass* as "a strange volume of what cannot be called poetry" (Willard, p. 132). In 1895, frankly identifying Whitman's methods of versification with "degenerative insanity as well as sexual perversion," a German scholar had even decided that Whitman's so-called poetry was really "prose gone mad" (Willard, p. 159). But even such early defenders of Whitman's art as Saintsbury and Howells conceded that "[a] page of his work has little or no look of poetry about it" because "he produced a new kind in literature, which we may or may not allow to be poetry" (Saintsbury, p. 788; Howells, p. 790). As late as 1937 their views were echoed by, among others, the poet Edgar Lee Masters, who declared that although "[n]o one says now with Emerson that Whitman is half song thrush and half alligator," there "may never be a time when . . . cultivated minds will not prefer Milton's 'Lycidas,' Tennyson's 'In Memoriam' and even Arnold's 'Thyrsis' to Whitman's 'When Lilacs Last in the Dooryard Bloom'd'" (pp. 296, 307).

7. In fact, even the highest praise Higginson offered Dickinson's prosody was vaguely censorious: "[W]e catch glimpses of a lyric strain, sustained perhaps but for a line or two at a time and making the reader regret its sudden cessation" (Higginson, p. vi).

8. Mrs. Todd went on to complain that Dickinson ignored "the simplest laws of verse-making" and that "what she called rhymes grated on me" (R. Miller, pp.

8–9). As for Bowles, he passionately admired the sort of "little poetic gems" offered him by one Collette Loomis, who was among the *Republican*'s "pet contributors" (for example, "We must all grow old, for time goes on; / The flowers will fade that we live among; / But the flowers of feeling their strength impart / to the genial heart, to the tender heart. . . .") (R. Miller, pp. 122–23). Similarly, Holland's 1873 *Illustrated Library of Favorite Song* didn't include any of Dickinson's work (or for that matter any of Whitman's). As late as 1924, indeed, Conrad Aiken, one of Dickinson's first major champions, apologized that "[h]er genius was . . . erratic. . . . Her disregard for accepted forms or for regularities was incorrigible." Thus, despite his chronological and intellectual distance from Higginson and Holland, he might well have agreed with these mentors that Dickinson wrote what Higginson called "poetry torn up by the roots"—or what Holland pronounced "not poetry" (Aiken, pp. 301–08). To be sure, a number of the "genteel critics" who reviewed the posthumous collection of Dickinson's poems that was edited by Higginson and Todd did share the editors' sense of the work's genius even while expressing wonder at its strangeness. Noted one reviewer in the November 23, 1890, *Boston Sunday Herald*: "Madder rhymes one has seldom seen—scornful disregard of poetic technique could hardly go farther—and yet there is about the book a fascination, a power, a vision that enthralls you" (Buckingham, p. 34, and for comparable comments, see Buckingham, passim). I am grateful to Joanne Feit Diehl for calling these reviews to my attention.

9. Whitman, *CPP,* pp. 192–94; unless otherwise indicated, all Whitman texts are as given in this edition.

10. "For all flesh is as grass . . .": 1 Peter 1, 24–25, 23.

11. For "leaves" as a printer's "verbal equivalent of doodling," see Delbanco; for further comments on Whitman as a printer, see Loving, pp. 36, 38. On the "Word made Flesh" see also Dickinson, J 1651/F 1715.

12. "Notes on New Books," *Washington Daily National Intelligencer* (February 18, 1856), p. 2.

13. All Dickinson texts are from *CP,* ed. Thomas Johnson; citations will be given (as here, in "J 731") by "Johnson" number—i.e., as numbered in this edition. For the convenience of readers who are using the newer, Franklin edition, Franklin numbers will also be given as alternatives (e.g., J 731/F 851).

14. L 86, p. 197. All Dickinson letters are from Dickinson, *Letters,* ed. Thomas Johnson; citations will be given (as here, in "L 86") by "Johnson" number—i.e., as numbered in this edition.

15. "Sentimental religious culture": see, e.g., St. Armand, who argues strongly for Dickinson's deep engagement with such a culture, especially in chapters 2 ("Dark Parade: Dickinson, Sigourney, and the Victorian Way of Death"); 4 ("Paradise Deferred: Dickinson, Phelps, and the Image of Heaven"); and 5 ("American Grotesque: Dickinson, God, and Folk Forms"), but see also, among others, Eberwein, p. 39 and passim; "sermons on unbelief": L 176.

16. J 1551. To be sure, this poem continues by noting: "The abdication of Belief /

Makes the Behavior small— / Better an ignis fatuus / Than no illume at all—"
But the notion that "an ignis fatuus" may be more comforting than "no illume
at all" hardly suggests Dickinson's adherence to the kind of "sentimental religious culture" that produced, say, Mrs. Sigourney.

17. For differing critical views on "I heard a Fly buzz," see Duchac, *Commentary* . . .
    1890–1977, pp. 203–10, and *Commentary* . . . *1978–1989*, pp. 161–65.

18. See "Death is the supple Suitor / That wins at last" by carrying his mortal bride
    "away in triumph / To Troth unknown / And Kindred as responsive / As Porce-
    lain" (J 1445/F 1470), as well as "It was a quiet way— / He asked if I was his . . .
    And then He bore me on / Before this mortal noise / With swiftness, as of Char-
    iots" (J 1053/F 573), and "The grave my little cottage is, / Where 'Keeping
    house' for thee / I make my parlor orderly / And lay the marble tea" (J 1743/F
    1784). To be sure, this last poem goes on to imagine "two" united for "everlast-
    ing life" in "strong society," but its examples of such "life" (the grave and, within
    it, the unnerving "marble tea") hardly suggest the celestial banqueting of con-
    ventional Christian piety.

19. Dickinson took voice lessons as a girl, played the piano expertly all her life, and
    was the most musical member of her family; see Small, pp. 206–24.

20. Leyda, vol. 2, p. 475.

21. Quoted in Sewall, vol. 2, pp. 273–74; Mrs. Todd reinforces the allegorical signif-
    icance of her reference to "the bars being lowered" between the fields and the
    cemetery" with a quote from Dickinson's poem beginning "Let down the Bars,
    Oh Death— / The tired Flocks come in" (J 1065), one of the poet's more con-
    ventionally pious verses.

22. See "Hugh Conway" (Frederick John Fargus).

23. For Whitman's funeral, see Kaplan, pp. 52–54.

24. For Whitman's tomb, see ibid., pp. 49–52.

25. Whitman, "The Million Dead, Too, Summ'd Up," *Specimen Days, CPP,* pp.
    777–78.

26. Eberwein, p. 39. Interesting extended discussions of these issues appear in
    Wolosky and St. Armand.

27. L 255, late March 1862, pp. 397–98, and L 245, December 31, 1861, p. 386.

28. L 263, early May, p. 407.

CHAPTER 13: "RATS' ALLEY" AND THE DEATH OF PASTORAL

1. See Darrell Hall, pp. 175–87, 215–21. Agamben also notes the origin of the concentration camp in the so-called *reconcentrado* camps established in Cuba by
   Spanish authorities; see Agamben, p. 166, and chapter 6 of this volume.

2. Hardy, *CP,* pp. 90–91.

3. Service, pp. 95–98.

4. W. Collins, p. 34.

5. Brooke, *CP,* p. 111; ironically, Brooke died of blood poisoning on a troopship

destined for Gallipoli (in 1915) before he had experienced very much significant action.

6. I use the words "ambitious," "distinguished," and "influential" to differentiate the World War I poets who have come to seem most powerful from a range of their often quite popular contemporaries—including, for instance, "Woodbine Willie," John Oxenham, Robert Service, and Major Owen Rutter, among others—who wrote more conventionally patriotic, upbeat, and sometimes jingoistic verse about the war; for more on these writers, see Winter; Stephen, *Price of Pity*; and Hynes, *A War Imagined.*

7. Owen, letter of August 8, 1917, in *SL*, p. 539

8. Stevens, "The Owl in the Sarcophagus," *CPP*, p. 374.

9. Stevens, *CPP*, p. 81. As a combatant in the Great War the Italian poet Giuseppe Ungaretti produced a famous haikulike piece entitled "Soldati," whose fatalistic and distanced vision of war death is notably similar to the stance of Stevens's "The Death of a Soldier": "*Si sta come / d'autunno / sugli alber / le foglie*" ("One is as / in autumn / on the trees / the leaves"). For a helpful historical discussion of the trope of the dead, especially the war dead, as leaves, see R. Harrison, pp. 125–33; as a vision of specifically "modern death," however, Ungaretti's poem, like Stevens's, seems to me to depart significantly from the Homeric, Virgilian, Dantesque, and Miltonic visions of the dead as leaves that Harrison traces; far from being an epic simile, Ungaretti's terse comparison is wistfully fragmentary, seemingly spoken out of nowhere and to no one, in the midst of the Great War's alienating No Man's Land. "After the first death": cf. Dylan Thomas's famous line "After the first death there is no other," which concludes another famous wartime elegy, "A Refusal to Mourn the Death, by Fire, of a Child in London."

10. Translation from Stevens, *CPP*, p. 1008.

11. Ibid., p. 545.

12. For these definitions of "pastoral," see the *American Heritage Dictionary*, 4th ed.

13. Sacks, p. 2 and passim.

14. The casualty statistics from the First World War are staggering: the British war dead numbered 908,371; the American dead numbered 126,000; the French dead numbered 1,357,800. Total casualties from the war (including the wounded and missing in action) came to 37,508,686, more than 50 percent of the many soldiers from around the world who were mobilized to serve in the conflict. (See the ENCYCLOPAEDIA OF THE FIRST WORLD WAR online.)

15. See Winter, who insists that a "process of re-sacralization marks the poetry of the war," for the "war poets did not turn away from the sacred. Theirs is not the poetry of 'demystification.'" On the contrary, "Many sought to reach the sacred through the metaphor of resurrection" (pp. 223, 221).

16. See Fussell, *Great War*. For the war as "future shock" and "apocalypse," see Bradbury, pp. 193–94.

17. On the "Angel of Mons," see Wilson, pp. 42, 161, and M. Gilbert, pp. 51, 61, 162.

See also David, p. 118—"Some beleaguered soldiers [at Mons] reported being rescued by angels and ghostly longbowmen"—and Whitehouse, pp. 20–21: after the battle on what is known as the retreat from Mons, some Coldstream Guards, the last to withdraw, got lost in the area of the Mormal Forest and had dug-in to make a last stand. Whitehouse reports that an "angel" then appeared: "The glowing nimbus moved in closer and the Coldstreamers perceived the dim outline of a female figure. As it became more distinct, they decided that they were looking at an angel. It looked exactly like any angel they had ever seen in a regimental chapel: tall, slim, and wearing a white flowing gown. She had a gold band around her hair and Eastern sandals on her feet, a pair of white wings were folded against her slim back." The guardsmen followed the glowing figure across an open field to a hidden, sunken road that enabled them to escape. For a discussion of this legend's derivation from Arthur Machen's popular tale "The Bowmen," see Coulson and Hanlon. On spiritualism and the First World War, see chapter 4 of this work ("E-mail to the Dead"), p. 74.

18. Aldington, p. 429; Brittain, pp. 252–53; and chapter 7 of the present work, pp. 147–52. For a treatment of these issues from a somewhat different perspective, see "Soldier's Heart," in Gilbert and Gubar, *Sexchanges* .

19. Ford Maddox Ford, "Arms and the Mind," cited in Hynes, *A War Imagined*, p. 106; Binding, pp. 216–17, cited in Hynes, *Soldiers' Tale*, p. 7. Adds Hynes: "I call this desolation 'landscape,' but it isn't that: it's *anti*-landscape, an entirely strange terrain with nothing natural left in it. It's the antithesis of the comprehensible natural world that travel writers inhabit" (p. 7). On the transformation of landscape to "anti-landscape," see also Blunden, pp. 213–14, on a return to "our old familiar place, Observatory Ridge, and Sanctuary Wood": "[N]ever was a transformation more surprising. The shapeless Ridge had lost every tree; the brown hummock [was] flayed and clawed up. . . . [W]e looked over the befouled fragments of Ypres, the solitary sheet of water, Zilleeke Lake, the completed hopelessness. The denuded scene had acquired a strange abruptness of outline; the lake and the ashy city lay unprotected, isolated."

20. Owen, *CL*.

21. For further discussion of Bone's paintings, see Hynes, *A War Imagined*, pp. 160–61.

22. D. Jones, *In Parenthesis*, p. 43.

23. Ibid., p. 54.

24. Silkin, p. 156; for "Counter-Attack," see Sassoon, p. 68.

25. Graves, "A Dead Boche," p. 27.

26. Rosenberg, pp. 73, 80; Herbert Asquith, "After the Salvo," in Gardner, pp. 80–81.

27. Owen, *CP*, p. 65.

28. "To His Love," Gurney, p. 41.

29. Quoted in Cannadine, p. 203.

30. Ibid., p. 204.

31. Webster, pp. 52–53; I am grateful to John Currie for bringing this work to my attention.

32. Sassoon, pp. 23–24; cf. J. C. Squire's wry comment on conventional theology, discussed in chapter 10 of this volume: "God heard the embattled nations sing and shout: / 'Gott strafe England'—'God save the King'— / 'God this'—'God that'—and 'God the other thing'. / 'My God,' said God, 'I've got my work cut out,'" (Silkin, p. 140). "[F]rom that moment," quoted in Dyer, pp. 126–27; Dyer adds: "In some ways, then, the Thiepval Memorial [to the 73,077 "missing" in that battle] is a memorial if not to death, then certainly to the superfluousness of God." In the course of this infamously devastating battle, which lasted from July 1 to November 13, 1916, the British suffered some 420,000 casualties, the French 195,000 and the Germans 650,000.

33. Owen, *CP*, p. 44; on the crucial importance of the soldier's testimony, see Hynes, *Soldiers' Tale*.

34. Felman and Laub, p. 5.

35. Freud, "Reflections upon War and Death," *Character and Culture*, pp. 109, 113, 124; for further discussion of this essay, see chapter 7 of this book.

36. Cannadine, p. 217.

37. Kipling, "Common Form," *Verse*, p. 446. See also "The Children: 1914–1918," pp. 590–92.

38. Freud, "Reflections upon War and Death," p.124; Cannadine, p. 218.

39. For discussions of spiritualism, see Cannadine, pp. 230–31, Winter, pp. 54–71, and chapter 4 of this work.

40. Owen, *CP*, pp. 34–35.

41. A passage from Shelley also seems to have influenced Owen: in *The Revolt of Islam* the speaker reports that "one whose spear had pierced me, leaned beside . . . and all / Seemed like some brothers on a journey wide . . . whom now strange meeting did befall / In a strange land." For further comment on the sources of "Strange Meeting," see Silkin, pp. 236–37; for "The Rear-Guard," see also Sassoon, pp. 69–70.

42. To put the question more Byronically, how would Shelley have shaped "Adonais" had he himself been the author of the article that snuffed out Keats's life, that "fiery particle"?

43. Eliot, *The Waste Land, Facs.*, p. 1.

44. Critics who have made this claim include J. Miller, Jay, and me. In 1977, for instance, Miller offered a particularly interesting analysis of the efforts at elegiac resolution embodied in "What the Thunder Said," while in 1983 Jay noted that the "corpus of the elegy lies buried in *The Waste Land*." Jay's reading was primarily Bloomian, with hardly any reference to the work's biographical context, but Miller's discussion evolved out of his still-underappreciated *T.S. Eliot's Personal Waste Land*, which made extensive use of John Peter's work. In what has since become a classic of literary censorship, the poet's solicitors had Peter's original essay suppressed, but Peter's argument is still the most incisive statement of what might be considered the text's covert "plot," for whether or not one would choose to claim that the speaker of *The Waste Land* had "fallen . . . irretrievably," in love, it is clear that *an* "object of his love was a young man."

See Peter, J. Miller, and Jay, pp. 156–62. My own earlier discussion of *The Waste Land* as fragmented elegy appears in *Sexchanges,* pp. 310–14, and in " 'Rats' Alley,' " pp. 179–201. For a different reading of *The Waste Land* that also acknowledges the centrality of Eliot's relationship to Verdenal in the poem's making, see Froula, pp. 235–53.

45. Eliot's comment about Verdenal was made in a review of Henri Massis, *Evocations*, that appeared in the *Criterion* (April 1934); the poet remembered "a friend coming across the Luxembourg Gardens in the late afternoon, waving a branch of lilac, a friend who was later (so far as I could find out) to be mixed with the mud of Gallipoli"; for further commentary see Miller, p. 19 and passim. For other analyses of the relationship, see both Watson and Mayer, pp. 199–202. Without entering into details about what some commentators have scathingly called "the homosexual interpretation of *The Waste Land*," I confess that I have long thought the argument about Verdenal's significance to Eliot is incontrovertible.

46. A number of the points I make here and in the next few paragraphs are drawn directly from Gilbert and Gubar, *Sexchanges.*

47. On the meaning of "Phlebas," see G. Smith, pp. 106–07; on another avatar of Verdenal, some of Eliot's own reminiscences together with the draft manuscripts of *The Waste Land* suggest that the "hyacinth girl" who appears in the poem's first section was originally a hyacinth *boy*. But such depersonalized vegetal rather than divine resurrection holds out considerably less hope for the posthumous fate of Eliot's drowned Phoenician sailor than, say, the heavenly assumption Milton imagines for his Lycidas.

48. Eliot, *Waste Land, Facs.*, p. 79.

49. Eliot, *Letters*, vol. 1, pp. 18, 32. Gide's homosexuality is not irrelevant here. Gide and Eliot exchanged letters expressing mutual admiration around the time the poet was writing and revising *The Waste Land.* See pp. 490–91, 494–95, 502–03, 516.

50. See note 45, this chapter.

51. J. Morris, pp. 188, 179.

52. Scott Herring, " 'Through the Grass and Flowers Came the Vile Streak': Dante, *The Waste Land*, and Pastoral Elegy," unpublished paper. I am grateful to Herring for allowing me to cite this fine essay, which was written for a seminar that I taught at the University of California, Davis, in the winter of 1997.

53. Another battle against the Turks, the struggle in Mesopotamia, also yielded imagery of a drought-stricken wasteland that Eliot may have associated with the rock-strewn terrain in which Verdenal died. An evocative, anonymous poem entitled "Home Thoughts" that appeared in the *Times* of London in 1916 offered some imagery the elegist of *The Waste Land* perhaps unconsciously echoed: "The *hot red rocks* of Aden / Stand from their burnished sea; / The bitter sands of Aden / Lie shimmering in their lee." See Stephen, ed., *Poems of the First World War*, pp. 185–86.

54. Masefield, *Gallipoli*, pp. 127–30; I am grateful to Scott Herring for directing me toward this illuminating work.

55. J. Miller, p. 21.

56. J. Morris, p. 193.

57. Winter, pp. 22–30.

58. For a discussion of this act of censorship and of Barbusse's book more generally, see ibid., pp. 178–86.

59. Eliot, *Waste Land, Facs.*, pp. 2, 125.

60. Fussell, *Great War*, p. 145; Fussell adds "Norse myth, Chaucer, *The Rime of the Ancient Mariner*, the poems of G. M. Hopkins, and even the works of Lewis Carroll" to his list, as he argues that *In Parenthesis* "can't keep its allusions from suggesting that the war, if ghastly, is firmly 'in the tradition'" (p. 146).

61. D. Jones, *In Parenthesis*, pp. ix, x. At least one commentator has spoken of this work's "quasi-documentary authority," and Jones himself considered the book "much more 'prosaic' " than some of his readers imagined, explaining that he had attempted to " 'proceed' from the known to the unknown"; see Dilworth, p. 50, and D. Jones, *Dai Greatcoat*, p. 189.

62. D. Jones, *In Parenthesis*, p. xiv.

63. Shakespeare, *Henry IV, Part I*, IV, 1.

64. D. Jones, *In Parenthesis*, p. 24.

65. Ibid., 185–86.

66. Fussell, *Great War*, p. 153. For more recent commentators who differ from Fussell in their assessment of the poem but do see *In Parenthesis* as striving to conclude with what is in some sense a redemptive view of the Great War, see, e.g., Ward—"*In Parenthesis* [achieves] the recovery of genuinely 'heroic,' even epic, form in a successful departure from the mode of 'personal lyric response' which had characterized the bulk of earlier war poetry" (p. 77)—and Whitaker: "*In Parenthesis* shapes a labyrinthine course and a synchronic form in rough harmony with other works of affirmative passage" (p. 33).

67. To be sure, some of these names (Balder, Lillywhite, even Fatty) have an allegorical/mythic ring. In this regard, Balder is particularly notable since he is the namesake of a Norse god who is described in Scandinavian folklore as handsome, wise, supposedly invulnerable, and even radiant (so bright, indeed, as to be a source of light). In the old myths, his death from a dart made of mistletoe—the only earthly substance that could wound him—and his ritual immolation on a funeral pyre was associated by Frazer with a sacred grove venerated in Norway and with traditional European festivals of fire intended to promote fertility (see Frazer, pp. 706–49). Yet ironically, along with the pure and flowery-sounding Lillywhite and the prosperous-sounding Fatty, Balder has now been assimilated into a far from sacred grove in the dead heart of the wasteland.

68. D. Jones, *In Parenthesis*, p. 186.

69. Ibid., p. 187.

70. See the *American Heritage Dictionary* definition of "geste" as a "notable adventure or exploit. **2a.** A verse romance or tale. **b.** A prose romance."

71. Fussell, *Great War*, p. 154. To be fair to Fussell, I should note that despite his many objections to *In Parenthesis*, he concludes that the book "remains in many ways a masterpiece impervious to criticism" (p. 154).

Chapter 14: Monsters of Elegy

1. See Stevens, "The Snow Man," *CPP*, p. 8.

2. See Iimura.

3. W. C. Williams, "To the Editor of *The Egoist*" (Vol. 3, No. 9, p. 137: 1915), *SL*, p. 30; the crude affairs of the war, Williams added, had gifted the New World with a number of refugees from the Old World, among them the experimental French painters Marcel Duchamp and Albert Gleizes, even while "in poetry the fiercest twitchings appeared," including the establishment of the innovative journal *Others,* and although by the end of his piece he ruefully recorded the "financial ruin" that ultimately faced *Others*, he was sufficiently encouraged by the creative flowering he'd witnessed to declare: "One turns at last to one's desk drawer and thumbs one's own verses with something of the feelings of a miser."

4. "Living on a rock": Whittemore, p. 130. On Williams's wartime responsibilities, see Mariani, p. 121. In "The Drill Sergeant" Williams produced a sketch about the guilt and horror of military killing that focused on the kind of trauma that combatants like Owen and Sassoon dramatized in their poems: the piece culminated in the ongoing nightmares—now we'd call them post-traumatic stress syndrome—of a soldier in Belleau Woods who "jammed his bayonet up behind the jaw of the [Prussian] boy facing him till it came out of the top of his head, he had to put his foot down on his face so he could pull it out again." See "The Drill Sergeant," pp. 243–45.

5. Stevens, *CPP*, p. 81 and chapter 13 of this book, pp. 368–71; Pound, pp. 61–64; Eliot, see chapter 13 of this book, pp. 384–90; Pound bitterly lamented in "Mauberly" that "There [in the Great War] died a myriad, / And of the best, among them, // For an old bitch gone in the teeth, / For a botched civilization." For an interesting comment on his mourning during and after the Great War, see Ramazani's claim that his "grief for Gaudier-Brzeska, though less submerged than Eliot's for Verdenal, was probably at least as determinative in his career" (p. 27); other American writers were of course to become combatants—most famously, perhaps, Ernest Hemingway and E. E. Cummings.

6. W. C. Williams, "The Dance," *CP*, vol. 2, p. 407, and "Death," in *CP*, vol. 1, p. 346. Mariani notes that an earlier version of "Death" more specifically described his father, who regularly traveled on business in the tropics: "his eyes / rolled up out of / the light— / calabashes— // such as he used to bring / home from South America when he would / go there on business trips— / in the years gone by" (p. 14). In both the earlier and later versions, however, the depiction of the cadaver is equally clinical, though perhaps its surgical objectivity is more

shocking in a biographical context. For "medical case histories," see Schott, Preface to *Kora in Hell*, in *Imaginations*, p. 5; "phraseology of science": Williams, *Imaginations*, p. 149; "no ideas but in things": "A Sort of a Song," *CP*, vol. 2, p. 55, and *Paterson*, pp. 6, 9.

7. Like Gertrude Stein, who identified the twentieth century as "the American century," Williams defined the future as American, the past as European. Thus "I had a violent feeling that Eliot had betrayed what I believed in," he confessed to an interviewer. "He was looking backward; I was looking forward"; see W. C. Williams, *I Wanted to Write a Poem*, p. 30; "the great catastrophe": see Tomlinson, Introduction to Williams, *SP*, p. vii. "Europe is nothing to us," Williams also pronounced. "Their music is death to us. . . . Every word we get must be broken off from the European mass" (*Imaginations*, pp. 174–75). "When we think of the body": "Water, Salts, Fat, etc.," a review of *The Human Body*, by Logan Clendening, M.D., in *Imaginations*, p. 359; "the practice of medicine": *Imaginations*, p. 365.

8. "Cool Tombs": Sandburg, p. 134; the poem first appeared in *Poetry* in 1917, after which Williams sent his comment to Harriet Monroe. He added: "Few men are making any progress in their art. They are adding new decoration or repeating the old stuff, but Sandburg is really thinking like an artist" (July 17, 1917, *SL*, p. 41); "approach death at a walk," *Imaginations*, p. 21; "death's canticle": ibid., p. 38.

9. "Jacob Louslinger": *Imaginations*, p. 31; "the enormity": ibid., pp. 45–46.

10. "Misery and brokenness": ibid., p. 57; Juana la Loca, see chapter 2 of this book, p. 36.

11. "The Accident": *Imaginations*, p. 307.

12. Ibid., p. 146.

13. Stevens, *CPP*, p. 50; Stevens later commented that "by contrast with the things in relation in the poem," the decorative words "concupiscent curds" were meant "to express or accentuate life's destitution" and that "the true sense of Let be be the finale of seem is let being come to the conclusion or denouement of appearing to be: in short, ice cream as an absolute good," though the poem "is obviously not about ice cream, but about being as distinguished from seeming to be" (*SL*, pp. 500, 341). On "ice cream," Ramazani comments that "the refrain forces together antithetical meanings: Sensuality rules, death rules. The pleasure principle is all (the *cream*), the reality principle is all (the *ice*)" (p. 93).

14. W. C. Williams, "Tract," *CP*, vol. 1, pp. 72–74.

15. Shapiro, "An Aesthetics of Inadequacy."

16. Ramazani, pp. 16–17.

17. To be sure, Williams's "Tract" includes many traditional trappings of the elegy—a complaint, a processional, flowers, even communal hopefulness— while his overtly materialist "Death" at least hints at a definition of death-as-expiration in its view of the dead body as "a godforsaken curio / without / any breath in it" because "Love's . . . come out of the man." But what is striking about Williams is that he evokes these elements specifically to repudiate them.

18. Blake, "The Divine Image," p. 111; Plath, "Apprehensions," *CP*, pp. 195–96.

19. For another mid-century view of the need for ceremonial mourning, see B. Jones, front flap, and "A Deathly Hush," review of Jones's book. I am grateful to Burton Benedict for introducing me to this book.

20. Not surprisingly, this particular strategy for closure doesn't usually character- ize the work of the World War I poets who, like Owen and Sassoon, were writ- ing a form of protest poetry; see chapter 13 of this volume, passim.

21. Shapiro, "The Accident," in *Song & Dance*, p. 25; "sumptuous destitution": Dickinson, J 1382/F 1404; "fire-fangled feathers": Stevens, "Of Mere Being," *CPP*, p. 477; "luckier": Whitman, "Song of Myself," *LG*, p. 194.

22. See Lowell, "William Carlos Williams: Paterson I" (1947), *CP*, p. 29. Ginsberg, quoted in Mariani, p. 604; eventually Ginsberg produced a poem entitled "Written in My Dream by W. C. Williams," in which the ghost of Williams— "writing" in very un-Ginsberg-like short lines—reassured the younger poet that "you're bearing // a common Truth // Commonly known / as desire // No need / to dress // it up / as beauty // No need / to distort // what's not / stan- dard // to be understandable" (*White Shroud*, p. 59).

23. W. C. Williams, Introduction to Ginsberg, *Howl*, pp. 7–8. Williams, who was not only moved by Ginsberg's visions of his era but also shocked by the younger poet's open homosexuality, saw "Howl" as wholly infernal in tone and substance, concluding his Introduction with the comment "Hold back the edges of your gowns, Ladies, we are going through hell." In a mostly grateful response, Ginsberg thanked Williams but commented that "there was also a strength and gaiety" in the work that the older poet had failed to detect (Mar- iani, p. 705).

24. Burke: 47, cited in Mariani, p. 846; Lowell, in Ostroff, p.108; W. C. Williams, who read *Life Studies* in manuscript, praised Lowell's new metrical freedom, noting that the younger poet "needed that break" because "rhyme would not contain [his ideas] any more" (see Mariani, p. 735).

25. In fact, although the poem that gives *Kaddish* its title is often conflated with the collection in which it appears, the book contains a number of elegies in the same mode, which together might be seen as a series of case histories.

26. From William Cowper and Thomas Hood to Thomas Hardy and John Mase- field, eighteenth- and nineteenth-century poets had from time to time pro- duced sorrowful poems about the deaths of mothers and grandmothers, but in the history of English-language elegy these works are unusual until the mid- twentieth century. See, e.g., Cowper, "On the Receipt of My Mother's Picture out of Norfolk," pp. 55–56; Hood, "The Death Bed," p. 64; Hardy, "One We Knew," *CP*, pp. 274–75; and Masefield, "C.L.M.," *SP*, pp. 70–71.

27. Lowell, *Life Studies*, pp. 77–78.

28. See (in this order) "My Last Afternoon with Uncle Devereux Winslow," "Dun- barton," "Grandparents," "Commander Lowell," "Terminal Days at Beverly Farms," "During Fever," and "For Sale," all ibid., pp. 59–80.

29. Ginsberg, *Kaddish*, pp. 7–36. Notably, even the "eyes" of the "corsets and eyes" that Naomi Ginsberg is "gone without" represent an inhuman *thingness* as well as a human subjectivity, since traditional corsets are fastened with hooks and *eyes*. For a different view of the relationship between "Kaddish" and "Adonais," see Ramazani, pp. 248–49; in particular, Ramazani argues that Ginsberg's use of a key line from Shelley's poem ("Die, / If thou wouldst be with that which thou dost seek!") implies a desire to emphasize "not only the self-destructiveness but also the erotics of mourning."

30. Ramazani notes that Ginsberg breaks "ancient taboos on the exposure and degradation of the dead [by flooding] the poem with graphic details that mimic the uncontrolled discharge he describes. Bursting through the dam of elegiac decorum, he reproduces at a literary level his mother's oral, anal, and urinary efflux" (p. 251).

31. On Renaissance *blazons*, see, for instance, Vickers, pp. 265–79; arguably Ginsberg's litany of *blazons* also derives (again ironically) from Andre Breton's famous "Freedom of Love," which celebrates the French poet's beloved through an incantatory accumulation of similar figures: "My wife with the hair of a wood fire / With the thoughts of heat lightning / With the waist of an hourglass / With the waist of an otter in the teeth of a tiger / My wife with the lips of a cockade and of a bunch of stars of the last magnitude / With the teeth of tracks of white mice on the white earth / With the tongue of rubbed amber and glass" (p. 11).

32. See chapter 9 of this volume, "Death and the Camera," pp. 218–22.

33. Rosenthal, "Poetry as Confession," pp. 71–75; later Rosenthal ruefully confessed that though the "term 'confessional poetry' came naturally to my mind when I reviewed . . . *Life Studies* in 1959 . . . it was a term both helpful and too limited, and very possibly the conception of a confessional school has by now done a certain amount of damage" (*New Poets*, p. 25).

34. W. C. Williams, *CP*, p. 140; the first version of this poem was far more explicit about the speaker's relationship to the grandmother: Williams as grandson is depicted as having insouciantly forgotten his beloved grandmother "for other things" until "she began to rave in the night," after which he fried "an egg for her . . . combed his whiskers . . . picked his pimples / and got busy with / a telegram for help" (see *CP*, vol. 1, pp. 253–55); his revision of the piece, omitting the earlier comic portrait of the artist as a young man, retained the graphic yet understated depiction of the dying woman with a few small improvements (i.e., the poet deftly transformed his description of her bed from a "stinking bed" to the less judgmental "rank, disheveled bed").

35. Frost, "Out, Out—," pp. 136–37; Lowell, "Terminal Days at Beverly Farms," *Life Studies*, p. 74.

36. Gunn, p. 64; Olds, pp. 7, 14, 15; Donald Hall, pp. 35–45.

37. Shapiro, *Song & Dance*: "Big Screen," p. 39; "Three Questions," p. 41.

38. Berryman, pp. 169, 170, 175; Stone, *Cheap*, p. 47; Bidart, pp. 75–76.

39. Lawrence, "The Bride," *CP*, p. 101; "a model for Williams": Williams was a great admirer of Lawrence's and wrote a major elegy for him (see "An Elegy for D. H. Lawrence," *CP*, pp. 393–95).

40. Olds, p. 47; Snodgrass, p. 59; Doty, *Bethlehem . . .* , p. 34.

41. Berryman, p. 175; Gunn, p. 51; Monette, *Love Alone*, pp. 4–5; Gallagher, p. 49; Stone, *Cheap*, pp. 15, 14.

42. Eliot, *Waste Land, Facs.*, p. 119; even the usually unflappable Ezra Pound found this passage too much, commenting, as Richard Ellmann notes, that this didn't "add anything, either to *The Waste Land* or to Eliot's previous work"; see Ellmann, "The First *Waste Land*, " p. 56.

43. Gallagher, p. 72; Gunn, p. 68; T. Harrison, "Marked with D.," p. 153.

44. Olds, p. 51.

45. Stevens, p. 445; for more on "Madame la Fleurie," see chapter 2 of this book.

46. Freud, *General Psychological Theory*, pp. 165–67.

47. Stone, "Turn Your Eyes Away," *Second-Hand Coat*, p. 47; Gallagher, p. 38.

48. Rich, "A Woman Mourned by Daughters," p. 57.

49. Feinstein, p. 80 ; T. Harrison, "Flood,"p. 135; Heaney, "Clearances #3," p. 285.

50. Kumin, "How It Is," p. 46; Garcia, p. 12; Hacker, "Autumn 1980," *SP*, p. 150; Meehan, "Child Burial," pp. 17–18.

51. Barker, "Trying To," p. 63; Dunn, "Dining," pp. 27–28; Donald Hall, p. 52; Olds, "One Year," *The Father*, p. 55; for an example of (in Ramazani's phrase) a "self-elegy" in this mode, see Alicia Ostriker's address to her surgeon in "Mastectomy": "Was I succulent? Was I juicy? . . . I dreamed you displayed me / In pleated paper like a candied fruit" (p. 204).

52. W. C. Williams, *CP*, vol. 1, p. 372.

53. Stone, "Curtains," *Second-Hand Coat*, p. 15; Hacker, *Winter Numbers*, pp. 11–15; Donald Hall, p. 52; Hughes, "Life after Death," *Birthday Letters*, p. 182.

54. Gluck, "Lullaby," pp. 28–29; Gunn, "Death's Door," p. 82; Heaney, "Clearances #2," p. 284. For more on "Death's Door," see chapter 4 of this volume, pp. 67–68.

55. Ginsberg, *White Shroud*, pp. 47–50.

56. Sexton, "The Truth the Dead Know," p. 49; Olds, "One Year," *The Father* p. 55; Hillman, "Quartz Tractate," pp. 48–49.

57. Merwin, "Lament . . . ," pp. 23–30; Dunbar, pp. 98–101.

58. Ginsberg, *Kaddish*, pp. 83–85; Lowell, "Epilogue," *Day by Day*, p. 127.

59. Whitman, "So Long!," p. 611; Dickinson, J 675/ F 772 ("Essential Oils—are Wrung").

60. See Holst-Warhaft, *Cue*, passim; more specifically on the AIDS elegy, see, e.g., Zeiger, pp. 107–34, and Woods.

61. For another poet-critic's formulation of what seems to me to be a similar point, see Shapiro, "Some Questions," in which he elaborates his notion of an "aesthetic of insufficiency": "If death is the mother of beauty, then I want the kind of beauty that acknowledges the insufficiency of beauty. I want the kind of art that admits it's giving us a song and dance when it transforms suffering into pleasure, pain into insight, life into clarifying images of life; the kind of art that

recognizes there is no good substitute for the precious flesh. And recognizing this apologizes for its own necessity" (p. 28).

Chapter 15: Apocalypse Now (and Then)

1. Even now, years after the non-Y2K-event, a Google search for "Y2K" yields 845,000 "hits," although one of the first of these to appear on my screen tells the whole story succinctly: "Y2K area has been closed; / any future Y2K events will be / posted if they ever occur"; see www.sba.gov/y2k/.

2. "Rough beasts . . .": Yeats, "The Second Coming," *CP*, p. 187; "old gang": Auden, *CP*, p. 36; Yeats, "Two Songs from a Play," *CP*, pp. 213–14 ; "swans . . .": Yeats, "Leda and the Swan," *CP*, pp. 214–15. Even in their theatrical disillusionment, the great modernists would seem to have trumped us in their trumpetings of doom as well as of transformation. "Signs are taken for wonders," declares T. S. Eliot's Gerontion, that dull head among the windy spaces of the pre-"postmodern," or as W. B. Yeats famously puts it, "The best lack all conviction, while the worst / Are full of passionate intensity." "Are we nothing, already, but the lapsing of a great dead past?" asks D. H. Lawrence in "To Let Go or To Hold On—?", one of the poetic *pensées* (called *Pansies*) that he published toward the end of his life, while in another he commented that "in their seething minds" the "living dead" have "phosphorescent teeming white words / of putrescent wisdom"; see "Gerontion," in Eliot, *CPP*, pp. 21–23; Yeats, "The Second Coming," *CP*, p.187; Lawrence, *CP*, pp. 429, 441. During the First World War, Lawrence actually saw a German Zeppelin, bombing London, as a "new world in the heavens" seeming to signal that "the cosmic order [had] gone, as if there had come a new order, a new heavens above us" (quoted in Hynes, *A War Imagined*, p. 140).

3. See Montgomery with Garland, and Creme. For an overview of "events and crises" in the second half of the twentieth century "that have fueled apocalyptic reflection by [Americans] expecting a sudden catastrophic close of the present order," see Stein, in Amanat and Bernhardsson, p. 207; Stein also notes, as have other scholars, that "the countless prophecies and predictions of the Web surrounding the Y2K problem demonstrated the almost total integration between religious and secular apocalypse" (p. 210).

4. Lindsey, p. 142; Fontaine, p. 7; for commentary on these and other popular prophetic writings, see Keller, passim; Stein, pp. 187–211; and Boyer, pp. 312–35. For "ghosts" and "bar codes," see Van Praagh. See also Tsvygun, in Manning, *Prophecies for the Millennium*, p. 91; convinced that she was an incarnation of Christ named Maria Devi Christos, Tsvygun argued that every "bar code contains three pairs of thin lines which are slightly longer than the rest" and therefore "represent '666,' the number of the Beast." For an overview of current fundamentalist apocalypticism online, see (among many other sites) www.armageddonbooks.com.

5. Included in Kamper and Wulf, p. 54; "paralyzed by irony" and further commentary: see Keller, pp. 13, 14.

6. Nor for that matter, would anyone have attended nervously to the Blakean *Howl* of warning with which the late Allen Ginsberg excoriated American capitalism, defining high-tech Manhattan as "Moloch whose eyes are a thousand blind windows! Moloch whose skyscrapers stand in the long streets like endless Jehovahs"; see *Howl*, pp. 21–22.

7. See Haflidason.

8. Kahane, in Greenberg, p. 107; as Kahane notes, the critic and theorist Slavoj Zizek also remarked on the uncanny confluence of the 9/11 catastrophe with what came to look like cinematic anticipations of the event; see Kahane, p. 108 and passim as well as Zizek.

9. Karr, p. B-1; Hazo, in Heyen, ed., *September 11, 2001,* p. 170. It's interesting to compare these optimistic claims with Alan Shapiro's skeptical "has a work of art ever averted an atrocity? Has it made us better? . . . The art I'm most interested in is the kind that cultivates compassion and sympathy [but] it *doesn't* insulate you from anything. It *doesn't* provide you with equipment for the worst things that could happen" ("Aesthetics of Inadequacy").

10. Antler, in Heyen, ed., *September 11*, p. 20; Kuhar, in Cohen and Matson, p. 68; Borenstein, ibid., p. 58; Foerster, ibid., p. 121; Giancola, ibid., p. 133.

11. Chappell, ibid., p. 72; Clifton, ibid., p. 80. A more complete description of "PHOENIX RISING" includes the information that the piece, an "Improvisation and Incantation for 911 and Beyond," will be performed by "Poet David Budbill and world renowned bassist, multi-instrumentalist and composer William Parker," that it is designed "for the spoken word, upright, acoustic bass, pocket trumpet, Gralle (Barcelonian double reed), Shakuhachi (vertical bamboo flute), and slit drum, various whistles, bells, wood blocks, noise makers, pots, pans, gongs and ringing bowls" and that "for future bookings" would-be audiences should "contact David Budbill at budbill@sover.net" (Heyen, pp. 70–71).

12. Pinsky, in Cohen and Matson, p. 94.

13. B. Collins.

14. Merwin, *New Yorker*. Spiegelman, too, comments on the inadequacy of poetry-as-solace in the immediate aftermath of 9/11, despite its ubiquity. Though New Yorkers were said to need "poetry to give voice to their pain, culture to reaffirm faith in a wounded civilization," he admits that his "mind kept wandering" and he found only "old comic strips . . . ephemera from the optimistic dawn of the 20th Century [sic]" appropriate for "an end-of-the-world moment" (*In the Shadow*, "The Comic Supplement," n.p.).

15. DeLillo, "In the Ruins of the Future"; On Stockhausen, see *New York Times*, September 19, 2001, p. E-3.

16. On *Piss Christ*, see Serrano; on the *Wrapped Reichstag* and other works, see Christo and Jeanne-Claude.

17. See Zizek, p. 12.

18. See Moyers, "Bill Moyers on Health . . ." and see also Spiegelman, *In the Shadow*, who describes feeling "like the world was ending" (p. 2).

19. From our late-twentieth-century perspective, therefore, John of Patmos's powerfully authored Apocalypse or Revelation is both sexually incorrect in its vehement vaunting of the empowered male gaze at the haplessly stripped female subject ("I John *saw*") and theoretically suspect in its egocentric and logocentric assumption that there *can* be *a* gaze, *a* Word, *a* singular and uniquely knowable subject.

20. Revelation, 21:2; 19:16, 15; 22:1–2.

21. Lawrence, *Apocalypse*, pp. 142–44.

22. Ibid., p. 125.

23. Phillip Marcus has examined these in some detail in an incisive analysis of "Lawrence, Yeats, and 'the Resurrection of the Body' " that deals primarily with "The Escaped Cock," while W. Y. Tindall long ago demonstrated Lawrence's use of occult sources on which Yeats also was heavily dependent. Marcus cites Tindall and others who noted Lawrence's reading of "Madame Blavatsky's *The Secret Doctrine*, Frazer's *The Golden Bough*, Burnet's *Early Greek Philosophy*, the *Upanishads* [and] even such less well known texts as Balzac's 'occult' novel *Seraphita*" (p. 217). Nevertheless, although he does discuss *Apocalypse* in some detail, Marcus's primary focus is on *The Escaped Cock*.

24. On fin de siècle visions of Leda and the Swan, see Dijkstra; for Yeats's comments on "Leda and the Swan," see *The Cat and the Moon*, p. 37; Lawrence, "Religion," *CP*, pp. 949–50.

25. Lawrence, *CP*, pp. 439–40.

26. Ibid., p. 959; brackets Lawrence's.

27. Ibid., pp. 112, 143–46.

28. See Allison, as quoted online. Others who set this text to music include Ernst Widmer and William Matthias.

29. For an account of this event, a party thrown by Basil Rathbone and his wife, to which guests were invited to "Come as the one you most admire," see Riva, pp. 350–51, 366. Notes Riva: "No film costume was ever worked on and perfected more than the one for Leda and her swan. When Dietrich was finally sewn into that costume, what an incredible sight! Clustered short 'greek statue' curls framed her face, leaving her neck bare for her swan to curl his neck gently around it and pillow his head on one swelling breast. Her body sheathed in sculpted white chiffon, she stood within his all-enveloping passionate embrace. They were truly 'one.' There might have been some who did not know the story of Leda and her swan, but no one could misunderstand the emotion my mother represented" (p. 351). In the meantime, as if to elaborate the theme of narcissism, the young actress Elizabeth Allan, Dietrich's "escort" for the evening, was dressed in top hat and trousers as "Marlene Dietrich." (I am grateful to Joan Schenkar for pointing me toward this episode.)

30. Benjamin, pp. 257–58.

31. Stamelman, in Greenberg, pp. 12–14.

32. MacLeish, p. 89; Hemingway, p. 383. See also chapter 6 of this volume, p. 124.

33. Sebald, *On the Natural History of Destruction*, pp. 10, 26–27.

34. DeLillo, "In the Ruins of the Future."
35. *Lear*, V, iii, 262–63.
36. Griffin, "How It Comes," in Heyen, p. 162.
37. Interestingly, as Boyer points out, throughout the nineties a number of con-temporary fundamentalist apocalypticists associated Saddam with the Antichrist, paying special attention to "Saddam's rebuilding of ancient Babylon [55 miles south of Baghdad][,] the symbol of wickedness in the Bible, whose destruction by fire is foretold in Isaiah 13 and again in Revelation 18" (pp. 326–27). Notes Boyer: "Charles H. Dyer of Dallas Theological Seminary in his bestselling *The Rise of Babylon: Sign of the End Times* (1991), with its cover illustration juxtaposing Saddam's image with that of King Nebuchadnezzar, reflected on Babylon's prophesied destruction: [W]ho will destroy it? The United States? Will America wipe out Iraq? Unfortunately, Isaiah does not give us any information about the United States. But the United States is a major world power—how could it *not* play a major role in the last days?"
38. For the full statement by Arad and Walker, along with their plans for the memorial as well as the other fifty-two hundred sets of plans entered in the competition, see Arad and Walker, online.

BIBLIOGRAPHY

Abrams, M. H. *The Correspondent Breeze: Essays on English Romanticism*. New York: W. W. Norton, 1984.

Adams, Ansel. Preface to Alexander Alland, *Jacob A. Riis: Photographer and Citizen*. New York: Aperture, 1974.

Adorno, Theodor. "Cultural Criticism and Society" (1949). *Prisms*. Trans. Samuel and Sherry Weber. Cambridge, Mass.: MIT Press, 1967.

———. *Engagement*. 1962. *Notes to Literature*. Trans. Sherry Weber Nicholsen. Ed. Rolf Tiedeman. New York: Columbia University Press, 1992.

———. *Negative Dialectics*. Trans. E. B. Ashton. New York: Continuum, 1983.

Agamben, Giorgio. *Homo Sacer: Sovereign Power and Bare Life*. Trans. Daniel Heller-Roazeni. Stanford: Stanford University Press, 1998.

———. *Language and Death: The Place of Negativity*. Trans. Karen E. Pinkus with Michael Hardt. Minneapolis: University of Minnesota Press, 1991.

Aiken, Conrad. "Emily Dickinson," *Dial*, vol. 76 (April 1924).

Albom, Mitch. *Tuesdays with Morrie*. London: Warner Books/Little, Brown UK, 1998.

Aldington, Richard. *Death of a Hero*. London: Chatto & Windus, 1929.

Alexiou, Margaret. *The Ritual Lament in Greek Tradition*. Cambridge, U.K.: Cambridge University Press, 1974.

Allison, Shawn. "Confessions of a Recovering Choir Director." Web blog. <http://www.cantemusdomino.net/blog/archives/000325.php>

Alvarez, A. *The Savage God: A Study of Suicide*. 1971. New York: W. W. Norton. 1990.

Amanat, Abbas, and Magnus Bernhardsson. *Imagining the End: Visions of Apocalypse from the Ancient Middle East to Modern America*. London and New York: I. B. Tauris, 2002.

American Heritage Dictionary, 4th ed. Boston and New York: Houghton Mifflin, 2000.

Andre, Dena; Philip Brookman; and Jane Livingston, eds. *Hospice: A Photographic Inquiry*. Photographs by Jim Goldberg, Nan Goldin, Sally Mann, Jack Radcliffe, Kathy Vargas. Boston: Little, Brown, 1996.

Angier, Natalie. "Century-Old Death Records Provide a Glimpse into Medicine's History." *New York Times*, May 25, 2004.

Aquinas, Thomas. *Basic Writings of Saint Thomas Aquinas,* vol. 1. Ed. Anton C. Pegis. New York: Random House, 1945.

Arad, Michael, and Peter Walker. "Reflecting Absence." WORLD TRADE CENTER SITE MEMORIAL COMPETITION. <http://www.wtcsitememorial.org/fin7.html>

Arbus, Diane. *Revelations*. New York: Random House, 2003.

Ariès, Philippe. *The Hour of Our Death*. Trans. Helen Weaver. New York: Knopf, 1981.

ARMAGEDDON BOOKS. West Jefferson, N.C. 2004. <http://www.armageddonbooks.com/>

Armstrong, Karen. *The Spiral Staircase: My Climb out of Darkness*. New York: Knopf, 2004.

Arnold, Matthew. *The Portable Matthew Arnold*. Ed. Lionel Trilling. New York: Viking Press, 1949.

Auden, W. H. *Collected Poetry of W. H. Auden*. New York: Random House, 1945.

———. *The English Auden: Poems, Essays and Dramatic Writings, 1927–1939*. Ed. Edward Mendelson. New York: Random House, 1977.

Austin, C. "Chaos Awaits in the Dark Season of Samhain." THE CELTIC CONNECTION. <http://merganser.math.gvsu.edu/myth/samhain-10-97.html>

Balbert, Peter, and Phillip Marcus. *D. H. Lawrence: A Centenary Consideration*. Ithaca: Cornell University Press, 1985.

Barker, Wendy. *Let the Ice Speak*. New York: Greenfield Review Press, 1991.

Barley, Nigel. *Grave Matters: A Lively History of Death around the World*. New York: Henry Holt, 1997.

Barr, Alfred H., Jr. *Picasso: 50 Years of His Art*. New York: Museum of Modern Art, 1955.

Barthes, Roland. *Camera Lucida: Reflections on Photography*. Trans. Richard Howard. New York: Farrar, Straus and Giroux, 1981.

Bataille, Georges. *Inner Experience*. Trans. and with intro. by Leslie Anne Boldt. Albany: State University of New York Press, 1988.

Bauby, Jean-Dominique. *The Diving Bell and the Butterfly*. Trans. Jeremy Leggatt. New York: Vintage, 1997.

Baudelaire, Charles. *The Painter of Modern Life and Other Essays*. Trans. and ed. Jonathan Mayne. London: Phaidon Press, 1964.

Baudrillard, Jean. *Symbolic Exchange and Death*. London: Sage Publications, 1993.

Bauman, Zygmunt. *Modernity and the Holocaust*. Ithaca: Cornell University Press, 1989, 2000.

———. *Mortality, Immortality and Other Life Strategies*. Stanford: Stanford University Press, 1992.

Beauvoir, Simone de. *A Very Easy Death*. Trans. Patrick O'Brian. New York: Pantheon, 1965.

———. Introduction. In Lanzmann.

Becker, Ernest. *The Denial of Death*. New York: Free Press, 1997. 1st pub. 1973.

Becker, Jillian. *Giving Up: The Last Days of Sylvia Plath*. London: Ferrington, 2002.

Beckett, Samuel. *Krapp's Last Tape and Other Dramatic Pieces*. New York: Grove/Evergreen, 1960.

———. *Waiting for Godot*. New York: Grove Press, 1954.

Benjamin, Walter. *Illuminations.* Trans. Harry Zohn. Ed. and with intro. by Hannah Arendt. New York: Schocken, 1968.

Bercovitch, Sacvan, ed. *Reconstructing American Literary History.* Cambridge, Mass.: Harvard University Press, 1986.

Berger, John. *Ways of Seeing.* London: Penguin, 1972.

Berger, Peter L.; Brigitte Berger; and Hansfried Kellner. *The Homeless Mind: Modernization and Consciousness.* New York: Random House, 1973.

Berlinger, Nancy. "Broken Stories: Patients, Families, and Clinicians after Medical Error." *Literature and Medicine,* 22.2 (2003).

Berryman, John. *The Dream Songs.* New York: Farrar Straus, 1982.

Bertman, Sandra L. *Facing Death: Images, Insights, and Interventions.* Bristol, Pa.: Taylor & Francis, 1991.

Bidart, Frank. *In the Western Night: Collected Poems 1965–90.* New York: Farrar Straus, 1990.

Binding, Rudolph. *A Fatalist at War.* Trans. Ian F. D. Morrow. Boston: Houghton Mifflin, 1929.

Blackstone, William. *Commentaries on the Laws of England,* vol. 1. Oxford: Clarendon Press, 1770.

Blake, William. *The Complete Poems.* Ed. Alicia Ostriker. London: Penguin, 1977.

Blanchot, Maurice. *The Gaze of Orpheus.* Trans. Lydia Davis. Barrytown, N.Y.: Station Hill, 1981.

Blaufox, Donald M., M.D. *An Ear to the Chest: An Illustrated History of the Evolution of the Stethoscope.* Boca Raton, Fla.: Parthenon Publishing, 2002.

Bloom, Harold. *Kabbalah and Criticism.* New York: Seabury, 1975.

———. *Wallace Stevens: The Poems of Our Climate.* Ithaca: Cornell University Press, 1977.

Blunden, Edmund. *Undertones of War.* 1928. London: Penguin, 1982.

Blythe, Ronald. *Akenfield.* New York: Pantheon, 1969.

Bondeson, Jan. *Buried Alive: The Terrifying History of Our Most Primal Fear.* New York: W. W. Norton, 2001.

Bosk, Charles. *All God's Mistakes: Genetic Counseling in a Pediatric Hospital.* Chicago: University of Chicago Press, 1992.

Bourke, Angela. "The Irish Traditional Lament and the Grieving Process." *Women's Studies in International Forum,* vol. 11, no. 4 (1988).

Boxer, Sarah. "Humiliating Photographs as Trophies of War." *New York Times,* May 20, 2004.

———. "Slogging through the Valley of the Shutter of Death." *New York Times,* July 23, 2004.

Boyer, Paul. "The Middle East in Modern American Popular Prophetic Belief." In Amanat and Bernhardsson.

Bradbury, Malcolm. "The Denuded Place: War and Form in *Parade's End* and *U.S.A.*" *The First World War in Fiction.* Ed. Holger Klein. London: Macmillan, 1976.

Brazeau, Peter. *Parts of a World: An Oral Biography*. New York: Random House, 1983.

Breton, André. *Young Cherry Trees Secured against Hares*. Trans. Édouard Roditi. New York: View Editions, 1946.

Brittain, Vera. *Testament of Youth*. New York: Macmillan, 1934.

Brodkey, Harold. *This Wild Darkness: The Story of My Death*. New York: Henry Holt Metropolitan, 1996.

Brody, Jane E. "A Doctor's Duty, When Death Is Inevitable." *New York Times*, August 10, 2004.

———. "Often, Time Beats Therapy for Treating Grief." *New York Times*, January 27, 2004.

Bronfen, Elisabeth. *Over Her Dead Body: Death, Femininity, and the Aesthetic*. New York: Routledge, 1992

———. *Sylvia Plath*. Plymouth, U.K.: *Writers and Their Work*, Northcote House, 1998.

Bronski, Michael. "Mourning in America." BOSTON PHOENIX. Boston, October 11, 2001. <http://www.bostonphoenix.com/boston/news_features/other_stories/documents/01860444.htm>

Brontë, Emily. *Gondal's Queen*. Ed. Fannie E. Ratchford, Austin and London: University of Texas Press, 1977.

———. *Wuthering Heights*. 1847. Modern Library. New York: Random House, 1994.

Brooke, Rupert. *Collected Poems*. New York: Dodd, Mead and Company, 1922.

Brown, Rebecca. *Excerpts from a Family Medical Dictionary*. London: Granta, 2001.

Browne, Sir Thomas. *Religio Medici, Urn Burial, Christian Morals, and Other Essays*. Ed. and with intro. by John Addington Symonds. London: W. Scott, 1886.

Browning, Christopher R. "The German Bureaucracy and the Holocaust." In Grobman and Landes.

Browning, Elizabeth Barrett. *The Complete Works of Elizabeth Barrett Browning*, vol. 3. New York: Thomas Y. Crowell, 1900.

Browning, Robert. *Poems of Robert Browning*. Ed. Donald Smalley. Boston: Houghton Mifflin, 1956.

Broyard, Anatole. *Intoxicated by My Illness: And Other Writings on Life and Death*. Comp. and ed. Alexandra Broyard. New York: Clarkson Potter, 1991.

Buchloh, Benjamin H. D. "Gerhard Richter's *Atlas*: The Anomic Archive." *Photography and Painting in the Work of Gerhard Richter: Four Essays on Atlas*. Ed. B. H. D. Buchloh et al. Barcelona: Museu d'Art Contemporani de Barcelona, 1998.

Buckingham, Willis J., ed. *Emily Dickinson's Reception in the 1890s: A Documentary History*. Pittsburgh: University of Pittsburgh Press, 1989.

Burke, Kenneth. "William Carlos Williams, 1883–1963." *New York Review of Books*, special issue (May 10, 1963).

Burns, Stanley B. *Sleeping Beauty: Memorial Photography in America*. Altadena, Calif.: Twelvetree Press, 1990.

Burress, Charles. "Laughter Eclipses Tears at Mitford Tribute." *San Francisco Chronicle*, July 30, 1996.

Byatt, A. S. *Angels and Insects*. New York: Random House, 1992.

Caine, Lynn. *Widow*. New York: William Morrow, 1974.

Caine, T. Hall. *Recollections of Dante Gabriel Rossetti*. London: Elliot Stock, 1882.

Cannadine, David. "War and Death, Grief and Mourning in Modern Britain." In Whaley.

Cantor, Jay. "Death and the Image." In Warren.

Carey, Benedict. "In the Hospital, a Degrading Shift From Person to Patient." *New York Times*, August 16, 2005.

Carver, Raymond. *All of Us: The Collected Poems*. New York: Random House, 1996.

The Catholic Encyclopedia. Ed. Charles G. Herbermann, Edward A. Pace, Conde B. Pallen, Right Reverend Thomas J. Shahan, and John J. Wynne. 1907. Online edition, ed. K. Knight, 2003. <http://www.newadvent.org/cathen/01315b.htm>

Celan, Paul. *Selected Poems and Prose of Paul Celan*. Trans. and ed. John Felstiner. New York: W. W. Norton, 2001.

Certeau, Michel de. *The Writing of History*. New York: Columbia University Press, 1988.

Chast, Roz. "For Their Own Good." *New Yorker* (November 8, 1999).

Choron, Jacques. *Death and Western Thought*. New York: Macmillan, 1963.

Christ, Carol. "Painting the Dead: Portraiture and Necrophilia in Victorian Art and Poetry." In Goodwin and Bronfen.

Christo and Jeanne-Claude. "Wrapped Reichstag, Berlin, 1971–95." *Stanford Presidential Lectures and Symposia in the Humanities and Arts*. Stanford University. <http://prelectur.stanford.edu/lecturers/christo/wrapped.html>

Clarke, Graham. *The Photograph*. Oxford and New York: Oxford University Press, 1997.

Coetzee, J. M. *The Lives of Animals*. Ed. and with intro. by Amy Gutmann. Princeton: Princeton University Press, 1999.

———. *Disgrace*. London: Vintage, 2000.

Cohen, Allen, and Clive Matson, eds. *An Eye for an Eye Makes the Whole World Blind: Poets on 9/11*. Oakland, Calif.: Regent Press, 2002.

Cole, Susan Letzler. *The Absent One: Mourning Ritual, Tragedy, and the Performance of Ambivalence*. University Park: Pennsylvania State University Press, 1985.

Cole, Thomas R., Robert Kastenbaum, and Ruth E. Ray, eds. *Handbook of the Humanities and Aging*, 2nd ed. New York: Springer, 2000.

Coleridge, Samuel Taylor. *The Complete Poetical Works of Samuel Taylor Coleridge*, vol. 1. Oxford: Clarendon Press, 1912.

Collins, Billy. "The Names." *New York Times*, Sept. 6, 2002: A25.

Collins, David. *My Louise: A Memoir*. Princeton: Ontario Review Press, 2002.

Collins, William. *The Works of William Collins*. Ed. Richard Wendorf and Charles Ryskamp. New York: Oxford University Press, 1979.

Conrad, Joseph. *Heart of Darkness*. 1899. New York: W. W. Norton, 1971.

Conway, Hugh (Frederick John Fargus). *Called Back*, aka *The Fatal House*. Chicago and New York: Belford, Clarke & Co., 1993. <http://gaslight.mtroyal.ab.ca/caldmenu.htm>

Cooper, Glenda. "Not a Heartbeat but a Whir: 'I'm Still Getting Used to It,' Recipient Says of Implant." *Washington Post Service/International Herald Tribune,* August 23, 2001.

Copeland, Libby. "A Dead Ringer for the Dearly Departed." *Washington Post,* December 30, 2002.

Coulson, Alan S., and Michael E. Hanlon. "The Case of the Elusive Angel of Mons." *Legends and Traditions of the Great War.* Ed. Michael Hanlon. The Great War Society. 2000. <http://www.worldwar1.com/heritage/angel.htm>

Cowan, Howard. "39 Carloads of Bodies on Track at Dachau." *Washington Post,* May 1, 1945.

Cowper, William. *The Poems of William Cowper,* vol. 3: *1785–1800.* Ed. John D. Baird and Charles Ryskamp. Oxford: Oxford University Press, 1995.

Crace, Jim. *Being Dead.* New York: Viking, 1999.

Creme, Benjamin. *Maitreya's Mission,* 3 vols. Amsterdam and London: Share International Foundation, 1993–97.

Croce, Benedetto. *Frammenti d'etica.* Bari: Gius, Laterza & Figli, 1922.

Cronin, Anne. "After the Attacks: The Voices; a Black Cloud. A Shower of Glass. A Glimpse of Hell. Run!" *New York Times,* September 16, 2001.

Cruttwell, C. R. M. F. *History of the Great War.* Oxford: Clarendon Press,1934.

The Cryonics Institute. Ed. Robert C. W. Ettinger. Clinton Township, Mich., 2002. <http://www.cryonics.org/>

CURRENT SCIENCE AND TECHNOLOGY CENTER. "Artificial Heart Pioneer Passes Away." 2002. <http://www.mos.org/cst/article/3737/10.html>

David, Daniel. *The 1914 Campaign.* Bryn Mawr: Combined Books, 1987.

Davis, Cortney, and Judy Schaefer, eds. *Between the Heartbeats: Poetry & Prose by Nurses.* Iowa City: University of Iowa Press, 1995.

Dawkins, Richard. *The Blind Watchmaker: Why the Evidence of Evolution Reveals a Universe Without Design.* New York: W. W. Norton, 1993.

"A Deathly Hush." Review of Barbara Jones's *Design for Death. The Observer,* September 10, 1967.

"Death Watch." *PBS Online NewsHour.* November 24, 1998. PBS.org. <http://www.pbs.org/newshour/bb/media/july-dec98/suicide_11-24.html>

Defoe, Daniel. *Serious Reflections during the Life and Surprising Adventures of Robinson Crusoe.* Ed. George A. Aitken. London: J. M. Dent, 1895.

Delbanco, Andrew. "Barbaric Yawp." *New York Times Book Review,* August 22, 1999.

Delbo, Charlotte. *Auschwitz and After.* Trans. Rosette C. Lamont, with intro. by Lawrence L. Langer. New Haven and London: Yale University Press, 1995.

DeLillo, Don. "In the Ruins of the Future." *Guardian,* December 22, 2001.

"The Democratization of Death." *Chronicle of Higher Education,* vol. 48, no. 21 (February 2, 2002).

Demske, James M. *Being, Man, & Death: A Key to Heidegger.* Lexington: University of Kentucky Press, 1970.

Derrida, Jacques. *Memoires: for Paul de Man.* Trans. Jonathan Culler, Cecile Lindsay, and Eduardo Cadava. New York: Columbia University Press, 1990.

————.*The Work of Mourning.* Ed. Pascale-Anne Brault and Michael Naas. Chicago: University of Chicago Press, 2001.

Des Pres, Terrence. *The Survivor: An Anatomy of Life in the Death Camps.* New York: Oxford University Press, 1976.

de Vries, Brian, ed. *End of Life Issues: Interdisciplinary and Multidisciplinary Perspectives.* New York: Springer, 1999.

Dickey, James. *Poems: 1957–1967.* Middletown, Conn.: Wesleyan University Press, 1967.

Dickinson, Emily. *The Complete Poems.* Ed. Thomas Johnson. Cambridge: Belknap Press of Harvard University Press, 1979.

————. *The Letters of Emily Dickinson.* Ed. Thomas Johnson. Cambridge: Belknap Press of Harvard University Press, 1986.

————. *The Poems of Emily Dickinson.* Ed. R. W. Franklin. Cambridge: Belknap Press of Harvard University Press, 1999.

Dijkstra, Bram. *Idols of Perversity: Fantasies of Feminine Evil in Fin-de-Siècle Culture.* New York: Oxford University Press, 1988.

Dilworth, Thomas. *The Shape of Meaning in the Poetry of David Jones.* Toronto: University of Toronto Press, 1988.

Doctor Assisted Suicide: A Guide to Websites and Their Literature. Janet D. Greenwood Library, Longwood University, Farmville, Va., 2004. <http://www .longwood.edu/library/suic.htm>

Donne, John. *The Poems of John Donne.* Ed. Sir J. C. Grierson. London: Oxford University Press, 1933.

Doty, Mark. *Bethlehem in Broad Daylight.* Boston: David R. Godine, 1991.

————. *Atlantis.* New York: Harper Perennial, 1995.

Doxiadis, Euphrosyne. *Mysterious Fayum Portraits.* New York: Harry Abrams, 1995.

Doyle, Arthur Conan. *The Vital Message.* New York: George H. Doran, 1919.

Duchac, Joseph. *The Poems of Emily Dickinson, an Annotated Guide to Commentary Published in English, 1890–1977.* Boston: G. K. Hall & Co., 1979.

————. *The Poems of Emily Dickinson, an Annotated Guide to Commentary Published in English, 1978–1989.* Boston: G. K. Hall & Co., 1993.

Dunbar, William. *Selected Poems.* Ed. with intro. by Harriet Harvey Wood. Manchester, U.K.: Carcanet, 1999.

Dunn, Douglas. *Elegies.* London: Faber, 1995.

Durdin-Robertson, Lawrence. "Juno Covella: Perpetual Calendar of the Fellowship of Isis." FELLOWSHIP OF ISIS. 2004. <http://www.fellowshipofisis.com/jc/jcoct31.html>

Dyer, Geoff. *The Missing of the Somme.* London: Penguin, 1995.

Eberwein, Jane Donahue. "Dickinson's Local, Global, and Cosmic Perspectives." In Grabher, Hagenbuchle, and Miller.

Ecksteins, Modris. "Pilgrimage and Tourism to the Western Front." In Mackaman and Mays.

———. *Rites of Spring: The Great War and the Birth of the Modern Age.* New York: Anchor Books. 1990.

Edson, Margaret. *Wit.* New York: Farrar Straus, 1999.

Eggers, Dave. *A Heartbreaking Work of Staggering Genius.* New York: Simon & Schuster, 2000.

Ehrenreich, Barbara. *Blood Rites: Origins and History of the Passions of War.* New York: Henry Holt, 1997.

El-Ghobashy, Tamer, and Bill Hutchinson. "Video of Pearl Slaying Showing Up on the Web." *Seattle Times,* May 16, 2002.

Elias, Norbert. *The Loneliness of the Dying.* Trans. Edmund Jephcott. Oxford: Basil Blackwell, 1985.

Eliot, T. S. *The Complete Poems and Plays: 1909–1950.* New York: Harcourt Brace, 1952.

———. *Four Quartets.* New York: Harcourt Brace, 1943.

———. *The Letters of T. S. Eliot, vol. 1, 1898–1922.* Ed. Valerie Eliot. New York: Harcourt Brace, 1988.

———. *The Waste Land: A Facsimile and Transcript of the Original Drafts Including the Annotations of Ezra Pound.* Ed. and with intro. by Valerie Eliot. New York: Harcourt Brace, 1971.

Ellin, Abby. "Freezing Time: Plans for a Giant Cryonics Facility Are Heating Up." *New York Times Magazine,* April 22, 2001.

Elliott, Jeff, and Laura McCreery. "Decca: the Making of a Muckraker." *Albion Monitor,* October 9, 1995. http://www.monitor.net/monitor/decca/churchill.html>

Ellmann, Richard. "The First *Waste Land.*" *Eliot in His Time: Essays on the Occasion of the Fiftieth Anniversary of The Waste Land.* Ed. A. Walton Litz. Princeton: Princeton University Press, 1973.

Empson, William. *The Gathering Storm.* London: Faber & Faber, 1940.

ENCYCLOPAEDIA OF THE FIRST WORLD WAR. "Casualties: First World War." Spartacus Educational. <http://www.spartacus.schoolnet.co.uk/FWWdeaths.htm>

Ewald, Richard. Review of Deidre Scherer, "The Last Year." *Hospice Magazine* (Fall 1991).

Faas, Ekbert. *Ted Hughes: The Unaccommodated Universe.* Santa Barbara, Calif.: Black Sparrow Press, 1980.

Fainlight, Ruth. "Jane and Sylvia." *Crossroads,* no. 64 (Spring 2004).

FANS OF FIEGER. "Mercitron." May 2, 2004. <http://www.fansoffieger.com/mercitron.htm>

Fears, Darryl. "Even the Dead Are Immigrating: Many Asians Import Ashes of Their Ancestors to U.S." *International Herald Tribune* and *Washington Post,* July 16, 2002.

Feingold, Henry L. "How Unique Is the Holocaust?" In Grobman and Landes.

Feinstein, Elaine. *Collected Poems & Translations.* Manchester, U.K.: Carcanet 2002.

Feldman, Karen. "The Shape of Mourning: Reading, Aesthetic Cognition and the Vietnam Veterans Memorial." *Word & Image,* vol. 19, no. 4 (2003).

Felman, Shoshana, and Dori Laub. *Testimony: Crises of Witnessing Literature, Psychoanalysis, and History.* New York: Routledge, 1992.

Ferguson, Margaret, Mary Jo Salter, and Jon Stallworthy, eds. *The Norton Anthology of Poetry*, 4th Edition. New York: W. W. Norton, 1970.

Field, Marilyn J., and Christine K. Cassel, eds. *Approaching Death: Improving Care at the End of Life.* Washington, D.C.: National Academic Press, 1997.

Figueira, Dorothy M. "Die Flambierte Frau: Sati in European Culture." In Hawley.

Flavel, John. *The Method of Grace in the Gospel Redemption.* London: Printed by M. White for Francis Tyton, 1681.

Foley, Kathleen M., and Herbert Hendin, eds. *The Case against Assisted Suicide: For the Right to End-of-Life Care.* Baltimore: Johns Hopkins University Press, 2002.

Folsom, Jack. "Death and Rebirth in Sylvia Plath's Berck-Plage." *Journal of Modern Literature*, vol. 17, no. 4 (1991).

Fontaine, Sonny. "Here's a Place Where Elvis Is God." *Boca Raton Sun*, August 8, 1995.

Ford, Ford Maddox. "Arms and the Mind." *Esquire*, 94 (December 1980).

Foucault, Michel. *The Birth of the Clinic: An Archaeology of Medical Perception.* Trans. A. M. Sheridan Smith. New York: Random House, 1965.

Frank, Victor. *From Camp to Existentialism.* Trans. Ilse Larch. Boston: Beacon Press, 1959.

Franks, Arthur W. *The Wounded Storyteller: Body, Illness, and Ethics.* Chicago: University of Chicago Press, 1995.

Frazer, Sir James George. *The Golden Bough: A Study in Magic and Religion. A New Abridgement from the Second and Third Editions.* Ed. and with intro. by Robert Fraser. 1922. London and New York: Oxford University Press, 1994.

Freud, Sigmund. *Character and Culture.* Ed. Philip Rieff. New York: Collier, 1963.

———. *Collected Papers*, vol. 4. Trans. and ed. Joan Riviere. New York: Basic Books, 1959.

———. "Mourning and Melancholia." 1917. Trans. Joan Riviere. *General Psychological Theory.* Ed. and with intro. by Philip Rieff. New York: Collier, 1963.

———. *The Standard Edition of the Complete Psychological Works of Sigmund Freud*, vol. 14: *1914–16.* Trans. and ed. James Stacey. London: Hogarth Press, 1957.

Friedlander, Saul, ed. *Probing the Limits of Representation: Nazism and the "Final Solution."* Cambridge: Harvard University Press, 1992.

Fritsch, Jane. "Please Order Your Last Meal Seven Days in Advance." "Week in Review," *New York Times*, April 22, 2001, p. 7.

Frost, Robert. *The Poetry of Robert Frost.* New York: Holt, Rinehart, 1969.

Froula, Christine. "Eliot's Grail Quest, or, The Lover, the Police, and *The Waste Land.*" *Yale Review*, vol. 78, no. 2 (Winter 1989).

Fry, Paul H. "The Absent Dead: Wordsworth, Byron, and the Epitaph," *Studies in Romanticism*, vol. 17, no. 4 (Fall 1978).

Frye, Northrop. *Anatomy of Criticism: Four Essays.* Atheneum: New York, 1970.

Frye, William. "Thousands Tortured to Death in Camp at Belsen," *Boston Globe*, April 21, 1945.

Fulton, Robert. ed. *Death and Identity.* New York: Wiley & Sons, 1965.

Furst, Peter. "Anti-Nazi Bavarians Helped to Seize Munich." *PM,* May 1, 1945.

Fuss, Diana. "Corpse Poem," *Critical Inquiry,* vol. 30, no. 1 (Autumn 2003).

Fussell, Paul. *The Great War and Modern Memory.* New York: Oxford University Press, 1975.

———. *The Norton Book of Modern War.* New York: W. W. Norton, 1991.

Gagnon, Monika. "A Convergence of Stakes: Photography, Feminism, and AIDS." *Fluid Exchanges: Artists and Critics in the AIDS Crisis,* ed. James Miller. Toronto: University of Toronto Press, 1992.

Gallagher, Tess. *Moon Crossing Bridge.* St. Paul: Graywolf Press, 1992.

Garcia, Richard. *The Flying Garcias.* Pittsburgh: University of Pittsburgh Press, 1993.

Gardner, Brian, ed. *Up the Line to Death: The War Poets 1914–1918.* Foreword by Edmund Blunden. London: Magnum Books, 1976.

Gay, John. *Poetry and Prose,* vol. 1. Ed. Vinton A. Dearing. Oxford and London: Oxford University Press, 1974.

Gewanter, David. " 'Undervoicings of Loss': Hardy's Elegies to His Wife." *Victorian Poetry* vol. 29, no. 3 (Autumn 1991).

Gil, Gideon. "First Heart Implant Patient Dies: 'He Has Been Able to Make a Difference for Mankind.' " *Louisville Courier-Journal,* December 1, 2001.

Gilbert, Elliot L. *A Guide: The World of Mystery Fiction.* San Diego: University of California at San Diego, 1978.

Gilbert, Martin. *The First World War.* New York: Henry Holt, 1994.

Gilbert, Roger. "From Anxiety to Power: Grammar and Crisis in 'Crossing Brooklyn Ferry.' " *Nineteenth Century Literature,* vol. 42, no. 3 (December 1987).

Gilbert, Sandra. "The American Sexual Poetics of Walt Whitman and Emily Dickinson." In Bercovitch.

———. "A Fine, White Flying Myth: The Life/Work of Sylvia Plath." In Gilbert and Gubar, *Shakespeare's Sisters.*

———. *Inventions of Farewell: A Book of Elegies.* New York: W. W. Norton, 2001.

———. *Kissing the Bread: New and Selected Poems 1969–1999.* New York: W. W. Norton, 2000.

———. " 'Rats' Alley': The Great War, Modernism, and the Anti-Pastoral Elegy," *New Literary History,* 30 (1999).

———. *Wrongful Death.* New York: W. W. Norton, 1995.

Gilbert, Sandra, and Susan Gubar, *No Man's Land: The Place of the Woman Writer in the Twentieth Century,* vol. 2: *Sexchanges.* New Haven: Yale University Press, 1989.

———. eds. *Shakespeare's Sisters: Feminist Essays on Women Poets.* Indiana University Press, 1979.

Gilbert, Susanna. " 'I Scream the Body Electric': Mark O'Brien's Cyborg Voice," in *"This Long Disease, My Life": Literary Responses to Illness in Contemporary America.* Dissertation, University of California at Santa Barbara, 2000.

———. " 'Some god got hold of me': The Medicalization of Silvia Plath," in *"This Long Disease, My Life."*

Ginsberg, Allen. *Howl and Other Poems*. San Francisco: City Lights, 1959.

———. *Kaddish and Other Poems, 1958–1960*. San Francisco: City Lights, 1961.

———. *White Shroud: Poems 1980–1985*. New York: Harper & Row, 1986.

Glaser, Barney G., and Anselm L. Strauss. *Awareness of Dying*. Chicago: Aldine, 1965.

———. *Time for Dying*. Chicago: Aldine, 1968.

Glass, Ira. "Birthdays, Anniversaries, and Milestones." *This American Life*. Public Radio International. December 29, 2000. <http://www.thislife.org/>

Gluck, Louise. *Ararat*. New York: Ecco, 1990.

Goldensohn, Lorrie. *Dismantling Glory: Twentieth-Century Soldier Poetry*. New York: Columbia University Press, 2003.

Gonzalez-Crussi, F. *The Day of the Dead and Other Mortal Reflections*. New York: Harcourt Brace, 1993.

Goodwin, Sarah Webster, and Elizabeth Bronfen, eds. *Death and Representation*. Baltimore and London: Johns Hopkins University Press, 1993.

Gopnik, Adam. "Crazy Piety." *New Yorker* (September 29, 1997).

Gorer, Geoffrey. *Death, Grief, and Mourning in Contemporary Britain*. London: Cresset Press, 1965.

Grabher, Gudrin; Roland Hagenbuchle; and Cristanne Miller, eds. *The Emily Dickinson Handbook*. Amherst: University of Massachusetts Press, 1999.

Graves, Robert. *The Complete Poems*. Ed. Beryl Graves and Dunstan Ward. Manchester, U.K.: Carcanet, 2000.

Greenberg, Judith, ed. *Trauma at Home: After 9/11*. Lincoln: University of Nebraska Press, 2003.

Greenblatt, Stephen. *Hamlet in Purgatory*. Princeton: Princeton University Press, 2001.

Greenfield, Meg. "Respecting the Dead," *Newsweek* (April 22, 1996).

Greenhalgh, Susanne. "Our Lady of Flowers: The Ambiguous Politics of Diana's Floral Revolution." In Kear and Steinberg.

Grider, Sylvia. "Spontaneous Shrines: A Modern Response to Tragedy and Disaster." *New Directions in Folklore*, vol. 5 (October 2001).

Grobman, Alex, and Daniel Landes, eds. *Genocide: Critical Issues of the Holocaust*. Los Angeles: Simon Wiesenthal Center, 1983.

Groddeck, Georg. *The Book of the It*. 1928. New York: Vintage, 1961.

Groopman, Jerome, M.D. *The Anatomy of Hope: How People Prevail in the Face of Illness*. New York: Random House, 2004.

———. "The Grief Industry." *New Yorker* (January 26, 2004).

Gross, Jane. "Seeking Solace with Final Gestures." *New York Times*, July 25, 1999.

———. "Alone in Illness, Seeking Steady Arm to Lean On." *New York Times*, August 26, 2005.

Gubar, Susan. *Poetry after Auschwitz: Remembering What One Never Knew*. Bloomington: Indiana University Press, 2003.

———. "Prosopopoeia and Holocaust Poetry in English: The Case of Sylvia Plath." In Miller and Tougaw.

Guide de Tourisme: Michelin, Nord de la France, Champagne, Ardennes. Paris: Pneu Michelin, 1980.

———. *Brittany.* Clermont-Ferrand: Michelin et Cie, 1991.

Gunn, Thom. *The Man with Night Sweats.* New York: Noonday, 1992.

Gunther, John. *Death Be Not Proud.* 1949. New York: Perennial Classics, 1998.

Gurney, Ivor. *Collected Poems of Ivor Gurney.* Ed. P. J. Kavanagh. Oxford and New York: Oxford University Press, 1982.

Hacker, Marilyn. *Selected Poems: 1965–1990.* New York: W. W. Norton, 1994.

———. *Winter Numbers.* New York: W. W. Norton, 1994.

Haflidason, Almar. "Review of *The Towering Inferno* (1974)." *BBC Film Reviews.* December 26, 2000. <http://www.bbc.co.uk/films/2000/09/26/towering_inferno_review.shtml>

Hall, Darrell. *The Hall Handbook of the Anglo Boer War.* Pietermaritzburg: University of Natal Press, 1999.

Hall, Donald. *Without.* New York: Houghton Mifflin, 1998.

Haraway, Donna. "A Cyborg Manifesto: Science, Technology, and Socialist Feminism in the Late Twentieth Century." *Simians, Cyborgs, and Women: The Reinvention of Nature.* New York: Routledge, 1991.

Hardie, Lance. "Plan Your Epitaph Day." <http://www.hardiehouse.org/epitaph/index.html>

Hardy, Thomas, *The Complete Poems.* Ed. James Gibson. New York: Macmillan, 1976.

———. *The Life and Work of Thomas Hardy.* (Florence Emily Hardy, 1928, 1930.) Ed. Michael Millgate. Athens: University of Georgia Press, 1985.

Harlan, Lindsey. "Perfection and Devotion: Sati Tradition in Rajasthan." In Hawley.

Harmon, Louise. *Fragments on the Deathwatch.* Boston: Beacon Press, 1998.

Harrison, Robert Pogue. *The Dominion of the Dead.* Chicago: University of Chicago Press, 2003.

Harrison, Sophie. "Diary." *London Review of Books,* vol. 26, no. 3 (February 2004).

Harrison, Tony. *Selected Poems.* New York: Viking/Penguin, 1984.

Hartman, Geoffrey. "The Book of the Destruction." In Friedlander.

Harvey, Charlotte Bruce. "I Might Not Be There." *Brown Alumni Magazine* (July–August 2003).

Haskell, Molly. *Love & Other Infectious Diseases.* New York: William Morrow, 1990.

Hawks, Peter. "Naming Names: The Art of Memory and the NAMES Project AIDS Quilt," *Critical Inquiry,* vol. 19, no. 4 (Summer 1993).

Hawley, John, ed. *Sati, the Blessing and the Curse: The Burning of Wives in India.* New York: Oxford University Press, 1994.

Hazo, Samuel. "September 11, 2001." In Heyen, *September 11, 2001.*

Heaney, Seamus. *Selected Poems. 1966–1996.* New York: Farrar Straus, 1998.

Heidegger, Martin. *Being and Time.* Trans. John Macquarrie and Edward Robson. New York: Harper, 1962.

———. *Poetry, Language and Thought.* Trans. Albert Hofstadter. New York: Harper, 1971.

Heinemann, Henry. "Human Values in the Medical Care of the Terminally Ill." In Schoenberg, Carr, Peretz, and Kutscher.

Hejinian, Lyn. *The Language of Inquiry.* Berkeley: University of California Press, 2000.

Hemingway, Ernest. *The Short Stories.* New York: Scribner, 1995.

Hemmer, Bill. "Bill Hemmer: For Most, Closure Will Take the Rest of Their Lives." *CNN.COM LAW CENTER: ON THE SCENE.* June 11, 2001. <http://archives.cnn.com/ 2001/LAW/06/11/mcveigh.hemmer.otsc.otsc/>

Henderson, Carol. *Losing Malcolm: A Mother's Journey through Grief.* Jackson: University Press of Mississippi, 2001.

Henig, Robin Marantz. "Will We Ever Arrive at the Good Death?" *New York Times Magazine,* August 7, 2005.

Hennezel, Marie de. *Intimate Death: How the Dying Teach Us How to Live.* Trans. Carol Janeway. New York: Vintage, 1998.

Héran, Emmanuelle. *Le Dernier Portrait,* catalog of an exposition at the Musée d'Orsay. Paris: Seuil, 2002.

Heyen, William. *Erika: Poems of the Holocaust.* St. Louis: Time Being Press, 1991.

———, ed. *September 11, 2001: American Writers Respond.* Silver Springs, Md.: Etruscan Press, 2002.

Hibberd, Dominic, and John Onions, eds. *Poetry of the Great War: An Anthology.* London: Macmillan, 1986.

Hibbs, Ben. "Journey to a Shattered World." *Saturday Evening Post* (June 9, 1945).

Higginson, Thomas Wentworth. Preface to *Poems by Emily Dickinson.* Ed. Mabel Loomis Todd and T. W. Higginson. Boston: Little, Brown, 1920.

Hillman, Brenda. *The Death Tractates.* Hanover and London: Wesleyan University Press, 1992.

Hills, Paul, ed. *David Jones: Artist and Poet.* Aldershot, U.K.: Scolar Press, 1997.

Hoffman, Eva. *After Such Knowledge: A Meditation on the Aftermath of the Holocaust.* London: Secker & Warburg, 2004.

Hoffman, Jan. "Awash in Information, Patients Face a Lonely, Uncertain Road." *New York Times,* August 14, 2005.

Holst-Warhaft, Gail. *Dangerous Voices: Women's Laments and Greek Literature.* London and New York: Routledge, 1992.

———. *The Cue for Passion: Grief and Its Political Uses.* Cambridge: Harvard University Press, 2000.

———. "Deathfugue: Intruding on Paul Celan," a review of John Felstiner's *Paul Celan: Poet, Survivor, Jew. Bookpress,* vol. 6, no. 2 (1996).

Homberger, Eric; William Janeway; and Simon Schama, eds. *The Cambridge Mind.* London: Jonathan Cape, 1969.

Hood, Thomas. *Selected Poems of Thomas Hood.* Ed. John Clubbe. Cambridge, Mass.: Harvard University Press, 1970.

Howells, William Dean. "Whitman in Retrospect." In Whitman, *Leaves of Grass.*

Hughes, Ted. *Moortown.* New York: Harper & Row, 1979.

———. *Birthday Letters.* New York: Harper, 1998.

————. *Winter Pollen: Occasional Prose.* Ed. William Scammell. London: Faber and Faber, 1994.

————. "Notes on the Chronological Order of Sylvia Plath's Poems." In C. Newman.

Huizinga, Johan. *The Waning of the Middle Ages.* New York: Anchor, 1954.

Humphry, Derek. *Final Exit: The Practicalities of Self-Deliverance and Assisted Suicide for the Dying.* New York: Dell, 1991.

Hynes, Samuel. *The Soldiers' Tale: Bearing Witness to Modern War.* New York: Penguin, 1997.

————. *A War Imagined: The First World War and English Culture.* New York: Atheneum, 1991.

Ignatieff, Michael. "The Terrorist as Auteur." *New York Times Magazine,* November 14, 2004.

Iimura, Takahiko. "A Note for *MA:* SpaceTime in the Garden of Ryoan-Ji." *Media World of Takahiko Iimura.* <http://www2.gol.com/users/iimura/review/notema.html>

Izzo, David Garrett. *The Auden Encyclopedia.* Jefferson, N.C.: McFarland & Co., 2004.

————. *W. H. Auden: A Legacy.* West Cornwall, Conn.: Locust Hill Press, 2002.

Jacobs, Joseph. "The Dying of Death." *Fortnightly Review,* vol. 66 (July–December 1899).

Jamison, Stephen. *Assisted Suicide: A Decision-Making Guide for Health Professionals.* San Francisco: Jossey-Bass, 1997.

Jay, Gregory. *T. S. Eliot and the Poetics of Literary History.* Baton Rouge and London: Louisiana State University Press, 1983.

Jeffords, Susan. "Rape & Resolution in Bosnia," unpublished paper presented at "A Day of Peace," University of California at Irvine, May 15, 1993.

Johnson, Barbara. "Apostrophe, Animation, Abortion." In Warhol and Herndl.

Johnson, George. "True Believers: Science and Religion Cross Their Line in the Sand." "Week in Review." *New York Times,* July 12, 1998.

Johnson, Richard. "Exemplary Differences: Mourning (and Not Mourning) a Process." In Kear and Steinberg.

Jones, Barbara. *Design for Death.* London: Deutsch, 1967.

Jones, David. *In Parenthesis.* London: Faber & Faber, 1937.

————. *Dai Greatcoat.* Ed. Rene Hague. London: Faber & Faber, 1980.

Jünger, Ernst. *The Storm of Steel.* Trans. Basil Creighton. London: Chatto & Windus, 1929.

Jury, Mark and Dan. *Gramp: A Man Ages and Dies. An Extraordinary Record of One Family's Encounter with the Reality of Dying. 1975–1976.* New York: Grossman, 1976.

Kahane, Claire. "Uncanny Sights: The Anticipation of the Abomination." In Greenberg.

Kamper, Dietmar, and Christoph Wulf, eds. *Looking Back on the End of the World.* Trans. David Antal. New York: Semiotext(e), 1989.

Kaplan, Justin. *Walt Whitman: A Life.* New York: Simon & Schuster, 1980.

Karr, Mary. "Negotiating the Darkness, Fortified by Poets' Strength." *New York Times,* Jan. 14, 2002.

Kayser-Jones, Jeanie, R.N., Ph.D., FAAN, et al. "Factors that Influence End-of-Life Care in Nursing Homes: The Physical Environment, Inadequate Staffing, and Lack of Supervision." *Gerontologist,* vol. 43, no. 2 (2003).

Kaufman, Sharon R. . . . *And a Time to Die: How American Hospitals Shape the End of Life.* New York: Scribner, 2005.

———. "In the Shadow of 'Death with Dignity': Medicine and the Cultural Quandaries of the Vegetative State." *American Anthropologist,* vol. 102, no. 1 (2000).

———. "Intensive Care, Old Age, and the Problem of Death in America." *Gerontologist,* vol. 38, 6 (1998).

———. "Narrative, Death, and the Uses of Anthropology." In Cole, Kastenbaum, and Ray.

Kear, Adrian, and Deborah Lynn Steinberg, eds. *Mourning Diana: Nation, Culture and the Performance of Grief.* London & New York: Routledge, 1999.

Keats, John. *Complete Poems and Selected Letters.* Intro. Edward Hirsch. New York: Random House, the Modern Library, 2001.

Keizer, Bert. *Dancing with Mr. D.* New York: Doubleday, 1997.

Keller, Catherine. *Apocalypse Now and Then.* Boston: Beacon Press, 1996.

Kendall, Tim. *Sylvia Plath: A Critical Study.* London: Faber and Faber, 2001.

Kenzer, Stephen. "Cincinnati, Art Bows to the Privacy of Death." *New York Times,* August 3, 2002.

Kingston, Maxine Hong. *China Men.* New York: Knopf, 1980.

Kipling, Rudyard. *Rudyard Kipling's Verse: Inclusive Edition 1885–1926.* New York: Doubleday, Page & Co., 1927.

———. *Selected Stories.* Ed. Sandra Kemp. London and Melbourne: J. M. Dent & Sons, 1987.

———. *Traffics and Discoveries.* 1904. London: Macmillan & Co., 1949.

Klawans, Stuart. "Dead Stars, Alive Again: Yes, Marilyn May Fall Love with Viggo." *New York Times,* August 1, 2004.

Kleinfeld, N. R. "Death Watch for Stranger, Becoming a Friend to the End." *New York Times,* January 25, 2004.

Kleinman, Arthur, M.D., *The Illness Narratives: Suffering, Healing, and the Human Condition.* New York: Basic Books, 1988.

Kluger, Ruth. *Still Alive: A Holocaust Girlhood Remembered.* Foreword by Lore Segal. New York: Feminist Press, 2001.

Knowles, James. "Aspects of Tennyson, II: A Personal Reminiscence." *Nineteenth Century,* vol. 33 (1983).

Kolata, Gina. "Extending Life, Defibrillators Can Prolong Misery." *New York Times,* March 25, 2002.

———. "Sick and Scared, and Waiting, Waiting, Waiting." *New York Times*, August 20, 2005.

Kristeva, Julia. *Powers of Horror: An Essay on Abjection*. Trans. Leon S. Roudiez. New York: Columbia University Press, 1982.

Kroll, Judith. *Chapters in a Mythology: The Poetry of Sylvia Plath*. New York: Harper & Row, 1976.

Krondorfer, Bjorn. "Innocence, Corruption, Holocaust." *Christianity and Crisis*, (August 11, 1986).

Kübler-Ross, Elisabeth. *On Death and Dying: What the Dying Have to Teach Doctors, Nurses, Clergy and Their Own Families*. New York: Macmillan, 1970.

———. *On Life after Death*. Berkeley: Celestial Arts, 1991.

———. *The Tunnel and the Light*. New York: Marlowe & Co., 1999.

Kumin, Maxine. *Selected Poems: 1969–1990*. New York: W. W. Norton, 1991.

Kurlander, Yitzchok. "Kaddish Related Definitions." Cleveland Heights, Ohio: Kaddish Foundation. <http://www.mnemotrix.com/kaddish/terms.html>

Kyle, Donald G. *Spectacles of Death in Ancient Rome*. New York: Routledge, 1998.

———. Review of D. S. Potter, D. J. Mattingly, "Life, Death, and Entertainment in the Roman Empire." *Bryn Mawr Classical Review*, vol. 10. no. 36 (1999).

Langone, John. "Paean to the Stethoscope." *New York Times*, November 12, 2002.

Lanzmann, Claude. *Shoah*. New York: Pantheon, 1995.

Laqueur, Thomas. "Closing Time." *London Review of Books* (August 18, 1994).

———, Maya Lin, Stanley Saitowitz, Stephen Greenblatt, and Andrew Barshay. "Grounds for Remembering." Doreen B. Townsend Center for the Humanities: Occasional Papers. Paper 3. March 6, 1995.

Larkin, Philip. *Collected Poems*. Ed. Anthony Thwaite. New York: Farrar Straus, 1989.

———. *Further Requirements: Interviews, Broadcasts, Statements, and Book Reviews*. Ed. and with intro. by Anthony Thwaite. London: Faber & Faber, 2001.

Lawrence, D. H. *Apocalypse*. Ed. Mara Kalins. New York: Penguin, 1995.

———. *The Collected Short Stories of D. H. Lawrence*. New York: Viking, 1994.

———. *The Complete Poems of D. H. Lawrence*. Ed. Vivian de Sola Pinto and Warren Roberts. New York: Viking, 1964.

———. *Letters of D. H. Lawrence*, vol. 1: 1901–13. Ed. James T. Boulton. Cambridge, U.K.: Cambridge University Press, 1979.

———. *Sons and Lovers*. New York: Viking, 1968.

Leed, Eric J. *No Man's Land: Combat and Identity in World War I*. London and New York: Cambridge University Press, 1979.

Léger, Fernand. *Une Correspondance de Guerre à Louis Poughon, 1914–1918*. Paris: Éditions du Centre Pompidou, 1990.

Lengyel, Olga. *Five Chimneys: The Story of Auschwitz*. Trans. Clifford Coch and Paul Weiss. Chicago: Ziff-Davis, 1947.

Leonard, Karen. "Decca's Last Request." (Letter to Robert Waltrip.) August 10, 1996. JESSICA MITFORD MEMORIAL SITE. <http://www.mitford.org/lastreq.htm>

Lest We Forget: The Horrors of Nazi Concentration Camps Revealed for All Time in the Most Terrible Photographs Ever Published. London: Daily Mail/Associated Newspapers, Ltd., 1945.

Levi, Primo. *The Drowned and the Saved.* Trans. Raymond Rosenthal. New York: Summit Books, 1998.

———. *Survival in Auschwitz: The Nazi Assault on Humanity.* Trans. Stuart Woolf. 1958. New York: Simon & Schuster, 1996.

Lévy, Bernard-Henri. *Who Killed Daniel Pearl?* Trans. James X. Mitchell. Hoboken, N.J.: Melville House, 2003.

Lewis, C. S. *A Grief Observed.* London and Boston: Faber & Faber, 1961.

———. *The Lion, the Witch and the Wardrobe.* New York: Harper Trophy, 1978.

Leyda, Jay. *The Years and Hours of Emily Dickinson,* vol. 2. New Haven: Yale University Press, 1960.

Lifton, Robert Jay. *Death in Life: Survivors of Hiroshima.* New York: Random House, 1967.

———. *The Nazi Doctors.* New York: Basic Books, 1986.

Lin, Maya. *Boundaries.* New York: Simon & Schuster, 2000.

Linder, Douglas. "An Introduction to the My Lai Courts-Martial." MY LAI COURTS-MARTIAL HOMEPAGE. <http://www.law.umkc.edu/faculty/projects/ftrials/mylai/mylai.htm>

Lindsey, Hal. *The Late Great Planet Earth.* New York: Bantam, 1973.

Liss, Andrea. *Trespassing through Shadows: Memory, Photography, and the Holocaust.* Minneapolis: University of Minnesota Press, 1998.

Louchheim, Rabbi Tom. "Jewish Customs of Mourning." RABBI SCHEINERMAN'S HOME PAGE. Tucson: 1997. <http://scheinerman.net/judaism/life-cycle/mourning.html>

Loving, Jerome. *Walt Whitman: The Song of Himself.* Berkeley: University of California Press: 1999.

Lowell, Robert. *Day by Day.* New York: Farrar Straus, 1977.

———. Introduction to Sylvia Plath, *Ariel.* New York: Harper & Row, 1966.

———. *Life Studies: and, For the Union Dead.* 1967. New York: Farrar Straus, 1977.

———. "On Robert Lowell's 'Skunk Hour.'" In Ostroff.

———. *Selected Poems.* New York: Farrar Straus, 1976.

———. "William Carlos Williams: Paterson I." *Collected Prose.* 1947. Ed. Robert Giroux. New York: Farrar Straus Giroux, 1987.

Lyall, Sarah. "Philip Pullman's Strange and Thrilling Worlds." *International Herald Tribune,* November 9, 2000.

Lynch, Thomas. *The Undertaking: Life Studies from the Dismal Trade.* New York: Penguin, 1998.

———. "Socko Finish." *New York Times Magazine.* July 12, 1998.

———. *Bodies in Motion and at Rest: On Metaphor and Mortality.* New York: W. W. Norton, 2000.

Lynn, Joanne, et al., "Perceptions by Family Members of the Dying Experience of Older and Seriously Ill Patients." *Annals of Internal Medicine,* vol. 126 (January 15, 1997).

McEwan, Ian. *Saturday*. London: Johnathan Cape, 2005.

McHenry, Eric. "An Aesthetics of Inadequacy." (Interview with Alan Shapiro). May 30, 2002. THE ATLANTIC ONLINE. <http://www.theatlantic.com/doc/prem/200205u/int2002-05-30>

Mackaman, Douglas, and Michael Mays, eds. *World War I and the Cultures of Modernity*. Jackson: University Press of Mississippi, 2000.

MacLeish, Archibald. *Collected Poems 1917–1982*. Boston: Houghton Mifflin, 1985.

MacMillan, R. L., M. D., FRCP, and K. W. G. Brown, M.D., FRCP. "Cardiac Arrest Remembered." *Canadian Medical Association Journal*, vol. 104 (May 1971).

Maddox, Brenda. *Yeats's Ghosts: The Secret Life of W. B. Yeats*. New York: Harper-Collins/Perennial, 1999.

Magnusson, Roger S., with Peter H. Ballis. *Angels of Death: Exploring the Euthanasia Underground*. New Haven: Yale University Press, 2002.

Mairs, Nancy. *A Troubled Guest: Life and Death Stories*. Boston: Beacon Press, 2001.

Mann, Sally. "Giving Up the Ghost." *Egg the Arts Show*. PBS. <http://www.pbs.org/wnet/egg/301/mann/>

Manning, James, ed. *Prophecies for the Millennium: Psychics, Seers, and Oracles Tell You What to Expect from the Next 1000 Years*. New York: HarperCollins, 1997.

Marcus, Phillip. "Lawrence, Yeats and 'the Resurrection of the Body.' " In Balbert and Marcus.

Mariani, Paul. *William Carlos Williams: A New World Naked*. New York: W. W. Norton, 1990.

Marinetti, F. T. *Selected Writings*. Trans. R.W. Flint and Arthur A. Coppotelli. Ed. R. W. Flint. New York: Farrar, Straus & Giroux, 1972.

Masefield, John. *Gallipoli*. 1916. New York: Macmillan, 1925.

———. *Selected Poems of John Masefield*. Ed. Donald Stanford. Manchester, U.K.: Carcanet, 1984.

Masters, Edgar Lee. *Whitman*. New York: Biblio and Tannen, 1968.

Mayer, John T. *T. S. Eliot's Silent Voices*. New York and Oxford: Oxford University Press, 1989.

Mechanic, David. *Medical Sociology*. New York: Free Press, 1968.

Meehan, Paula. *Mysteries of the Home*. Newcastle-upon-Tyne, U.K.: Bloodaxe, 1996.

Menand, Louis. "The Reluctant Memorialist." *New Yorker* (July 8, 2002).

Merleau-Ponty, Maurice. *The Phenomenology of Perception*. Trans. Colin Smith. London: Routledge, 1962.

Merrill, James. *The Changing Light at Sandover*. New York: Atheneum, 1982.

Merwin, W. S. *The River Sound*. New York: Knopf, 1999.

———. "To the Words (9/17/01)." *The New Yorker* (Oct. 8, 2001):65.

Metcalf, Peter, and Richard Huntington. *Celebrations of Death: The Anthropology of Mortuary Ritual*, 2nd ed. Cambridge, U.K.: Cambridge University Press, 1991.

Middlebrook, Diane. *Her Husband: Hughes and Plath—A Marriage*. New York: Viking, 2003.

Miles, Randy. "The Elvis Seance." 1994. <http://www.ibiblio.org/elvis/seance.html>

Millay, Edna St. Vincent. *Collected Poems*. Ed. Norma Millay. New York: Harper & Row, 1981.

Miller, James. *T. S. Eliot's Personal Waste Land: Exorcism of the Demons*. University Park and London: Pennsylvania State University Press, 1977.

Miller, Nancy. *Bequest and Betrayal: Memoirs of a Parent's Death*. Bloomington: Indiana University Press, 2000.

———, and Jason Tougaw, eds. *Extremities: Trauma, Testimony, and Community*. Urbana: University of Illinois Press, 2002.

Miller, Ruth. *The Poetry of Emily Dickinson*. Middletown, Conn.: Wesleyan University Press, 1968.

Milton, John. "Lycidas." *Paradise Regained, The Minor Poems & Samson Agonistes*. Ed. Merritt Y. Hughes. New York: Odyssey Press, 1967.

Milton, Sybil. "Images of the Holocaust—Part I." *Holocaust and Genocide Studies, 1*, 1 (1986).

———. "The Camera as Weapon: Documentary Photography and the Holocaust." *Simon Wiesenthal Center Annual*, vol. 1, no. 1 (1984).

Mitford, Jessica. *The American Way of Death*. New York: Simon & Schuster, 1963.

———. *The American Way of Death Revisited*. New York: Knopf, 1998.

Moaveni, Azadeh. "How Images of Death Became Must-See TV." *Time* (April 29, 2002).

Mohr, Richard. *Gay Ideas: Outing and Other Controversies*. Boston: Beacon Press, 1992.

Moller, David Wendell. *Confronting Death: Values, Institutions, & Human Mortality*. New York: Oxford University Press1996.

———. *On Death without Dignity: The Human Impact of Technological Dying*. Perspectives on Death & Dying Series. Amityville, N.Y.: Baywood Publishing Co., 1990.

Monette, Paul. *Love Alone: Eighteen Elegies for Rog*. New York: St. Martin's Press, 1988.

———. *Borrowed Time: An AIDS Memoir*. New York: Avon, 1990.

Montgomery, Ruth, with Joanne Garland. *Herald of the New Age*. London: Grafton, 1987.

"The Most Terrible Example of Organized Cruelty in the History of Civilization." *Illustrated London News* (October 14, 1944).

Moreno, Jonathan D. *Arguing Euthanasia: The Controversy over Mercy Killing, Assisted Suicide, and the "Right to Die."* New York: Simon & Schuster, 1995.

Morin, Edgar. *L'Homme et la Mort*. Paris: Seuil, 1970.

Morris, Dan. "Unforgettable Morrie." ABCNEWS.COM <http://204.202.137 .114/onair/nightline/nl1990225_morrie.html>

Morris, David. "Gothic Sublimity." *New Literary History*, vol. 16 (Winter 1985).

Morris, James. *Farewell the Trumpets: An Imperial Retreat*. New York and London: Harcourt Brace Jovanovich, 1978.

Morrison, Toni. *Beloved*. New York: Knopf, 1987.

———. *Sula*. New York: Knopf, 1973.

Moyers, Bill. "Bill Moyers on Health and the Global Environment." <http://yubanet.com/artman/publish/article_15874.shtml> December 4, 2004.

———, and Judith Davidson Moyers, eds. *On Our Own Terms: Bill Moyers on Dying.* PBS THIRTEEN ONLINE. 2000. <http://www.pbs.org/wnet/onourownterms/index.html>

Müller, Filip, with literary collaboration by Helmut Freitag. *Eyewitness Auschwitz: Three Years in the Gas Chambers.* Trans. and ed. Susanne Flatauer. Chicago: Ivan R. Dee, 1999.

Murray, John, M.D. *Intensive Care: A Doctor's Journal.* Berkeley: University of California Press, 2000.

Murray, T. Jock. "Reflections: Illness and Healing, the Art of Robert Pope." *Humane Medicine* (July 1994).

Myers, Steven Lee. "Explosives Round Russian Crash." *International Herald Tribune*, August 28–29, 2004.

Nagel, Thomas. *Mortal Questions.* New York: Cambridge University Press, 1979.

Narasimhan, Sakuntala. *Sati: Widow Burning in India.* New York: Doubleday Anchor, 1990.

National Council on Disability. *Assisted Suicide: A Disability Perspective Position Paper.* Washington, D.C.: 1997.

Nelson, Emmanuel S., ed. *AIDS: The Literary Response.* New York: Twayne, 1992.

Nemerov, Howard. *Figures of Thought: Speculations on the Meaning of Poetry and Other Essays.* Boston: David R. Godine, 1978.

The New American Bible. New York: Oxford University Press, 1995.

The New Cassell's German Dictionary. New York: Funk & Wagnalls, 1962.

Newman, Charles, ed. *The Art of Sylvia Plath.* Bloomington: Indiana University Press, 1970.

Newman, Judith Sternberg. *In the Hell of Auschwitz.* New York: Exposition, 1964.

New-York Historical Society, with City Lore: The New York Center for Urban Folk Culture. "Missing: Streetscape of a City in Mourning." 2002. <http://www.nyhistory.org/missing/index.html>

Niebuhr, Gustav. "In Search of Holy Ground." *New York Times Magazine*, December 7, 1997.

Nietzsche, Friedrich. *The Gay Science.* 1882. Trans. and ed. Walter Kaufmann. New York: Vintage, 1974.

Nixon, Nicholas, and Bebe Nixon. *People with AIDS.* Boston: David R. Godine, 1991.

Norris, Margot. *Writing War in the Twentieth Century.* Charlottesville and London: University Press of Virginia, 2000.

Not Dead Yet. Founder Diane Coleman. <http://www.notdeadyet.org/>

"Notes on New Books." *Washington Daily National Intelligencer*, February 18, 1856.

Nuland, Sherwin. *How We Die.* New York: Knopf, 1994.

Nussbaum, Emily. "Good Grief! The Case for Repression." *Lingua Franca* (October 1997).

O'Brien, Mark. *The Man in the Iron Lung.* Berkeley: Lemonade Factory, 1997.

————. "A High Quad Defends Quality of Life—Kevorkian Argues I Would Be Better Off Dead Than Alive." PACIFIC NEWS SERVICE, October 1, 1996. <http://www.pacificnews.org/jinn/stories/2.20/961001-kevorkian.html>

————. "A Quack Remedy for the Terminally Ill." PACIFIC NEWS SERVICE, March 3, 1995. <http://www.pacificnews.org/marko/950324-death.html>

Olds, Sharon. *The Father.* New York: Knopf, 1993.

On Our Own Terms: Bill Moyers on Dying. Ed. Judith Davidson Moyers, Bill Moyers. PBS/Thirteen Online. 2000. <http://www.pbs.org/wnet/onourownterms/index.html>

Ostriker, Alicia. *The Little Space: Poems Selected and New, 1968–1998.* Pittsburgh: University of Pittsburgh Press, 1998.

Ostroff, Anthony. *The Contemporary Poet as Artist and Critic.* Boston: Little, Brown, 1964.

Owen, Wilfred. *Collected Letters.* Ed. Harold Owen and John Bell. Oxford and New York: Oxford University Press, 1967.

————. *The Collected Poems of Wilfred Owen.* Ed. and intro. by C. Day Lewis. Memoir by Edmund Blunden. New York: New Directions, 1963.

Ozeki, Ruth. "A Vacation with Ghosts." *New York Times*, August 11, 2004.

Parkes, Colin Murray. *Bereavement; Studies of Grief in Adult Life.* Foreword by John Bowlby. London: Tavistock; Harmondsworth: Pelican, 1978.

Parlette, Alicia. "Alicia's Story." *San Francisco Chronicle*, June 5–10, 2005; July 31, 2005; August 17, 2005, and <http://www.sfgate.com/alicia>

Pascal, Blaise. *Pascal's Pensées.* Trans. Martin Turnell. London: Harvill Press, 1962.

Peter, John. "A New Interpretation of *The Waste Land.*" *Essays in Criticism,* vol. 2 (1952).

Pflieger, Pat. "Death and the Readers of *Robert Merry's Museum.*" Paper presented at American Culture Association Convention. Chicago, 1994. <http://www.merrycoz.org/papers/DEATH.HTM>

Phillips, Adam. *Darwin's Worms: On Life Stories and Death Stories.* New York: Perseus, 2000.

Pinsky, Robert. *The Figured Wheel: New and Collected Poems 1966–1996.* New York: Farrar Straus, 1996.

Plath, Sylvia. *Ariel.* New York: Harper & Row, 1966.

————. *Collected Poems.* Ed. Ted Hughes. New York: Harper & Row, 1981.

————. *Johnny Panic and the Bible of Dreams.* 1977. London: Faber & Faber, 2001.

————. *Sylvia Plath: Letters Home.* Ed. Aurelia S. Plath. New York: Harper & Row, 1975.

————. *The Unabridged Journals.* Ed. Karen V. Kukil. New York: Anchor, 2000.

Poe, Edgar Allan. *Tales of Mystery & Imagination.* Baltimore: Garamond Press, 1941.

Pope, Alexander. *Pope's Essay on Man.* Intro. and notes by F. Ryland. London: G. Bell & Sons, 1915.

Pope, Robert. *Illness and Healing: Images of Cancer.* Hantsport, Nova Scotia: Lancelot, 1995.

Pound, Ezra. *Selected Poems*. New York: New Directions, 1957.

Praz, Mario. *The Romantic Agony*. Oxford and New York: Oxford University Press, 1970.

Price, Jonathan. *Readings in Literary Criticism 17: Critics on Robert Lowell*. 1959. Coral Gables: University of Miami Press, 1972.

Price, Reynolds. *A Whole New Life*. New York: Scribner, 1994.

Proulx, E. Annie. "Dead Stuff." *Aperture*, vol. 149 (Fall 1997).

Publishers Weekly. Review of Euphrosyne Doxiadis, *Mysterious Fayum Portraits*. November 22, 1995.

Ramazani, Jahan. *The Poetry of Mourning: The Modern Elegy from Hardy to Heaney*. Chicago: University of Chicago Press, 1994.

Reich, Wilhelm. *The Cancer Biopathy*. New York: Farrar, Straus & Giroux, 1973.

Redfield, James. *Nature and Culture in the Iliad: The Tragedy of Hector*. Chicago: University of Chicago Press, 1975.

Replansky, Naomi. *The Dangerous World: New and Selected Poems 1934–1994*. Chicago: Another Chicago Press, 1994.

Rich, Adrienne. *Poems Selected & New 1950–74*. New York: W. W. Norton, 1975.

Rich, Frank. "It's Closure Mongering Time." *New York Times*, April 22, 2001.

Richards, Frank. *Old Soldiers Never Die*. London: Faber, 1933.

Richardson, Ruth. *Death, Dissection, and the Destitute*. Chicago: University of Chicago Press, 2000.

Ricks, Christopher. *Beckett's Dying Words*. Oxford and New York: Oxford University Press, 1993.

Riva, Maria. *Marlene Dietrich: By Her Daughter*. New York: Knopf, 1993.

Roach, Mary. *Stiff: The Curious Lives of Human Cadavers*. New York: W. W. Norton, 2003.

Roberts, Pamela. "Tangible Sorrow, Virtual Tributes: Cemeteries in Cyberspace." In de Vries.

————, and Lourdes A. Vidal. "Perpetual Care in Cyberspace: A Portrait of Memorials on the Web," *Omega: Journal of Death and Dying*, 40, 4 (1999).

Robinson, Henry Peach. *Pictorial Effect in Photography, being hints on composition and chiaroscuro for photographers*. With an intro. by Robert A Sobieszek. Pawlet, Vt.: Helios, 1971.

La Rochefoucauld, *The Maxims of François duc de la Rochefoucauld*. Trans. F. G. Stevens. London: Oxford University Press, 1940.

Rogak, Lisa. *Death Warmed Over: Funeral Food, Rituals, and Customs from around the World*. Berkeley, Calif.: Tenspeed Press, 2004.

Rose, Gillian. *Love's Work*. London: Vintage, 1997.

Rose, Jacqueline. *The Haunting of Sylvia Plath*. Cambridge: Harvard University Press, 1992.

Rosenbaum, Ron. "Turn On, Tune In, Drop Dead." *Harper's* (July 1982).

Rosenberg, Isaac. *The Collected Poems of Isaac Rosenberg*. Ed. Gordon Bottomley and Denys Harding. Foreword by Siegfried Sassoon. New York: Schocken, 1949.

Rosenthal, M. L. *The New Poets*. New York: Oxford University Press, 1967.

————. "Poetry as Confession: *Life Studies* by Robert Lowell." In Price.

Rossetti, Dante Gabriel. *The Poetical Works of Dante Gabriel Rossetti*. Ed. William M. Rossetti. London: Ellis & Elvey, 1891.

Roszak, Theodore. *The Gendered Atom: Reflections on the Sexual Psychology of Science*. Berkeley, Calif.: Conari Press, 1999.

Roth, Philip. *Patrimony: A True Story*. New York: Vintage, 1996.

Rothenberg, Laura. *Breathing for a Living*. New York: Hyperion, 2003.

Rotman, Brian. *Signifying Nothing: The Semiotics of Zero*. Stanford: Stanford University Press, 1987.

Rowland, Anthony. *Tony Harrison and the Holocaust*. Liverpool: Liverpool University Press, 2001.

Russell, Bertrand. *The Collected Papers of Bertrand Russell*, vol. 12: *Contemplation and Action, 1902–14*. London: Routledge, 1985.

Sacks, Peter. *The English Elegy: Studies in the Genre from Spenser to Yeats*. Baltimore and London: Johns Hopkins University Press, 1985.

Saintsbury, George. "Leaves of Grass." In Whitman, *Leaves of Grass*.

St. Armand, Barton Levi. *Emily Dickinson and Her Culture: The Soul's Society*. Cambridge, U.K.: Cambridge University Press, 1984.

Salamon, Julie. "Briefly Back from the Dead to Give Mourners Some Words of Advice." *New York Times*, December 29, 2000.

Sampson, Martin C. "When the Curtains of Death Parted." *The Vestibule*. Ed. Jess E. Weiss. New York: Pocket Books, 1974.

Sand, Michael. "Interview with Joel-Peter Witkin." *World Art* (January 1996).

Sandburg, Carl. *Collected Poems*. New York: Harcourt, 1970.

Sassoon, Siegfried. *Collected Poems*. New York: Viking, 1949.

Saunders, Cicily, and Mary Baines. *Living with Dying: A Guide to Palliative Care*. Oxford: Oxford University Press, 1983.

Scarry, Elaine. *The Body in Pain*. New York: Oxford University Press, 1985.

Scherer, Deidre. *Work in Fabric and Thread*. New York: Watson-Guptill, 1998.

Schnell, Lisa. "A Lament and a Lesson: I Am Still Claire's Mom," *PDIA Newsletter*, vol. 7 (April 2000).

Schoenberg, Bernard; Arthur C. Carr; David Peretz; and Austin H. Kutscher, eds. *Psychosocial Aspects of Terminal Care*. New York: Columbia University Press, 1972.

Scholes, Robert. *Structural Fabulation*. Notre Dame: University of Notre Dame Press, 1975.

Schopenhauer, Arthur. *The World as Will and Representation*. Trans. E. F. J. Payne, 2 vols. New York: Dover Publications, 1969.

Schwartz, Vanessa R. *Spectacular Realities: Early Mass Culture in Fin-de-Siècle Paris*. Berkeley and Los Angeles: University of California Press, 1998.

Schwenger, Peter. "Corpsing the Image," *Critical Inquiry*, vol. 26, no. 3 (Spring 2000).

Sconce, Jeffrey. *Haunted Media*. Durham, N.C.: Duke University Press, 2000.

Scruggs, Jan C., and Joel L. Swerdlow. *To Heal a Nation: The Vietnam Veterans Memorial*. New York: Harper, 1985.

Scully, Vincent. "The Terrible Art of Designing a War Memorial." *New York Times*, July 14, 1991.

Seale, Clive. *Constructing Death*. Cambridge, U.K.: Cambridge University Press, 1998.

Sebald, W. G. *Austerlitz*. Trans. Anthea Bell. New York: Random House, 2001.

———. *On the Natural History of Destruction*. Trans. Anthea Bell. New York: Random House, 2003.

———. *Campo Santo*. Ed. Sven Meyer, trans. Anthea Bell. London: Hamish Hamilton, 2005.

Seltzer, Richard. *Mortal Lessons: Notes on the Art of Surgery*. New York: Simon & Schuster, 1976.

Serrano, Andres. "Piss Christ." 1989. *USC Annenberg School of Communication.* <http://www.usc.edu/schools/annenberg/asc/projects/comm544/library/images/502.html>

Service, Robert. *The Spell of the Yukon and Other Verses*. New York: Barset Hopkins, 1907.

Sewall, Richard B. *The Life of Emily Dickinson*, vol. 2. New York: Farrar, Straus & Giroux, 1974.

Sexton, Anne. *Collected Poems*. Boston: Houghton Mifflin, 1981.

Shakespeare, William. *Hamlet*. Ed. Harold Jenkins. London: Arden Shakespeare, 1982.

———. *King Henry V.* Ed. T. W. Craik. London: Arden Shakespeare, 1995.

———. *King Lear.* Ed. R. A. Foakes. London: Arden Shakespeare, 1997.

Shapiro, Alan. "An Aesthetics of Inadequacy." *Atlantic Online* (May 30, 2002).

———. *The Dead Alive and Busy*. Chicago: University of Chicago Press, 2000.

———. "Some Questions Concerning Art and Suffering." *Tikkun* (January–February 2004).

———. *Song and Dance*. Boston: Houghton Mifflin, 2002.

———. *Vigil.* Chicago and London: University of Chicago Press, 1997.

Sharpe, Virginia A., ed. *Accountability: Patient Safety and Policy Reform*. Washington, D.C.: Georgetown University Press, 2004.

Shelley, Percy Bysshe. *Poetical Works*. London: Oxford University Press, 1967.

Siegel, Bernie. *Love, Medicine and Miracles*. New York: Harper & Row, 1986.

Sigourney, Lydia. *The Weeping Willow*. Hartford, Conn.: Henry S. Parsons, 1847.

Silkin, Jon. *Out of Battle: The Poetry of the Great War*. Oxford and New York: Oxford University Press, 1972.

Silverthorne, Jeffrey. *Photographs*. Oak Park, Mich.: Book Beat Gallery, 1994.

Simpson, David. "The Mourning Paper," *London Review of Books*, vol. 26, no. 10 (May 20, 2004).

Six Feet Under. Home Box Office, Inc. 2004. <http://www.hbo.com/sixfeetunder/about/index.shtml>

Sleutelaar, Armando and Hans. *De SS-ers. Nederlandse vrijwilligers in de tweede wereldoorlog*. 1967. Amsterdam: De Bezige Bij, 1990.

Small, Judy Jo. "A Musical Aesthetic." *Emily Dickinson: A Collection of Critical Essays*. Ed. Judith Farr. Upper Saddle River, N.J.: Prentice Hall, 1996.

Smith, Craig S. "A Love that Transcends Death Is Blessed by the State." *New York Times*, February 19, 2004.

Smith, Dinitia. "Battling Failing Health, Her Own Words." *New York Times*, August 5, 2002.

Smith, Grover. *The Waste Land*. London: Allen & Unwin, 1983.

Smith, Ian Haydn. Review of Tony Harrison's *Prometheus*. Institute of Film Studies, University of Nottingham. November 8, 1999. <http://www.nottingham.ac.uk /film/journal/filmrev/prome.htm>

Snodgrass, W. D. *Selected Poems: 1957–1987*. New York: Soho Press, 1988.

Snyder, Lois, and Arthur Kaplan. *Assisted Suicide: Finding Common Ground*. Bloomington: Indiana University Press, 2002.

THE SOCIETY FOR PSYCHICAL RESEARCH. London. <http://www.spr.ac.uk/>

Sontag, Susan. *Illness as Metaphor/AIDS and Its Metaphors*. New York: Penguin, 1991.

———. *On Photography*. New York: Penguin, 1977.

———. *Regarding the Pain of Others*. New York: Farrar Straus, 2003.

———. "Regarding the Torture of Others." *New York Times Magazine*, May 23, 2004.

Spiegelman, Art. *Maus, A Survivor's Tale*. New York: Pantheon, 1986.

———. *Maus II: A Survivor's Tale: And Here My Troubles Began*. New York: Pantheon, 1991.

———. *In the Shadow of No Towers*. New York: Pantheon, 2004.

Stamelman, Richard. "September 11: Between Memory and History." In Greenberg.

Stanley, Edith, and Stephanie Simon. "Grieving Families' Hearts Lie in Ashes." *San Francisco Chronicle*, February 18, 2002.

Stein, Gertrude. *Everybody's Autobiography*. 1937. Cambridge: Exact Change, 1993.

Stein, Stephen J. "American Millennial Visions: Toward a Construction of a New Architectonic of American Apocalypticism." In Amanat and Bernhardsson.

Steinberg, Jacques. "Kidnappings, Beheadings and Defining What's News." *New York Times*, August 1, 2004.

Steiner, George. *Bluebeard's Castle*. New Haven: Yale University Press, 1971.

———. "In Extremis." In Homberger, Janeway, and Schama.

Stephen, Martin. *The Price of Pity: Poetry, History and Myth in the Great War*. London: Leo Cooper, 1996.

———, ed. *Poems of the First World War: "Never Such Innocence."* London: Dent/Everyman, 1993.

Stephenson, John S. *Death, Grief, and Mourning: Individual and Social Realities*. New York: Free Press, 1985.

Stevens, Wallace. *The Collected Poems and Prose*. New York: Library of America, 1997.

———. *Letters of Wallace Stevens*. Ed. Holly Stevens. Berkeley: University of California Press, 1996.

Stevenson, Anne. *Bitter Fame: A Life of Sylvia Plath*. Boston: Houghton Mifflin, 1989.

Stewart, Garrett. *Death Sentences: Styles of Dying in British Fiction.* Cambridge: Harvard University Press, 1984.

Stillman, Edmund, and William Pfaff. *The Politics of Hysteria.* New York: Harper & Row, 1964.

Stolberg, Sheryl Gay. "On Medicine's Frontier: The Last Journey of James Quinn." *New York Times,* October 8, 2002.

Stone, Ruth. *Cheap: New Poems and Ballads.* New York: Harcourt Brace Jovanovich, 1972.

———. *Second-Hand Coat: Poems New and Selected.* Boston: Godine, 1987.

SUPPORT Principal Investigators. "A Controlled Trial to Improve Care for Seriously Ill Hospitalized Patients; the Study to Understand Prognoses and Preferences for Outcomes and Risks of Treatments." *Journal of the American Medical Association,* vol. 274 (1995).

Sweeney, Camille, ed. "The Afterlife, As I See It." *New York Times Magazine,* December 7, 1997.

Sword, Helen. *Ghostwriting Modernism.* Ithaca, N.Y.: Cornell University Press, 2001.

Szasz, Thomas. *The Second Sin.* New York: Anchor, 1974.

Talbot, Margaret. "A Desire to Duplicate." *New York Times Magazine,* February 4, 2004.

TANGBEN. <http://www.tangben.com/message/message.cfm?ID=2117>

Tanner, Laura E. "Haunted Images: Photographic Representations of People with AIDS." *Genre,* vol. 29 (Spring–Summer 1996).

Tappan, Eva March, ed. *The World's Story: A History of the World in Story, Song and Art,* vol. 2: *India, Persia, Mesopotamia, and Palestine.* Boston: Houghton Mifflin, 1914.

Tarlow, Sarah. *Bereavement and Commemoration: An Archaeology of Mortality.* Oxford, U.K.: Blackwell, 1999.

Tatum, James. *The Mourner's Song: War and Remembrance from the* Iliad *to Vietnam.* Chicago: University of Chicago Press, 2003.

Taylor, Diana. "Downloading Grief: Minority Populations Mourn Diana." In Kear and Steinberg.

Tennyson, Alfred Lord. *Tennyson's Poetry: A Norton Critical Edition,* 2nd ed. Ed. Robert W. Hill, Jr. New York: W. W. Norton, 1999.

———. *Poems of Tennyson.* Ed. Jerome H. Buckley. Boston: Houghton Mifflin, 1958.

Tennyson, Hallam. *Alfred Lord Tennyson: A Memoir by His Son.* London: Macmillan, 1897.

Thomas, Dylan. *Collected Poems.* New York: New Directions, 1953.

Tiedeman, Rolf, ed. *Notes to Literature.* Trans. Sherry Weber Nicholsen. New York: Columbia University Press, 1992.

Todorov, Tzvetan. *Facing the Extreme: Moral Life in the Concentration Camps.* Trans. Arthur Denner and Abigail Pollak. New York: Holt/Owl Books, 1996.

Tolchin, Neal L. *Mourning, Gender, and Creativity in the Art of Herman Melville.* New Haven: Yale University Press, 1988.

Tolstoy, Leo. *The Death of Ivan Ilyich and Other Stories.* Trans. and with intro. by Rosemary Edmonds. London: Penguin, 1960.

Tsvygun, Marina. *Prophecies for the Millennium.* Ed. James Manning. New York: HarperCollins, 1997.

Twain, Mark. *The Adventures of Huckleberry Finn.* Ed. James K. Bowen and Richard Vanderbeets. Glenview, Ill.: Scott, Foresman and Co., 1970.

Updike, John. "Nelson and Annabelle, II." *New Yorker* (October 9, 2000).

Valentine, Douglas. *The Phoenix Program.* New York: William Morrow, 1990.

Valentine, Stephen, ed. *Timeship.* New York. 2004. <http://timeship.org/>

Van Biema, David. "Does Heaven Exist?" *Time* (March 24, 1997).

Van Praagh, James. *Heaven and Earth: Making the Psychic Connection.* New York: Pocket Books, 2002.

Vernant, Jean Pierre. *Myth and Thought among the Greeks.* 1965. Trans. Janet Lloyd. London: Routledge, 1983.

Vickers, Nancy. "Diana Described: Scattered Woman and Scattered Rhyme." *Critical Inquiry*, vol. 8 (1981).

VIRTUAL MUSEUM OF THE IRON LUNG. Ed. Richard Hill. <http://www.newsplus .enta.net/ironlung.htm>

Von Alphen, Ernest. *Caught by History: Holocaust Effects in Contemporary Art, Literature, and Theory.* Stanford: Stanford University Press, 1997.

von Trier, Lars. *The Kingdom.* DVD. Denmark: 1994.

———. *The Kingdom II.* DVD. Denmark: 1997.

Walker, Susan. *Ancient Faces: Mummy Portraits in Roman Egypt.* London: Routledge, 2000.

Walkerdine, Valerie. "The Crowd in the Age of Diana: Ordinary Inventiveness and the Popular Imagination." In Kear and Steinberg.

Wallace, Jonathan. "An Auschwitz Alphabet." <http://www.spectacle.org/695/ ausch.html>

Ward, Elizabeth. *David Jones: Mythmaker.* Manchester, U.K.: Manchester University Press, 1983.

Warhol, Robin, and Diane Herndl, eds. *Feminisms.* New Brunswick, N.J.: Rutgers University Press, 1997.

Waring, Belle. "Euthanasia." In Davis and Schaefer.

Warren, Charles, ed. *Beyond Document: Essays on Nonfiction Film.* Hanover and London: Wesleyan University Press, 1996.

Washington, Peter, ed., *Poems of Mourning.* New York: Knopf, Everyman's Library, 1998.

Watson, George. "Quest for a Frenchman." *Sewanee Review*, vol. 84 (1976).

Waugh, Evelyn. *The Loved One.* 1948. London: Penguin, 2000.

———. "Evelyn Waugh in His Own Words: Forest Lawn." EVELYN WAUGH WEB SITE.

Ed. David Cliffe. December 8, 2000. <http://www.abbotshill.freeserve.co.uk/Forest%20Lawn.htm>

Webster, Donovan. *Aftermath: The Remnants of War.* New York: Pantheon, 1996.

Weil, Simone. *The* Iliad *or the Poem of Force.* 1941. Ed. James P. Holoka. New York: Peter Lang, 2003.

Weinberg, Steven. *The First Three Minutes: A Modern View of the Origin of the Universe.* New York: Bantam, 1979.

Weiss, Reska. *Journey through Hell.* London: Valentine, Mitchell, 1961.

Whaley, Joachim, ed. *Mirrors of Mortality: Studies in the Social History of Death.* New York: St. Martin's Press, 1981.

Whitaker, Thomas. "*In Parenthesis* and the Poetics of Passage." In Hills.

Whitehouse, Arch. *Heroes and Legends of World War I.* New York: Doubleday, 1964.

Whitman, Walt. *Complete Poetry and Collected Prose.* Ed. Justin Kaplan. New York: Penguin/Putnam, Library of America, 1982.

———. *Leaves of Grass.* Norton Critical Edition. Ed. Sculley Bradley and Harold W. Blodgett. New York: W. W. Norton, 1973.

Whittemore, Reed. *William Carlos Williams: Poet from Jersey.* Boston: Houghton Mifflin, 1975.

Wilde, Oscar. *The Importance of Being Earnest and Other Writings.* Ed. Joseph Bristow. London and New York: Routledge, 1992.

Willard, Charles B. *Whitman's American Fame: The Growth of His Reputation in America after 1892.* Providence, RI: Brown University Studies, vol. 12, American Series no. 3, 1950.

Williams, C. K. *The Vigil.* New York: Farrar Straus, 1998.

Williams, William Carlos. *The Collected Poems of William Carlos Williams,* vol. 1, 1909–1939. Ed. A. Walton Litz and Christopher MacGowan. New York: New Directions, 1986.

———. *The Collected Poems of William Carlos Williams,* vol. 2, 1939–1962. Ed. A. Walton Litz and Christopher MacGowan. New York: New Directions, 1988.

———. *Imaginations.* Ed. Webster Schott. New York: New Directions, 1971.

———. *I Wanted to Write a Poem: The Autobiography of the Works of a Poet.* Reported and ed. by Edith Heal. New York: New Directions, 1978.

———. *Paterson.* Ed. Christopher MacGowan. New York: New Directions, 1992.

———. *The Selected Letters of William Carlos Williams.* Ed. John C. Thirlwall. 1957. New York: New Directions, 1984.

———. "The Drill Sergeant." *New Directions in Prose & Poetry 1939.* Norfolk, Va.: New Directions, 1939.

Wilson, Trevor. *The Myriad Faces of War.* Cambridge, U.K.: Polity Press, 1986.

Winner, Lauren F. "Goodbye to God. Also Hello." *New York Times Book Review,* April 25, 2004.

Winter, Jay. *Sites of Memory, Sites of Mourning: The Great War in European Cultural History.* Cambridge, U.K.: Cambridge University Press, 1995.

Winterton, Paul. "Biggest Murder Case in History." *British News Chronicle,* August 30, 1944.

Wolosky, Shira. *Emily Dickinson: A Voice of War*. New Haven: Yale University Press, 1984.

Woods, Gregory. "AIDS to Remembrance: The Uses of Elegy." In Nelson.

WORLD WIDE CEMETERY. Founder Michael Kibbee. 1995. 2004. <http://www .cemetery.org/>

Wright, Judith. *Collected Poems 1942–85*. Manchester, U.K.: Angus & Robertson, 1944.

Wuthnow, Robert. *After Heaven: Spirituality in America Since the 1950s*. Berkeley: University of California Press, 1998.

Wyschogrod, Edith. *Spirit in Ashes: Hegel, Heidegger, and Man-Made Mass Death*. New Haven: Yale University Press, 1985.

Yeats, W. B. *The Cat and the Moon and Certain Poems*. Dublin: Cuala Press, 1924.

———. *Collected Poems*. Ed. Richard J. Finneran. New York: Collier, 1989.

———. *Collected Plays, New Edition*. 1934. New York: Macmillan, 1952.

Zaroff, Larry, M.D. "One Last Recipe from Mother, for the Good Death." *New York Times*, August 30, 2005.

Zeiger, Melissa F. *Beyond Consolation: Death, Sexuality, and the Changing Shapes of Elegy*. Ithaca, N.Y.: Cornell University Press, 1997.

Zelizer, Barbie. *Remembering to Forget: Holocaust Memory through the Camera's Eye*. Chicago: University of Chicago Press, 1998.

Zizek, Slavoj. *Welcome to the Desert of the Real: Five Essays on September 11 and Related Dates*. London and New York: Verso, 2002.

Zola, Emil. *Thérèse Raquin*. Trans. Leonard Tancock. New York: Penguin, 1973.

ILLUSTRATION CREDITS

Frontispiece: *La Victoire* by René Magritte. Private Collection. © 2005 C. Herscovici, Brussels/ Artists Rights Society (ARS), New York. Photo: Herscovici/Art Resource, NY

p. 108   *La Crucifixion*: Musée d'Unterlinden Colmar. Photograph: O. Zimmerman

p. 116   Detail of Grünewald, *La Crucifixion*: Musée d'Unterlinden Colmar. Photograph: O. Zimmerman

p. 118   Detail of Grünewald, *La Resurrection*: Musée d'Unterlinden Colmar. Photograph: O. Zimmerman

p. 131   *Le Miracle de la résurection des poulets rôtis*: Musée d'Unterlinden Colmar. Photograph: O. Zimmerman

p. 180   *X-Ray Viewing Room*: Robert Pope, Robert Pope Foundation

p. 191   *Doctors*: Robert Pope, Robert Pope Foundation

p. 205   *Gramp Holding Dan* and *Dan Holding Gramp*: Dan Jury

p. 206   *Tom Moran*: Nicholas Nixon, Nicholas and Bebe Nixon

p. 212   George Rodger's picture of a little boy, *Bergen-Belsen Concentration Camp*: George Rodger, Time & Life Pictures, Getty Images

p. 214   *People About to Be Shot*: Ron Haeberle, Time & Life Pictures, Getty Images

p. 225   *Fading Away*: HP Robinson, NMPFT, Royal Photographic Society, Science & Society Picture Library

p. 231   *Bigger Than Just Each Other*: Deidre Scherer

p. 263   *Family*: Robert Pope, Robert Pope Foundation

p. 282   Three selections from *Missing: Gallery of Images*: Martha Cooper

p. 285   Thiepval Monument: Joanna Legg, www.greatwar.co.uk

p. 287   *Maya Lin's Vietnam Veterans Memorial*, Leah Asofsky

p. 289   *Man Sitting Beside AIDS Quilt*: Louise Gubb, © Louise Gubb / CORBIS SABA

p. 356   *Death and the Maiden*: Hans Baldung Grien, *Death and the Maiden*. Kunstmuseum Basel. Photograph: Martin Bühler

p. 361   *Emily Dickinson's Grave*: Dietrich Christian Lammerts

p. 362   *Walt Whitman's Tomb*: Dietrich Christian Lammerts

p. 362   Blake's engraving of "Death's Door": Louis Schiavonetti, Italian, 1765–1810, after William Blake, British, 1757–1827. Illustration from "The Grave, A Poem" by Robert Blair: *Death's Door*, 1808, etching. 23.9 x 13.8 cm (image). Purchased, 1954. National Gallery of Victoria, Melbourne, Australia

INDEX

Page numbers in *italics* refer to illustrations.